The Protection of Geographical Indications in China

The Protection of Geographical Indications in China

Challenges of Adopting the European Approach

Xinzhe Song

Wolters Kluwer

Published by:
Kluwer Law International B.V.
PO Box 316
2400 AH Alphen aan den Rijn
The Netherlands
E-mail: international-sales@wolterskluwer.com
Website: www.wolterskluwer.com/en/solutions/kluwerlawinternational

Sold and distributed by:
Wolters Kluwer Legal & Regulatory U.S.
7201 McKinney Circle
Frederick, MD 21704
United States of America
E-mail: customer.service@wolterskluwer.com

ISBN 978-94-035-3400-8

e-Book: ISBN 978-94-035-3401-5
web-PDF: ISBN 978-94-035-3402-2

About the Author

Dr Xinzhe Song is an Associate Professor in Intellectual Property at the Law School of Hainan University, People's Republic of China. In 2017, he was awarded the highest distinction (*Mention très honorable avec les félicitations du jury à l'unanimité*) for his doctoral dissertation on geographical indications (GIs) defended at the University of Toulouse, France. His research projects on GIs have received grants from China's most prestigious funders, including China Scholarship Council (CSC) and National Social Science Foundation (NSSF). He is the author and editor of several books and numerous articles on GIs in publications including Queen Mary Journal of Intellectual Property, Journal of World Intellectual Property, Journal of World Trade, Propriété Industrielle (in French), and Intellectual Property (in Chinese).

Table of Contents

List of Abbreviations

AIPPI	International Association for the Protection of Intellectual Property
AO	Appellation of Origin/Appellation d'Origine
AOC	Appellation d'Origine Contrôlée
AOCE	Appellation d'Origine Contrôlée d'Excellence
AOVDQS	Appellation d'Origine Vin délimité de Qualité supérieure
AQSC	Agricultural Quality Safety Centre (China)
AQSIQ	General Administration of Quality Supervision, Inspection and Quarantine of the People's Republic of China
C. consom.	Code de la Consommation
C. rur.	Code Rural et de la Pêche Maritime
C.A.	Cour d'Appel
C.E.	Conseil d'État (France)
CAP	Common Agricultural Policy
Cass. civ.	Chambre Civile de la Cour de Cassation
Cass. com.	Chambre Commerciale de la Cour de Cassation
Cass. crim.	Chambre Criminelle de la Cour de Cassation
CCP	Product Conformity Certificate/Certification de Conformité
CFI	Court of First Instance/General Court of the Court of Justice of the European Union
CIVC	Comité Interprofessionnel du Vin de Champagne
CJEU	Court of Justice of the European Union
CMO	Common Market Organization
CNIPA	China National Intellectual Property Administration
COFRAC	Comité Français d'Accréditation

CPC	Communist Party of China
CPI	Code de la Propriété Intellectuelle
DGCCRF	Direction Générale de la Concurrence, de la Consommation et de la Répression des Fraudes
EC	European Communities
EU	European Union
EUIPO	European Union Intellectual Property Office
FITFIR	First in Time, First in Right
GATT	General Agreement on Tariffs and Trade
GI	Geographical Indication
ICH	Intangible Cultural Heritage
IGPIA	Indication Géographique protégeant les Produits Industriels et Artisanaux
INAO	Institut National des Appellations d'Origine/Institut National de l'Origine et de la Qualité
INPI	National Institute of Industrial Property/Institut National de la Propriété Industrielle
IP	Intellectual Property
IS	Indication of Source
L.	Loi/Law
MAFF	Ministry of Agriculture, Forestry and Fisheries (Japan)
MARA	Ministry of Agriculture and Rural Affairs of the People's Republic of China
MOA	Ministry of Agriculture of the People's Republic of China
OC	Organisme de Contrôle
ODG	Organization for Defence and Management/Organisme de Défense et de Gestion
OHIM	Office for Harmonization in the Internal Market
OJ	Official Journal
PDO	Protected Designation of Origin
PEOP	Protected Eco-Origin Product
PGI	Protected Geographical Indication
QWpsr	Quality Wine Produced in a Specified Region
RMB	Renminbi
SAIC	State Administration for Industry and Commerce of the People's Republic of China
SAMR	State Administration of Market Regulation (China)
SCT	Standing Committee on the Law of Trademarks, Industrial Designs and Geographical Indications

SFA	State Forestry Administration of the People's Republic of China
SIQO	Identification Sign of Quality and Origin/Signe d'Identification de la Qualité et de l'Origine
SME	Small- and Medium-sized Enterprise
T.G.I.	Tribunal de Grande Instance
TCM	Traditional Chinese Medicine
TK	Traditional Knowledge
TRAB	Trademark Review and Adjudication Board (China)
TRIPS	Agreement on Trade-Related Aspects of Intellectual Property Rights
TSG	Traditional Speciality Guaranteed
TTAB	Trademark Trial and Appeal Board (the United States)
TW	Table Wine
UK	United Kingdom
UNESCO	United Nations Educational, Scientific and Cultural Organization
US	United States
VDP	Vin de Pays
WIPO	World Intellectual Property Organization
WTO	World Trade Organization

Preface

The European approach to protecting geographical indications (GIs) is characterized by a distinct sui generis legal system with a high level of protection. The European Union (EU) has long been 'selling' the approach worldwide. As early as in the Uruguay Round of multilateral trade negotiations (1986-1994), the EU's proposal succeeded in adding a separate chapter on GI protection in the World Trade Organization (WTO) Agreement on Trade-Related Aspects of Intellectual Property Rights. Accordingly, all WTO Members have an obligation to provide protection to GIs, although not necessarily in the same way as the EU. In recent years, the EU has exerted influence on the design of many countries' GI protection systems through bilateral agreements, which have intensified the debate over whether other countries should adopt the European approach.

This book joins the debate from the perspective of the Chinese GI systems. Inspired by the EU, China established a sui generis system in the 1990s to protect GIs, which operates in parallel with the trademark system modelled on the United States (US) approach. The Agreement between the EU and China on Cooperation on, and Protection of, Geographical Indications concluded in November 2019 (entered into force on 1 March 2021) is expected to expand the influence of the European sui generis approach in China.

On 22 September 2021, China released a fifteen-year plan (2021-2035) on the development of intellectual property (IP) rights. The guideline, which demands stricter IP rights protection, maps out a number of key tasks including '*exploring* the formulation of sui generis laws and regulations for GI protection'. China seems to take a step closer towards the European approach since currently the EU-inspired Chinese sui generis regime is only governed by administrative rules promulgated by agencies under the State Council, which are at a lower level in the hierarchy of legislation than laws and regulations. However, the term 'exploring' used in the guideline suggests that difficulties and challenges lie ahead and that China may after all choose not to legislate specifically in the field of GIs but allow the US-modelled Chinese trademark regime to play a major role.

This book aims to study why China has struggled over the last three decades to decide whether the European sui generis approach would be more suitable compared with the US approach. If the European approach is not an appropriate option for China with more than 8,000 GIs (exceeding twice the number of European GIs), why do other countries follow it? Alternatively, if the European system is more suitable, what difficulties and challenges have impeded the adoption?

To find the answers, this book not only compares the systems of China and the EU but also traces the 'spirit' (reasoning) behind GI legislation. Chapter 1 reviews the genesis of the GI concept in the EU and reveals the 'spirit' behind the sui generis GI protection: the *terroir* idea. Chapter 2 shows the multifaceted nature of the Europe-originated concept, which brings difficulties to China when adopting it. In Chapters 3 and 4, this book analyses the extent to which China has adopted the European approach by comparing the differences of protection systems between China and the EU in detail. Chapter 5 focuses on the competition between the EU and US approaches in China. Chapter 6 analyses why the European sui generis approach has been accorded low priority in China relative to the US approach. Finally, in Chapters 7 and 8, based on the *terroir* idea, the book demonstrates that the EU-inspired sui generis regime rather than the US-modelled trademark regime should be designated as the primary system for GI protection in China. The sui generis regime should provide a high level of protection for all GI products.

By taking China as an example, this book seeks to provide considerations for countries that have developed or are considering developing GI systems. It is intended to enrich the reflection on the different approaches for GI protection. In addition, this book provides access to detailed practical information on GI registration requirements, quality control requirements, and level of protection in China, France, and the EU in order to support international legal practitioners in filing international GI registration applications and taking legal actions.

Acknowledgements

This book is based on research conducted in France (2013-2017) and China (2018-2021), with the assistance of the China Scholarship Council (201308500092) and the National Social Science Fund of China (21CFX080). I wish to express my special appreciation to Jacques Larrieu who was my PhD supervisor during my time in France and who remains a constant source of support and encouragement during my research work in China. I would like to extend my sincere gratitude and appreciation for the advice and comments of Alexandra Mendoza-Caminade, Jacques Raynard, Nicolas Bouche, Mingde Li, Weixing Shen, Xiuqin Lin, Yinliang Liu, Shujie Feng, Zuming Li, Wenting Cheng, Chuanjuan Zhang, and Xiaoyan Wang.

A special note of gratitude is owed to the experienced team members of Kluwer Law International for providing significant support in the preparation of this book.

Last but certainly not least, I want to express my deepest acknowledgement to my wife, Xiaoxuan Yi, and my parents, Lihua Dong and Xiangjin Song, for being with me every step of the way.

Introduction

Chinese producers in the agriculture and handicraft sectors are facing increasing competition due to the spread of globalization. Low-cost mass production by a handful of very large multinational agribusiness groups is placing heavy pressure on Chinese farmers. China's traditional agriculture – with small-scale, independent, decentralized forms of production – is struggling to compete with foreign large-scale, modernized agriculture.[1] While globalization has made China 'the factory of the world' by expanding its access to markets and resources,[2] rural areas in China's central and western regions are at the risk of being marginalized by the large cities in eastern China, such as Guangzhou and Shanghai, which are much more deeply integrated into the global market.[3] When economic conditions are unfavourable, farmers and artisans – especially those who consider that their efforts in sustaining traditional ways of producing quality products are not being fairly rewarded – abandon their land and migrate to cities in hopes of increasing their incomes and living standards. Their departure causes several problems, including unused lands, underdeveloped rural infrastructures, ageing rural populations, vacant villages, and disappearing traditional *savoir-faire*.[4]

However, the global marketplace also provides opportunities for the diversification of agricultural products, foodstuffs, and handicrafts. The proliferation of large companies with standardized products and the homogenization of quality have led

1. Jonathan Rigg, Albert Salamanca & Eric C. Thompson, *The Puzzle of East and Southeast Asia's Persistent Smallholder*, 43 J. Rural Stud. 118, 126 (2016).
2. Léon Vandermeersch, *La Chine et la mondialisation*, Archives de Philosophie du Droit, Vol. 47, 2003, p. 99.
3. Yanhai Zhao, *L'insertion de la Chine dans la mondialisation, les flux d'investissements directs étrangers et la disparité économique régionale en Chine*, thèse, Université Sorbonne Nouvelle-Paris 3, 2009, p. 112.
4. Xia Liyan, Nongcun Laodongli Liushi dui Nongcun Jingji Fazhan de Yingxiang ji Duice [Negative Effects of Labor Force Drain on Rural Economy], NANJIN NONGYE DAXUE XUEBAO [JOURNAL OF NANJING AGRICULTURAL UNIVERSITY], March 2009, 14-19; Xu Zengwen, Nongcun Laodongli de Liudong yu Nongye Laodongli de Liushi [Rural Labor Movement and Rural Labor Drain], ZHONGGUO NONGCUN JINGJI [CHINESE RURAL ECONOMY], January 1995, 51-53.

many consumers to 'turn back',[5] as they begin to doubt whether the quality of a McDonald's burger is really superior to that of local food[6] and become increasingly attached to and value products that are closely linked to their place of origin.[7] This preference rests on the belief that products sourced from a given location have not only utilitarian values (e.g., safety, health, and nutritional value) but also a special taste, desirable style, tradition, authenticity, or quality.[8] These origin-based attributes thus constitute the most potent among the weapons local producers can use to insert their products into globalization schemes.

Local producers are unlikely to be satisfied with a single sale. To generate repeat sales, they need to make the products easier to identify in the marketplace. Two instruments are useful for achieving this objective: trademarks and geographical indications (GIs).[9] These tell consumers where the products come from and allow them to distinguish one line of products from others in the marketplace. They reduce consumer search costs and incentivize producers to maintain consistent quality.

However, GIs overlap with trademarks only partially. If Sanka coffee had no trademark, consumers would have to order it in a restaurant or grocery store by asking for the 'decaffeinated coffee made by General Foods'.[10] If the GI '*Bayerisches* Bier' had no name, then consumers would have to ask for the 'beer produced in the German Land of Bavaria, in accordance with a particular method of production that originated

5. Nuria Ackermann & Fabio Russo, *Adding Value to Traditional Products of Regional Origin: A Guide to Creating a Quality Consortium* 1 (United Nations Industrial Development Organization 2010).
6. A study carried out by the Shanghai Institute for Food and Drug Safety shows that more than 70 per cent of Shanghai residents worry about the quality of mass-produced domestic agri-foods. *See* Tang Minhui, SHIPIN YAOPIN ANQUAN YU JIANGUAN ZHENGCE YANJIU BAOGAO [REPORT FOR FOOD AND DRUG SAFETY AND REGULATORY POLICIES] (Social Science Academic Press, 2012); *See also* Petra van de Kop, Denis Sautier & Astrid Gerz, *Origin-Based Products: Lessons for Pro-poor Market Development* 9 (The Royal Tropical Institute-KIT 2006).
7. Koert van Ittersum et al., *Consumers' Appreciation of Regional Certification Labels: A Pan-European Study*, 58 J. Agric. Econ. 1 (2007); Ramona Teuber, *Protecting Geographical Indications: Lessons Learned from the Economic Literature*, Presentation at the EAAE 2011 Congress (30 August 2011).
8. Jean-Louis Rastoin, *Créer un label méditerranéen pour les produits agroalimentaires d'origine: quelques justifications théoriques et empiriques*, Séminaire international sur Les produits de terroir, les indications géographiques et le développement local durable des pays méditerranéens, No. 89, CIHEAM, 2008, pp. 19-27; Tomer Broude, *Taking Trade and Culture Seriously: Geographical Indications and Cultural Protection in WTO Law*, 26 U. Pa. J. Int'l Econ. L. 623 (2005); Ramona Teuber, *Consumers' and Producers' Expectations Towards Geographical Indications: Empirical Evidence for a German Case Study*, 113 Brit. Food J. 900 (2011).
9. It must be noted that there is no harmonized GI definition across the world. Instead, GI definitions in domestic laws can vary significantly: some being very broad, some very narrow. Furthermore, an abundance of the terminology used in this area may fall into the umbrella of GIs, such as *appellation d'origine contrôlée*, protected designations of origin, protected geographical indications, indications of geographical origin or even indications of provenance. The term 'geographical indication', which will be used in this book, corresponds to the definition given by the TRIPS Agreement, as we will discuss later. Unless otherwise specified, it covers terminologies *appellations d'origine (contrôlée), indications géographiques protégeant les produits industriels et artisanaux*, protected designations of origin, protected geographical indications, geographical indication products and geographical indications for agricultural products.
10. William M. Landes & Richard A. Posner, *Trademark Law: An Economic Perspective*, 30 J.L. & Econ. 265, 269 (1987).

during the nineteenth century in Bavaria, and there is a direct link between the quality of the beer and the place Bavaria'. GIs do not merely designate by whom the product was made[11] but also where and how it was made, so as to provide a guarantee regarding the product's quality. This function rests upon the qualitative link between the local product and its place of origin, which could be articulated through the French idea of *terroir*.

The *terroir* idea was originally associated with viticulture, which relates the attributes of a wine to geographically specific conditions of soil and climate in the place where the grapes are grown. However, this is not a static idea. Both in France and globally, it has been progressively reinterpreted over time. It is departing significantly from the model of a purely natural link and is gradually acknowledging that collective, intergenerational human *savoir-faire* may play a significant role in the shaping of a local speciality. The anchoring to place and human knowledge of production account for the multiple objectives behind the protection of GIs: in addition to protecting consumers against fraud and of producers against unfair competition, the goals include the preservation of rural development, cultural heritage, and traditional knowledge (TK), as well as environmental/ecological protection.

Given the extensive information that GIs convey and the multiple objectives that GI protection seeks to achieve, legal systems are being challenged by the question of how best to protect them, both nationally and internationally.

GI protection at the national level is marked by the diversity of approaches adopted by different countries. These include regulations focusing on business practices (such as unfair competition, passing off, consumer protection, and labelling), trademark law, and special protection.[12] The two largest trade and investment partners for virtually all other countries in the global economy, the EU and the United States utilize 'fundamentally different philosophies and approaches'.[13] The EU (including France) has established a comprehensive body of laws and regulations specifically dedicated to the protection of GIs. Often referred to as 'sui generis GI protection regimes', they are designed not only to regulate the use of distinctive signs in the marketplace but also to verify (in the application process) and establish (via approved product specifications or *cahiers des charges*) the linkages between a product's characteristics and its place of origin. It is believed that EU/French sui generis regimes are based on the *terroir* idea.

By contrast, the United States views GIs as a subset of trademarks and incorporates GI protection under its trademark law. This is usually achieved through two

11. A GI usually does not identify a good or service as originating from a particular commercial source.
12. WTO, *Review under Article 24.2 of the Application of the Provisions of the Section of the TRIPS Agreement on Geographical Indications*, IP/C/W/253/Rev.1 (24 November 2003); Carlos M. Correa, *Protection of Geographical Indications in CARICOM Countries* (Caribbean Regional Negotiating Machinery Technical Papers 2002).
13. The EU and the United States are the primary parties in the debate over the protection of geographical indications. *See* Philippe Zylberg, *Geographical Indications v. Trademarks: The Lisbon Agreement – A Violation of TRIPS*, 11 U. Balt. Intell. Prop. L.J. 1 (2002); Daniele Giovannucci et al., *Guide to Geographical Indications: Linking Products and Their Origins* 56 (International Trade Centre 2009).

trademark subcategories: 'collective marks' and 'certification marks'. The law allows operators wide discretion in their decisions about which products should be designated by the mark. Thus, operators can use trademarks to designate GI products or certify a place of origin, methods of production, and/or origin-based quality attributes. Therefore, trademarks, like GIs, can also have a *terroir* dimension, but this is due to trademarks' self-enforcing feature: they have this dimension because their owners want them to have it. The owner of a certification mark can, for example, select place of origin and other attributes to be certified and can change them at any time. The trademark law 'does not care what the certification standards are'.[14]

After more than a century at the negotiating table,[15] the international discussion on protection levels continues. Various protection levels have been developed via multilateral agreements. These include protection against the 'direct or indirect use of a false indication of the source of the goods', as provided under Article 10(1) of the Paris Convention;[16] protection against any use that constitutes an act of unfair competition, as provided for Article 10bis of the Paris Convention; protection against the use of indications that are deceptive or misleading, as established by the Madrid Agreement[17] and by Article 22(2) of the Agreement on Trade-Related Aspects of Intellectual Property Rights ('TRIPS Agreement' hereinafter);[18] and so-called *absolute* protection, as established under the Lisbon Agreement[19] and Article 23(1) of the TRIPS Agreement. The most controversial issue concerns absolute protection.

The Lisbon Agreement has defined the content of absolute protection. The Agreement was originally applied only to the 'appellation of origin'/Appellation d'Origine (AO) concept (a subcategory of GIs), which was defined as the 'geographical denomination of a country, region, or locality, which serves to designate a product originating therein, the quality or characteristics of which are due exclusively or essentially to the geographical environment, including natural and human factors'.[20] The AO thus requires a strong link between the product and its place of origin. Provided that the AO was recognized and protected 'as such' in the country of origin and registered at the International Bureau of Intellectual Property (IP),[21] the contracting

14. *Geographical Indication Protection in the United States*, United States Patent and Trademark Office (USPTO) (1 May 2021), https://www.uspto.gov/sites/default/files/web/offices/dcom/olia/globalip/pdf/gi_system.pdf; Justin Hughes, *Champagne, Feta, and Bourbon: The Spirited Debate about Geographical Indications*, 58 Hastings L.J. 299, 310 (2006).
15. Amy P. Cotton, *123 Years at the Negotiating Table and Still No Dessert: The Case in Support of TRIPS Geographical Indication Protections*, 82 Chi.-Kent L. Rev. 1295 (2007).
16. Paris Convention for the Protection of Industrial Property, 20 March 1883 as revised at Stockholm on 14 July 1967, 828 U.N.T.S 305 (1972) ('Paris Convention' hereinafter).
17. Madrid Agreement for the Repression of False or Deceptive Indications of Source of Goods, 14 April 1891, 828 U.N.T.S. 389 (1972) ('Madrid Agreement' hereinafter).
18. Agreement on Trade-Related Aspects of Intellectual Property Rights, 15 April 1994, 33 I.L.M. 1125, 1197 (1994) ('TRIPS Agreement' hereinafter).
19. Lisbon Agreement for the Protection of Appellations of Origin and Their International Registration Article 2, 31 October 1958, 923 U.N.T.S. 205 (as amended on 28 September 1979) ('Lisbon Agreement' hereinafter).
20. *Ibid.*, Article 2.
21. *Ibid.*, Article 1.

States had the obligation to protect the name in their own jurisdiction.[22] The content of protection was specified in Article 3, which provided protection against 'any usurpation or imitation, even if the true origin of the product is indicated or if the appellation is used in translated form or accompanied by terms such as "kind", "type", "make", "imitation", or the like'. This protection level is higher than that provided by traditional trademark protection standards, as protection is ensured regardless of whether the public may be misled or not or whether the use of the AO is likely to impair, dilute, or take advantage of the reputation of the AO.

The 'old' Lisbon Agreement is more in line with the European approach of using sui generis regimes to protect GIs. The need for the AO to be recognized and protected 'as such', as required by Article 1, might require that Lisbon members have specific legislation for the AO, or at least have the 'AO' concept or an equivalent in their national law. This requirement may be unpalatable to those states that protect this form of IP under competition, consumer protection, or trademark laws.[23] This partially explains why the Lisbon Agreement received little international support.

The Lisbon Agreement has been reformed to make it more attractive.[24] The Geneva Act,[25] adopted on 20 May 2015, widens the Agreement's scope to cover all GIs, the definition of which closely models the language of the TRIPS Agreement.[26] As defined in Article 2, a GI is any indication consisting of or containing the name of a geographical area, or another indication that is known to refer to such an area (a GI is not necessarily a name), 'which identifies a good as originating in that geographical area, where a given quality, reputation or other characteristic of the good is essentially attributable to its geographical origin'. The requirement regarding the connection between the product and its place of origin is relaxed, as the Geneva Act employs 'reputation' criteria for GI protection. The expression 'as such' is deleted from the Agreement. Contracting parties are free to 'choose the type of legislation under which it establishes the protection stipulated in this Act'.[27] Though the new Act introduces a number of flexibilities that may be attractive for a variety of legal systems, many non party States that protect GIs as trademarks still question the compatibility of the Act with their national laws, arguing that the higher level of protection for AOs/GIs stipulated in the Act is inconsistent with trademark protection standards.[28]

22. However, a contracting party may declare within one year of receiving the notice of registration that it cannot ensure the protection of a registered appellation within its territory. *See ibid.*, Article 5(3).
23. Danielle Dudding, *The Lisbon Agreement: Why the United States Should Stop Fighting the Geneva Act*, 18 Vand. J. Ent. & Tech. L. 167 (2015).
24. Anna G. Micara, *The Geneva Act of the Lisbon Agreement for the Protection of Appellations of Origin and Their International Registration: An Assessment of a Controversial Agreement*, 47 IIC-Int'l Rev. Intell. Prop. & Competition L. 673 (2016).
25. Geneva Act of the Lisbon Agreement on Appellations of Origin and Geographical Indications, 20 May 2015, *entered into force* 26 February 2020 ('Geneva Act' hereinafter).
26. Daniel J. Gervais, *Irreconcilable Differences? The Geneva Act of the Lisbon Agreement and the Common Law*, 53 Hous. L. Rev. 358 (2015).
27. *See* Article 10 of the Geneva Act.
28. Article 11 of the Geneva Act revises and replaces provisions of the old Lisbon Agreement (Stockholm Act) on the content of protection. Where the AO or GI is used in respect of goods of the same kind, the protection is still 'absolute', irrespective of consumer confusion or GI

Article 23 of the TRIPS Agreement also establishes a high level of protection for GIs, defined by Article 22(1) as 'indications which identify a good as originating in the territory of a Member, or a region or locality in that territory, where a given quality, reputation or characteristic of the good is essentially attributable to its geographical origin'. This Article requires World Trade Organization (WTO) members to restrict the use of GIs to products that actually originate from the place they indicate. The Article applies even where measures preventing public confusion have been undertaken (such as when the true origin of the good is indicated or the use of the GI is accompanied by expressions such as 'kind', 'type', 'style', or 'imitation').[29] It protects GIs regardless of whether their use would be likely to result in consumer confusion, unfair competition, or the appropriation or weakening of the reputation of the GI. Since the only test is 'correctness',[30] the level of protection might be higher even than that afforded to well-known trademarks.[31]

---

dilution. *See* Article 11 of the Geneva Act: 'Subject to the provisions of this Act, in respect of a registered appellation of origin or a registered geographical indication, each Contracting Party shall provide the legal means to prevent: (a) use of the appellation of origin or the geographical indication (i) in respect of goods of the same kind as those to which the appellation of origin or the geographical indication applies, not originating in the geographical area of origin or not complying with any other applicable requirements for using the appellation of origin or the geographical indication; (ii) in respect of goods that are not of the same kind as those to which the appellation of origin or geographical indication applies or services, if such use would indicate or suggest a connection between those goods or services and the beneficiaries of the appellation of origin or the geographical indication, and would be likely to damage their interests, or, where applicable, because of the reputation of the appellation of origin or geographical indication in the Contracting Party concerned, such use would be likely to impair or dilute in an unfair manner, or take unfair advantage of, that reputation; (b) any other practice liable to mislead consumers as to the true origin, provenance or nature of the goods. (2) Paragraph (1)(a) shall also apply to use of the appellation of origin or geographical indication amounting to its imitation, even if the true origin of the goods is indicated, or if the appellation of origin or the geographical indication is used in translated form or is accompanied by terms such as "style", "kind", "type", "make", "imitation", "method", "as produced in", "like", "similar" or the like.' *See also* Daniel J. Gervais & Matthew Slider, *The Geneva Act of the Lisbon Agreement: Controversial Negotiations and Controversial Results, in The Importance of Place: Geographical Indications as a Tool for Local and Regional Development* 15 (William van Caenegem ed., Springer International Publishing 2017).

29. Article 23 also applies where the GI is used in translation. *See* Agreement on Trade-Related Aspects of Intellectual Property Rights Article 23(1), 15 April 1994, 33 I.L.M. 1125, 1197 (1994) ('TRIPS Agreement' hereinafter): 'Each Member shall provide the legal means for interested parties to prevent use of a geographical indication identifying wines for wines not originating in the place indicated by the geographical indication in question or identifying spirits for spirits not originating in the place indicated by the geographical indication in question, even where the true origin of the goods is indicated or the geographical indication is used in translation or accompanied by expressions such as "kind", "type", "style", "imitation" or the like.'
30. WTO, *Issues Related to the Extension of the Protection of Geographical Indications Provided for in Article 23 of the TRIPS Agreement to Products Other than Wines and Spirits and Those Related to the Relationship Between the TRIPS Agreement and the Convention on Biological Diversity*, WT/GC/W/633 (21 April 2011).
31. Gail Evans and Michael Blakeney argue that the scope of exclusivity granted by Article 23 to GIs approximates dilution-style protection for well-known trademarks. However, the bar that Article 23 establishes on the use of GIs does not depend on the GIs' reputation and consumer understandings of the terms in the country where protection is sought. Where a GI is unknown in a place, there would not any risk of reputation dilution. Thus Justin Hughes observes that the protection afforded by Article 23 may be understood as 'dilution plus' standard. *See* Gail Evans

However, this strong protection is available only for GIs identifying wines and spirits. The protection of GIs for other products is ensured on the basis of Article 22, which prevents the use of GIs that mislead the public as to the true geographical origin of the goods.[32] The likelihood of confusion, the usual test for trademark infringement, is the standard that determines whether the use of the GIs should be prohibited.[33] Therefore, if the issue of generic use is not considered, 'New Zealand Feta Cheese' can be used legitimately in circumstances where consumers are not misled, while 'New Zealand *Cognac*' would be caught by the prohibition in Article 23.

The two different levels of protection are outcomes of the General Agreement on Tariffs and Trade (GATT) Uruguay Round negotiations. As many have pointed out, this differential treatment of GIs is not based on logical reasoning or material evidence.[34] Rather, it is a compromise between the common law approach of protecting GIs as trademarks and the European approach of using sui generis GI regimes. The higher level of protection was introduced at the request of the EU, but the EU's proposal at the Uruguay Round was to provide the same high level of protection for all products, not just to wines and spirits. The proposal was that GIs should be protected against 'any usurpation, imitation or evocation, even where the true origin of the product is indicated or the appellation or designation is used in translation or accompanied by expressions such as "kind", "type", "style", "imitation" or the like'.[35] This proposal reflects the EU's regional policy and the EU member countries' national legal frameworks, which protect GIs as sui generis IP rights and applies standalone standards of protection, distinct from those of trademarks.[36] However, certain common law countries that treat GIs as trademarks – such as the US, Canada, and Australia – opposed the introduction of a provision that could lead to a level of GI protection higher than that offered by trademark laws. Not surprisingly, they also opposed the inclusion of GI

& Michael Blakeney, *The International Protection of Geographical Indications Yesterday, Today and Tomorrow*, 9 J. Int'l Econ. L. 575 (2006); Hughes, *supra* n. 14, at 319.

32. Article 22(2) of the TRIPS Agreement: 'In respect of geographical indications, Members shall provide the legal means for interested parties to prevent: (a) the use of any means in the designation or presentation of a good that indicates or suggests that the good in question originates in a geographical area other than the true place of origin in a manner which misleads the public as to the geographical origin of the good; (b) any use which constitutes an act of unfair competition within the meaning of Article 10bis of the Paris Convention (1967).'
33. When disputes over the GIs occur, the GI holders must prove that the public was misled.
34. WTO, *Proposal from Bulgaria, Cuba, the Czech Republic, Egypt, Iceland, India, Jamaica, Kenya, Liechtenstein, Mauritius, Nigeria, Pakistan, Slovenia, Sri Lanka, Switzerland, Turkey and Venezuela*, IP/C/W/247/Rev.1 (17 May 2001).
35. GATT Secretariat, *Guidelines and Objectives Proposed by the European Community for the Negotiations on Trade Related Aspects of Substantive Standards of Intellectual Property Rights*, MTN.GNG/NG11/W/26 (7 July 1988).
36. Michael Handler, *Rethinking GI Extension, in Research Handbook on Intellectual Property and Geographical Indications* 146 (Dev Gangjee ed., Edward Elgar Publishing 2016); Watson K. William, *Reign of Terroir: How to Resist Europe's Efforts to Control Common Food Names as Geographical Indications* (Cato Institute 5 May 2021), https://www.cato.org/policy-analysis/reign-terroir-how-resist-europes-efforts-control-common-food-names-geographical.

protection in the TRIPS Agreement, arguing that the provisions on trademarks provided GIs with sufficient protection.[37]

The compromise allows the common law countries to continue protecting GIs through their existing trademark systems while giving the EU its desired high-level protection for wines and spirits, which are particularly important to several EU member countries.[38] However, two fundamental questions have been left hanging in the air: to what extent do GIs differ from trademarks, and why do GIs deserve a standard of protection different from that set out in trademark laws? These questions continue to be the subject of debate in the current negotiations regarding modifications to the TRIPS rules.[39]

The dual standards set out in Articles 22 and 23 are the minimum standards that must be met by WTO members, but the Agreement allows for a high degree of flexibility.[40] First, since nothing in the Agreement stipulates how the protection shall be afforded, members are free to choose the legal means by which they meet their obligations. Second, as the Article 22 standard applied to most GIs is not incompatible with trademark and consumer protection laws, protection through their application can meet the TRIPS requirements. Therefore, the choice of whether to use specific GI laws is left entirely to WTO members.

Accordingly, Chinese authorities have decided to transplant the French/EU sui generis GI regime into their soil in the hopes of 'ensuring effective protection of China's "recognized AO products", regulating the signs of the products, and guaranteeing the quality and characteristics of the products'.[41] The former General Administration of Quality Supervision, Inspection and Quarantine of the People's Republic of China (AQSIQ) established two sui generis systems in 1999 and 2001, which were merged in 2005 into a single system, the 'GI product' regime. In the context of the 2018 institutional reform of the State Council, the China National Intellectual Property Administration (CNIPA) replaced the former AQSIQ as the managing authority of the 'GI product' regime.[42] Moreover, the Ministry of Agriculture (merged into the Ministry of Agriculture and Rural Affairs (MARA) in 2018; hereinafter jointly referred to as

37. GATT Secretariat, *Draft Agreement on the Trade-Related Aspects of Intellectual Property Rights: Communication from the United States*, MTN.GNG/NG11/W/70 (11 May 1990); Teshager Dagne, *The Identity of Geographical Indications and Their Relation to Traditional Knowledge in Intellectual Property Law*, 5 WIPO J. 137 (2014); Stacy D. Goldberg, *Who Will Raise the White Flag: The Battle Between the United States and the European Union over the Protection of Geographical Indications*, 22 U. Pa. J. Int'l Econ. L. 107 (2001); Justin M. Waggoner, *Acquiring a European Taste for Geographical Indications*, 33 Brook. J. Int'l L. 569 (2007).
38. Friederike Frantz, *Twenty Years of TRIPS, Twenty Years of Debate: The Extension of High Level Protection of Geographical Indications: Arguments, State of negotiations and Prospects*, 21 Ann. Surv. Int'l & Comp. L. 93 (2016).
39. The proposed modifications include, notably, creating a multilateral register for wines and spirits and extending the higher (Article 23) level of protection beyond wines and spirits.
40. WIPO, *Introduction to Geographical Indications and Recent Developments in the World Intellectual Property Organization*, WIPO/GEO/SFO/03/1 (9 July 2003); Matthijs Geuze, *The Provisions on Geographical Indications in the TRIPS Agreement*, 10 Estey Ctr. J. Int'l L. & Trade 50 (2009).
41. Provisions on the Protection of Products with Appellations of Origin, Article 1 (1999).
42. Di Shisanjie Quanguo Renmin Daibiao Dahui Diyici Huiyi Guanyu Guowuyuan Jigou Gaige Fangan de Jueding (Decision of the First Session of the Thirteenth National People's Congress on the Plan for Institutional Reform of the State Council), 17 March 2018.

'MOA') developed a parallel, partially overlapping GI system specifically for agricultural products in 2008.[43]

The authorities claim that the transplanted sui generis systems afford the same level of protection to Chinese products as is afforded to European products by the original laws. Nevertheless, contrary to what the authorities assert, there are several reasons to believe that transplantation has suffered a major setback in the face of challenges and that the Chinese systems cannot be equated with their counterparts in Europe.

The French/EU systems are built around the following main elements: GIs classified into different subcategories and defined on the basis of the linkage (strong or weak) between the product and its *terroir*; an administrative process independent of trademark registration systems that verifies whether the names for which protection is sought meet the linkage requirements prescribed in the definitions; product specifications (*cahier des charges*) laying down the geographical area delimited, the methods of obtaining the product, and the product's characteristics, etc.; monitoring systems via official controls that ensure the verification of compliance with the product specifications; a high level of protection ('absolute' protection); and coexistence between GIs and prior trademarks.[44]

While the registration processes are similar, the European and Chinese special systems are significantly different. They do not use the same terminology, and some of the terms they share have different meanings. This leads to different link requirements. Their inspection structures are also different. Protection is not 'absolute' but is limited to prevent misleading uses of registered GIs and is subject to the principle of 'speciality'. The coexistence of GIs and prior trademarks is not provided for in Chinese sui generis GI regulations. Although the Agreement between the EU and China on Cooperation on and Protection of Geographical Indications (concluded in November 2019; the 'EU-China GI Agreement' hereinafter) stipulates that China shall provide a higher level of protection for GIs, this provision is limited to certain GIs listed in Annex III and IV of the Agreement.[45]

Thus, several main elements of the French/EU GI systems have not been transplanted in China. This flawed transplantation and the challenges of adopting the European sui generis approach are even clearer when the Chinese sui generis systems are in conflict with the trademark system. Under the influence of the practices in common law countries, particularly the US, China relies heavily on the trademark system to protect GIs. Special rules have been set out in the trademark law for the registration of collective and certification marks containing or consisting of GIs. The functions of those trademarks are considered equivalent to those of GIs. Contrary to the French and EU models, the trademark system is not intended to complement the sui generis systems but to replace them. Since 2018, the CNIPA has been the sole authority

43. *Ibid.*
44. European Commission, *Paper on Geographical Indications (GIs) in the EU-US Transatlantic Trade and Investment Partnership* (21 March 2016).
45. This provision also covers geographical indications added to the list pursuant to Article 3 of the Agreement.

responsible for GI protection under the Trademark Law and the Regulations on the Protection of GI Products; however, the Draft Provisions on the Protection of Geographical Indications issued by the CNIPA in 2020 show no intention of merging the trademark system and the sui generis GI system. The ongoing battle between GIs recognized by the sui generis systems and conflicting signs registered as individual, collective, or certification marks is fierce, and rights conferred by the former are often compromised.[46]

Do these challenges mean that China should abolish the sui generis GI systems? Do they imply that the regimes arising in the European *terroir* cannot be successfully transplanted in China, or, conversely, should China look into the reasons for the system failure in order to overcome the challenges?

These questions are important because China faces the difficult choice of either to improve the sui generis systems or use the trademark system as the primary means of protecting GIs. The current dual protection – utilising a sui generis regime as in the EU and a trademark system similar to the US approach – is not meeting expectations. It has been widely criticized for wasting resources, creating conflicts of interest, confusing consumers, and adding costs for producers. This is not surprising, as the two approaches are not compatible.[47] One possible solution for China would be to take one approach while discarding the other. Since China's legislators are considering a reform of national regulations on GIs, there is an urgent need to settle this issue.

These questions are also important from a global perspective. The protection of GIs is subject to the principle of territoriality, but the market for GI products is global. This means that GIs will not necessarily be afforded the same level of protection in every country when products are traded across borders and protection is sought internationally.[48] The EU is seeking to overcome the limitations of the territoriality principle by undertaking efforts to expand the geographical scope of its own model of protection at the multilateral, bilateral, and national levels. By contrast, the United States is competing with the EU by promoting a different approach.[49]

At the multilateral level, the EU is pushing for amendments to the TRIPS Agreement so that the Article 23 level of protection applies to GIs for all goods (not merely wines and spirits) and a multilateral register for GIs is established.[50] This proposal has been staunchly opposed by a number of the so-called New World

46. Issued in May 2021 by the CNIPA, the Guidelines on Strengthening the Protection of Geographical Indications have pointed out the need for a harmonic relationship between GIs registered under the sui generis GI systems and signs registered under the trademark system. This need is reaffirmed by the Central Committee of the Communist Party of China (CPC) and the State Council in a 15-year plan (2021-2035) on the development of IP rights. *See* Guojia Zhishi Chanquan Ju Guojia Shichang Jiandu Guanli Zongju Guanyu Jinyibu Jiaqiang Dili Biaozhi Baohu de Zhidao Yijian [Guidelines on Strengthening the Protection of Geographical Indications], 21 May 2021; ZhiShi Chanquan Qiangguo Jianshe Gangyao (2021-2035) [Guidelines for Building a Powerful Country with Intellectual Property Rights (2021-2035)], 22 September 2021.
47. Bernard O'Connor, *The European Union and the United States Conflicting Agendas on Geographical Indications: What's Happening in Asia?*, 9 Global Trade & Cust. J. 66 (2014).
48. WIPO, *Geographical Indications and the Territoriality Principle*, SCT/9/5 (1 October 2002).
49. *See* O'Connor, *supra* n. 47.
50. WTO, *Geographical Indications (Communication from the European Communities)*, TN/IP/W/11 (14 June 2005); WTO, *Draft Modalities for TRIPS Related Issues (Communication*

countries, such as the United States, Australia, New Zealand, Argentina, Chile, and Canada.[51] To achieve its goal, the EU needs allies at the negotiations. Is China an ally of the EU? China's position is mixed, reflecting its dual system of GI protection (i.e., sui generis regime and trademark system). In a case against the EU GI regulation initiated by the United States and Australia under the WTO dispute settlement system, China joined the US–Australia side as an independent party.[52] Since 2011, China has supported the EU's push for amendments to the TRIPS Agreement.[53] While the EU has welcomed the adoption of the Geneva Act on a revised Lisbon Agreement, China recently re-joined the US–Australia side and, as an observer at the diplomatic conference on revising the Agreement, questioned the compatibility of the Geneva Act with its existing national law (i.e., the trademark law), which protects GIs as collective and certification marks.[54] If China were ultimately to decide to abolish national sui generis GIs laws and protect GIs only through trademark law, China could turn its back on the EU on both the 'GI extension' and 'multilateral GI register' issues at the negotiation table; GI extension would no longer be necessary for China if Chinese GIs were to be protected only on the basis of domestic trademark law since the provisions of the TRIPS Agreement on trademarks would provide sufficient protection. In this case, the multilateral GI register would become redundant because this type of agreement already exists for trademarks (the Madrid Agreement Concerning the International Registration of Marks), including those containing or consisting of GIs.

At the bilateral level, the EU has been negotiating for a higher level of GI protection, which has so far not been achieved in the TRIPS Agreement. It has successfully concluded many 'TRIPS-plus' bilateral agreements with various countries, such as Australia,[55] Canada,[56] Switzerland,[57] Chile,[58] South Africa,[59] and Mexico.[60]

from the Albania et al.), TN/C/W/52 (19 July 2008); WTO, *Multilateral System of Notification and Registration of Geographical Indications for Wines and Spirits*, TN/IP/21 (21 April 2011).

51. WTO, *Proposed Draft TRIPS Council Decision on the Establishment of a Multilateral System of Notification and Registration of Geographical Indications for Wines and Spirits (Submission by Argentina et al.)*, TN/IP/W/10/Rev.4 (31 March 2011); WTO, *Proposed Report from the Council for TRIPS to the TNC Regarding Article 23 of the TRIPS Agreement: Issues Related to the Extension of the Protection of Geographical Indications Provided for in Article 23 to Products Other than Wines and Spirits (Communication from Argentina et al.)*, IP/C/W/395 (10 December 2002); WTO, *Implications of Article 23 Extension (Communication from Argentina et al.)*, IP/C/W/386 (8 November 2002).
52. WTO Panel Report on *European Communities Protection of Trademarks and Geographical Indications for Agricultural Products and Foodstuffs (Complaint by the United States)*, WT/DS174/R/Add.3, adopted 15 March 2005, Annex C (Arguments from the third parties).
53. WTO, *Draft Modalities for TRIPS Related Issues*, *supra* n. 50; WTO, *Draft Decision to Amend Section 3 of Part II of the TRIPS Agreement (Communication from Albania et al.)*, TN/C/W/60 (19 April 2011).
54. *Revised WIPO Lisbon Agreement to Cover Geographical Indications*, International Centre for Trade and Sustainable Development (7 May 2021), https://ictsd.iisd.org/search?f%5B0%5D=field_tag%3A542.
55. *Agreement Between the European Community and Australia on Trade in Wine*, OJ L 86, 31.3.1994, p. 3.
56. *Agreement Between the European Community and Canada on Trade in Wines and Spirit Drinks*, OJ L 35, 6.2.2004, p. 3.
57. *Agreement Between the European Community and the Swiss Confederation on Trade in Agricultural Products*, OJ L 114, 30.4.2002, p. 132.

Those agreements, reached at an early stage, concerned wines and spirits and contained specific provisions on the protection of names considered semi-generic in the contracting countries. The EU's recent efforts have been directed at all products. The negotiation objectives are multiple and include extending the GI protection provided by Article 23 of the TRIPS Agreement to products other than wines and spirits, allowing coexistence with prior trademarks, and phasing out prior uses of EU names.[61] This can be seen in the recent free trade agreements (FTA) with countries such as Korea,[62] Canada,[63] and Singapore.[64] In November 2019, the EU concluded with China the 'EU-China GI Agreement', aiming to ensure that China provides a high level of protection for European GIs; this came into force in March 2021. Meanwhile, in January 2020, the United States concluded with China the Economic and Trade Agreement ('US-China Agreement' hereinafter), which contains several provisions designed to challenge the GI protection status by alleging generic-ness so as to undermine the EU *terroir* philosophy and efforts in China.[65] The EU and the United States are reshaping China's laws and policies on GIs through bilateral agreements. China's solution of reconciling the competing approaches can be used as a reference by other countries who need to conclude bilateral trade agreements with the EU or the United States.

At the national level, the EU is encouraging the transposition of its internal legislation on GIs onto third countries. One of the many examples of this can be seen in Article 12(1) of Regulation 2081/92, which sets out the equivalence and reciprocity conditions for third countries. To register third-country GIs under the Regulation, third countries were required to adopt a GI system equivalent to that used in the EU and provide reciprocal protection to EU products.[66] However, since these conditions were

58. *Agreement Establishing an Association Between the European Community and Its Member States, of the One Part, and the Republic of Chile, of the Other Part*, OJ L 352, 30.12.2002, p. 3.
59. *Agreement Between the European Community and the Republic of South Africa on Trade in Wine*, OJ L 28, 30.1.2002, p. 4.
60. *Agreement Between the European Community and the United Mexican States on the Mutual Recognition and Protection of Designations for Spirit Drinks*, OJ L 152, 11.6.1997, p. 15.
61. *Working Document on International Protection of EU Geographical Indications: Objectives, Outcome and Challenges* (Directorate-General for Agriculture and Rural Development, Working Paper Ref. Ares(2012)669394, 2012).
62. *Free Trade Agreement Between the European Union and Its Member States, of the One Part, and the Republic of Korea, of the Other Part*, OJ L 127, 14.3.2011, p. 6.
63. Council of the European Union, *Comprehensive Economic and Trade Agreement Between Canada, of the One Part, and the European Union and Its Member States, of the Other Part*, 2016/0206 (NLE) (14 September 2016).
64. *Free Trademark Agreement Between the European Union and the Republic of Singapore*, OJ L 294, 14.11.2019, p. 3-755.
65. *See* Alberto Ribeiro de Almeida, *Geographical Indications Versus Trade Marks and Generic Terms: The US-China Agreement*, 51 IIC-Int'l Rev. Intell. Prop. & Competition L. 277 (2020); Weinian Hu, *Dinner for Three: EU, China and the US Around the Geographical Indications Table* (Centre for European Policy Studies 2021), https://espas.secure.europarl.europa.eu/orbis/node/1430; Danny Friedmann, *Grafting the Old and New World: Towards a Universal Trademark Register That Cancels Generic IGO Terms, in Wine Law and Policy: From National Terroir to a Global Market* 311 (Julien Chaisse et al. eds, Brill Nijhoff 2020).
66. *Council Regulation (EEC) No 2081/92 of 14 July 1992 on the protection of geographical indications and designations of origin for agricultural products and foodstuffs*, OJ L208,

found to violate the national treatment obligations under the TRIPS Agreement,[67] the EU now promotes its sui generis legal model by advocating the role and benefits of the model for third-country products.[68] Nevertheless, if transplantation in China were to fail, the EU's argument would be less convincing.

In the face of global competition, each country faces the question as to whether GIs can be better protected through the trademark system, whether using that system should be encouraged, and whether the sui generis system of GIs should be replaced by the system of trademarks. Even the EU, which has indicated a clear preference for the sui generis regime of GIs over the system of collective and certification marks,[69] cannot avoid asking those questions.[70]

Therefore, this book addresses the questions that China and other countries must face by examining the case of China's GI legislation. It first looks at the transplantation of GI laws in China in order to point out the various subcategories of GIs and systems for their protection and to highlight the EU's (France) and China's different preferences for the sui generis GI regime versus the trademark regime. Given the fact that China has encountered several challenges in adopting the European sui generis approach to GI protection, it is appropriate to determine what the challenges are, before finding a solution (i.e., making a choice between replacing the sui generis systems with the trademark system or strengthening the sui generis systems).

24.7.1992. Article 12(1) of Regulation 2081/92: 'Without prejudice to international agreements, this Regulation may apply to an agricultural product or foodstuff from a third country provided that: the third country is able to give guarantees identical or equivalent to those referred to in Article 4, the third country concerned has inspection arrangements equivalent to those laid down in Article 10, the third country concerned is prepared to provide protection equivalent to that available in the Community to corresponding agricultural products for foodstuffs coming from the Community.'

67. WTO Panel Report, *supra* n. 52.
68. William A. Kerr, *Enjoying a Good Port with a Clear Conscience: Geographic Indicators, Rent Seeking and Development*, 7 Estey Ctr. J. Int'l L. & Trade Pol'y 1 (2006).
69. Jacques Larrieu, *Indications géographiques et marques en droit français, in Indications géographiques: perspectives globales et locales* 81 (Jacques de Werra ed., Schulthess Éditions Romandes 2016).
70. European Commission, *Impact Assessment on Geographical Indications: Accompanying Document to the Proposal for a Regulation of the European Parliament and of the Council on Agricultural Product Quality Schemes* (Working Paper); European Commission, *Green Paper on Agricultural Product Quality: Product Standards, Farming Requirements and Quality Schemes*, COM(2008)641 final (15 October 2008); European Parliament, *Agricultural Product Quality Policy: What Strategy to Follow?*, 2009/2105(INI) (25 March 2010).

CHAPTER 1

Emergence of the Notion of 'Geographical Indications' in Europe

An abundant terminology has been used to denote GIs, including Appellation d'Origine Contrôlée (AOC), Indication Géographique protégeant les Produits Industriels et Artisanaux (IGPIA), Protected Designations of Origin (PDOs), Protected Geographical Indications (PGI), and Geographical Indications for Agricultural Products (one of the expressions used in Chinese GI regulations). This chapter examines the fundamental reasons behind this terminological diversity through a historical review of the development of European laws and policies for GIs, focusing on whether we can find a commonly accepted basis. The discussion begins by analysing the role of the 'terroir' idea in the creation of the French AOC and IGPIA. It then focuses on the incentives associated with the genesis of the EU's PDO and PGI. The discussion then examines a possible new EU notion for non-agricultural products. The chapter concludes by suggesting that the reinterpreted 'terroir' idea may bring coherence to the various approaches to defining and protecting GIs and pave the way for the protection of industrial products under GI law.

France is known to be the cradle of Geographical Indication (GI) protection.[1] The origin of GI laws can be traced back to French statutes designed to fight against fraudulent claims regarding the provenance of wines in the Middle Ages.[2] Over time, the French approach to GI protection has been progressively transposed to other European

1. William van Caenegem, *Registered Geographical Indications: Between Intellectual Property and Rural Policy – Part 2*, 6 J. World Intell. Prop. 861, 865 (2003).
2. Michel Menjucq & Jean-Marc Bahans, *Droit de la vigne et du vin*, 2e éd., Paris, Litec, 2010, p. 72; François-Xavier Kalinda, *La protection des indications géographiques et son intérêt pour les pays en développement*, thèse, Université de Strasbourg, 2010, p. 19.

countries and has been adopted in China.[3] During the transplantation process, each jurisdiction has invented its own terminology for GIs.

France and the EU have placed a high value on natural links, based on the strictly defined *terroir* concept, which relates the quality attributes of a product to the conditions of its place of production. For instance, in France, indications of geographical origin are traditionally divided between indications of provenance and appellations of origin. Indications of provenance have never been expressly defined, although several of them fall within the scope of the GIs delimited within the meaning of Article 22 of the TRIPS Agreement. This lack of definition reflects the low priority that has been given to this category. It shows a lack of interest in the links built on human inputs (as opposed to natural inputs) and the reputation of the product (as opposed to its quality or characteristics). At the EU level, the initial proposal for Regulation 2081/92 was directed at regulating only the use of the designations of origin (PDO), without mentioning the protected geographical indications (PGI) category, whose links with the natural conditions in a particular location are weaker. The EU-wide GI protection is not available for non-agricultural products, the specific qualities and reputation of which are usually due to human factors found in the place of origin.

The concept of *terroir* has been reinvented not only in France but also across the EU. Localized skills have been acknowledged alongside geographical features. The French legal regime has recognized the importance of human contributions by imposing strict controls on production standards (the Appellation d'Origine Contrôlée (AOC) system) and by creating in 2014 a new system for industrial products, allowing the links to be established on the basis of human factors or reputation. In the EU framework, localized production skills and traditional *savoir-faire* are seen as one of the main arguments for developing unitary GI protection for non-agricultural products.[4]

Not only does the reinvented *terroir* concept respond to the 'new frontier' of GIs, but it may also provide a doctrinal basis for the inclusion of the PGI category in the EU GI scheme. This inclusion has long been criticized for 'exploiting GIs' commercial value at the expense of geographical accuracy'.[5]

It is argued that the link to place is what sets GIs apart from trademarks.[6] Therefore, it is imperative to know what the link is and how it gives rise to the different categories of GIs in French law (§1.01) and EU law (§1.02).

---

3. Bernard Dutoit et al., *La protection des indications de provenance et des appellations d'origine en France, en Italie, en République fédérale d'Allemagne et en Suisse, in Les indications de provenance et les appellations d'origine en droit comparé, Actes du colloque de Lausanne*, Genève, Librairie Droz, 1983, p. 127.
4. The Geneva Act of the Lisbon Agreement on Appellations of Origin and Geographical Indications differentiates between appellations of origin and geographical indications. The latter requires a weaker link, including 'reputation' as an element for GI protection.
5. Irene Calboli, *In Territorio Veritas: Bringing Geographical Coherence in the Definition of Geographical Indications of Origin under TRIPS*, 6 WIPO J. 57, 60 (2014).
6. Dev Gangjee, *Introduction: Timeless Signs or Signs of the Times?, in Research Handbook on Intellectual Property and Geographical Indications* 1 (Dev Gangjee ed., Edward Elgar Publishing 2016).

§1.01 GI NOTION IN FRENCH LAW

An indication of a product's geographical origin may refer to a certain quality, characteristic, or reputation in consumers' minds. Therefore, these designations are the subjects of a protection that responds to the interests of both consumers, who desire genuine products with specific qualities and characteristics, and local producers, who might suffer damage due to unfair competition.[7]

The traditional French legal regime governing these designations focuses on the quality or characteristics of the product. A duality is maintained according to whether the product possesses an origin-related quality or attribute (i.e., indications of provenance and appellations of origin).[8]

Through the reinterpretation of the *terroir* concept, the TK (*savoir-faire*) component in *terroir* is considered an independent value to be protected. It justifies creating a new category of GIs, namely 'geographical indications for the protection of industrial and artisanal products'.[9]

[A] Traditional Duality of Indications of the Geographical Origin

The distinction between indications of provenance and appellations of origin was made in the traditional French GI regime according to the 'quality standard'.[10] The indication of provenance does not constitute a guarantee of quality or of particular characteristics; Dean Paul Roubier concluded that it is merely an indication of production area. However, the AO is something else: 'it constitutes a recall of qualities which are due essentially to the origin in a certain *terroir*'.[11]

7. Consumer protection and repression of unfair competition are among the earliest justifications for the protection of geographical indications. On the one hand, the justifications refer to the protection of fair competition for the benefit of producers, and on the other hand, to the protection of consumers. However, they are not the only reason why geographical indications should be protected.
8. Ladas pointed to a distinction between 'indication' and 'appellation'. Grammatically, 'indication' is what serves to indicate or point at something or informs. 'Appellation' means a name given to a person or thing. Therefore 'appellation' evokes the idea of the susceptibility of appropriation or the idea of a property right. *See* Stephen P. Ladas, *Patents, Trademarks, and Related Rights: National and International Protection* 1574 (Harvard University Press 1975).
9. Article 73 of the Law of 17 March 2014 (*Loi du 17 mars 2014*) has instituted a new category of geographical indications: the 'geographical indications for the protection of the industrial and artisanal products (*indications géographiques protégeant les produits industriels et artisanaux*, IGPIA)'.
10. Paul Roubier argued that the 'quality standard' refers to qualities that correspond to a given origin. Thus, the appellation of origin defines and protects the qualities of origin, opposed to both the indication of provenance, which is simply a matter of origin, and the collective mark, which is essentially a matter of quality. Paul Roubier, *Le droit de la propriété industrielle*, Tome 2, Paris, Sirey, 1954, p. 768.
11. Roubier, *supra* n. 10, at 763.

[1] Indications of Provenance: A Fruitful Source of Confusion

Indications of provenance (*indication de provenance*), along with appellations of origin, have been expressly recognized as one object of the industrial property protection provided in the Paris Convention for the Protection of Industrial Property,[12] one of the earliest international frameworks of IP protection. However, its role in France is secondary relative to that played by the AO.[13] The term 'indication of provenance' is employed in French legal texts but not frequently.[14] Moreover, no definition has ever been given in these few legal instruments and documents. It is thus not unreasonable to doubt the legal status of indications of provenance.[15]

Legal arrangements made in recent years may support this suspicion. Article L. 640-2 of the French Rural Code lists several modes of adding value to products.[16] As one of three categories of value enhancement, the 'signs of identification of the quality and the origin' (*signes d'identification de la qualité et de l'origine*) are composed of the '*label rouge*', the 'appellation of origin', the 'geographical indication', the 'traditional specialities guarantee', and the mention of 'biologic agriculture'. Indications of provenance are not mentioned in this category; meanwhile, both 'appellations of origin' and 'geographical indications' earn positions in the list of enumeration. Furthermore, after the amendment introduced by the Law of 2014 (*Loi du 17 mars 2014*), Article L. 722-1 of the French Intellectual Code provides that 'geographical indications' refer to (1) the 'appellations of origin', (2) the 'geographical indications for the protection of industrial and artisanal products', and (3) the 'designations of origin' and the 'geographical indications' protected pursuant to the law of the EU.[17] Again, no indication of provenance is mentioned.

12. Paris Convention for the Protection of Industrial Property, 20 March 1883 as revised at Stockholm on 14 July 1967, 828 U.N.T.S 305 (1972) ('Paris Convention' hereinafter). Article 1(2): 'The protection of industrial property has as its object patents, utility models, industrial designs, trademarks, service marks, trade names, indications of source or appellations of origin, and the repression of unfair competition.'
13. Hélène Gaumont-Prat, *Droit de la propriété industrielle*, 2e éd., Paris, LexisNexis, 2009, p. 249.
14. Only a few French legal texts directly address the protection of indications of provenance, mainly the former Article L. 217-1 and L. 217-6 (since 2016, Article L. 413-4 and L. 413-8) of the Consumer Code.
15. Dominique Denis, *Appellation d'origine et indication de provenance*, Paris, Dalloz, 1995, p. 114: '*L'indication de provenance n'a pas de statut juridique en France, et n'est pas définie en tant que telle.*'
16. Article L. 640-2 of the French Rural Code: '*Les produits agricoles, forestiers ou alimentaires et les produits de la mer peuvent, dans les conditions prévues par le présent titre et lorsqu'il n'y a pas de contradiction avec la réglementation communautaire, bénéficier d'un ou plusieurs modes de valorisation appartenant aux catégories suivantes: Les signes d'identification de la qualité et de l'origine : le label rouge, attestant la qualité supérieure; l'appellation d'origine, l'indication géographique et la spécialité traditionnelle garantie, attestant la qualité liée à l'origine ou à la tradition; la mention "agriculture biologique", attestant la qualité environnementale.*'
17. Article L. 722-1 of the French Intellectual Property Code: '*Pour l'application du présent chapitre, on entend par "indication géographique": a) Les appellations d'origine définies à l'article L. 115-1 du code de la consommation; b) Les indications géographiques définies à l'article L. 721-2; c) Les appellations d'origine et les indications géographiques protégées en vertu du droit de l'Union européenne.*'

Since the indication of provenance has not been expressly classified as 'the signs of identification of the quality and the origin' in Article L. 640-2 of the French Rural Code or as 'geographical indications' in Article L. 722-1 of the IP Code, its nature is in question. It is not disputed that the indication of provenance indicates places where the products are cultivated or fabricated. Unlike the AO, it is not a guarantee of quality or of particular characteristics.[18] However, if the indication of provenance merely indicates the place of origin,[19] which means that its function is geographically descriptive,[20] then why should it be included within the ambit of industrial property, where exclusive rights could be conferred?[21] After all, all the fabricants could print the name of the locality where the products are cultivated or fabricated. Those fabricants who are the first users of a geographical name do not necessarily enjoy the right to prohibit others from using it.

One response to this question is the identification of the valuable intangible (reputation) that was collectively generated around a geographically descriptive term. We commence with a review of the historical evidence. Article L. 413-4 (the former Article L. 217-1) of the French Consumer Code, which penalizes the fraudulent use of place of production (*nom d'un lieu*), codified the dispositions of the Law of 1824 (*Loi du 28 juillet 1824*). Article 1 of the Law of 1824 provided the following:

> Anyone who has, either affixed, or displayed by addition, retrenchment or by any alteration whatsoever, on manufactured objects, the name of a manufacturer other than that of its author, or the name of a manufactory other than that where the said objects were manufactured, or finally, the name of place other than that where the said objects were manufactured, shall be punished by the penalties provided for in Article L. 423 of the Penal Code, without prejudice to compensation, where appropriate.[22]

The text remained silent about whether the name of the place is associated with a reputation. However, the preparatory discussions (*travaux préparatoires*) for the Law of 1824 may provide clues.[23] When the statement of reasons (*exposé des motifs*) was discussed at the Chamber of Deputies, it was argued that 'they [the dispositions]

18. Frédéric Pollaud-Dulian, *Droit de la propriété industrielle*, Paris, Economica, 2011, p. 1119.
19. Jacques Audier, *Protection of Geographical Indications in France and Protection of French Geographical Indications in Other Countries*, Lecture presented at the Symposium on the Protection of Geographical Indications in the Worldwide Context (WIPO/GEO/EGR/97/8/Rev, 1997).
20. *Code de la consommation 2014 commenté*, 19e éd., Paris, Dalloz, p. 49: '*Elles ne constituent alors qu'en renseignement sur l'origine du produit, aucune protection ne pouvant être accordée.*'
21. The CJEU concluded in a judgment that the objective of preventing the producers of a Contracting State from using geographical indications should be regarded as falling within the sphere of the protection of industrial property. *See* Case C-3/91 *Exportur SA v. LOR SA and Confiserie du Tech SA* [1992] I-05529, para. 37.
22. Article 1, Loi du 28 juillet 1824 relative aux altérations ou suppositions de noms sur les produits fabriqués: '*Quiconque aura, soit apposé, soit fait apparaître, par addition, retranchement, ou par une altération quelconque, sur les objets fabriqués, le nom d'un fabricant autre que celui qui en est l'auteur, ou la raison commerciale d'une fabrique autre que celle où lesdits objets auront été fabriqués, ou enfin le nom d'un lieu autre que celui de la fabrication, sera puni des peines portées en l'article 423 du code pénal, sans préjudice des dommages-intérêts, s'il y a lieu.*'
23. Paul Vallé, *De la fausse indication de lieu de provenance en matière de produits vinicoles*, Paris, Arthur Rousseau, 1904, p. 84.

should be aimed at providing new guarantees to the manufacturing, for our industrial products, and aimed at increasing the reputation [of the products] in the foreign countries like in the UK territory'.[24] In the statement of reasons of the Chamber of Paris, it was argued that 'the reputation of a manufacturer, for the fabricant, is a property'.[25] With the illustration of the sheets from Louviers and Sedan,[26] the *rapporteur* Minister Lemoine des Mares stated that 'there are some manufacturing cities whose products have a reputation which we could call collective, and this [the reputation] is still property'.[27] As the manufacturer's or factory's name can possess valuable intangible assets, a place name can also acquire a reputation. The preparatory works for the Law of 1824 revealed the collective reputation dimension of place names.

More direct support for the collective reputation dimension of the indication of provenance can be found in judicial practices. A ruling of the Paris Court of Appeal has clearly distinguished an indication of provenance from a simple geographical name according to this collective reputation dimension. The court reasoned that:

> A geographical name is an indication of provenance when, in the mind of the public, it has established a link between the place of production and characteristics which are attributed to the principal raw materials obtained in a region or a country, or attributed to processes and cares of production, by which throughout ages the value is found, owing to the implementation (of production processes and cares) in practice by numerous manufactures devoted in the same geographical zone.[28]

In other words, a geographical name can be referred to as an indication of provenance when it acquires a certain reputation among the public. The term '*Brésil*' is considered an indication of provenance for Brazil's coffee because of its reputation.[29] As a negative example, the geographical location '*Mont Roucous*' is not well-known to

24. However, the protection of the indication of provenance is indirect. It relies on laws against unfair competition or misleading advertising. Therefore, the legitimate users of the indication of provenance cannot claim an exclusive right. *See* Eugène Pouillet, *Traité des marques de fabrique de la concurrence déloyale en tous genres*, 2e éd., Paris, Marchal et Billard, 1883, p. 807: '*Vous les accueillerez, nous n'en doutons pas, avec une égale sollicitude, puisqu'elles doivent avoir pour objet de donner de nouvelles garanties à la fabrication, au débit de nos produits industriels, et d'accroître par là, à l'étranger comme dans l'intérieur du royaume, la juste réputation dont ils jouissent.*'
25. *See Ibid.*, 812: '*La réputation d'un manufacturier est, pour le fabricant, une propriété à laquelle il tient justement.*'
26. In the Middle Age, Louviers had a cloth-making industry of a certain reputation. In this example of Louviers and Sedan sheets, manufacturers in these two cities engaged in preventing confusion with the cloth produced elsewhere. *See* Jean-François Belhoste, *La maison, la fabrique et la ville. L'industrie du drap fin en France (XVe-XVIIIe siècles)*, Histoire, économie et société, Vol. 13, n° 3, 1994, p. 460.
27. *See* Pouillet, *supra* n. 24, at 808: '*Il est des villes de fabrique dont les produits ont aussi une réputation qu'on peut appeler collective, et c'est encore une propriété.*'
28. C.A. Paris, 6 févr. 1986, PIBD 1986, III, p. 196: '*Il y a indication de provenance seulement lorsque, dans l'esprit du public s'est établi un lien entre le lieu de fabrication et des caractéristiques tenant à des facteurs soit géographiques, soit humains, la qualité reconnue du produit étant attachée à la matière première procurée par une région ou un pays déterminé ou encore à des procédés et soins de fabrication dont la valeur s'est trouvée au long des âges consacrée grâce à leur mise en pratique par de nombreux fabricants concentrés dans une même zone géographique.*'
29. C.A. Paris, 16 juin 1988, D. 1989, p. 282, note Jean-René Gusmao.

the general public and thus is not likely to constitute an indication of provenance with reference to a particular quality. Hence, the name '*Mont Roucous*' was assessed as being 'neutral'.[30] Based on reputation, the Court of Justice of the European Union (CJEU) intervened to justify the French instruments for protecting indications of provenance. By comparing with the AO, the court pointed out that 'a more or less considerable reputation may attach to that geographical provenance' and that the indication of provenance is protected to suppress 'the abusive exploitation of another's reputation'.[31]

Although some scholars have argued that the indication of provenance is equivalent to simple information about the place where a product has been created or prepared,[32] the evolution of the case law has led us to interpret the indication of provenance as something more than a simple reference of address.[33] An increasing number of scholars have noticed the collective reputation dimension of the indication of provenance. Professor Jacques Azéma observes that the indication of provenance involves a certain reputation for the product in the mind of customers.[34] Similarly, Professor Frédéric Pollaud-Dulian asserts that the indication of provenance informs the customer that the product has a particular geographical origin wherein local producers' efforts have resulted in creating a certain degree of reputation.[35] In the definition of 'indication of provenance' given by Professor Jérôme Passa, a certain reputation among the public is also required as an essential element.[36]

After considering the collective reputation dimension of the indication of provenance, it is helpful to consider how this collective reputation could be acquired, maintained, and handed down from one generation to another without quality control regimes like the AOC. Under the AOC system, the requirement fixed in the product specification (*cahier des charges*) must be satisfied by the producers who are demanding the usage of the appellation, and an organization approved by the government monitors the fulfilment of the requirement.[37] Without state involvement in guaranteeing the quality of the product, the reputation maintenance of the indication of provenance relies on the market: if the quality of the product declines, the punishment

30. Cass. com., 24 oct. 2000, PIBD 2000, III, p. 33.
31. Case C-3/91, *Exportur SA v. LOR SA*, *supra* n. 21, para. 11.
32. *See* Roubier, *supra* n. 10, at 810-811. Dean Roubier treats the *indication de provenance* as a reference of identification of goods in the international trade.
33. Norbert Olszak, *Appellations d'origine et indications de provenance*, Répertoire Dalloz de droit pénal et de procédure pénale, 2008 (actualité 2015), para. 11.
34. Jacques Azema & Jean-christophe Galloux, *Droit de la propriété industrielle*, 7e éd., Paris, Dalloz, 2012, p. 979. Examples are given, such as nougat from *Montélimar*, mustard from *Dijon*, and silk fabric production from *Lyon*.
35. Pollaud-Dulian, *supra* n. 18, at 1119.
36. *See* Jérôme Passa, *Droit de la propriété industrielle: Tome 1, Marques et autres signes distinctifs, dessins et modèles*, 2e éd., Paris, LGDJ, 2009, p. 787: '*Elle peut se définir comme le nom d'un lieu, plus ou moins étendu, désignant les produits qui en sont originaires lorsque ceux-ci jouissent, en raison de cette origine géographique, d'une certaine réputation du public, résultant d'une association que celui-ci opère entre cette origine et une qualité des produits.*'
37. *See* Article L. 642-1, L. 642-2, and L. 642-3 of the French Rural Code.

will be consumer defection.[38] Consumers expect the same quality level under identical commercial forms, and they deserve to get it. Local producers who fail to meet consumers' expectations will likely lose their consumers and collective reputation. On this point, the essence of the 'quality function' of trademarks seems to be applicable to that of the indication of provenance:[39] an important ingredient inheres in the consumer's belief as measured by past satisfaction and market reputation.[40] A valuable trademark would be reluctant to lower its quality because it would suffer from a capital loss on its investment in the trademark.[41] Just as trademark protection gives producers an incentive to provide products of consistent quality,[42] the indication of provenance protection provides local producers with an incentive to generate as much goodwill toward their geographical origin as possible by producing products of consistent quality.

We have revealed two dimensions of the indication of provenance: (1) the communicative dimension, wherein the indication of provenance deserves protection to operate as an indicator of geographical source; and (2) the collective reputation dimension, wherein the indication of provenance deserves protection because it involves a certain reputation for the product in consumers' minds and this reputation results from a collective effort to deliver quality products to meet consumers' expectations. Trademarks serve two similar functions: (1) an origin function, in which marks deserve protection because they indicate the trade source; and (2) a quality or guarantee function, in which marks deserve protection because they symbolize quality and guarantee that the goods or services measure up to expectations.[43] Discussions of proper legal protection often take these functions as a starting point.[44] Their similar functions imply that the justifications for their protection are also similar. The question arises: why not include the indication of provenance within the ambit of trademarks in the first place, considering the apparent similarities in their functions?

In fact, indications of provenance differ from trademarks in two significant respects. First, there is a collective interest in their accessibility to all legitimate producers in the same area. Second, geographical names are by nature geographically

38. *See* Passa, *supra* n. 36, at 790: '*La garantie d'une qualité constante existe surtout dans l'esprit du public, qui a tendance à déduire de la constance de la provenance géographique une permanence de la qualité. Mais si la qualité des produits de l'un des producteurs de la zone diminue, la sanction sera essentiellement de nature économique, se traduisant par une perte de clientèle.*'
39. *See* James M. Treece, *Trademark Licensing and Vertical Restraints in Franchising Arrangements*, 116 U. Pa. L. Rev. 435, 438 (1967): 'It seems likely that sometimes trademark will be associated with a general reputation for quality and sometimes with specific production process assumed to have a particular relation to quality.'
40. J. Thomas McCarthy, *McCarthy on Trademarks and Unfair Competition* § 3:11 (5th ed. Thomson West 2021 update).
41. William M. Landes & Richard A. Posner, *Trademark Law: An Economic Perspective*, 30 J.L. & Econ. 265 (1987).
42. *See* McCarthy, *supra* n. 40, § 3:11: 'That is, the customer assumes that products and services sold under the same trademark will be of an equal nature and quality regardless of the actual physical location of producer of the goods or of the persons performing the services.'
43. William R. Cornish, *Intellectual Property: Patents, Copyright, Trade Marks and Allied Rights* 644 (Sweet & Maxwell 8th ed. 2013): 'These functions of trademark may be distinguished: (1) origin function; (2) quality or guarantee function; (3) investment or advertising function.'
44. *Ibid.*, 643.

descriptive and usually do not comply with the general rules of the validity of trademarks: they must be vacant, distinctive (not descriptive), and not deceptive.[45] The early trademark system rooted in private law could not solve the collective interest puzzle.[46] The exclusive use of a geographical name by a single producer would disturb other producers in the same area. The common denomination of a product must be left accessible to all producers as a way to designate their products. Moreover, the early trademark system in France prohibited the registration of a locality name by itself.[47] A geographical name could serve as a trademark only if it were presented in a distinct, special form. It was a particular appearance that was claimed as a trademark, not the name of a locality.[48] Finally, the concept of the quality function of trademarks arose only in the 1930s in some countries.[49] Prior to that, the primary and proper function of a trademark was considered to 'identify the origin or ownership of the goods to which it is affixed'.[50] Thus, how could the collective reputation dimension of the indication of provenance seek a satisfactory solution in the early trademark system, where the origin function was the primary justification for legal protection?[51]

The indication of provenance designates the place where a product is obtained or produced. This communicative dimension is not in dispute.[52] However, its collective

45. Nicolas Bouche, *Intellectual Property Law in France* 189 (Kluwer Law International 2nd ed. 2014).
46. *See* Joanna Schmidt-Szalewski & Jean-Luc Pierre, *Droit de la propriété industrielle*, 4e éd., Paris, 2007, p. 291: '*Le régime spécifique de ces marques (marques collectives) fut introduit par la loi du 31 décembre 1964.*'
47. *See* Alessandro Stanziani, *Wine Reputation and Quality Controls: The Origin of the AOCs in 19th Century France*, 18 Eur. J.L. & Econ. 149, 157 (2004).
48. Pouillet, *supra* n. 24, at 76: '*Un nom de ville, ou plus généralement un nom de localité, peut, comme un nom patronymique, servir de marque de fabrique; toutefois, ici encore, c'est à la condition que le nom se présentera sous une forme distincte, spéciale, toujours la même: c'est cette physionomie particulière qui fait la marque et non pas le nom pris isolément et pour lui-même.*'
49. It was introduced in France more recently. *See* McCarthy, *supra* n. 40, § 3:11: 'Starting in the 1930s a new theory of trademarks arose. This new approach abandoned sole reliance on a physical concept of the source theory in favor of the view that a trademark does not necessarily indicate physical source, but can also indicate the source of quality standards.'
50. Frank I. Schechter, *Rational Basis of Trademark Protection*, 40 Harv. L. Rev. 813 (1926); Yann Basire, *Les fonctions de la marque: essai sur la cohérence du régime juridique d'un signe distinctif*, Paris, LexisNexis, 2015.
51. Trademark traditionally has been viewed as functioning to identify the origin or source of the goods to which it is affixed. However, in more recent times, trademarks have been recognized as serving a second function that assures the purchaser a certain degree of uniformity or quality in the products to which they are attached. *See* Elmer William Hanak III, *The Quality Assurance Function of Trademarks*, 43 Fordham L. Rev. 363 (1974).
52. The WIPO defines indications of provenance as 'any name, designation, sign or other indication which refers to a given country or to a place located therein, which has the effect of conveying the notion that the goods bearing the indication originate in that country or place'. *See* WIPO, *Introduction to Intellectual Property: Theory and Practice*, paras 18, 145 (Kluwer Law International 1997); WIPO, *Comité permanent du droit des marques, des dessins et models industriels et des indications géographiques*, WIPO Publication SCT/9/4 (1 October 2002). The expression '*indication de provenance*' is used in Article 1.2 and Article 1.0 of the Paris Convention and throughout the Madrid Agreement for the Repression of False or Deceptive Indications of Source on Goods. The *indication de provenance* is defined in neither of these two treaties. However, Article 1 of the Madrid Agreement sheds light on the meaning of this term: 'All goods bearing a false or deceptive indication by which one of the countries to which this Agreement applies, or

reputation dimension remains controversial. While legal practitioners are increasingly defining the indication of provenance with an additional condition that it must possess a collective reputation dimension, a significant proportion of them asserts that 'it merely indicates the place of origin'.[53] As a 'middle-ground' approach, Professor Norbert Olszak splits indications of provenance into two groups: simple indications and indications with a qualitative dimension.[54] Indeed, without a legal definition in French law, 'the terminology used in this area itself risks being a fruitful source of confusion'.[55] Given that the collective reputation dimension serves to justify the indication of provenance as an object of IP protection, we make a distinction between the indication of provenance and a simple geographically descriptive term: geographical names can be referred to as the indication of provenance only if they possess both a communicative dimension and collective reputation dimension. In this sense, the indication of provenance can be defined as follows:

> The name of a place, large or small, designates the products are originated from that place when they enjoy, because of this geographical origin, a certain reputation within the public, resulting from an association between this origin and quality of products.[56]

This definition reminds us of the GI notion, which shares certain elements. Without tackling the complex problem of distinguishing between the two notions, we could *at least* say that some indications of provenance belong to the family of GIs when they have a certain degree of reputation. Traditionally, however, France has paid less attention to reputation-based indications and more attention to the objective link between a product and its place of origin. The discussion below will shed light on the notion based on the objective link.

---

a place situated therein, is directly or indirectly indicated as being the country or place of origin shall be seized on importation into any of the said countries.'

53. *See* Laure Marino, *Droit de la propriété industrielle*, 8e éd., Paris, Mémentos, 2013, p. 126: '*Il s'agit simplement d'indiquer le lieu où le produit a été fabriqué ou cultivé*'; WIPO, *Standing Committee on the Law of Trademarks, Industrial Designs and Geographical Indications*, WIPO Publication SCT/8/4 (2 April 2002) p. 3: 'Consequently an indication of source can be defined as an indication referring to a country, or to a place in that country, as being the country or place of origin of a product.'
54. *See* Olszak, *supra* n. 33, para. 11: '*Il y aurait donc deux catégories d'indications de provenance: les indications simples, qui se bornent à préciser l'origine douanière ou le lieu d'établissement du producteur, et les indications qualifiantes, qui comportent une dimension qualitative.*'
55. *See* Case C-312/98 *Schutzverband gegen Unwesen in der Wirtschaft eV v. Warsteiner Brauerei Haus Cramer GmbH &Co. KG* [2000] ECR I-09187, para. 2 (Opinion of Advocate General). In this case, the Federal Court of Justice, Germany, asks the Court whether Regulation 2081/92 precludes applying a national provision that prohibits the misleading use of a simple geographical indication of source. In Germany, there is a legal distinction between simple geographical indications of source and a geographical indication of source that enjoys a particular reputation. Correspondingly, the scope of protection for these two categories of indications of source differs from each other.
56. Passa, *supra* n. 36, at 787.

[2] Appellations of Origin: Origin Alone Does Not Guarantee Quality

Article L. 431-1 (the former Article L. 115-1) of the French Consumer Code defines the 'appellation of origin (AO)' as 'the name of a country, of a region or of a locality serving to designate a product which originates from there and the quality or character of which is due to the geographical location, comprising natural and human factors'.[57] This definition reflects the *terroir* concept that originated in France: the existence of a link between a product and its place of origin. Nevertheless, the link between product and *terroir* (place) alone does not explain the creation of the AO. Before the emergence of the AO in France, such links were systematically studied and documented in China.[58] However, the early Chinese studies did not produce a similar legal notion.[59] The question then arises as to how the *terroir* idea gradually generated the notion of the AO in France. A historical review may provide some clues.

In the late nineteenth century, French wine-producing regions confronted the challenges known as 'the wine crisis' (*crise du vin*),[60] the responses to which resulted in a systematic reorganization of the wine industry and the regulations governing it. Originating in the United States, phylloxera was inadvertently imported into France in the 1860s.[61] While many French vineyards were destroyed as a result of the phylloxera invasion, the demand for wine did not slump. The supply–demand imbalance caused ideal conditions for fraud. Foreign producers and vineyards reconstructed in the south of France usurped prestigious appellations to sell products of inferior quality.[62]

Amid this fraud via counterfeit goods (in which producers in other regions used a prestigious appellation fraudulently), loss in quality (relative to the authentic product) was not uncommon.[63] The supply shortage encouraged French producers to adopt new techniques that provoked an important redistribution of the properties, to the benefit of former tradesmen.[64] In terms of the winemaking process, adulteration

57. Article L. 431-1 of the French Consumer Code: '*Constitue une appellation d'origine la dénomination d'un pays, d'une région ou d'une localité servant à désigner un produit qui en est originaire et dont la qualité ou les caractères sont dus au milieu géographique, comprenant des facteurs naturels et des facteurs humains.*'
58. For example, dating back to 1505, the term '*Daodi* medical materials' has been formally put into use in a Chinese medical book (Collected Essentials of Species of Medical Materials). In this book, many records of medical materials are accompanied by a description of the place of origin, and some records are especially supplemented with the '*Daodi*' description to indicate that medical materials originating in a particular location are of higher quality. *See* Liu Wentai, BENCAO PINHUI JINGYAO [COLLECTED ESSENTIALS OF SPECIES OF MEDICAL MATERIALS] (Beijing Science and Technology Press, 2019).
59. The case of China is an example where a perception of a close link will not automatically transform itself into the concept of *appellation d'origine.*
60. Philip Whalen, '*Insofar as the Ruby Wine Seduces Them*': *Cultural Strategies for Selling Wine in Inter-war Burgundy*, 18 Contemp. Eur. Hist. 67, 68 (2009).
61. Michael G. Mullins et al., *Biology of the Grapevine* 183 (Cambridge University Press 1992).
62. *See* Hugh Johnson & Claude Dovaz, *Une histoire mondiale du vin: de l'Antiquité à nos jours*, Paris, Hachette literatures, 2009.
63. Pascale Tréfigny, *Les principe du droit, brève histoires juridique*, Lamy droit des affaires, n° 68, 2004, p. 17.
64. *See* Stanziani, *supra* n. 47, at 164.

(including the addition of water, sugar, and artificial colouring) was widespread.[65] In a similar vein, the adulteration of raw materials (grapes) was another way wine producers faced with phylloxera dealt with the production deficiency relative to consumption.[66] As senator A. Mathey affirmed, 'since the invasion of the phylloxera which has largely decreased the production of wine in France, a lucrative industry has been established, which consists of producing wines without the intervention of vine, replacing the juice of fresh grape by water, dry grapes, sugars, alcohol and very often colorants'.[67] The final characteristics of the wine could reflect completely different technical solutions with no guarantee of quality. The widespread fraudulent misrepresentation of origin and compromised quality led to government interventions.[68]

Several attempts were made to address practices that affected wine quality. The Law of 1889 set out that 'no one will be able to deliver, sell or put on sale under the denomination of wine, a product other than this product made from the fermentation of fresh grapes'.[69] Several fraudulent practices were targeted, such as the watering of wine and choosing dry grapes as raw materials. The Law of 1905 was issued to combat fraud in the sale of goods and falsification of products; this law made it possible to suppress the fraud and deceptive practices regarding the origin of the goods.[70] Article 1 stated that:

> Anyone who has misled or attempted to mislead a contracting party as to nature, substantial qualities, composition and content of the useful features of any good, or mislead with regard to their variety or origin, where the false designation of variety or origin was considered the main cause for the sale, is liable to imprisonment for a term of three months to one year and a fine of one hundred to five thousand francs, or only one of these two penalties.[71]

---

65. Alfred Bedel, *Traité complet de manipulation des vins*, Paris, Garniers frères, 1887.
66. Henry Sempé, *Régime économique du vin*, thèse, Université de Bordeaux, 1898, p. 96.
67. Archives Nationales, F12 6873, Sénat, n° 400, séance du 22 juin1888: '*Depuis que l'invasion du phylloxéra (...) a diminué dans une large mesure la production de vin en France, il s'est établi une industrie très lucrative, qui consiste à fabriquer du vin sans l'intervention de la vigne, en remplaçant le jus du raisin frais par de l'eau, des raisins secs, du sucre, de l'alcool et trop souvent des colorants.*' *See also* Alessandro Stanziani, *La falsification du vin en France, 1880-1905: un cas de fraude agro-alimentaire*, Revue d'histoire moderne et contemporaine, 2003, p. 172.
68. A certain amount of less honest producers or merchants usurped the prestigious appellations like '*Bordeaux*' or '*Bourgogne*'. The task before the government was to address origin fraud, ensure quality and repress overproduction. *See* Gordon Wright, *The Winegrowers of France and the Government since 1875 by Charles K. Warner*, 33 J. Mod. Hist. 210 (1961); Jean-François Gautier, *Le droit vitivinicole*, Revue de droit rural, n° 212, 1993, p. 175.
69. Loi du 14 août 1889 sur les vins, J.O. du 15 août 1889, p. 4001: '*Nul ne pourra expédier, vendre ou mettre en vente, sous la dénomination de vin, un produit autre que celui de la fermentation des raisins frais.*'
70. Loi du 1er août 1905 sur la répression des fraudes dans la vente des marchandises et des falsifications des denrées alimentaires et des produits agricoles, J.O. du 5 août 1905, p. 4813. This law has been in force until the promulgation of the French Consumer Code, but its dispositions have been conserved in the former Article L. 213-1 (since 2016, Article L. 441-1) of the French Consumer Code.
71. Article 1, Loi du 1er août 1905: '*Quiconque aura trompé ou tenté de tromper le contractant : soit sur la nature, les qualité substantielles, la composition er la teneur en principes utiles de toutes marchandises; soit sur leur espèce ou leur origine lorsque, d'après la convention ou les usages, la désignation de l' espèce or de l'origine faussement attribuées aux marchandises, devra être considérées comme la cause principale de la vente ... Sera puni de l'emprisonnement pendant*

The Law of 1905 identified truthful information on 'origin' as one method of ensuring the authenticity of products. However, one key issue left unresolved by the Law of 1905 was which criteria should be used to delimit 'origin'.

This defect had been addressed by the Law of 1908, which established that administration regulations could define the boundaries of 'origin' entitled to the use of an appellation of provenance 'on the basis of constant local usages'.[72] In the implementation of the Law of 1908, a number of decrees were adopted between 1908 and 1911.[73] These decrees delimited regions of production for appellations, such as '*Champagne*',[74] '*Cognac*', '*eau-de-vie de Cognac*',[75] and '*Armagnac*'.[76] Some decisions on delimitation were readily accepted,[77] but others provoked conflicts. According to the Decree of 1908, winemakers from Aube were deprived of the right to sell their wines under the name of *Champagne*, whereas their neighbours in Marne were recognized as having this right.[78] This contradiction led to furious protests and demonstrations.[79] In fact, it was the nature of the land and the quality of the wine that resulted in the exclusion of Aube from the '*Champagne*' region.[80] As the conflict between Marne and Aube had become severe, the Council of State intervened to deal with this controversy. The proposed distinction between 'High' and 'Low' Champagne

trois mois au moins, un an au plus, et d'une amende de cent francs au moine, de cinq mille francs au plus, ou de l'une de ces deux peines seulement.'

72. Loi modifiant l'article 11 de la loi du 1er août 1905 sur la sur la répression des fraudes dans la vente des marchandises et des falsifications des denrées alimentaires et des produits agricoles et complétant cette loi par un article additionnel, J.O. du 11 août 1908, p. 5637: '*La dénomination des régions pouvant prétendre exclusivement aux appellations de provenance des produits. Cette délimitation sera faite en prenant pour base les usages locaux constants.*'
73. Eugène Pouillet, *Traité des marques de fabrique et de la concurrence déloyale en tous genres (6e éd. entièrement refondue et mise au courant de la législation, de la doctrine et de la jurisprudence)*, 6e éd., Paris, Marchal et Godde, 1912, p. 582.
74. Décret du 17 décembre 1908 délimitant les territoires vinicoles de la 'Champagne', J.O. du 4 janv. 1909.
75. Décret du 1er mai 1909 portant règlement d'administration publique pour la délimitation de la région ayant pour ses eaux-de-vie un droit exclusif à la dénomination 'Cognac', J.O. du 3 mai 1909.
76. Décret du 25 mai 1909, J.O. du 26 mai 1909.
77. For example, in regions of Cognac, Banyuls, and Armagnac, the delimitation had been accepted without much difficulty.
78. Giulia Meloni & Johan Swinnen, *Trade and Terroir: The Political Economy of the World's First Geographical Indications*, 81 Food Pol'y 1, 13 (2018).
79. Since the Decree of 1908, the journals of the *Aube* were filled with appeals inviting the winemakers to participate in protestations and demonstrations. It is worth mentioning that claims of protestors had been made mainly from two aspects: (1) For the aspect of origin, the *Aube* was always one part of *Champagne* province, and there was a history of production there; (2) For the aspect of quality, wines produced in the *Aube* shared with those produced in the *Marne* the same production process, the same taste and the same bouquet. While the first aspect could be covered in the scope of constant local usages provided by the Law of 1908, the second aspect seems to extend beyond it: it contained a direct reference to particular qualities or characteristics. *See* Étienne Clémentel, *Un drame économique, les délimitations, le passé, l'avenir*, Paris, Pierre Lafitte & Cie, 1914, p. 160: '*Notre arrondissement a toujours fait partie de la province de Champagne: de quel droit voudrait-on empêcher ses vignerons de vendre leurs vins pour la fabrication du Champagne? … Nos vins, ajoutaient les Aubois, ressemblent d'une façon extraordinaire à ceux du département de la Marne; ils ont même saveur, même bouquet et se champagnisent d'une manière parfaite.*'
80. Pouillet, *supra* n. 73, at 585.

(*Haute et Basse Champagne*) was considered unacceptable.[81] Finally, the Decree of 1911 designated a region, including a large part of Aube, referred to as 'Champagne Second Zone' (*Champagne deuxième zone*), which was 'entirely distinct from the region "*Champagne*" delimited by the Decree of 1908'.[82] This solution fully reflects the doctrine of quality control under the framework of the Law of 1905:[83] ensuring the authenticity of the product by simply delimiting its 'origin'. Shortly afterwards, however, this doctrine proved insufficient to guarantee quality.

The delimitation of regions under the Law of 1905 did not satisfy the wine producers and led to furious protests and demonstrations.[84] As a response to the law's shortcomings, the Law of 1919 concerning the protection of *appellations d'origine* was enacted,[85] which stipulated that 'any person alleging that an appellation of origin is applied in a prejudicial manner ... could bring a lawsuit to prohibit the usage of this appellation'.[86] The Law of 1919 started a new era where *AO* was confirmed by the judicial process. Producers had a free choice of using an *AO* for their products; when a conflict emerged on this usage, the courts could intervene to regulate the use of names,[87] according to 'the origin of the product or local, loyal and constant usages'.[88]

The geographical origin or 'local, loyal and constant usages' thus constitutes the criterion of right to the appellation. The theory of '*cumulation*' emerged as a way to interpret this criterion: the right to an appellation demanded the fulfilment of the dual condition of being obtained in the geographical origin and being in accordance with 'local, loyal and constant usages'.[89] In a judgment delivered by the Court of Saint-Affrique on 21 December 1921, related to the appellation '*Roquefort*', the judge confirmed that 'for acquiring an appellation, it is not only necessary that the cheese should be produced in Roquefort, with milk from this community, but also the cheese should be refined exclusively in natural stores, subjected to cold and humid air, coming from fractures of the mountain of Combalou in Roquefort'.[90] In another judgment on 27

81. *Ibid.*
82. Décret du 7 juin 1911 délimitant les territoires de la 'Champagne deuxième zone', Propriété industrielle : organe mensuel du bureau international de l'union pour la protection de la propriété industrielle, 31 mai 1912, p. 63.
83. The Law of 1908 could be considered under the framework of the Law of 1909. The Law of 1908 aimed to modify Article 11 of the Law of 1905 and complete it with an additional article. *See* Loi du 5 août 1908, J.O. du 11 août 1908, p. 5637.
84. There were many protests and demonstrations on the delimitation of the region by the administration, particularly regarding the delimitation of the appellation *Champagne* and the delimitation of Appellation *Bordeaux.*
85. Loi du 6 mai 1919 relative à la protection des appellations d'origine, J.O. du 8 mai 1919, p. 4726.
86. Article 1, Loi du 6 mai 1919: '*toute personnes qui prétendra qu'une appellation d'origine est appliquée à son préjudice direct ou indirect et contre son droit à un produit naturel ou fabriqué et contrairement à l'origine de ce produit, ou à des usages locaux, loyaux et constants, aura une action en justice pour faire interdire l'usage de cette appellation*'.
87. Denis, *supra* n. 15, at 69.
88. Article 1 of the Law of 1919.
89. P. Max Bernard, *Le régime des vins à appellation d'origine*, thèse, Université de Montpellier, 1932, p. 16.
90. *Gazette du Palais*, 2e partie, 1921, p. 81: '*Il faut, pour que cette appellation soit acquise, non seulement que le fromage soit fabriqué à Roquefort, avec du lait provenance de cette commune, mais aussi qu'il s'agisse de lait de brebis et que le fromage ait été affiné exclusivement dans des*

July 1923, the Court of Tonnerre affirmed that 'the origin of wine and its appellation were determined by the climate, the grape growing and winemaking process, the mode of plantation, the exposure, and above all the vine as well as nature of soil'.[91] While some believed that this established direct quality control over production practices, the decision rendered by the Court of Cassation in 1925 dashed their hopes by putting an immediate stop to attempts by the trial court to make 'local, loyal and constant usages' a condition of confirming geographical origin.[92]

Professor Frédéric Pollaud-Duliar asserted that this system was based above all on a purely geographic delimitation, tempered by taking account of usages that exceeded the limits of an administrative boundary, but it was not founded on considerations of product quality or characteristic.[93] The Law of 1919 continued to rely on origin as the touchstone for prohibiting fraud. However, ensuring truthful origin labelling ensures quality for only a handful of natural products, such as mineral water or particular varieties of clay.[94] With scrupulous respect for the rules established by the Law of 1919, winemakers were able to use an appellation signifying a high-quality wine for inferior-quality, high-yield wines and to grow vines in unsuitable conditions.[95] The judicial process was not designed to eliminate such practices, and the problem of compromised quality remained unaddressed.[96] Moreover, since judges were not competent to specify other production criteria for an appellation, all kinds of areas could be, and were, declared to be appellations. The outcome was a significantly larger number of appellations of origin throughout the wine industry.[97]

Before the establishment of the AOC system, specific provisions moved closer to the ideal of direct quality control by inserting requirements governing production techniques and fabrication conditions. The Law of 1925,[98] aiming to guarantee the AO of cheese from Roquefort, prohibited use of the appellation of 'Roquefort' unless the cheese had 'been prepared and produced exclusively with the sheep's milk' and 'in

caves naturelles, parcourues par des courants d'air froids et humides, provenant des fissures ou fleurines de la montagne du Combalou, à Roquefort.'

91. *Gazette du Palais*, I, 1923, p. 685: '... *attendu que l'origine d'un vin, et par la suite appellation, sont déterminées par le climat, les procédés de culture et de vinification, le mode de plantation, l'exposition, mais surtout le cépage et la nature du sol*'.
92. *Gazette du Palais, 2e partie*, 1925, p. 245. At first instance, the addition of a criterion could be accepted, like the grade varieties or winemaking techniques, but before courts of appeal, the theory of '*cumulation*' was often not accepted. *See* Roubier, *supra* n. 10, at 310-314; Olszak, *supra* n. 33, para. 27.
93. Pollaud-Dulian, *supra* n. 18, at 1137.
94. *See* Roubier, *supra* n. 10, at 785.
95. Joseph Capus, *L'évolution de la législation sur les appellations d'origine : Genèse des appellations contrôlées*, Paris, Louis larmat, 1947.
96. *See* Olszak, *supra* n. 33, para. 26: '*Ces délimitations judiciaires sont donc impuissantes à enrayer les pratiques de certains viticulteurs stimulés par l'euphorie du début des "années folles": pour répondre à la forte demande, ils plantent des cépages hybrides à gros rendement et réclament malgré cela le bénéfice de l'appellation d'origine.*'
97. Sabrina Lucatelli, *Appellation of Origin and Geographical Indications in OECD Member Countries: Economic and Legal Implications* 8 (Report by OECD, Directorate for Food, Agriculture & Fisheries 2000).
98. Loi ayant pour but de garantir l'appellation d'origine du fromage de Roquefort, J.O. du 30 juill. 1925, p. 7190.

conformity with local, loyal, and constant usages in respect of both the place of ripening and the method used'.[99] Despite the attempt at quality control, no minimum standards were established by the Law of 1925; these were to be determined by the judicial system on the basis of 'local, loyal, and constant usages'.[100]

In the field of wine, against the background of massive overproduction caused by the plantation of hybrid vines, there was a pressing need to incorporate the production conditions for guaranteeing the quality of the product. The Law of 1927 declared that the right of a regional or local appellation should not be conferred to any wine if 'it did not come from the vine and a production area established by local, loyal, and constant usages'.[101] It provided that wine coming from hybrids did not have the right to an appellation.[102] It further addressed the problem of the method of fabrication. Article 17 of the Law of 1927 was precise on this point: 'the appellation of origin (*Champagne*) could only apply to wines that are made sparkling by fermentation in the bottle'.[103] During the discussions on the Law of 1927, Roux (the director of the Service of Fraud Repression) stated that there was great danger facing the '*Champagne*' wines due to the absence of regulations on the methods used to make sparkling wine. Two methods were available, but only the classic method could guarantee quality.[104] Cumulatively, the requirements in the Law of 1925, as well as the Law of 1927, were based on a demand for control over production practices. They reflect a gradual acknowledgement

---

99. Article 1, Loi du 26 juillet 1925: '*Il est interdit de fabriquer, exposer, transporter, mettre en vente ou vendre, détenir, importer, exporter, sous le nom de roquefort, avec ou sans addition nominale ou qualificative, un fromage autre que celui qui aura été: a) Préparé et fabriqué exclusivement avec du lait de brebis; b) Fabriqué et affiné conformément aux usages locaux, loyaux et constants, en ce qui concerne tant le lieu de cet affinage que la méthode employée.*'
100. Whereas under the AOC system, detailed minimum standards for the benefit of the appellation of origin '*Roquefort*' were specified in the '*cahier des charges*'. For example, as for the mode of refining cheeses, the methods have been documented as follows: '*Le fromage est affiné et maturé pendant une période minimale de quatre-vingt-dix jours à compter de son jour de fabrication. Au cours de cette période, il est procédé à un affinage, suivi d'une maturation à température dirigée. L'affinage est réalisé dans les caves situées dans la zone des éboulis de la montagne du Combalou (commune de Roquefort-sur-Soulzon), délimitée par le jugement du tribunal de grande instance de Millau du 12 juillet 1961, parcourues naturellement par les courants d'air frais et humide provenant des failles calcaires, dites "fleurines" de cette montagne.*' *See* Décret du 22 janvier relatif à l'appellation d'origine contrôlée 'Roquefort', J.O. du 25 Janv. 2001, p. 1284.
101. Article 3 of the Law of 1927: '... *aucun vin n'a droit à une appellation régional ou locale s'il ne provient de cépages et d'une aire de production consacrée par des usages locaux, loyaux et constants*'. Loi tendant à compléter la loi du 6 mai 1919 relative à la protection des appellation d'origine, J.O. du 27 juill. 1927, p. 7762.
102. Article 3 of the Law of 1927: '*Les vins provenant des hybrides producteurs directs n'ont, en aucun cas, droit à une appellation d'origine.*'
103. Article 17 of the Law of 1927: '... *l'appellation d'origine Champagne n'est applicable qu'aux vins rendus mousseux par fermentation en bouteilles*'.
104. *See Séance du 12 juillet 1927*, J.O. du 13 juill. 1927, p. 932: '*Il y aurait de très graves dangers pour la réputation des vins de Champagne à ne pas préciser, de façon assez étroite, la méthode employée pour les rendre mousseux ... dans la vielle méthode classique, méthode Champenoise, on peut tout au plus gagner plus d'un degré d'alcool, ce pourquoi il faudrait ajouter plus de vingt et quelques grammes de sucre, la bouteille ne manquerait pas de sauter. La vieille méthode Champenoise offre des garanties de qualité tout à fait précieuses et auxquelles il ne faut pas toucher.*'

of the inefficiency of quality control endeavours within a framework wherein delimiting 'origin' was the only way to ensure the authenticity of the product.

The main flaw of the early legislation was that it concerned only provenance, paying no attention to the human or technical dimension.[105] With a view to guaranteeing both origin and quality, Joseph Capus put forward a draft law (*proposition de loi*) based on the rationale that it was necessary not only to make it easier for consumers to distinguish appellations of origin but also to establish production discipline, a control, and a guarantee of quality for the appellations.[106] This is the starting point of the AOC regime.[107]

Instituted on 30 July 1935, the AOC regime was initially designed to determine the conditions for producing a product, including the area of production, the grape variety, the yield per hectare, the minimum degree of alcohol, the culture process, and the method of vinification or distillation.[108] At present, the products that qualify under this regime must not only satisfy the conditions of the *AO* fixed by Article L. 431-1 of the French Consumer Code[109] but also have a duly established reputation. The production must be subjected to procedures involving an entitlement of operators, the control of production conditions, and the control of products. The scope of products includes agricultural, forestry, and food products, as well as those drawn from the sea, both processed and non-processed.[110] Industrial products are not covered within the ambit of the AOC.[111] However, it is possible to protect names designating industrial products as a simple *AO* according to Article L. 431-1 of the Consumer Code, or as an *Indication Géographique protégeant les Produits Industriels et Artisanaux* (IGPIA) under the Law of 2014.[112] The Law of 1935 also established the National Committee of Appellations of Origin of Wines or Spirits (*Comité national des appellations d'origine*

105. Amy B. Trubek, *The Taste of Place: A Cultural Journey into Terroir* 27 (University of California Press 2008).
106. Capus, *supra* n. 95.
107. Décret-loi du 30 juillet 1935 relatif à la défense du marché du vin et au régime économique de l'alcool, J.O. du 31 juill. 1935, p. 8314.
108. Article 21, Décret-loi du 30 juillet 1935: '... *Le comité national déterminera, après avis des syndicat intéressés les conditions de production auxquelles devra satisfaire le vin ou l'eau-de-vie de chacune de ces appellations contrôlées. Ces condition sont relatives à l'aire de production, aux cépages, au rendement à l'hectare, au degré alcoolique minimum du vin* ...'.
109. It was not until 1966 that French legislators had defined the notion of appellations of origin.
110. Article L. 641-5 of the French Rural Code: '*Peuvent bénéficier d'une appellation d'origine contrôlée les produits agricoles, forestiers ou alimentaires et les produits de la mer, bruts ou transformés, qui remplissent les conditions fixées par les dispositions de l'article L. 115-1 du code de la consommation, possèdent une notoriété dûment établie et dont la production est soumise à des procédures comportant une habilitation des opérateurs, un contrôle des conditions de production et un contrôle des produits.*'
111. The Law of 1966 created an administrative recognition system of simple appellations of origin available for industrial products and agricultural products. However, since the Law of 1990 decided that the agricultural or food products could exclusively be recognized as the *appellation d'origine contrôlée,* almost only industrial products could be identified as simple appellations of origin. *See* Loi n° 66-482 du 6 juillet 1966 modifiant et complétant la loi du 6 mai 1919 relative à la protection des Appellations d'Origine, J.O. du 7 juill. 1966, p. 5781; Loi n° 90-558 du 2 juillet 1990 relative aux appellations d'origine contrôlées des produits agricoles ou alimentaires, bruts ou transformés, J.O. du 6 juill. 1990, p. 7912.
112. Loi n° 2014-344 du 17 mars 2014 relative à la consommation, J.O. du 18 mars 2014, p. 5400.

des vins ou eaux-de-vie, CNAO).[113] In 1947, the CNAO became the National Institute of Appellations of Origin (*Institut national des appellations d'origine*, INAO),[114] then the National Institute of Origin and Quality (*Institut national de l'origine et de la qualité*) in 2006, which continues to be responsible for the recognition of AOC and the monitoring of product specifications (*cahier des charges*).[115]

A historical review of the establishment of the French AO/AOC regime allows us to appreciate that the notion of appellations of origin is not based solely on the link between products and the physical conditions of climate and soil. The importance of collectively generated and intergenerational *savoir-faire* has been gradually acknowledged, and direct quality control over production practices has ensued. With the gradual acknowledgement of human factors, the link between product and *terroir* has been reconstructed, enabling us to extend GI protections to industrial and artisanal products. This aspect will be discussed in the paragraphs below.

[B] Making the Most out of Traditional Savoir-Faire: GIs for the Protection of Industrial and Artisanal Products

Article 73 of the Law of 2014 (*Loi du 17 mars 2014*) has instituted a new category of GIs, 'geographical indications for the protection of industrial and artisanal products (IG-PIA)'.[116] The necessity of this creation is doubtful since it seems that the system of appellations of origin (AO) already provides protection for industrial and artisanal products if their quality or character is due to the geographical location, comprising natural and human factors.

On this issue, through a reinterpretation of the *terroir* concept, we argue that the TK component in *terroir* paves the way for protecting industrial and artisanal products under the regime of GIs. In return, the IGPIA regime keeps traditional and precious *savoir-faire* alive.

[1] A Reinterpretation of the Terroir Concept: Making Space for Non-agricultural GIs

The term *terroir* originates etymologically from the Latin word *territorium* ('territory') and *terra* ('the land').[117] It was used primarily in a technical sense during the

113. Décret-loi du 30 juillet 1935 relatif à la défense du marché du vin et au régime économique de l'alcool, J.O. du 31 juill. 1935, p. 8314.
114. Décret du 16 juillet 1947 fixant la composition du comité national des appellations d'origine des vins et eaux-de-vie, J.O. du 19 juill. 1947, p. 6948.
115. The INAO is a public administrative institution under the Ministry of Agriculture, Food, and Forest. *See* Ordonnance n° 2006-1547 du 7 décembre 2006 relative à la valorisation des produits agricoles, forestiers ou alimentaires et des produits de la mer, J.O. du 8 déc. 2006, p. 18607.
116. Loi n° 2014-344 du 17 mars 2014 relative à la consommation, J.O. du 18 mars 2014, p. 5400.
117. *Le Grand dictionnaire François-latin*, Paris, J. Cottereau, 1609, p. 904; Auguste Brachet, *Dictionnaire étymologique de la langue française*, 3e éd., Paris, J. Hetzel, 1870, p. 524; Martine Tabeaud, *Le changement en environnement: Les faits, les représentations, les enjeux*, Paris, Publications de la Sorbonne, 1995.

development of soil science in the nineteenth century.[118] Hence, from the very beginning, the physical geography component, particularly the soil or the land, was in the blood of the word *terroir*.[119]

A link between *terroir* and products was progressively established: 'The quality of soils is communicated in plants which are planted there; it forms the so-called taste of place (*goût de terroir*).'[120] Since each production area is unique, the taste of a place allows us to recognize the common characteristics shared by a large region and distinguish the speciality added by the local elements limited to a smaller area. The uniqueness of a *terroir* was attributed mainly to soil and climate factors at that time. Joseph Capus, one of the first writers to talk about *terroir*, once wrote that 'a *terroir*, it is a soil and the climatic factors whose combination makes an area of production'.[121]

Elizabeth Barham noted that, 'historically *terroir* refers to an area or terrain, usually rather small, whose soil and microclimate impart distinctive qualities to food products'.[122] A demarcation of plots of land could therefore be made based on the climate and soil factors in a *terroir* to ensure the distinctive qualities of products. Producers argued that their unique products needed to be protected by creating delimitations around the production area.[123] Their success led to the first modern law on GIs: the Law of 1905 and its complement, the Law of 1908.

However, a historical review of France's legislative evolution regarding the AO indicates that the physical environment alone is insufficient to guarantee quality.[124] Truth-telling rules on geographical provenance cannot deal with the quality-compromising problems, such as hybrid vines and the '*vase clos*' method of fabrication.[125] Human factors intervened: choices of vegetal raw materials, schedules of

118. Conseil général de l'alimentation, de l'agriculture et des espaces ruraux (France), Conseil général du développement agricole (Maroc), *Terroirs et origine: leçons d'une lecture croisée des expériences du Maroc et de la France pour une Méditerranée durable*, Ministère de l'alimentation, de l'agriculture et de la pêche, 2011, p. 20.
119. This initial interpretation of *terroir*, narrowly suggesting a link between land and product quality, is still taken by authors today, but in the articles which criticize the foundation of geographical indications protection. *See* Michael Blakeney, *Geographical Indications: What Do They Indicate?*, 6 WIPO J. 50 (2014); Kal Raustiala & Chris Sprigman, *Eat, Drink and Be Wary: Why the U.S. Should Oppose the WTO's Extending Stringent Intellectual Property Protection of Wine and Spirit Names to Other Products*, Findlaw (11 June 2021), https://supreme.findlaw.com/legal-commentary/eat-drink-and-be-wary.html; Warren Moran, *The Wine Appellation as Territory in France and California*, 83 Annals Ass'n Am. Geographers 694 (1993).
120. Émile Littré, *Le dictionnaire de la langue française*, Paris, Hachette, 1872, p. 276.
121. Capus, *supra* n. 95; Jacques Audier, *Réflexions juridiques sur la notion de terroir*, Bulletin de l'OIV (747-748), 1993, p. 21.
122. Elizabeth Barham, *Translating Terroir: The Global Challenge of French AOC Labeling*, 19 J. Rural Stud. 127, 131 (2003).
123. Trubek, *supra* n. 105, at 26.
124. On the one hand, some authors summarize that geographical names were traditionally served not only as a statement of origin but also as a guarantee of quality and the maintenance of certain characteristics. However, on the other hand, the quality-origin link, which said to be the foundation of GI legislation, has been largely criticized. *See* Bernard O'Connor, *The Law of Geographical Indications* 171 (Cameron 2004); Blakeney, *supra* n. 119.
125. During the discussion of the Law of 1927, the director of the Service of the Fraud Repression, Roux explained two methods available for making *Champagne* wines sparkling. With the '*vase clos*' method, producers were technically able to use as much sugar as they want to make wines

activities, and winemaking methods. Established production conditions and production methods were gradually integrated as requirements for the right to the AO according to the 'the origin of the product or local, loyal and constant usages'. Direct quality control over production practices ensued, and the AOC system was established. The human contribution had finally become part of the vision of legislators.[126]

The acknowledgement of the human factors is often traced back to Roger Dior's work on the history of grapevines and wine in France.[127] Addressing the existence of both wild and cultivated vines, Dion believed that cultivated vines could not have descended from the sky and that technical and human elements had fostered and directed the revolution from wild vines to cultivated vines over the course of history. This led Dion to study viticulture further, particularly the human dimension. He concluded that French viticulture owed much more to human factors than to natural factors: what had been explained as occurring under the influence of geographic determinism, by the climate and soil, actually stemmed much more from the imperative of commerce, the trial-and-error scientific study of viticulture activities, and the will of vineyard owners.[128]

The development of the AOC regime after 1935 allows us to appreciate the gradual acknowledgement of human contributions. Initially created for wines and spirits, this system was extended to all agricultural products and foodstuffs.[129] The first extension was to cheese in 1955.[130] The Law of 1955 applied the rationale established by the Law of 1935 and confirmed that appropriate production practices were imperative for a cheese to be eligible for appellations of origin.[131] The Law of 1990 extended the AOC concept to encompass all agricultural and alimentary products 'which had duly established a reputation and were subject to supervision or approval by the authority'.[132] It further stipulated that agricultural and alimentary products

---

sparkling, which may lead to low quality. In contrast, the traditional '*Champenoise*' method was considered to be a guarantee of the product. *See Séance du 12 juillet 1927*, J.O. du 13 juill. 1927, p. 932.

126. Professor Jacques Audier asserted that producers had systematically, empirically and scientifically researched how to achieve the highest quality products after the invasion of phylloxera. The human and natural factors are the basis of an appellation of origin. *See* Audier, *supra* n. 121.
127. *See* Dev Gangjee, *Relocating the Law of Geographical Indications* 89 (Cambridge University Press 2012).
128. Roger Dion, *Histoire de la vigne et du vin en France: des origines au 19e siècle*, Paris, CNRS, 2010.
129. Audier, *supra* n. 19.
130. Loi 55-1533 du 28 novembre 1955 relative aux appellations d'origine des fromages, J.O. du 30 nov. 1955, p. 11580.
131. Article 3 of the Law of 1955: '*Chaque appellation d'origine est, à l'exclusion de toute autre procédure, définie par un décret pris sur avis conforme du comité national des appellations d'origine des fromages. Ce décret précise l'aire géographique de production, les conditions de fabrication et d'affinage, les qualités, les caractères du fromage, ainsi que les mesures imposées aux professionnels intéressés en vue d'assurer le respect de l'ensemble de ses prescriptions.*'
132. Article 7-4 de la loi n° 90-558 du 2 juillet 1990: '*... ces produits peuvent bénéficier d'une appellation d'origine contrôlée s'ils répondent aux dispositions de l'article A, possèdent une notoriété dûment établie et font l'objet de procédures d'agrément ...*'. Loi n° 90-558 du 2 juillet 1990 relative aux appellations d'origine contrôlées des produits agricoles ou alimentaires, bruts ou transformés, J.O. du 6 juill. 1990, p. 7912.

could be recognized as AOC only on the advice of the INAO.[133] For the simple appellations of origin defined by the judicial process before 1990, they had to be recognized under the AOC regime where established production practices and control systems were required; otherwise, they would expire.[134] It is evident that the ideal of guaranteeing both origin and quality was broadly accepted and that the 'human factors were progressively more visible'.[135]

More direct evidence of the acknowledgement of human contributions can be found in the Law of 1966, which defined the French notion of *AO* for the first time.[136] It defined the *AO* as 'the name of a country, of a region or of a locality serving to designate a product which originates from there and the quality or character of which is due to the geographical location, comprising natural and human factors'.[137] In this definition, the human factors associated with natural factors were expressly identified as capable of conferring on the product its quality or character. Furthermore, one of the objectives of the Law of 1966 was to carry out structural changes permitting the execution of the Lisbon Agreement signed in 1958.[138] In the Conference of Lisbon, France proposed a draft definition wherein the quality or character of a product was affirmed as being due exclusively to 'the place and the method of production, fabrication or extraction'.[139] Thus, Laurence Bérard and Philippe Marchenay noted:

133. Article 7-4 de la loi n° 90-558 du 2 juillet 1990: '*Les produits agricoles ou alimentaires, bruts ou transformés, peuvent se voir reconnaître exclusivement une appellation d'origine contrôlée ....*'
134. Article 7-6 de la loi n° 90-558 du 2 juillet 1990: '*Les appellations d'origine définies par voie législative ou réglementaire avant le 1er juillet 1990 sont considérées comme répondant aux conditions de l'article 7-5. Toute modification ultérieure des textes définissant ces appellations doit intervenir conformément à la procédure prévue au même article. Avant le 1er juillet 1995, les produits dont l'appellation d'origine a été définie par voie judiciaire avant le 1er juillet 1990 ou a été acquise en application des articles 14 et 15 de la présente loi dans leur rédaction antérieure à la loi no 90-558 du 2 juillet 1990 feront l'objet, s'ils satisfont aux conditions fixées à l'article 7-4, d'un décret leur attribuant une appellation d'origine contrôlée selon la procédure prévue à l'article 7 5. A défaut, ces appellations seront caduques.*'
135. Gangjee, *supra* n. 127, at 112.
136. The definition provided by the Law of 1966 had adapted the terms in the Lisbon Agreement, where the appellation of origin is defined by Article 2 as 'the geographical denomination of a country, region, or locality, which serves to designate a product originating therein, the quality or characteristics of which are due exclusively or essentially to the geographical environment, including natural and human factors'. Although some authors believe that the French Law of 1966 used the same definition as the Lisbon Agreement, the French definition is not exactly the same as the Lisbon Agreement for the absence of wordings 'exclusively or essentially'. *See* O'Connor, *supra* n. 124, at 168.
137. Loi n° 66-482 du 6 juillet 1966 modifiant et complétant la loi du 6 mai 1919 relative à la protection des Appellations d'Origine, J.O. du 7 juill. 1966, p. 5781.
138. Loi n° 60-1352 du 17 décembre 1960 autorisant la ratification, J.O. du 18 déc. 1960, p. 11370; Décret n° 68-309 du 26 mars 1968 portant publication de l'arrangement de lisbonne concernant la protection des appellation d'origine et leur enregistrement international et de son règlement du 31 octobre 1958, J.O. du 6 avr. 1968, p. 3552. *See* Jean Touscoz & Pierre-François, *Les conventions internationales conclues par la France et publiées au journal officiel de la république française en 1968*, Annuaire français de droit international, 1968, p. 803.
139. Actes de la conférence réunie à Lisbonne du 6 au 31 octobre 1958, Bureau de l'Union internationale pour la protection de la propriété industrielle, 1963, p. 833: '*On entend par appellation d'origine au sens du présent Arrangement la dénomination géographique d'un pays, d'une région ou d'une localité servant à designer ou à qualifier un produit qui en est originaire*

> The natural environment cannot solely account for the speciality of products. It is the human activities, through the local and indigenous *savoir-faire*, the forms of social organization, the practices and performances, which give meaning to this relation'.[140]

A product's speciality or particular quality lies in a combination of criteria: space, time, and local *savoir-faire*.[141] Under the AOC regime, producers who choose to engage in the process of protection have to jointly prepare the product specifications (*cahier des charges*) in which the production conditions to be satisfied by the operators are recorded down to the last detail.[142] Codifying these practices is not easy. We can see how hard it is to identify the range of knowledge, traditional *savoir-faire*, and definitions required in the drawing up of the product specifications.[143] Implementing practices is even more challenging, as it involves collective human efforts under the control of regulatory bodies. It is through these efforts that producers built links between the product characteristics, the identity of each community, its history, and shared collective rules.[144] The specific characteristics of the products, which were initially considered almost exclusively due to natural conditions, are now increasingly seen as the fruit of the interaction of a human community and its locale.[145]

---

et dont l'emploi correspond à des qualité ou à une nature particulière de ce produit, dues exclusivement au lieu et à la méthode de production, de fabrication ou d'extraction de ces produits.'

140. Laurence Bérard & Philippe Marchenay, *Produits de terroir: comprendre et agir*, Ressources des terroirs – Cultures, usages, sociétés, 2007, p. 17.
141. Laurence Bérard & Philippe Marchenay, *Les produits de terroir. Entre cultures et règlements*, Paris, CNRS, 2004, p. 229.
142. The EU regulations related to the protection of appellations of origin lays down the dispositions of product specifications (*cahier des charges*). According to the regulations, the product specifications must include the following sections: (1) the name to be protected as a designation of origin; (2) a description of the product; (3) the definition of the geographical area; (4) evidence that the product originates in the defined geographical area; (5) a description of the method of obtaining the product and, where appropriate, the authentic and unvarying local methods as well as information concerning packaging; (6) the link between the quality or characteristics; (7) the name and address of the authorities. At the national level, it is the same *cahier des charges* that would be examined in order to obtain legal recognition as AOC. *See Regulation (EU) No 1151/2012 of European Parliament and of the Council of 21 November 2012 on quality schemes for agricultural products and foodstuffs*, OJ L343, 14.12.2012, p. 9, Article 7; INAO, *Guide du demandeur d'AOC/AOP*, INAO Publication, 2009, p. 13.
143. Laurence Bérard, *Savoirs et savoir-faire naturalistes locaux: l'originalité française*, La revue en sciences de l'environnement, Vol. 6, 2005, p. 8.
144. *Terroirs et origine*, *supra* n. 118, at 22.
145. Professor Jacques Audier justified the additional protection of geographical indications for wines and spirits in the TRIPS Agreement on the ground that the products were steeped in history, cultural significance, and economic interest. *See* Jacques Audier, *Accord ADPIC: Indication Géographique*, Office des publications officielles des communautés européennes, 2000, p. 29. The Food and Agricultural Organization of the United Nations also proposes that specific quality linked to the geographical origin is associated with the *valorization* of local resources, which may be physical (soil, climate, conditions of drying places, etc.), genetic (especially indigenous plant varieties and livestock breeds) and cultural (know-how, traditions in relation with farming and processing, etc.). Context available at, http://www.fao.org/food-quality-origin/what-is-it/the-link-to-origin/en/ (last accessed on 11 June 2021).

Underlying the development of the AOC regime was the evolution of the *terroir* concept,[146] which ultimately included, in addition to the natural environment, the human skills, TK, local *savoir-faire*, and other aspects of producers.[147] On the one hand, as Hugh Johnson pointed out, the land itself chooses the crop that suits it best. If this were not so, why have all the French growers not settled on the same vines, the same winemaking skills, or the same idea of what the best wine is?[148] On the other hand, the land input is more than just a medium for holding the plant in place while fertilizer is applied.[149] Local producers have collectively adapted their techniques and production practices to suit the particular condition of the natural environment, allowing the geographical resources to express themselves. It is precisely the human activities (traditional *savoir-faire* and methods of social organization, practice, and representation) that make sense of this link.[150] Elizabeth Barham argued that: 'The production practice is a complex dance with the goal of interpreting or translating the local ecology, displaying its qualities to best advantage.'[151]

This interaction between natural geographical factors and local producers was noted in the case of Feta, where the status of Feta as a protected designation of origin (PDO) was maintained.[152] The preamble to the regulation registering the name 'Feta' provides as follows:

> Extensive grazing and transhumance, central to the method of keeping the ewes and goats used to provide the raw material for making Feta cheese, are the result of an ancestral tradition allowing adaptation to climate changes and their impact on the available vegetation. This has led to the development of small native breeds of sheep and goats which are extremely tough and resistant, fitted for survival in an environment that offers little food in quantitative terms but, in terms of quality, is endowed with an extremely diversified flora, thus giving the finished product its own specific aroma and flavour. The interplay between the above natural factors and the specific human factors, in particular the traditional production method, which requires straining without pressure, has thus given Feta Cheese its remarkable international reputation.[153]

In this sense, it is not difficult to understand why France stated that 'without people, *terroir* would not exist'.[154] Nevertheless, the emphasis on human contributions

146. Tomer Broude, *Taking 'Trade and Culture' Seriously: Geographical Indications and Cultural Protection in WTO Law*, 26 U. Pa. J. Int'l Econ. L. 623, 651 (2005).
147. Delphine Marie-Vivien, *The Protection of Geographical Indications for Handicrafts or How to Apply the Concepts of Natural and Human factors to All Products*, 4 WIPO J. 191 (2013).
148. Hugh Johnson & Jancis Robinson, *The World Atlas of Wine* (Mitchell Beazley 7th ed. 2013).
149. Tim Josling, *The War on Terroir: Geographical Indications as a Transatlantic Trade Conflict*, 57 J. Agric. Econ. 337 (2006).
150. Bérard & Marchenay, *supra* 141, at 229.
151. Barham, *supra* n. 122, at 131.
152. '*Feta*' had been registered as a protected designation of origin (PDO) in 1996 at the request of Greece. However, in 1999 the CJEU annulled the registration. In 2002, the Commission once again registered the name '*Feta*' as PDO. Germany and Denmark, supported by France and the United Kingdom, have applied for the annulment of this registration. *See* Joined Cases C-465/02 & C-466/02 *Kingdom of Denmark v. European Commission* [2005] ECR I-09115.
153. *Ibid.*, para. 36.
154. *Terroirs et origine*, *supra* n. 118, at 22.

raises more questions than it answers. Registered AOC/PDO products are subject to a standard of 'absolute protection'.[155] They are protected against 'any misuse, imitation or evocation'.[156] It is explicitly forbidden for a producer outside the region to even mention a protected AOC/PDO, even if the true origin of the product is clearly indicated. Conceptually, appellations of origin rest fundamentally on a connection between the product and its geographical location (including natural and human factors). It is not disputed that the climate–soil factor cannot be duplicated elsewhere, whereas the production methods and professional *savoir-faire* are reproducible.[157] Therefore, the greater is the emphasis on human factors, the weaker is the rationale for granting a GI an 'absolute protection'.[158] Suppose producers, with their production methods and traditional *savoir-faire*, migrate to new locales far from the original area. Should they be allowed to use the previous geographical appellation or use it accompanied by an expression such as 'style' or 'type'?[159]

The human–nature interplay in a *terroir* gives a product its unique quality, characteristics, or reputation. This is why it is possible to ensure the authenticity of a product by regulating the geographical area of production and codifying all the production practices. In this sense, human factors function as a tool for achieving authentic goods. More importantly, a community may have constructed collective knowledge through this interaction throughout their history, which also forms an integral part of *terroir*. The International Trade Centre describes *terroir* as a delimited geographic space where a human community has constructed collective intellectual or tacit production know-how over the course of history, based on a system of interactions between a physical and biological milieu and a set of human factors.[160] In its

155. In the text of the TRIPS Agreement, 'absolute protection' is referred to as 'additional protection'. Under Article 23, use of a protected GI for wine and spirits must be prevented 'even where the true origin of the goods is indicated or the geographical indication is used in translation or accompanied by expressions such as "kind", "type", "style", "imitation" or the like'.
156. Article L. 643-1 of the French Rural Code provides that '*l'appellation d'origine ne peut jamais être considérée comme présentant un caractère générique et tomber dans le domaine public. Le nom qui constitue l'appellation d'origine ou toute autre mention l'évoquant ne peuvent être employés pour aucun produit similaire, sans préjudice des dispositions législatives et réglementaires en vigueur le 6 juillet 1990. Ils ne peuvent être employés pour aucun établissement et aucun autre produit ou service, lorsque cette utilisation est susceptible de détourner ou d'affaiblir la notoriété de l'appellation*'. For the purpose of this paragraph, we choose the EU regulation as a starting point. *See* Article 13 of Regulation 1151/2012.
157. Federico Castellucci, *Geographical Indications: The Italian Scenario for the Wine Sector*, Worldwide Symposium on Geographical Indications, WIPO/GEO/SFO/03/10 (9 July 2003) p. 4.
158. Kal Raustiala & Stephen R. Munzer, *The Global Struggle over Geographic Indications*, 18 Eur. J. Int'l L. 337, 340 (2007).
159. Delphine Marie-Vivien, *Do Geographical Indications for Handicrafts Deserve a Special Regime? Insights from Worldwide Law and Practice, in The Importance of Place: Geographical Indications as a Tool for Local and Regional Development* 221, 243 (William van Caenegem & Jen Cleary eds, Springer 2017).
160. It further explained that this French term '*terroir*' indicates a place where the combination of particular agroecology and 'traditional *savoir-faire*' yield unique characteristics. *See* Daniele Giovannucci et al., *Guide to Geographical Indications: Linking Products and Their Origins* (Organization for an International Geographical Indications Network 11 June 2021), https://www.origin-gi.com/images/stories/PDFs/English/E-Library/geographical_indications.pdf.

Applicant's Guide released in 2011, the INAO provides a similar definition: 'A *terroir* is a determined geographical area, in which a human community constructed, along with its history, a collective knowledge of production, based on a system of the interaction between physical and biological milieu and a set of human factors involved'.[161] Together, these definitions clearly indicate an immaterial knowledge component in the '*terroir*' concept. Furthermore, within this collectively accumulated knowledge, there are skills and understandings possessed by indigenous or local peoples over a significant period of time, passed from one generation to another, which is now frequently referred to as 'traditional knowledge',[162] or intangible cultural heritage' (ICH).[163]

A domino effect took place. The acknowledgement of the TK or ICH components in *terroir* enables politicians and legislators to orient the objectives of GI protection. As a superstructure founded on the *terroir* concept, GI protection can (1) not only cater to the interests of local skilled producers who fabricate distinctly authentic products in a *terroir* combining traditional techniques with the unique climate-soil factor of geographical location[164] (2) but also accommodate the need to preserve TK and cultural heritage. The European Commission states that 'GIs are key to EU and developing countries' cultural heritage, traditional methods of production and natural resources.'[165] During the TRIPS Council meeting, the representative from Thailand

161. INAO, *Guide du demandeur d'une appellation d'originc(AOC/AOP)*, INAO Pulication, 2011, p. 26: '*Un terroir est un espace géographique délimité, dans lequel une communauté humaine, construit, au cours de son histoire, un savoir collectif de production, fondé sur un système d'interactions entre un milieu physique et biologique, et un ensemble de facteurs humains. Les itinéraires socio-techniques ainsi mis en jeu, révèlent une originalité, confèrent une typicité, et aboutissent à une réputation, pour un bien originaire de cet espace géographique.*'
162. Local communities have always generated specific knowledge used for shorter and longer periods, and informally passed from generation to generation or from group to group. This traditional knowledge can be defined as the knowledge, innovations and practices of indigenous peoples and local communities. *See* Bernard O'Connor, *Protecting Traditional Knowledge: An Overview of a Developing Area of Intellectual Property Law*, 6 J. World Intell. Prop. 677 (2003).
163. The United Nations Educational, Scientific and Cultural Organization (UNESCO) set the standard definition for intangible cultural heritage (ICH) in their 2003 Convention for the Safeguarding of Intangible Cultural Heritage. Its Article 2 states: 'The "intangible cultural heritage" means the practices, representations, expressions, knowledge, skills – as well as the instruments, objects, artifacts and cultural spaces associated therewith – that communities, groups and, in some cases, individuals recognize as part of their cultural heritage. This intangible cultural heritage, transmitted from generation to generation, is constantly recreated by communities and groups in response to their environment, their interaction with nature and their history, and provides them with a sense of identity and continuity, thus promoting respect for cultural diversity and human creativity.' *See* General Conference of United Nations Educational, Scientific and Cultural Organization (UNESCO), *Convention for the Safeguarding of the Intangible Cultural Heritage*, MISC/2003/CLT/CH/14 (17 October 2003).
164. Teshager W. Dagne, *The Identity of Geographical Indications and Their Relation to Traditional Knowledge in Intellectual Property Law*, 54 IDEA 255, 271 (2013-2014).
165. European Commission, *Why Do Geographical Indications Matter to Us?*, Memo/03/160 (30 July 2003). The European Commission further explained: 'Similarly, "Basmati Rice", "Long-Ging Tea" and "Jasmine Rice" are at the heart of the national identities of India, China and Thailand.' Among these products, 'Long-Ging Tea' has been registered as a protected designation of origin (PDO) in 2011 through the '10 plus 10' project, a cooperation program entre EU and China.

supported the extension of additional protection under the TRIPS Agreement on the grounds that 'GIs were often related to culture and ancestors' traditional knowledge.'[166] Switzerland noted that, unlike private trademark rights, GIs 'form part of the national, cantonal or communal heritage'.[167]

TK, or ICH, once considered a tool for guaranteeing the quality of products, has become an independent value to be protected by the GI regime. To 'make the most out of Europe's traditional *savoir-faire*',[168] the European Commission is currently studying a possible extension of GI protection to non-agricultural products, particularly industrial and handicraft products.[169] In 2012, an external study showed that 'a better protection (of non-agricultural GI products) would maintain local identities and traditions linked to these products as well as traditional knowledge'.[170] Michel Barnier, vice president of the European Commission for Internal Market and Services, claimed that 'the European Union is rich in products based on traditional knowledge and production methods, which are often rooted in the cultural and social heritage of a particular geographical location ... Extending EU-wide GI protection to such products could help preserve our unique and diverse heritage'.[171] Here, the principal argument is not that traditional *savoir-faire* leads to product characteristics but the opposite – that GI products keep traditional and precious *savoir-faire* alive.

To conclude, although *terroir* is not a legal notion,[172] it operates as an explanation of why a place name should be protected in two different ways. (1) First, the interaction

166. Council for Trade-Related Aspects of Intellectual Property Rights, *Minutes of Meeting Held in the Centre William Rappard on 25-27 and 29 November, and 20 December 2002*, IP/C/M/38 (5 February 2003).
167. WTO, *Review under Article 24.2 – Switzerland's Response to the Checklist*, IP/C/W/117/Add.13 (16 February 1999) p. 10.
168. The European Commission launched a Green Paper titled 'Making the Most out of Traditional Know-How' consultation on a possible extension of geographical indication protection to non-agricultural products on 15 July 2014. The Green Paper consists of two parts. The first part asks about the current means of protection provided at the national and EU level and the potential economic, social and cultural benefits that could be achieved by improved GI protection in the EU. The second part includes more technical questions to seek the views of interested parties on possible options for EU-level GI protection for non-agricultural products. *See* European Commission, *Green Paper on Making the Most of Europe's Traditional Know-How: A Possible Extension of Geographical Indication Protection of the European Union to Non-agricultural Products*, COM(2014)469 final (15 July 2014).
169. On 22 March 2013, the Commission published the 'Study on Protection via Geographical Indications for Non-agricultural Products in the Internal Market'. On 22 April 2013, a public hearing on geographical indication protection for non-agricultural products in the internal market took place in Brussels. On 15 July 2014, the European Commission launched a green paper consultation on a possible extension of geographical indication protection to non-agricultural products. On 19 January 2015, the European Commission organized a conference to present and discuss the results of the public consultation on its Green Paper. On 29 April 2021, the Commission launched a detailed stakeholders consultation.
170. Insight Consulting et al., *Study on Geographical Indication Protection for Non-agricultural Products in the Internal Market*, Final report (18 February 2013) p. 149.
171. European Commission, *Making the Most of Europe's Traditional Know-How: Commission Launches Public Consultation on the Protection of Geographical Indications for Non-agricultural Products*, Press release (15 July 2014).
172. The meaning of the word '*terroir*' is primarily used in a technical sense, and it has no legal meaning in texts and judiciary decisions. *See* Audier, *supra* n. 121.

of non-reproducible soil–climate factors and indispensable human contributions in a *terroir* may result in particular qualities or characteristics. In this case, natural and human factors could be considered tools for establishing a link between origin and quality. This rationale can be seen in the French AOC regime. (2) Second, the interaction of natural factors and indigenous communities in a *terroir* may also accumulate traditional *savoir-faire* or ICH. In this sense, traditional *savoir-faire*, or ICH, is an independent value to be safeguarded. With the goal of 'keeping traditional and precious know-how alive and be passed on from generation to generation',[173] the GI regime could thus take the cultural heritage aspect into account – particularly in order to respect and promote its diversity.[174] In short, the traditional *savoir-faire*, or ICH, component in *terroir* paves the way for the creation of GIs for industrial products. However, this may prompt a question: is that a good way to protect traditional *savoir-faire* under the GI regime? The regime itself is problematic: the scope of protection remains an unsolved international issue; the establishment of multinational registration has been subject to a prolonged discussion; and sui generis GI protection is being seriously challenged by proponents of trademark protection. This question will be pursued in subsequent chapters.[175]

[2] Creation of GIs for the Protection of Industrial and Artisanal Products

The new French GI regime concerns industrial and artisanal products. A new category of GIs has been created: 'geographical indications for the protection of the industrial and artisanal products' (*indications géographiques protégeant les produits industriels et artisanaux*; IGPIA). Introduced by Article 73 of the Law of 2014,[176] Article L. 721-2 of the French IP Code defines IGPIA as:

> The denomination of a geographical area or a given place serving to designate a product, other than agricultural, forestry, food product or product from the sea, which originates therein and a given quality, a reputation or other characteristics of which are essentially attributable to this geographical origin. The conditions for production or transformation of products, such as cutting, extraction or fabrication, respect a product specification which is approved by a decision taken in accordance with Article L. 411-4.[177]

173. European Commission, *Green Paper on Making the Most of Europe's Traditional Know-How*, *supra* n. 168, at 10.
174. For example, according to Article 167 of the Treaty on the Functioning of the European Union, the European Union shall contribute to the flowering of the cultures of the Member States, while respecting their national and regional diversity and at the same time bringing the common cultural heritage to the fore … conservation and safeguarding of cultural heritage of European significance. *See Consolidated Version of the Treaty on the Functioning of the European Union*, OJ C 202/1.
175. *See* Chapter 5 and Chapter 6 *infra*.
176. Loi n° 2014-344 du 17 mars 2014 relative à la consommation, J.O. du 18 mars 2014, p. 5400.
177. Article L. 721-2 of the French Intellectual Property Code: '*Constitue une indication géographique la dénomination d'une zone géographique ou d'un lieu déterminé servant à désigner un produit, autre qu'agricole, forestier, alimentaire ou de la mer, qui en est originaire*

This definition of IGPIA is significantly closer to that of GI laid down in Article 22.1 of the TRIPS Agreement[178] and is similar to that of PGI set out in Article 5.2 of EU Regulation 1151/2012.[179] Despite dissimilarities in the scope of products covered and their choice of words, these three definitions share one essential element: a link between the product and *terroir*.[180]

The creation of IGPIA raises doubts since the French AO regime and the EU provisions concerning PDO and PGI already provide protection for local products that are linked with *terroir* to varying degrees.[181] At the national level, the AO system is available for non-agricultural products as long as the requirement is met under Article L. 431-1 of the Consumer Code.[182] Moreover, some industrial products have been protected under the AO regime,[183] such as *'Poterie de Vallauris'*, *'Dentelle du Puy'*, *'Emaux de Limoges'* and *'Mouchoirs et Toiles de Cholet'*.[184] At the EU level, there are two different types of GIs: PDO, which is closely connected with geographical origin, and PGI, whose link with *terroir* is weaker. Considering the abundant availability of GI regimes at different levels, what is the necessity of creating this new GI category?

One response to this question is the imperfection of the previous GI regimes. The EU-wide protection of GIs is currently limited to agriculture-related products,[185] even

et qui possède une qualité déterminée, une réputation ou d'autres caractéristiques qui peuvent être attribuées essentiellement à cette origine géographique. Les conditions de production ou de transformation de ce produit, telles que la découpe, l'extraction ou la fabrication, respectent un cahier des charges homologué par décision prise en application de l'article L. 411-4.'

178. Article 22.1 of the TRIPS Agreement: 'Geographical indications are, for the purposes of this Agreement, indications which identify a good as originating in the territory of a Member, or a region or locality in that territory, where a given quality, reputation or other characteristic of the good is essentially attributable to its geographical origin.'

179. Article 5.2 of Regulation 1151/2012: 'For the purpose of this Regulation, "geographical indication" is a name which identifies a product: (a) originating in a specific place, region or country; (b) whose given quality, reputation or other characteristic is essentially attributable to its geographical origin; and (c) at least one of the production steps of which take place in the defined geographical area.'

180. *See* Nicolas Bouche, *Les indications géographiques protégeant les produits industriels et artisanaux*, Propriété industrielle, n° 4, 2016, étude 7.

181. Jacques Azéma, *Législation: Loi relative à la consommation*, RTD Com., 2014, p. 355.

182. Two French researches, one conducted by the *Direction générale de la concurrence, de la consommation et de la répression des fraudes* (DGCCRF) in 1995 and the other made by the *Directions régionales des entreprises, de la concurrence, de la consommation, du travail et de l'emploi* (DIRECCTE) in 2011, have shown that a number of local industrial products, identified by the name of their geographical origin, represent a manifestation of localized traditional *savoir-faire*. However, not all of them are protected under the French GI systems. *See* Étude d'impact, *Projet de loi relatif à la consommation*, EFIX1307316L/Bleue-1, 2013.

183. The Annex A of the Agreement Between France and German on the Protection of Indications of Provenance and Appellations of Origin on 8 March 1960 mentioned only four French appellations for industry products: *'Poterie de Vallauris'*, *'Dentelle du Puy'*, *'Emaux de Limoges'*, and *'Mouchoirs et Toiles de Cholet'*. *See* Décret 61-547 du 26 mai 1961 portant publication de L'accord entre la France et l'Allemagne sur la protection des indications de provenance, des appellations d'origine et d'autres dénominations géographiques, signé le 8 mars 1960, J.O. du 3 juin 1961, p. 5022; Dutoit et al., *supra* n. 3, at 71.

184. *Dentelles du Puy* (T. du Puy, 19 févr. 1931); *Mouchoirs et toiles de Cholet* (C.A. Angers, 17 nov. 1936); *Poterie de Vallauris* (Cass. crim., 18 nov. 1930); *Emaux de Limoges* (Cass. crim., 14 nov. 1950).

185. EU legislation on agricultural products includes: (1) EU Regulation 1151/2012 for agricultural products and foodstuffs, (2) Regulation 1308/2013 for geographical indications in the wine

though the European Commission may extend GIs to non-agricultural products, in the name of 'making the most of traditional *savoir-faire*'.[186] At the national level, the definition of 'appellations of origin' is said to be too strict, 'requiring a link with *terroir* too restrictive to apply for industrial and artisanal products'.[187] However, indications of geographical origin for non-agricultural products have been protected under the AO regime for almost a hundred years.[188] If this link required by the AO definition is too restrictive, it is by its very nature unsuitable for industrial and artisanal products. Then, the question arises: why did local producers not seek to redress the situation over that hundred-year period? Why was the IGPIA regime not created earlier?

The national procedure for AO protection stipulated in the French Consumer Code is seemingly no longer in line with the interests of local producers.[189] With the globalization of trade and commerce, very few industrial products appear likely to qualify for a definition of AO that requires a robust link with *terroir*. The judgment of the French Council of State of 31 January 1973 confirmed that the protection of the denomination '*Porcelaine de Limoges*' is not possible under the AO regime because the raw materials are no longer local.[190] This deficiency has enabled third parties to register GIs as trademarks to designate all categories of products in a non-geographically descriptive sense.[191] For example, the community of Laguiole failed to prevent third parties from using the place name as a trademark, as the Paris Court of Appeal held that the public does not necessarily associate the term '*Laguiole*' with the community: it is primarily a designation of one type of knife so that this term becomes generic.[192]

---

sector, (3) Regulation 2019/787 on the protection of geographical indications for spirit drinks, and (4) Regulation 251/2014 on the protection of GIs of aromatized wine products.

186. European Commission, *Green Paper on Making the Most of Europe's Traditional Know-How*, *supra* n. 168, at 10.
187. Caroline Le Goffic, *Les apports de la loi du 17 mars 2014 au Code de la propriété intellectuelle*, Propriété industrielle, n° 5, 2014, p. 3.
188. The Law of 1919, which gave the court the task of defining appellation of origin in case of conflicts between users, did not discriminate between various kinds of products. Instead, they allowed for handicraft appellations to be protected.
189. Jérôme Ferrando, *La consécration d'un nouveau droit de propriété industrielle – Embouteillages à l'INPI*, Revue Lamy droit de l'immatériel, n° 102, 2014, p. 89.
190. This is the same for '*Linge basque*'. *See* T.G.I. Paris, 8 mars 1957, D. 1957, somm. 118; *L'étude d'impact du projet de loi relatif à la consommation*, NOR: EFIX1307316L/Bleue-1, 2013, p. 49.
191. In French law, before the Law of 2014, a geographical name could be registered as a trademark (former Article L. 711-1, a of the Intellectual Property Code), provided that the concerned trademark is not deceptive (former Article L. 711-3, c, which has become Article L. 711-2, 8° since the Ordinance No. 2019-1169 of 13 November 2019) or descriptive (former Article L. 711-2, b, which has become Article L. 711-2, 3°), and that it is not prejudicial to a protected designation of origin (former Article L. 711-4, d, which has now become L. 711-3, 5°). Modified by the Law of 2014, Article L. 711-4(d) is completed by the words: 'or a geographical origin' so that the concerned trademark shall not infringe the right of geographical indications. *See* Jacques Larrieu, *Un an de protection des noms des communes*, Propriété industrielle, n° 4, 2008, chron. 3; André-R. Bertrand, *Droit des marques: Signes distinctifs, Noms de domaine*, Paris, Dalloz, 2005, p. 37.
192. The Court of Cassation overruled the judgment from the Paris Court of Appeal. T.G.I. Paris, 13 sept. 2012, n° 10/08800; C.A. Paris, 4 avr. 2014, n° 12/20559; Cass. com., 4 oct. 2016, n° 14-22.245; C.A. Paris, 5 mars 2019, n° 17/04510; Jacques Larrieu, *À couteaux tirés*, Propriété industrielle, n° 4, 2013, comm. 29; Christian le Stanc, *Laguiole Bazar*, Propriété industrielle, 2013, repère 4; Jacques Larrieu, *Laguiole: le match retour*, Propriété industrielle, n° 12, 2016,

The setback for the Laguiole community demands a thoughtful reflection not only on the relationship between geographical denominations and other distinctive signs (particularly trademarks)[193] but also on the relationship between geographical denominations and the traditional *savoir-faire* component in a given *terroir*. The impact assessment of the draft law of 2011 justified the possible extension of GI protection to non-agricultural products mainly on the basis of the fight against counterfeiting.[194] At that time, the deficiency of the previous laws for protecting traditional *savoir-faire* was not fully revealed, and this draft law failed to produce results.[195]

Another attempt to extend GI protection to industrial and artisanal products was made by the law proposal of 2012.[196] The basis of the proposal for the possible extension of GIs was the 'maintenance of the reputation of products … which were often linked with a *savoir-faire*, a history and a tradition'.[197] The justification for the law proposal of 2012 seems to treat traditional *savoir-faire* as a means of obtaining a reputation rather than an independent value to be safeguarded. Except for a single reference to '*savoir-faire*' in the explanatory memorandum (*Exposé de motif*) in the sense of 'tool', there is no other mention of '*savoir-faire*' or 'traditional *savoir-faire*' in the proposal, which is an entirely different situation from that of the Law of 2014. Again, this law proposal has failed to produce results.[198]

The *Laguiole* case reminded legislators of the independent value of preserving traditional *savoir-faire* and the intangible heritage component in *terroir*. According to Arnaud Montebourg, Minister of Economy, and Valérie Fourneyron, Secretary of State for Commerce, 'the history of *Laguiole* has shown up the loopholes in the legal

comm. 89; Jacques Larrieu, *Guerre des étoiles contre la fraude à Laguiole*, La semaine juridique entreprise et affaires, n° 10, 2018, 1124.

193. Marie Blanchart, *L'optimisation du patrimoine immatériel des collectivités territoriales: la protection offerte par le droit des marques*, Revue Lamy collectivités territoriales, 2014, p. 101; Jean-Christophe Galloux, *Les lois n° 2014-315 du 11 mars 2014 renforçant la lutte contre la contrefaçon et n° 2014-344 du 17 mars 2014, relative à la consommation*, RTD Com., 2014, p. 579: 'The law of 2014 strengthens the protection of names of territorial authorities against other distinctive signs, and in particular trademarks.'

194. *L'étude d'impact du projet de loi renforçant les droits, la protection et l'information des consommateurs*, 1er juin 2011: '*L'absence de protection du nom de ces produits contribue à l'essor de produits similaires fabriqués notamment à l'étranger, ce qui crée une concurrence déloyale pour les entreprises concernées.*'

195. Assemblée nationale, *Compte rendu intégral 1re séance du jeudi 6 décembre 2012*, No 91 A.N. (C.R.), 2012.

196. Assemblée nationale, *Proposition de loi visant à mieux protéger les indications géographiques et les noms des collectivités territoriales*, n° 329, déposée le 24 oct. 2012.

197. *Ibid.*, p. 3: '*Afin de préserver la notoriété des produits fabriqués sur notre territoire, produits qui sont souvent liés à un savoir-faire, une histoire, une tradition, il est essentiel que les pouvoirs publics mettent en place un système de protection simple et efficace.*'

198. In the Law Proposal of 2012 (*Proposition de loi visant à mieux protéger les indications géographiques et les noms des collectivités territoriales*), the dispositions of geographical indications for the protection of industrial and artisanal products was arranged in the Consumer Code *(Code de la consommation)*, whereas the disposition of IGPIA in the Law of 2014 constitute a new section in the Intellectual Property Code (*Code de la propriété intellectuelle*). The Law Proposal of 2012 has not adopted by the National Assembly in the session of 6 December 2012. *See* Assemblée nationale, *Proposition de loi visant à mieux protéger les indications géographiques et les noms des collectivités territoriales*, texte n° 127.

protection of traditional French *savoir-faire* and the products derived from *savoir-faire*'.[199] It is precisely the growing awareness of the value of preserving and promoting TK in a *terroir* that finally gave birth to the IGPIA. The impact assessment of the draft law relating to consumption confirmed that 'a certain amount of industrial and artisanal products, containing an origin in their denomination, reflect a recognized and specific *savoir-faire* in a region'.[200] It further justified legal intervention on the basis that:

> The lack of protection of the products' names contributes to the development of similar products produced in foreign countries, which may give rise to unfair competition for the concerned companies in their efforts to ensure continuity of production ... and to guarantee traditional *savoir-faire* in the development of products.[201]

Thus, the new measures on GIs have been adopted to address this lack and, more precisely, to encourage the preservation and enhancement of the value of traditional *savoir-faire* embedded in a given terroir. Consequently, the TK dimension of GIs has been adopted in the Law of 2014. The second half of the definition of the IGPIA requires that 'the conditions for the production or transformation of products, such as cutting, extraction or fabrication, respect a product specification (*cahier des charges*) which is approved by a decision taken in accordance with Article L. 411-4'.[202] The question then is 'What should be contained in the product specification?' According to the new Article L. 721-7 of the IP Code, the product specification of an IGPIA should specify 'the quality, the reputation, the traditional *savoir-faire* or other characteristics that the concerned products possess and which could be essentially attributable to this geographical area or the given place'.[203] Thus, French legislators have for the first time

---

199. Arnaud Montebourg & Valérie Fourneyron, *Situation du village de Laguiole: La loi Consommation apporte désormais les protections nécessaires*, Communiqué de presse, n° 016, 16 avr. 2014: '*Le dossier de Laguiole est révélateur des lacunes quant à la protection juridique des savoir-faire français traditionnels et des produits issus de ces savoir-faire particuliers. Pleinement conscient de ces difficultés, le Gouvernement s'est mobilisé pour remédier à de telles situations. Ainsi, la loi Consommation du 17 mars 2014 contient une disposition qui protège les entreprises employant un savoir-faire traditionnel pour fabriquer des produits présentant un lien fort avec une zone géographique déterminée.*'
200. *L'étude d'impact du projet de loi relatif à la consommation*, NOR: EFIX1307316L/Bleue-1, 2013, p. 49.
201. *See Question écrite n° 5277 au Ministère de l'artisanat du 14 mars 2013*, PIBD 2013, p. 187: '*L'absence de protection du nom de ces produits contribue à l'essor de produits similaires fabriqués principalement à l'étranger, ce qui crée une concurrence déloyale pour les entreprises concernées lorsqu'elles s'efforcent de maintenir la production et donc les emplois dans la zone historique de production et de garantir des savoir-faire de tradition dans l'élaboration de ces produits.*'
202. Article L. 721-2 CPI: '*Les conditions de production ou de transformation de ce produit, telles que la découpe, l'extraction ou la fabrication, respectent un cahier des charges homologué par décision prise en application de l'article L. 411-4.*'
203. Article L. 721-7 CPI: '*Le cahier des charges d'une indication géographique précise: ... 4° La qualité, la réputation, le savoir-faire traditionnel ou les autres caractéristiques que possède le produit concerné et qui peuvent être attribués essentiellement à cette zone géographique ou à ce lieu déterminé, ainsi que les éléments établissant le lien entre le produit et la zone géographique ou le lieu déterminé associé.*'

given equal weight to each of these four elements: quality, reputation, traditional *savoir-faire*,[204] and other characteristics. In the traditional GI regime – particularly the French AO/AOC instrument – traditional *savoir-faire* has always been treated as a tool for giving the product a particular quality or other characteristics. The underlying philosophy seems to favour 'product value', where no protection will be conferred without a particular product quality or other characteristics, regardless of the existence of traditional methods of production. However, Article L. 721-7 indicates a critical innovation: in addition to the traditionally emphasized 'product value', the independent value of preserving and promoting traditional *savoir-faire* becomes the purpose of legal protection. Furthermore, the new Article L. 721-6 of the IP Code continues to pursue the aim of the IGPIA. It provides that 'the organizations for the defence and management [should] contribute to the fulfilment of the general interest of the preservation and enhancement of territories, local traditions and *savoir-faire* as well as products processed from them'.[205] Therefore, as several authors have commented, the creation of the IGPIA is intended not only for the protection of legitimate producers and the information of consumers but also for the preservation and enhancement of territories, local traditions, and local *savoir-faire*.[206]

At the end of 2020, the IGPIA system allowed the *Syndicat des Fabricants Aveyronnais du Couteau de Laguiole* to submit an application to the French National Institute of Industrial Property (INPI) for protection of the name '*Couteau de Laguiole*'.[207] Before the application, twelve names associated with local *savoir-faire* have already been registered as an IGPIA,[208] and two applications concerning Marseille soap are pending.

In conclusion, since the creation of the IGPIA, a new duality of GIs in the French national system has been established. The system includes the controlled appellations of origin (AOC) for agrifood products on the one hand and the IGPIA applicable to industrial and artisanal products on the other.[209] This duality corresponds to two

---

204. On 14 April 2021, the Court of Cassation has ruled that the traditional *savoir-faire* is not required to be unique or have a secret character. *See* Cass. com., 14 avr. 2021, n° 19-10.327. However, some authors contend that the *savoir-faire* must be secret. *See* Marie Malaurie-Vignal, *La protection des savoir-faire et motifs traditionnels – Pour la défense d'une mode éthique*, Propriété industrielle, n° 2, 2019, étude 4.
205. Article L. 721-6 CPI: '*L'organisme de défense et de gestion contribue à la mission d'intérêt général de préservation et de mise en valeur des territoires, des traditions locales et des savoir-faire ainsi que des produits qui en sont issus.*'
206. *See* Galloux, *supra* n. 193, at 579; Le Goffic, *supra* n. 187, at 3.
207. The public inquiry period closed on 30 March 2021. The application is still pending at the time of writing.
208. The registered names are: Absolue Pays de Grasse, Linge basque, Pierre d'Arudy, Pierres marbrières de Rhône-Alpes, Charentaise de Charente-Périgord, Tapis d'Aubusson, Tapisserie d'Aubusson, Grenat de Perpignan, Siège de Liffol, Granit de Bretagne, Pierre de Bourgogne and Porcelaine de Limoges. *See IG homologuées*, INPI (7 July 2021), https://base-indications-geographiques.inpi.fr/fr/ig-homologuees.
209. With the enactment of the Law of 29 October 2007 (*loi n° 2007-1544 du 29 octobre 2007 de lutte contre la contrefaçon*), the Title II of Volume VII of the Intellectual Property Code has been entitled now with 'geographical indications', not 'appellations of origin' anymore. Furthermore, the Law of 2014 has created a new section under Title II of Volume VII of the Intellectual Property Code, namely 'geographical indications for the protection of industrial and artisanal

approaches to interpreting *terroir*. In the AOC regime, the traditional *savoir-faire* in *terroir*, combined with natural geographical features and resources, contributes to the quality and other characteristics of the product. However, a gradual acknowledgement of human factors led traditional *savoir-faire* to be considered an integral part of ICH that deserved to be recognized, preserved, and promoted. This view has led to the creation of the IGPIA.

§1.02 GI NOTION IN EU LAW

At the European level, GIs have been considered an industrial property right since the 1970s.[210] However, sui generis provisions concerning this right were established only in 1992, with Regulation 2081/92 on the protection of geographical indications (PGI) and designations of origin (PDO) for agricultural products.[211] Regulation 2081/92 created the concept of PDO/PGI, which was subsequently extended to other product sectors (wines, spirits, aromatized wines, and possibly non-agricultural products).

[A] Creation of the EU Notion of GI: The PDO/PGI Dichotomy for Agricultural Products and Foodstuffs

In response to concerns about quality, the European authorities envisaged harmonizing diverse national protection instruments of geographical denominations, establishing a *terroir*-based link between product quality and geographical origin. However, the conceptual duality between PDO and PGI was defined even though the PGI category is suspected of not being premised on the *terroir* logic.

products'. From then on, the duality between AO and IGPIA has been built. *See* Loi n° 2007-1544 du 29 octobre 2007 de lutte contre la contrefaçon, J.O. du 30 oct. 2007, p. 17775.

210. The principle of the free movement of products is the bedrock of the Treaty establishing the European Economic Community. For free circulation, Article 30 of the Treaty prohibits not only quantitative import restrictions but also all measures with equivalent effect. Regarding product designations, Directive 70/50 treated it as measures with an equivalent effect that 'confine names which are not indicative of origin or source to domestic products only (French text: *appellation d'origine et indication de provenance*)'. That is to say, if the geographical name constitutes *appellation d'origine* or *indication de provenance*, reserving the said name would not be necessarily considered as measures with equivalent effect. Why? According to Article 36, restrictions could be justified on the ground of the protection of industrial property. Therefore, Professor Frédéric Pollaud-Dulian concludes that *appellation d'origine* or *indication de provenance* constitutes without any doubt the subject matter of intellectual property right. In 1975, the CJEU confirmed *appellation d'origine* and *indication de provenance* as industrial property rights. *See* Article 30 of the Treaty establishing the European Economic Community; *Commission Directive 70/50/EEC of 22 December 1969 based on the provisions of Article 33 (7), on the abolition of measures which have an effect equivalent to quantitative restrictions on imports and are not covered by other provisions adopted in pursuance of the EEC Treaty*, OJ L 13, 19.1.1970, p. 29; Frédéric Pollaud-Dulian, *Appellation d'origine*, Rép. dr. comn. D., 1998; Case 12/74 *Commission of the European Communities v. the Federal Republic of German* [1975] ECR 00181, paras 14-15.

211. Michael Blakeney, *The Protection of Geographical Indications: Law and Practice* 69 (Edward Elgar 2014).

[1] Genesis of PDO/PGI: A Response to Concerns about Quality

Based on Article 43 of the Treaty establishing the European Economic Community,[212] Regulation 2081/92 established two European instruments with which to identify the link between the product and its geographical origin: PDO and PGI.[213] These two GI subcategories were not created in the field of Competition Policy[214] but were introduced along with the adjustment of the Common Agricultural Policy (CAP),[215] in 'a movement towards more qualitative concerns than mere productivity'.[216] However, product quality had been a matter of concern to EU legislators since at least 1969.[217] It is worth pursuing this issue by asking why we had to wait years for a specific European regulation related to the distinctive signs of quality. A historical review of the establishment of the PDO/PGI system may provide us with an answer.

In the absence of harmonized community rules, it is up to the Member States to regulate quality requirements, which specify the composition of certain foodstuffs or their manufacturing characteristics. Given the differences between them, national laws concerning 'compositional rules' or 'recipe standards' may constitute an obstacle to intra-Community trade when they apply to products imported from a Member State in which they are lawfully manufactured and marketed.[218] On 28 May 1969, the Council therefore launched a general programme to eliminate technical barriers to trade in the foodstuffs sector.[219]

212. Article 43 of the Treaty establishing the European Economic Community: 'In order to formulate the guiding lines of a common agricultural policy, the Commission shall, upon the date of the entry into force of this Treaty, convene a conference of Member States, with a view to comparing their agricultural policies by drawing up, in particular, a statement of their resources and needs ...'. According to the preamble to Council Regulation 2081/92, the council of the European Community intervenes, 'having regard to the Treaty establishing the European Economic Community, and in particular Article 43'.
213. *Council Regulation (EEC) No 2081/92 of 14 July 1992 on the protection of geographical indications and designations of origin for agricultural products and foodstuffs*, OJ L 208, 24.7.1992, p. 1.
214. Both designations of origin and geographical indications within the meaning of Regulation 2081/92 are geographical indications as defined in Article 22.1 of the TRIPS Agreement. *See* WTO Panel Report on *European Communities: Protection of Trademarks and Geographical Indications for Agricultural Products and Foodstuffs*, WT/DS174/R/Add.2, adopted 15 April 2005, p. B-34.
215. Joanna Schmidt-Szalewski, *La protection des noms géographiques en droit communautaire*, La semaine juridique entreprise et affaires, n° 44, 1997, p. 703.
216. Claude Blumann, *Politique agricole commune: Droit communautaire agricole et agro-alimentaire*, Paris, Litec, 1996, p. 238.
217. Gabrielle Rochdi Talbot, *L'harmonisation européenne des législations nationales relatives aux produits agro-alimentaires*, thèse, Université de Poitiers, 1994, p. 432.
218. *See* Case C-196/89 *State (Italy) v. Nespoli & Crippa* [1990] ECR I-03647. The Court considered that in the absence of community rules, Italy could establish whatever compositional standards it felt were appropriate for cheese. However, the compositional rules may hinder the sale of products lawfully traded in the other Member States, including low-fat varieties of cheese that failed to adhere to minimum fat content.
219. Conseil des communauté européennes, *Programme général du 28 mai 1969 en vue de l'élimination des entraves techniques aux échanges résultant de disparités entre les dispositions législatives, réglementaires et administratives des États membres*, JO C 76, 17.6.1969, p. 5.

A community provision of the same nature has been relied on to approximate the laws of the Member States, which apply vertically only to particular sectors. This has approach aimed at determining the composition and manufacturing characteristics of certain foodstuffs marketed in the European Community, such as sugar,[220] honey,[221] fruit juices and similar products,[222] and cocoa and chocolate products.[223] It was proposed that this approach should be extended, which would enable more products to benefit from the collective 'EUR' mark if they met several specific conditions.[224]

However, this approach was revised rather than extended. The 'principle of proportionality' laid down in the '*Cassis de Dijon*' case requires that future Community legislation on foodstuffs be limited to satisfy 'essential requirements' in the general interest: the protection of public health, the need for consumer information and protection in matters other than heath, the safeguarding of fair trade, and the demand for necessary public controls.[225] In the White Paper of 8 November 1985, the Commission affirmed that it was no longer necessary to develop 'recipe laws'[226] unless it was required to protect public health.[227] As for the matters not related to health, only adequate information on the nature and composition of foodstuffs was deemed necessary for the protection of consumers.[228]

This new approach was severely criticized by several Member States, particularly France, Germany, and Italy, who estimated that the *Cassis de Dijon* law would

220. *Council Directive 73/437/EEC of 11 December 1973 on the approximation of the laws of the Member States concerning certain sugars intended for human consumption*, OJ L 356, 27.12.1973, p. 71.
221. *Council Directive 74/409/EEC of 22 July 1974 on the harmonization of the laws of the Member States relating to honey*, OJ L 221, 12.8.1974, p. 10.
222. *Council Directive 75/726/EEC of 17 November 1975 on the approximation of the laws of the Member States concerning fruit juices and certain similar products*, OJ L 311, 1.12.1975, p. 40.
223. *Council Directive 75/155/EEC of 4 March 1975 amending, for the third time, Council Directive No 73/241/EEC on the approximation of the laws of the Member States relating to cocoa and chocolate products intended for human consumption*, OJ L 64, 11.3.1975, p. 21.
224. For example, to legally bear this mark, 'the emulsified sauces must be manufactured from raw materials of sound merchantable quality, and shall be stored and handled under conditions that chemically and bacteriologically maintain the said characteristics. They must comply with the given bacteriological characteristics. Additives, other than those listed in Annex, shall not be used ...' *See Amended proposal for a Council Directive on the approximation of the laws of the Member States relating to mayonnaise, sauces derived from mayonnaise and the other emulsified condiment sauces*, OJ C 54, 8.3.1976, p. 1. In 1976, the Commission decided to withdraw these proposals on which the Council had not reached a decision and which was no longer of topical interest. *See Withdrawal of certain proposals and drafts from the Commission to the Council*, OJ C 26, 3.2.1977, p. 5.
225. In the case of '*Cassis de Dijon*', the judge considered that obstacles to movement within the Community resulting from disparities between the national laws must be justified to satisfy mandatory requirements relating in particular to the effectiveness of fiscal supervision, the protection of public health, the fairness of commercial transactions, and the defence of the consumer. *See* Case 120/78 *Rewe v. Bundesmonopolverwaltung für Branntwein* [1979] ECR 00649, para. 8.
226. The term 'recipe law' refers to highly detailed regulations on each foodstuff's composition and manufacturing characteristics.
227. European Commission, *Completion of the Internal Market: Community Legislation on Foodstuffs*, COM(85)603 final (8 November 1985) p. 11.
228. *Ibid.*, 9.

inevitably lead to a reduction in the quality of foodstuffs.[229] According to the judgment of the *Cassis de Dijon* case, a Member State should not prohibit the marketing in its territory of foodstuffs that are compositionally different from those generally marketed there unless the prohibition can be recognized as being necessary in order to satisfy mandatory requirements.[230] This has permitted the marketing of products of a quality standard lower than that to which consumers have become accustomed.[231] Thus, it is believed that a system has been developed that permits the lowest quality variant of a foodstuff to be legitimately marketable in any Member State.[232]

Since product quality was not envisaged as an 'essential requirement',[233] meeting a minimum level of quality – namely the sanitary quality of the products – became the objective of quality requirements after the foodstuffs legislation was reoriented.[234] However, it must be noted that the Member States were divided over the concept of 'quality'. In countries in northern Europe, preference was given to the health and safety aspects of product quality. Contrariwise, due to their strong agricultural tradition, southern countries wished to go beyond the northern interpretation of quality and take into account more subjective aspects of quality, such as specific characteristics generated by the geographical origin and the typical features linked to a traditional local *savoir-faire*.[235]

---

229. Onno Brouwer, *Community Protection of Geographical Indications and Specific Character as a Means of Enhancing Foodstuff Quality*, 28 Common Mkt. L. Rev. 615, 618 (1991).
230. The principle of the judgment in the '*Cassis de Dijon*' case has been confirmed in a large number of subsequent decisions by the Court of Justice. Case 27/80 *Criminal proceedings against Anton Adriaan Fietje* [1980] ECR 03839; Case 130/80 *Criminal proceedings against Fabriek voor Hoogwaardige Voedingsprodukten Kelderman BV* [1981] ECR 00527; Case 178/84 *Commission of the European Communities v. Federal Republic of Germany* [1987] ECR 01227.
231. Caoimhin MacMaolain, *Free Movement of Foodstuffs, Quality Requirements and Consumer Protection: Have the Court and the Commission Both Got It Wrong?*, 26 Eur. L. Rev. 413, 414 (2001).
232. Onno Brouwer, *Free Movement of Foodstuffs and Quality Requirements: Has the Commission Got It Wrong?*, 25 Common Mkt. L. Rev. 237 (1998); Von Heydebrand, *Free Movement of Foodstuffs, Consumer Protection and Food Standards in the European Community: Has the Court of Justice Got It Wrong?*, 16 Eur. L. Rev. 391 (1991).
233. Ludwig Krämer, *La CEE et la protection au consommateur*, Bruxelles, Story Scientia, 1988.
234. Gabrielle Rochdi Talbot, *L'harmonisation européenne des législations nationales relatives aux produits agro-alimentaires*, thèse, Université de Poitiers, 1994, p. 435.
235. Does quality relate to geographical origin? The understanding of the term 'quality' in Northern countries is that it refers to a minimum standard that acts as a health guarantee for consumers. In this perspective, quality is not related to geographical origin, and the role of the state is limited to intervening only for health and safety matters. However, the southern understanding of 'quality' is based on a wider conception of the term, including superior qualities, notably the sensorial quality, which can be appreciated by the consumers. The various aspects of superior quality allow the differentiation of marketed products, and some of the differentiation is based on the area of origin. In this sense, a quality highly relates to geographical origin. *See* Dominique Barjolle & Bertil Sylvander, *Protected Designations of Origin and Protected Geographical Indications in Europe: Regulation or policy? Recommendations* 7 (Euorpean Commission, Final Report FAIR1-CT95-0306, 2000); Denis Rochard, *L'adoption d'un cadre juridique communautaire de protection de la qualité des produits agro-alimentaires: un système de protection du vocabulaire*, Revue de droit rural, n° 246, 1996, p. 362; Denis Rochard, *La protection internationale des indications géographique*, thèse, Université de Poitiers, 1999, p. 338.

In a move unfavourable to the southern countries, the French government submitted a memorandum entitled 'Contribution to the Completion of the Internal Market in the Field of Foodstuffs', which suggested the establishment of a Community quality certification arrangement and community invention to ensure EU-wide protection of appellations of origin. While the Member States generally supported the French view, the United Kingdom (UK) strongly opposed it. It believed that there was no need for Community legislation on GIs since the labelling Directive 79/112/EEC already provided consumers with sufficient protection.[236]

It is true that the Commission did state on several occasions that labelling requirements, together with other measures on the protection of health, could provide sufficient protection for the consumer.[237] Directive 79/112 on the labelling of foodstuffs provided that the consumer must not be misled as to product origin or provenance[238] and required that very detailed information be given on the label.[239] However, the labelling Directive alone may not be enough to protect certain geographical denominations of origin.[240] For example, it does not appear to contravene the Directive for a producer who resides in an 'appellation of origin' area to use the appellation even though their products are not in accordance with the product speciation (*cahier des charges*).[241] The dispositions concerning GIs in the labelling Directive are similar to those of the French law of 1905,[242] which relied upon truthful information of 'origin' as the method of ensuring the authenticity of products. However, as French experience illustrated, provisions premised on the communicative function of geographical descriptions do not guarantee quality.[243]

European authorities soon realized the insufficiency of the 'labelling approach'. A communication on 'the future of rural society'[244] revealed their intention to promote a policy of product quality at the community level. In another communication, on 'the

236. *Council Directive 79/112/EEC of 18 December 1978 on the approximation of the laws of the Member States relating to the labelling, presentation and advertising of foodstuffs for sale to the ultimate consumer*, OJ L 33, 18.12.1978, p. 1; *See also* Brouwer, *supra* n. 229, at 618-619.
237. *Writing Question No 407/88 by Mr. Roger Partrat to the Commission of the European Communities*, OJ C 151, 13.6.1988, p. 10.
238. Article 2 of Council Directive 79/112/EEC: 'The labelling and methods used must not be such as could mislead the purchaser to a material degree, particularly: as to the characteristics of the foodstuff and, in particular, as to its nature, identity, properties, composition, quantity, durability, of method origin or provenance, manufacture or production ... .'
239. Article 3 of Council Directive 79/112/EEC: '... indication of the following particulars alone shall be compulsory on the labelling of foodstuffs: (7) particulars of the place of origin or provenance in the cases where failure to give such particulars might mislead the consumer to a material degree as to the true origin or provenance of the foodstuff ...'.
240. Economic and Social Committee, *Opinion on the Proposal for a Council Regulation (EEC) on the Protection of Geographical Indications and Designations of Origin for Agricultural Products and Foodstuffs*, OJ C 269, 14.10.1991, p. 19.
241. Grégoire Salignon, *La jurisprudence et la réglementation communautaire relatives à la protection des appellations d'origine, des dénominations géographiques et des indications de provenance*, Revue du marché unique européen, 1994, p. 108.
242. Loi du 1er août 1905 sur la répression des fraudes dans la vente des marchandises et des falsifications des denrées alimentaires et des produits agricoles, J.O. du 5 août 1905, p. 4813.
243. *See supra* n. 124.
244. European Commission, *The Future of Rural Society*, COM(88)501 (29 July 1988).

free movement of foodstuffs within the Community',[245] the Commission admitted that common rules for labelling, including Directive 79/112, were not as clear and effective as one could wish. It thus promised to take measures relating to labels and designations of origin as part of its policy on agricultural product quality. Since concerns about product quality had led to the appearance of controlled AOC in the Member States, a harmonized community approach – namely a general framework for the use of quality marks – was considered necessary to establish a 'clear link between product quality and geographical origin'.[246]

As a result, on 21 December 1990, a proposition on protecting GIs and designations of origin for agricultural products and foodstuffs[247] was submitted to the Council. In the preamble to the proposition, the Commission justified the intervention in the following manner.

It argued that, from the traditional perspective, it is essential to implement a community quality policy with a twofold purpose: on the one hand, to protect the interests of the consumers against deceptive and misleading labelling ('provide clear and succinct information regarding the origin of the product') and,[248] on the other hand, to protect the interests of producers against unfair competition ('ensure fair competition between the producers of products bearing such indications and enhance the credibility of the products in the consumers' eyes').[249] We are not strangers to these two objectives since they were identified in the case of '*Sekt*' as the objectives of GI protection.[250]

245. *Communication on the Free Movement of Foodstuffs Within the Community*, OJ C 271, 24.10.1989, p. 3.
246. Article 4(a) of the Communication on the Free Movement of Foodstuffs Within the Community: '... the same approach ought to be followed for the granting of controlled origin designations. The approval procedures for recognition at Community level ought to enable a clear link to be established between product quality and geographical origin (soil, herbage cover, vine variety, know-how, etc.) ...' *See Communication on the free movement of foodstuffs within the Community*, OJ C 271, 24.10.1989, p. 6; European Commission, *Proposal for a Council Regulation on the Protection of Geographical Indications and Designations of Origin for Agricultural Products and Foodstuffs*, COM(2005)698 final/2 (5 January 2006) p. 2.
247. European Commission, *Proposal for a Council Regulation (EEC) on the Protection of Geographical Indications and Designations of Origin for Agricultural Products and Foodstuffs SEC (90) 2415 final*, OJ C 30, 6.2.1991, p. 6.
248. European Commission, *Proposal for a Council Regulation SEC (90) 2415 final*, *supra* n. 247, Recital 4.
249. *Ibid.*, Recital 7.
250. In the '*Sekt*' case, the CJEU has determined the objectives of geographical indications protection: 'To the extent to which these appellations are protected by law they must satisfy the objectives of such protection, in particular the need to ensure not only that the interests of the producers concerned are safeguarded against unfair competition, but also that consumers are protected against information which may mislead them.' *See* Case 12/74, *Commission v. German*, *supra* n. 210, para. 7. The specific objectives of GI protection are expressly indicated by Regulation 1151/2012/EU as to 'secure a fair return for farmers and producers for the qualities and characteristics of a given product, or of its mode of production, and provide clear information on products with specific characteristics linked to geographical origin, thereby enabling consumers to make more informed purchasing choices'. This approach can also be found in the French Law of 1 August 1905. *See* Loi du 1 août 1905 sur la répression des fraudes dans la vente des marchandises et falsifications des denrées alimentaires et des produits agricoles, J.O. du 5 août 1905, p. 4813.

More importantly, the Commission put forward two new rationales. First, by creating market segmentation, product differentiation could be an effective market-intervention and supply-control method: 'The diversification of agricultural production should be encouraged so as to achieve a better balance between supply and demand on the markets.'[251] Second, 'the promotion of products having certain characteristics could be of considerable benefit to the rural economy, by improving the income of farmers and retaining the rural population.'[252] From this perspective, GIs serve as a vector for implementing a set of goals relating to agricultural policy and rural development.[253] In this sense, the role of GIs appears to be distinct from that of trademarks, the latter serving merely to 'guarantee the identity of the origin of the product'.[254]

Although the motives were generally accepted, it took about two years of difficult negotiations to finally adopt Regulation 2081/92, which created two different concepts for identifying the link between a product and its geographical origin: PDO and PGI.[255] Before discussing what led to the distinction between PDO and PGI, we should appreciate what that distinction is.

[2] Distinction Between PGI and PDO: Terroir v. Reputation

In response to the dispute at the WTO level concerning conformity with the TRIPS Agreement and GATT 1994,[256] European authorities amended the terms of Regulation

---

251. The EU wishes to shift the emphasis from quantity to quality or speciality, and Gis play an important part in this transformation. The proposal stated, 'Consumers are tending to attach greater importance to the quality of foodstuffs rather than to quantity; whereas this quest for specific products generates a growing demand for agricultural products or foodstuffs with an identifiable geographical origin.' *See* European Commission, *Proposal for a Council Regulation SEC (90) 2415 final, supra* n. 247, Recital 3; Quality food specificity has been introduced as the cornerstone of the EU's proposition at the WTO Agricultural Negotiations. *See* WTO, *Food Quality: Improvement of Market Access Opportunities*, G/AG/NG/W/18 (28 June 2000). Furthermore, a central feature of the EU's growth strategy for the decade from 2010 to 2020 is the prioritization of innovation. In this area, agricultural product quality policy is identified as 'to provide producers with the right tools to better identify and promote those of their products having specific characteristics'. *See* Recital 5 of Regulation 1151/2012.
252. European Commission, *Proposal for a Council Regulation SEC (90) 2415 final, supra* n. 247, Recital 2.
253. Dev Gangjee, *Quibbling Siblings: Conflicts Between Trademarks and Geographical Indications*, 82 Chi.-Kent L. Rev. 1253, 1267 (2007).
254. Case C-102/77 *Hoffman-La Roche v. Centrafarm* [1978] ECR 01139, p. 1145.
255. Jean-Marie Bailly, *Appellation d'origine protégées et indications géographiques protégées*, Revue de droit rural, n° 215, 1993, p. 319.
256. WTO Panel Report on *European Communities: Protection of Trademarks and Geographical Indications for Agricultural Products and Foodstuffs*, WT/DS174/R, WT/DS/290/R, adopted 15 April 2005. The United States and Australia contended that EC Regulation 2081/92 does not provide national treatment with respect to geographical indications and does not provide sufficient protection to pre-existing trademarks that are similar or identical to a geographical indication. They considered this situation to be inconsistent with the EC's obligations under the TRIPS Agreement. The European Community's response implicitly acknowledged those points and modified the dispositions in 2003. However, the complaints had not been withdrawn and resulted in two decisions, recommending reform of the community system. In consequence, the authorities have revoked the system of 1992 and adopted the system of 2006. *See* Joanna

2081/92 in 2003[257] and replaced it with Regulation 510/2006 in 2006.[258] The latter was subsequently repealed and replaced by Regulation 1151/2012 for the achievement of 'quality schemes for agricultural products and foodstuffs', which incorporated the 'geographical indications scheme for agricultural products and foodstuffs' and the scheme of 'Traditional Specialities Guaranteed (TSG)'.[259] Nonetheless, despite some non-substantive modifications to the definitions that occurred during the evolution of the regulations,[260] the distinction between PDO and PGI was maintained.

[a] Protected Designation of Origin

Article 5(1) of Regulation 1151/2012 defines PDO as follows:

> a name which identifies a product: originating in a specific place, region or, in exceptional cases, a country, whose quality or characteristics are essentially or exclusively due to a particular geographical environment with its inherent natural and human factors; and the production steps which all take place in the defined geographical area.[261]

Schmidt-Szalewski, *Droit de la propriété industrielle*, 7e éd., Paris, Dalloz, 2009; Gail E. Evans & Michael Blakeney, *The Protection of Geographical Indications after Doha: Quo Vadis?*, 9 J. Int'l Econ. L. 575 (2006).

257. *See Council Regulation (EC) No 692/2003 of 8 April 2003 amending Regulation (EEC) No 2081/92 on the protection of geographical indications and designations of origin for agricultural products and foodstuffs*, OJ L 99, 17.5.2003, p. 1; Denis Rochard, *AOP-IGP: Protection communautaire – Évolution de la réglementation*, Revue de droit rural, n° 314, 2003, p. 357.
258. *See Council Regulation (EC) No 510/2006 of 20 March 2006 on the protection of geographical indications and designations of origin for agricultural products and foodstuffs*, OJ L 93, 31.3.2006, p. 12; European Commission, *Proposal for a Council Regulation on the Protection of Geographical Indications and Designations of Origin for Agricultural Products and Foodstuffs*, *supra* n. 246, at 2.
259. The first comprehensive European legislation for the protection of geographical indications and designations of origin, Regulation 2081/92 was adopted the same day with the first legislation on certificates of specific character for agricultural products and foodstuffs, Regulation 2082/92. Subsequently, on the same day that the GI Regulation 2081/92 was replaced by Regulation 510/2006, Regulation 509/2006 on traditional specialities guaranteed replaced Regulation 2082/92. Ultimately, the two schemes were amalgamated into the single legal work considering that they have common objectives and provisions, and there is a priority for the EU to achieve greater coherence and consistency of agricultural product quality policy. It is not a coincidence that the two schemes were simultaneously promulgated, modified and merged. It reflects what degree the European agricultural policy on protecting the product quality could affect the legislation on geographical indications. *See Council Regulation (EEC) No 2082/92 of 14 July 1992 on certificates of specific character for agricultural products and foodstuffs*, OJ L 208, 24.7.1992, p. 9; *Council Regulation (EC) No 509/2006 of 20 March 2006 on agricultural products and foodstuffs as traditional specialities guaranteed*, OJ L 93, 20.3.2006, p. 1; Recital 9-14 of Regulation 1151/2012.
260. According to the EU, the modifications to the definitions have been adopted in order to better take into account the definition of geographical indications laid down in the TRIPS Agreement and make them simpler and clearer for operators to understand. However, PDO and PGI definitions are maintained substantially unaltered with only a few slight changes. Matteo Gragnan, *The EU Regulation 1151/2012 on Quality Schemes for Agricultural Products and Foodstuffs*, 8 Eur. Food & Feed L. Rev. 376 (2013).
261. In the former Regulation 510/2006, the PDO definition (and PGI definition) referred to 'the name of a region, a specific place or a region, a specific place or, in exceptional cases, a country'. Regulation 1151/2012 simplified this expression and replaced it with 'a name'. That

This definition is similar to that given by Article 2 of the Lisbon Agreement of 1958 and Article 1 of the French Law of 1966.[262] Several commenters observed that the PDO definition was obviously inspired by the former definitions.[263] Thus, why did the European legislators not simply repeat the former definitions despite their apparent similarity? Unquestionably, the concept of PDO, like its former definitions, includes both a 'geographical link' and a 'qualitative link' between the product and the territory of its production.

On the one hand, in addition to the general requirement that a product must originate in a specific place, the geographical link of the PDO demands that 'the production steps of the product all take place in the defined geographical area'.[264] While the previous definitions provided by Regulation 2081/92 and Regulation 510/2006 are specific in referring to 'production, processing and preparation',[265] Regulation 1151/2012 refers simply to 'the production steps'. Is it only a question of simplified wording? In the drafting process, the Commission used the expression 'production steps' to describe the PDO definition under Regulation 510/2006. In other words, at least in the eyes of the law drafters, 'production steps' would be equal to 'production, processing and preparation'.[266] However, the Commission explains in the same context that the 'production steps' include but are not limited to the 'sourcing of

is to say, a traditional geographical name or non-geographical name (e.g., *Feta*) could satisfy this requirement. However, this amendment does not really constitute an extension of the subject matter. Because Article 2(2) of Regulation 510/2006 has already provided that 'traditional geographical or non-geographical names ... shall also be considered as designations of origin or geographical indications'. This article has been removed in Regulation 1151/2012. Therefore, removing Article 2(2) and modifying the 'name' requirement that follows in Regulation 1151/2012 does not substantially change the scope of the 'name'. *See* Article 2 of Regulation 510/2006; Article 5 of Regulation 1151/2012.

262. Article 2 of the Lisbon Agreement: 'Appellation of origin means the geographical denomination of a country, region, or locality, which serves to designate a product originating therein, the quality or characteristics of which are due exclusively or essentially to the geographical environment, including natural and human factors'. Article 1 of the Law of 1966: '*Constitue une appellation d'origine la dénomination d'un pays, d'une région ou d'une localité servant à désigner un produit qui en est originaire et dont la qualité ou les caractères sont dus au milieu géographique, comprenant des facteurs naturels et des facteurs humains.*' *See* loi n° 66-482 du 6 juillet 1966 modifiant et complétant la loi du 6 mai 1919 relative à la protection des appellations d'origine, J.O. du 7 juill. 1966, p. 5781.
263. Passa, *supra* n. 36, at 870.
264. Dominique Denis criticized this additional requirement as empty words. He considered it hard to imagine that a product whose quality is due to the geographical environment is not elaborated on the spot. Denis, *supra* n. 15, at 44.
265. Both Regulation 2081/92 and Regulation 510/2006 define PDO as 'the name ... used to describe an agricultural product or a foodstuff: originating in that region, specific place or country, the quality or characteristics of which are essentially or exclusively due to a particular geographical environment with its inherent natural and human factors, and the production, processing and preparation of which take place in the defined geographical area'.
266. *See* European Commission, *Green Paper on Agricultural Product Quality: Product Standards, Farming Requirements and Quality Schemes*, COM(2008)641 final (15 October 2008) p. 11; European Commission, *Impact Assessment of Geographical Indications: Accompanying Document to the Proposal for a Regulation of the European Parliament and of the Council on Agricultural Product Quality Schemes* 7 (Commission Staff Working Paper, 2010).

raw materials, cleaning and grading, processing, maturing, preparation or final product'.[267] It seems that the Commission's explanation of the 'production steps' is more comprehensive than the previous expression. Thus, Evans notes that it is an open question whether the simplification of the wording in Regulation 1151/2012 may have unintended consequences.[268]

On the other hand, the PDO definition requires a clear qualitative link: the quality or the characteristics of the product must be essentially or exclusively due to a particular geographical environment.[269] This qualitative link is closely associated with the French idea of *terroir*: the authenticity and typicality derived from a combination of natural conditions (soil, climate, etc.) and accumulated *savoir-faire* in a given place of origin. The Commission noted:

> The special characteristics of the foods involved derive from their origin, soil conditions, geographical and climatic environment, the varieties and species used, and the way they are prepared or produced. It is these factors that give the product its name and reputation in the market place.[270]

Michael Blakeney questioned the existence of the quality–place relationship on the grounds that there are virtually no examples of proof of this relationship in any GI litigation.[271] However, lack of proof in litigation does not mean that the relationship has never been proven: it might have been objectively measured somewhere else (e.g., in the GI application process). A helpful resource addressing the causal link between geographical area and a specific quality is the Applicant's Guide for the PDO published by France's INAO. The authority suggests that 'the purpose is to show what role the natural factors and human factors might play in the specific characteristics'.[272] The INAO illustrates this suggestion with the example of the PDO '*Fin gras/Fin gras du Mézenc*':[273]

267. *See* European Commission, *Green Paper on Agricultural Product Quality*, *supra* n. 266, at 11.
268. Gail E. Evans, *The Simplification of European Legislation for the Protection of Geographical Indications: The Proposed Regulation on Agricultural Product Quality Schemes*, 34 Eur. Intell. Prop. Rev. 770, 774 (2012).
269. Christophe Geiger el at., *Toward a Flexible International Framework for the Protection of Geographical Indications*, 1 WIPO J. 147, 152 (2010); Denis Rochard, *La protection internationale des indications géographiques*, Paris, Presses Universitaires de France, 2002, p. 318; Gail E. Evans, *The Strategic Exploitation of Geographical Indications and Community Trade Marks for the Marketing of Agricultural Products in the European Union*, 1 WIPO J. 159 (2010).
270. *Opinion on the Proposal for a Council Regulation (EEC) on the Protection of Geographical Indications and Designations of Origin for Agricultural Products and Foodstuffs*, OJ C 269, 14.10.1991, p. 63.
271. Blakeney, *supra* n. 119, at 51.
272. INAO, *Guide du demandeur d'une appellation d'origine (AOC/AOP)*, INAO Publication, 2011, p. 25.
273. The INAO provides this example anonymously. However, after comparing the description given by the INAO and the product specification of '*Fin gras*', we can identify that the INAO's example is '*Fin gras/Fin gras du Mézenc*' designation. *See* INAO, *Guide du demandeur d'une appellation d'origine (AOC/AOP)*, 2011, p. 25: '*Les conditions d'altitude, géologiques et climatiques d'un plateau permettent la présence d'une flore variée particulièrement adaptée à la production d'un foin d'excellente qualité séché sur pré. Les habitants du plateau ont développé un élevage adapté aux rudes conditions climatiques et notamment ont pratiqué un engraissement d'hiver basé sur le foin. Une conduite et une sélection pointue des animaux permet d'en*

> The geological conditions of the *Mézenc* plateau, the altitude and the weather combine to produce varied flora, which is particularly well adapted to producing hay of excellent quality, dried in the meadows. The farmers of the plateau have developed for a long time rearing practices suitable for harsh climatic conditions (production of high-quality hay, sorting of the animals, long hay-based fattening period during the winter).[274]

In short, the characteristics of the *Fin gras du Mézenc* are linked to environmental conditions, the resulting natural flora, and rearing practices. The French AOC regime, often appreciated as the original version of PDO,[275] is traditionally justified by the *terroir* logic:[276] where there is a link between product quality and geographical area, exclusive use of a geographical denomination should be allowed so that the geographical name can express the characteristics of the product linked to the geographic origin, for the protection both of consumers who desire authentic goods and of producers who produce goods meeting certain quality standards.[277]

At the European level, before the formal establishment of the PDO notion, the CJEU followed similar logic in justifying appellation laws. In the '*Sekt*' case, the CJEU observed:

> To the extent to which these appellations are protected by law they must satisfy the objectives of such protection, in particular the need to ensure not only that the interests of the producers concerned are safeguarded against unfair competition, but also that consumers are protected against information which may mislead them. These appellations only fulfil their specific purpose if the product, which they describe, does in fact possess qualities and characteristics, which are due to the fact that it originated in a specific geographical area. As regards indications of origin in particular, the geographical area of origin of a product must confer on it a specific quality and specific characteristics of such a nature as to distinguish it from all other products.[278]

---

faire des animaux d'exception et de produire une viande savoureuse. La notoriété de ce produit autour de cette production saisonnière est avérée.'

274. Cahier des charges de l'appellation d'origine 'Fin gras' ou 'Fin gras du Mézenc', J.O. du 23 févr. 2012; *Publication of an Application Pursuant to Article 6(2) of Council Regulation (EC) No 510/2006 on the Protection of Geographical Indications and Designations of Origin for Agricultural Products and Foodstuffs*, OJ C 180, 21.6.2012, p. 26; *Commission Implementing Regulation (EU) No 422/2013 of 7 May 2013 entering a name in the register of protected designations of origin and protected geographical indications [Fin Gras/Fin Gras du Mézenc (PDO)]*, OJ L 127, 9.5.2013, p. 3.
275. Audier, *supra* n. 19.
276. Justin Hughes, *Champagne, Feta, and Bourbon: The Spirited Debate about Geographical Indications*, 58 Hastings L.J. 299, 301 (2006).
277. More strictly speaking, the traditional *terroir* theory emphasizes that particular land is a key input for a particular product. The natural and human conditions of the GI-denominated regions are inimitable. The local producers are entitled to exclusive use of a product name because no one outside the locale can genuinely make the same product. Registered names shall be protected against any misuse, imitation or evocation, even if the true origin of the products or services is indicated because anyone outside of the concerned area cannot possibly imitate products with similar quality. *See* Hughes, *supra* n. 276, at 367; Calboli, *supra* n. 5, at 61; Roubier, *supra* n. 10, at 762.
278. Case 12/74, *Commission v. German*, *supra* n. 210, para. 7. In this regard, the court did not distinguish the appellation of origin and the indication of origin.

Such observations were unarguably in line with the *terroir* logic underlying the AOC system. The court requires the geographical denominations to meet two criteria, with which Dean Paul Roubier constructed his notion of the AO: the 'exclusivity of origin' and the 'quality of origin'.[279]

During the legislative process of the 1990s, the European Commission expressed its determination to grant designations of origin (PDO), enabling a *terroir*-based link to be established between product quality and geographical origin (e.g., soil, herbage cover, vine variety, *savoir-faire*).[280] Surprisingly, despite the European authorities' efforts to justify protecting a *terroir*-based link, when the Proposal reached the Council, the other category, PGI, was proposed, which requires a looser link between product and place.[281]

[b] Protected Geographical Indication

According to Article 5(2) of Regulation 1151/2012, PGI is a name which identifies a product: originating in a specific place, region or country; whose given quality, reputation or other characteristic is essentially attributable to its geographical origin; and at least one of the production steps of which take place in the defined geographical area. The product-place relationship in PGI is different from that in PDO in two ways.[282]

First, it would be sufficient for only one of the protection steps (among production, processing, and preparation) to be carried out in the concerned area,[283] unlike PDO, which requires that all production steps be carried out. This means that raw materials may come from outside the area.[284] For example, the designation '*Spreewälder Gurken*' has been identified by the CJEU as a qualified PGI even though the

279. *See* Paul Roubier, *supra* n. 10, at 762; Pollaud-Dulian, *supra* n. 210.
280. *Communication on the Free Movement of Foodstuffs Within the Community*, OJ C 271, 24.10.1989, p. 6.
281. European Commission, *Proposal for a Council Regulation SEC (90) 2415 final*, *supra* n. 247.
282. Gail E. Evans and Michael Blakeney affirm that the requirements for a PGI are less stringent than those pertaining to a PDO, since the product need not originate entirely from the designated region and need only have one particular quality, rather than the majority of the food's characteristics, that is attributable to, rather than exclusively due to, the geographical area. *See* Evans & Blakeney, *supra* n. 256, at 585; Alberto Francisco & Ribeiro de Almeida, *The Legal Nature of Geographical Indications and Designations of Origin*, 36 Eur. Intell. Prop. Rev. 640, 642 (2014).
283. However, the requirement to package a product covered by a PGI in its geographical area of production is allowed if it constitutes a necessary and proportionate means to safeguard the quality of the product, to guarantee its origin or to ensure the verification of the specification of the protected geographical indication. *See* Case C-367/17 *S v. EA and Others* (ECJ 19 December 2018) para. 36.
284. Compared to PGI, PDO asks for a stronger link to the area and all production steps taking place in the concerned region. However, by way of derogation from the rule that raw materials must come from the area (Article 3 of Regulation 1151/2012), some sourcing from outside the production zone has been possible for a PDO (e.g., Roquefort, Prosciutto di Parma, West Country farmhouse Cheddar, Jerez).

specification did not require that all the raw materials come from the defined geographical area.[285]

However, GIs are protected 'because they provide useful information to consumers in an established market'.[286] When producers turn to outside resources, GIs do not accurately reflect the geographical origin of the products. According to a study financed by the Commission, PGI may mislead consumers into believing that the ingredients come from an area much smaller than that specified.[287] The Commission admitted that outside-sourced raw materials of PGI might not be what the consumer is expecting.[288]

European authorities have considered two approaches to reducing the tension caused by the possibility of consumer confusion. One approach is based on the logic that 'consumers are able to make better choices due to clear information on product origin'[289] and thus that consumers should be informed that some raw materials might be sourced from outside the geographical area to which the PGI refers. In 2006, the Commission declared that it would undertake a policy review concerning the 'identification of the origin of raw materials in a PGI'.[290] It then released a green paper outlining the advantages and disadvantages of identifying the origin of raw materials.[291] Subsequently, in a communication on agricultural product quality policy, the Commission reaffirmed its intention to recast the legislation concerning 'information on the place of farming of raw materials where this is different from the place indicated by the geographical indication'.[292]

The other approach is based on the logic that 'consumers are confused because the product–place link of a PGI is not strong enough'. This is more fundamentally revolutionary because it considers introducing additional criteria in PGI 'to emphasize the link between the product and the geographical area'.[293] For example, it could be mandated that a PGI whose raw materials are sourced elsewhere can be registered only if it is not contrary to consumer expectations.[294] On this issue, instead of adding criteria

285. *See* Case C-269/99 *Carl Kühne and Others* [2001] ECR I-09517, para. 62.
286. Gangjee, *supra* n. 127, at 182.
287. London Economics, *Evaluation of the CAP Policy on Protected Designations of Origin (PDO) and Protected Geographical Indications (PGI)* 269 (Final Report, 2008).
288. For instance, consumers may expect that the pig meat for Mortadella Bologna or Jambon d'Ardenne is sourced from the local region. *See* European Commission, *Green Paper on Agricultural Product Quality, supra* n. 266, at 13; DG AGRI, *Background Paper to Green Paper on Agricultural Product Quality* (Working Document, 2008).
289. London Economics, *supra* n. 287, at 256.
290. European Council, *2720th Meeting of the Council of the European Union (Agriculture and Fisheries)*, 7702/06 ADD1 (5 April 2006) p. 4. The European Economic and Social Committee also gave his opinion that the new issues of identification of the origin of raw materials need to be explored. *See Opinion of the European Economic and Social Committee on Geographical Indications and Designations*, OJ C 204, 9.8.2008, p. 63.
291. European Commission, *Green Paper on Agricultural Product Quality, supra* n. 266, at 15.
292. European Commission, *Communication from the Commission to the European Parliament, the Council, the European Economic and Social Committee and the Committee of the Regions on Agricultural Product Quality Policy*, COM(2009)234 final (28 May 2009) p. 11.
293. European Commission, *Green Paper on Agricultural Product Quality, supra* n. 266, at 13.
294. According to the background paper to the green paper on the agricultural quality scheme, consumer expectations on the origin of raw materials may vary from one product to another. For instance, consumers may not expect that all the components of a '*Turrón de Jijona*' come from the area of Jijona, but they may expect that the pigmeat for '*Mortadella Bologna*' or

to restrict PGI application, the Commission seems to be interested in a more flexible solution, suggested by France, in which the origin of raw materials must be indicated where there is a risk of consumer confusion.[295]

Unlike the two proposed approaches, the legislative response is more cautious concerning placing additional controls on the loose product–place link in PGI.[296] The original proposal on the agricultural product quality scheme tended to place closer supervision on both 'the production steps which shall take place in the defined geographical area' and 'the sourcing of raw materials'.[297] However, the final version of Regulation 1151/2012 allows the Commission only to adopt delegated acts concerning restrictions and derogations with regard to 'the slaughtering of live animals' and 'the sourcing of raw materials',[298] by reference to quality or usage and recognized *savoir-faire* or natural factors.[299] Of course, legislators' cautious attitudes are not helpful in easing the tension between the meaning of the term 'originating' in the minds of consumers and the fact that the ingredients of a PGI product might be sourced somewhere else. To borrow Irene Calboli's words, the PGI under current legislation might be 'a vehicle for consumer confusion and deception through the offering of inaccurate information about the products' geographical origin'.[300]

According to the powers provided by the delegated acts, Regulation 664/2014 allows restrictions regarding the sourcing of raw materials to be provided in the product specification of PGI products.[301] In the future, the demander of the PGI could

---

'*Jambon d'Ardenne*' is sourced from the local region. Therefore, we could conclude that a certain number of PGI products whose raw materials are outsourced do not necessarily contravene the expectation of consumers. *See* DG AGRI, *Background Paper to Green Paper on Agricultural Product Quality*, *supra* n. 288, at 3.

295. European Commission, *Impact Assessment of Geographical Indications*, *supra* n. 266, at 29.

296. The EU's hands are tied because it is bound to respect the TRIPS Agreement, and it is not easy to delist the existing PGI names that did not meet the possible new criteria. The margin of manoeuvre to modify the definition of the protected geographical indication is narrow. *See* European Commission, *Impact Assessment of Geographical Indications*, *supra* n. 266, at 31.

297. Article 5(3) of the Proposal: 'In order to take into account the specificities related to certain sectors or areas, the Commission may, by means of delegated acts, adopt restrictions and derogations regarding the steps of production which shall take place in the defined geographical area or regarding the sourcing of raw materials.' *See* European Commission, *Proposal for a Regulation of the European Parliament and the Council on Agricultural Product Quality Schemes*, COM(2010)733 final (10 December 2010) p. 25.

298. Article 5(4) of Regulation 1151/2012: 'In addition, in order to take into account the specific character of certain products or areas, the Commission shall be empowered to adopt delegated acts in accordance with Article 56, concerning restrictions and derogations with regard to the slaughtering of live animals or with regard to the sourcing of raw materials.'

299. The original proposal from the Commission only authorizes the Commission to adopt restrictions and derogations regarding the sourcing of raw materials. It is then amended that these restrictions and derogations shall, based on objective criteria, take into account quality or usage and recognized know-how or natural factors. *See* European Commission, *Proposal for a Regulation of the European Parliament and the Council on Agricultural Product Quality Schemes*, *supra* n. 297, at 25; European Council, *Proposal for a Regulation of the European Parliament and of the Council on Agricultural Product Quality Schemes: Outcome of the European Parliament's First Reading*, 13668/12 (14 September 2012) p. 16.

300. *See* Calboli, *supra* n. 5, at 62.

301. Preamble to Regulation 664/2014: 'Having regard to Regulation (EU) No 1151/2012 of the European Parliament and of the Council of 21 November 2012 on quality schemes for agricultural products and foodstuffs, and in particular the first and second subparagraphs of

state the restrictions on the origin of the raw materials used.[302] However, since such restrictions may represent obstacles to the single market, they must be justified by the link between a given product quality, reputation, or other characteristic and the geographical origin required by the PGI definition.[303] This is the second, and more fundamental, difference between PDO and PGI.

Instead of requiring that the quality or characteristic be 'essentially or exclusively due to' a particular place, according to the previous Regulation 510/2006, it is sufficient that a specific quality, reputation, or other characteristic be 'attributable'[304] to the geographical origin in the case of PGI. Since Regulation 1151/2012 has added the word 'essentially' in the new PGI definition, the given quality, reputation, or other characteristic has to be 'essentially attributable' to its geographical origin.[305] Although the legislators indicate that the objective of this slight modification is to take into account the definition of GIs laid down in the TRIPS Agreement,[306] some commentators worry that adding the word 'essentially' weakens the link between the product and its place of origin.[307]

Article 5(4) ... restrictions with regard to the sourcing of raw materials for protected geographical indications should be allowed in the product specification of such products.' *See Commission Delegated Regulation (EU) No 664/2014 of 18 December 2013 supplementing Regulation (EU) No 1151/2012 of the European Parliament and of the Council with regard to the establishment of the Union symbols for protected designations of origin, protected geographical indications and traditional specialties guaranteed and with regard to certain rules on sourcing, certain procedural rules and certain additional transitional rules*, OJ L 179, 19.6.2014, p. 17.

302. *Commission Implementing Regulation (EU) No 668/2014 of 13 June 2014 laying down rules for the application of Regulation (EU) No 1151/2012 of the European Parliament and of the Council on quality schemes for agricultural products and foodstuffs*, OJ L 179, 19.6.2014, p. 36.
303. Article 1(2) of Regulation 664/2014: 'Any restrictions to the origin of raw materials provided in the product specification of a product the name of which is registered as a protected geographical indication shall be justified in relation to the link referred to in point (f)(ii) of Article 7(1) of Regulation 1151/2012.'
304. Article 2(1) of Regulation 510/2006.
305. Article 5(2) of Regulation 1151/2012.
306. Similarly, the effort of bringing closer the GI definition in the TRIPS Agreement and the PGI definition could be seen in the legislative process of Regulation 510/2006. Article 22 of the TRIPS Agreement provides that 'geographical indications are, for the purposes of this Agreement, indications which identify a good as originating in the territory of a Member, or a region or locality in that territory, where a given quality, reputation or other characteristic of the good is essentially attributable to its geographical origin'. The proposal of Regulation 510/2006 defines PGI as 'an indication serving to identify an agricultural product or a foodstuff originating in a region, specific place or country, which possesses a specific quality, reputation or other characteristic essentially attributable to that geographical origin, and the production, processing or preparation of which take place in the defined geographical area'. Here the scope of the wording 'indication' is broader than the wording 'the name of region' in previous Regulation 2081/92 and 'names' in subsequent Regulation 1151/2012. Unlike the notion of an appellation, which relates to geographical games, the indication is considered more accommodating. A broad range of signs could fit within the 'indication' category, for example, indirect indications, the shape of the *Bocksbeutel*. In addition, the proposal recommended the criterion of 'essentially attributable'. However, it was not accepted in Regulation 510/2006. *See* European Commission, *Proposal for a Council Regulation on the Protection of Geographical Indications and Designations of Origin for Agricultural Products and Foodstuffs*, *supra* n. 246, at 2.
307. Gragnan, *supra* 260, at 376.

Indeed, at its most attenuated point, the definition of PGI simply requires that the reputation of the product be attributable to the geographical area.[308] In this case, the actual quality or characteristics of the product is not the determining factor for registration; it is enough for the name of the product to enjoy a reputation associated with a specific geographical area. The Commission explained that these rules are based on the idea that 'a geographical indication deserves protection even where it cannot be proven that the product owes its special features to its region of origin'.[309] Nonetheless, as illustrated above, GI protection is traditionally justified by the *terroir* logic, whereby the combination of natural and human conditions in the GI regions is inimitable anywhere else so that the authentic product cannot possibly be made outside the locale. Thus, exclusive use of GIs shall be entitled to GI producers for the protection of consumers who desire products with specific characteristics and of producers who meet consumers' expectations. However, why does a GI still deserve protection when no qualitative linkage between special features and origin exists?

Early European jurisprudence addressed the justification of such protection. In the case of '*Exportur*', the CJEU held that 'such names [indications of provenance] may nevertheless enjoy a high reputation amongst consumers and constitute for producers established in the places to which they refer an essential means of attracting custom. They are therefore entitled to protection'.[310] The exclusive right to the geographical names of their actual place of origin is entitled because others might try to exploit the *reputation* of that indication of provenance.[311] The Advocate General in the '*Feta*' case further explained that:

> Such protection entails a reward for the effort invested by the multiple holder of the registered name, who, by manufacturing the product concerned in a particular manner, ensures that the product acquires a reputation worthy of protection under that form of industrial property right the protection ensures that the holders of the designation do not suffer financial loss and also precludes unjust enrichment on the part of other individuals.[312]

When the link between a product and a place is a matter of reputation, then the justification for protection appears to protect intangible assets and reward the efforts of the local producers who ensure that the product maintains its reputation and prevent people from outside from fraudulently exploiting that reputation. Where a locality's reputation forms the basis, the protection logic of the PGI is different from that of PDO, which is based on the idea of *terroir*. Thus, we contest Schmidt-Szalewski's conclusion that 'the difference between the PDO and PGI is not a fundamental difference in nature,

---

308. Christophe Geiger, *Constructing European Intellectual Property: Achievements and New Perspective* 186 (Edward Elgar Publishing 2013); Case T-43/15 *CRM Srl v. European Commission* (CFI 23 April 2018) paras 42-48.
309. European Commission, *Protection of Geographical Indications, Designations of Origin and Certificates of Specific Character for Agricultural Products and Foodstuffs* 7 (Working Document of the Commission, 2nd ed., 2004).
310. Case C-3/91, *Exportur SA v. LOR SA*, *supra* n. 21, para. 28.
311. *Ibid.*, para. 15 (Opinion of Advocate General).
312. Joined Cases C-465/02 & C-466/02, *Germany and Denmark v. Commission*, *supra* n. 152, para. 27 (Opinion of Advocate General).

but a matter of degree'.[313] Instead, we argue that they differ fundamentally according to the nature of the link and the protection logic based on it.[314]

This difference is shown in the difficulties that emerge over the delimitation of the geographical area.[315] To justify a link involving a PDO product, producers invoke the *terroir* concept to prove that the qualities crucially depend on the distinctiveness of a combination of soil–climate conditions and production methods in the place of origin, which forms the basis for demarcating regions. Therefore, it is possible to define the limits of the production area objectively. However, with the PGI category, as one jurist explained, 'The causal link between the place of origin and the quality of the product may be a matter of reputation rather than verifiable fact.'[316] Without verifiable fact, what criteria must be applied in delimiting the geographical area? In the case of 'Melton Mowbray Pork Pie', the product enjoyed a reputation associated with a place. However, consumers' perception of the geographical boundaries of the 'Melton Mowbray Pork Pie' extends beyond the administrative boundaries of Melton Mowbray.[317] When the product–place link is based simply on a reputation, it is challenging to clarify the extent to which the public perception of the geographical boundaries plays a part in shaping the actual boundaries, making establishing clearly defined boundaries even more problematic.[318]

Apart from the weakest 'reputation linkage', the PGI application could also be approved if the given quality or other characteristic is 'essentially attributable' to its geographical origin. Here 'essentially attributable' is understood to require a causal connection between product qualities or other distinctive features and the region of origin. Article 7(f) of Regulation 1151/2012 provides that the product specification shall include details establishing 'the link' between a given quality or other characteristics of the product and the geographical origin.[319] Regulation 668/2014, which lays down detailed rules for the application of Regulation 1151/2012, further illustrates that the link has to be 'a causal link'.[320] What is a causal link? According to the EU's Guide for Application under Regulation 1151/2012, the causal link requires that 'the

313. *See* Schmidt-Szalewski, *supra* n. 215, at 704; Caroline Le Goffic, *Indication géographique en droit international*, J.-Cl. Marques: Dessins et modèles, fasc. 8120, p. 21.
314. WIPO, *EU System for Geographical Indications for Agricultural Products and Foodstuffs*, Worldwide Symposium on Geographical Indications, WIPO/GEO/SOF/09/4 (10 June 2009) p. 3.
315. Gail E. Evans, *The Comparative Advantage of Geographical Indications and Community Trade Marks for the Marketing of Agricultural Products*, 41 IIC-Int'l Rev. Intell. Prop. & Competition L. 645 (2010).
316. *Consorzio Del Prosciutto Di Parma v. Asda Stores Limited and Others* [2001] UKHL 7.
317. *Northern Foods Plc v. The Department for Environment, Food and Rural Affairs & Anor* [2005] EWHC 2971 (Admin).
318. Dev Gangjee, *Melton Mowbray and the GI Pie in the Sky: Exploring Cartographies of Protection*, 3 Intell. Prop. Q. 291 (2006).
319. Article 7(f) of Regulation 1151/2012.
320. Annex I of Regulation 668/2014.

specificities of the geographical area influence those of the product'.[321] In this context, is the 'causal link' requirement of PGI identical to that of PDO?

Once again, the INAO's guide provides a helpful reference. For the application of PGI, the INAO suggests specifying the environmental and human factors that have an impact on the product's specific nature: 'It is critical to explain why the location results in a different quality.'[322] It illustrates this critical point with the example of the 'Corsican clementine' (*Clémentine de Corse*): 'There is a correlation between the temperatures, a high rainfall level, and a high humidity and the organoleptic characteristics of the product.'[323] The exemplary correlation reflects the idea that soil–climate conditions in a given area influence product specificities, which is rooted in the very essence of the *terroir* concept and forms the basis of the PDO link. Thus, another question arises: is there really a fundamental difference between the PGI link and the *terroir*-based PDO link?

Carlos Correa suggests that 'essentially attributable' may be understood to imply that 'the production of the relevant goods may partially take place outside the designated territory'.[324] On this matter, we have already concluded that the PGI link is looser since it is sufficient for only one of the protection steps to be carried out in the region of origin. However, this does not necessarily change the nature of the link. One could argue that the PGI link need not include the combination of natural and human contributions contained in the PDO.[325] Practice shows that PGIs are registered and that result only from the collective *savoir-faire* of local producers.[326] Again, attaching less importance to natural factors weakens the strength of the link to the origin, but the nature of the causal link remains the same. Furthermore, a study by Knöferl analysing all available product specifications concludes that there are practically no differences between PDO and PGI specifications concerning specificity and quality.[327]

---

321. *Guild to Applicants: How to Compile the Single Document*, European Commission (10 June 2021), https://ec.europa.eu/info/food-farming-fisheries/food-safety-and-quality/certification/quality-labels/registration-name-quality-product/applications-food-and-agricultural-products_en.
322. Article 1.3.8.3 of Guide of Applicants of PGI: '*Il convient ici de rappeler les facteurs du milieu et les facteurs humains qui ont une incidence sur la spécificité du produit et d'établir la corrélation entre les deux qui matérialise la nature du lien. Il est impératif d'expliquer pourquoi la localisation entraîne une qualité différente; il s'agit de l'influence de la localisation du produit sur ses caractéristiques propres.*' *See* INAO, *Guide du demandeur d'une indication géographique protégée*, 2009, p. 24.
323. *See Publication of an Application for Registration Pursuant to Article 6(2) of Regulation (EEC) No 2081/92 on the Protection of Geographical Indications and Designations of Origin*, OJ C 240, 30.9.2005, p. 34; *Commission Regulation (EC) No 148/2007 of 15 February 2007 Registering Certain Names in the Register of Protected Designation of Origin and Protected Geographical Indications (Clémentine de Corse)*, OJ L 46, 16.2.2007, p. 14.
324. Carlos Correa, *Trade-Related Aspects of Intellectual Property Rights: A Commentary on the TRIPS Agreement* 218 (Oxford University Press 2007).
325. Giovannucci et al., *supra* n. 160.
326. *See Arrêté du 12 février 2010 portant homologation du cahier des charges de l'indication géographique protégée 'Rillettes du Mans'*, J.O. du 23 févr. 2010, p. 3340; Marie-Vivien, *supra* n. 147.
327. *See* Adriano Profeta et al., *The Protection of Origins for Agricultural Products and Foods in Europe: Status Quo, Problems and Policy Recommendations for the Green Book*, 12 J. World Intell. Prop. 622 (2009); Geiger, *supra* n. 269, at 147-158.

[c] *Duality of Geographical Descriptions*

It appears that, when the 'reputation linkage' is not triggered in the PGI application,[328] the distinction of the GI scheme depends mainly on the degree of association with a specific geographical area.[329] As the measurement of this degree is subjective in theory and practice,[330] the distinction between PDO and PGI is often deemed to be inexact, subtle and unclear.[331] What is worse is that the distinction may prove impenetrable to consumers because it might confuse them.[332]

In response, to simplify and clarify the GI system, European authorities expressed in a 2009 communication their intention to eliminate the controversial distinction between PDO and PGI by merging the two instruments into one.[333] This 'invention' is only old wine in a new bottle, however. In fact, owing to the amendments implemented after numerous meetings of the Council Working Group and the Special Committee of Agriculture,[334] when the proposal of Regulation 2081/92 first reached the European Parliament in 1991, GI protection was only limited to one category: PDO. Although most Member States were prepared to accept this version, the European Parliament did not adopt it.[335]

History repeated itself. During the legislative process for Regulation 1151/2012, a simplification of the scheme by merging the two instruments was deemed to be

328. In the case of the PGI, one single criterion attributable to a geographical origin is sufficient: a quality or the reputation or a characteristic. According to Regulation 668/2014, applicants for the PGI should state explicitly on which one of the given factors (reputation, given quality, other characteristic of the product) the causal link is based and give information only with respect to the relevant factors. Therefore, when producers only invoke given quality or other characteristic of the product for applying the PGI, the information concerning reputation and the causal link between product and reputation would not be considered relevant. In this case, the reputation linkage is not triggered. *See* Annex I of Regulation 668/2014.
329. *See* Catherine Seville, *EU Intellectual Property Law and Policy* 296 (Edward Elgar Publishing 2009).
330. Knöferl observed unequal treatment of applications by different national examination authorities. Similar products with comparable specificity (e.g., asparagus, lamb) are approved as PDO in one Member State and as PGI in another. In addition, there are cases where profiles of quality and specificity are higher for a PGI than for a similar PDO. *See* Adriano Profeta, *Protected Geographical Indications and Designations of Origin: An Overview of the Status Quo and the Development of the Use of Regulation (EC) 510/06 in Europe, With Special Consideration of the German Situation*, 22 J. Int'l Food & Agribus. Mark. 179 (2010).
331. *See* Geiger, *supra* n. 269, at 147-158; Charles Lister, *Protectionism and Integration: Designations of Origin for Foodstuffs in the European Community*, 47 Food & Drug L.J. 639 (1992).
332. Both the European Commission and the European Court of Auditors indicated that two different links might confuse consumers. *See* Michael Koenig et al., *Public Consultations on Geographical Indication Protection for Non-agricultural Products in the EU: Summary of Results* 14 (European Commission, Industrial Property Unit J1, DG Growth Working Paper, 2015); European Court of Auditors, *Do the Design and Management of the Geographical Indications Scheme Allow It to Be Effective* 26 (Special Report n° 11, 2011).
333. European Commission, *Communication from the Commission to the European Parliament, the Council, the European Economic and Social Committee and the Committee of the Regions on Agricultural Product Quality Policy*, *supra* n. 292, at 10.
334. There were many suggestions during the legislative process that the two geographical designations should be combined. *See* Lister, *supra* n. 331, at 651.
335. Marina Kolia, *Monopolising Names: EEC Proposal on the Protection of Trade Descriptions of Foodstuffs*, 14 Eur. Intell. Prop. Rev. 238 (1992).

difficult: if the merged definition adopted the looser criteria of the PGI, merging the two definitions would eliminate the PDO category and diminish the added-value benefits of the PDO identification.[336] Contrariwise, if the new criteria were close to that of the PDO, it would likely contravene the terms of GI protection in the TRIPS Agreement, and it would be challenging to delist existing PGI names that did not meet the new criteria.[337] In the end, the legislators of Regulation 1151/2012 abandoned the merging proposition and maintained the distinction between PDO and PGI 'in the light of existing practice'.[338] Indeed, it was precisely the 'existing practice' that made 'it appropriate to define the two different types of geographical description' in Regulation 2081/92 and Regulation 510/2006.[339]

Strangely enough, while we have walked 'in the light of existing practice' for over thirty years, none of the three legal texts explained why the 'existing practice' made the duality of definitions 'appropriate'. In the '*Haus Cramer*' case, the Advocate General Jacobs regrouped the seventh, ninth and tenth recitals in the preamble to Regulation 2081/92 and seemed to imply that 'existing practice' referred to the fact that 'there is diversity in the national practices for implementing registered designations of origin and geographical indications'.[340] Consistent with this view, Professor Dominique Denis noted that the disparity between the French model, based on *AO*, and the German model, based on indications of provenance, made it necessary to create a PDO and a PGI.[341] Dev Ganjee's remark is more explicit in pointing out that the duality was 'a compromise informed by two sets of national experiences (i.e., French experience and German experience)'.[342]

We would not go so far as to speak of the 'superpower' of these two countries in promoting EU policy, but there is definitely an inevitable compromise linked to the fact that the French model of protecting *AO* has been adopted across the EU. We have to bear in mind that the European protection of GIs at the national level is characterized

336. *See* European Commission, *Proposal for a Regulation of the European Parliament and the Council on Agricultural Product Quality Schemes*, *supra* n. 297, at 6.
337. *See* European Commission, *Impact Assessment of Geographical Indications*, *supra* n. 266, at 31.
338. Recital 22 of Regulation 1151/2012: 'In the light of existing practice, the two different instruments for identifying the link between the product and its geographical origin, namely the protected designation of origin and the protected geographical indication, should be further defined and maintained.'
339. Preamble to Regulation 2081/92: 'Whereas existing practices make it appropriate to define two different types of geographical description, namely protected geographical indications and protected designation of origin.' Recital 9 of Regulation 510/2006: 'In the light of existing practices, two different types of geographical description should be defined, namely protected geographical indications and protected designations of origin.'
340. The seventh, ninth and tenth recitals in the preamble to Regulation 2081/92: 'There is diversity in the national practices for implementing registered designations of origin and geographical indications; ... The scope of this Regulation is limited to certain agricultural products and foodstuffs for which a link between product or foodstuff characteristics and geographical origin exists; ... however, this scope could be enlarged to encompass other products or foodstuffs ... existing practices make it appropriate to define two different types of geographical description'. *See* Case C-312/98, *Haus Cramer*, *supra* n. 55, at 22 (Opinion of Advocate General).
341. Denis, *supra* n. 15, at 31.
342. Gangjee, *supra* n. 318.

by the diversity of national systems.[343] Only a few EU members are accustomed to *AO* or PDO protection based on the French idea of *terroir*. The best example of this is the negligible attractiveness of another *terroir*-based international agreement,[344] the Lisbon Agreement for the Protection of Appellations of Origin.[345] As of January 2021, only ten out of seventy-seven EU Member States have signed the Agreement, and all of them are from southern Europe (Italy, France, Spain, Portugal and Greece).[346] Similarly, after around thirty years of the EU's PDO/PGI system, 77 per cent of the registered product names (PDO and PGI) originate from only five southern Member States – Italy, France, Spain, Portugal and Greece[347] – where PDO registration is more densely concentrated.[348]

Obviously, in the cases of both the Lisbon Agreement and the EU's GI protection, the figures show a cleavage in the EU between northern states and southern states over AO/PDO protection.[349] However, what is strange is that the northern Member States, who have shown no interest in joining the Lisbon Agreement, voted to establish the European sui generis system of PDO protection, even though it requires more national obligations for the protection of AO/PDO.[350] If the northern EU members find the

343. *See* Geiger, *supra* n. 269, at 152; Francis Gurry (Director General of WIPO), *Ceremony to Mark the 50th Anniversary of the Adoption of the Lisbon Agreement*, WIPO (11 June 2021), http://www.wipo.int/about-wipo/en/dgo/speeches/gurry_lisbon_08.html.
344. Daniel Gervais, *The Lisbon Agreement's Misunderstood Potential*, 1 WIPO J. 87 (2009).
345. Lisbon Agreement for the Protection of Appellations of Origin and Their International Registration, 31 October 1958, 923 U.N.T.S. 205 (as amended on 28 September 1979) ('Lisbon Agreement' hereinafter).
346. The Lisbon Agreement has thirty contracting parties, seven of which are the EU Member States (Bulgaria, Czech Republic, Hungary, France, Italy, Portugal and Slovakia). Greece, Romania and Spain have signed but not ratified the Agreement. *See* Toshiyuki Kono, *Intellectual Property and Private International Law: Comparative Perspectives* 977 (Hart Publishing 2012); Matteo Gragnani, *The European Union and the Lisbon Agreement for the Protection of Appellations of Origin and Their International Registration*, Centre d'études juridiques européennes (11 June 2021), https://www.ceje.ch/fr/actualites/action-exterieure/2010/08/european-union-and-lisbon-agreement-protection-appellations-origin-and-their-international-registration/.
347. *See* DG AGRI, *International Protection of EU Geographical Indications: Objectives, Outcome and Challenges* 3 (Working Paper, Ref. Ares (2012) 669394, 2012); European Court of Auditors, *Do the Design and Management of the Geographical Indications Scheme Allow It to Be Effective*, *supra* n. 332, at 26.
348. Michael Erhart, *The EU Agricultural Quality Policy: Opportunities and Perspectives* 22 (European Flour Millers Conference 2013); Tania G. Albuquerque et al., *25 Years of European Union (EU) Quality Schemes for Agricultural Products and Foodstuffs Across EU Member States*, 98 J. Sci. Food & Agric. 2475, 2486 (2018).
349. A study shows that the southern Mediterranean countries, including Portugal, have the highest number of products registered as PDO/PGI. The number of products registered in Germany, Austria, the United Kingdom and Ireland is far lower than the number of products registered in the Mediterranean countries. In the more northern countries of Europe (i.e., the Benelux countries and the Scandinavian countries), only a few products are registered as PDO/PGI. *See* Tilman Becker & Alexander Staus, *European Food Quality Policy: The Importance of Geographical Indications, Organic Certification and Food Quality Assurance Schemes in European Countries*, 10 Estey Ctr. J. Int'l L. & Trade Pol'y 111 (2009). *See also* Martijn Huysmans & Johan Swinnen, *No Terroir in the Cold? A Note on the Geography of Geographical Indications*, 70 J. Agric. Econ 550 (2019).
350. The EU-wide system for the protection of certain geographical denomination is not original in principle. The Lisbon Agreement of 1958, aimed at protecting appellation of origin, is significantly close to PDO/PGI protection. Once an appellation of origin is registered within the

Lisbon Agreement unattractive because 'these countries have virtually no commercially valuable appellations of origin and therefore nothing to gain from joining such international agreement',[351] then why have they decided to join a similar one?

We argue that the duality between PDO and PGI helped attract more northern states, making the EU-wide sui generis GI protection possible. This may explain why, in the negotiations for Regulation 2081/92, Germany pressured for an extensive category under which all geographical names, including PDO and PGI, would be protected.[352] Not coincidentally, this is also the case with the Lisbon Agreement, where the Geneva Act has extended the international register currently covering appellations of origins to GIs in order to 'make it more attractive to states and users'.[353] The conceptual duality between AO and GI is replicated in the regime of the Lisbon Agreement.[354]

Lisbon union, fellow Lisbon members must protect it in their countries. They do, however, have the option of saying that they cannot guarantee the AO within one year of that appellation being registered, as long as they alert the International Bureau and explain the grounds for that decision. Nonetheless, the EU system leads to an extension of national obligations. The protection is 'immediate' and 'automatic' insofar as the denomination is listed in the European Commission's Register. Member States are obliged to ensure the protection without having the power to select which can be protected or which one not. *See* Article 5(3) of the Lisbon Agreement: 'The Authority of any country may declare that it cannot ensure the protection of an appellation of origin whose registration has been notified to it, but only in so far as its declaration is notified to the International Bureau, together with an indication of the grounds therefor, within a period of one year from the receipt of the notification of registration.'

351. Jim Chen, *A Sober Second Look at Appellations of Origin: How the United States Will Crash France's Wine and Cheese Party*, 5 Minn. J. Global Trade 29, 55 (1996).
352. Kolia, *supra* n. 335, at 239.
353. In 2008, a working group was established to explore possible improvements under the Lisbon Agreement and make it 'more attractive to states and users, while preserving the principles and objectives of the Lisbon Agreement'. A year later, the working group was given the mandate to begin a full review of the system. The revisions in the diplomatic conference in May 2015 have changed the subject matter covered by the Lisbon registry to include GIs, not just AOs. *See* WIPO, *Special Union for the Protection of Appellations of Origin and Their Inferential Registration (Lisbon union)*, LI/A/25/2 (19 June 2009) p. 1; WIPO, *Diplomatic Conference for the Adoption of a New Act of the Lisbon Agreement for the Protection of Appellations of Origin and Their International Registration: Basic Proposal for the New Act of the Lisbon Agreement on Appellations of Origin and Geographical Indications*, LI/DC/3 (14 November 2014) p. 5.
354. Article 2(1) of the Geneva Act of the Lisbon Agreement: 'This Act applies in respect of: (i) any denomination protected in the Contracting Party of Origin consisting of or containing the name of a geographical area, or another denomination known as referring to such area, which serves to designate a good as originating in that geographical area, where the quality or characteristics of the good are due exclusively or essentially to the geographical environment, including natural and human factors, and which has given the good its reputation; as well as (ii) any indication protected in the Contracting Party of Origin consisting of or containing the name of a geographical area, or another indication known as referring to such area, which identifies a good as originating in that geographical area, where a given quality, reputation or other characteristic of the good is essentially attributable to its geographical origin.' *See also* WIPO, *Basic Proposal for the New Act of the Lisbon Agreement on Appellations of Origin and Geographical Indications*, LI/DC/3 (14 November 2014) p. 5; WIPO, *Draft Revised Lisbon Agreement on Appellations of Origin and Geographical Indications*, LI/WG/DEV/8/2 (11 October 2013) p. 4.

In conclusion, as a member of the broader family of unfair competition law,[355] the European notion of GIs was created amid the background of adjustments of the CAP, rather than in the field of competition policy. As a result, their informative function for consumers is no longer GI's baseline for protection (e.g., Directive 79/112 on the labelling of foodstuffs). Instead, GI protection in the EU can be viewed as a vector for improving agricultural product quality, encouraging diversification in agricultural production (thereby achieving a better balance between supply and demand), identifying products with specific characteristics in the marketplace, improving farmers' incomes (to help rural economies) and, last but not least, addressing the diversity across national systems in terms of GI protection. Because of this reconciliation, reputation alone may trigger PGI protection, which is not based on the *terroir* idea.[356] This lack of justification based on the *terroir* idea leads us to doubt if 'GIs are a genuine quality signal or a rent for producers.'[357] However, it has to be borne in mind that the *terroir* concept has been reinterpreted by putting more emphasis on human contributions, as in the case of France. We argue that the 'looser link' requirement in PGI protection may be justified by the need to accommodate traditional production methods, the *savoir-faire* of producers who, due to their intergenerational occupancy, are identified with a particular territory.[358] This rationale is also reflected in the discussion on the extension of EU-wide GI protection to industrial products. We will explore the EU's changed attitude towards the objectives of and basis for GI protection in the following section.[359]

[B] Extension of the GI Notion to Other Product Sectors

The EU legislation concerning GI protection initially applied to the wine sector in the 1970s as part of the Common Market Organization (CMO) of wine. It once even served as a reference for Regulation 2081/92.[360] However, the PDO/PGI concept was not created until Regulation 2081/92, which limited the scope of protection to certain agricultural products and foodstuffs.[361] It was the reform of the wine CMO in 2008 that finally adopted the principles of the regulation on agricultural products and foodstuffs.

355. Annette Kur, *Quibbling Siblings: Comments to Dev Gangjee's Presentation*, 82 Chi.-Kent. L. Rev. 1317, 1318 (2007).
356. Justin Hughes advocates that if the link between a place and a product is just a matter of reputation, the GIs function no differently than a trademark. *See* Hughes, *supra* n. 276, at 368.
357. *See* Marion Desquilbet & Sylvette Monier-Dilhan, *Are Geographical Indications a Worthy Quality Signal? A Framework with Endogenous Quality Choice*, 42 Eur. Rev. of Agric. Econ. 129, 130 (2015); Josling, *supra* n. 149.
358. *See* Dagne, *supra* n. 164.
359. *See infra* n. 439.
360. The preamble to Regulation 2081/92: 'Whereas the planned rules should take account of existing Community legislation on wines and spirit drinks, which provide for a higher level of protection.'
361. According to Article 2(1) of Regulation 1151/2012, it applies to basic agricultural products intended for human consumption listed in Annex I to the Treaty of Rome (e.g., meat, dairy and fish products, honey, fruits, vegetables), other agricultural products (not in Annex I to the Treaty) listed in Annex I of Regulation (e.g., essential oils, hay, cotton) and foodstuffs (not necessarily agricultural products) referred to in Annex I of Regulation (e.g., beer, bread, pastry,

The GI notion was also extended to spirits and aromatized wine products. European authorities are considering a possible extension of GI protection to non-agricultural products in order to accommodate traditional *savoir-faire*.

[1] PDO/PGI for Wines, Spirits, and Aromatized Wines

In 1962, the objectives of quality policy were set as the cornerstone of European wine legislation,[362] via Regulation 24 of 4 April 1962, which established a common organization for the wine market.[363] The unitary GI protection for wines begins in 1970.[364] A different dichotomy from that used in the GI protection developed for other agricultural products was made as a starting point and remained until 2008: quality wine produced

salt). It is worth noting that the list is not always the same but tends to expand. For example, cork and cochineal were added in 1997. Wine vinegar was included in the scope in 2003. Salt and cotton were added in 2008. Moreover, Regulation 1151/2012 provided that this list could be supplemented, taking into account international commitments or new production methods or material. Thus, some commenters note that the broad formulation leaves an open door for the Commission to add goods that are not fully understood as agricultural goods or foodstuffs. *See* Vadim Mantrov, *EU Law on Indications of Geographical Origin: Theory and Practice* 157 (Springer 2014); *Commission Regulation (EC) No 1068/97 of 12 June 1997 amending Annex II to Council Regulation (EEC) No 2081/92 on the protection of geographical indications and designations of origin for agricultural products and foodstuffs*, OJ L 156, 13.6.1997, p. 10; *Commission Regulation (EC) No 417/2008 of 8 May 2008 amending Annexes I and II to Council Regulation (EC) No 510/2006 on the protection of geographical indications and designations of origin for agricultural products and foodstuffs*, OJ L 125, 9.5.2008, p. 27; European Commission, *Overview of the EU GIs System of Protection and Its Benefits*, WIPO-IPOPHL Seminar (28-29 February 2012) p. 4; Gesa Wesseler, *PDO and PGI Schemes in the EU: Present and Future Legal Framework* 9 (DG AGRI Working Document 2010); O'Connor, *supra* n. 124, at 128. Conversely, formerly protectable under Regulation 2081/92, mineral waters and spring waters were removed from the list in 2003 by Regulation 692/2003. *See Council Regulation (EC) No 692/2003 of 8 April 2003 amending Regulation (EEC) No 2081/92 on the protection of geographical indications and designations of origin for agricultural products and foodstuffs*, OJ L 99, 17.5.2003, p. 1; Gail Evans & Michael Blakeney, *The International Protection of Geographical Indications Yesterday, Today and Tomorrow, in Emerging Issues in Intellectual Property* 250, 279 (Guido Westkamp ed., Edward Elgar 2007).

362. Quality regulations were part of the initial wine policy in 1962 and have been strengthened since the Regulations of 1970, 1979, 1987, 1999 and 2008 to increase quality. *See* Giulia Melonia & Johan Swinnena, *The Political Economy of European Wine Regulations*, 8 J. Wine Econ. 244, 248 (2013).
363. The first regulations concerning quality policy or GI protection were related to wines because of the common organization of markets. Regulation 24 on the Progressive Establishment of a Common Organization of the Market in Wine provided for creating EU-wide rules for quality wines produced in specific regions, under the policy of encouraging quality production. *See* R. Van Der Stappen, *L'OCM vitivinicole: genèse, évolution et défis actuels*, Revue du droit rural, n° 335, 2005, p. 22; *Regulation No 24 on the progressive establishment of a common organisation of the market in wine*, OJ 30, 20.4.1962, p. 989.
364. In 1970, the EU published two concrete CMO regulations relating to quality wine (Regulation 817/70) and table wine (Regulation 816/70). These two regulations remained separate until 1999 with Regulation 1493/1999. Regulation 816/1970 provided a scheme of intervention for table wine, and Regulation 817/90 provided the rules for the production of quality wine. *See* Davide Gaeta & Corsinovi Paola, *Economics, Governance, and Politics in the Wine Market: European Union Developments* 34 (Palgrave Macmillan 2014).

in a specific region (QWpsr),[365] on the one hand, and table wine (TW),[366] on the other. This distinction was the result of a spirit of compromise between the Member States in favour of the notion of appellations of origin and members that were not.[367]

The concept of QWpsr was similar to that of appellations of origin.[368] Regulation 1493/1999 only specified in Article 54 that 'QWpsr shall mean wines which comply with the provisions of this Title and the Community and national provisions adopted in this connection.'[369] Although this definition was not accurate, the QWpsr clearly indicated that the wine's quality was inseparable from its geographical origin. It was also specified in Annex VI that 'specified region shall mean a wine-growing area or a combination of wine-growing areas which produces wines with particular quality characteristics and whose name is used to designate QWpsr'.[370]

By contrast, Annex I of Regulation 1493/1999 first defined the TW as a wine other than QWpsr and then explained this through a series of technical specifications concerning authorized grape varieties, alcoholic strength and acidity content. As long as the wines were produced in the EU, geographical origin was not relevant in the assessment.[371] However, a TW could also be designated by a GI if quality standards were met. In this case, the wine had to be produced 'wholly from certain clearly specified vine varieties and coming exclusively from the territory, precisely demarcated, whose name it bears'.[372] Therefore, TW includes two subcategories: TW with GIs and TW without.

Far from harmonizing national legislations and choosing a common definition of appellations of origin in the wine sector, the regulation on QWpsr and TW could be

365. *Regulation (EEC) No 817/70 of the Council of 28 April 1970 laying down special provisions relating to quality wines produced in specified regions*, OJ L 99, 5.5.1970, p. 20.
366. *See Regulation (EEC) No 816/70 of the Council of 28 April 1970 laying down additional provisions for the common organization of the market in wine*, OJ L 99, 5.5.1970, p. 1.
367. *See* Jean-Marc Bahans, *La nouvelle OCM vitivinicole: une réforme communautaire sous l'inspiration de l'OMC. – (commentaire des titres II, III et IV du règlement (CE) n° 479/2008 du Conseil du 29 avril 2008 et du règlement (CE) n° 555/2008 de la Commission du 27 juin 2008)*, Droit rural, n° 366, 2008, dossier 33, p. 2; *Réforme de l'OCM vitivinicole: sauvons notre filière et nos viticulteurs*, Sénat (11 June 2021), http://www.senat.fr/rap/r06-348/r06-3484.html.
368. The French expressions '*Appellation d'origine contrôlée*', '*Appellation contrôlée*', '*Champagne*' and '*Vin délimité de qualité supérieure*' have been recognized by Regulation 817/70 as expressions traditionally used in France to designate QWpsr. *See* Article 12 of Regulation 817/70.
369. *Council Regulation (EC) No 1493/1999 of 17 May 1999 on the common organization of the market in wine*, OJ L 179, 14.7.1999, p. 29.
370. *Ibid.*, 60.
371. *Ibid.*, 40.
372. Article 28 of Regulation 753/2002 provides more specifically that the national rules on the use of certain geographical indications for TW must require the terms concerned to be linked to the use of a specified geographical indication smaller than the Member State and reserved for table wines meeting certain production requirements, notably regarding the vine variety, minimum natural alcoholic strength by volume and an evaluation or indication of the organoleptic characteristics. *See Commission Regulation (EC) No 753/2002 of 29 April 2002 laying down certain rules for applying Council Regulation (EC) No 1493/1999 as regards the description, designation, presentation and protection of certain wine sector products*, OJ L 118, 4.5.2002, p. 1; *See also* Article 30 of Regulation 816/70; Article 51 of Regulation 1493/1999.

considered a mutual recognition of national regulations that define wine quality.[373] Member States retained the power to define QWpsr/TW, and they only had to forward to the Commission the list of QWpsr/TW they had recognized.[374] It is therefore no wonder that the two EU definitions tell us almost nothing because they do not in fact exist: the Member States enjoyed a broad competence to make their own selections.[375] Thus, France was able to maintain its strict approach of reinforcing the link with the region for the wines concerned, particularly via its classification (AOC, Vin délimité de qualité supérieure (AOVDQS),[376] and *Vins de pays* (VDP)).[377] Nonetheless, the QWpsr/TW system also allowed a less strict approach, which was adopted by Germany and Luxembourg, who have opted to classify almost all manufactured wines as QWpsr.[378] The increase in the number of QWpsr/TW, which did not necessarily reflect the quality of the wine,[379] led to consumer confusion, weakened the community

---

373. *See* François Barque, *Le droit communautaire des appellations d'origine et indications géographiques en matière vinicole*, Revue trimestrielle de droit européen, 2009, p. 743; Norbert Olszak, *Droit des appellations d'origine et indications de provenance*, Paris, Tec & Doc, 2001, pp. 147-151.
374. Article 54(4) and 54(5) of Regulation 1493/1999: 'Member States shall forward to the Commission the list of quality wines psr which they have recognized, stating, for each of these quality wines psr, details of the national provisions governing the production and manufacture of those quality wines psr. The Commission shall publish the list in the C series of the Official Journal of the European Communities.' Article 28 of Regulation 753/2002: '... The producer Member States may adopt stricter rules on the use of these terms (geographical indications) for wine produced in their territory ... .'
375. Articles 55 and 57 of Regulation 1493/1999 conferred the Member States the possibility to determine other conditions of production and characteristics that shall be obligatory for the QWpsr. *See* Article 51 of Regulation 1493/1999.
376. The '*Vin délimité de qualité supérieure (AOVDQS)*' was enshrined in the Law of 1949, after the Second World War, for designating the wines benefiting an *appellation d'origine non-contrôlée* claimed according to the Law of 1919 and the Law of 1927. The AOVDQS belongs to QWpsr with respect to European classification. Article L. 644-12 laid down by the Law of 2007 has put an end to the AOVDQS. All AOVDQS hence should submit a claim of transformation for the AOC or *Vins de pays*. *See* Loi n° 49-1603 du 18 décembre 1949 relative à la reconnaissance officielle, dans le statut viticole, des vins délimités de qualité supérieure, J.O. du 21 déc. 1949, p. 12198; Loi n° 2007-1821 du 24 décembre 2007 ratifiant l'ordonnance n° 2006-1547 du 7 décembre 2006 relative à la valorisation des produits agricoles, forestiers ou alimentaires et des produits de la mer, J.O. du 27 déc. 2007, p. 21210.
377. The *Vins de pays* corresponded to the TW and was once classified as a *mention valorisante* (mention that adds value to the products). Article 64 of the Law of 2009 suppressed the *Vins de pays* from the *mention valorisante* and inserted them in the PGI category. *See* Loi n° 2009-526 du 12 mai 2009 de simplification et de clarification du droit et d'allègement des procédures, J.O. du 13 mai 2009, p. 7920.
378. In practice, 90–95 per cent of wines in Germany and Luxembourg are classed as quality wines psr each year, with a lower percentage in Austria and the United Kingdom, where the system was introduced at a later date. *See* European Commission, *Annex to the Communication from the Commission to the Council and the European Parliament: Towards a Sustainable European Wine Sector COM(2006)319*, at 9 (Commission Staff Working Document, SEC (2006) 770, 2006).
379. The Commission notes that the distinction between QWpsr and TW does not necessarily reflect the quality of the wines. Moreover, there is no reference in the QWpsr definition of geographical indications as defined by the TRIPS Agreement. *See* European Commission, *Annex to the Communication from the Commission to the Council and the European Parliament: Towards a*

quality policy, and thus contributed to the decline of the market situation.[380] As a consequence, the dichotomy between QWpsr and TW no longer provided the appropriate framework in which to promote quality wines.[381]

Since 'the concept of EU quality wines is based on a geographical origin approach and the EU wants to confirm, adapt, promote and enhance this concept worldwide',[382] a substantial revision of the EU classification system for wines is envisaged, considering the insufficiency of the former regime in this respect.[383] The old system of the 1970s should be updated in light of the GI definitions of the TRIPS Agreement in order not only to achieve better international protection for EU GIs[384] but also to strengthen the EU position on GIs, which would provide the EU with a sound and credible position in international negotiations on GI protection.[385] Thus, an alternative has been considered – to restructure the wine categories on the basis of the TRIPS Agreement into 'wines without GI' and 'wines with GI'.[386]

This formula could have helped to simplify the old complex classification of wines.[387] However, the European legislators considered that the new classification should also be consistent with the horizontal quality policy (former Regulation 510/2006) and that therefore 'wines with GI' should be further divided into 'wines with PDO' and 'wines with PGI'.[388] The justification the legislators offered for this

Sustainable European Wine Sector COM(2006)319, *supra* n. 378, at 9. European Commission, *Impact Assessment: Towards a Sustainable European Wine Sector COM(2006)319*, SEC (2006) 770 (22 June 2006) p. 9.

380. European Commission, *Communication from the Commission to the Council and the European Parliament: Towards a Sustainable European Wine Sector*, COM(2006)319 final (22 June 2006) p. 5.
381. European Commission, *Accompanying Document to the Proposal for a Council Regulation on the Common Organization of the Market in Wine and Amending Certain Regulations* 6 (Commission Staff Working Document, SEC (2007) 893/2, 2007).
382. European Commission, *Communication from the Commission to the Council and the European Parliament: Towards a Sustainable European Wine Sector*, *supra* n. 380, at 10.
383. European Commission, *Proposal for a Council Regulation on the Common Organization of the Market in Wine*, COM(2007)372 final (4 July 2007) p. 6.
384. The concept of geographical indication is linked only with the category of TW with a geographical indication (but makes no reference to the TRIPS Agreement). QWprs are linked with specified regions, and there is no reference in the QWpsr definition of geographical indications as defined by the TRIPS Agreement. Thus, geographical wine names are not necessarily recognized as geographical indications under the TRIPS Agreement. It is therefore not easy to defend wine names in the light of the WTO Agreements. *See* European Commission, *Wine: Common Market Organization* 54 (Working Paper, 2006).
385. European Commission, *Accompanying Document to the Proposal for a Council Regulation on the Common Organization of the Market in Wine and Amending Certain Regulations*, *supra* n. 381, at 33-34.
386. *See* European Commission, *Wine: Common Market Organization*, *supra* n. 384, at 54; European Commission, *Towards a Sustainable European Wine Sector*, AGRI – C3 MD (2 June 2006) p. 25.
387. The European Commission noted that EU regulations are too complex, notably on definitions and classification (i.e., QWpsr, TW with GI and TW without GI). *See* European Commission, *EU Wine Reform: Background Information on the Wine Sector*, MEMO/06/245 (22 June 2006).
388. European Commission, *Proposal for a Council Regulation on the Common Organization of the Market in Wine*, *supra* n. 383, at 6.

complementary criterion was that 'quality wines are identified for consumers via protected designations of origin and geographical indications'.[389]

According to Article 34 of Regulation 479/2008 (as the wine sector is now governed by Regulation 1308/2013, but the definitions are the same),[390] the definition of the PDO for wine repeats the general definition of appellations of origin; it concerns 'the name of a region, a specific place or, in exceptional cases, a country used to describe a wine whose quality and characteristics are essentially or exclusively due to a particular geographical environment with its inherent natural and human factors'. By contrast, the definition does not contain the general threefold requirement laid down in Regulation 510/2006 for other PDO agricultural products ('the production, processing and preparation shall take place in the defined geographical area')[391] but instead substitutes the following specific threefold requirement. First, the wine must be produced from grapes originating exclusively in the designated geographical zone. Second, the production of the wine should take place in the geographical area but not necessarily in the processing and preparation. Although the term 'production' is interpreted in Regulation 607/2009 as 'all the operations from the harvesting of the grapes to the completion of the winemaking process',[392] it is believed to be possible to market bulk wine produced in the area of production but assembled outside it (e.g., other Member States or non-EU countries).[393] Finally, the wine must be obtained from vine varieties belonging to *Vitis vinifera*.[394]

389. Recital 27 of Regulation 479/2008: 'The concept of quality wines in the Community is based, inter alia, on the specific characteristics attributable to the wine's geographical origin. Such wines are identified for consumers via protected designations of origin and geographical indications, although the current system is not fully developed in this respect.' *See Council Regulation (EC) No 479/2008 of 29 April 2008 on the common organization of the market in wine, amending Regulations (EC) No 1493/1999, (EC) No 1782/2003, (EC) No 1290/2005, (EC) No 3/2008 and repealing Regulations (EEC) No 2392/86 and (EC) No 1493/1999*, OJ L 148, 6.6.2008, p. 4.
390. Regulation 479/2008 had been repealed and integrated into Regulation 1234/2007, which, in turn, was repealed by Regulation 1308/2013. *See Council Regulation (EC) No 491/2009 of 25 May 2009 amending Regulation (EC) No 1234/2007 establishing a common organization of agricultural markets and on specific provisions for certain agricultural products (Single CMO Regulation)*, OJ L 154, 17.6.2009, p. 1; *Regulation (EU) No 1308/2013 of the European Parliament and the Council establishing a common organisation of the markets in agricultural products and repealing Council Regulations 922/72, 234/79, 1037/2001 and 1234/2007*, OJ L 148, 6.6.2008, p. 671, Article 93.
391. Article 2 of Regulation 510/2006.
392. *Commission Regulation (EC) No 607/2009 of 14 July 2009 laying down certain detailed rules for the implementation of Council Regulation (EC) No 479/2008 as regards protected designations of origin and geographical indications, traditional terms, labelling and presentation of certain wine sector products*, OJ L 193, 24.7.2009, p. 63, Article 6.
393. Bahans & Menjucq, *supra* n. 2, at 90; Caroline Le Goffic, *Indications géographiques en droit Européen*, J.-Cl. Europe Traité, fasc. 1810, p. 20; Mélanie Gros, *Les signes d'origine et de qualité des vins*, thèse, Université de Toulouse, 2009, p. 230.
394. *See* Article 34 of Regulation 479/2008; *Council Regulation (EC) No 1234/2007 of 22 October 2007 establishing a common organization of agricultural markets and on specific provisions for certain agricultural products (Single CMO Regulation)*, OJ L 299, 16.11.2007, p. 1, Article 118b.

The definition of PGI for wine is closer to the GI definition adopted in the TRIPS Agreement.[395] A causal interaction between the geographical area and the quality, reputation, or other specific characteristics of the product is required.[396] It is worth noting that the causation is not purely physical but is also social: 'The products should have a minimum of the history grounded in the region for establishing this link.'[397] Furthermore, similar to the wine sector PDO, it does not repeat the former threefold requirement for other PGI agricultural products, whereby at least one of the production steps (production, processing, or preparation) must take place in the defined geographical area, but concerns only the 'production' step.[398] It is also indicated that the wine should be from grapes at least 85 per cent of which come exclusively from the geographical area. The wine should be obtained from vine varieties belonging to *Vitis vinifera* or a cross between the *Vitis vinifera* species and other species of the *genus Vitis*.[399]

Overall, the connection with *terroir* is generally more robust in the wine sector than it is in the PDO/PGI for other agricultural sectors. For both the PDO and PGI for wines, all the production stages must take place in the geographical area,[400] and there is a requirement governing the source of the raw materials (100 per cent of the grapes for a PDO and 85 per cent or more for a PGI). By contrast, for PGI in other agricultural sectors, only one of the production steps is required to take place in the concerned region, and there is no minimum requirement for raw materials sourcing.[401]

Since the establishment of Regulation 479/2008, the distinction between QWpsr and TW has become history. The names of QWpsr and TW are protected as PDO and PGI for wines.[402] A similar approach is adopted for spirits and aromatized wine products. However, Regulation 2019/787 (which repealed Regulation 110/2008) and Regulation 251/2014 made no distinction between PDO and PGI but provided a unitary notion of GI whose definition is a very faithful copy of that adopted in the TRIPS Agreement.[403] As there is nothing to prevent the Member States from laying down

395. PGI for wine does not have the 'essentiality' requirement and only requires that 'it possesses a specific quality, reputation or other characteristics *attributable* to that geographical origin'. *See* Vincent Ruzek, *La stratégie communautaire de protection des indications géographiques en question*, Droit rural, n° 373, 2009, étude 7.
396. Article 7 of Regulation 607/2009.
397. *See* C. E., 26 avr. 2013, n° 355941; C. E., 26 avr. 2013, n° 355942; Jean-Marc Bahans, *Un an de jurisprudence en droit de la vigne et du vin (2013 -2014)*, Droit rural, n° 429, 2015, chron. 1.
398. Article 2 of Regulation 510/2006.
399. *See* Article 34 of Regulation 479/2008; Article 118b of Regulation 1234/2007.
400. It covers all the operations involved but with the exception of any post-production processes. *See* Article 6 of Regulation 607/2009.
401. European Commission, *Green Paper on Making the Most of Europe's Traditional Know-How*, *supra* n. 168, at 16.
402. Articles 46 and 51 of Regulation 479/2008.
403. Article 3(4) of Regulation 2019/787: '... "geographical indication" means an indication which identifies a spirit drink as originating in the territory of a country, or a region or locality in that territory, where a given quality, reputation or other characteristic of that spirit drink is essentially attributable to its geographical origin'; Article 2(3) of Regulation 251/2014: 'Geographical indication means an indication which identifies an aromatized wine product as originating in a region, a specific place, or a country, where a given quality, reputation or other characteristics of that product is essentially attributable to its geographical origin.' *See*

stricter rules fostering a much closer quality-*terroir* link,[404] the French AOC '*Cognac*'[405] – which requires special characteristics, a history of a link with *terroir* factors, and a history linked to a product reputation – could be classified only in the vague category of GIs at the EU level.[406] The notion of appellations of origin vanished. Therefore, Professor Jean-Marc Bahans has questioned whether it is fair that the more stringent AOC '*Cognac*' belongs to the same category as 'Scotch Whisky', whose link with *terroir* is obviously weaker.[407]

The remarks of Professor Bahans raise the question of how European GI definitions should be made. Should they be fully harmonized with the definition of the TRIPS Agreement, as is the case of the GIs for spirits? Alternatively, should they be further divided into PDO and PGI? Despite the long-standing unsolved problems, other issues deserve further reflection. First, the current European GI legislative regime continues to be complex[408] because it is split into four frameworks[409] depending on the product it is addressed to (agricultural products and foodstuffs, wines, spirits, and aromatized wines),[410] and each framework has its own understanding of what a GI is.[411] Second, the relationship between GI protection at the EU level and that at the national level (e.g., AOC) needs to be articulated. Although European authorities indicated in the proposal for Regulation 479/2008 that 'protecting geographical names

---

Regulation (EU) 2019/787 of the European Parliament and of the Council of 17 April 2019 on the definition, description, presentation and labelling of spirit drinks, the use of the names of spirit drinks in the presentation and labelling of other foodstuffs, the protection of geographical indications for spirit drinks, the use of ethyl alcohol and distillates of agricultural origin in alcoholic beverages, and repealing Regulation (EC) No 110/2008, OJ L 130, 17.5.2019, p. 1; *Regulation (EU) No 251/2014 of the European Parliament and of the Council of 26 February 2014 on the definition, description, presentation, labelling and the protection of geographical indications of aromatised wine products and repealing Council Regulation (EEC) No 1601/91*, OJ L 85, 20.3.2014, p. 14.

404. Member States may lay down stricter rules on production, description, presentation and labelling in so far as they are compatible with Community law. *See* Article 45 of Regulation 2019/787.
405. Décret n° 2015-10 du 7 janvier 2015 relatif à l'appellation d'origine contrôlée Cognac ou Eau-de-vie de Cognac ou Eau-de-vie des Charentes, J.O. du 9 janv. 2015, p. 423.
406. Cahier des charges de l'appellation d'origine contrôlée 'Cognac' ou 'Eau-de-vie de Cognac' ou 'Eau-de-vie des Charentes' homologué par le décret n° 2015-10 du 7 janvier 2015 relatif à l'appellation d'origine contrôlée 'Cognac' ou 'Eau-de-vie de Cognac' ou 'Eau-de-vie des Charentes', J.O. du 9 janv. 2015.
407. Bahans & Menjucq, *supra* n. 2, at 91.
408. European Commission, *Impact Assessment of Geographical Indications*, *supra* n. 266, at 22.
409. The merger of the existing systems (for wine, spirits, aromatized wines and agricultural products and foodstuffs) is viewed positively by the Commission. *See* European Commission, *Proposal for a Regulation of the European Parliament and the Council on Agricultural Product Quality Schemes*, *supra* n. 297, at 5.
410. *Council Regulation (EEC) No 1601/91 of 10 June 1991 laying down general rules on the definition, description and presentation of aromatized wines, aromatized wine-based drinks and aromatized wine-product cocktails*, OJ L 149, 14.7.1991, p. 1.
411. In several cases, EU cannot avoid a burdensome work of explication that EU GIs refers to PDO/PGI as referred in Regulation 1151/2012 (PDO/PGI for agricultural products); Regulation 1234/2007 (PDO/PGI for wine); Regulation 2019/787 (GI for spirit); and Regulation 1601/91 (geographical designations for aromatized drinks based on wine products). *See Free Trade Agreement Between the European Union and Its Member States, of the One Part, and the Republic Korea, of the Other Part*, OJ L 127, 14.5.2011, p. 46.

as PDO/PGI at national level should no longer be possible',[412] this passage was erased in the final text and replaced by the claim that 'quality policy regulated at national level may continue'.[413] Considering the 'exhaustive nature' of the EU's uniform system of protection for GIs,[414] the question therefore arises: to what extent does the national quality policy on GIs such as the AOC system exist? It seems that, while the EU escaped from the old GI jungle, it has fallen into another peril, a new conceptual maze.

[2] GIs for Non-agricultural Products in the EU

It is not a coincidence that France has been revising its position on the interpretation of the link to *terroir* since 2010[415] while a uniform approach to GI protection for non-agricultural products is being considered in the EU. A vivid example is the case of '*Laguiole*', which contributed to the creation of the IGPIA in France[416] and continues to have an impact at the European negotiation table.[417]

In the EU, the unitary protection of GIs is limited to agricultural products, foodstuffs, wines, and other alcoholic beverages. The European vision can be explained by the traditional interpretation of the *terroir* idea,[418] which emphasizes the physical aspects of a defined territory (land and soil) as a result of wine production

412. European Commission, *Proposal for a Council Regulation on the Common Organization of the Market in Wine, supra* n. 383, at 17.
413. *See* Recital 37 of Regulation 479/2008.
414. The CJEU demonstrates that Regulation 510/2006 is exhaustive in nature so that it precludes national protection of geographical indications. However, it does not preclude the application of domestic rules protecting designations containing specific geographical references (e.g., the use of the description 'mountain' in relation to agricultural products or foodstuffs). Also, it does not preclude the application of national legislation that prohibits the potentially misleading use of a simple geographical indication of source where there is no link between the characteristics of the product and its geographical provenance. *See* Case C-478/07 *Budějovický Budvar* [2009] ECR I-07721, para. 129; Case C-312/98, *Haus Cramer, supra* n. 55, para. 54; Joined Cases C-321/94, C-322/94, C-323/94 & C-324/94 *Criminal proceedings against Jacques Pistre* [1997] ECR I-02343, para. 55; Case C-35/13 *Assica -Associazione Industriali delle Carni e dei Salumi and Kraft Foods Italia SpA v. Associazioni fra produttori per la tutela del 'Salame Felino' and Others* (ECJ 8 May 2014) para. 28; Maryline Boizard, *Régime communautaire de protection des indications géographiques et des appellations d'origine protégées et dispositifs nationaux de protection des dénominations géographiques: une application distributive stricte*, Droit rural, n° 429, 2015, comm. 17.
415. *See* Delphine Marie-Vivien et al., *Are French Geographical Indications Losing Their Soul? Analyzing Recent Developments in the Governance of the Link to the Origin in France*, 98 World Dev. 25 (2017).
416. *See* Laurence Bineau, *Une extension attendue de l'indication géographique protégée aux produits manufacturés*, Contrats concurrence consommation, n° 2, 2013, étude 3; Delphine Marie-Vivien, *La protection de l'indication géographique de produits industriels et artisanaux: le choix d'un régime juridique spécifique en question*, Contrats concurrence consommation, n° 12, 2013, étude 15.
417. European Parliament, *Draft Report on a Possible Extension of European Union Geographical Indication Protection to Non-agricultural Products*, 2015/2053(INI) (21 April 2015) p. 7, available at, https://www.europarl.europa.eu/doceo/document/JURI-PR-554895_EN.pdf (last accessed on 11 June 2021).
418. Marie-Vivien, *supra* n. 147.

governance in France during the early twentieth century.[419] As human factors become gradually acknowledged amid the evolution of the French AOC regime, the *terroir* concept is increasingly regarded as a hybrid model that connects both natural and human factors in a specific area.[420] On this issue, the Commission also noted that:

> GIs are self-evidently relevant to agricultural products where their geographical origin is linked with qualities stemming either directly from the soil or climate (e.g. wines) or a combination of natural factors and traditional processing methods applied in the region.[421]

Nevertheless, GIs do not by nature place non-agricultural products outside the range of protection. The TRIPS Agreement protects GIs regardless of whether the products are agriculture-related, thus allowing the contracting countries to protect handicrafts under their national regimes.[422] In China, for instance, according to a report released by the Trademark Office in 2014, 105 GIs for handicrafts have been registered as collective or certification marks, which makes up 3.89 per cent of the GI registration under the trademark regime.[423] Furthermore, the Lisbon Agreement, which is more restrictive regarding the definition of geographical ascriptions requiring a solid link to *terroir*, does not discriminate against non-agricultural products.[424] Even in France, where the *terroir* concept was elaborated, non-agricultural products can be protected under the AO regime or the new IGPIA regime.[425]

In the absence of common rules governing the production and marketing of non-agricultural products, it is up to the Member States to regulate such matters (including product description and labelling) in their territory.[426] Aside from France, fourteen other Member States provide a sui generis system of GI protection for non-agricultural products,[427] while the other Member States mainly rely on trademark

419. Emily C. Creditt, *Terroir v. Trademarks: The Debate over Geographical Indications and Expansions to the TRIPS Agreement*, 11 Vand. J. Ent. & Tech. L. 425, 427 (2008).
420. *See* Matthew J. Rippon, *Traditional Foods, Territorial Boundaries and the TRIPS Agreement: The Case of the Melton Mowbray Pork Pie*, 16 J. World Intell. Prop. 262, 292 (2013); François Casabianca et al., *Terroir et typicité: propositions de définitions pour deux notions essentielles à l'appréhension des Indications Géographiques et du développement durable*, Actes du Vième Congrès International des Terroirs Viticoles, 2006, pp. 3-7. This understanding of *terroir* is now widely accepted by several organizations. *See* Filippo Arfini et al., *Linking People, Places and Products: A Guide for Promoting Quality Linked to Geographical Origin and Sustainable Geographical Indications* (FAO Document 2009).
421. European Commission, *Green Paper on Making the Most of Europe's Traditional Know-How*, *supra* n. 168, at 4.
422. Josef Drexl et al., *EU Bilateral Trade Agreements and Intellectual Property: For Better or Worse?* 144 (Springer 2013).
423. *Tables and Records on Geographical Indication Registration in China*, Trademark Office of China (11 June 2021), http://sbj.cnipa.gov.cn/dlbz/xwbd/201503/t20150317_229104.html.
424. About 100 non-agricultural Gis are governed under the Lisbon Agreement. *See* Massimo Vittori, Managing Director of origin, *Geographical Indications for Non-agricultural Products* (Presentation at the Worldwide Symposium on Geographical Indications 27-29 March 2013).
425. Séverine Visse-Causse, *L'appellation d'origine*, thèse, Université de Reims, 2004, pp. 79-88.
426. *See* Case 27/80 *Criminal proceedings against Anton Adriaan Fietje* [1980] ECR 03839, para. 1; Case C-312/98, *Haus Cramer*, *supra* n. 55, para. 54.
427. Belgium (Wallonia), Bulgaria, Croatia, Czech Republic, Estonia, Germany, Hungary, Latvia, Poland, Portugal, Romania, Slovakia, Slovenia, and Spain (Region of Murcia). *See* Insight

law or unfair competition law. As a result, non-agricultural GIs are subject to a diversity of protections granted through different national legal instruments, which may not be in line with the objective of the free movement of products in the internal market.[428] As identified in the 'Cost of Non-Europe' report released in 2019, introducing EU-wide GI protection would have an overall positive effect on trade, employment, and rural development.[429] However, despite an intense debate, the Commission has not put forward a specific proposal.[430]

One of the core issues concerns how strong the link with the territory should be. In this respect, French experience regarding the creation of the IGPIA shows that the link to *terroir* required by the AO definition is too close to be applied to industrial products and handicrafts. A study carried out on behalf of the Commission arrived at a similar conclusion, finding that few non-agricultural products could meet the strict PDO requirements.[431] Two types of links – namely those in the PDO/PGI dichotomy – are also viewed unfavourably since two different links might confuse consumers.[432] Instead, a new approach was proposed to establish a link more strongly focused on human inputs: a locally developed *savoir-faire*.[433]

Even if human inputs did not constitute the primary goal of the European GI policies, they have never been forgotten. In justifying the creation of the PDO/PGI for agricultural products in 1992, the Commission noted that the know-how factor, combined with other factors such as herbage, cover, vine variety, and soil, could serve as a tool for maintaining the quality of products produced in a defined area.[434] Practice shows that certain GIs may be based entirely on human, rather than natural, inputs (e.g., '*Rillettes du Mans*').[435] As these human inputs are increasingly found to have a cultural heritage dimension,[436] GI protection has the potential to serve as a vector for rewarding those who produce traditional cultural expressions and keep traditions alive.[437]

Consulting et al., *Study on Geographical Indication Protection for Non-agricultural Products in the Internal Market*, *supra* n. 170, at 30.

428. *See* Catherine Barnard, *The Substantive Law of the EU: The Four Freedoms* (Oxford University Press 2010).
429. *See* Cecilia Navarra & Elodie Thirion, *Cost of Non-europe Report on Geographical Indications for Non-agricultural Products*, PE 631.764 (November 2019) p. 59.
430. *See* Andrea Zappalaglio et al., *Sui Generis Geographical Indications for the Protection of Non-agricultural Products in the EU: Can the Quality Schemes Fulfil the Task?*, 51 IIC-Int'l Rev. Intell. Prop. & Competition L. 31 (2020).
431. Insight Consulting et al., *Study on Geographical Indication Protection for Non-agricultural Products in the Internal Market*, *supra* n. 170, at 298.
432. Michael Koenig et al., *Public Consultations on Geographical Indication Protection for Non-agricultural Products in the EU: Summary of Results*, *supra* n. 332, at 14.
433. *Ibid.*
434. *Communication on the Free Movement of Foodstuffs Within the Community*, OJ C 271, 24.10.1989, p. 6.
435. *See* Bineau, *supra* n. 416; *Arrêté du 12 février 2010 portant homologation du cahier des charges de l'indication géographique protégée 'Rillettes du Mans'*, J.O. du 23 févr. 2010, p. 3340.
436. Giovanni Belletti & Andrea Marescotti, *Link Between Origin Labelled Products and Rural Development* 11 (Dolphins Final Report July 2002).
437. Dev Gangjee, *Geographical Indications and Cultural Heritage*, 4 WIPO J. 92 (2012).

In light of this valuable potential, European authorities' tone about human inputs is changing, even in the agricultural sector. One of the justifications for GI protection used in the earlier regulations (Recital 2 of Regulation 2081/92 and Regulation 510/2006) referred to 'the encouragement of agricultural production diversification' as a starting point, followed by the argument that 'the promotion of products having certain characteristics can be of considerable benefit to the rural economy'.[438] However, over the last decade, the Commission has made a 180-degree turn and has started to take the view that 'immaterial elements (e.g. the know-how of producers, cultural values, traditions) that have helped to build the reputation of a particular production area are the main reason behind the creation of a GI (rather than soil and climate factors)'.[439] More persuasive evidence is provided by Regulation 1151/2012, which replaced Recital 2 of the previous regulations with a brand new justification. Recital 1 of Regulation 1151/2012 states:

> The quality and diversity of the Union's agricultural, fisheries and aquaculture production is one of its important strengths, giving a competitive advantage to the Union's producers and making a major contribution to its living cultural and gastronomic heritage. This is due to the skills and determination of Union farmers and producers who have kept traditions alive while taking into account the developments of new production methods and material.[440]

As a logical consequence, the justification of GI protection turns out to be the need to reward the efforts of producers with traditional *savoir-faire*.[441] The Commission commented that '(one of) the main objectives of GI systems is to preserve traditional know-how in the sector',[442] whereas no GI legislation had ever explicitly acknowledged traditional know-how preservation as its 'main objective'.[443]

As the importance attached to cultural heritage preservation increases, there is a growing demand to make the most out of human inputs – specifically, Europe's traditional *savoir-faire*. This new vision paves the way for the extension of GI

438. Recital 2 of Regulation 2081/92: 'Whereas, as part of the adjustment of the common agricultural policy the diversification of agricultural production should be encouraged so as to achieve a better balance between supply and demand on the markets; whereas the promotion of products having certain characteristics could be of considerable benefit to the rural economy, in particular to less-favoured or remote areas, by improving the incomes of farmers and by retaining the rural population in these areas.' Recital 2 of Regulation 510/2006: 'The diversification of agricultural production should be encouraged so as to achieve a better balance between supply and demand on the markets. The promotion of products having certain characteristics can be of considerable benefit to the rural economy, particularly in less favored or remote areas, by improving the incomes of farmers and by retaining the rural population in these areas.'
439. Areté & Directorate-General for Agriculture and Rural Development, *Study on Assessing the Added Value of PDO/PGI Products* 11 (Final Report, KF-02-14-448-EN-N, 2014).
440. Recital 1 of Regulation 1151/2012.
441. DG AGRI, *Working Document on International Protection of EU Geographical Indications: Objectives, Outcome and Challenges*, Ref. Ares(2012)669394 (25 June 2012) p. 1.
442. European Commission, *Green Paper on Making the Most of Europe's Traditional Know-How*, *supra* n. 168, at 7; European Commission, *EU Protection of Geographical Indications for Non-agricultural Products*, Ref. Ares(2020)7158775 (27 November 2020) p. 4.
443. Regulation 479/2008 reformed the wine regime to preserve the best traditions of Community wine production.

protection to non-agricultural products in the EU.[444] In the communication titled 'Making the Most out of Europe's Traditional Know-How', the role of human contributions is recognized as having three broad dimensions: first, a combination of natural factors and traditional processing methods can give the product its speciality; second, specific qualities of a product may be due to specific manufacturing skills and traditions that exist in the place of origin (rather than natural factors alone or a combination of human and natural factors); third, traditional and precious *savoir-faire* itself should be kept alive and passed on from generation to generation (cultural heritage dimension).[445]

The last two dimensions could help to justify a looser link that focuses more on human inputs. Since the creation of the French IGPIA is based on a similar logic, French practices could be drawn on to produce results for the EU-wide GI protection of non-agricultural products. We argue that the European notion of the GI for non-agricultural products could build upon the experience of France and provide a loose link wherein it is sufficient that 'a given quality, a reputation or other characteristics of products are essentially attributable to this geographical origin'.[446]

However, the French definition of IGPIA cannot be duplicated at the EU level. The IGPIA notion is applied to 'industrial and artisanal products', which means 'products other than agricultural, forestry, alimentary or seafood products',[447] because agricultural products are governed under the AOC regime. Nevertheless, at the European level, the application scope of the IGPIA seems to be too large to be copied. The historical review of the PDO/PGI has shown that the EU preferred a sector-specific approach, establishing specific rules for different product categories. In each sector, products covered within the ambit of unitary protection are always listed. It remains an open question whether there is a need to differentiate between schemes depending on the categories of non-agricultural products.[448]

In conclusion, the evolution of the European GI notion discussed in Chapter 1 allows us to observe the expansion of the GI protection system. Geographically speaking, the practice of protecting GIs as a separate category of IP rights began in France and has been accepted as a uniform measure applied in all EU Member States. A more recent development is the expansion of product coverage. Industrial products and handicrafts are being integrated into a GI regime initially designed for the agricultural and food sectors.

444. The Commission identified this issue and proposed a thorough analysis of the existing legal framework for GI protection. Then it released a Green Paper in 2014 aiming at sparking discussion and feedback from all stakeholders. *See* European Commission, *Green Paper on the Protection of Geographical Indications for Non-agricultural Products – Frequently Asked Questions*, MEMO IP/14/832 (15 July 2014) p. 3.
445. European Commission, *Green Paper on Making the Most of Europe's Traditional Know-How*, *supra* n. 168.
446. Article L. 721-2 of the French Intellectual Property Code.
447. Christian le Stanc, *Agitation legislative*, Propriété industrielle, n° 5, 2014, repère 5.
448. The definition of non-agricultural products has not reached a common ground at international or European levels. *See* UNESCO & WIPO, *World Forum on the Protection of Folklore* 162 (WIPO Publication No. 758 (E/F/S) 1998).

The geographical expansion has created tension between the EU Member States with dissimilar national GI practices. The EU has created two categories of GIs – PDO and PGI – to allow for the coexistence of two distinct protection logics: the *terroir* logic and the reputation logic. However, this coexistence may lead to disorder, as can be seen in the unceasing criticism of the PGI category and the EU's efforts to harmonize the two GI categories.

However, the expansion of the product scope may bring coherence to the two logics. Localized production methods could lay the cornerstone of an industrial product's reputation and be considered a significant component in the *terroir* concept. Historically, France stood out for its preference for the quality–place link; since the Law of 2014, it has recognized the link between the reputation of the industrial product and its place of origin. If the rationale behind this recognition works for industrial products, it can also serve as a justification for agricultural products. The PGI category may be justified on the basis of the need to preserve and promote traditional production methods.

The GI notion evolved in a different way during the expansion into China, which will be explored in Chapter 2.

CHAPTER 2

Introduction of the European GI Notion in China

This chapter discusses the introduction and development of the GI concept in China. Despite the richness of its local specialities, China has invented no GI concepts or relevant regulations of its own. When the GI concept migrated from France/EU to the East, China had to understand the GI concept and face the question as to how regulations governing GIs could be adapted to China's context. The French/EU law (the TRIPS Agreement) and the US approach (protecting GIs through the trademark system) have each influenced China's 'learning process'. As a result, GIs are defined in both sui generis regulations and trademark law in China and are thus protected through both regimes. After the GI concept was introduced as a response to the demand from other nations to protect their GIs, Chinese authorities became aware of the value of domestic terroir products linked to a geographical origin. Efforts have been made to harmonize the diverse GI concepts and create new terminologies in specific product sectors. The historical review in this chapter reflects the multifaceted and complex nature of the GI concepts.

GIs may seem to be a foreign or even exotic notion for China. The concept has its roots in France and dates back to the beginning of the twentieth century.[1] The idea that products from a specific region may possess certain qualities or a reputation due to their origin is not new in China. For example, at least since the sixteenth century, traditional Chinese medicinal materials originating from certain locations have been found to be more effective in curing diseases because of qualities resulting from natural and human factors.[2] The concept of '*daodi*' ('geo-authentic'), which is very similar to

1. Peter-Tobias Stoll, Jan Busche & Katrin Arend, *WTO: Trade-Related Aspects of Intellectual Property Rights* 359 (Martinus Nijhoff Publishers 2009).
2. *See* Hu Shilin, ZHONGGUO DAODI YAOCAI [CHINESE GENUINE MEDICAL MATERIALS] (Heilongjiang Science and Technology Press, 1989); Xiao Xiaohe et al., Zhongguo Daodi Yaocai

the French concept of '*terroir*',[3] was created to describe crude traditional Chinese drugs with specific germ plasma, production sites, or specific production techniques and processing methods.[4] Moreover, for thousands of years, skilled artisans possessing traditional needlework techniques and operating in four different regions have crafted China's most famous embroidery styles, which have been recently nominated as 'National Intangible Cultural Heritage'.[5]

Although scholars in both the East and West credit China with having contributed paper, movable type, and ink to humankind, IP concepts such as copyright, patents and trademarks did not exist in ancient China.[6] As with other types of IP, ancient imperial China did not develop the notion of GIs.[7] Many 'geo-authentic' products were offered as royal tribute to emperors instead of becoming GI products used for the benefit of both consumers and producers.[8]

After the Opium Wars, as foreign economic and other activities progressively expanded into China's quasi-colonial territory in the late nineteenth century, complaints about the unauthorized use of foreign business identifiers increased.[9] Western countries put pressure on China, resulting in several commercial treaties in which the protection of their business identifiers in China was the core issue (e.g., Mackay Treaty).[10] In order to fulfil the obligations of the treaties, China's first trademark law

---

Yanjiu Ershinian Gailun [Survey of Investigations on Daodi Chinese Medicinal Materials in China Since 1980s], ZHONGGUO ZHONGYAO ZAZHI [CHINA JOURNAL OF CHINESE MATERIA MEDICA], March 2009, 519.

3. Josef A. Brinckmann, *Geographical Indications for Medicinal Plants: Globalization, Climate Change, Quality and Market Implications for Geo-authentic Botanicals*, 1 World J. Traditional Chinese Med. 16 (2015).
4. State Drug Administration (China), Good Agricultural Practice for Chinese Crude Drugs (interim) (2002).
5. The four famous Chinese embroidery styles are the Su embroidery from Suzhou, the Xiang embroidery from Changsha, the Yue embroidery from Guangzhou & Ganzhou, and the Shu embroidery from Chengdu. *See* Guowuyuan Guanyu Gongbu Diyipi Guojiaji Feiwuzhi Wenhua Yichan Mulu de Tongzhi [State Council (of China)' Notice on First Publication of National Intangible Cultural Heritage], 20 May 2006.
6. *See* William P. Alford, *To Steal a Book Is an Elegant Offense: Intellectual Property Law in Chinese Civilization* (Stanford University Press 1995).
7. Li Yi, NONGCHANPIN DILI BIAOZHI GUANLI SHIWU [MANAGEMENT PRACTICE OF AGRICULTURAL GEOGRAPHICAL INDICATIONS], at 2 (Hunan Science and Technology Press, 2011).
8. *See* Hu Shilin, Daodi Yaocai yu Fangzhi he Gongpin [Geo-herbals with Geographies and Medical Tributes], ZHONGGUO YAOXUE ZAZHI [CHINESE PHARMACEUTICAL JOURNAL], August 1996, 496; Liang Fei, Daodi Yaocai Kao [Daodi Chinese Medicinal Materials], Doctoral Thesis, Beijing University of Chinese Medicine, 2013.
9. Alford, *supra* n. 6, at 34-38.
10. Mackay Treaty is also known as the Commercial Treaty of 1902 between Britain and China. In fact, three commercial treaties were signed in 1902 and 1903 (Sino-British, Sino-US and Sino-Japanese) in compliance with Article 11 of the Final Protocol for the Settlement of the Disturbances of 1900. The Mackay Treaty of 1902 with Great Britain and China's 1903 treaty with the United States both allowed for the protection of foreign trademarks. Article 7 of the Mackay Treaty provided that the Chinese government would establish registration offices under the control of the Imperial Maritime Customs Service. *See* Wang Dong, *China's Unequal Treaties: Narrating National History* 19-24 (Lexington Books 2005); Sumner J. La Croix & Denise Eby Konan, *Intellectual Property Rights in China: The Changing Political Economy of Chinese-American Interests*, 25 World Econ. 759, 761 (2002).

was drafted in 1904. It was subsequently modified,[11] and legal references to geographical denominations made their first appearance in China. It was proposed that 'indications of provenance and geographical appellations (associated with a trade name) should be protected and … not need to be registered as a trademark'.[12]

The birth of New China (the People's Republic of China) in 1949 marked the end of the quasi-colonial state, but the use of Western notions of GIs continued in response to the demand to fulfil the obligations of international treaties (§2.01). After the GI concept was introduced, Chinese authorities have made efforts to harmonize the diverse GI concepts and create new terminologies in specific product sectors (§2.02).

§2.01 INTRODUCING THE GI CONCEPT AS A RESPONSE TO FOREIGN DEMANDS

China's legislation has been deeply affected by the 'battle' in the international arena between the 'Old world' and the 'New world' concerning the notion of GIs and protection approaches. Thus, China's GI concept has been defined in terms of both the sui generis system and the trademark system.

[A] Appellations of Origin

China's efforts to legislate on GIs started quite late, in around 1985.[13] The first IP law,[14] the Trademark Law of 1982, contains no regulations on GIs, nor on the registration of a trademark containing a geographical name.[15] China began fulfilling its obligations under international instruments in 1985 by using the notion of appellations of origin in several administrative cases, primarily for the protection of foreign denominations; the notion was subsequently introduced in legislation.

[1] Appellations of Origin in Administrative Cases

Following the launch of China's Reform and Opening Policy, China became a full member of the Paris Convention for the Protection of Industrial Property – twelve days

11. Robert Heuser, *The Chinese Trademark Law of 1904: A Preliminary Study in Exterritoriality, Competition, and Late Ch'ing Law Reform*, 22 Oriens Extremus 183 (1975).
12. *See* Rules on Trade Marks in China, Article 1 (1905); Feng Xiaoqing & Yang Lihua, ZHONGGUO SHANGBIAOFA YANJIU YU LIFA SHIJIAN [RESEARCH AND LEGISLATIVE PRACTICE ON TRADE MARKS IN CHINA], at 86 (China University of Political Science and Law Press, 2013).
13. Wang Han, Woguo Dili Biaozhi Chuji Nongchanpin Fazhan Moshi Yanjiu (Study on Development Mode of our Country's Elementarily Agricultural Products Concerning Geographical Indications), Doctoral Thesis, University of Tianjin, 2008, pp. 11-13.
14. Zheng Chengsi, Zhishi Chanquan Falu Zhidu [Intellectual Property Law System, the National People's Congress of the People's Republic of China (11 June 2021), http://www.npc.gov.cn/npc/xinwen/2001-02/28/content_1459919.htm.
15. Trademark Law of the People's Republic of China (1982), promulgated by Order No. 10 of 23 August 1982 of Standing Committee of the National People's Congress, English version available at, http://www.wipo.int/wipolex/en/text.jsp?file_id = 131395, accessed 11 June 2021.

before the implementation of the Patent Law in 1985[16] – to accelerate the introduction of foreign technologies and implement newly established IP laws (Patent Law of 1984 and Trademark Law of 1982).[17] Apart from provisions on patents, utility models, and industrial designs, the Paris Convention contains provisions on indications of source (IS) and appellations of origin. As a result, even though protecting geographical denominations of origin was not the reason why China wished to join the Paris Convention, the accession imposed an obligation on China to protect them within its territory.

Since then, a case-by-case approach had been adopted for the protection of appellations of origin, primarily foreign ones.[18] For example, in a 1987 communication to the Administration for Industry and Commerce of Beijing, the Trademark Office pointed out that 'as a State Party of the Paris Convention, China is bound to respect its provisions ... for the protection of foreign appellations of origin in China; the unauthorized use of Danish butter cookies should be discontinued'.[19]

Another case in point concerns the French geographical name '*Champagne*'. In 1989, the State Administration for Industry and Commerce (SAIC) notified its local bureaus at provincial and city levels that Chinese companies should not use on alcoholic products the term '*Champagne*' or its Chinese translation (including expressions such as 'Big *Champagne*', 'Small *Champagne*', and 'Ladies *Champagne*').[20] It indicated that '*Champagne* is a French appellation of origin, not a generic term for alcoholic products. The generic use of Champagne would violate the right of others to

16. *See* Guanyu Woguo Jiaru Baohu Gongye Chanquan Bali Gongyue de Qingshi Baogao [Report of China's Accession to the Paris Convention], 1984; Huang Kunyi, Guanyu Jianyi Woguo Jiaru Baohu Gongye Chanquan Bali Gongyue de Shuoming [Report on the Proposition of China's Accession to the Paris Convention], Delivered at the Eighth Session of the Sixth National People's Congress, 9 November 1984; Zhao Yuanguo, Zhongguo Jiaru Baohu Gongye Chanquan Bali Gongye Huimou [A Retrospective Analysis of China's Accession to the Paris Convention], ZHONGGUO ZHISHI CHANQUAN BAO [CHINA REPORT OF INTELLECTUAL PROPERTY], 19 March 2010, 1-5; Zhu Jinqing & Zhao Yuanguo, Zhongguo Zhuanlifa yu Bali Gongyue [China's Patent Law and Paris Convention], FAXUE YANJIU [CHINESE JOURNAL OF LAW], February 1987, 24.
17. On 19 March 1985, the Paris Convention entered into force in China. On 1 April 1985, China's Patent Law formally took effect. *See* Patent Law of People's Republic of China, Article 69 (1984); Zhao Yuanguo, Huigu Zhongguo Zhuanlifa de Yunyu yu Dansheng [The Birth of China's Patent Law], ZHONGGUO FAMING YU ZHUANLI [CHINA INVENTION & PATENT], February 2007, 24.
18. *See* Tian Furong, DILI BIAOZHI FALU BAOHU ZHIDU YANJIU [LEGAL PROTECTION OF GEOGRAPHICAL INDICATIONS], at 238 (Intellectual Property Publishing House, 2009).
19. Trademark Office was established directly under the former State Administration for Industry and Commerce ('SAIC' hereinafter). Guojia Gongshang Xingzheng Guanliju Shangbiaoju Guanyu Baohu Yuanchandi Mingcheng de Han [Communication from Trademark Office of State Administration for Industry and Commerce Concerning the Protection of Appellations of Origin], 29 October 1987.
20. Guojia Gongshang Xingzheng Guanliju Guanyu Tingzhi zai Jiulei Shangpin shang Shiyong Xiangbin Ziyang de Tongzhi [Notice of the State Administration for Industry and Commerce on the Cessation of the Use of the Word Champagne on Alcoholic Products], 26 October 1989.

appellation of origin,[21] ... China is a member of the Paris Convention and is therefore under obligation to protect appellations of origin.'[22] In a written reply of 1996, concerning how to determine the appropriate basis for the protection of '*Champagne*', the trademark Office reaffirmed the need to fulfil the obligation under the Paris Convention to protect appellations of origin.[23] On this basis, administrative sanctions were imposed against *Yantai Changyu* Pioneer Wine Company in 1997, which had marketed Chinese wine under the '*Champagne*' appellation.[24]

China took the protection of Chinese appellations of origin into account while protecting foreign interests pursuant to the Paris Convention, although the number of such cases was limited relative to that of cases involving foreign interests. In 1987, the Trademark Office made the following observation concerning the usage of a Chinese geographical name: '*Longkou* is an appellation of origin used traditionally on pasta products. It is not appropriate for enterprises to register it as a trademark.'[25]

Even though the term 'appellation of origin' appeared several times in administrative cases during the first decade following China's accession to the Paris Convention, neither a definition nor a special mechanism of protection was stipulated in national legislation. This lack of regulation led to much uncertainty about the rules in this area.[26]

As a result, several alternatives were explored. The 1998 revision of the Regulations for the Implementation of the Trademark Law prohibited the use of geographical names of Chinese administrative divisions at or above the county level and of well-known foreign geographical names as trademarks. According to the Trademark Office, one of the main reasons for this prohibition was that the use of administrative division names or famous foreign geographical names as trademarks would effectively create conflicts with the protection of appellations of origin.[27] In 1993, a second clause

21. Guojia Gongshang Xinzheng Guanliju Shangbiaoju Guanyu Zhengdun Jiulei Shangbiao Gongzuo Zhong Jige Wenti de Tongzhi [Notice of the Trademark Office of the State Administration for Industry and Commerce on Several Issues in Rectification of Trademarks on Alcoholic Products], 2 August 1989.
22. Notice of the State Administration for Industry and Commerce on the Cessation of the Use of the Word Champagne on Alcoholic Products, *supra* n. 22.
23. Guanyu Yinfa Zhizhi zai Jiulei Shangpin shang Shiyong Xiangbin huo Champagne Ziyang Xingwei de Pifu [Official Letter Concerning Prohibition on the Use of Champagne Term on Alcoholic Products], 29 July 1996.
24. *See* State Administration for Industry and Commerce Trademark Office, Shangbiao Qinquan Dianxing Anli Pingxi [Analysis of Typical Cases of Trademark Infringement], at 161 (China Industry and Commerce Press, 1999); Liu Chengwei, Jiaqiang Dili Biaozhi de Shangbiao Baohu [Strengthening Trademark Protection on Geographical Indications], ZHISHI CHANQUAN [INTELLECTUAL PROPERTY], March 2002, 34.
25. Guojia Gongshang Xingzheng Gunaliju Shangbiaoju Guanyu Longkou Mingcheng de Yijian [State Administration for Industry and Commerce Trademark Office's Opinion on Longkou Appellation], 9 May 1988.
26. *See* Guanyu Dui Yong Xiangbin Zuo Jiulei Shangpin Mingcheng Xingwei Jinxing Chufa Shiyong Hezhong Yiju de Qingshi [Sichuan Industrial and Commercial Administrative Bureau's Request for Instructions on the Legal Basis for the Punishment for Those Who Use Champagne Appellation], 1996; Dili Biaozhi Anli [Cases of Geographical Indications], QINGDAO RIBAO [QINGDAO DAILY], 17 August 2006.
27. Regulations for the Implementation of the Trademark Law of the People's Republic of China, Article 6 (1988).

was added to Article 8 of the Trademark Law, which prohibited the use of geographical names in trademarks.[28]

This helped to provide a legal basis for the protection of appellations of origin. For example, '*Champagne*' could be considered a well-known foreign geographical name. Therefore, its use in commercial activities as an individual mark would constitute a breach of Article 8 of the Trademark Law.[29]

With China's accession to the Madrid Agreement Concerning the International Registration of Marks in 1989, special categories of foreign marks (i.e., collective, certification or guarantee marks) were introduced into the country.[30] Since the ordinary mark was found to be inconsistent with AO protection,[31] a new paradigm based on special categories of marks was expected to address the problem.

[2] Appellations of Origin in Legislation

[a] Appellations of Origin in Trademark Regime

Article 8 of the Trademark Law of 1993 explicitly prohibited the use of geographical names as trademarks. However, as the Trademark Law of 1982 contained no such restrictions, many place names had *already* been registered as ordinary trademarks from 1982 to 1993,[32] some of which have long enjoyed a good reputation both at home and abroad (e.g., *Qingdao* Beer) and even constitute appellations of origin (e.g.,

28. Trademark Law of the People's Republic of China, Article 8 (1993). The Second Clause of Article 8: 'Geographic names of administrative divisions at or above the county level or foreign geographic names known to the public shall not be used as trademarks, with the exception, however, of those geographic names having other meanings. Registered trademarks in which geographic names are used shall remain valid.'
29. Official Letter Concerning Prohibition on the Use of Champagne Term on Alcoholic Products, *supra* n. 23.
30. Zhongguo Dili Biaozhi Falu Zhidu Ji Chengjiu [Geographical Indications in China: Systems and Achievements], Trademark Office of China National Intellectual Property Administration (11 June 2021), http://sbj.cnipa.gov.cn/dlbz/zsjt/201203/t20120312_229181.html.
31. According to the Trademark Office, it is not appropriate for geographical names to be used as trademarks. The reasons are as follows: (1) It is commonly accepted in the world that administrative division names cannot be used as a trademark; (2) Registration of such names would exclude others from using them on the same kind or similar kind of products; (3) Conflict with the protection of appellations of origin; (4) Since such names can only indicate the origin of goods, lack of distinctiveness makes them unable to be used as trademarks. Moreover, regarding the revision of Article 8 of the Trademark Law, the drafting statements show that registration of geographical names would lead to confusion among consumers and cause a monopoly of the identifier of geographical origin. *See* Guojia Gongshang Xingzheng Guanliju Shangbiaoju Jiu Xianji Yishang Xingzheng Quhua Mingcheng Zuo Shangbiao Deng Wenti de Fuhan [State Administration for Industry and Commerce Trademark Office's Official Reply Concerning the Usage of Administrative Division Names as Trademarks], 6 November 1986; Liu Minxue, Guanyu Zhonghua Renmin Gongheguo Shangbiaofa Xiuzheng'an Cao'an de Shuoming [Drafting Instructions for the Revision of the Trademark Law], Twenty-Ninth Meeting of the Standing Committee of the Seventh National People's Congress, 22 December 1992.
32. Minxue, Drafting Instructions for the Revision of the Trademark Law, *supra* n. 31; Wang Zhiben, Yuanchan Diyu Chanpin Baohu yu Tigao Woguo Nongchanpin Guoji Jingzhengli [Protecting Appellations of Origin and Improving the International Competitiveness of Agricultural Products in China], SHIJIE NONGYE [WORLD AGRICULTURE], May 2002, 7.

Guizhou Maotai).[33] In light of the existing practices, Article 8 set out an exception: 'Registered trademarks, in which geographic names had *already* been used, shall remain valid.'

Influenced by China's integration into the Paris Union and Madrid System, the Implementing Regulations of the Trademark Law were amended the same year the Trademark Law (Article 8) was revised, in 1993, in order to bring it in line with international practices.[34] The revised Article 6 of the Implementing Regulations provided that: 'Collective trademarks and certification trademarks that have been approved and registered by the Trademark Office shall be protected by the law.'[35]

In accordance with the revised law and regulations, the SAIC promulgated the Measures for the Registration and Administration of Collective Marks and Certification Marks in 1994.[36] Under Article 2 of the Measures, a certification mark was defined as 'a mark ... for the purpose of certifying the place of origin, material, manufacturing process, quality, accuracy or other specified characteristics of the goods or services'.[37] Although the meaning of 'place of origin' was not clarified in this text, it can be deduced from the Guide for the Registration of Collective Marks and Certification Marks that it was intended for AO protection.[38]

Therefore, Article 2 opened the way for the protection of appellations of origin through the special category of trademarks. The use of certification marks meets the needs of both Chinese and foreign enterprises to protect their famous and high-quality

33. Zhang Huiping, Yuanchandi Mingcheng yu Diming de Bianxi Guizhou Maotai yu Maotai Zhen de Falu Dingwei [Analysis of Appellation of Origin and Place Name: Legal Definition of Guizhou Maotai Liquor and Maotao Town], NIANGJIU KEJI [LIQUOR MAKING SCIENCE & TECHNOLOGY], April 2007, 142; State Administration for Industry and Commerce, 2009 Nian Gongshang Xingzheng Guanli Jiguan Baohu Guonei Qiye Zhuce Shangbiao Zhuanyongquan Dianxing Anli [Typical Cases of the Protection of Registered Trademarks in 2009], May 2010.
34. This enactment has brought the Chinese trademark law up to the international standard required by the Paris Convention and Madrid Agreement. *See* Minxue, Drafting Instructions for the Revision of the Trademark Law, *supra* n. 31; Annie J. De Roo & Robert W. Jagtenberg, *Yearbook Law and Legal Practice in East Asia (1997-1998)* 64 (Kluwer Law International 1998).
35. Regulations for the Implementation of the Trademark Law of the People's Republic of China (1993), promulgated by Order No. 14 of 28 July 1993 of the State Administration for Industry and Commerce of the People's Republic of China.
36. Measures for the Registration and Administration of Collective Marks and Certification Marks (1994).
37. Collective marks and certification marks are defined as follows: 'Collective mark' means a trademark or service mark used by the members of a society of industrial or commercial enterprises or an association or other collective organization to indicate membership of the business operators of goods or services in the same organization; 'Certification mark' means a trademark or service mark under the control of organization which has the capacity of conducting inspection and supervision over the goods or services in respect of which the mark is used by the person other than the organization to certify the origin, material, mode of manufacture, quality, accuracy or other characteristics of such goods and services.
38. *See* Trademark Office, Jiti Shangbiao yu Zhengming Shangbiao Zhuce Zhinan [Guide for the Registration of Collective Marks and Certification Marks], 13 July 1995. The fourth Part: 'Appellations of origin are objects of legal protection in China. At present, there is no special legislation in our country regarding Aos protection. Since geographical names shall not be used as trademarks, a more practical way is needed for the protection of Aos. With the enactment of Collective and Certification Measures, protecting appellations of origin via certification marks has become a reality.'

native products, such as '*Shaoxing* yellow rice wine', '*Fuling* mustard', '*Florida* citrus' (US), and '*Pulque*' (Mexico). Over fifty applications for the registration of marks certifying place of origin were approved between the launch of the Measures in March 2001 and the end of the year.[39]

[b] Appellations of Origin in Sui Generis Regime

In the mid-1990s, in addition to the promulgation of the Certification Marks Measures, another system started to emerge. Scholars in both the West and East argue that this emergence was largely due to the influence of the French vision of appellations of origin.[40]

In 1995, the former State Bureau of Technical Supervision began cooperating with the French Ministry of Agriculture, the French Ministry of Finance, and the *Bureau national interprofessionnel du Cognac* with a view to building bridges and enhancing the protection of AOs.[41] On 16 May 1997, French president Jacques Chirac and Chinese president Jiang Zemin signed the French–Chinese Declaration on a Comprehensive Partnership in Beijing.[42] Under the framework of this declaration,[43] a French–Chinese committee on agriculture and agri-food was created to facilitate cooperation in the agricultural and the agri-foodstuffs sector, particularly 'the protection of appellations of origin and the fight against counterfeiting'.[44]

39. *See* De Roo & Jagtenberg, *supra* n. 34, at 65; Ding Manli, Zhengchu Duomen Fachu Duomen Yuanchandi Biaozhi Baohu Xianzhuang Hunluan [Each Department Acting on Its Own Law: Status Quo of Geographical Indications Protection], RENMIN RIBAO [PEOPLE'S DAILY], 29 May 2002.
40. Liu Zhaobin, Faguo Dili Biaozhi Chanpin Baohu Zhidu de Qishi [Inspirations from the French Instruments for Geographical Indication Protection], GUANGMING RIBAO [GUANGMING DAILY], 25 January 2015, 5; Frederic Wallet, *La protection des produits sous indication géographique en Chine: une analyse du processus d'émergence d'une régulation de la qualité agro-alimentaire*, Colloque SFER Toulouse, 2012.
41. Feng Liming, Zhongguo Dili Biaozhi Baohu Zhidu [The Protection System of Geographical Indications in China], Presentation at the Symposium on Geographical Indications & Appellations of Origin (Chongqing), 13 November 2009.
42. Déclaration conjointe sino-française pour un partenariat global. Voir Bureau de l'information du conseil des affaires d'Etat de la République Populaire de Chine, *Chine – France*, China Intercontinental Press, 2004, Annexes.
43. The Declaration of 1997 also made clear that both sides would reinforce the cooperation on the protection of appellations of origin and the fight against counterfeiting.
44. The Founding Declaration of the French-Chinese Committee on Agriculture and Ari-Food has been signed on 24 September 1998 by the French and Chinese prime ministers. For the French side, the aim of the creation of the committee is for the greatest benefit of French operators who carry on their activities in China. *See* Zhongfa Guanyu Chengli Nongye ji Nongye Shipin Hezuo Weiyuanhui de Shengming [Constitution of the Franco-Chinese Agri-Food Committee], RENMIN RIBAO [PEOPLE'S DAILY], 24 September 1988; Réponse du ministère de l'agriculture, *Création d'un comité agro-alimentaire franco-chinois*, JO Sénat du 29 oct. 1998, p. 3439: 'La mise en œuvre de cette déclaration devrait relancer la coopération agricole et agro-alimentaire entre les deux pays, pour le plus grand bénéfice des opérateurs exerçant leur activité sur le marché chinois'; Réponse du ministère de l'agriculture, *Comité agro-alimentaire franco-chinois*, JO Sénat du 8 juill. 1999, p. 2311.

After having assessed and drawn lessons from the French experience through this cooperation,[45] the State Bureau of Technical Supervision promulgated the Provisions on the Protection of Products with Appellations of Origin on 17 August 1999, which effectively created China's first sui generis GI regime; this was a separate system parallel to the trademark regime.[46] According to Article 2 of the Provisions, a 'product with Appellations of Origin' is defined as:

> A product (1) whose raw materials come from a specific region; (2) produced in a specific region according to traditional production methods; (3) the quality, speciality or reputation[47] of which is essentially attributable to geographical features of origin; (4) approved to be named from its geographical origin.[48]

Though not repeating the French definition of AOC, the definition of 'products with appellations of origin' clearly reflects the '*terroir*' concept, the basis of the French notion. For one thing, this definition obviously requires a stronger link between the product and the origin than that laid down in the TRIPS Agreement. Moreover, the raw materials must originate from a particular place,[49] and the quality must be essentially attributable to the 'geographical features' of that place. Climate-soil factors are thus seen as key in shaping the specific quality of the products, which corresponds exactly to the traditional understanding of '*terroir*'. Furthermore, the use of the expression 'traditional production methods' is in line with the method suggested by the French delegation to define 'appellations of origin' in the drafting of the Lisbon Agreement.

At the end of 1999, the General Requirements for Products with Appellations of Origin was promulgated for the implementation of the Provisions. The preamble makes more explicit the source of the Chinese sui generis GI regulation. It clearly states that: 'These Requirements have been built upon regulations of European and French laws concerning the protection of designations of origin and geographical indications.'[50] The

45. State Bureau of Technical Supervision, Shaoxingjiu yu Faguo Ganyi Xiangshou Tongyang Daiyu [Shaoxing Rice Wine Receives the Same Treatment as French Cognac], ZHONGGUO ZHILIANG JISHU JIANDU [CHINA QUALITY SUPERVISION], 15 February 2000, 28.
46. The Provisions on the Protection of Products with Appellations of Origin was the first governmental regulation specifying the system of Gis (appellations of origin). *See* Wang Xiaobing, LUN DILI BIAOZHI DE FALU BAOHU [LEGAL PROTECTION OF GEOGRAPHICAL INDICATIONS], at 225 (China Renmin University Press, 2006).
47. The provision does not adopt the expression used in the TRIPS Agreement: 'a given quality, reputation or other characteristic'. Instead, it slightly changes the order and the wording: 'the quality, speciality or reputation'. The reason for the modification is linked to the purpose of the regulation. Article 1 describing the objectives only mentioned the quality and speciality of products, not the reputation.
48. Provisions on the Protection of Products with Appellations of Origin (1999), Zhongguo Zhiliang Jishu Jiandu [China Quality Supervision], 15.
49. The implementing rule of the Provisions weakens this requirement. Two types of products of appellations of origin are provided in the implementing rule: on the one hand, products whose raw materials come from the local area; on the other hand, products whose raw materials come from a geographical area larger than or different from the processing area. *See* State Bureau of Technical Supervision of the People's Republic of China, Yuanchan Diyu Chanpin Tongyong Yaoqiu [General Requirements for Products with Appellations of Origin], GB17924-1999, 7 December 1999, Article 3.
50. *Ibid.*, para. 1 to the Preamble.

fundamental principles for determining legitimate products set by Article 4 of the Requirements are as follows:

> (1) The quality, speciality and reputation shall reflect a particular geographical environment with its inherent natural and human factors;[51] (2) The product has a consistent quality, a long history, a peculiar flavour, and enjoying a great reputation; (3) Stages of production take place in the defined area using traditional *savoir-faire* or traditional production equipment.[52]

The principles demonstrate the extent to which the French '*terroir*' concept has influenced the Chinese notion of 'products with appellations of origin'.

During the 1999-2000 pilot phase, the first product ('*Shaoxing* rice wine') was granted registration as a product with an AO.[53] The authority in charge proudly announced that 'Shaoxing rice wine finally received the same treatment in China as what French Cognac received (in France).'[54] In other words, the authority believed that the Chinese version of the French AOC regime had been formally established.

However, not everyone was happy. Academics, producers, and government officials (especially the Trademark Office), who favoured using the trademark system as the main instrument of protection, severely criticized the sui generis system that coexisted with the trademark regime for causing disorder in the GI protection system and compromising the exclusive rights of trademarks.[55] For example, the *Dong-e-e-jiao* Company, owner of a prior trademark containing the geographical name '*Dong'e*', opposed the registration of '*Dong'e*' as an AO under the sui generis system on the grounds that the collective usage of the later GI would terminate the exclusivity granted to the trademark owner.[56] While the United States brought a claim against the EU in the international arena for a similar reason (alleging that EU Regulation 2081/92 deprived

51. According to Article 3(1) of the General Requirement, the quality, speciality and reputation of the product should be attributed to a particular geographical environment with its inherent natural and human factors.
52. General Requirements for Products with Appellations of Origin, *supra* n. 49, Article 4.
53. Liu Zhaobin, Woguo Yuanchan Diyu Chanpin Baohu Zhidu Shishi de Xianzhuang yu Fazhan [The Status Quo and Development of the Protection System of Appellations of Origin Products in China], ZHONGGUO BIAOZHUNHUA [CHINA STANDARDIZATION], December 2001, 7.
54. State Bureau of Technical Supervision, Shaoxing Rice Wine Receives the Same Treatment as French Cognac, *supra* n. 45, at 28.
55. Chen Jintao, Xi TRIPS Xieyi yu Woguo Dili Biaozhi de Falu Baohu [TRIPS Agreement and Legal Protection of Geographical Indications in China], DANGDAI FAXUE [CONTEMPORARY LAW REVIEW], April 2003, 129-132.
56. The former AQSIQ conducted the formality examination of the applications of registering '*Dong'e E'jiao*' and published a notice of acceptance on 25 February 2002. Within one month from the date of publication, Dong-e Company raised opposition to the application. *See* Guojia Zhiliang Jiandu Jianyan Jianyi Zongju Gonggao 2002 Nian di 17 Hao [State General Administration of Quality Supervision, Inspection and Quarantine Announcement No. 17, 2002], 25 February 2002; Zhang Weijun, Diming Shangbiao yu Dili Biaozhi Chongtu de Falu Tiaozheng [The Legal Adjustment of the Conflict Between Trademarks Containing Geographical Names and Geographical Indications], ZHONGHUA SHANGBIAO [CHINA TRADEMARK], August 2002, 44.

the owners of existing registered trademarks of their exclusive rights by allowing prior trademarks and later GIs to coexist),[57] the war in China had just begun.

[B] Geographical Indications

In 1986, China officially applied for accession to the GATT.[58] After fifteen years of negotiations, it became a member of the WTO in 2001. As a result of the negotiations, China agreed to undertake a series of important commitments, including efforts to revise its domestic laws and enact new legislation fully in compliance with the WTO Agreement.[59] Among the laws revised or enacted in order to implement the WTO rules concerning denominations of origin are the Trademark Law and the Provisions on Marks of Origin.

[1] GIs in Trademark Regime

[a] Meeting Minimum Standards: Implementation of the TRIPS Agreement

As part of the package of WTO agreements, the TRIPS Agreement requires all WTO members to establish 'minimum protections' for GIs through their national laws.[60] Articles 22-24 of the TRIPS Agreement define GIs, establish several operative requirements, contemplate extended protection for wines/spirits, and provide exceptions.[61] Since China had failed to meet these minimum standards prior to its adherence,[62] it was necessary to modify and adapt the existing legal systems in order to be consistent with the TRIPS Agreement.

---

57. The United States first requested consultations regarding this matter on 1 June 1999. *See Summary of the Report of the Panel (WT/DS174/R) of March 15, 2005 regarding the Complaint by the United States against the European Communities on the Protection of Trademarks and Geographical Indications for Agricultural Products and Foodstuffs*, United States Patent and Trademark Office (8 May 2021), https://www.uspto.gov/sites/default/files/web/offices/dcom/olia/globalip/pdf/case_summary.pdf.
58. China was one of the original contracting parties when the GATT was concluded in 1947. Nevertheless, the Chiang Kai-shek government in Taiwan, which still represented China in the GATT, announced the withdrawal decision in 1950. China took the view that the withdrawal had been illegal because the Taiwan government had not been the legitimate representative of China. In 1986, China requested the resumption of membership as a contracting party in the GATT. *See* Henry G. Schermers & Niels M. Blokke, *International Institutional Law: Unity Within Diversity* 87 (Martinus Nijhoff Publishers 5th ed. 2011).
59. WTO, *WTO Successfully Concludes Negotiations on China's Entry*, Press/243 (17 September 2001).
60. Irene Calboli, *Expanding the Protection of Geographical Indications of Origin under TRIPS: Old Debate or New Opportunity?*, 10 Marq. Intell. Prop. L. Rev. 181, 183 (2006).
61. Kevin M. Murphy, *Conflict, Confusion, and Bias under TRIPs Articles 22-24*, 19 Am. U. Int'l L. Rev. 1181 (2003).
62. Chinese and French scholars described this situation as a 'legal desert'. *See* Cao Jianming, Jiaru WTO dui Zhongguo Sifa Gongzuo de Yingxiang ji Sikao [The Impact of the WTO on China's Judicial Work], FAXUE [SCIENCE OF LAW], June 2001, 59; Zheng Chengsi, WTO Zhong de Shangbiao yu Dili Biaozhi [Trademarks and Geographical Indications in the WTO], ZHONGHUA SHANGBIAO [CHINA TRADEMARK], April 1997, 10; Joanna Schmidt-Szalewski, *La propriété intellectuelle dans la mondialisation*, Propriété industrielle, n° 6, 2006, étude 20.

In October 2001, the Standing Committee of the National People's Congress ratified the Second Amendment to the Trademark Law,[63] which added three notions: 'collective marks', 'certification marks', and 'geographical indications'.[64] Article 16 for the first time gives a legal definition of GIs: 'GIs are indications which identify a good as originating in a place, where the specific quality, reputation or other characteristics of the good are primarily attributable to the natural factors or human factors of the place indicated.' In fact, like a number of other countries, China uses the TRIPS definition as the basis for its national legislation.[65] The only significant difference is that, whereas Article 22.1 of the TRIPS Agreement makes no mention of natural and/or human factors,[66] Article 16 adds the phrase 'natural factors or human factors'.[67]

Article 2(1)(i) of the Lisbon Agreement refers explicitly to 'a combination of natural and human factors'.[68] For wine appellation, physical geography plays a role so important that the land could virtually be considered a co-author of the products.[69] However, this dual requirement sometimes seems to be too ambiguous to be enforceable, as it seems to be for the 'industrial' appellations, which may depend primarily or

63. Trademark Law of the People's Republic of China (2001), amended for the second time in accordance with the Decision on Revising the Trademark Law of the People's Republic of China adopted at the Twenty-Fourth Meeting of the Standing Committee of the Ninth National People's Congress on 27 October 2001.
64. Before 2001, Implementing Regulations of the Trademark Law (1993) and Measures for the Registration and Administration of Collective Marks and Certification Marks (1994) dealt with collective marks and certification marks. Administrative methods were used to protect the place of origin. After several years of implementation, authorities demonstrated that it was ready to enact it as national law. *See* Wang Zhongfu, Guanyu Zhonghua Renmin Gongheguo Shangbiaofa Xiuzheng'an Cao'an de Shuoming [Drafting Instructions for the Revision of the Trademark Law], Nineteenth Meeting of the Standing Committee of the Ninth National People's Congress, 22 December 2000.
65. A number of countries now use the TRIPS definition as the basis for their national legislation on geographical indications. WIPO, *The Definition of Geographical Indications*, SCT/9/4 (1 October 2002).
66. Unlike the definition of appellations of origin under the Lisbon Agreement, geographical indications as defined in the TRIPS Agreement do not explicitly refer to a combination of natural and human factors forming the distinctive quality and characteristics of the product. Article 22.1 of the TRIPS Agreement requires that a quality, reputation or other characteristic of the good should be essentially attributable to its geographical origin. In other words, whether the cause is natural or human factors or a combination of both, a given quality, reputation or other characteristic can provide the essential factor justifying the link with the indicated geographical origin. *See Ibid.*, at 7; Daniel J. Gervais, *Reinventing Lisbon: The Case for a Protocol to the Lisbon Agreement (Geographical Indications)*, 11 Chi. J. Int'l L. 67, 86 (2010).
67. Despite the variations, commenters believe the definition of geographical indications in the Trademark Law is consistent with that in the TRIPS Agreement. *See* Liu Yajun, Wanshan Woguo Dili Biaozhi Falu Baohu Shizheng Fenxi [Positive Analysis on Our Amelioration of Geographical Indication], DANGDAI FAXUE [CONTEMPORARY LAW REVIEW], March 2004, 47.
68. The appellation of origin is defined in the Lisbon Agreement as 'any denomination protected in the Contracting Party of Origin consisting of or containing the name of a geographical area, or another denomination known as referring to such area, which serves to designate a good as originating in that geographical area, where the quality or characteristics of the good are due exclusively or essentially to the geographical environment, including natural and human factors, and which has given the good its reputation'. *See* Article 2(1) of the Geneva Act of the Lisbon Agreement on Appellations of Origin and Geographical Indications.
69. Dev Gangjee, *Relocating the Law of Geographical Indications* 142 (Cambridge University Press 2012).

even solely on traditional techniques accumulated within the region of production throughout history. Thus, the World Intellectual Property Organization (WIPO) suggested a definition of AO applicable to developing countries that replaced 'natural and human factors' with 'natural factors, human factors, or both natural and human factors'.[70] This proposed formula was refined and integrated into China's definition of GIs, which aimed at creating a wider space to enhance the protection of both agricultural and industrial products.

Though the expression 'both natural and human factors' does not appear in Article 16, the Guideline for Trademark Examination bridged the gap between the Model Law for developing countries and China's Trademark Law. The Guideline shows that (1) the quality, reputation, or other characteristics can be mainly attributable to 'natural factors' (e.g., 'Turpan Grape', '*Anxi Tieguanyin* Tea'); (2) the specialities can result mainly from 'human factors' (e.g., '*Nanjing* Brocade'); and (3) the place–product relationship can be built on 'both natural and human factors' (e.g., '*Shaoxing* Yellow Rice Wine').[71]

Furthermore, Article 3 contains a provision allowing certification marks to certify the 'place of origin' of the products.[72] Professor Zheng Chengsi remarked that the 'place of origin' can be understood here as a *synonym* for 'geographical indications', 'like author's right is synonymous with copyright'.[73] Although not everyone agrees,[74] his interpretation is in tune with regulations promulgated later. The Implementing Regulations of the Trademark Law, which were revised in 2002, provided in Article 6 that 'applications may be filed to register geographical indications as certification or collective marks'.[75] The next year, the 2003 Measures for the Registration and Administration of Collective and Certification Marks were published, which specify the conditions under which GIs per se can be registered as collective or certification

70. WIPO, *Model Law for Developing Countries on Appellations of Origin and Indications of Source*, section 1 (WIPO Publication No. 809 € 1975). Appellations of origin are defined as 'the geographical name of a country, region or specific place which serves to designate a product originating therein the characteristic qualities of which are due exclusively or essentially to the geographical environment, including natural factors, human factors, or both natural and human factors'. *See also* Konrad E. Zweigert et al., *Droit de la propriété intellectuelle et de la concurrence*, Alphen aan den Rijn, Sijthoff & Noordhoff, 1979, p. 283.
71. Trademark Office & Trademark Review and Adjudication Board, Shangbiao Shencha ji Shenli Biaozhun [Trademark Review Standard], December 2016, p. 133.
72. Article 3 of the Trademark Law.
73. Zheng Chengsi, Cong Rushi ji Faxue Yanjiu Jiaodu Kan Zhongguo Liangbu Fa de Xiugai [Two Laws Modified: Insights from Acceding to the WTO and Legal Research], ZHONGHUA SHANGBIAO [CHINA TRADEMARK], December 2001, 14.
74. Wu Chunqi, Dili Biaozhi ji Yuanchandi Mingcheng deng Xiangguan Gainian de Tanjiu [The Relationship Among Geographical Indications, Indications of Source and Appellations of Origin], SHANDONG DAXUE XUEBAO [JOURNAL OF SHANDONG UNIVERSITY], August 2003, 94.
75. Regulations for the Implementation of the Trademark Law of the People's Republic of China (2002), promulgated by Order No. 358 of 3 August 2002, of the State Council of People's Republic of China.

marks.[76] Thus, China has revisited the Trademark Law and redesigned the system of collective and certification marks in order to implement the WTO rules concerning GIs.

[b] *Orthodox or Loopholes: Why Are Obligations Fulfilled in the Neighbourhood?*

The question may arise as to why the minimum protection requirements of GIs have been fulfilled within the neighbourhood (i.e., in the trademark regime rather than China's established sui generis GI regime)[77] despite the fact that GIs and trademarks are treated as separate areas by the TRIPS Agreement.[78]

Perhaps the best perspective on this issue is from the standpoint of the global struggle between the 'Old' world and the 'New',[79] as well as the progressive efforts towards a broadly accepted definition of 'GI'. Prior to the TRIPS Agreement, the most significant attempts to establish consistent worldwide protection of GIs could be found in three agreements: the Paris Convention, Madrid Agreement, and Lisbon Agreement.[80] However, none of them established a definition of 'GI'. In the mid-1970s, in an attempt to create an international consensus,[81] the WIPO released the draft Treaty on the Protection of GIs, where the concept of GIs was first introduced as a compound term covering not only appellations of origin (AO) but also IS.[82] It intended to underline that both AO and IS were covered and that levels of protection could differ.[83] Thus, two

76. The Measures of 2003 replaced the Measures of 1994. *See* Measures for the Registration and Administration of Collective Marks and Certification Marks (2003).
77. *See* Paul Torremans et al., *Intellectual Property and TRIPS Compliance in China: Chinese and European Perspectives* 19 (Edward Elgar Publishing 2007).
78. The areas of intellectual property that the TRIPS Agreement covers are: copyright and related rights (i.e., the rights of performers, producers of sound recordings and broadcasting organizations); trademarks including service marks; geographical indications including appellations of origin; industrial designs; patents including the protection of new varieties of plants; the layout-designs of integrated circuits; and undisclosed information including trade secrets and test data. *See* WTO, *Overview: The TRIPS Agreement* (8 May 2021), https://www.wto.org/english/tratop_e/trips_e/intel2_e.htm.
79. GIs were some of the most difficult to negotiate in the Uruguay Round: on the one side, there were countries like the EU and their Member States, India, and Switzerland, and on the other side, countries such as Australia, Canada and the United States. *See* Felix Addor & Alexandra Grazioli, *Geographical Indications Beyond Wines and Spirits: A Roadmap for a Better Protection for Geographical Indications in the WTO TRIPS Agreement*, 5 J. World Intell. Prop. 865, 883 (2002).
80. Paris Convention for the Protection of Industrial Property; Madrid Agreement for the Repression of False or Deceptive Indications of Source of Goods; Lisbon Agreement for the Protection of Appellations of Origin and Their Registration.
81. WIPO, *Revision of the Lisbon Agreement or Conclusion of a New Treaty*, TAO/II/3 (25 August 1975); *See also* Lee Bendekgey & Caroline H. Mead, *International Protection of Appellations of Origin and Other Geographical Indications*, 82 Trademark Rep. 765 (1992).
82. *See* WIPO, *Draft Treaty on the Protection of Geographical Indications*, TAO/II/2 (25 August 1975), Article 2: 'The expression geographical indications covers indications of source and appellations of origin as defined below.'
83. WIPO, *The Need for a New Treaty and Its Possible Contents*, GEO/CE/I/2 (9 April 1990) p. 4: 'The term geographical indication seems to be preferable to the expression indication of source because the latter expression frequently is understood to imply a lower level of protection, in comparison with the strong protection of appellations of origin. The use of the term geographical

distinct levels of protection were explored: low protection (Paris-Madrid type, preventing deceptive practices)[84] for simple indications of origin and high protection (Lisbon-type, not limited to misleading use)[85] for appellations of origin;[86] this kind of differential treatment has been traditionally justified on the basis of the link between quality and *terroir*.

The umbrella term re-emerged in the Diplomatic Conference on the Revision of the Paris Convention (1979), the purpose of which was to ensure more extensive protection of AO and IS against their use as trademarks.[87] The 1990 WIPO Committee of Experts on the International Protection of GIs then evoked the GI concept in order to make the treaty attractive to all States party to the Paris Convention.[88] Nevertheless, since the projects were never realized, this broader concept (relative to the definition of 'AO') could not be formally adopted.

The 'GI' definition in the TRIPS Agreement is also derived from the 'AO' definition established in the Lisbon Agreement,[89] but it adopts another approach to broaden its restrictiveness.[90] One of the main features of the TRIPS definition is the availability of three alternative ways (quality, reputation, or other characteristics) to establish the link between product and place. It relaxes the product–place link requirement, and reputation alone – based solely on human factors – is allowed to satisfy the requirement.[91] Along with the construction of a substantial definition, it

indications is intended to underline that both appellations of origin and indications of source are covered and that the protection to be established is not limited to the protection which at present exists with respect to indications of source.'

84. Article 22.2 prevents the use of GIs that misleads the public or constitutes an act of unfair competition. This approach has developed historically, starting from the limited prohibition to use false indications of source only in cases where they were used together with false trade names (as provided for by the original text of the Paris Convention), evolving to a prohibition of the use of false and deceptive indications of source (Lisbon Act of the Paris Convention and the Madrid Agreement on Indications of Source). *See* WIPO, *Geographical Indications: Historical Background, Nature of rights, Existing System for Protection and Obtaining Effective Protection in Other Countries*, SCT/6/3 (25 January 2001) p. 22.
85. Prohibition is also valid for the use of protected appellations of origin in connection with the indication of the true place of origin of the product, in translated form or accompanied by terms such as 'kind', 'type', 'make', 'imitation', or the like. *See Ibid.*, at 23.
86. WIPO, *Report Adopted by the Committee of Experts*, TAO/I/8 (15 November 1974): 'The new system should provide for protection on two levels ... prohibiting deceptive practices in relation to the geographical origin of a product; in addition, a special system of protection should be set for specific geographical indications (appellations of origin) and for those kinds of indications of source specially defined as being included in the special system.'
87. WIPO, *The Need for a New Treaty and Its Possible Contents*, *supra* n. 83.
88. WIPO, *Basic Proposals (Supplement to Document PR/DC/3)*, PR/DC/4 (30 August 1979).
89. WIPO, *The Definition of Geographical Indications*, *supra* n. 65.
90. WIPO, *Possible Solutions for Conflicts Between Trademarks and Geographical Indications and for Conflicts Between Homonymous Geographical Indications*, SCT/5/3 (8 June 2000) p. 6.
91. The original proposal by EU (1988) defined GIs as those 'which designate a product as originating from a country, region or locality where a given quality, reputation or other characteristic of the product is attributable to its geographical origin, including natural and human factors'. However, in the Draft Final Act of 1990, geographical indications were limited to products 'where a given quality or other characteristic on which its reputation is based is essentially attributable to its geographical origin'. In this case, reputation alone does not satisfy the link. At the end of the game, the Dunkel Draft of 1991 renewed the definition proposed by the EU with some alterations: 'Geographical indications are, for the purposes of this Agreement,

recognized two levels of protection: Paris-Madrid type protection for GIs generally and additional (Lisbon-type) protection for GIs with regard to wines and spirits.[92] This mechanism brings together, in an unjustified manner (or merely the result of compromise), both the *terroir* logic born out of the French wine industry and the consumer-deception logic that US trademark law has traditionally been concerned with.[93] It would not exclude those who preferred collective marks or certification marks as an adequate means of GI protection[94] nor prevent others from establishing a sui generis regime such as AOC. As a consequence, the absence of any prescribed form of protection (which may be a loophole) allows flexibility in the development of domestic legislation,[95] and thus breeds various types of national configurations.[96]

Due to this flexibility (or loophole), China had a choice of how to legislate the protection of GIs. The drafting history shows that protecting GIs through collective and certification marks was not always China's preferred option. In the original drafting amendment of the Trademark Law, 'place of origin' was not even listed among the factors that could be certified by certification marks (the initially proposed factors included raw materials and mode of manufacture). It was due to the recommendation of several committee members, government ministries, and experts that 'place of

---

indications which identify a good as originating in the territory of a Party, or a region or locality in that territory, where a given quality, reputation or other characteristic of the good is essentially attributable to its geographical origin.' The requirement of a combination of natural and human influences has disappeared in the Dunkel Draft, which was adopted in the final version of the TRIPS Agreement. *See Guidelines and Objectives Proposed by the European Community for the Negotiations on Trade-Related Aspects of Substantive Standards of Intellectual Property Rights*, MTN.GNG/NG11/W/26 (7 July 1988) p. 9; Trade Negotiations Committee, *Draft Final Act Embodying the Results of the Uruguay Round of Multilateral Trade Negotiations*, MTN.TNC/W/35/Rev.1 (3 December 1990) p. 205; Trade Negotiations Committee, *Draft Final Act Embodying the Results of the Uruguay Round of Multilateral Trade Negotiations*, MTN.TNC/W/FA (20 December 1991); Stoll et al., *supra* n. 1, at 379.

92. Daniel Gervais, *The TRIPS Agreement: Drafting History and Analysis* 294-300 (Sweet & Maxwell 3rd ed. 2008).
93. *See* Stacy D. Goldberg, *Who Will Raise the White Flag: The Battle Between the United States and the European Union over the Protection of Geographical Indications*, 22 U. Pa. J. Int'l Econ. L. 107 (2001); Molly Torsen, *Apples and Oranges (and Wine): Why the International Conversation Regarding Geographic Indications Is at a Standstill*, 87 J. Pat. & Trademark Off. Soc'y 31, 33 (2005).
94. The United States advocated that there could be no doubt that geographical indications as defined by TRIPS Article 22.1 could be protected as certification marks. *See* WIPO, *Report Adopted by the Standing Committee*, SCT/7/4 (27 May 2002) p. 5.
95. Carlos M. Correa, *Intellectual Property Rights, the WTO and Developing Countries: The TRIPS Agreement and Policy Options* 21 (Zed Books 2000).
96. The main existing concepts of protection are as follows: Unfair competition and passing off, protected appellations of origin and registered geographical indications, collective and certification trademarks, and administrative schemes of protection. Moreover, since the mechanisms described do not necessarily apply on an exclusive basis, the combination of mechanisms makes a choice even more varied. *See* WIPO, *Addendum to Document SCT/6/3 (Geographical Indications: Historical Background, Nature of Rights, Existing System for Protection and Obtaining Effective Protection in Other Countries)*, SCT/8/5 (2 April 2002); WIPO, *Introduction to Geographical Indications and Recent Developments in the World Intellectual Property Organization*, WIPO/GEO/SFO/03/1 (9 July 2003) p. 4.

origin' was included in the enumeration and protected as an 'intellectual property right'.[97] One question then remains: on what basis was that recommendation made?

It is worth noting that, at this stage, the United States was very concerned about the implementation of the WTO commitments that China had made.[98] Early in the APEC-IPR International Symposium held in June 1999 in Korea, the US Patent and Trademark Office wrote a report to try to influence the implementation model of the GI provisions made in Asian countries.[99] During the drafting of the second amendment of the Chinese Trademark Law, an official in the Chinese Trademark Office translated the US report, whose main argument was that 'GIs serve the same functions as trademarks; the system of protecting GIs as trademarks, collective or certification marks fulfils all of the requirements of substantive GIs obligations in TRIPS.'[100] This argument was fully accepted by the Chinese Trademark Office and therefore laid the foundation for China's new trademark system designed to be in charge of GI protection.[101] Furthermore, the Trademark Office drew a comparison between GI legislation in France and legislation in other countries (i.e., the US, Germany, the UK, Australia, and Canada), and came to the conclusion that most countries rely on the trademark system as an adequate means of GI protection. Professor Zheng Chengsi used the US legislation as a reference model in his comments on the Trademark Law amendment.[102] As we can see from the arguments and remarks made by officials and specialists at that time, it is clear that the US model, as well as its justifications, strongly influenced China's choice of legal instrument for providing TRIPS-level protection to GIs.[103] The practice of protecting GIs through the trademark system has thus been formalized in China.

---

97. Hu Guangbao, Guanyu Zhonghua Renmin Gongheguo Shangbiaofa Xiuzheng'an Cao'an de Shuoming [Drafting Instructions for the Revision of the Trademark Law], Twenty-Fourth Meeting of the Standing Committee of the Ninth National People's Congress, 22 October 2001.
98. Tomoko Sugiyama, *Intellectual Property Rights and Prospects for U.S.-Japan Cooperation in Asia* (Columbia University Libraries 8 May 2021), https://academiccommons.columbia.edu/doi/10.7916/D8FR04F4.
99. Robert Stoll, US Patent and Trademark Office, *TRIPS Implementation on Geographical Indications*, Presentation at the APEC-IPR International Symposium (June 1999). In twenty-nine years with the Patent and Trademark Office, Robert Stoll has held several leadership posts, such as training foreign officials on all aspects of intellectual property.
100. Robert Stoll & Wang Ze (trans.), TRIPS Youguan Dili Biaozhi Guiding de Shishi [TRIPS Implementation on Geographical Indications], ZHONGHUA SHANGBIAO [CHINA TRADEMARK], March 2000, 38-41.
101. Xie Dongwei, Rushi yu Woguo Yuanchandi Mingcheng Dili Biaozhi de Baohu [WTO and the Protection of China's Geographical Indications], ZHONGHUA SHANGBIAO [CHINA TRADEMARK], May 2001, 14-16.
102. Zheng Chengsi, Manzu Zuidi Yaoqiu Zhongguo Rushi yu Zhishi Chanquan Baohu [Fulfilling Minimum Requirements: WTO and the Protection of Intellectual Property Rights], GUOJI MAOYI [INTERNATIONAL TRADE], January 2001, 38.
103. Having compared the examples of China, Japan, and Taiwan, Min-Chiuan Wang noted that the Asian countries, not having their own geographical indication norm in the past, have to implement the TRIPS Agreement in their domestic laws, understand what GIs mean and how these rules concern them. In enacting their geographical indication laws, many Asian countries have relied primarily on trademark law. The influence of the United States has gained the upper hand. China is a significant exception that adopts both the trademark law model and the appellation of origin model. *See* Min-Chiuan Wang, *The Asian Consciousness and Interests in Geographical Indications*, 96 Trademark Rep. 906, 920 (2006).

[2] GIs in Sui Generis Regime

In order to ensure consistency with the Agreement on Rules of Origin and other relevant provisions of the WTO Agreement (including the TRIPS Agreement),[104] the former State Administration for Entry-Exit Inspection and Quarantine promulgated the Provisions on the Administration of 'Marks of Origin' upon China's accession to the WTO in 2001,[105] the scope of which was extended beyond 'indications of the country of origin'[106] to include 'geographical indications'.

Article 4(2) of the Provisions defined GIs as:

> The geographical name of a country, region or a specific place, used to indicate that a product originates from that place, where the *quality and characteristics* of the product are *essentially or exclusively* due to the geographical environment, natural conditions, human culture backgrounds and other factors.

Since this definition resembles the Lisbon definition of 'appellations of origin' more closely than it does the TRIPS definition of 'geographical indications', many commentators argued that Article 4(2) did not provide an accurate 'GI' definition and was not consistent with international practice.[107]

Despite this criticism, one has to wonder if the restrictive formula in Article 4(2) is the result of a misunderstanding of the TRIPS Agreement or if it was done intentionally to serve a different purpose. In fact, Article 5 clearly specified that GIs, thus defined, were to be used for 'well-known, excellent, and special products'.[108] These products are traditionally known as 'Local and Special Products', a Chinese expression frequently used to describe agricultural products and handicrafts (1) originating from various places and (2) possessing unique characteristics, styles, or skills.[109] We are likely to gain a better understanding of this expression if we consider its French counterpart, '*produits de terroir*'. Just as the French AOC system is designed

---

104. Determining the origin of goods is also the goal of the WTO Agreements on Rules of Origin. However, the basic role of rules of origin is the determination of the economic nationality as opposed to the geographical nationality of a given good. *See Rules of Origin – Handbook*, World Customs Organization (8 May 2021), http://www.wcoomd.org/~/media/wco/public/global/pdf/topics/origin/overview/origin-handbook/rules-of-origin-handbook.pdf.
105. Provisions on the Administration of Marks of Origin and the Implementing Measures (2001).
106. According to Article 4.1 of the Provisions, an indication of the country of origin refers to marks, labels, signs, characters, graphics and various certificates relating to the place of origin that are used to indicate that a product or service originates from the corresponding country or area.
107. *See* Su Ping, Yu Dili Biaozhi Xiangguan de Falu Shuyu Yujing Kaobian (Textual Research on the Contexts for Legal Terms Related to Geographical Signs), CHONGQING GONGXUEYUAN XUEBAO [JOURNAL OF CHONGQING INSTITUTE OF TECHNOLOGY], January 2007, 123; Zhong Changyuan, Qianxi Yuanchandi Biaoji he Dili Biaozhi Jiqi Xiangguan Gainian [Analysis on the Marks of Origin and Geographical Indication and Relevant Concepts], KEJI QINGBAO KAIFA YU JINGJI [SCI-TECH INFORMATION DEVELOPMENT & ECONOMY], September 2009, 124.
108. Article 5 of Provisions on the Administration of Marks of Origin: 'The legible products of marks of origin include: ... (2) well-known, excellent and special products and traditional handicrafts.'
109. *See* Xia Zhengnong & Cheng Zhili, CIHAI [WORD & PHRASE DICTIONARY], at 3963 (6th ed., Zhonghua Book Company, 2010); National People's Congress, Quanguo Nongye Fazhan Gangyao [Agricultural Development Outline], 11 April 1960, Article 17.

to help the development of '*produits de terroir*',[110] the 'Marks of Origin' regime was designed to be a control system guaranteeing specific qualities and providing a labelling tool for the promotion of 'local and special products'.[111] According to Pei Xiaoying, Chief of the Division of Geographical Indications at the National Bureau of Quality Inspection, the Marks of Origin regime drew inspiration from both the TRIPS Agreement and the sui generis protection system of GIs in the EU, while considering the particular conditions in China.[112] The increasing consumer interest in local and special products, as well as the motivation of producers in the sector, may explain why China chose to imitate France and the EU, who have a successful experience of valorizing *produits de terroir*. This may also partially explain why the definition of 'GI' in Article 4(2) is more in line with that of 'AO', reflecting the spirit of the French '*terroir*' concept.

Besides agricultural products and foodstuffs, the Marks of Origin regime was also available for traditional handicrafts once the requirements of the GI definition were met.[113] Clearly, the conditions set out in Article 4(2) are too challenging to be applied to handicrafts. The Implementing Measures for the Provisions relaxed the purely qualitative linkage requirement. It required only that 'a specific quality, characteristic *or reputation* shall be attributable to the natural environment and human factors of the concerned area; and production steps shall take place in this area adopting traditional production methods'.[114] This relaxation opened the door for traditional and artisanal products such as 'Satin from *Suzhou*'[115] and 'Porcelain from *Jingdezhen*'.[116]

---

110. Ministère de l'Alimentation, de l'Agriculture et de la Pêche, Décret n° 2009-1268 du 19 octobre 2009 relatif à l'appellation d'origine contrôlée 'Oignon de Roscoff', J.O. du 22 oct. 2009, n° 245, pp. 17565-17572.
111. Shen Feilong, Tutechan Pinpai de Chengwei Tanxi [Appellation of Local and Special Products], FAZHAN [DEVELOPMENT], November 2007, 111; Cao Xinming, Woguo Dili Biaozhi Baohu Zhidu zhi Wanshan [On Improving the System of Geographical Indications in China Based on Promoting China's Agricultural Economy Development], ZHISHI CHANQUAN [INTELLECTUAL PROPERTY], January 2007, 26; Zhang Weike, Liu Zhenlei & Gao Dacheng, Dili Biaozhi Baohu yu Mingyoute Nongchanpin de Fazhan [The Geographical Indication Protection and the Development of Famous Agricultural Products], QINGDAO XINGZHENG XUEYUAN XUEBAO [JOURNAL OF QINGDAO ADMINISTRATIVE INSTITUTE], August 2004, 85; Xu Fang & Wu Guoying, Mingyoute Chanpin Dili Biaozhi de Baohu Zhanlue Yanjiu [Geographical Indications Protection for Famous, Excellent and Special Products], JIANGSU SHANGLUN [JIANGSU FORUM], February 2005, 15; Zhang Yumin, Dili Biaozhi Baohu de Jige Guanxi [Several Relations on Geographical Indications Protection], GONGSHANG XINGZHENG GUANLI [BI-WEEKLY OF ADMINISTRATION FOR INDUSTRY AND COMMERCE], March 2012, 12-13.
112. Pei Xiaoying, Liu Hongchun & Qiao Hong, Dili Biaozhi Diyu Techan de Huwei Shen [Geographical Indications: Guardian of Local Products], ZHONGGUO ZHILIANG JISHU JIANDU [CHINA QUALITY SUPERVISION], March 2006, 48.
113. Provisions on the Administration of Marks of Origin, Article 5.
114. Implementing Measures for the Provisions on the Administration of Marks of Origin, Article 6.
115. *See* Guojia Zhiliang Jiandu Jianyan Jianyi Zongju Gonggao 2002 Nian di 16 Hao [State General Administration of Quality Supervision, Inspection and Quarantine Announcement No. 16, 2002], 25 February 2002.
116. *See* Guojia Zhiliang Jiandu Jianyan Jianyi Zongju Gonggao 2001 Nian di 10 Hao [State General Administration of Quality Supervision, Inspection and Quarantine Announcement No. 10, 2001], 30 July 2001.

The Marks of Origin regime (administered by the former State Administration for Entry-Exit Inspection and Quarantine)[117] actually constituted a third parallel system for GI protection,[118] coexisting with the trademark regime (administered by the Trademark Office)[119] and the sui generis regime of products with appellations of origin (administered by the former State Bureau of Quality and Technical Supervision).[120] As each regime had its own understanding of what a GI was and how it should be protected, the lack of harmonization resulted in the underperformance of China's GI scheme, as will be discussed later.[121]

§2.02 CONCEPTUAL MUTATION OF GI AFTER CHINA'S ACCESSION TO THE WTO

After China had fulfilled its commitments set out in international treaties, there were three different concepts of indications of geographical origin by the time it accede to the WTO (in 2001),[122] defined respectively under the authority of the Trademark Office of SAIC, the former State Administration of Quality and Technical Supervision, and the former State Administration for Entry-Exit Inspection and Quarantine. The latter two bodies merged, in 2001, to form the former General Administration of Quality Supervision, Inspection and Quarantine (AQSIQ).[123] After the merger, the former AQSIQ effectively operated two parallel mechanisms with similar purposes or effects, namely the system of 'products with appellations of origin' and the system of 'marks of

117. Article 3 of the Provisions on the Administration of Marks of Origin: 'The State Administration for Entry-Exit Inspection and Quarantine shall administer the management of marks of origin of the whole country uniformly and shall be responsible for the formulation of administration measures, the organization, coordination, supervision, and administration of marks of origin.'
118. Lu Qi, Zhongfa Dili Biaozhi Falu Baohu Bijiao Yanjiu [Comparative Study on Geographical Indications Protection: France-China], FAZHI LUNCONG [LAW FORUM], March 2004, 25; Gu Xiaodong & Liu Weiming, WTO-TRIPS Xieyi Zhong Dili Biaozhi Zai Woguo de Falu Baohu Yanjiu [China's Legal Protection of Geographical Indications of the TRIPS Agreement], QIYE JINGJI [ENTERPRISE ECONOMY], July 2006, 174.
119. Article 2 of the Trademark Law (2001): 'The Trademark Office of the Administrative Authority for Industry and Commerce under the State Council shall be responsible for the registration and administration of trademarks throughout the country.'
120. Article 6 of the Provisions on the Protection of Products with Appellations of Origin: 'The State Bureau of Quality and Technical Supervision shall establish the Office for the Protection of AO Products, dealing specifically with the administrative work relating to the protection of AO products.'
121. *See* Chapter 6 *infra*.
122. 'Geographical indications' set out in Article 16 of the Trademark Law; 'Products with appellations of origin' in Article 2 of the Provisions on the Protection of Products with Appellations of Origin; 'Geographical indications' in Article 4.2 of the Provisions on the Administration of Marks of Origin.
123. Guowuyuan Guanyu Guojia Gongshang Xingzheng Guanliju Xinwen Chubanshu Guojia Zhiliang Jishu Jianduju Guojia Churujing Jianyan Jianyi Ju Jigou Tiaozheng de Tongzhi [State Council's Notice of Restructuring the State Administration for Industry and Commerce, the General Administration of Press and Publication, the State Bureau of Quality and Technical Supervision and the State Administration for Entry-Exit Inspection and Quarantine], 30 April 2001.

origin (which include GIs)'. A restructuring of the two systems under the former AQSIQ was accompanied by a harmonization of terminologies.

While the battle between the Trademark Office and the former AQSIQ remained intense, the MOA waded into the fray in 2007 by creating a new notion, 'geographical indications for agricultural products'. Moreover, the former State Forestry Administration (SFA) (which has become the National Forestry and Grassland Administration since 2018) studied a draft proposal for another notion, 'geographical indications for forest products'. We observe a trend towards the extension of GI concepts based on a sector-specific approach: 'These have contributed to form the consciousness of GIs at the second stage.'[124]

[A] Evolution of GI Concepts under the AQSIQ

Starting in 2004, the former AQSIQ initiated the integration of the two GI systems under its governance. As a result, the dual concepts of 'products of appellations of origin' and 'geographical indications', both inspired by the French 'AO' concept, were replaced and merged into a single and unified notion, 'geographical indication products'. Meanwhile, as indications of geographical origin are increasingly tied to ecological considerations,[125] the former AQSIQ created in 2012 the notion of 'protected eco-origin products' (PEOP), which combines both 'origin' and 'ecology' factors. Although the CNIPA replaced the former AQSIQ in 2018 to exercise the nationwide administration of the 'GI products' regime, the concepts developed by the former AQSIQ continue to be employed.

[1] GI Products

The merger of governmental bodies into the former AQSIQ has led to a situation where two similar mechanisms of protection are governed by the same body, AQSIQ, and could be used jointly. It was possible to protect a GI jointly as a 'product with appellation of origin' and as a 'mark of origin' if protection were sought under both mechanisms (e.g., 'Aged Vinegar from *Shanxi*').[126] Since this dualistic structure proved to be complex and cumbersome,[127] a rationalization was to be undertaken. In 2004, the

124. Wang, *supra* n. 103, at 930.
125. *See* Sarah Bowena & Ana Valenzuela Zapata, *Geographical Indications, Terroir, and Socioeconomic and Ecological Sustainability: The Case of Tequila*, 25 J. Rural Stud. 108 (2009); Giovanni Belletti et al., *The Effects of Protecting Geographical Indicators: Ways and Means of Their Evaluation* (Swiss Federal Institute of Intellectual Property 2011).
126. Guojia Zhiliang Jiandu Jianyan Jianyi Zongju Gonggao 2002 Nian di 19 Hao [State General Administration of Quality Supervision, Inspection and Quarantine Announcement No. 19, 2002], 1 March 2002; Guojia Zhiliang Jiandu Jianyan Jianyi Zongju Gonggao 2004 Nian di 104 Hao [State General Administration of Quality Supervision, Inspection and Quarantine Announcement No. 104, 2004], 9 August 2004.
127. Bai Huiying, Woguo Dili Biaozhi Zhidu Ruogan Wenti Tanxi [Several Issues of the System of Geographical Indications in China], HENANSHENG ZHENGFA GUANLI GANBU XUEYUAN XUEBAO [JOURNAL OF HENAN ADMINISTRATIVE INSTITUTE OF POLITICS AND LAW], July 2006, 143.

former AQSIQ established the Geographical Indications Management Unit under the Science and Technology Department to harmonize efforts to protect products of appellations of origin and marks of origin.[128] Subsequently, in 2005, the AQSIQ promulgated the Provisions on the Protection of GI Products,[129] which replaced the former Provisions on the Protection of Products with Appellations of Origin (1999) and were understood to prevail where there were discrepancies with the Provisions on the Administration of Marks of Origin (2001).[130] The new GI regulation provides a unified concept that replaces the former notions of 'products with appellations of origin' and 'geographical indications (defined in Article 4(2) of the Provisions for Marks of Origin)'.[131]

According to Article 2 of the new regulation, 'geographical indication products' are defined as products '(1) which are named after a geographical name, after being examined and approved; (2) originated from a specific region; and (3) whose quality, reputation or other characteristics are essentially attributable to the place of production, including natural and humane factors'. Since the products must be named after the *name* of a place, symbols capable of indicating the origin of goods without literally naming the place of origin (indirect GIs) cannot qualify as GI products.[132] This constitutes a considerable difference from the notions of 'geographical indications' laid down in the Trademark Law and the TRIPS Agreement.[133] Yet another difference lies in the requirement for a combination of 'natural and human factors' for GI products. As a matter of fact, although 'both natural and human influences' once appeared in the original proposal for the TRIPS definition of 'GI' made by the EU,[134] they were not

128. Before the adjustment, the Regulation Department had born the primary obligation to protect and manage products of appellations of origin, and the Customs Department had been in charge of marks of origin. *See* Guojia Zhiliang Jiandu Jianyan Jianyi Zongju Bangongting Guanyu Dili Biaozhi Zhineng Tiaozheng Youguan Shiyi de Tongzhi [State General Administration of Quality Supervision, Inspection and Quarantine's Notice on the Adjustment of the Administrative Functions of the Geographical Indications], 1 November 2004.
129. Provisions on the Protection of Geographical Indication Products (2005), Promulgated by the General Administration of Quality Supervision, Inspection and Quarantine of the People's Republic of China.
130. Provisions on the Protection of Geographical Indication Products, Article 28.
131. Yang Lei, Zhuazhu Rushi Jiyu Chuangxin Zhijian Gongzuo Woguo Jiaru WTO Wunian Lai Guojia Zhijian Zongju Caiqu Youxiao Cuoshi Luxing Chengnuo Qude Xianzhu Chengxiao [Seizing the Opportunity to Innovate Quality Inspection Work: AQSIQ Took Effective Measures to Fulfil the WTO Commitments], ZHONGGUO ZHILIANG BAO [CHINA QUALITY REPORT], 11 December 2006, 3.
132. Li Yaqin, Lun Dili Biaozhi de Falu Baohu [Legal Protection of Geographical Indications], KEJI YU FALU [SCIENCE & LAW], April 2008, 54.
133. Geographical indications in the TRIPS Agreement may be classified as direct and indirect. Although geographical indications generally consist of geographical names (direct indications), they may also be based on non-geographical names or symbols (indirect indications). Indirect indications may be capable of indicating the origin of the goods without literally naming their place of origin. Examples are the *Eiffel* Tower for Paris, the Matterhorn for Switzerland, the Tower Bridge for London, the colours of the French flag for cigarettes, the statue of Liberty, etc. *See* Carlos M. Correa, *Protection of Geographical Indications in CARICOM Countries* (Caribbean Regional Negotiating Machinery Technical Papers 2002); WIPO, *Recent Developments at International Level in the Field of Trademarks*, WIPO/GEO/SBZ/03/2 (1 May 2003).
134. GATT Secretariat, *Guidelines and Objectives Proposed by the European Community*, *supra* n. 91, at 9: 'Geographical indications are, for the purpose of this agreement, those which designate a

adopted in the final version of the TRIPS Agreement, nor were they fully accepted in the Second Amendment of China's Trademark Law.[135]

The Implementing Rules for the Provisions on the Protection of GI Products promulgated in 2006 further specified the strength of the connection between the product and the geographical area. First, under the Rules, GI products include (1) products grown, cultivated, or bred in the local region, and whose specific quality, speciality *and* reputation are essentially attributable to 'natural factors'; (2) products whose raw materials all come from that region, whose specific quality, speciality *and* reputation are essentially attributable to 'natural and human factors', and whose production steps take place in this area using specific process; and (3) products whose raw materials are all or partly sourced from other regions, whose specific quality, speciality, *and* reputation are essentially attributable to 'natural and human factors', and they are produced in the area through a specific process.[136] Second, applications for GI products are ruled inadmissible if the product is not well-known to the public.[137] They must enjoy a certain amount of consumer recognition.[138] Finally, GI products must have a 'historic connection to the land', which requires that the products be produced for a long period in the same social and cultural environment.[139]

These rules are more detailed and stricter than those in the TRIPS Agreement and are actually derived from the General Requirements for Products with Appellations of Origin (1999),[140] the enactment of which was encouraged by the French AOC system

product as originating from a country, region or locality where a given quality, reputation or other characteristic of the product is attributable to its geographical origin, including natural and human factors.'

135. There is no reference to natural and/or human factors in Article 22.1 of the TRIPS Agreement. Article 16 of the Trademark Law only requires 'natural factors or human factors'.
136. Implementing Rules for the Provisions on the Protection of Geographical Indication Products, Article 7 (2006).
137. *Ibid.*, Article 9.
138. *Ibid.*, Article 19(2).
139. *Ibid.*, Article 11.4.3: 'Supporting documents for GI products include: ... a description of the visibility of the product ... as well as the historical root of the product'; Article 19: 'the registration application shall be verified by means of a formal investigation following the principles: ... (2) the product has a quality, speciality and reputation which could reflect a particular geographical environment with its inherent natural and human factors, it enjoys a certain amount of consumer recognition, and it is produced for a long period.'
140. General Requirements for Products with Appellations of Origin, Article 3.1: '[Products with appellations of origin include:] (1) Products named after the name of a region, whose raw materials all come from that region, whose specific quality, speciality and reputation are essentially attributable to natural and human factors and the production steps of which take place in this area using traditional production methods; (2) Products named after the name of a region, whose raw materials are all/partly sourced from other regions, whose specific quality, speciality and reputation are essentially attributable to natural and human factors and the production steps of which take place in this area adopting traditional production methods; (3) Certain products not named after geographical names, which fulfil the conditions referred to in the paragraph (1) shall also be considered as products with appellations of origin'; General Requirements, Article 4.2: 'The product must have a consistent quality, a long history, a peculiar flavour, and enjoying a great reputation'; General Requirements, Article 5.1: 'the AOs area is determined based on historical connection to the land and natural and human factors in the given land'.

and European PDO system.[141] Thus, Professor Zhu Lanye notes that the definition of 'geographical indication products' is the same as that of 'products of appellations of origin'.[142]

We admit that both the definitions stick firmly to the traditional philosophy of *terroir*, wherein natural links are more strongly emphasized. However, we would not go so far as to say that they are identical. While a great deal of importance is attached to 'traditional *savoir-faire*'[143] in the notion of 'products of appellations of origin', the notion of 'geographical indication products' uproots itself and gradually relocates to take advantage of the TRIPS framework, in which there is no such mandatory requirement for traditional production processes. Whereas the Provisions of AO Products (1999) were applied to goods 'produced in a specific region adopting *traditional* production methods',[144] the Provisions of GI Products (2005) are intended to apply generally to all products 'whose quality, reputation or other characteristics are attributable to the region of production, including both natural and *human* factors'.[145] Since 'human factors' refers here to 'specific techniques',[146] the production methods used for GI products are not restricted to traditional ones: GI products may include traditional as well as non-traditional products.[147]

Nevertheless, the similarities between the notion of AO products and that of GI products far outweigh the differences. That is why the vast majority of undertakings which had formerly been granted the right to use the AO product logo were granted the right to use the official GI product logo immediately after the 2005 Provisions came into force,[148] although the 2005 Provisions contain no transitional clauses. Given their similarities, we could conclude that the definition of GI products 'inherits' the features

141. *See* §2.01 *supra*.
142. Zhu Lanye, *An Analysis of China's System of Protecting Geographical Indications*, 1 Asian J. Comp. L. 1, 6 (2006).
143. Provisions on the Protection of Products with Appellations of Origin (1999), Articles 2, 10; General Requirements for Products with Appellations of Origin, Articles 3-4.
144. Provisions on the Protection of Products with Appellations of Origin (1999), Article 2
145. Provisions on the Protection of Geographical Indication Products (2005), Article 2.
146. Implementing Rules for the Provisions on the Protection of Geographical Indication Products, Article 2: 'GI products include: (1) products grown, raised or bred in the designated region; (2) products produced and processed from raw materials coming entirely from a region or partly from elsewhere according to the specific techniques of this region.'
147. *Ibid.*, Article 8: 'GI products generally include planting, breeding and processing products, processing products, processing food, wine, tea, Chinese medicinal materials, handicrafts and traditional products.'
148. Guojia Zhiliang Jiandu Jianyan Jianyi Zongju Gonggao 2005 Nian di 108 Hao [State General Administration of Quality Supervision, Inspection and Quarantine Announcement No. 108, 2005], 29 July 2005; Guojia Zhiliang Jiandu Jianyan Jianyi Zongju Gonggao 2005 Nian di 125 Hao [State General Administration of Quality Supervision, Inspection and Quarantine Announcement No. 125, 2005], 25 August 2005; Guojia Zhiliang Jiandu Jianyan Jianyi Zongju Gonggao 2005 Nian di 152 Hao [State General Administration of Quality Supervision, Inspection and Quarantine Announcement No. 152, 2005], 17 October 2005; Guojia Zhiliang Jiandu Jianyan Jianyi Zongju Gonggao 2005 Nian di 158 Hao [State General Administration of Quality Supervision, Inspection and Quarantine Announcement No. 158, 2005], 2 November 2005; Guojia Zhiliang Jiandu Jianyan Jianyi Zongju Gonggao 2005 Nian di 210 Hao [State General Administration of Quality Supervision, Inspection and Quarantine Announcement No. 210, 2005], 31 December 2005.

of the AO concept, which mirrors the close ties between sui generis GI systems in China and those in Europe.

Unsurprisingly, the sui generis regime of GI products continued to be criticized for being parallel to the trademark regime.[149] The war between the supporters of the special regime, represented by the former AQSIQ, and the supporters of the trademark regime, represented by the Trademark Office of the former SAIC, does not end with the AQSIQ's simplification of the GI terminology.

In March 2018, the former AQSIQ and the former SAIC merged to become the State Administration of Market Regulation (SAMR). Under the authority of the SAMR, the CNIPA became the sole body responsible for the 'GI product' regime established by the former AQSIQ and the trademark system. However, the two systems, along with their terminologies, continue to coexist. In September 2020, the CNIPA released the Draft Provisions on the Protection of GIs, which continue to use the concept of 'GI product' and shows no intention of replacing it.

[2] Protected Eco-Origin Products

Concerns regarding ecology, the environment, and biodiversity may be directly and indirectly associated with GIs. These concerns can be explicitly addressed in national requirements for GI recognition. In China, an application for GI protection will be refused if the product has a negative effect on the environment, ecology, or natural resources.[150] Moreover, even though environmental protection is not mentioned as a primary motivation in GI protection schemes,[151] the French and European experiences show a trend towards the enhancement of agro-ecosystem sustainability. The reform of the wine market organization of 2008, which established PDO/PGI concepts in the wine sector, aimed 'to create a wine regime ... ensuring all production respects the environment'.[152] The Green Paper on agricultural product quality stated concerning PGI criteria that 'sustainability criteria can also make an important contribution to the

149. The General Office of the former State Administration for Industry and Commerce on 28 April 2005 had sent a communication to the former AQSIQ, clearly opposed to the establishment of a parallel sui generis system alongside the trademark system under the circumstance where the latter had already been regulated by the Trademark Law. *See* Yao Fan, Yiyou Shangbiaofa You Lingjian Xin Guizhang Liangzhong Zhuce Qudao Weinan Quanliren [Existing Trademark Law and Other New Rules: Two Kinds of Registration Channels for Right Holders], FAZHI RIBAO [LEGAL DAILY], 5 August 2005 (cited by the Legal Affairs Office of the State Council of P. R. China).
150. Provisions on the Protection of Geographical Indication Products, Article 7: 'The products in respect of which an application is filed for protection of a geographical indication shall meet the requirements of safety, hygiene and environmental protection. Where a product jeopardizes the environment, ecology, or resources, application for the protection thereof shall be refused.'
151. For example, EU legislation on geographical indications for agricultural products (Regulation 1151/2012) does not mention environment protection among the specific objectives of the legislation.
152. Recital 5 of Council Regulation 479/2008 on the common organization of the market in wine.

quality of the product and in meeting consumer expectations, such as environmental sustainability of farming methods'.[153]

A new paradigm is emerging in which 'gastronomy' and environmental concerns are being linked.[154] Numerous researchers argue that GIs may act as a means of improving environmental quality in affected ecosystems.[155] The evidence suggests that GI systems may offer farmers the opportunity to establish environmentally sustainable farming systems[156] while taking account of the combination of cultural and biological diversity.[157] In this case, these products, identified by their geographical origin, may derive a quality or reputation from the ecosystem.[158]

Therefore, for products that comply with both GI and ecological criteria, two mechanisms may be available with which to 'transfer value from landscape to product':[159] the GI scheme and an environmental labelling scheme.[160] Using GIs makes a clear reference to the place of origin and guarantees quality and/or reputation. While it is generally admitted that GIs are related to biodiversity issues, environmental requirements are rarely explicitly included in the specification of a protected GI.[161] By contrast, the criteria for eco-labelling focus on the impact of consumption and production on the environment, allowing the promotion of 'products which have a high level of environmental performance'.[162] However, labelled products can be produced anywhere.

---

153. *See* European Commission, *Green Paper on Agricultural Product Quality: Product Standards, Farming Requirements and Quality Schemes*, COM(2008)641 final (15 October 2008) p. 13.
154. Erik Thévenod-Mottet, *Geographical Indications and Biodiversity, in Agriculture, Biodiversity and Markets: Livelihoods and Agroecology in Comparative Perspective* 206 (Stewart Lockie & David Carpenter eds, Earthscan 2010).
155. For example, European Commission funded the IPDEV project (Trade, intellectual property rights and sustainable development), to assess the impact of geographical indications on environmental quality. *See* Mariano Riccheri et al., *Assessing the Applicability of Geographical Indications as a Means to Improve Environmental Quality in Affected Ecosystems and the Competitiveness of Agricultural Products* (eSocialSciences, Working Papers 2007).
156. The GI registration system provides the opportunity to incorporate the environmental attributes of products into the product specifications. *See* Michael Blakeney, *Geographical Indications and Environmental Protection*, 12 Frontiers L. China 162, 172 (2017).
157. The IPDEV project studied the following cases: Arroz de Valencia, Borsac Mineral Water, Gulf Region Olive Oil, West Country Farmhouse Cheddar, Hisarska Mineral Water, Idiázabal Cheese, Jersey Royal Potatoes, Diepholzer Moorschnucke, Bulgarian Rose Oil, Schwäbisch Hall Quality Pork, Sierra Mágine Olive Oil, and Spreewald Gherkins. It concluded that environmental quality had been a secondary motivation in GI-related strategies.
158. Laurence Bérard & Philippe Marchenay, *Local Products and Geographical Indications: Taking Account of Local Knowledge and Biodiversity*, 58 Int'l Soc. Sci. J. 109 (2006).
159. Delphine Marie-Vivien et al., *Trademarks, Geographical Indications and Environmental Labelling to Promote Biodiversity: The Case of Agroforestry Coffee in India*, 32 Dev. Pol'y Rev. 379 (2014).
160. GIs scheme and eco-label award scheme are among the product quality schemes in operation in the EU, regulated by the EU legislation on food labelling rules. *See* European Commission, *Impact Assessment Report: Commission Staff Working Document Accompanying the Communication from the Commission to the European Parliament, the Council, the European Economic and Social Committee and the Committee of Regions on Agricultural Product Quality Policy*, SEC (2009) 670 (28 May 2009) p. 11.
161. *Ibid.*, at 21.
162. Recital 5 of Regulation (EC) No 66/2010 of the European Parliament and the Council on the EU ecolabel.

Like in the case of '*Agroforestry* Coffee' in India, since the GI scheme and environmental labelling scheme can both be used to differentiate products in the market to overcome information asymmetry and create added value,[163] producers may choose different strategies, based on marketing either the quality or reputation of the goods linked to the origin (to register a trademark or GI) or their environmentally friendly practices (to apply for the ecolabel).[164]

The first environmental label was the Blue Angel label, established in Germany for industrial goods in 1977.[165] Based on the environment policy for clean products, the EU launched the Ecolabel award programme in 1992, which covers environmental impacts during the entire life cycle of the product.[166] Environmental labelling programs are now in operation in more than fifty countries,[167] including China.

The Report to the Eighteenth National Congress of the Communist Party of China (CPC) highlighted the importance of making ecological progress.[168] In 2012, the former AQSIQ founded the PEOP label[169] which is intended to combine 'the goal of protecting the ecology with that of guaranteeing the origin'.[170]

According to Article 4 of the General Rules on PEOP, the notion of 'PEOP' covers ecological products (1) that are in conformity with energy-efficient, resource-saving, and other environmental requirements during their entire life cycle and (2) the quality or characteristic of which is linked to the particular features of the place of origin. The

163. Ulrike Grote, *Environmental Labelling, Protected Geographical Indications and the Interests of Developing Countries*, 10 Estey Ctr. J. Int'l L. & Trade Pol'y 99 (2009).

164. Delphine Marie-Vivien et al., *Trademarks, Geographical Indications and Environmental Labelling to Promote Biodiversity*, *supra* n. 159, at 382.

165. European Economic and Social Committee, *Opinion of the European Economic and Social Committee on a Community Ecolabel Schemes*, COM(2008)401 final – 2008/0152 (COD), OJ C 218, 11.9.2009, p. 53.

166. *Council Regulation 880/92 on a Community Eco-label Award Scheme*, OJ L 99, 11.4.1992, p. 1.

167. In Asia, for example, Japan founded the Eco Mark Programme in 1898, operated by the Japanese Environment Association. The Korea Eco-Label Program was initiated in 1992. The Thai Green Label Scheme was formally launched in 1994. *See Guidance for the Eco Mark*, Japan Environment Association (8 May 2021), https://www.ecomark.jp/english/pdf/tebiki_E.pdf; Xavier Leflaive, *Eco-Innovation Policies in the Republic of Korea*, OECD (8 May 2021), https://www.oecd.org/korea/42876970.pdf; *A Guide to The Thai Green Label Scheme*, Open Development Thailand (8 May 2021), https://data.opendevelopmentmekong.net/library_record/a-guide-to-the-thai-green-label-scheme.

168. Hu Jintao, former General Secretary of the Central Committee of the Communist Party of China (CPC) and Chinese president, delivered the report during the opening ceremony of the eighteenth CPC National Congress at the Great Hall of the People in Beijing, 8 November 2012.

169. Guojia Zhijian Zongju Guanyu Yinfa Shengtai Yuanchandi Chanpin Baohu Xiangguan Guiding ji Weituo Pingding Jigou Mingdan Diyipi de Tongzhi [Notice of the General Administration of Quality Supervision, Inspection and Quarantine on the Issuance of Relevant Regulations on the Protection of Ecological Products of Origin and the List of Entrusted Assessment Agencies], 29 September 2012.

170. While from the French perspective, the Protected Eco-Origin Product is considered more of a guarantee of origin (a means of fighting counterfeiting) than a scheme of encouraging businesses to market products and services that are kinder to the environment. *See* Alexandre Abellan, *Chine: les vins français bientôt au banc d'essai d'un label officiel anti-contrefaçon*, Vitisphere, actualités, 7 mai 2014; Zhao Junqi, Jianshe Meili Zhongguo Shengtai Yuanchandi Chanpin Baohu Dayou Kewei [Building a Beautiful Country: The Role of Protected Eco-origin Products], ZHONGGUO JIANYAN JIANYI [CHINA INSPECTION AND QUARANTINE], May 2013, 16.

PEOP criteria are actually based on both the environmental performance of products (ecology criteria) and the inherent connection between the product and its provenance (geographical origin criteria).[171] The ecology criteria include impacts on the environment, energy and resource consumption, carbon dioxide emissions, and health and safety aspects.[172] Regarding geographical origin criteria, the focus is on the natural, geographical, cultural, and historical aspects of the place where the products are made, grown, produced, processed, and manufactured. In order to qualify as PEOP, products should have a quality or other characteristic that is inherently linked to geographical elements, such as topography, soil conditions, hydrological data, meteorological conditions, historical origin, cultural background, production technology, and formulation.[173]

Many Chinese officials and scholars argue that PEOP is a subcategory of GIs.[174] Kong Xiangjun, an official responsible for GI protection at the Guangxi Province Entry-Exit Inspection and Quarantine Bureau, noted that PEOP is an upgraded version of GIs, featuring additional 'ecology criteria' that enable better environmental outcomes.[175] By incorporating a set of environmental practices into its definition, PEOP becomes more than simply an ecolabel and appears to be a 'Green GI'.[176]

The drafting history of the General Rules on PEOP supports this view. The TRIPS Agreement and the Provisions on the Administration of Marks of Origin, both of which contain clauses dealing with GI protection, have been used as a reference in defining PEOP.[177] Furthermore, through the implementation of the General Rules, many GI products have been granted the PEOP label and have become a member of the eco plan (e.g., '*Xixia* mushroom', '*Lushi* black fungus', '*Lingbao* apple').[178]

---

171. Hu Shen et al., Shengtai Yuanchandi Renzheng Tanxi [Analysis on Ecology Origin Certification], XIANDAI NONGYE KEJI [MODERN AGRICULTURAL SCIENCE AND TECHNOLOGY], September 2013, 301-302; Liang Siya & Liu Guining, Shengtai Yuanchandi Chanpin Baohu Zhidu de Fazhan yu Zhanwang [Development and Prospect of Protection System of PEOP], DI SHIYI JIE ZHONGGUO BIAOZHUNHUA LUNTAN LUNWENJI [THE ELEVENTH CHINA STANDARDIZATION FORUM], September 2014, 739-743.
172. The critical assessment factors with regard to environmental performance require that products be green and environmental, low-carbon and energy-efficient, resource-saving, healthy and safe. *See* General Rules on PEOP, Article 5.1.2 (2012).
173. General Rules on PEOP, Article 4.2.3 (2012).
174. *See* Kong Xiangjun & Su Yuejuan, Dili Biaozhi Baohu yu Shengtai Yuanchandi Baohu Buke Hunxiao [GIs and Protected Eco-Origin Products Are Not to Be Confused], ZHONGGUO JIANYAN JIANYI [CHINA INSPECTION AND QUARANTINE], December 2014, 78-79.
175. Huang Xin, Guangxi Qiye Da Shengtai Yuanchandi Pai Tingjin Dongmeng [The Role of Protected Eco-Origin Products as an Asset for Guangxi Enterprises], GUANGXI RIBAO [GUANGXI DAILY], 12 March 2014.
176. In a Green Paper, the European Commission also addressed whether environmental criteria should be included as part of the product specification of a PGI. *See* European Commission, *Green Paper on Agricultural Product Quality*, *supra* n. 153, at 13.
177. General Rules on PEOP, Article 3.
178. '*Xixia* mushroom', '*Lushi* black fungus', and '*Lingbao* apple' were included in the list of PEOP, first published in 2012. Among them, '*Xixia* mushroom' had been registered as GI products in 2008; '*Lushi* black fungus' had been registered as GI products in 2005; '*Lingbao* apple' had been registered as GI products in 2003. *See* Guojia Zhiliang Jiandu Jianyan Jianyi Zongju Gonggao 2008 Nian di 140 Hao [State General Administration of Quality Supervision, Inspection and Quarantine Announcement No. 140, 2008], 24 December 2008; Guojia Zhiliang Jiandu Jianyan Jianyi Zongju Gonggao 2005 Nian di 270 Hao [State General Administration of Quality

Nevertheless, what is noticeable is that not all registered PEOP belongs to the GI family, despite the link between the product's quality and place of origin. The reason for the exclusion is that a number of the registered products are not identified in the marketplace by their geographical origin; in other words, they are not marketed under names indicating their place of origin. For instance, a PEOP marketed under the company name '*Hongjiu* ginseng' cannot be classified among GI products because '*Hongjiu*' identifies only the company that produces or cultivates ginseng.[179] Again, taking as an example the case of '*Gongyiyuan* black soya bean oil',[180] although this oil is obtained from a unique variety of black soya beans in a region in Northeast China, it is marketed under the name '*Gongyiyuan*', which is actually a privately owned trademark capable only of distinguishing between goods of the legal person and those of others.

We must conclude that, while the PEOP regime can be a tool for valorizing products with a particular quality or characteristics linked to the place of production, not all PEOPs are GI products defined in the AQSIQ's Provisions on the Protection of GI Products because PEOP are not necessarily named after the name of their place of origin.

Finally, we also question whether the GI is, by its nature, an environmental tool. Care should be taken when introducing an additional environmental obligation into an already exceptionally complex scheme.[181]

[B] Sector-Specific Approach to GI Extension

Chinese consumers have a special interest in the quality and origin of the goods they purchase.[182] For this reason, state intervention is intensifying in this area. Though both the trademark regime and the sui generis regime are in place to protect GIs, China adopts a sector-specific approach to adding sui generis GI laws to the legal arsenal. In 2007, the MOA established its own preferred method of protection, intended for

Supervision, Inspection and Quarantine Announcement No. 270, 2005], 31 December 2005; Guojia Zhiliang Jiandu Jianyan Jianyi Zongju Gonggao 2003 Nian di 59 Hao [State General Administration of Quality Supervision, Inspection and Quarantine Announcement No. 59, 2003], 17 June 2003; Guojia Zhiliang Jiandu Jianyan Jianyi Zongju Gonggao 2012 Nian di 160 Hao [State General Administration of Quality Supervision, Inspection and Quarantine Announcement No. 160, 2012], 22 October 2012.

179. Guojia Zhiliang Jiandu Jianyan Jianyi Zongju Gonggao 2014 Nian di 91 Hao [State General Administration of Quality Supervision, Inspection and Quarantine Announcement No. 91, 2014], 18 August 2014.
180. Guojia Zhiliang Jiandu Jianyan Jianyi Zongju Gonggao 2015 Nian di 9 Hao [State General Administration of Quality Supervision, Inspection and Quarantine Announcement No. 9, 2015], 19 January 2015.
181. In 2010, the European Commission cautioned the introduction of environmental elements into the PDO/PGI requirements. *See* European Commission, *Impact Assessment of Geographical Indications: Accompanying Document to the Proposal for a Regulation of the European Parliament and of the Council on Agricultural Product Quality Schemes* 16 (Commission Staff Working Paper 2010).
182. YIN Huijing & Audrey Drummond, *La protection des indications géographiques en Chine*, Le blog sur la propriété intellectuelle en Chine (13 June 2021), http://chinepi.com/protection-indications-geographiques-en-chine/.

agricultural products. Moreover, the former SFA proposed a draft regulation aimed at establishing a new regime to protect GIs for forest products. Along with the enrichment of the legal arsenal, subcategories of GIs have been or will be created.

[1] GIs for Agricultural Products

GIs can be considered a collective tool for producers to use to promote the products made in their territory and, to a larger extent, to represent a factor of rural development.[183] The notion of 'GIs for agricultural products' was created to respond to the needs of agriculture modernization in China.[184]

In 2004, the former SAIC and the MOA jointly announced their intention to enhance the protection of agricultural GIs for the implementation of the Opinions of the CPC and the State Council concerning Several Policies on Promoting the Increase of Farmers' Income.[185] In 2007, the CPC and the State Council reaffirmed the importance of GI protection for agricultural products as a public policy tool with which to 'modernize agriculture' and 'build new socialist villages'.[186] In this context, on 25 December 2007, the MOA issued an ordinance on the protection of 'GIs for agricultural products',[187] which created the third parallel system of GI protection.

Article 2(2) of the Measures for the Administration of GIs for Agricultural products defines 'GIs for agricultural products' as:

> Indications that are (1) named after geographical names, (2) used to describe agricultural products originating from a specific area, and (3) whose quality and

183. WIPO, *The Lisbon Agreement: International Protection for Identifiers of Typical Products from a Defined Geographical Area* 2 (WIPO Publication No. 942(E) 2018).
184. Several Chinese scholars note that the creation of the notion 'GIs for agricultural products' is linked to the orientation of agricultural development. *See* Shao Weijie, Nongchanpin Dili Biaozhi Baohu de Yiyi ji Lujin [The Significance of Protecting GIs for Agricultural Products and How to Protect], QILU XUEKAN [QILU JOURNAL], January 2009, 105-110; Huang Huajun, Nongye Xiandaihua yu Dili Biaozhi de Zhishi Chanquan Baohu [The Modernization of Agriculture and Geographical Indication Protection], SHEHUI KEXUE ZHANXIAN [SOCIAL SCIENCE FRONT], January 2006, 224-227; Wang Han & Chen Tong, Woguo Nongchanpin Dili Biaozhi Fazhan Xianzhuang Fenxi [Development of Geographical Indications of Agricultural Products in China], XIAN DIANZI KEJI DAXUE XUEBAO [JOURNAL OF XIDIAN UNIVERSITY], July 2008, 101-105.
185. Guojia Gongshang Xingzheng Guanli Zongju Nongyebu Guanyu Jiaqiang Nongchanpin Dili Biaozhi Baohu yu Shangbiao Zhuce Gongzuo de Tongzhi [Notice of the State Administration for Industry and Commerce and the Ministry of Agriculture on Strengthening the Protection of Geographical Indications and the Registration of Trademarks for Agricultural Products], 7 December 2004.
186. The modernization of agriculture in China tends to ensure the supply of agricultural products, improve farmers' incomes, and facilitate sustained development of agriculture. *See* Zhonggong Zhongyang Guowuyuan Guanyu Jiji Fazhan Xiandaihua Nongye Zhashi Tuijin Shehui Zhuyi Xinnongcun de Ruogan Yijian [Opinions of the CPC Central Committee and the State Council on Developing Modern Agriculture Actively and Promoting the Construction of a New Socialist Countryside], 31 December 2006. Shiqida Baogao Jiedu Zou Zhongguo Tese Nongye Xiandaihua Daolu [Seventeenth National Congress Report Interpretation: Take the Road of Agricultural Modernization with Chinese Characteristics], Xinhua News Agency (15 June 2021), http://www.gov.cn/jrzg/2007-11/30/content_821057.htm.
187. Measures for the Administration of Geographical Indications for Agricultural Products (2007).

other characteristics are essentially attributable to the natural and ecological environment as well as cultural and historical factors of the area.

The coverage of the MOA's system is narrower than that of the other regimes:[188] it covers only 'agricultural products'. Furthermore, according to Article 2(1), the term 'agricultural products' refers to agricultural raw materials,[189] such as vegetables, fruits, cereals, mushrooms, oil, spices, and herbs (raw materials used for medical purposes).[190] Its scope is even more limited than one might expect based on the literal meaning of the term 'agricultural products'. For example, although wine is covered by the EU's CAP, it is not included in the product coverage of the Measures in China. However, the Measures can be applied to grapes, the raw material used for the production of wine (e.g., '*Wuwei* Vitis vinifera').[191]

Again, consideration should be given to the sort of link that is required by the definition. For an application for 'GIs for agricultural products', it is necessary to demonstrate a linkage between the speciality of the product and the particularity of the landscape.[192] The description of product specialities should include the main organoleptic (e.g., aroma, texture, flavour, shape, colour), physical-chemical (e.g., the amount of dietary fibre, sugar content), or microbiological characteristics of the product. However, the defined geographical area should have special characteristics that contribute to the causal link between the geographical area and the quality or characteristics of the product, relating to 'the natural and ecological environment' (e.g., sunlight, temperature, humanity, rainfall, hydrology, geology, topography, pedology)[193] and 'cultural and historical factors' (relating to the specific *terroir*, its people, and their history).[194]

188. The term 'other regimes' refers to the trademark regime and the GI products regime created by the former AQSIQ. Both two regimes have adopted a general law on GIs with a broad definition. As a result, all categories of products are covered if the requirements of GIs are met.
189. Article 2(1) of the Measures for Geographical Indications for Agricultural Products: 'The term agricultural product as mentioned in the Measures refers to primary products sourced from agriculture, namely, plants, animals, microorganisms, and the products thereof obtained in agricultural activities.'
190. Agricultural Product Quality Safety Centre under the Ministry of Agriculture, Nongchanpin Dili Biaozhi Wushi Wen [Fifty Questions about GIs for Agricultural Products], 25 February 2013, 2-3.
191. '*Wuwei* Vitis vinifera' has been recognized as 'GIs for agricultural products' in 2014. *See* Nongyebu Gonggao di 2105 Hao [Ministry of Agriculture Announcement No. 2105], 22 May 2014.
192. Article 7 of the Measures for Geographical Indications for Agricultural Products: 'An agricultural product whose geographical indication is applied for registration shall meet the following requirements: (1) its name is composed of the name of the geographic area and the general name of the agricultural product; (2) the product has unique characteristics or special mode of production; (3) the quality and characteristic of the product mainly lie on the unique natural and ecological environment as well as cultural and historical factors; (4) the product has a limited producing area; and (5) the environment of its producing area and its quality satisfy the state's compulsory technical norms.'
193. The Agricultural Product Quality Safety Centre, responsible for the preliminary examination of GIs applications under the Ministry of Agriculture, has given an example of '*Beiyijing* Muskmelon', where the physical geography components, in particular the soil and the geomorphology of the *Xinding* Basin, are essential in shaping the characteristics of the

Despite several differences in wording, the Chinese definition of 'GIs for agricultural products' is very close to the AO notion established in the Lisbon Agreement and French Consumer Code. In this definition, the link to *terroir* (both natural and human factors) must be essential, or even exclusive, which leads us to consider that the *terroir* imprints its characteristics onto the product, thus rendering it typical. The MOA's regime resembles the French AOC regime more closely than do other Chinese systems in use for GI protection, in that the objective link between the speciality of the product and its geographical origin is the only route for protection (a link based simply on a collective reputation would be inadmissible).

[2] GIs for Forest Products

Given the lack of an independent system for the protection of GIs for forest products, the responsibility for protecting such products has been mainly assigned to the existing three divisions (i.e., the trademark system, the GI product regime, and the system of GIs for agricultural products).[195] According to the statistics compiled by the China Forestry Intellectual Property Website,[196] 272 denominations of forest products have been registered as collective marks or certification marks under the trademark system, 231 have been recognized under the GI product regime, and 170 have been recognized under the system of GIs for agricultural products.

Article 32 of the Outline of the National Intellectual Property Strategy made a commitment to improve the protection system for GIs – specifically, to 'give support to products with GIs, and promote the transformation of natural and humanistic advantages with regional characteristics into practical productivity'.[197] In this context, the former SFA intended to establish a system for facilitating the protection of forest products with distinctive regional characteristics.[198]

The draft Measures propose a new subcategory of GIs, namely 'GIs for forest products', which are defined as '(1) indications which are named after geographical

muskmelon. *See* Agricultural Product Quality Safety Centre, Fifty Questions about GIs for Agricultural Products, *supra* n. 190, at 4.

194. *Ibid.*, at 3-5.

195. Fan Shengming, Wang Zhongming & Zhou Dawei, Woguo Linchanpin Dili Biaozhi Zhishi Chanquan Baohu Wenti Tantao [Discussions on the Protection of Forestry Products' Intellectual Property of Geographical Indications], GUANGDONG NONGYE KEXUE [GUANGDONG AGRICULTURAL SCIENCES], January 2012, 186.

196. The China Forestry Intellectual Property Website is sponsored by the State Forestry Administration of China (the National Forestry and Grassland Administration since 2018). Available at, http://www.cfip.cn, accessed 8 May 2021.

197. Guowuyuan Guanyu Yinfa Guojia Zhishi Chanquan Zhanlue Gangyao de Tongzhi [Notice of the State Council on Issuing the Outline of the National Intellectual Property Strategy], 5 June 2008.

198. *See* Guojia Linyeju 2014 Nian Gongzuo Yaodian [Key focus of the work of the State Forestry Administration of 2014], 20 January 2014; Former State Forestry Administration, 2014 Nian Linye Shishi Zhishi Chanquan Zhanlue Tuijin Jihua [Implementation of Intellectual Property Strategy in Forestry Sector in 2014], 4 June 2014; Former State Forestry Administration, 2015 Nian Linye Shishi Zhishi Chanquan Zhanlue Tuijin Jihua [Implementation of Intellectual Property Strategy in Forestry Sector in 2015, 6 May 2015.

names, (2) used to describe forest products originating from a specific region, and (3) whose the quality and other characteristics are essentially attributable to the natural and ecological environment as well as cultural and historical factors of the area'.[199]

It is not coincidental that the definition elaborated by the former SFA is virtually identical to that in the MOA regime, except as regards the scope of the products covered. In fact, the former SFA acknowledges that it has learnt a great deal from the experience of the 'GIs for agricultural products' regime under the MOA.[200] However, the question arises as to whether it is reasonable to separate the two notions ('GIs for agricultural products' and 'GIs for forest products') simply because of the division of jurisdiction (the MOA supports the development of agriculture, whereas the former SFA was responsible for the development of forestry).[201]

The conclusion of Chapter 2 pointed out that the Chinese GI laws were formed under the influence of Europe and the United States as well as international agreements in the context of the war between the 'Old' and 'New' worlds. China has adopted both the sui generis approach championed by France and the EU[202] and the trademark approach proposed by the United States.[203] A number of national concepts, generally known under the broad term 'geographical indications', describe a relationship between a product and its place of origin. From the west to the east of Eurasia, a long list of concepts and terminologies are used in this area, including AO, AOC, IGPIA, PDO, PGI, and GI. The multifaceted nature of the GI concept led to different understandings of the concept when it was introduced in China.

It seems appropriate to use the story of the 'blind men and an elephant' to illustrate a variety of different understandings in China of the GI concept. In this tale, six blind men are asked to figure out what an elephant looks like by touching it. Depending on which part is touched, they perceive the elephant to be a wall (side), spear (tusk), snake (trunk), tree (leg), fan (ear), or rope (tail). They compare notes and learn that they are in complete disagreement. Here, the concept of GIs is our elephant. The evolution of the concept in France/EU shows its multidimensional nature: GIs are intended not only to protect consumers (even though the French definition of AO is

199. Former State Forestry Administration, Linchanpin Dili Biaozhi Guanli Banfa Zhengqiu Yijiangao [Draft Measures for the Administration of Geographical Indications for Forest Products], 15 August 2013.
200. Former State Forestry Administration, Linchanpin Dili Biaozhi Guanli Banfa Zhengqiu Yijiangao Qicao Shuoming [Drafting Instruction of the Measures for the Administration of Geographical Indications for Forest Products], 15 August 2003.
201. In a short period (May 1970-February 1979), the Ministry of Agriculture and Forestry of China existed. However, since 16 February 1979, it has been separated into the Ministry of Agriculture and the Ministry of Forestry. Subsequently, in March 1998, the Ministry of Forestry was renamed State Forestry Administration. *See* Fan Baomin, ZHONGGUO LINYE SIXIANG YU ZHENGCE SHI [CHINESE FORESTRY IDEOLOGY AND POLICY HISTORY (1644-2008)] (Science Press, 2009).
202. Hélène Ilbert, *Products with Denominations of Origin and Intellectual Property Rights: The International Bargaining Process, in Geographical Indications and International Agricultural Trade: The Challenge for Asia* 91, 92 (Louis Augustin-Jean ed., Palgrave Macmillan 2012).
203. David Snyder, *Enhanced Protections for Geographical Indications under TRIPs: Potential Conflicts under the US Constitutional and Statutory Regimes*, 18 Fordham Intell. Prop. Media & Ent. L.J. 1297, 1308 (2008).

located in the Consumer Code) or maximize the profits of producers but also to serve as a public tool with which to support rural development, enhance the sustainability of ecosystems, and add value to TK. The concept of 'GI' is a blend of all these features.

When the 'GI' concept spread from France/EU to China, Chinese governmental bodies made every effort to understand what the European notion meant, but each one felt a different part, and only one part while learning what the concept meant.[204]

The trademark regime has given a definition to GIs on the grounds that GIs are source-identifiers like any other distinctive sign. The AQSIQ created 'products with AOs' (later renamed 'GI products') because of the link to *terroir* or traditional *savoir-faire*. To promote rural development, the MOA created 'GIs for agricultural products'. A 'green GI' (PEOP) was also established in view of GIs' association with ecology. The reinterpretation of the 'GI' concept is ongoing, as the former SFA continues to add 'GIs for forest products'.

As a consequence of the 'blind men and an elephant' method, many parallel protection systems have been established, creating chaos in subsequent stages.[205] The unification of the different regimes is to be expected, but what slows the process down is the disagreement among the government bodies about what GIs are and how best to protect them. In order to facilitate improvements in current and future operating practices, a compressive understanding of GIs and their protection instruments is urgently needed.

The historical approach that our study adopts sheds light on the stimulus for this conceptual diversity. The driving forces behind this diversity are, not surprisingly, various and often competing. We first illustrated a confrontation between the traditional *terroir* logic (premised on a qualitative link) and the reputation logic (premised on a more subjective link). This dichotomous logic may be one of the main causes of the AO/GI duality. Contracting obligations serve as another incentive for amplifying the conceptual arsenal (e.g., China defines GIs within the trademark regime to ensure compliance with its TRIPS obligations).

There are hints suggesting that the competing forces which drove the conceptual mess are starting to achieve some coherence. The *terroir* and reputation logics no longer act upon each other like water and fire, as more emphasis is being placed on the human factors in the *terroir*. Production skills can make products that not only have unique features but are also famous. If the goal of GI protection includes the protection of these production skills, which form part of TK and ICH, both quality and reputation – as the fruits of human innovation and investments – should be regarded as criteria for GI protection. Moreover, China has moved away from its initial aim of just fulfilling its international obligations and has expressed the need for a more coherent conceptual framework.

---

204. Zhao Xiaoping, *Whither China's Protection of Geographical Indications? A Case Study of Qinzhouhuang Millet*, 7 Queen Mary J. Intell. Prop. 25 (2017).
205. *See* Zhang Chi, Bumen Boyi Dili Biaozhi Chanpin Baohu Yu Ganga [A Boxing Match among Government Bodies: The Riddle of Geographical Indication Protection], FAREN ZAZHI [LEGAL JOURNAL], February 2006, 100.

However, in spite of this trend, views on the design of national protection systems remain unlikely to reach a consensus. We will discuss this issue in the following chapters.

CHAPTER 3

GI Protection under the Trademark Regime: A Comparison Between the EU and Chinese Approaches

This chapter analyses the regimes of collective marks and certification marks in France, the EU, and China in order to understand the European and Chinese approaches to the protection of GIs within the trademark system. It assesses whether China has adopted the European approach to GIs (i.e., a preference for the sui generis regime as opposed to the trademark regime). It discusses the differences in the designs of the trademark systems and their role in protecting GIs. The European (French) regime of collective and certification marks is used as a tool for ensuring 'additional' protection for GIs, whereas the Chinese regime is one of China's primary means of GI protection. Within the Chinese regime of collective and certification marks, which is a special regime, a sub-divisional special regime has been introduced for collective and certification marks that contain or consist of GIs.

Countries can be broadly classified into two groups: those that protect GIs as collective or certification marks (the US approach) and those that prefer a sui generis system (the EU approach). The latter verifies and ensures the link between the special qualities of the product and its place of origin through public intervention during the registration process as well as during commercial use, while the former ensures only that there is no conflicting user of the sign.[1] For the legislation of one jurisdiction, the choice is then whether to protect GIs through the trademark system or establish a sui generis GI system.

However, this assumption proves to be inaccurate. The trademark system and the sui generis GI system do not necessarily apply on an exclusive basis. In any given

1. Daniel J. Gervais, *Reinventing Lisbon: The Case for a Protocol to the Lisbon Agreement (Geographical Indications)*, 11 Chi. J. Int'l L. 67, 87 (2010).

country, a joint application of the two mechanisms is possible. France and the EU, the main proponents of sui generis protection for GIs, do not preclude the possibility of using the trademark system to protect and add value to GI products. In China, both mechanisms are the main instruments used for the protection of GIs. Moreover, countries that protect GIs through the trademark system differ in 'how' the trademark system is used. For example, China allows GIs to be protected as collective or certification marks but requires that evidence of the link between the special characteristics of the product and the geographical origin be submitted by the applicants. No such requirement is contained in either European trademark law or US trademark law.

Both GIs and trademarks can serve to indicate the source of goods and a certain quality. Regimes for protecting GIs are thus essentially 'labelling regimes'.[2] However, GIs differ from trademarks in that GIs cannot be owned by the individuals who actually use them for their products. While GIs sit awkwardly with the system of ordinary trademarks, which takes an 'individual ownership' approach,[3] collectively used marks have proven a useful instrument for promoting regional goods with specific common characteristics.[4]

GIs can be protected in the form of collectively used marks,[5] which can be divided into two categories: marks used to indicate that the goods come from members of a certain group (collective marks) and those used to certify that the goods possess certain characteristics and qualities (certification marks).[6] The function of collective marks is close to that of individual marks. A trademark, which is initially registered as an individual mark, can be used collectively and even used like a collective mark. The function of certification marks is different, yet both types of marks can help a small- and medium-sized enterprise (SME) to market its products and build and enhance a product reputation among consumers.[7] Special rules or regimes are therefore used in

2. WIPO, *Symposium on the International Protection of Geographical Indications* 45 (WIPO Publication No. 764(E)).
3. The International Association for the Protection of Intellectual Property (AIPPI) recommends that as a general rule, because of its nature, an indication of source or an appellation of origin cannot be registered or protected as an individual mark for the goods or services to which the indication or appellation applies. *See Question 118: Trade and Service Marks and Geographical Indications* 408 (AIPPI Yearbook 1994/II); Inessa Shalevich, *Protection of Trademarks and Geographical Indications*, 6 Buff. Intell. Prop. L.J. 67 (2008).
4. *See Directive (EU) 2015/2436 of the European Parliament and of the Council of 16 December 2015 to approximate the laws of the Member States relating to trade marks*, OJ L 336, 23.12.2015, p. 1, Recital 35.
5. WIPO, *Introduction to Intellectual Property, Theory and Practice* 234 (Kluwer Law International 1997).
6. Different terms are used to identify the subject matter of protection: French law refers to '*marques collectives* (ordinary collective marks)' and '*marques collectives de certification* (collective certification marks, which has now become guarantee marks)'; EU law speaks of 'collective marks' and, since the EU's trademark reform in 2015, 'certification marks'; China law, from the very beginning, distinguishes between 'collective marks' and 'certification marks'.
7. Amarjit Singh, *The Role of Collective Marks, Certification Marks and Geographical Indications*, Presentation made at WIPO Asia Sub Regional Workshop on the Use of Intellectual Property (IP) by SME Support Institutions for the Promotion of Competiveness of SMEs in the Food Processing Sector (5 June 2007).

France, the EU, and China to make sure that these marks fulfil their functions and economic potential.

However, GIs also differ from collective marks. GIs do not necessarily differentiate the goods of members of an association from those of other undertakings; they distinguish goods according to their geographical origin. In other words, GIs do not necessarily perform the trademark (collective mark) function of indicating a precise commercial origin. They are regarded as lacking a distinctive character according to the trademark doctrine. Furthermore, GIs guarantee a link between the characteristics of the product and its geographical origin. They must incorporate a link to *terroir*. 'The protection of GIs is, above all, a protection of a typical product and its land, including people, cultures, traditions, *savoir-faire* and *terroir*.'[8]

Where a GI is registered as a collective mark, the problem is that the function of the collective geographical mark is not clear. Does it perform the same function as other ordinary collective marks (to distinguish the product of members of a particular association), or does it perform the function of GIs (to indicate regional origin and product characteristics linked to it, rather than to distinguish the product according to its commercial origin)? In short, would the GI's function be transferred to that of the mark containing it?

Both France and the EU suggest that a collective mark, wholly or partly composed of a GI, has the same function as ordinary marks. Provisions applied to ordinary marks are equally applicable to collective marks containing a GI. By contrast, China's law implies that the collective mark containing a GI has the same function as the GI. Special rules are thus applied to accommodate the uniqueness of the collective geographical mark.

However, certification marks share more similarities with GIs. They can serve to certify that the product comes from a certain region and has certain characteristics. A certification mark composed of a GI may continue to indicate the geographical origin, material, mode of manufacture, or other features of the product upon which it is used.[9] However, European legislators largely preclude the use of certification marks for the protection of GIs, as is apparent in the EU's trademark reform of 2015.

Due to the differences in the approaches, while the regime of collective and certification marks is used in France and the EU as a tool for ensuring 'additional' protection for GIs, it is one of China's primary means for GI protection. Within the Chinese regime of collective and certification marks, which is *already* a special regime, a sub-divisional special regime has been introduced for the collective and certification marks that contain or consist of GIs (e.g., the addition of a product–place link requirement for the registration of GIs as a mark).

We therefore consider it appropriate to analyse the regime of collective marks (§3.01) and the regime of certification marks (§3.02) in France, the EU, and China in

---

8. Dorothée Boyer-Paillard, *Essai sur les notions d'origine et de provenance en droit du commerce: la reconnaissance juridique des 'territoires des productions typiques'*, Droit rural, n° 435, 2015, étude 16.
9. *Community of Roquefort v. William Faehndrich, INC.*, 303 F. 2d 494 (2d. Cir. 1962).

order to understand the European and Chinese approaches to the protection of GIs within the trademark system.

§3.01 REGIME OF COLLECTIVE MARKS

Owing to the collective nature of GIs, those who produce and market GI products must engage in collective action.[10] The collective mark may provide a useful basis for such an association between producers. Once a GI is registered as a collective mark, the protection of that GI can be enforced in accordance with the applicable rules of trademark law.

[A] Registration of GIs in the Form of Collective Marks

'The GIs are, in a way, a collective mark.' They are collectively held and used by thousands of small producers.[11] However, it is difficult to distinguish collective marks from individual marks. An individual mark can be used collectively, even like a collective mark. It is also difficult to distinguish them from certification marks[12] since they both set up rights for collective use by those who comply with defined rules.[13]

Some countries have opted to protect GIs under trademark law, through collective or certification marks, instead of establishing a sui generis system of protection. However, this does not mean that GIs cannot be registered or protected as collective marks in countries where a sui generis system is established.[14]

In order to appreciate the role of the collective mark regime in GI protection in the countries with sui generis GI systems, it is necessary to understand the nature of collective marks.

10. WIPO, *Geographical Indications: An Introduction* 7 (WIPO Publication No. 952E 2017); Xiomara F. Quinones-Ruiz, *Why Early Collective Action Pays Off: Evidence from Setting Protected Geographical Indications*, 32 Renewable Agric. & Food Sys. 179, 188 (2016).
11. European Commission, *Why Do Geographical Indications Matter to Us?*, MEMO/03/160 (30 July 2003).
12. WIPO, *Geographical Indications: Historical Background, Nature of Rights, Existing Systems for Protecting and Obtaining Protection in Other Countries*, SCT/8/4 (2 April 2002) p. 9.
13. The use of both collective marks and certification marks depends on the fulfilment of the regulations governing use. Some parties might seek to avoid the more rigorous burden of a certification mark by opting to register a collective mark. *See* Gary Myers, *Principles of Intellectual Property Law* 212 (Concise Hornbook Series 2nd ed. 2012).
14. Article L. 711-3 (since the Order of 2019) of the French Intellectual Property Code prohibits the registration of a trademark, which is likely to infringe prior rights, particularly protected appellations of origin and geographical indications. However, not every use of a GI in a trademark constitutes an infringement. For example, it is permissible to register a trademark consisting of two parts (one part containing a GI and one part containing other distinguishing signs) to designate products having rights to the GI.

[1] Collective Marks: Indistinguishable from Certification Marks?

Collective marks should not be confused with certification marks, nor with individual marks.[15] The distinction between them is, however, somewhat unclear.[16] McCarthy notes, 'The problem with collective trademarks and service marks is that they are almost indistinguishable from certification marks.'[17] Not surprisingly, France, the EU, and China all have difficulties distinguishing between these different types of marks.

[a] Ordinary Collective Marks in French Law

French collective trademarks may trace their origins to ancient corporate marks, which traditionally served to ensure compliance with the corporation rules governing the fabrication of the product, with the objective of identifying their origin and guaranteeing quality.[18] They were rigorously protected and highly controlled. Professor Bahans considers this regime an ancestor of that of appellations of origin.[19] The French Revolution brought down the whole system of corporate marks, by removing the corporations and their privileges and calling for freedom in commerce and industry. However, there was soon an urgent need to defend distinctive signs against the excesses of freedom of commerce (individual freedom led to a failure to guarantee quality standards). As a result, the law of 1824[20] was enacted for the protection of trade names, trademarks, and indications of provenance.[21]

Half a century after the revision of the Paris Convention in Washington (1911),[22] the Law of 1964 introduced the regime of collective trademarks (*marques collectives*),[23]

15. Sheldon W. Halpern, Craig Allen Nard & Kenneth L. Port, *Fundamentals of United States Intellectual Property Law: Copyright, Patent, and Trademark* 315 (Kluwer Law International 2nd ed. 2006).
16. *See* Arnaud Folliard-Monguiral, *Arrêt Gözze: marques de certification et fonction essentielle*, Propriété industrielle, n° 9, 2017, alerte 52: '*Si la frontière entre marque individuelle et marque de certification semble relativement aisée à tracer, il n'en est pas de même vis-à-vis de la marque collective dans la mesure où la fonction essentielle de cette dernière est beaucoup plus floue.*'
17. J. Thomas McCarthy, *McCarthy on Trademarks and Unfair Competition* § 19:99 (Thomson West 5th ed. 2021); Frederick Breitenfeld, *Collective Marks: Should They Be Abolished?* 47 Trademark Rep. 1 (1957).
18. Raymond Dusolier, *Les Marques collectives et les marques de qualité dans l'ancien droit et dans le droit moderne*, Paris, Librairies techniques, 1974, p. 29.
19. *See* Michel Menjucq & Jean-Marc Bahans, *Droit de la vigne et du vin*, 2e éd., Paris, Litec, 2010, p. 75.
20. Loi du 28 juillet 1824 relative aux altérations ou suppositions de noms sur les produits fabriqués, J.O. du 20 août 1944, p. 541, Article 1: '*Quiconque aura, soit apposé, soit fait apparaître, par addition, retranchement, ou par une altération quelconque, sur les objets fabriqués, le nom d'un fabricant autre que celui qui en est l'auteur, ou la raison commerciale d'une fabrique autre que celle où lesdits objets auront été fabriqués, ou enfin le nom d'un lieu autre que celui de la fabrication, sera puni des peines ... .*'
21. *See* Frédéric Pollaud-Dulian, *Droit de la propriété industrielle*, Paris, Economica, 2010, pp. 722, 1136.
22. At the Washington Conference of the Convention, Article 7bis was adopted. This article requires the protection of collective marks belonging to associations, the existence of which is not contrary to the law of the country of origin, even if such associations do not possess an industrial or commercial establishment. This modification was the outcome of the demand of the

though without distinguishing between ordinary collective marks (*marques collectives simples*) and collective certification marks (*marques collectives de certification*).[24] These two types of marks were hence placed together in the same regime, a special regime.[25]

This special regime had four main aspects: an obligation to file the rules and regulations for the use of collective marks (Article 19);[26] a prohibition against assignment, pledge, or any measure of enforcement (Article 20);[27] a list of particular cases in which nullity can arise and the particular grounds for revocation of rights (Article 21);[28] and supplementary rights (Article 34).[29]

However, why were ordinary collective marks not distinguished from certification marks in the first place? In fact, the Law of 1964 also introduced the system of individual marks. A differentiation was made, however, between individual marks and

---

Anglo-Saxon countries that already had the collective or certification marks. *See* Jeffrey Belson, *Certification and Collecitve Marks* 40 (Edward Elgar Publishing 2017); Jeanne Boucourechliev, *Presentation de la marque collective, in Les Marques collectives, Journée d'étude, Faculté de droit, Lyon, 12 janvier 1979*, Paris, Librairies techniques, 1979, p. 16.

23. Article 7bis of the Paris Convention has progressively led several European countries (including France) to adopt special provisions for collective marks. *See* Charles Gielen & Verena Von Bomhard, *Concise European Trademark and Design Law* 351 (Kluwer Law International 2011).
24. Loi n° 64-1360 du 31 décembre 1964 sur les marques de fabrique, de commerce ou de service, J.O. du 1 janv. 1965, p. 3.
25. Under the law of 1964, collective marks (including ordinary collective marks and collective certification marks were generally subject to the regime of trademarks (classic individual marks). However, the regime of collective marks had some special dispositions, contained in Articles 16-23, 34, and 36.
26. Article 19, Loi du 31 décembre 1964: '*Le dépôt d'une marque collective doit comprendre le règlement déterminant les conditions auxquelles est subordonné l'emploi de la marque.*'
27. Article 20, Loi du 31 décembre 1964: '*La marque collective ne peut faire l'objet ni de cession, ni de concession de gage, ni d'aucune mesure d'exécution forcée.*'
28. Article 21, Loi du 31 décembre 1964: '*La nullité du dépôt d'une marque collective ou la déchéance des droits du déposant est prononcée: 1° Lorsque la personne morale ou la collectivité cesse d'exister; 2° Lorsqu'elle ne satisfait pas aux prescriptions du présent titre; 3° Lorsqu'elle a employé ou sciemment laissé employer sa marque dans des conditions autres que celles prescrites au règlement; 4° Lorsque le règlement contient des dispositions contraires à l'ordre public et aux bonnes moeurs. En cas de nullité ou de déchéance, la marque collective ne peut pas être appropriée pour les mêmes produits ou services par un nouveau dépôt, ni être employée à un titre quelconque. Toutefois, à l'expiration d'un délai de dix ans, la marque collective peut être à nouveau déposée à ce titre par une personne morale ou collectivité de même nationalité.*'
29. Article 34, Loi du 31 décembre 1964: '*Les pénalités prévues par les articles 422 à 423-3 sont applicables en matière de marques collectives de fabrique, de commerce ou de service. En outre, seront punis des peines prévues à l'article 422: 1° Ceux qui auront sciemment fait un usage quelconque d'une marque collective dans les conditions autres que celles prescrites au règlement d'emploi accompagnant le dépôt prévu par la réglementation sur les marques collectives de fabrique, de commerce ou de service; 2° Ceux qui auront sciemment vendu ou mis en vente un ou plusieurs produits revêtus d'une marque collective irrégulièrement employée au regard de la réglementation des marques de fabrique, de commerce ou de service; 3° Ceux qui sciemment auront fait un usage quelconque, dans un délai de dix ans à compter de la date d'annulation d'une marque collective, d'une marque reproduisant ou imitant ladite marque collective; 4° Ceux qui, dans un délai de dix ans à compter de la date d'annulation d'une marque collective, auront sciemment vendu, mis en vente, fourni ou offert de fournir des produits ou des services sous une marque reproduisant ou imitant ladite marque collective.*'

all collectively used marks.[30] Individual marks, as defined in Article 1 of the 1964 Law, are signs that serve to distinguish the goods or services of 'one person'.[31] Collective marks are not defined. However, according to Article 17 concerning their use, collective marks are used either by a variety of traders whose products meet the standards established by the trademark owner or by the members of the owner.[32] Thus, they can be used by more than one person. Then, how can a mark that is collectively used by more than one person be a kind of individual trademark, which by definition is used by one person? Following this logic, the Law of 1964 only distinguished between individual trademarks and all collectively used marks and merged ordinary collective marks and collective certification marks into a single class, *marques collectives*.[33]

However, this logic might be mistaken. A reading of Article 16 suggests that collectively used marks have two parallel objectives: to protect the 'general interest' (e.g., to protect consumers by providing a guarantee of quality) and to 'encourage the development of members' common interests'.[34] While it is true that some collectively used marks serve to guarantee quality, certifying that the products or services covered by the mark meet the specifications in the regulations governing use (relating to quality, geographical origin, composition, and other characteristics), many collectively used marks have nothing to do with the 'quality promise': they are used by the members of the trademark owner for their own interests.[35] These marks constitute an

30. The features of the 1964 system were based on the understanding of legislators on the difference between individual marks and collective marks, particularly in relation to the modality of exploitation (collectively used or not) and their goals (public interest or private interest).
31. Article 1, Loi du 31 décembre 1964: '*Sont considérés comme marques de fabrique, de commerce ou de service les noms patronymiques, les pseudonymes, les noms géographiques, les dénominations arbitraires ou de fantaisie, la forme caractéristique du produit ou de son conditionnement, les étiquettes, enveloppes, emblèmes, empreintes, timbres, cachets, vignettes, lisières, lisérés, combinaisons ou dispositions de couleurs, dessins, reliefs, lettres, chiffres, devises et, en général, tous signes matériels servant à distinguer les produits, objets ou services d'une entreprise quelconque.*'
32. Article 1, Loi du 31 décembre 1964: '*Les marques collectives sont apposées soit directement par la personne morale ou collectivité à titre de contrôle sur certains produits ou objets, soit par ses membres, sous sa surveillance et à des conditions déterminées, sur les produits de leur fabrication ou de leur industrie ou sur les objets de leur commerce.*'
33. In contrast, the neighbouring country of England has distinguished two categories of marks under the Trade Mark Act of 1938, namely, on the one hand, the 'trademark', which indicates a trade connection between the product and the trademark owner(s) but does not offer any guarantee to consumers that the product has a particular quality; on the other hand, 'certification trademark', which allows a distinction to be made between common products and certified products, regarding the origin, the quality or other characteristics. As Denis Rochard observed, the English distinction between trademark and certification mark is based on the function exercised by the mark, not on the users (collective or individual), as adopted by the French legislators in the Law of 1964. *See* Denis Rochard, *La protection internationale des indications géographiques*, Paris, Presses Universitaires de France, 2002, p. 182.
34. Article 16, Loi du 31 décembre 1964: '*Les personnes morales, Etat, département, communes et établissement publics, ainsi que les syndicats, unions de syndicats, associations, groupements ou collectivités de producteurs, d'industriels et de commerçants, pourvus d'une administration légalement constituée et de la capacité juridique, peuvent, dans un but d'intérêt général, industriel, commercial ou agricole, ou pour favoriser le développement du commerce ou de l'industrie de leurs membres posséder des marques de fabrique, de commerce ou de service.*'
35. Jérôme Passa, *Marques Collectives*, J.-Cl. Marques Dessins et modèles, fasc. 7450, 2021, para. 7.

instrument of competition, like a private trademark, and make no commitment to consumers with regard to quality.[36] In other words, their function is to identify the origin of the product, which is no different from that of the individual mark.[37]

By way of comparison, it is interesting that, in roughly the same period, the neighbouring UK also distinguished between two categories of marks under the Trade Mark Act: the 'trademark', which indicates an association between the product and the trademark owner(s) but does not offer any guarantee to consumers that the product has a particular quality; and the 'certification trademark', which allows a differentiation between common products and certified products regarding the origin, quality, or other characteristics.[38] Thus, Denis Rochard observes that the UK distinction between trademarks and certification marks is based on the function exercised by the mark rather than on the mode of use (i.e., used by one person versus more than one person).[39]

By contrast, the French distinction in the Law of 1964 seemed more based on the mode of use.[40] This approach soon led to difficulties and uncertainty for trademark owners. An individual mark can, in fact, be used like a collective mark. That is to say, a mark initially registered as an individual trademark can be licensed to the members of the trademark owner. In the absence of formal regulations governing use, the licensing agreements can play such a role by providing the conditions to which the use of the mark is subject. In this case, does the mark remain an individual mark, or does it become a collective mark?

This is not merely a theoretical question. Bear in mind that, under Article 19 of the 1964 Law, applicants must submit the regulations governing the use of a collectively used mark during the application. Otherwise, the mark is likely to be declared invalid (Article 21). Therefore, an individual trademark used like a collective mark might be declared invalid if the regulations governing its use were not submitted, as in the case of '*Ecole de conduite française*'.[41]

---

36. Jacques Azéma, *Marque Collective de Certification*, RTD Com., 2014, p. 358.
37. Individual trademarks enable the consumer to distinguish the goods or service from others that have another origin without any possibility of confusion. They also indicate the commercial origin of the goods or services. Se Paul Mathé, *Marques collectives et de certification, Mélanges offerts à Albert Chavanne*, Paris, Litec, 1990, p. 243; Albert Chavanne, *Caractère facultatif ou obligatoire de la marque collective, in Les Marques collectives, Journée d'étude, Faculté de droit, Lyon, 12 janvier 1979*, Paris, Librairies techniques, 1979, p. 59.
38. Trade Marks Act 1938, 1 & 2 Geo. 6. Chapter 22.
39. Rochard, *supra* n. 33, at 182.
40. The legislators of the 1964 Law seemed to emphasize too much on the difference between individual marks and collective marks regarding the modality of exploitation. A duality between individual marks and collective marks was made just because the latter are collectively used, although collective marks might serve different goals and have distinct functions.
41. In this particular case, an association had registered an individual trademark consisting of the name '*Ecole de conduite française*'. It had authorized its members to use the mark in the course of carrying out their economic activity. The Aix-en-Provence Court of Appeal considered that this mark was actually a collective mark and no longer an individual mark. Therefore, it has annulled the mark on the ground that the registration was not accompanied by the regulations governing use, as required by Article 19 of the Law of 1964. *See* C.A. Aix-en-Provence, 24 oct. 1974 et Cass. com., 28 juin 1976, n° 75-10.193, JCP 1977. II, n° 18700.

However, Article 19 was made in the 'general interest', falling within the objective of the protection of consumers:[42] 'The regulation governing use is a commitment to consumers and links the mark to the quality promises.'[43] However, as mentioned, some collectively used marks only distinguish between products or services provided by members belonging to the same association. Their function is close to that of individual marks, indicating the commercial source of goods. Thus, why should Article 19 be applied to those collective marks[44] if the 'quality promise' is not involved?[45]

The 1964 system was reformed by the Law of 1991,[46] which distinguishes between two separate categories: 'ordinary collective marks', whose function is close to that of individual marks, and 'collective certification marks', which concern a quality promise (exercising a certifying function).[47] Owing to this distinction, the reform subjects ordinary collective marks to the same regime as that which governs individual marks. The special regime imposed by the 1964 system no longer applies to ordinary collective marks.

It is worth mentioning here that ordinary collective marks are subject again to a special regime, as imposed by European Directive 2015/2436. Special rules are provided for collective marks concerning regulations governing use, refusal of an application, and grounds for revocation or invalidity.[48] We will discuss this later on.[49]

---

42. Martine Dehaut and Natalie Pacaud remark that the French law on collective marks is one of the most draconian in Europe and hence more of a protector of consumers' interests. The neighbouring countries of France, for example, the United Kingdom, have certification marks but only require that the mark owner himself should not deliver the products and services which the mark covers. *See* Martine Dehaut & Natalie Pacaud, *Les marques de certification: apports du décret du 1er mars 2007 modifiant le Code de la propriété intellectuelle*, Propriété industrielle, n° 6, 2007, alerte 79.
43. Chavanne, *supra* n. 37, at 34.
44. From another perspective, the individual mark constitutes the property of its owner. Nothing prevents the private trademark owner from granting licenses to many companies or individuals or fixing several conditions in the licensing agreement. A mark registered as an individual mark owned by the association could be used by its members under specific conditions fixed in the license contract. The licensing agreement could be effectively considered as the regulations governing use of a collective trademark. There is also no reason why this licensing agreement must be submitted during the registration process.
45. Although the ordinary collective mark enables consumers to identify the product 'of certain quality', the scope of the guarantee, given by the second type, is limited to link the mark to the company that exploits it. *See* Thibault Lancrenon, *Ballade dans la brume des marques collectives*, Propriété intellectuelle, n° 13, 2004, p. 848.
46. Loi n° 91-7 du 4 janvier 1991 relative aux marques de fabrique, de commerce ou de service, J.O. du 6 janv. 1991, p. 316.
47. This distinction is directly influenced by the doctrinal works, particularly that of Paul Mathély. It is based on the function of marks, not on the choice of applicants during the registration process. As a recent case concerning the collective mark '*Palace*' shows, despite the fact that the box 'collective certification mark' was not marked in the application form, the Paris First Instance Court considered it as a 'collective certification mark', after having analysed the functioning of the mark concerned. *See* T.G.I. Paris, 21 juin 2013, PIBD 2013, n° 994, III, p. 1568; Pascale Tréfigny, *Palace pour tous ...*, Propriété industrielle, n° 1, 2014, comm. 3; Jean Foyer, *Commentaire de la loi du 4 janvier 1991 relative aux marques de fabrique, de commerce et de service*, Recueil Dalloz, 1991, p. 57.
48. *See* Articles 30-36 of Directive 2015/2436.
49. *See* §3.02 *infra*.

A key issue that has yet to be resolved is the definition of 'ordinary collective mark'. Former Article L. 715-1 of the IP Code provides that 'a mark shall be known as a collective mark if it may be used by any person who complies with regulations for use issued by the owner of the registration'.[50] This definition is broad enough to cover not only ordinary collective marks but also collective certification marks. Jérôme Passa suggests that ordinary collective marks are those that satisfy the definition in former Article L. 715-1 of the IP Code but do not perform the certifying function certification marks do.[51] That would be tantamount to saying that what does not constitute a certification mark is an ordinary collective mark.

In transposing Directive 2015/2436, the Order of 13 November 2019, created the French notion of 'collective marks', which is inserted into the IP Code. Article L. 715-6 of the Code defines the French collective mark as follows: 'a mark is described as such when the mark is applied for and is capable of distinguishing the goods or services of the persons authorized to use it according to the regulations governing use (translation added)'.[52] This definition is slightly different from that of Directive 2015/2436, which requires that the collective mark distinguish the goods or services of 'the members of an association which is the proprietor of the mark from the goods or services of other undertakings'.[53]

[b] EU Collective Marks

European law provides a means of protecting collective marks throughout the EU through the filing of a single application. With the amendment of Regulation 207/2009 in 2015 (Regulation 2015/2424, codified and repealed by Regulation 2017/1001), the term 'community collective marks' was replaced by 'EU collective marks'.[54] The first paragraph of Article 74 of Regulation 2017/1001 (Article 66 of the former Regulation 207/2009) describes EU collective marks as a trademark 'which is applied for and is capable of distinguishing the goods or services of the members of the association which is the proprietor of the mark from those of other undertakings'.[55] Literally interpreted, the EU collective mark seems more like an ordinary collective mark than a collective certification mark (guarantee mark) in French Law: it identifies the commercial origin

50. Article L. 715-1 CPI: '*La marque est dite collective lorsqu'elle peut être exploitée par toute personne respectant un règlement d'usage établi par le titulaire de l'enregistrement.*'
51. Jérôme Passa, *Marques Collectives*, J.-Cl. Marques Dessins et modèles, fasc. 7450, 2014, para. 12.
52. Article L. 715-6 CPI: '*Une marque collective est une marque ainsi désignée lors de son dépôt et propre à distinguer les produits ou les services des personnes autorisées à l'utiliser en vertu de son règlement d'usage.*'
53. Article 27 of Directive 2015/2436.
54. *Regulation (EU) 2015/2424 of 16 December 2015 amending Council Regulation (EC) No 207/2009 on the Community trade mark and Commission Regulation (EC) No 2868/95 implementing Council Regulation (EC) No 40/94 on the Community trade mark, and repealing Commission Regulation (EC) No 2869/95 on the fees payable to the Office for Harmonization in the Internal Market (Trade Marks and Designs)*, OJ L 341, 24.12.2015, p. 21, Article 1; *Regulation (EU) 2017/1001 of the European Parliament and of the Council of 14 June 2017 on the European Union trade mark*, OJ L 154, 16.6.2017, p. 1.
55. Article 74(1) of Regulation 2017/1001.

'by informing the consumer that the producer of the goods provider belongs to a certain association'.[56]

Under Article 66 of the former Regulation 207/2009, in addition to associations of producers, legal persons governed by public law are also authorized to apply for EU collective marks.[57] The paradox is that legal persons governed by public law (a public body such as the EU, Member State, or municipality) do not have an associative structure; so, how can a mark owned by a public body be used 'only by members of an association to indicate that they form part of that group'?[58] Neither the provision nor the recitals provide any useful clarification. The old Guidelines of the Office for Harmonization in the Internal Market (OHIM) ('European Union Intellectual Property Office' (EUIPO) hereinafter)[59] concerning trademark examination required that a public body (applicant) 'must have members' who have the right to influence the use of the mark.[60] According to this solution, the 'Organic Farming Community collective mark' was not acceptable, not only because the public body applicant (the EU) does not have an association link with the intended users (i.e., the intended users are not members of an association) but also because the aim of the mark is to certify that the producer has met the quality standards with regard to organic farming (i.e., the mark does not indicate membership).[61] In other words, the old Guidelines prevented certification marks from being registered as EU collective marks.

However, this solution was found to be inconsistent with the legislative intent of the former Article 66. In the appeal proceeding of the 'Organic Framing' case,[62] the Board of Appeal interpreted the legislators' intentions based on the legislative history of the provision:

> The initial proposal for the CTMR, on the one hand expressly provided for guarantee marks and, on the other hand, did not include legal persons governed by

56. OHIM (EUIPO), *Guidelines for Examination in the Office*, Part B Examination, Final Version (1 August 2015) p. 72.
57. Article 66 of Regulation 207/2009: '... Associations of manufacturers, producers, suppliers of services, or traders ..., as well as legal persons governed by public law, may apply for Community collective marks.' *See Council Regulation (EC) No 207/2009 of 26 February 2009 on the Community trade mark*, OJ L 78, 24.3.2009, pp. 1-42.
58. European Commission, *Impact Assessment Accompanying Document to the Proposal for a Regulation Amending Council Regulation (EC) No 207/2009 of 26 February 2009 on the Community Trade Mark and the Proposal for a Directive to Approximate the Laws of the Member States Relating to Trade Marks (Recast)*, SWD(2013) 95 final (27 March 2013) p. 70.
59. The European Union Intellectual Property Office (EUIPO) is established by Regulation 2015/2424. All references in Union law to the Office for Harmonization in the Internal Market (OHIM) shall be read as references to the European Union Intellectual Property Office. *See* Article 2 of Regulation 2015/2424.
60. OHIM (EUIPO), *The Manual Concerning Proceedings Before the Office for Harmonization in the Internal Market*, Part B Examination, Final version (April 2008) p. 58: 'If it is a public body, it must have members who have the right to influence the regulations of use of the mark.'
61. Case R 1007/2011-2 *Decision of the Second Board of Appeal of 10 May 2012* (EUIPO) para. 4; *See also* Case R 828/2011-1 *Decision of the First Board of Appeal of 22 November 2011* (EUIPO).
62. The 'Organic Farming Community collective mark' application was refused by the decision of 11 March 2011. The decision was contested. The Board of Appeal ruled that the contested decision refusing to register the trademark applied for based on an incorrect interpretation of the conditions required by Article 66 of the trademark regulation must therefore be annulled.

> public law among possible proprietors of a collective mark. However, the removal of the specific rules on certification marks in the final version of the CTMR, resulted in the scope of collective marks, which were initially reserved for associations of producers, being expanded to include legal persons governed by public law, in order to cover the situations existing in certain Member States where persons governed by public law were the proprietors of (collective) quality guarantee marks.[63]

Taking account of the above analysis, it can be concluded that the EU collective marks system was introduced as a compromise formula, intended for the protection of both ordinary collective marks and, under certain conditions, guarantee or certification marks.

Following this case, the 2015 Guidelines expressly acknowledge that EU collective marks may 'sometimes' serve to certify the quality of the goods[64] and imply that they are not required to be used by members of an association when the applicant is a public body.[65] These marks are effectively certification marks, used to guarantee that the goods possess specific features. Paradoxically, in explaining their quality guarantee function, the OHIM (EUIPO) nevertheless gives an example of an ordinary collective mark: 'regulations governing use frequently contain provisions to certify the quality of the goods and services of the members of the association, and this is acceptable'.[66] Since the mark in the example is reserved to certify the goods of affiliated entities, it is not open to anyone whose product quality satisfies the conditions laid down in the regulations. Lacking 'openness', to what extent could the mark exercise the function of quality assurance?[67] This contradiction reveals the shortcoming of the compromise formula adopted in Article 66: the hybrid structure mixing the ordinary collective mark with the certification mark is likely to be misunderstood.

The 'Trademark Package' may correct this deficiency by bringing forward a new formula.[68] Regulation 2015/2424 distinguishes between 'EU collective marks' and 'EU certification marks' in two distinct sections. Specific rules are added regarding the protection of certification marks.

The 2021 Guidelines delete all references to EU collective marks' potential use for certifying quality. The Guidelines confirm that the marks should fulfil the essential function of indicating the collective commercial origin of the goods sold under the trademark or indicating that the companies using the mark are members of a certain

63. Case R 1007/2011-2 *Decision of the Second Board of Appeal of 10 May 2012* (EUIPO) para. 16.
64. OHIM (EUIPO), *Guidelines for Examination in the Office*, Part B Examination, Final Version (1 August 2015) p. 73.
65. *Ibid.*, at 74: 'When the applicant for a CCTM is a legal person governed by public law which does not necessarily have a corporative or an associative structure, such as the European Union, a State or a municipality, the regulations governing use of the mark need not contain details concerning membership.'
66. *Ibid.*, at 73.
67. The open character (openness) lies at the heart of the mechanism of certification marks. Lack of openness, even the regulations governing use provide quality standard, it is still an ordinary collective mark and cannot exercise its quality insurance function. *See* Cass. com., 3 juin 2008, n° 07-15.050.
68. Yann Basire, *La réforme du droit des marques en Europe: quid novi?* Europe, n° 5, 2016, étude 4.

association.[69] The function of certifying quality is now exercised by the newly created EU certification marks.

[c] Collective Marks in Chinese Law

In 1993, China introduced a regime for collectively used marks. From the very beginning, a distinction has always been made between collective marks and certification marks.[70]

Collective marks are defined as those registered in the name of a group, an association, or other organizations and used by the members of the organization in commercial activities to indicate their membership.[71]

By definition, the function of a collective mark is to indicate, in trade, that the user of the mark is a member of a particular organization: 'It does not indicate that a good or service originates from a supplier.'[72] This might distinguish the collective mark from the individual trademark.

However, China has experienced the same difficulty as France[73] in its attempts to clarify this distinction. This distinction is not always clear because an individual mark may be used like a collective mark.[74] In the '*Jinjiunmei*' case, an individual mark was ruled to be not registrable because it would be used by the members of an association according to the licensing agreement. The judge reasoned, 'While the function of the individual mark is to indicate the commercial origin, that of the collective mark is to indicate the membership, not to indicate a product comes from a particular supplier.' Where an individual mark is licensed to members of an association, it will 'lose its function of origin identification and become a collective mark',[75] and 'thus it should have been registered as a collective mark, instead of an individual mark'.[76]

69. EUIPO, *Guidelines for Examination*, Part B (1 March 2021) p. 642.
70. Regulations for the Implementation of the Trademark Law of the People's Republic of China (1993), promulgated by Order No. 14 of 28 July 1993 of the State Administration for Industry and Commerce of the People's Republic of China.
71. Article 3(2) of the Trademark Law.
72. *Wuyishan Tongmu Tea Co. Ltd. v. State Administration for Industry and Commerce Trademark Review and Adjudication Board*, Beijing High People's Court (12 December 2013).
73. It seems that the distinction made by China between collective marks and individual marks is similar to that made by France under the 1964 Law.
74. Where a proprietor of a private trademark licenses its members to use the mark, the mark is actually used as a collective mark.
75. *Wuyishan Tongmu Tea Co. Ltd. v. State Administration for Industry and Commerce Trademark Review and Adjudication Board*, Beijing High People's Court (12 December 2013).
76. *See Ibid*. This solution is nevertheless debatable. Under China's Trademark Law (Article 43), a trademark owner may license other parties to use its registered trademark. Nothing prevents the licensees from being members of an association. Then would it be appropriate to make a judgement that the mark will preserve the function of indicating commercial origin when licensed to independent parties, whereas it will lose this function when licensed to parties who are members of a group? What if the independent licensees become members of a group at a later date? If this question were answered in the affirmative, the result would be that the licensees should not be members of a group or become members of a group in the future. Such a result would not be consistent with the very nature of the trademark licence.

In conclusion, it is common practice in these jurisdictions (France, the EU, and China) to distinguish between collective marks and certification marks. This distinction is welcome because there is a gap between them in terms of legal function. The function of collective marks is close to that of individual marks because both serve to identify and distinguish between goods or services based on commercial origin. We will discuss below how collective marks could support the protection of GIs.

[2] GIs: A Registrable Collective Mark?

By definition, GIs serve to designate the geographical origin of goods or services. The problem with seeking to protect GIs through collective marks is that trademark law considers geographical names to be descriptive.[77] As GIs do not describe any particular trade or business source, they lack the requisite distinctiveness. Hence, they might be unregistrable as a trademark or collective mark.[78]

The US, a strong advocate of protecting GIs under trademark law, provides a solution. Under US Federal Lanham Act, a GI may be registered as a collective mark if it acquires a 'secondary meaning'. The GI's 'secondary meaning' would satisfy the distinctiveness requirement of a trademark.

However, the secondary meaning route is not the only one that would make a GI a registrable collective mark. The distinctiveness requirement can also be satisfied by associating the GI with other distinctive elements. This practice is not uncommon in France. The distinctiveness requirement can even be relaxed via a derogation from the ordinary rules governing trademarks. In fact, the EU Trademark Regulation and China Trademark Law allow geographically descriptive terms to be registered as collective marks without requiring a secondary meaning.

A question may arise as to what function is played by the mark registered through each of these routes. If a GI's secondary meaning to consumers is a trade or business source,[79] there is little doubt that the mark registered on this basis indicates the trade source. However, a mark registered 'by way of derogation' is not necessarily able to indicate a commercial origin because there may be no secondary meaning. Furthermore, one also wonders what the point is of associating the GI with other distinctive elements. These questions require a detailed examination.

---

77. *See* Joined Cases C-108/97 & C-109/97 *Windsurfing Chiemsee* [1999] ECR I-2779, para. 25; Gail E. Evans, *The Comparative Advantage of Geographical Indications and Community Trade Marks for the Marketing of Agricultural Products*, 41 IIC-Int'l Rev. Intell. Prop. & Competition L. 645 (2010).
78. WIPO, *Summary of Replies to the Questionnaire on Trademark Law and Practice*, SCT/14/5 Rev. (1 November 2005).
79. Lynne Beresford, *Geographical Indications: The Current Landscape*, 17 Fordham Intell. Prop. Media & Ent. L.J. 979 (2006).

[a] *Registering GIs in the Form of Ordinary Collective Marks in French Law*

The conditions of the protection of ordinary collective marks are the same as those of individual marks.[80] The only difference is in the mode of use:[81] ordinary collective marks are used by anyone complying with the regulations governing use.[82]

In order to serve as a valid trademark, a sign must be distinctive.[83] Article L. 711-2, point 3 of the IP Code, excludes from the registration process signs or names 'which may serve to designate the characteristics of the goods or services, particularly the type, quality, quantity, purpose, value, geographical origin, time of production of the goods or furnishing of the service'.[84] Their 'geographical origin' is expressly listed as one of the characteristics of goods. 'Geographically descriptive' signs or names thus cannot serve as a valid trademark per se.[85]

The CJEU has underlined that the exclusion of geographically descriptive signs 'pursues an aim which is in the public interest'.[86] These signs may be an indication of the quality or other characteristics of the goods and may also influence consumer tastes in various ways. It is in the public interest that they remain available to everyone equally and not be monopolized.[87] Furthermore, geographically descriptive signs serve to describe the product as originating from a geographical area, and not to identify the product as originating from a particular undertaking. Considering that there might be a number of different undertakings in a given area marketing their products under the same geographical name, the name can hardly be used to distinguish the goods of one undertaking from those of another.[88] Trademark law does not give monopoly rights over a sign that does not perform the function of a trademark.[89]

In most cases, GIs are used collectively by different undertakings to identify a good as originating in a locality; consumers would not recognize it as identifying a good

80. Article L. 715-6 CPI: '*Les dispositions du présent livre sont applicables aux marques collectives sous réserve des dispositions particulières prévues dans la présente section.*'
81. Joanna Schmidt-Szalewski, *Le droit des marques*, Paris, Dalloz, 1997, p. 63.
82. Former Article L. 715-1 of the French Intellectual Property Code.
83. *See* Nicolas Bouche, *Intellectual Property Law in France* 189 (Kluwer Law International 2nd ed. 2014).
84. Article L. 711-2(3) CPI: '*Une marque composée exclusivement d'éléments ou d'indications pouvant servir à désigner, dans le commerce, une caractéristique du produit ou du service, et notamment l'espèce, la qualité, la quantité, la destination, la valeur, la provenance géographique, l'époque de la production du bien ou de la prestation du service.*'
85. In other words, if a trademark consists exclusively of indications that may serve to designate the geographical origin of the goods, it is devoid of the distinctive character and thus liable to be declared invalid.
86. *See* Joined Cases C-108/97 & C-109/97 *Windsurfing Chiemsee* [1999] ECR I-2779, para. 25.
87. A geographically descriptive term must be freely used by all traders who legitimately require that term to describe the goods.
88. Pascale Tréfigny, *D'utiles précisions: déchéance et intérêt légitime à l'action ...*, Propriété industrielle, n° 7-8, 2006, comm. 55.
89. The right to a trademark is a right of occupancy, not a right of creation. The mere registration of a sign allows the reservation of it to assist customers in identifying the origin of the products. The monopoly shall not be entitled if the sign does not perform the function of distinguishing the goods of one enterprise from those of another. *See also* Case C-383/99 P *Procter & Gamble v. OHIM* [2001] ECR I-06251.

from a particular undertaking. GIs cannot be reserved to one undertaking alone[90] and thus would not be registrable as an individual trademark.[91]

As mentioned, the function of ordinary collective marks is similar to that of individual marks. Ordinary collective marks are also an indication of a commercial origin, but they distinguish the goods of a member of 'a particular association' from those of other traders. GIs cannot be reserved to one association alone because there might be several different associations to which producers belong. Moreover, the conditions for registering an ordinary collective mark are no different from those for an individual trademark. GIs do not identify a particular group of producers.[92] A mark consisting exclusively of a GI would not meet the distinctiveness requirement.[93] For these reasons, a GI per se would not be registrable as an ordinary collective mark.[94]

However, a GI can be contained in an ordinary collective mark when combined with other words or graphic components if the combination, taken as a whole, serves to distinguish the commercial source of the product.[95] For example, the complex mark composed of the word '*Châteauneuf du Pape*' (AOC) and other figurative elements (a stylized picture of the Papal tiara and two crossed keys) has been held valid.[96]

Since nothing prevents collective marks from being cumulatively used with GIs,[97] the legitimate users of a GI can make use of an ordinary collective mark (containing or consisting of a GI) in order to inform consumers of their affiliation with a particular association[98] and provide additional, attractive information to consumers.[99] The mark '*Les Champagnes de Vignerons*', a mark collectively used by the members of the

90. C.A. Paris, 4 avr. 2014, n° 12/20559: '*... cela afin d'en laisser la libre disposition à tous ceux qui proposent des produits ou services revêtant la même caractéristique et de permettre au signe d'assurer sa fonction d'identification de l'origine des produits et services ...*'; Cass. com., 1 déc. 1987, PIBD, 1989, III, p. 14.
91. Former Article L. 711-1 of the Intellectual Property Code provides that geographical names could constitute a trademark, but the names must be distinctive, lawful and available.
92. A GI can identify a particular company, manufacturer or collectivized group of producers if it has acquired a secondary meaning through use. However, to establish acquired distinctiveness, a company or group must use it exclusively and continuously as a trademark for a period of time. The lack of retroactive collectivization by, and control over, all producers in a region may make it difficult.
93. On the validity of a collective mark, the District Court of Carpentras notes that it is a common practice that the name constituting an appellation of origin cannot be registered as a trademark (or a collective mark). *See* T.G.I. Carpentras, 5 September 2000, n° 2531/97.
94. According to the answers given by the French Group in the AIPPI, ordinary collective marks, subject to a privative appropriation, are too distant from GIs. Thus, GIs alone cannot be privately reserved to one association. *See Question Q191 Relationship Between Trademarks and Geographical Indications* 467-468 (AIPPI Yearbook 2006/II).
95. Case R 218/2006-2 *Decision of the Second Board of Appeal of 24 November 2006* (EUIPO) p. 9.
96. T.G.I. Carpentras, 5 September 2000, n° 2531/97; C.A. Nîmes, 16 avr. 2002, n° 2000/4426; Cass. com., 21 September 2004, n° 02-15.435; Jérôme Passa, *Droit de la propriété industrielle: Tome 1, Marques et autres signes distinctifs, dessins et modèles*, 2e éd., Paris, LGDJ, 2009, p. 769; Jacques Audier, *Marques et indications géographiques da la filière vitivinicole*, Revue de droit rural, n° 312, 2003, p. 241.
97. For example, the '*Roquefort*' benefits both from the AOP official label and the collective mark '*Label Brebis Rouge*' containing the term '*Roquefort*', owned by the *Confédération générale des producteurs de lait de brebis et des industriels de Roquefort*.
98. Norbert Olszak, *Marques et indications géographiques, in Les défis du droit des marques au XXIe siècle: Actes du colloque en l'honneur du Professeur Yves Reboul*, Paris, Lexis Nexis, 2011, p. 76.

Syndicat Général des Vignerons de la Champagne, aims to inform the consumer about their family-farm production method.[100]

Furthermore, during the last decade, there has been a boom in what is known as '*marque ombrelle territoriale*' ('territorial umbrella mark'),[101] which is essentially a collective mark used for a wide range of heterogeneous products originating from the same region.[102] Products bearing different GIs, along with other regional products (without GIs), can be marketed under the same banner.[103] In the umbrella mark '*Sud de France*' for example, the first feature of the mark is that it is intended for use by its members drawn from a variety of product sectors, so products bearing the mark include agriculture, wine, fish, aquaculture, food, wood, and cosmetic products. The second feature is that the members can be drawn only from the *Occitanie/Pyrénées-Méditerranée* region.[104] This aims at ensuring the '*link to the territory*', to ensure that the products to which the mark applies are produced, harvested, or/and prepared in the aforementioned place.[105]

In the Occitanie region, there are more than forty-three AOC, twenty-four IGP, a dozen Label Rouge, and countless other regional products without Identification Signs of Quality and Origin (SIQOs). Producers, artisans, and distributors working with these products all have access to '*Sud de France*'. The umbrella mark thus no longer focuses on one single product whose characteristics are attributable to some aspects of its geographical origin, as GIs do. Rather, its brand image is based on a '*basket of*

---

99. Case C-487/07 *L'Oréal and Others* [2009] ECR I-05185, para. 54 (AG Opinion): 'With regard to the trade mark's communication functions ... there can be no doubt that the trade mark acts as a vehicle for providing consumers with various kinds of information on the goods identified by them.'
100. The vineyard is cultivated by the winegrowers themselves and vinified on their own land or within the winegrower' union. *See Champagne de Vignerons: la bannière collective du vignoble champenois*, Champagne de Vignerons (9 May 2021), http://www.champagnesdevignerons.com/Les-champagnes-de-vignerons/Une-marque-collective.html.
101. Examples: '*Bienvenue en Gourmandie*', '*Saveurs en'Or*', '*Un peu beaucoup Franche Comté*', '*Saveurs Paris Ile de France*', '*Sud Ouest France*', '*Sud de France*', '*Produit en Bretagne*', '*Produit en Poitou-Charentes*', '*Esprit de Poitou-charentes*', '*Signé Poitou-Charentes*', '*Produit en Limousin*', '*Midi Pyrénées, prenez goût au Sud-Ouest*', '*Buy Normandie*', '*Marque Parc*', '*Marque Savoie*', '*Pays Cathare*', '*Qualité Landes*', '*Saveurs du Périgord*', '*Terres d'Eure et Loir*', '*Goûtez l'Ardèche*'. *See* Julien Frayssignes, *Marques territoriales et développement rural: lecture critique pour la construction d'un programme de recherche, in Labellisation et mise en marques des territoires*, Clermont-Ferrand, Presses Universitaires Blaise Pascal, 2014, p. 56.
102. Chambre d'agriculture de la Dordogne, *Bilan comparé: Marques ombrelles territoriales*, déc. 2012, p. 7.
103. Daniel Richard & Laurent Rieutort, *Les processus récents de valorisation de la qualité et de l'origine des produits agroalimentaires: marques territoriales ou labels? in Labellisation et mise en marques des territoires*, Clermont-Ferrand, Presses Universitaires Blaise Pascal, 2014, p. 24.
104. The members' registered office (*siège social*) and the production, processing or packaging sites must be located inside the region *Occitanie/Pyrénées-Méditerranée.*
105. *Règlement d'usage de la marque Sud de France*, Sud-de-France (9 May 2021), http://www.sud-de-france.com.

products'[106] obtained from all the resources of the land, such as the sun, sea, ponds, mountains, scrubland, beaches, tourism, heritage, and culture.[107]

Territorial umbrella marks immediately remind us of the 'Regional Labels', which were the preferred means of identifying and promoting regional products in the 1980s.[108] However, those labels were soon abolished due to their incompatibility with the exhaustive nature of the PDO/PGI regime.[109] Given the failure to implement an official labelling system, it is not unreasonable for regional producers (including GI producers) to resort to ordinary collective marks, particularly territorial umbrella marks. One example will suffice here. The *Comité de promotion des produits régionaux de Franche-Comté* was the holder of the former Regional Label '*Franche-Comté*', which covered several local products with and without a GI. After the Regional Label was discontinued, the Comité launched its ordinary collective mark '*Un Peu Beaucoup Franche-Comté*' in 2011, which covered almost all the products embraced by the former Regional Label.[110] Thus, umbrella marks are cited by some researchers as the 'second generation of quality labels'.[111]

On the basis of the above, it must be concluded that the official labelling scheme is not the only pathway for enhancing the value of GI products. This can also be achieved through ordinary collective marks. A good example is '*Châtaignier d'Ardèche*', which benefits from an AOC/AOP label and several ordinary collective

106. Richard & Rieutort, *supra* n. 103, at 24.
107. Anne Lacroix, Amédée Mollard & Bernard Pecqueur, *Politiques de développement local et rente de qualité territoriale des produits alimentaires, in Journées internationales de la recherche pour la gestion des territoires ruraux sensibles*, Paris, Cemagref Éditions, 1998, pp. 165-182.
108. Around the 1980s, there was a growing number of '*Labels Régionaux*' approved for products from different areas: '*Savoie*', '*Franche-Comté*', '*Midi-Pyrénées*', '*Limousin*', '*Normandie*', '*Languedoc-Roussillon*' ... These regional labels were generally used to add value to regional products by the implementation of collective promotions.
109. The law of 1994 concerning the recognition of the quality of agricultural products and foods has decided the abolition of regional labels after an eight-year transitional period. This period was also considered to be excessive by the CJEU. France has taken the judgment into consideration, and the two decrees of 2003 finally abolished regional labels. *See* Loi n° 94-2 du 3 janvier 1994 relative à la reconnaissance de qualité des produits agricoles et alimentaires, J.O. du 4 janv. 1994, p. 131; Case C-6/02 *Commission v. France* [2003] ECR I-02389; Arrêté du 27 mai 2003 portant abrogation de labels agricoles, J.O. du 5 juin 2003, p. 9577; Arrêté du 28 mai 2003 portant abrogation de labels agricoles, J.O. du 5 juin 2003, p. 9577; Mai-Anh Ngo, *Quel avenir pour les labels au regard de la libre circulation des marchandises?*, Droit rural, n° 356, 2007, étude 34.
110. The products covered by the mark '*Un Peu Beaucoup Franche-Comté*' highly overlap with those covered by the former region labels: '*Jambon fumé du Haut Doubs*', '*Véritable jambon de Luxeuil*', '*Saucisse de Montbéliard (IGP)*'... *See* Arrêté du 25 juin 1998 portant homologation de cahiers des charges de labels agricoles, agrément d'un organisme certificateur et retrait d'agrément d'organismes certificateurs, J.O. du 8 juill. 1998, p. 10426.
111. Eduardo Ramos Real & Dolores Garrido Garcia, *Towards a Second Generation of Quality Labels: A Proposal for Evaluation of Territorial Quality Marks, in Labellisation et mise en marques des territoires* 71-88 (Clermont-Ferrand, Presses Universitaires Blaise Pascal 2014).

marks, such as '*Goutez L'Ardèche*', '*Site Remarquable du Goût*', and '*Parc Naturel Régional des Monts d'Ardèche*'.[112]

[b] Registering GIs in the Form of EU Collective Marks

Under Article 7(1)(c) of Regulation 2017/1001, 'trademarks which consist exclusively of signs or indications may serve, in trade, to designate ... geographical origin ... or other characteristics of goods or services' are not to be registered. Thus EU law also prohibits the registration of descriptive signs relating to the characteristics of goods or services. However, in contrast to French law, Article 74(2) introduces an exception. It provides that 'in derogation from Article 7(1)(c), signs or indications which may serve, in trade, to designate the geographical origin of the goods or services may constitute EU collective marks'. The registration conditions for a mark have been relaxed.[113] It follows that the EU collective mark can consist solely of geographically descriptive signs and GIs.[114]

As mentioned, the function of EU collective marks is to distinguish the goods or services of association members who are their proprietors from those of other associations or undertakings.[115] The essential function of GIs is 'to guarantee to consumers the geographical origin of the goods and the special qualities inherent in them'.[116] The question that needs to be asked is, therefore 'What is the function of the collective mark consisting exclusively of a GI, registered through "derogation" provisions?'

Some authors argue that the collective mark containing a GI does not differentiate the products of one producer from those of another. It identifies the geographical origin of the products as well as a set of characteristics attached to their origin. If these collective marks are reproduced or imitated by an unauthorized third party, they consider that 'the risk is not linked to confusion as to the commercial origin of products, but rather to confusion as to the geographical origin of products and their characteristics attached'. By the same reasoning, it is recommended that the 'likelihood of confusion' concept should evolve: the risk that the public might believe that the

112. These marks are registered as ordinary collective marks, but their exploitation is the decisive factor for assessing their status (ordinary collective marks or collective certification marks). They are likely to be interpreted as collective certification marks (guarantee marks) if they are exploited like them.
113. Case T-534/10 *Organismos Kypriakis Galaktokomikis Viomichanias v. OHMI* (CFI 13 June 2012) para. 51; Case C-393/12 P *Foundation for the Protection of the Traditional Cheese of Cyprus Named Halloumi v. OHIM* (ECJ 21 March 2013); Case T-627/13 *The Tea Board v. OHMI* (CFI 2 October 2015) para. 42.
114. Case T-295/01 *Nordmilch v. OHIM* [2003] ECR II-4378, para. 32; Case T-379/03 *Peek & Cloppenburg v. OHIM (Cloppenburg)* [2005] ECR II-04633, para. 35.
115. *See* §3.01(A)(1) *supra; See also* Case T-138/09 *Muñoz Arraiza v. OHMI* [2010] ECR II-02317, paras 26-27.
116. Case C-96/09 P *Anheuser-Busch v. Budějovický Budvar* [2011] ECR I-02131, para. 147.

goods come from the same geographical origin and have the same characteristics constitutes a likelihood of confusion.[117]

This theory is not completely unreasonable. Registering a GI as a collective mark will not automatically eliminate the GI's function. 'The public would still not perceive the geographical indication as an indication of the collective commercial origin of the product.'[118] The GI, of which the mark is entirely composed, may continue to have a descriptive meaning, which could be understood as a reference to the producing region by the public. It has been held that the word '*Rioja*' contained in an EU collective figurative mark refers directly to Rioja wine.[119] Similarly, the consumer will understand that the word '*Halloumi*' refers to a speciality cheese from Cyprus,[120] rather than a designation of (individual or collective) commercial origin.

However, there is no reason to believe that the descriptive meaning might preclude the possibility that a geographical term may identify the product as originating from a particular undertaking or economically linked undertakings. The continuous and exclusive use of the geographical reference as a mark by one entity (or one producer group) may create a connection in the minds of consumers between the goods of the entity and the geographical term.[121] At this point, the term has two meanings: the 'primary meaning' is the place described by the term; its 'secondary meaning' transcends the mere geographical connotation since consumers recognize the term as identifying the commercial origin (a particular entity).[122]

The secondary meaning can form the basis for a grant of exclusivity to one entity. For instance, under US trademark law, GIs are not registrable as trademarks or collective marks because they are descriptive of the good's place of origin. However, there is an exception: a GI that has acquired a secondary meaning through use can be registered.[123] In this case, the registered name has two meanings and thus indicates both the geographical origin and the trade origin, but the protection afforded by trademark law only guarantees the name as an indication of the trade origin:[124] 'If no

117. Benjamin Fontaine, *La défense des indications géographiques protégées à titre de marques communautaires collectives: Quelques réflexions inspirées du jugement du Tribunal de l'Union européenne du 9 juin 2010*, Propriété industrielle, n° 2, 2011, étude 4.
118. Case C-766/18 P *Foundation for the Protection of the Traditional Cheese of Cyprus Named Halloumi v. European Union Intellectual Property Office* (ECJ 5 March 2020) para. 75 (AG Opinion).
119. Case T-138/09 *Muñoz Arraiza v. OHMI, supra* n. 115, para. 52.
120. Case T-534/10 *Organismos Kypriakis Galaktokomikis Viomichanias v. OHMI, supra* n. 113, para. 41. *See also* Case T-358/09 *Sociedad Agricola Requingua Ltda v. OHIM* [2011] ECR II-00105, para. 39; Case R 218/2006-2 *Decision of the Second Board of Appeal of 24 November 2006* (EUIPO) p. 8.
121. Joined Cases C-108/97 & C-109/97 *Windsurfing Chiemsee, supra* n. 86, para. 49.
122. WIPO, *Key Ingredients for Geographical Indications: Collectivization and Control*, WIPO/GEO/BEI/07/9 (14 June 2007) p. 5.
123. *See* 15 U.S.C. § 1052 (e)(f) (2018).
124. Stacy D. Goldberg, *Who Will Raise the White Flag: The Battle Between the United States and the European Union over the Protection of Geographical Indications*, 22 U. Pa. J. Int'l Econ. L. 107 (2001).

secondary meaning exists, then exclusivity is not granted.'[125] Therefore, the function of the mark registered on this basis is no different from that of other ordinary marks.

Nevertheless, the same argument would not be valid for collective marks registered under Article 74(2). As noted above, the exception provided for in Article 74(2) applies as long as the GIs are registered as EU collective marks (not individual marks), without requiring the existence of a secondary meaning. In the case where the secondary meaning does not exist, the function of the mark registered under 74(2) becomes blurred.

In a judgment issued on 2 October 2015, the CJEU acknowledged that the GI '*Darjeeling*' may serve to designate the geographical origin of the product and that the function of the GI is to guarantee to consumers the geographical origin. However, the court then observed that the fact a collective mark consists of a GI 'does not affect the essential function of all collective marks', arguing that 'the function of a Community collective mark is not altered as a result of its registration under Article 66.2 (now Article 74.2)'. Consequently, it was held that the essential function of the mark consisting of a GI is 'to distinguish the goods covered according to the specific body from which they originate and not according to their geographical origin'.[126] On appeal, the CJEU observed that only trademarks that have the ability to distinguish the goods of association members from the goods of other undertakings may constitute EU collective marks.[127]

Where the precise commercial origin is unknown to the consumers (i.e., when the mark holder is an administrative body and the consumer would not think that the goods come from the body or its members), a collective mark that is composed exclusively of a GI is still considered an indication of the commercial origin, not of the geographical origin.[128]

The CJEU reaffirmed in its judgment of 5 March 2020, that Article 66(2) of Regulation 207/2009 is not an exception to the requirement for a trademark function.[129]

It logically follows that the CJEU would not allow the evolution of the 'likelihood of confusion' notion, as advocated by several authors. It has been noted that, in assessing the likelihood of confusion under trademark law, account must be taken of the risk that the consumer might believe that the goods come from the same producer or group of producers,[130] instead of the risk that the public might believe that the goods come from the same geographical origin. Thus, any assessment concerning a collective geographical mark must be carried out using the same criteria as those applicable to ordinary collective marks or individual marks.[131]

125. WIPO, *Key Ingredients for Geographical Indications: Collectivization and Control*, *supra* n. 122, at 5.
126. Case T-627/13 *The Tea Board v. OHMI*, *supra* n. 113, paras 41-43.
127. Joined Cases C-673/15 P-C-676/15 P *The Tea Board v. EUIPO* (ECJ 20 September 2017).
128. Case T-138/09 *Muñoz Arraiza v. OHMI*, *supra* n. 115, paras 26-27.
129. Case C-766/18 P *Halloumi v. EUIPO*, *supra* n. 118, para. 73.
130. Case T-162/01 *Laboratorios RTB v. OHMI* [2003] ECR II-02821, para. 30.
131. Case T-627/13 *The Tea Board v. OHMI*, *supra* n. 113, para. 76.

Following the judgments of the CJEU, the Guidelines of the EUIPO emphasize that Article 7(1)(b) and Article 7(3) of the EU Trademark Regulation apply also to EU collective marks. Therefore, where an association applies to register as an EU collective mark a sign that may designate a geographical origin, it must ensure that the sign has *elements* that enable the consumer to distinguish the goods or services of its members from those of other undertakings.[132] In other words, the signs must contain not only geographically descriptive terms (including GIs) but also elements that are sufficient to render the mark distinctive as a collective mark. This requirement is contrary to that of the 2015 Guidelines, which stated that a sign that exclusively describes the geographical origin of the goods or services can be accepted as an EU collective mark.[133]

Finally, the geographical connotation of GIs will not disappear as a result of its registration as a trademark. On the contrary, the descriptive meaning is used on an ongoing basis as a factor considered in the assessment of the likelihood of confusion.[134] For instance, since the words '*Halloumi*' and '*Hellim*' both refer to the same speciality cheese from Cyprus, some conceptual similarity may be present depending on the prior translation.[135] In a similar vein, the court has held that there is a high degree of conceptual similarity between '*Riojavina*' and '*Rioja*', which refers directly to grapevine products and specifically to Rioja wine.[136]

[c] Registering GIs in the Form of Collective Marks in Chinese law

Under Article 10 (paragraph 2, sentence 1) of China's Trademark Law, registration will be refused for the 'geographical names of (China's) administrative divisions at or above the county level'. The former vice president and judge of the Supreme People's Court, Kong Xiangjun, explained as follows:

> Geographical names indicate a particular location and therefore are not capable of distinguishing goods or services as to their commercial origin. Registering geographical names as trademarks would mislead the consumer as to the true origin and put other operators in the same area at a disadvantaged position. The restriction provided in Article 10 is necessary to ensure the function of the trademark and fair competition.[137]

---

132. EUIPO, *Guidelines for Examination*, Part B (1 March 2021) pp. 647-648.
133. EUIPO, *Guidelines for Examination*, Part B (1 August 2015) p. 75.
134. The likelihood of confusion between a collective geographical mark and other trademarks is determined in the same way as between two ordinary marks: by means of a global appreciation of the visual, aural or conceptual similarity. *See* Case T-534/10 *Organismos Kypriakis Galaktokomikis Viomichanias v. OHMI, supra* n. 113, para. 36; Case C-251/95 *SABEL BV v. Puma AG* [1997] ECR I-06191, para. 23.
135. Case T-534/10 *Organismos Kypriakis Galaktokomikis Viomichanias v. OHMI, supra* n. 113, paras 41-42.
136. Case T-138/09 *Muñoz Arraiza v. OHMI, supra* n. 115, para. 52.
137. Kong Xiangjun, Xia Junli & Zhou Yunchuan, Guanyu Shenli Shangbiao Shouquan Quequan Xingzheng Anjian Ruogan Wenti de Lijie yu Shiyong [Understanding and Application of the Opinions on Several Issues Concerning the Trial of Administrative Cases Involving the Authorization and Determination of Trademark Rights], RENMIN SIFA [PEOPLE'S JUSTICE], June 2010, 21.

It thus appears that Article 10 pursues the same objectives as Article L. 711-2, point 3 of the French IP Code and Article 7(1)(c) of EU Regulation 2017/1001.

As in EU law, the second sentence of Article 10 introduces an exception. It allows geographical names to be registered as *part* of a collective mark (and certification mark) without requiring a secondary meaning.[138] The other part of that collective mark could be a distinctive element or the common name of a product.[139] Thus, a GI composed of a geographical name and a common name (e.g., '*Fuling* Mustard') may serve as a valid collective mark.

The Implementing Regulation of the Trademark Law further relaxes the conditions for registration, since its Article 4 provides in a general manner that 'GIs as referred to in Article 16 of the Trademark Law may be registered as collective marks or certification marks.' Thus, a GI, which would be registrable as a collective mark, may be not only the name of a geographical region but also any other sign capable of indicating the place of origin.[140]

The same question will be asked regarding the function of the 'GI collective marks' registered under the derogatory provision.[141] There is reason to believe that these marks are recognized as a separate category with their own unique set of rules. First, to register GIs as collective marks, the applicant must provide information to show that the quality or reputation of the product is due to its geographical origin. This requirement does not exist for other marks (except for GI certification marks). Second, as specified in the guidelines issued in 2014 by Beijing's High People's Court for the trial of cases concerning the grant of trademark rights, 'the plea, alleging that a subsequent GI collective (or certification) mark should not have been registered or should be declared invalid because of the existence of an earlier (identical or similar) ordinary mark (for identical or similar goods), must be rejected'.[142] In other words, a later GI collective mark can be registered even if there might be an identical or similar earlier ordinary mark. This guideline is somewhat contrary to Article 30 of the Trademark Law, which provides that registration shall be refused 'if the trademark in

138. Trademark Law, Article 10(2): 'The geographical names of administrative divisions at or above the county level and foreign geographical names well-known to the public shall not be used as trademarks, except for geographical names that have other meaning or constitute part of a collective mark or certification mark ....'
139. Wu Shan, Dili Biaozhi he Chiming Shangbiao Chongtu de Falu Tiaozheng [The Resolution of the Conflict Between Geographical Indications and Geographical Marks], ZHONGGUO LUSHI [CHINA LAWYER], October 2008, 23.
140. Zheng Haiyan, *Geographical Indications Protection in China, in Research Handbook on Intellectual Property and Geographical Indications* 327, 331 (Dev Gangjee ed., Edward Elgar Publishing 2016).
141. Although 'GI collective mark' is not a terminology in the legislative text, it is used in practice by governments to describe collective marks composed of GIs. *See* Guojia Zhishi Chanquanju Bangongshi Guanyu Kaizhan 2012 Niandu Zhishi Chanquan Fuwuye Tongji Diaocha Gongzuo de Tongzhi [State Intellectual Property Office's Notice on Carrying out the 2012 Annual Survey on Intellectual Property Services], 29 September 2012.
142. *See* Beijing Gaoji Renmin Fayuan Guanyu Shangbiao Shouquan Quequan Xingzheng Anjian de Shenli Zhinan [Beijing High People's Court's Guide to the Trial of Administrative Cases Concerning Trademarks], 22 January 2014, Article 5.

question is identical with or similar to a registered trademark used in connection with the same or similar goods'.[143]

In justifying this guideline, the judge of the High People's Court pointed out that the function of ordinary trademarks and that of GI collective marks are so different that 'the assessment of the similarity between the two categories of marks would be unnecessary'.[144] He added that 'while ordinary trademarks serve to distinguish the commercial source of the product, GI collective marks indicate the geographical origin and other features of the product that are linked to its *terroir*'. On the basis of the difference in function, the judgment concluded that the registration or use of a later GI collective mark would be unlikely to cause confusion with the prior ordinary trademark (despite the similarity between the signs and products).[145]

It can be seen that the function of the GI collective mark has been equated with that of the GI. That is to say, when a collective mark is composed of a GI, it is considered to be performing the same function as the GI contained in it. This idea is echoed by the Supreme People's Court, which considered adopting a similar provision that would permit the registration of a later GI collective mark.[146] However, the Supreme Court did not adopt the provision in the final version of 1 March 2017.[147]

In the guidelines issued in 2019 by the Beijing High People's Court, a restriction is provided for the coexistence between subsequent GIs and the prior trademarks. Article 13(5) stipulates that if the application for the GI collective or certification trademark comes after the application for the ordinary trademark, the objective existence of the GI, its reputation, distinctiveness and the cognition of the relevant public shall be taken into account to determine whether the relevant public is likely to be confused about the source of commodities or services.[148]

To conclude, unlike the practice in Europe, GI collective marks are recognized in China as a separate category whose uniqueness lies in its function. Accordingly, while, in Europe, collective geographical marks are subject to the same regime of protection

143. Trademark Law, Article 30: 'Where a trademark application does not comply with the relevant provisions in this Law or is identical with or similar to a registered trademark used in connection with the same or similar goods, its registration shall be refused by the Trademark Office after examination, and the mark shall not be published.'
144. Zhou Bo, Jiaqiang Shenli Zhidao Tongyi Shenpan Chidu Zhiyi [Strengthening the Guide of Trials and Unifying Judgment Standard], ZHONGGUO ZHISHI CHANQUAN BAO [CHINA INTELLECTUAL PROPERTY NEWS], 7 March 2014.
145. *See Changsha Yulu Enterprise Marketing Planning Co. Ltd. v. the Trademark Review and Adjudication Board of the State Administration for Industry and Commerce*, Beijing High People's Court (5 July 2013).
146. *See* Zuigao Renmin Fayuan Guanyu Shenli Shangbiao Shouquan Quequan Xingzheng Anjian Ruogan Wenti de Guiding Zhengqiu Yijiangao [Draft Provisions of the Supreme People's Court on Several Issues Concerning the Administrative Cases of Trademark], 14 October 2014, Article 13.
147. *See* Zuigao Renmin Fayuan Guanyu Shenli Shangbiao Shouquan Quequan Xingzheng Anjian Ruogan Wenti de Guiding [Provisions of the Supreme People's Court on Several Issues Concerning the Administrative Cases of Trademark], 1 March 2017.
148. *See* Beijing Gaoji Renmin Fayuan Guanyu Shangbiao Shouquan Quequan Xingzheng Anjian de Shenli Zhinan [Beijing High People's Court's Guide to the Trial of Administrative Cases Concerning Trademarks], 24 April 2019, Article 13(5).

as are other ordinary collective marks, GI collective marks in China are governed by 'a regime of exception'. The following sections discuss this difference in detail.

[B] Protection of GIs Through Collective Marks

The regime of collective marks could be used to protect GIs due to certain features of the regime and the protection afforded to the marks.

[1] Special Regime of Collective Marks

Both in Europe and in China, collective marks are subject to certain special rules with regard to matters such as applicants, the regulations governing use, and the use of the marks. These rules constitute a basis for the functioning of collective marks. By contrast, China has adopted another set of rules with the aim of accommodating the uniqueness of the GI collective mark, in addition to the special regime for all collective marks.

[a] Special Regime of Ordinary Collective Marks in French Law

The first paragraph of Article L. 715-6 of the IP Law provides that the general regime of trademarks applies to ordinary collective marks. Collective marks in France were not subject to any special rules before the Order of 2019.[149] However, under Directive 2015/2436, the European Parliament and the Council require the Member States to set up a special regime to be applied to collective marks. According to Articles 30-36 of the Directive, the special regime shall include the obligation to submit the regulations governing use,[150] additional grounds for the refusal of a collective mark application,[151] the right to bring an action for infringement,[152] and additional grounds for revocation[153] and invalidity.[154] A comparison with Regulation 2017/1001 would show that the regime to which national collective marks will be subject is very similar to the regime applicable to EU collective marks.

However, why should collective marks be subject to a special regime when their function is close to that of individual marks? The introduction of this special system is not based on the legal function of collective marks but on an economic rationale. Recital 8 in the preamble to the Directive expressly states, 'Collective trademarks have proven a useful instrument for promoting goods or services with specific common properties. It is therefore appropriate to subject national collective trademarks to rules similar to the rules applicable to European Union collective marks.'

149. Formerly Article L. 715-2 of the French Intellectual Property Code.
150. Article 30 of Directive 2015/2436.
151. Article 31 of Directive 2015/2436.
152. *Ibid.*, Article 34.
153. *Ibid.*, Article 35.
154. *Ibid.*, Article 36.

In the context of the European trademark law reform, the Order of 13 November 2019, created a special regime for French collective marks.[155] Article L. 715-6-Article L. 715-10 of the IP Code govern the function of the collective marks. Given the strong similarity between the rules applicable to national collective marks and those applicable to EU collective marks, a discussion of the regime at the EU level will suffice.

[b] Special Regime of EU Collective Marks

Under the EU regime, regulations governing use must be attached to an application for the EU collective mark[156] regardless of whether the mark guarantees a particular quality.[157] Several limitations have been placed on the contents of the regulations: 'The regulations shall specify the persons authorized to use the mark, the conditions of membership and, where they exist, the conditions of use of the mark, including sanctions.'[158] While Article 74(2) leaves open the door to registering the signs or indications that serve to designate the geographical origin, the regulations governing the use of that collective mark registered under Article 74(2) must authorize any person whose goods originate in the geographical area concerned to become a member of the association, in order to prevent GIs or signs from being monopolized by the applicant.[159]

The question arises as to whether the use of the mark is open to all persons who establish in the area of the geographical origin designated by the mark. In this regard, it should be noted that 'the conditions of membership' and the 'conditions of use of the mark' are enumerated in two separate clusters (Article 75). This may indicate that becoming a member is not the same as having the right to use the mark. In fact, there is nothing preventing the regulations from setting out supplementary criteria in the conditions of use apart from the geographical location. With respect to collective marks containing a PGI/PDO, the EUIPO provides that the regulations governing use should reflect the fact that 'they refer to the use of the trademark for goods complying with the

155. Ordonnance n° 2019-1169 du 13 novembre 2019 relative aux marques de produits ou de services, J.O. du 14 nov. 2019, texte n° 12.
156. The regulations must be contained in the application for an EU collective mark or subsequently submitted to the EUIPO within a period of two months after the date of filing. *See* Article 75 of Regulation 2017/1001.
157. In France, before the Order of 2019, only collective certification marks guaranteeing a particular quality or other characteristics were required to submit the regulations governing use in the application process. However, the Order of 2019 has made it compulsory for both collective marks and guarantee marks to submit the regulations governing use.
158. Article 75 of Regulation 2017/1001; *Commission Implementing Regulation (EU) 2018/626 of 5 March 2018 laying down detailed rules for implementing certain provisions of Regulation (EU) 2017/1001 of the European Parliament and of the Council on the European Union trade mark, and repealing Implementing Regulation (EU) 2017/143*, OJ L 104, 24.4.2018, pp. 37-56, Article 16.
159. Article 75 of Regulation 2017/1001: '... The regulations governing use of a mark referred to in Article 74(2) must authorize any person whose goods or services originate in the geographical area concerned to become a member of the association which is the proprietor of the mark.'

PGI/PDO'.[160] Since the mark should be used in a manner compatible with the conditions of use,[161] there is reason to believe that the proprietor of the mark can maintain controls on the conformity of the products.[162] Manufacturers whose goods do not comply with the conditions of use consequently would not have the right to use the mark, even if their goods originate directly from the geographical area concerned.

This is not to say, however, that the use of the geographical name is reserved to members whose products comply with the conditions of use and that non-member local businesses would be unable to use the place name to indicate the geographical provenance of the category of goods concerned. As a matter of fact, local producers who are not yet a member of the association that owns the collective geographical mark can use the name to indicate the geographical origin of their goods provided the use is in accordance with honest practices in industrial or commercial matters. In particular, 'Such a mark may not be invoked against a third party who is entitled to use a geographical name.'[163] It is thereby ensured that a GI may not be monopolized and thus remains available to local users.[164]

As for the second distinctive feature, the special grounds for revocation or invalidity have been expressly incorporated into European law. A declaration of revocation of a collective mark may be based not only on the general grounds for revocation (e.g., failure to use a trademark properly)[165] but also on special grounds, wherein the proprietor would be deprived of the right to the mark if 'he does not take reasonable steps to prevent the mark being used in a manner incompatible with the conditions of use'. A disqualification may be ordered if 'the manner in which the mark has been used by the proprietor has caused it to become liable to mislead the public'.[166] Moreover, a declaration of invalidity may be based not only on general grounds[167] but also on special grounds.[168] Furthermore, regarding the collective geographical mark referred to in Article 74(2), a decision declaring it invalid may be ordered if the membership is not open to any person whose products originate in the geographical area concerned.[169]

160. EUIPO (OHIM), *Guidelines for Examination in the Office,* Part B Examination (1 August 2015) p. 74.
161. Article 81(a) of Regulation 2017/1001.
162. Kalliopi Dani, *Community Collective Marks: Status, Scope and Rivals in the European Signs Landscape* 15 (Nomos Verlagsgesellschaft mbH 2014).
163. Article 74(2) of Regulation 2017/1001: '... A collective mark shall not entitle the proprietor to prohibit a third party from using in the course of trade such signs or indications, provided he uses them in accordance with honest practices in industrial or commercial matters; in particular, such a mark may not be invoked against a third party who is entitled to use a geographical name.'
164. Jan Rosén, *Individualism and Collectiveness in Intellectual Property Law* 251 (Edward Elgar 2012).
165. Article 58 of Regulation 2017/1001.
166. Article 81 of Regulation 2017/1001.
167. Articles 59-60 of Regulation 2017/1001.
168. Article 82 of Regulation 2017/1001.
169. An EU collective mark that is registered in breach of Article 76 shall be declared invalid. Article 76 provides that the EU collective mark shall satisfy the provisions of Article 74 or 75. The latter

[c] *Special Regime of Collective Marks in Chinese Law*

In China, collective marks are primarily governed by a special regulation: the Measures for the Registration and Administration of Collective Marks and Certification Marks. The Measures provide for general rules that apply to all collective marks, whereby the ownership of a collective mark is limited to collective organizations, such as a group, an association, or other organizations. Thus, private companies without an associative structure cannot be owners of a collective mark. Where an application is filed for a collective mark, the applicant must present a document certifying its status as a collective organization.[170] The application requires regulations governing the use of the mark.[171]

China's trademark system imposes a set of additional requirements on the functioning of the GI collective mark based on the understanding that it forms a category separate from that of the ordinary collective mark.[172]

First, the applicant for the registration of a GI collective mark must be a collective organization whose members come from the region indicated by the GI. It must be capable of supervising the particular quality of the GI products.[173] In order to acquire the supervision capacity, the applicant must have its own supervision units or assign this role to other bodies with specialized technical personnel and testing equipment.[174] For foreign applicants, proof must also be submitted that the GI is under protection in the country of origin.[175] This rule complies with the terms of the TRIPS Agreement,

---

requires that the regulations governing use of a collective geographical mark must authorize any person whose goods originate in the geographical area concerned to become a member of the association.

170. China's Guidelines for Examination of Trademark Applications provide that the supporting documents can include the business license of an enterprise, the approval document for the establishment of a public institution or a social group. It seems to indicate that an enterprise, a public institution or a social group, which does not necessarily have a corporation or an association structure, can obtain the ownership of a collective mark. However, how can collective marks owned by an enterprise or a public institution perform its function of indicating membership? *See* Trademark Office & Trademark Review and Adjudication Board, Shangbiao Shencha ji Shenli Biaozhun [Trademark Review Standard], December 2016, p. 130.
171. Article 13(5) of the Regulations for the Implementation of the Trademark Law: 'If applying for the registration of a collective mark or a certification mark, the applicant shall make a statement in the application and submit the documents certifying the qualification of the applicant and the regulations governing use of that mark.'
172. *See* §3.01 *supra*; *See also* Zhou Bo, Ruhe Shencha Butong Leixing de Jiti Shangbiao [How to Examine Different Types of Collective Trademarks], ZHONGGUO ZHISHI CHANQUAN BAO [CHINA INTELLECTUAL PROPERTY NEWS], 11 September 2015.
173. Article 4 of the Measures for the Registration and Administration of Collective and Certification Marks: 'The applicant shall submit the detailed information of the professionals and special testing equipment that it has or that is owned by any other organization authorized by it, to show its capability of supervising the particular quality of the goods to which the said geographical indication applies.'
174. *Shandong Tourism Industry Association v. Trademark Review and Adjudication Board of State Administration for Industry and Commerce*, Beijing Intellectual Property Court (20 April 2015).
175. Article 6(2) of the Measures for Collective and Certification Marks: 'Any foreign person or enterprise applying for the registration of a geographical indication as a collective mark or a certification mark shall furnish documents certifying that the geographical indication in question is under the legal protection, in his or its name, in the country of origin.'

wherein protection is open to foreign GIs except those not protected in their country of origin.[176] It is also in line with internationally accepted practices. For instance, where an application for the registration of a PDO/PGI relates to a geographical area in a foreign country, it must be proved that the geographical name is protected in its country of origin.[177]

Second, as with other collective marks, regulations governing use must be submitted with the application. The regulations include the purpose, the quality of the product, the procedural rules governing the use of the mark, users' rights and obligations, sanctions, and rules concerning the supervisory system and controls over the product.[178] The content of the regulations must be published in the Trademark Gazette as an abstract or full text.[179] If a collective mark is composed entirely of a GI, special rules will be applied only for this category of collective marks.[180] According to the case law, the applicant for the registration of a GI as a collective mark must specify in the regulations that the product possesses 'a level of quality which is higher than that of similar products'.[181] In addition, it must present the following information in the application dossier: the particular quality, reputation or other characteristics of the product; the link between the given product quality, reputation, or other characteristic and the geographical origin; and the boundary of the region indicated by the GI in question.[182] These details, which are usually examined for GI registration, are required in the trademark examination procedure.[183] This leaves us wondering about the nature of the registration: what we have registered is a mark containing a GI or simply a GI?

Third, collective marks must be used exclusively by the members of the association that is the proprietor of the mark.[184] The name and address of the members must be specified in the application dossier and subsequently published.[185] If there is any change with regard to accession to or withdrawal of membership at a later stage,[186] the registrant shall apply to the Bureau to modify the list of members, and this modification will also be published by the Bureau.[187] The registrant is responsible for controls over

176. *See* Article 24(9) of the TRIPS Agreement.
177. Under the PDO/PGI regime, an application shall, in addition, prove that the name of the product is protected in its country of origin. *See* Regulation Article 8(1)(c) of 1151/2012.
178. Measures for Collective and Certification Marks, Article 10.
179. Any amendment to the regulations governing the use of the mark shall be submitted to the Trademark Office for examination and approval, and the amendments shall come into effect on the date of publication. *See* Implementing Regulations of the Trademark Law, Article 96; Measures for Collective and Certification Marks, Article 13.
180. *Shandong Tourism Industry Association v. Trademark Review and Adjudication Board of State Administration for Industry and Commerce*, Beijing High People's Court (19 August 2015).
181. *Ibid.*
182. Measures for Collective and Certification Marks, Article 7.
183. *See* Trademark Office & Trademark Review and Adjudication Board, Shangbiao Shencha ji Shenli Biaozhun [Trademark Review Standard], December 2016, pp. 132-135.
184. The collective mark may not be licensed to persons who are not members of the association. If the 'closeness' is violated, a period of time will be ordered by the administrative body to rectify the situation. If the registrant refuses to do so, a fine will be imposed. *See* Measures for Collective and Certification Marks, Articles 17 and 22.
185. Measures for Collective and Certification Marks, Article 4.
186. Measures for Collective and Certification Marks, Article 14.
187. *Ibid.*

the use of the mark and product quality compliance with the regulations governing use. Fines will be imposed for non-compliance.[188] Where a GI is registered in the form of a collective mark, any person whose products satisfy the conditions of use (of the GI) may submit a membership request, which should be accepted. Local producers who are unwilling to become a member of the association can still use the GI in accordance with honest practices.[189] However, under the trademark regime, the GI notion is not restricted to geographical names but also includes signs or symbols capable of graphic representation.[190] Only the fair use of geographical *names* is allowed.[191]

Finally, the previous Administrative Measures (1994) included special grounds for the revocation of a collective mark:[192] 'The trademark rights shall be revoked where the proprietor has lost control over the use of the mark.'[193] Within a period of two years following the revocation of a collective mark, any application for the registration of an identical or similar mark should not be approved,[194] while the unavailability period is only one year following the revocation of an individual mark.[195] However, the current Measures (2003) have no special provisions regarding the grounds for revocation or the unavailability period, subjecting collective marks to the general regime of individual marks in this respect.

[2] Defence of Collective Marks

By registering a GI as a collective mark, the affiliated producers acquire a right over the sign that constitutes both the GI and the mark. The trademark regime enables the trademark owner or those who have the right to use the mark with the 'exclusive right' to prevent the use of the mark by unauthorized parties.

Nevertheless, the exclusive right afforded by a collective mark is not absolute. As with ordinary trademarks, the right to prevent the illegal use of the collective mark is limited by the 'principle of speciality'. Furthermore, it seems that collective geographical marks with a prima facie weak distinctive character enjoy a narrower protection

188. Measures for Collective and Certification Marks, Article 21.
189. The organization that is the mark owner is not entitled to prohibit them from using, as long as the use is considered a 'fair use', the geographical name in that mark. *See* Trademark Law, Article 59; Implementing Regulations of the Trademark Law, Article 4(2).
190. Measures for Collective and Certification Marks, Article 8.
191. Measures for Collective and Certification Marks, Article 18(2): 'The fair use of a geographical indication under paragraph 2 of Article 6 of the Implementing Regulations shall refer to the fair use of the geographical name of the said geographical indication.' *See also Aksu Apple Association v. Wang Yushan, New Wu District Shangya Fruit Store*, Jiangsu Wuxi Intermediate People's Court (15 April 2021).
192. This special ground for revocation also applies to certification marks.
193. Measures for Collective and Certification Marks, Article 14 (1994).
194. Measures for Collective and Certification Marks, Article 15 (1994).
195. The purpose of the unavailability period is to avoid confusion among consumers. Considering the lifecycle of the products, the cancellation of the mark does not mean that the mark will disappear immediately: the products with that mark will not be out of the market immediately but will exist in circulation for a period of time. *See* Wang Yingchao & Zhang Hui, ZHONGHUA RENMIN GONGHEGUO SHANGBIAOFA SHIYI [INTERPRETATION OF THE TRADEMARK LAW OF THE PEOPLE'S REPUBLIC OF CHINA] (China Industry and Commerce Press, 2013); Trademark Law, Article 50.

than ordinary trademarks with an average or even highly distinctive character. It is therefore important to carefully analyse the protection afforded by the collective mark– and particularly the geographical collective mark – in France, the EU, and China.

[a] Defence of Ordinary Collective Marks in French Law

In the scope of protection conferred by the French trademark system, there is generally no difference between individual trademarks and ordinary collective marks. The exclusive right to use collective marks is not absolute,[196] being limited by the principle of speciality[197] whereby collective marks are not protected in themselves but in their relationships with certain goods.[198] Accordingly, the law imposes two types of prohibitions on the unauthorized use of the distinctive signs used to designate identical or similar products or services.[199]

First, the collective mark is protected against any misuse of the same sign in respect of goods/services that are identical. Under the former Article L. 713-3 of the IP Code, the reproduction or use of the authentic mark constitutes infringement without any consideration for other requirements, especially the likelihood of confusion in the minds of consumers. The adjunction of words such as 'formula', 'style', 'system', 'imitation', 'type', or 'method' does not disqualify these actions as a form of counterfeit.[200] It is worth noting that 'reproduction' should be understood as a 'slavish copying'.[201] If the mark has been added with a minor modification,[202] leading to differences that are not insignificant and do not go unnoticed by an average consumer, the infringement claim then must be addressed in light of former Article L. 713-3 of the IP Code.[203] Since the Order of 13 November 2019, was promulgated, Article L. 713-2 of

196. The trademark owner cannot prohibit the use of the trademark by an unauthorized third party unless the three conditions are met: the use should take place in the course of trade; the use is for designating identical or similar goods or services; it should affect or be liable to affect the functions of the trademark. Therefore, if the collective mark is not used as a mark to indicate an origin, infringement of such a right is excluded from the scope. *See* Cass. com., 4 mai 2010, n° 09-14.435; T.G.I. Paris, 15 mai 2014, n° 12/16452; T.G.I. Paris, 4 déc. 2007, PIBD 2008, n° 869, III, p. 169; C.A. Paris, 1 avr. 2009, n° 07/20719.
197. *See* Adrien Bouvel, *Principe de spécialité et signes distinctifs*, Paris, Litec, 2004.
198. C.A. Paris, 3 nov. 1999, Ann. propr. Ind., 2000, p. 115: '*La Marque de certification n'étant destinée à protéger que les produits ou services qu'elle désigne précisément … le titulaire est mal fondé à en solliciter l'extension à des produits autres que ceux (couvert par la marque).*'
199. *See* Séverine Visse-Causse, *Droit de la propriété intellectuelle*, Paris, Lextenso, 2015, p. 165.
200. Ancien Article L. 713-2 CPI: '*Sont interdits, sauf autorisation du propriétaire: a) La reproduction, l'usage ou l'apposition d'une marque, même avec l'adjonction de mots tels que: "formule, façon, système, imitation, genre, méthode", ainsi que l'usage d'une marque reproduite, pour des produits ou services identiques à ceux désignés dans l'enregistrement ….*'
201. Case C-291/00 *LTJ Diffusion SA v. Sadas Vertbaudet SA* [2003] ECR I-02799, para. 54: '*Article 5(1)(a) of the directive must be interpreted as meaning that a sign is identical with the trade mark where it reproduces, without any modification or addition, all the elements constituting the trade mark or where, viewed as a whole, it contains differences so insignificant that they may go unnoticed by an average consumer.*'
202. *See* Catherine Verneret, *Évolution jurisprudentielle en matière d'appréciation de la contrefaçon de marque*, La semaine juridique entreprise et affaires, n° 12, 2001.
203. C.A. Paris, 12 déc. 2014, n° 13/22467: '*… les signes "Papounet" (marque collective simple) et "Le Papounet" sont différents en ce que la dénomination "Le Papounet" comporte un article*

the French IP Code has replaced the former Article L. 713-3 and employs wording similar to that used in Directive 2015/2436. Article L. 713-2 provides that 'unless authorized by the trademark holder, the use of a sign identical to the trademark and used for products or services identical to those for which the trademark is registered in the course of trade for products or services is prohibited'.[204]

On the other hand, pursuant to the former Article L. 713-3 mentioned above, the infringement is constituted on the condition that there exists a likelihood of confusion on the part of the public.[205] This includes cases where the authentic mark is reproduced for similar products (not for identical products) or the mark is imitated for identical or similar products.[206] In the same vein, since the Order of 13 November 2019, Article L. 713-2 prohibits the use of a sign identical or similar to the mark and used for goods or services identical or similar to those for which the mark is registered if there is, in the mind of the public, a likelihood of confusion, including the risk of association of the sign with the mark.[207] Furthermore, when the collective mark is well-known, it enjoys the special protection accorded by Article L. 713-3.[208] Well-known collective marks are protected against misuse in respect of products that are identical, similar, or even different if such use is likely to 'cause a prejudice to the owner of the mark' or if it 'constitutes unjustified exploitation of the mark'.[209]

Regarding procedures, Article 22 of the Law of 1964 provided that persons with the right to use the collective mark could institute infringement proceedings. However, the Law of 1991, which reformed the 1964 system, deleted this rule. We can therefore assume that, under the Law of 1991, the general trademark law does not allow

défini qui détermine le genre du groupe nominal qu'il précède, lequel n'est pas insignifiant et ne passera pas inaperçu aux yeux du consommateur moyen de sorte que c'est au regard de l'article 713-3 du code de la propriété intellectuelle qu'il convient d'apprécier la demande en contrefaçon concernant les actes ....'

204. Article L. 713-2 CPI: '*Est interdit, sauf autorisation du titulaire de la marque, l'usage dans la vie des affaires pour des produits ou des services: 1° D'un signe identique à la marque et utilisé pour des produits ou des services identiques à ceux pour lesquels la marque est enregistrée.*'
205. Ancien Article L. 713-3 CPI: '*Sont interdits, sauf autorisation du propriétaire, s'il peut en résulter un risque de confusion dans l'esprit du public: a) La reproduction, l'usage ou l'apposition d'une marque, ainsi que l'usage d'une marque reproduite, pour des produits ou services similaires à ceux désignés dans l'enregistrement; b) L'imitation d'une marque et l'usage d'une marque imitée, pour des produits ou services identiques ou similaires à ceux désignés dans l'enregistrement.*'
206. T.G.I. Paris, 30 nov. 2004, PIBD 2005, n° 803, III, p. 150.
207. Article L. 713-2 CPI: '*Est interdit, sauf autorisation du titulaire de la marque, l'usage dans la vie des affaires pour des produits ou des services: ... 2° D'un signe identique ou similaire à la marque et utilisé pour des produits ou des services identiques ou similaires à ceux pour lesquels la marque est enregistrée, s'il existe, dans l'esprit du public, un risque de confusion incluant le risque d'association du signe avec la marque.*'
208. Article L. 713-3 CPI: '*Est interdit, sauf autorisation du titulaire de la marque, l'usage dans la vie des affaires, pour des produits ou des services, d'un signe identique ou similaire à la marque jouissant d'une renommée et utilisé pour des produits ou des services identiques, similaires ou non similaires à ceux pour lesquels la marque est enregistrée, si cet usage du signe, sans juste motif, tire indûment profit du caractère distinctif ou de la renommée de la marque, ou leur porte préjudice.*'
209. T.G.I Paris, 12 déc. 2007, PIBD, 2008, n° 869, III, p. 152.

infringement proceedings to be brought by member users of a French collective mark except if they benefit from an exclusive right of exploitation.[210]

However, since the Order of 13 November 2019, Article L. 716-4-2 of the IP Code provides that the persons authorized to use a collective mark may bring an action for infringement with or without the consent of the owner if specified in the regulations governing use.[211]

[b] Defence of EU Collective Marks

The scope of protection of the EU collective mark is the same as that of individual marks[212] as set out in Articles 9-14 of Regulation 2017/1001. If the sign used by the third party is identical to the registered mark and designates the same products, its use can be prohibited without needing to prove a risk of confusion in the mind of the public. Instead, the risk of confusion must be established to prevent the use of a similar sign for similar products. When the mark has a reputation in the EU, the effective scope of his protection will be extended to different products if the use of that sign 'takes unfair advantage of, or is detrimental to, the distinctive character or the repute of the mark'.[213]

It is important to note that the EU Regulation emphasizes the protection of the interests of persons who have the right to use a collective mark. Proceedings for infringement of a collective mark may be brought by, in addition to the proprietor, any person who has the authority to use the mark provided that they obtain the consent of the proprietor.[214] Lacking such consent, users of a collective mark can intervene in infringement proceedings brought by the proprietor to seek compensation for any damage suffered by them.[215] The proprietor is also entitled to claim compensation on behalf of users who sustained damages.[216]

While the EU regime of collective marks appears to be a good tool for the protection of GIs, there are substantive differences between the two that might impact its effectiveness.[217]

As mentioned, due to their functional equivalence, provisions applicable to ordinary marks are equally applicable to marks registered in derogation from Article 7(1)(c) under Article 74 of the EU Trademark Regulation.[218] This makes proving the

210. Article L. 716-4-2 CPI.
211. *Ibid.*, para. 2: '*La personne habilitée à faire usage d'une marque de garantie ou d'une marque collective ne peut engager une action en contrefaçon qu'avec le consentement du titulaire de celle-ci, sauf mention contraire du règlement d'usage.*'
212. The fact that a mark is a collective mark does not imply that its scope of protection is broader than ordinary marks. *See* Case T-143/11 *Consorzio vino Chianti Classico v. OHMI* (CFI 5 December 2012) para. 61.
213. Joanna Schmidt-Szalewski, *Droit de la propriété industrielle*, 7e éd., Paris, Dalloz, 2009, p. 396.
214. Article 80 of Regulation 2017/1001: 'The provisions of Article 25(3) and (4) concerning the rights of licensees shall apply to every person who has authority to use an EU collective mark.'
215. Article 25(4) of Regulation 2017/1001.
216. Article 80(2) of Regulation 2017/1001.
217. *See* Evans, *supra* n. 77.
218. *See* §3.01 *supra*.

risk of confusion more difficult for collective geographical marks. It is not disputed that the risk of confusion largely depends on the degree of distinctiveness:[219] The more distinctive the earlier trademark, the greater the likelihood of confusion between the two signs at issue.[220] Therefore, marks with a highly distinctive character enjoy a broader protection than marks with a less distinctive character.[221]

An individual trademark consisting exclusively of a GI shall not be registered because it would lack distinctiveness.[222] Although Article 74(2) relaxes the non-descriptiveness requirement at the registration stage by allowing a geographically descriptive term to be registered, it cannot give rise to a presumption that the mark has acquired an average distinctive character.[223] Its inherent distinctiveness is to be assessed in the usual way.[224] Therefore, at a later stage, any challenge by the proprietor of an earlier collective geographical mark is likely to fail if a certain degree of distinctiveness cannot be proven.

An illustration of this inconvenience is provided by the '*Halloumi*' case, where the earlier collective geographical mark '*Halloumi*' was considered as not having a particularly distinctive character on the grounds that the Greek term '*Halloumi*' designates a speciality cheese from Cyprus; 'in view of its descriptive character', the court ruled out the likelihood of confusion despite the conceptual similarity between the earlier mark and the contested mark '*Hellim*' (the Turkish translation of '*Halloumi*').[225]

219. WTO Panel Report on *European Communities: Protection of Trademarks and Geographical Indications for Agricultural Products and Foodstuffs*, WT/DS174/R, adopted 15 April 2005, p. 121.
220. Case C-251/95 *SABEL BV v. Puma AG*, *supra* n. 134, para. 24.
221. Case C-39/97 *Canon Kabushiki Kaisha v. Metro-Goldwyn-Mayer* [1998] ECR I-05507, para. 18.
222. WTO Panel Report, *supra* n. 219, at 121.
223. Case C-393/12 P *Foundation for the Protection of the Traditional Cheese of Cyprus Named Halloumi v. OHIM*, *supra* n. 113, para. 36.
224. OHIM (EUIPO), *Guidelines for Examination in the Office*, Part C Opposition (2 January 2014) p. 20. However, the European way in which the distinctiveness of a collective geographical mark might be assessed is different from the US way. In a case concerning a geographic certification mark 'Darjeeling' registered in the US, the Tea Board of India, owner of the certification mark, brought an opposition against an application to register 'Darjeeling Nouveau' by the Republic of Tea, a Californian distributor. The US Trademark Trial and Appeal Board (TTAB) began by noting that 'geographically descriptive terms are generally regarded as inherently weak and entitled to less protection than arbitrary or suggestive marks'. Ordinarily, a term that describes the geographic source is not protectable without a showing of acquired distinctiveness. However, section 2(e)(2) of the Trademark Act prohibits registration of a mark that is primarily geographically descriptive of an applicant's goods and provides a specific exception for marks used to certify indications of regional origin under section 4 of the Act. Thus, the TTAB considered that 'the presumption that a geographic term is inherently weak does not attach to geographic terms used to certify regional origin'. As a mark registered on the Principal Register, 'Darjeeling' was presumed to be inherently distinctive as a certification mark indicating geographic origin as it inherently identifies the geographic source of the tea. *See Tea Board of India v. The Republic of Tea*, 80 USPQ2d 1881 (TTAB 2006); Toshiko Takenaka, *Intellectual Property in Common Law and Civil Law* 276 (Edward Elgar 2013).
225. Case T-534/10 *Organismos Kypriakis Galaktokomikis Viomichanias v. OHMI*, *supra* n. 113, para. 55.

Although there may be a likelihood of confusion even due to an earlier mark of weak distinctive character,[226] established case law gives us the impression that collective geographical marks with a prima facie weak distinctive character enjoy narrower protection than other ordinary marks with an average or even highly distinctive character.

[c] Defence of Collective Marks in Chinese Law

As set forth above,[227] there are two main sets of requirements for the registration of GIs in the form of collective marks: first, the general rules concerning all collective marks;[228] second, the special rules governing the GI collective marks, namely collective marks composed exclusively of GIs. According to the latter, no registration would be accepted where the applicant failed to prove a link between the product's characteristics (or reputation) and the delimited geographical production area,[229] which is nevertheless an essential requirement[230] (i.e., the *terroir* link requirement) often set out under the sui generis system for the registration of GIs (e.g., the PDO/PGI regime). One is then made to wonder whether what we protect under China's trademark system is a trademark containing a GI or simply a GI.

In a judgment of 28 July 2015, concerning a GI registered through the trademark system, Beijing's High People's Court ruled that 'GIs protection is based on the fact that the natural and human factors in a given area have formed an objective thing (the product feature), which consumers can count on when making purchasing choices.'[231] While it is true that the rights conferred on the proprietor of a trademark (including the collective or certification mark composed entirely of a GI) begin on the date of approval of registration,[232] the protection of the GI of which the mark is entirely composed does not begin on that date: 'this state of protection lasts a long time'.[233] By separating the protection of a GI from the protection of a mark consisting of the GI, this judgment

226. Case T-358/09 *Sociedad Agricola Requingua Ltda v. OHIM, supra* n. 120, para. 45; Case T-112/03 *L'Oréal v. OHMI* [2005] ECR II-00949, para. 61.
227. *See* §3.01 *supra.*
228. For example, the regulations governing use must be submitted regardless of whether or not signs of which a trademark may consist constitute GIs.
229. *State Administration for Industry v. Commerce Trademark Review and Adjudication Board and Ning'an Jingpo Lake Soybean Association*, Beijing High People's Court (12 June 2016).
230. Article 7 of the Measures for Collective and Certification Marks: 'Any party applying for the registration of a geographical indication as a collective mark or a certification mark shall present the following information in the application documents: (i) the given quality, reputation or any other characteristic of the goods indicated by the geographical indication; (ii) the correlation between the given quality, reputation or any other characteristic of the goods and the natural and human factors of the region indicated by the geographical indication; (iii) the boundary of the region indicated by the geographical indication.'
231. *Chen Jianhua v. Trademark Review and Adjudication Board of the State Administration for Industry and Commerce*, Beijing High People's Court (28 July 2015); Bo, *supra* n. 172.
232. Trademark Law, Article 39: 'A trademark registration shall remain valid for a period of ten years from the date of approval for registration.'
233. *Guan Zhihuan et al. v. Trademark Administrative Disputes of the Trademark Review and Adjudication Board of the State Administration for Industry and Commerce*, Beijing First Intermediate People's Court (20 December 2010).

suggests that the subject matter of protection concerns a trademark containing a GI rather than the GI itself.[234] A GI's protection nevertheless does not depend on the registration but on the fact that the geographical environment has given the product its characteristics.

Inevitably, this raises another question: does China's trademark law protect GIs that are not yet registered in the form of collective or certification marks? Article 16(1) of the Law provides that 'it shall be prohibited to register or use a trademark that contains a GI with respect to products not originating in the region indicated, if (use of the indication in the trademark) misleads the public'. Since it does not require that the GI be registered under the trademark regime, Article 16(1) applies to all GIs, including those not registered in China;[235] thus, it is often used for the protection of foreign GIs. However, the registration of a GI in a foreign county does not give rise to the assumption that the sign or indication should be recognized as a GI in China. The plaintiff then bears the burden of proof in demonstrating that it meets the definition of GI as set forth in Article 16(2).[236] Their pleas based on an infringement of Article 16(1) would be rejected if it could not be proved that the 'products originated in a delimited geographical area possess a particular quality, reputation, or other characteristic, which is essentially attributable to natural or human factors of the area of production'.[237]

It is important to note that Article 16(1) seems to apply only in identical or similar goods situations, where the sign is used on 'the specific categories of goods concerned' not originating from the place in question.[238] In an opinion issued in 2017, the Supreme

234. It should be noted that this conclusion does not contradict the conclusion that a GI can be registered as a collective or certification mark. A trademark may consist of any signs capable of being represented graphically, including personal names, designs, letters, numerals, the shape of goods and geographical indications under certain conditions. Thus, we can say that personal names, designs, letters, or geographical indications could be registered as a trademark. However, they are just signs of which a trademark may consist. What is registered is still a trademark, which can distinguish the goods or services of one undertaking from those of other undertakings or indicate membership in an association in the case where a collective mark consists exclusively of a geographical indication.

235. *France National Office of Appellations of Origin v. Huang Xiaodong*, Beijing High People's Court (16 October 2015).

236. Although the necessity of proof always lies with the person who lays charges, China's case law also imposes some burden of proof on the defendant (after the plaintiff has proved that the trademark contains a GI). It should be the defendant's duty to make sure that his products originate in the region indicated by the GI and use of the indication in the mark does not mislead the public. *See Chen Jianhua v. Trademark Review and Adjudication Board of the State Administration for Industry and Commerce, supra* n. 231; *France National Office of Appellations of Origin v. Huang Xiaodong, supra* n. 235; *Chongqing Nantong Mining Co. Ltd. Jiuguoqing Forestry Comprehensive Branch v. the State Administration for Industry and Commerce Trademark Review and Adjudication Board*, Beijing High People's Court (5 March 2012).

237. *Ibid.*

238. In a case concerning '*Champagne*', the court in the first instance even considered that Article 16(1) only applies to identical goods situation, 'not including similar and dissimilar goods'. The analysis is not endorsed by the court in the second instance. *See France Champagne Industry Commission v. Trademark Review and Adjudication Board of the State Administration for Industry and Commerce of the People's Republic of China*, Beijing High People's Court (2 March 2012).

Court of China provided that, if the goods for which a subsequent trademark is registered is 'not identical' to the GI's goods, the party claiming infringement must prove that the use of the GI in the trademark would mislead the public and lead them to believe that the goods bearing that mark come from the area indicated by the GI and possess a particular quality, reputation, or other characteristics due to the place of origin. It is questionable if the terms 'not identical' could be understood to include 'dissimilar' goods.[239]

Article 16(1), embodying the requirements established by Article 22 of the TRIPS Agreement,[240] is constructed around the unfair competition justification. It is designed to prevent the use of a GI that misleads the public as to the geographical origin of the goods.[241] However, signs or indications may serve to designate the place of origin as well as the quality and characteristics attached solely when they are used in relation to the specific categories of goods: 'This function would not be extended to other categories.' In other words, the public is unlikely to understand the term used in connection with other categories of goods as a reference to the place of origin and thus believe that the goods originate there.[242] This introduces a limitation to the scope of protection.[243] An illustration of this limitation can be found in a series of decisions wherein French *Champagne* producers unsuccessfully resorted to Article 16(1) in a situation in which the wine appellation '*Champagne*' was registered as a trademark by third parties for dissimilar goods (e.g., cafés, hair lotions).[244]

---

239. *See* Zuigao Renmin Fayuan Guanyu Shenli Shangbiao Shouquan Quequan Xingzheng Anjian Ruogan Wenti de Guiding [Provisions of the Supreme People's Court on Several Issues Concerning the Administrative Cases of Trademark], 10 January 2017, Article 17.
240. *See* Tian Furong, DILI BIAOZHI FALU BAOHU ZHIDU YANJIU [LEGAL PROTECTION OF GEOGRAPHICAL INDICATIONS], at 259 (Intellectual Property Publishing House, 2009).
241. Article 16(1) embodies the requirements of Article 22(3) of the TRIPS Agreement. Nevertheless, the TRIPS Agreement prevents the use that misleads the public 'as to the true place of origin'. China's Trademark Law does not specify what constitutes the 'misleading use'. In 2019, Beijing High People's Court published the Guidelines for trademark cases, according to which the trademark shall be prohibited to register or use if it misleads the consumer and 'leads him to believe that the goods come from the region indicated by the GI'. In other words, in assessing the likelihood of confusion under Article 16(1), account must be taken of risk that the public might believe that the goods come from the same geographical origin, instead of the risk that the consumer might believe that the goods come from the same producer. *See* Beijing Gaoji Renmin Fayuan Guanyu Shangbiao Shouquan Quequan Xingzheng Anjian de Shenli Zhinan [Beijing High People's Court's Guide to the Trial of Administrative Cases Concerning Trademarks], 24 April 2019, Article 13.
242. *France Champagne Industry Commission v. Trademark Review and Adjudication Board of the State Administration for Industry and Commerce of the People's Republic of China*, Beijing High People's Court (6 July 2010).
243. In assessing the scope, much will depend on the interpretation of the 'the specific categories of goods concerned'. *See* Hector Mac Queen & Charlotte Waelde, *Contemporary Intellectual Property: Law and Policy* 748 (Oxford University Press 2nd ed. 2011).
244. *See France Champagne Industry Commission v. Trademark Review and Adjudication Board of the State Administration for Industry and Commerce of the People's Republic of China*, *supra* n. 242; *France Champagne Industry Commission v. Trademark Review and Adjudication Board of the State Administration for Industry and Commerce of the People's Republic of China*, Beijing First Intermediate People's Court (18 November 2010); *France Champagne Industry Commission v. Trademark Review and Adjudication Board of the State Administration for Industry and Commerce of the People's Republic of China*, Beijing High People's Court, *supra* n. 238.

Given the uncertainty surrounding the status of unregistered GIs (the link to *terroir* must be proven before protection is applied) as well as the limited scope of protection (Article 16.1 does not apply to dissimilar goods), registering GIs in the form of collective or certification marks will be a practical option.

The registration of a GI as a collective (or certification) mark will confer on the proprietor of the mark an exclusive right to use that mark in relation to the goods designated.[245] In the absence of special provisions for the GI collective mark concerning its scope of protection, general provisions governing ordinary trademarks are applicable. The mark is thus protected, in a classic way, against the use of an identical mark in respect of the same goods,[246] against the use of a similar mark in respect of the same goods,[247] or the use of an identical or similar mark in respect of goods that are similar to those goods designated in the registration, where its use is likely to cause confusion.[248]

For well-known marks, two levels of protection are afforded: Paris-type protection[249] for well-known marks that have not been registered in China (protection against the use of a mark which constitutes a reproduction, an imitation, or a translation of a well-known mark for identical or similar goods if its use is liable to create confusion);[250] and TRIPS-type protection[251] for well-known marks that have been registered in China (protection against the use for dissimilar goods if its use misleads the public and may cause damage to the interests of the registrant of the well-known mark).[252] Therefore, where a GI has been registered in China as a collective or certification mark that is well-known to the public, the scope of protection can be extended beyond 'the specific categories of goods concerned' (protection provided by Article 16.1) to dissimilar goods.

245. Trademark Law, Article 56.
246. *See* Trademark Law, Article 57(1); *Zhenjiang Vinegar Industry Association v. Xu Linjiang*, Jiangsu Suzhou Intermediate People's Court (5 June 2008); *Zhenjiang Vinegar Industry Association v. Anhui Tengfei Food Co. Ltd.*, Anhui Fuyang Intermediate People's Court (2010); *Rice Association of Sheyang County Jiangsu Province v. Ge Zhucun*, Jiangsu Yancheng Intermediate People's Court (4 September 2014).
247. *See Chengdu Pidu District Food Industry Association v. Nanjing Jiangning District Lao Menggan Store, Pixian Qiaoshufang Trading Co., Ltd.*, and Pingxiang County Kangjia Pickle Factory, Sichuan Pixian People's Court (2019 CHUAN 0124 MIN CHU 6851 HAO); *Conseil Interprofessionnel du Vin de Bordeaux v. Penglai Yunque Winery Co. Ltd*, Shandong High People's Court (13 May 2019).
248. *See* Trademark Law, Article 57(2); *Sheyang County Rice Association v. Dafeng City Baiju Town Jian Feng Rice Factory*, Jiangsu Dafeng Intermediate People's Court (20 June 2014).
249. Article 6bis of the Paris Convention prohibits the use of a reproduced, imitated, or translated well-known mark if there is a likelihood of confusion in the public's mind and it is used for 'identical or similar goods'.
250. Trademark Law, Article 13(2).
251. Article 16(3) of the TRIPS Agreement provides that Article 6bis of the Paris Convention shall apply to goods or services 'which are not similar' to those in respect of which a trademark is registered, if the use of that trademark in relation to those goods or services would indicate a connection between those goods or services and the owner of the registered trademark and provided that the interests of the owner of the registered trademark are likely to be damaged by such use.
252. Trademark Law, Article 13(3).

Lastly, account must also be taken of the special treatment of GIs for wines and spirits, which is known as the 'additional protection' as set forth in Article 23 of the TRIPS Agreement. Article 12 of the Measures for Collective and Certification Marks prevents the use of a GI identifying wines/spirits for wines/spirits not originating in the place indicated by the GI in question, even if the true origin of the goods is indicated or the GI is used in translation or the GI is accompanied by expressions such as 'kind', 'type', 'style', or 'imitation'.[253] Regarding the scope of Article 12, its main feature is the absence of any requirement for misleading use and of any need to establish confusion.[254] However, this rule applies only to GIs that have been registered as collective or certification marks.[255] It is thus questionable whether the enhanced protection is granted to GIs or to marks containing them. As Li Yahong observed, under the Trademark Law of 2003, 'no (additional) protection is provided for geographical indications for wines and spirits'.[256] This might be at least partially true considering that unregistered GIs are not within the ambit of Article 12.

To conclude, we note that, while GIs can be protected in the form of collective marks, they act as a brand but also indicate the geographical origin of the goods:[257] They can be both distinctive and descriptive of a geographical origin. The distinguishing function explains why an exclusive right should be granted, whereas the descriptive function (where the term has a descriptive meaning about the place of origin) explains why fair use should be allowed. However, the descriptive meaning of the place name is likely to dilute the distinctiveness of the mark, which may impede judicial remedies. Perhaps that is why the European trademark system plays only a minor role in protecting GIs.[258] By contrast, China's trademark system has constantly evolved its rules to protect not only collective marks containing GIs but also GIs themselves. This is evident from the fact that the link to *terroir* serves as a basis for the protection of both the GI collective marks and of the unregistered GIs under Article 16(2) of the Trademark Law. As GI collective marks are *terroir*-based, their function is perceived as equivalent to that of GIs. A sub-divisional special regime is introduced for those marks within the special regime of collective marks.

253. Article 12 of the Measures for Collective and Certification Marks only applies to GIs that are used for wines and spirits, not including dissimilar goods.
254. Wang Xiaobing, LUN DILI BIAOZHI DE FALU BAOHU [LEGAL PROTECTION OF GEOGRAPHICAL INDICATIONS], at 224 (China Renmin University Press, 2006).
255. Measures for Collective and Certification Marks, Article 12: 'Where any party uses another party's geographical indication for wines or spirits registered as a collective mark or certification mark to identify wines or spirits not originating in the place indicated by the geographical indication in question ... Article 16 of the Trademark Law shall apply.'
256. Li Yahong, *The Wolf Has Come: Are China's Intellectual Property Industries Prepared for the WTO*, 20 UCLA Pac. Basin L.J. 77, 88 (2002); Peter K. Yu, *From Pirates to Partners (Episode II): Protecting Intellectual Property in Post-WTO China*, 55 Am. UL Rev. 901 (2005).
257. Dev Gangjee, *Protecting Geographical Indications as Collective Trademarks: The Prospects and Pitfalls*, Institute of Intellectual Property (10 May 2021), https://www.iip.or.jp/e/summary/pdf/detail2005/e17_14.pdf.
258. *See* Fontaine, *supra* n. 117.

§3.02 REGIME OF CERTIFICATION MARKS

A certification mark can send a message to consumers that the product is certified as having certain characteristics, which may also include the geographical origin. The function of certification marks could thus support the function of GIs. GIs can also be registered as certification marks, and their protection is enforced in accordance with the applicable rules of trademark law.

[A] Registration of GIs in the Form of Certification Marks

'The function of certification marks can be seen as complimentary to a GI.'[259] A certification mark can be used to certify the geographical origin, material, production method, or other characteristics of a good. More importantly, the same mark can be used to certify more than one characteristic. For instance, the mark '*Darjeeling*' (registered in the United States as a regional certification mark) certifies that the tea originates from a specific region of India and that the quality meets other specifications established by the certifier.[260] Similarly, the mark '*Roquefort*' is used to indicate that the cheese has been manufactured from sheep's milk and cured in the Roquefort area of France in accordance with traditional production methods.[261]

There is no doubt that a certification mark is capable of informing purchasers that the products possess certain characteristics linked to their place of origin. The link to the *terroir* can be included in the regulations governing the use of the certification mark and be the object of certification. To appreciate the role of the certification mark regime in GI protection, it is necessary to understand the nature of certification marks.

[1] Certification Marks

Certification marks belong to an independent category of marks that have a function different from that of ordinary trademarks. Those marks are specially regulated in the French and Chinese trademark systems, as well as the EU-wide system since Regulation 2015/2424 amended Regulation 207/2009 (codified and repealed by Regulation 2017/1001).

259. Intellectual Property Office (UK), *Guidance on Collective and Certification Trade Marks*, UK Government (10 May 2021), https://www.gov.uk/government/publications/collective-and-certification-trade-marks.
260. McCarthy, *supra* n. 17, § 14:21.
261. *Geographical Indication Protection in the United States*, United States Patent and Trademark Office (USPTO) (10 May 2021), https://www.uspto.gov/sites/default/files/web/offices/dcom/olia/globalip/pdf/gi_system.pdf.

[a] Collective Certification Marks (Guarantee Marks) in French Law

It should first be observed that French legislation differed from EU terminology ('guarantee or certification marks')[262] by referring to 'collective certification mark (*marque collective de certification*)'. Former Article L. 715-1 of the IP Code defined it as a mark 'applied for goods or services which present, especially as to their nature, properties or qualities, the characters listed in the regulation of use'.[263] Without indicating the commercial origin of goods, the collective certification mark informs purchasers that the goods or services to which the mark applies satisfy certain requirements laid down in the regulation of use, especially as regards their nature, components, manufacture process, or quality. In short, it certifies the presence of characteristics that make the goods different from those with ordinary collective marks or individual marks.[264]

Although the geographical origin is not expressly listed as one of the characteristics being certified, this does not preclude a collective certification mark from certifying the place of origin (e.g., '*Laguiole Origine Garantie*' or '*Origine France Garantie*').

In the Order of 13 November 2019, the French IP replaced the term 'collective certification mark' with 'guarantee marks', which is used in Directive 2015/2436. The French guarantee mark is defined in Article L. 715-1 as 'a mark so designated when it is filed and capable of distinguishing the products or services for which the material, method of manufacture or service, quality, precision or other characteristics are guaranteed'.[265] Again, the geographical origin is not expressly mentioned as a quality that can be guaranteed by French guarantee marks. It is questionable if the geographical origin can be classified as 'other characteristics' that can be certified.[266]

262. Article 27 of Directive 2015/2436: '"guarantee or certification mark" means a trade mark which is described as such when the mark is applied for and is capable of distinguishing goods or services which are certified by the proprietor of the mark in respect of material, mode of manufacture of goods or performance of services, quality, accuracy or other characteristics, from goods and services which are not so certified'.
263. Ancien Article L. 715-1(2) CPI: '*La marque collective de certification est appliquée au produit ou au service qui présente notamment, quant à sa nature, ses propriétés ou ses qualités, des caractères précisés dans son règlement.*' The English translation is by Nicolas Bouche. *See* Bouche, *supra* n. 83, at 188.
264. It should be noted that an ordinary collective mark might have the regulations governing use, which could be simple (containing only one term) or be elaborate (containing a certain number of requirements with regard to the characteristics of products. The Court of Cassation has held that it is seen as an ordinary collective mark if it is not available to any person whose products/services meet the requirement of the regulations governing use, as the case of a collective certification mark. In other words, an ordinary collective mark could be associated with regulations governing use in which quality requirements are provided. It should not be considered as collective certification marks as long as it is reserved to affiliated entities of the trademark owner. *See* Cass. com., 3 juin 2008, n° 07-15.050.
265. Article L. 715-1 CPI: '*Une marque de garantie est une marque ainsi désignée lors de son dépôt et propre à distinguer les produits ou les services pour lesquels la matière, le mode de fabrication ou de prestation, la qualité, la précision ou d'autres caractéristiques sont garantis.*'
266. Nicolas Binctin, *Marque collective et marque de garantie: Ordonnance et décret d'application issus de la transposition du 'Paquet Marques'*, Communication commerce électronique, n° 5, 2020, étude 10: 'Cette liste n'est pas limitative et il est possible qu'un déposant de marque de

[b] EU Certification Marks

Since the introduction of Regulation 2015/2424, the EU-wide trademark system provides protection to EU certification marks. One wonders if those marks can be used to certify the specific geographical origin of the goods.

The draft Regulation defines the EU certification mark as a European trademark 'which is capable of distinguishing goods or services which are certified by the proprietor of the mark in respect of geographical origin, material, mode of manufacture of goods or performance of services, quality, accuracy or other characteristic from goods and services which are not so certified'.[267] The definition includes 'geographical origin' as one of the characteristics that can be certified by the owner of the certification mark.

Nevertheless, the definition given in the final text of Regulation 2015/2424 expressly excludes 'geographical origin'. According to the newly added Article 74a (now Article 83 of Regulation 2017/1001), an EU certification mark is an EU trademark that is capable of distinguishing goods certified by the proprietor of the mark in respect of material, mode of manufacture, quality, accuracy, or other characteristics 'with the exception of geographical origin' from goods that are not so certified.[268] This clear exclusion is contrary to the expectation that the use of certification marks can be more actively encouraged for GI protection.[269]

[c] Certification Marks in Chinese Law

According to Article 3(3) of the Trademark Law, a certification mark is a mark that is controlled by an organization capable of supervising specific categories of goods or services and used by a party or parties other than the owner of the mark to certify some aspect of the third parties' goods/services, particularly with regard to their *geographical origin*, material, mode of manufacture, quality, or other characteristics.

Unlike in the European legislation, the definition given in China's trademark law clearly mentions the role that the certifications mark can play in certifying the geographical origin.

---

garantie identifie un aspect spécifique d'un produit ou service et qu'il souhaite le mettre en avant pour tous les opérateurs grâce à ce signe collectif.'

267. European Commission, *Proposal for a Regulation of the European Parliament and of the Council Amending Council Regulation No 207/2009 on the Community Trade Mark*, COM(2013)161 final (27 March 2013).
268. Olivier Thrierr, *Quel(s) nouveau(x) droit(s) des marques dans l'Union européenne?*, Propriété industrielle, n° 7, 2016, étude 14.
269. *See* European Commission, *Green Paper on Agricultural Product Quality: Product Standards, Farming Requirements and Quality Schemes*, COM(2008)641 final (15 October 2008) p. 13; Vincent Ruzek, *La stratégie communautaire de protection des indications géographiques en question*, Droit rural, n° 373, 2009, étude 7.

This brief review of the definition of certification marks shows that they are an instrument for distinguishing products that are certified to possess certain characteristics or qualities from those that are not so certified.[270] Their quality guarantee function might be attractive for the protection of GIs.

[2] Certification Marks: An Alternative Instrument for GI Protection?

While it might be possible to protect GIs as certification marks (as advocated by the US), European legislators are so strongly in favour of the sui generis system of GIs that they essentially preclude the use of the regime of certification marks.[271] By contrast, under the influence of the US, greater importance has been attached by China's government to protecting GIs within the trademark system with the aim of adding value to agricultural products and boosting the rural economy.[272]

[a] Registering GIs in the Form of Collective Certification Marks (Guarantee Marks) in French Law

The use of collective certification marks (French guarantee marks) for GIs protection is restricted in France. The first reason for this relates to the fact that those certification marks are subject to the same requirement for distinctive characteristics as those that apply to ordinary trademarks.

Regarding the 'distinctiveness' requirement, Article 15(2) of the former Directive 2008/95/EC (also Article 28(4) of Directive 2015/2436)[273] allows the Member States to adopt special rules for certification marks by way of derogation from the general rules applying to ordinary trademarks.[274] This means that, in a Member State where the

270. Since the Law of 1991, the French legislation has made a difference, based on their functions, between a mark that is used to distinguish the products or services of the members of an association from those of others (individual mark or ordinary collective mark), and a mark that is used to distinguish the products or services that present some special features from those that do not have such features (collective certification mark).

271. Some authors note that European countries are hostile towards certification marks because they view them as threatening the European system of protecting geographic indications. *See* B. Brett Heavner & Michael R. Justus, *Worldwide Certification-Mark Registration: A Certifiable Nightmare*, 2 Landslide 21 (2009).

272. WIPO, *Symposium Promotes Better Understanding of GIs as Tool for Wealth Creation*, UPD/2007/295 (2 July 2007).

273. Article 28(4) of Directive 2015/2436: 'By way of derogation from Article 4(1)(c), Member States may provide that signs or indications which may serve, in trade, to designate the geographical origin of the goods or services may constitute guarantee or certification marks.'

274. Article 15(2) of Directive 2008/95/EC: 'By way of derogation from Article 3(1)(c), Member States may provide that signs or indications which may serve, in trade, to designate the geographical origin of the goods or services may constitute collective, guarantee or certification marks. Such a mark does not entitle the proprietor to prohibit a third party from using in the course of trade such signs or indications, provided he uses them in accordance with honest practices in industrial or commercial matters; in particular, such a mark may not be invoked against a third party who is entitled to use a geographical name.' *See Directive 2008/95/EC of the European Parliament and of the Council of 22 October 2008 to approximate the laws of the Member States relating to trade marks*, JO L 299, 8.11.2008, p. 25.

special provisions have been adopted, indications that are purely descriptive of the geographical origin of the goods (including GIs) can be registered as a guarantee or certification marks.[275]

This is the case in the UK, for instance, where a certification mark may be registered even if it consists of indications that may serve to designate the geographical origin of the goods or services,[276] 'notwithstanding section 3(1)(c) of Trade Mark Act' aiming at keeping descriptive indications free for legitimate use by other traders.[277] In order to justify this derogation, the UK IP Office notes, 'When considering the distinctiveness of a mark, it is important to appreciate that the distinguishing function of certification marks differs from that of ordinary trademarks.'[278] Then, it provides an example to illustrate this argument: the geographical name '*Bordeaux*' would not be registrable as an individual trademark or a collective mark, as there are a number of different producers and producer associations; it is unlikely that the consumer would regard it as pointing towards a specific trade source. On the other hand, '*Bordeaux*' appears to be capable of distinguishing wines that are certified from those that are not because French wine region names have been used for decades to certify geographical origin.[279] Thus, a GI that is considered to lack a distinctive character as an ordinary trademark may be acceptable as a certification mark if it is capable of performing the special function.

As Professor Jérôme Passa noted, geographical certification marks, on account of their special function, could derogate from the general distinctiveness requirement applying to individual marks.[280] The International Association for the Protection of Intellectual Property (AIPPI) also suggests that certification marks could consist solely of ISs or GIs even though they actually designate the geographical origin of the goods or services.[281]

Since the certification mark referred to in Article 15(2) can be exploited together with the PDO/PGI,[282] it may serve as a complementary tool for ensuring additional

275. *See* Gielen & Bomhard, *supra* n. 23, at 352.
276. Trade Marks Act 1994, s. 2, Article 3(1).
277. Section 3(c) of Trade Marks Act 1994: 'trade marks which consist exclusively of signs or indications which may serve, in trade, to designate the kind, quality, quantity, intended purpose, value, geographical origin, the time of production of goods or of rendering of services, or other characteristics of goods or services'.
278. *See* Intellectual Property Office (UK), *Trade Marks Manual*, 3 March 2009 (last updated at 31 March 2016), p. 302. The Manual provides us with an example: the mark '100% minced beef' may not be acceptable as an ordinary trademark in respect of meat or meat products (it is unlikely that the average consumer will regard it as pointing towards a single trade source for these goods) but would be acceptable as a certification mark as it is capable of performing that particular distinguishing function.
279. *See* Intellectual Property Office (UK), *Guidance on Collective and Certification Trade Marks*, UK Government (10 May 2021), https://www.gov.uk/government/publications/collective-and-certification-trade-marks.
280. Passa, *supra* n. 35, para. 44.
281. *Question 118: Trade and Service Marks and Geographical Indications*, *supra* n. 3, at 408-412.
282. Article 12(5) of Regulation 1151/2012: 'Without prejudice to Directive 2000/13/EC, the collective geographical marks referred to in Article 15 of Directive 2008/95/EC may be used on labels, together with the protected designation of origin or protected geographical indication.'

protection for GIs.[283] Moreover, it could also be used each time the requirements for GI registration (which are burdensome) are not met, which is particularly relevant for the defence of handicrafts.

Nevertheless, French legislators have chosen not to adopt special provisions under Article 15(2). This means that the 'distinctiveness' criterion applicable to individual trademarks applies equally to certification marks.[284] As a logical consequence, given the lack of distinctive character, a GI per se would not be registrable as a French guarantee mark.[285] However, since the distinctiveness should be assessed in light of all the elements of which the mark is composed,[286] a mark that partly contained a geographically descriptive reference could be regarded as having a distinctive nature if the other part of the mark included a distinctive sign[287] or other descriptive signs provided that they were configured in a manner that distinguished the resultant whole from the usual way of designating the geographical origin of the goods concerned or their essential characteristics.[288] In this respect, the collective mark '*Qualité France*' was judged distinctive in relation to the designated goods or services.[289] Similarly, the French guarantee mark '*Laguiole Origine Garantie*' was accepted as valid since the geographical reference '*Laguiole*', which could be regarded as descriptive, was accompanied by other distinctive elements (i.e., a figure).[290]

The second reason why the use of French guarantee marks is restricted is that they are deemed to threaten the protection of GIs. This perception has manifested itself in the evolution of the official certification signs '*Label Rouge*' ('Label' hereinafter), 'Regional Label', and 'Product Conformity Certificate' ('CCP' hereinafter).[291] Label was created in the 1960s as a collective mark to attest that a product conformed to certain qualities and characteristics.[292] It is worth pointing out that the first products benefiting from it were designated by their geographical origins: the '*Poulet des Landes*' and the

283. WIPO, *Study on the Relationship Between Regional Systems for the Protection of Geographical Indications and the Lisbon System; and on the Conditions for Accession to the Lisbon Agreement by Intergovernmental Organizations*, LI/WG/DEV/2/3 (6 August 2010) p. 23.
284. The mark '*Palace*' (collective certification mark) has been cancelled for lack of distinctiveness when it designates the hotel services. *See* C.A. Paris, 13 Janv. 2015, n° 13/12820: '*... le signe "Palace" est étroitement lié aux services hôteliers visés en classe 43 en désignant une de leurs caractéristiques, en l'espèce la qualité et la valeur de la prestation de service au sens de l'article L 711-2 sous b) du code de la propriété intellectuelle ...*'.
285. Laurence Bineau, *Une extension attendue de l'indication géographique protégée aux produits manufacturés*, Contrats concurrence consommation, n° 2, 2013, étude 3.
286. Case C-383/99 P *Procter & Gamble v. OHIM*, *supra* n. 89, para. 40.
287. Case C-353/03 *Société des produits Nestlé SA v. Mars UK Ltd* [2005] ECR I-06135, para. 32.
288. For example, trademarks such as '*Laguiole innove la tradition*', '*Laguiole Shopper*', '*Baron Laguiole*', '*Laguiole Cuisinier de Père en Fils*', '*Domaine Laguiole*', '*Laguiole Generation*', '*Laguiole Le Jardinier*' and '*Laguiole Premium*' have been considered valid even though the terms added may also be descriptive. *See* C.A. Paris, 4 avr. 2014, n° 12/20559.
289. C.A. Paris, 4 déc. 1978, Ann. Propr. Ind. 1980, p. 123.
290. C.A. Paris, 3 nov. 1999, Ann. Propr. Ind. 2000, p. 115.
291. *See* Denis Rochard, *Labels et certifications de conformité*, J.-Cl. Qualité des produits, fasc. 20.
292. Loi n° 60-808 du 5 août 1960 d'orientation agricole, J.O. du 07 août 1960, p. 07364: '*Le label agricole est une marque collective qui s'applique aux produits agricoles, attestant que le produit qui en bénéficie possède un ensemble distinct de qualités et de caractéristiques spécifiques.*'

'*Poulet de Loué*'.[293] The geographical approach continued with the creation of the Regional Label (1970s), certifying that regional agricultural products had specific features 'due in particular to their origin'[294] and with the arrival of the CCP (1990s),[295] certifying that a product was compliant with specific regulations that distinguished it from ordinary products and that related to production, processing, packaging, and, since the Law of 1994, the 'geographical origin of the food or the product'.[296] Following the emergence of the PDO/PGI system, Label and CCP were further anchored in the geographical dimension since they were required as a precondition for the PGI application.[297]

However, this trend has been reversed in favour of a simplified regime for the protection of GIs. The Regional Label was gradually phased out because GI protection can be afforded only within the uniform PDO/PGI framework.[298] However, this effort alone was not deemed enough: 'The system is too complex, not understandable to the market ... There is a chaos in geographical appellations.'[299] In order to simplify and clarify the system, the Order of 2006 established the 'principle of separation' between GI and Label/CCP:[300] producers no longer need to get the Label/CCP in applying for the PGI since the reform affords direct access to each of the signs.[301] The geographical reference must not appear on the Label/CCP unless the reference has become a generic term for the product. The Label/CCP cannot be used jointly with an AO.[302] However,

293. Norbert Olszak, *Appellations d'origine et indications de provenance*, Répertoire Dalloz de droit pénal et de procédure pénale, 2008 (actualité 2015), para. 116.
294. Décret n° 76-974 du 28 octobre 1976 relatif aux marques collectives régionales assimilées à des labels agricoles, J.O. du 30 oct. 1976, p. 6328, Article 1er: '*Toute marque collective tendant à attester que des produits agricoles régionaux présentent des caractères spécifiques, dus en particulier à leur origine ...*'.
295. Loi n° 88-1202 du 30 décembre 1988 relative à l'adaptation de l'exploitation agricole à son environnement économique et social, J.O. du 31 déc. 1988, p. 16748.
296. The Product Conformity Certificate (CCP) identified by their geographical origin includes, for example, '*Géraniums d'Alsace*' and '*Sel de Guérande*'. *See* Loi n° 94-2 du 3 janvier 1994 relative à la reconnaissance de qualité des produits agricoles et alimentaires, J.O. du 4 janv. 1994, p. 131, Article 1er: '*La certification de conformité atteste qu'une denrée alimentaire ou qu'un produit agricole non alimentaire et non transformé est conforme à des caractéristiques spécifiques ou à des règles préalablement fixées dans un cahier des charges portant, selon le cas, sur la production, la transformation ou le conditionnement et, le cas échéant, l'origine géographique de la denrée ou du produit lorsque cette origine est enregistrée comme indication géographique protégée.*'
297. Loi n° 94-2 du 3 janvier 1994, Article 4: '*La demande d'enregistrement d'une indication géographique ou d'une attestation de spécificité ne peut s'effectuer que dans le cadre des dispositions de la section II du présent chapitre (Labels et certification des produits alimentaires et agricoles).*'
298. *See* Case C-6/02 *Commission v. France* [2003] ECR I-02389, para. 20.
299. Philippe Vasseur, *La future loi d'orientation agricole*, France Agricole, 14 févr. 1997, p. 10.
300. Assemblé Nationale, *Rapport sur le projet de loi, adopté par le Sénat, ratifiant l'ordonnance n° 2006-1547 du 7 décembre 2006 relative à la valorisation des produits agricoles, forestiers ou alimentaires et des produits de la mer*, n° 437, 28 nov. 2007, pp. 20 and 37.
301. *Ibid.*, p. 41.
302. *See* Ordonnance n° 2006-1547, Chapitre Ier, section 1, Sous-section 1: '*Une denrée ou un produit peut bénéficier simultanément d'un label rouge et d'une indication géographique protégée ou d'une spécialité traditionnelle garantie mais non d'un label rouge et d'une appellation d'origine ou de la dénomination "vins de pays". Un label rouge ne peut comporter de mention géographique, à moins que celle-ci figure dans la dénomination devenue générique du*

considering their historic linkage with the PGI, a joint application remains possible between the Label/CCP and a GI in a narrower sense.[303] It is obvious that this separation reduces the geographical approach adopted in the early years.

In summary, the role of French certification (guarantee) marks, official or unofficial, is limited as a result of the 'distinctiveness' requirement under the common law of trademarks and the reform that has simplified the systems of GI protection.

[b] Registering GIs in the Form of EU Certification Marks

As mentioned,[304] Article 83 of Regulation 2017/1001 excludes 'geographical origin' from the list of product characteristics that can be certified by the proprietor of the certification mark. As a logical corollary, the rules governing certification marks do not provide for any derogation from the grounds for refusal set out in Article 7(1)(c). In other words, signs describing the geographical origin of the goods cannot be registered as certification marks, and, even if the signs are distinctive, they cannot certify geographical origin.[305] However, descriptive EU collective marks can be registered under Article 74(2).

The Guidelines of the EUIPO of 2021 state that the following signs should not be accepted as EU certification marks:

(1) where the sign will be perceived by the relevant public as an indication that the goods or services at issue will be certified in respect of their geographical origin;
(2) where the Regulations of use indicate that the characteristic being certified is the geographical origin of the goods or services or impose an obligation of a geographical nature (e.g., the location of the place of production);
(3) where the list of goods and services explicitly specifies that the goods and services have a geographical origin or comply with a PDO/PGI.

---

produit'; Ordonnance n° 2006-1547, Chapitre Ier, section 3: '*Les produits bénéficiant d'une appellation d'origine, d'un label rouge ou de la mention "vin de pays" ne peuvent faire l'objet d'une certification de conformité. Le certificat de conformité ne peut comporter de mention géographique, à moins que celle-ci figure dans la dénomination devenue générique du produit.*' *See* Ordonnance n° 2006-1547 du 7 décembre 2006 relative à la valorisation des produits agricoles, forestiers ou alimentaires et des produits de la mer, J.O. du 8 déc. 2006, p. 18607; *See also* Ordonnance n° 2010-459 du 6 mai 2010 modifiant les livres Ier, V et VI du code rural, J.O. du 7 mai 2010, texte n° 43.

303. As a response to numerous claims raised by operators producing both under the Label and the PGI, the Law of 2007 sets out another exception to the 'principle of separation'. Today, when associated with the PGI, the Label is entitled to incorporate geographical reference in its name or *cahier des charges*. *See* Loi n° 2007-1821 du 24 décembre 2007 ratifiant l'ordonnance n° 2006-1547, Article 3: '*Un label rouge ne peut comporter de référence géographique ni dans sa dénomination ni dans son cahier des charges, sauf: si le nom utilisé constitue une dénomination devenue générique du produit; ou si le label rouge est associé à une indication géographique protégée enregistrée ….*'

304. *See* §3.01 *supra*.

305. *See* Folliard-Monguiral, *supra* n. 16.

In particular, the EUIPO points out that a certification mark that contains a GI in its sign, list of goods, and services and/or regulations governing use will be objected to under Article 83 of Regulation 2017/1001.[306]

It appears that the Regulation excludes the option of using the certification mark instrument to protect GIs at the EU level. This shows that the EU is distancing itself from the 'New World' countries' policy for protecting GIs.[307]

[c] Registering GIs in the Form of Certification Marks in Chinese Law

China attaches greater importance to protecting GIs through certification marks than do France or the EU. Although it is, in principle, forbidden to register as a trademark the geographical name of a Chinese administrative division at or above the county level, one exemption applies to certification marks.[308]

As can be seen from the definition, the certification mark does not serve to guarantee the identity of the commercial origin of the product or service covered by it, which is the essential function of the individual trademark. Rather, it serves to certify some aspect of the third parties' goods or services. Based on its special function, 'the certification mark can consist exclusively of geographical signs or indications'.[309]

In several cases, Chinese Courts have observed that the 'GI certification mark'[310] indicates the place of origin and certifies the quality or other characteristics of the good that are essentially attributable to the climate/soil, the ecological environment, or special processing methods.[311] The purpose of the protection afforded to the mark is not to grant the proprietor a monopoly on a geographical term but to protect the '*terroir* resources' by virtue of the special function of the mark.[312]

Since the function of the GI certification mark is seen as complementary or equivalent to that of a GI, an additional requirement is imposed for registering certification marks containing GIs: the applicant must prove that quality, reputation, or other feature of the product is essentially attributed to its place of origin. The same

306. EUIPO, *Guidelines for Examination*, Part B (1 March 2021) p. 656.
307. In New World countries such as Australia, the US and Canada, certification marks have been used for years to protect geographical indications.
308. Trademark Law, Article 10.
309. *Guzhang Tea Industry Development Research Centre v. Hunan Huaming Tea Industry Co. Ltd.*, Hunan Changsha Tianxin District People's Court (23 October 2009).
310. Like the 'GI collective mark', 'GI certification mark' is not a terminology in the legislative text. However, it is frequently used in practice to describe certification marks composed of GIs.
311. *Changsha Yulu Enterprise Marketing Planning Co. Ltd. v. the Trademark Review and Adjudication Board of the State Administration for Industry and Commerce*, *supra* n. 145; *Zhoushan Fishery Circuits and Processing Industry Association v. Beijing Shenmaren Food Sales Co. Ltd. and Beijing Huaguan Trading Co. Ltd.*, Beijing High People's Court (8 November 2012); *Hangzhou Xihu District Longjing Tea Industry Association v. Beijing Yonghui Supermarket Co. Ltd.*, Beijing Dongcheng District People's Court (14 October 2014); *Xuzhouren Heju Food Factory v. Panjin Rice Association*, Jiangsu High People's Court (5 September 2013); *Beijing Hualian Comprehensive Supermarket Co. Ltd. Harbin First Branch Company v. Bayingolin Mongolian Autonomous Prefecture Korla Fragrant Pear Association*, Heilongjiang High People's Court (12 November 2019).
312. *Guzhang Tea Industry Development Research Centre v. Hunan Huaming Tea Industry Co. Ltd.*, *supra* n. 309.

requirement applies to collective marks, as we have already seen.[313] In sum, the practice of recognizing GIs within the regime of certification marks and collective marks is well-established in China.

[B] Protection of GIs Through Certification Marks

The regime of certification marks could be used to protect GIs due to certain features of the regime and the protection afforded to the marks.

[1] Special Regime of Certification Marks

In order to ensure a quality guarantee, the rules of certification marks differ from the rules for general trademarks.[314] Besides the special regime for all certification marks, China has adopted another set of rules for GI certification marks.

[a] Special Regime of Collective Certification Marks (Guarantee Marks) in French Law

Unsurprisingly, the special dispositions applied to French guarantee marks have many similarities with the rules protecting GIs.

The first special rule concerns the requirements of the right holder. In order to avoid an absurd quality control system in which the controlled and the controller are one and the same,[315] the right to file a French guarantee mark is reserved to legal persons who are not the manufacturer, importer, or seller of the goods or services (i.e., the right holder is not engaged in an activity relating to the supply of products or services of the same type as those guaranteed).[316] Furthermore, the certification requirements governed by the Rural Code and the Consumer Code might affect the applicant,[317] who must then be accredited.[318] In the agri-food sector, the certificate of

313. *See* § 3.01 *supra*.
314. Certification marks are generally subject to the common regime of the trademark system. However, several special dispositions may apply to these marks on specific issues to ensure their certification function. These special rules primarily consist of obligations and restrictions, such as the additional requirement of applicants, the deposition of regulations governing use, and the restricted transmissibility. They are justified by the policy goal of certification marks: for general interests or the protection of consumers.
315. Under a reasonable control system, the controlled cannot be the controller. *See* Jean Foyer, *Commentaire de la loi du 4 janvier 1991 relative aux marques de fabrique, de commerce et de service*, Actualités législatives Dalloz, 1991, p. 69.
316. Article L. 715-2(1) CPI: '*Peut déposer une marque de garantie toute personne physique ou morale y compris une personne morale de droit public, sous réserve que cette personne n'exerce pas une activité ayant trait à la fourniture de produits ou de services du même type que ceux qui sont garantis.*'
317. Article L. 641-20-L. 641-24 of the Rural Code (*La certification de conformité*) and Article L. 433-3-L. 433-11 of the Consumer Code (*Certification des services et des produits autres qu'agricoles, forestiers, alimentaires ou de la mer*).
318. *See* Article R. 715-1(8) CPI: '*Le règlement d'usage mentionné à l'article L. 715-2 comprend: … Le cas échéant, lorsque la législation l'impose, le nom, le numéro d'accréditation et l'attestation*

compliance is issued by a certification body accredited on the basis of standards relating to the requirements for certification bodies: impartiality, competence, confidentiality and openness, responsiveness to complaints and appeals, and responsibility.[319] For bodies certifying industrial products and services, accreditation is also required in the Consumer Code.[320] Thus Professor Pascale Tréfigny observes, 'It seems necessary that collective certification marks (French guarantee marks) must be filed by an independent certification body.'[321] This is an attempt to impose a neutrality that ensures the protection of the general interest: the right holder must be competent in the task of certification and be able to implement an objective and impartial control over the use of his mark. It is also for this reason that the applicant must receive approval from the Ministry concerned.

The second rule relates to the regulations governing use,[322] which must be included in the documents submitted for the registration of a French guarantee mark. Failing this, the mark will be declared invalid.[323] These regulations remind us of the '*cahier des charges* (product specification)' required in the GI regime. However, despite the importance placed on such regulations, the law does not specify what details they should contain. Does this mean that the content of the regulations depends on the free will of the applicant? From the doctrinal standpoint, the French guarantee mark aims

---

d'accréditation du ou des organismes de certification. L'accréditation doit être en lien avec l'objet du dépôt de la marque. Dans le cas où l'organisme de certification n'est pas encore accrédité, le document attestant de la recevabilité de la demande d'accréditation et de la portée d'accréditation demandée doit également être fourni.' See also WIPO, *Contribution de la France: Aspects Techniques et Procéduraux de L'enregistrement des Marques de Certification et des Marques Collectives*, SCT/21 (22 July 2009).

319. According to Article L. 641-23 and L. 641-24 of the Rural Code, the certificate of compliance shall be issued by a certification body, which is accredited under the conditions fixed by under conditions laid down by decree of the *Conseil d'Etat*. Article R. 641-61 (*Modifié par Décret n° 2017-775 du 4 mai 2017 relatif à la valorisation des produits agricoles, forestiers ou alimentaires et des produits de la mer*) specifies that 'the certification bodies are accredited by an accreditation body signatory to the multilateral agreement made within the framework of the European coordination of accreditation bodies, on the basis of the standard relating to the requirements for bodies certifying products, processes and services applicable to bodies carrying out product certification'.

320. Loi n° 2008-776 du 4 août 2008 de modernisation de l'économie, Article 137 (Article L. 433-4 du Code de la consommation): '*Peuvent seuls procéder à la certification de produits ou de services les organismes qui bénéficient d'une accréditation délivrée par l'instance nationale d'accréditation ....*' In France, the *Comité français d'accréditation* (COFRAC) has been designated as the only national body of accreditation (*Décret n° 2008-1401 du 19 décembre 2008 relatif à l'accréditation et à l'évaluation de conformité pris en application de l'article 137 de la loi n° 2008-776 du 4 août 2008 de modernisation de l'économie*). The COFRAC exercises its power of accreditation in many areas such as industrial products and services included in the scope of Article L. 433-3 of the Consumer Code, the compliance certification products (the Rural Code, Article L. 640-2, L. 641-20-24, and Article R. 641-58-R. 641-68), and the PDO/PGI products.

321. Pascale Tréfigny, *Conditions d'obtention du droit de marque*, J.-Cl. Marques Dessins et modèles, fasc. 600.

322. Article L. 715-2(2) CPI: '*Le dépôt d'une demande d'enregistrement de marque de garantie est accompagné d'un règlement d'usage. Toute modification ultérieure du règlement d'usage est portée à la connaissance de l'Institut national de la propriété industrielle.*'

323. *See* T.G.I. Paris, 15 mai 2014, n° 12/16452, PIBD 2014. III. 780.

to provide the customer with guarantees regarding the product's specific characteristics. 'This is indeed a quality promise', which therefore should be contained in the regulations governing use.[324] Albert Chavanne even describes collective certification marks (French guarantee marks) as marks 'whose regulations specify the nature, the characteristics or the qualities of products or services'.[325] Similarly from the implementation standpoint, the INPI states that 'The regulations should point out the characteristics of the goods or services.' It further suggests that regulations may take the form of a '*cahier des charges*'.[326]

Third, the properly filed regulations, not the free will of the owner, govern the exploitation of the mark. Under paragraph 3 of the former Article L. 715-2, all persons (other than the owner) may make use of the French guarantee mark as long as their goods or services satisfy the conditions laid down in the regulations.[327] However, this does not mean that there is no room for prior approval from the owner.[328] In fact, the owner is responsible for monitoring compliance with the regulations. This could require an agreement with the user as a prerequisite for granting authorization to use the mark (e.g., *Marque NF Environnement*).[329] In contrast to an individual trademark licence agreement, however, this agreement must be concluded if the conditions laid down in the regulations are met, which is beyond the control, and independent of, the will of the owner. This feature lies at the heart of the mechanism of the French guarantee mark, since the lack of openness of the mark's usage may preclude its classification as such.[330] In this sense, this mechanism appears to be very similar to that of a GI, where everyone is entitled to use the GI if the product fulfils the criteria. However, paragraph 3 disappeared from Article L. 715-2 with the Order of 13 November 2019.

The fourth feature of the mechanism is non-transferability, which is also a special characteristic in the GI regime. Unlike individual trademarks, GIs cannot be assigned or mortgaged because they are not 'owned' by private parties.[331] Similarly, as the French guarantee mark was considered 'more of a professional police institution than as a

324. Chavanne, *supra* n. 37, at 33.
325. Albert Chavanne, *La loi du 4 janvier 1991 sur les marques de fabrique*, La semaine juridique entreprise et affaires, n° 16, 1991, p. 45.
326. *Le formulaire marque – Comment remplir votre dossier de dépôt de marque*, INPI (11 May 2021), https://www.inpi.fr/sites/default/files/formulaire_marque_170202.pdf. Taking into account the law applicable to certification, when an accredited certification body decides to register a collective certification mark, which puts the certification into practice, it is possible that the regulations governing usage merge with the 'rules on production, processing or packaging' (Article L. 641-20 of the Rural Code or with a 'certification reference document' (Article L. 433-3 of the Consumer Code). *See* Anne Penneau, *La certification*, J.-Cl. Environnement et développement durable, fasc. 5300.
327. Ancien Article L. 715-2(3) CPI: '*L'usage de la marque collective de certification est ouvert à toutes les personnes, distinctes du titulaire, qui fournissent des produits ou des services répondant aux conditions imposées par le règlement.*'
328. Jérôme Passa, *Marques Collectives*, J.-CL. Marques, fasc. 7450, p. 18.
329. *Règles générales de la marque NF Environnement*, AFNOR (12 May 2021), http://cdn.afnor.org/download/reggen/FR/Marque%20NF%20Environnement.pdf.
330. *See* Cass. com., 3 juin 2008, n° 07-15.050.
331. *See* Andras Jokuti, *Where Is the What if the What Is in Why? A Rough Guide to the Maze of Geographical Indications*, 31 Eur. Intell. Prop. Rev. 118 (2009).

private good',[332] the free transfer of such marks was not acceptable. Paragraph 4 of the former Article L. 715-2 provided that 'a collective certification mark may not be subject to assignment, pledge or any measure of enforcement'.[333] The only exception was the transfer to another legal person in the case of the dissolution of the previous owner, but the conditions were stringent:[334] The transfer was subject to the conditions laid down by a Conseil d'Etat decree, whereby the transferee had to be a certification body or a legal person who was the main owner of the certification body to which it granted an exclusive licence for the mark.[335] However, with the Order of 13 November 2019, paragraph 3 disappeared from Article L. 715-2. The current Article L. 715-3 provides that a guarantee mark may be assigned or transmitted only to a person meeting the conditions set out in the first paragraph of Article L. 715-2.[336]

Finally, while trademark rights may be perpetual,[337] they can be lost under certain circumstances. Like an individual trademark, a French guarantee mark may be declared invalid or revoked.[338] However, there are additional grounds of invalidity wherein the owner carries on a business concerning the goods or services certified (Article L. 715-2, 1°, CPI), the regulations governing usage have not been properly submitted (Article L. 715-2, 2°, CPI), the owner fails to take reasonable measures to prevent a use of the mark that is not compatible with the regulations governing use (Article L. 715-5, 2°, CPI), or the mark has become liable to mislead the public (Article L. 715-5, 3°, CPI). Once the mark has been used, a link between the products covered by the mark and their quality would be established in the minds of consumers. Under paragraph 4 of the former Article L. 715-2, where such a mark has ceased to be protected, it may be neither registered nor used during a period of ten years[339] since the newly registered mark may not ensure the same quality and is thus likely to lead to confusion among consumers.

332. *See* Foyer, *supra* n. 315, at 70.
333. Ancien Article L. 715-2(4) CPI: '*La marque collective de certification ne peut faire l'objet ni de cession, ni de gage, ni d'aucune mesure d'exécution forcée; toutefois, en cas de dissolution de la personne morale qui en est titulaire, elle peut être transmise à une autre personne morale dans des conditions fixées par décret en Conseil d'Etat.*'
334. Martine Dehaut, *Les marques de certification: apports du décret du 1er mars 2007 modifiant le Code de la propriété intellectuelle*, Propriété industrielle, n° 6, 2007, alerte 79.
335. Ancien Article R. 715-2 CPI (*Décret n° 2007-280 du 1er mars 2007 modifiant le code de la propriété intellectuelle, art. 28*): '*En cas de dissolution de la personne morale titulaire d'une marque collective de certification, la transmission de cette marque ne peut intervenir qu'au profit d'un autre organisme certificateur ou d'une personne morale détenant majoritairement, directement ou indirectement, un organisme certificateur auquel elle (en) concède une licence exclusive de cette marque.*'
336. Article L. 715-3 CPI: '*Une marque de garantie ne peut être cédée ou transmise qu'à une personne répondant aux conditions énoncées au premier alinéa de l'article L. 715-2.*'
337. Article L. 712-1(2) CPI: '*L'enregistrement produit ses effets à compter de la date de dépôt de la demande pour une période de dix ans indéfiniment renouvelable.*'
338. WIPO, *Contribution de la France: Aspects Techniques et Procéduraux de L'enregistrement des Marques de Certification et des Marques Collectives*, *supra* n. 318, at 12-13.
339. Ancien Article L. 715-2(4) CPI: '*Lorsqu'une marque de certification a été utilisée et qu'elle a cessé d'être protégée par la loi, elle ne peut, sous réserve des dispositions de l'article L. 712-10, être ni déposée ni utilisée à un titre quelconque avant un délai de dix ans.*'

[b] *Special Regime of EU Certification Marks*

Due to its particular operating rules, the EU certification mark has the potential to be a useful tool by which GI producers may inform purchasers that the products possess certain characteristics (except regarding geographical origin). The specific rules governing how the EU certification mark should operate are contained in Articles 83-93 of Regulation 2017/1001.

The basic feature of the EU certification mark is that it is not used by the proprietor of the mark. The proprietor (no matter if it is the applicant or the person to whom the mark has been transferred) should not carry on a business involving the supply of goods or services of the kind certified.[340] Instead, it is used by 'any person who has authority to use it according to the regulations governing use'.[341]

To guarantee the presence of certain characteristics, the regulations governing the use of the certification mark must be submitted no later than two months from the filing of the application.[342] Those regulations must specify 'the persons authorized to use the mark, the characteristics to be certified by the mark, how the certifying body is to test those characteristics and to supervise the use of the mark'.[343] Marks failing to meet the above conditions will be refused registration[344] or be declared invalid.[345] Furthermore, the proprietor must ensure that the mark is used in a way compatible with the conditions of use laid down in the regulations; otherwise, the mark will be revoked.[346]

[c] *Special Regime of Certification Marks in Chinese Law*

Like collective marks, certification marks are also governed by a special regulation in China, the Measures for the Registration and Administration of Collective Marks and Certification Marks. In addition, since a certification mark containing a GI is seen as having the same function as the GI, there are special provisions regulating how those GI certification marks should operate, in order to ensure their special function.

The first special rule concerns the conditions of the proprietor. The applicant for the registration of a GI certification mark must be an organization with the capacity to supervise the particular quality of the categories of goods in relation to which

340. Article 83 of Regulation 2017/1001: 'Any natural or legal person, including institutions, authorities and bodies governed by public law, may apply for EU certification marks provided that such person does not carry on a business involving the supply of goods or services of the kind certified'; Article 89 of Regulation 2017/1001: 'By way of derogation from Article 20(1), an EU certification mark may only be transferred to a person who meets the requirements of Article 83(2).'
341. Article 87 of Regulation 2017/1001.
342. *Ibid.*, Article 84.
343. *Ibid.*; *See also* Article 17 of Commission Implementing Regulation (EU) 2018/626.
344. *Ibid.*, Article 85.
345. *Ibid.*, Article 92.
346. *Ibid.*, Article 91.

registration of the mark is applied for.[347] If the applicant does not have the professionals or testing equipment required for the supervision, this task can be entrusted to a qualified organization through the signing of an entrustment agreement.[348]

Second, regulations governing the use of a certification mark must be submitted and subsequently published in the Gazette. They contain almost the same information as that contained in the regulations governing the use of a collective mark, except that the former also includes the requirements for using the mark.[349] In practice, where a GI is registered as a certification mark, origination in a specific place and the possession of a particular quality are required for the use of that mark.[350] The authorized production area delimited by the regulations governing use should not differ from the boundary of the region indicated by the GI, although it sometimes does. Where the region specified in the mark application is smaller than the original area of production of the GI products, some existing users of the GI will be excluded from using it. An illustration is provided by '*Korla* Fragrant Pear', a GI registered as a certification mark in early 1995. Its regulations governing use limit the production area to the Peacock River Basin and the Tarim Basin, whereas the pear in question is also cultivated elsewhere (in the Ili River Basin).[351] While this problem may be resolved under Article 49 of the Implementation Regulation (the registrant cannot prohibit a third party from using indications concerning the kind of goods), no guidance has been provided for delimiting the boundary of production in cases like that of '*Korla* Fragrant Pear'.

Third, the registrant is prohibited from using the certification mark for goods provided by itself.[352] This constitutes a principle that is fundamental to the concept of the certification mark in most countries: it is in the public interest for an independent person to act as a certifier.[353] Another notable feature is that the use of the mark is permitted to anybody who satisfies the requirements provided in the regulations.[354] The openness of access to certification marks distinguishes them from individual marks, to which access is determined by the will of the registrant,[355] as well as from

347. *See* Measures for Collective and Certification Marks, Article 5.
348. *Changsha Yulu Enterprise Marketing Planning Co. Ltd. v. the Trademark Review and Adjudication Board of the State Administration for Industry and Commerce, supra* n. 145.
349. Regulations governing use of a certification mark shall include the purpose of the mark, the quality of the goods, the requirements for using the mark, the procedural rules governing use of the mark, users' rights and obligations, sanctions, and the rules concerning the supervisory system and controls over the product. *See* Measures for Collective and Certification Marks, Article 11.
350. *Hangzhou Xihu District Longjing Tea Industry Association v. Guangzhou Guangyi Tea Expo Garden Trading Co. Ltd.*, Guangdong Guangzhou Liwan People's Court (2 September 2015).
351. *Korla Pear Association of Bayingolin Mongolian Autonomous Prefecture of Xinjiang Uygur Autonomous Region v. Korla Hebrew Paper Industry Co. Ltd.*, Xinjiang High People's Court (26 June 2005).
352. Measures for Collective and Certification Marks, Article 20.
353. *See* Belson, *supra* n. 22, at 62.
354. Certification marks are often recognized as 'Open Marks'. *See* Wang Xiaobing & Irina Kireeva, *Q&A Manual: China Legislation on Geographical Indications*, V&S NEWS (11 May 2021), https://www.vsnews.fr/images/etudes/QA_Manual_Chinese_legislation_on_GIs1012.pdf; Measures for Collective and Certification Marks, Article 18.
355. *Zhoushan Fishery Circulation and Processing Industry Association v. Beijing North Fisherman Food Co. Ltd.*, Beijing Chaoyang District People's Court (22 July 2011).

collective marks, to which access is limited to the members of an association. It is worth mentioning that permission cannot be granted without going through the prescribed regulatory process, according to which the potential users shall submit a request for the use of the mark.[356] This process allows for the registrant to supervise the product as well as its qualification for using the mark. Regarding the GI certification mark, Article 4 of Implementation Regulations provides that a request may not be refused to anyone 'whose goods satisfy the conditions for using the GI'.[357] If local producers are unwilling to submit the request or their goods do not satisfy the requirements for using the mark, the registrant of that mark cannot prevent them from using the geographical name in good faith in its descriptive sense 'if the goods indeed originate from the region indicated by the GI'.[358]

To conclude, special provisions are necessary in order to take into account the particularities of certification marks. In Europe and China, certification marks are subject to a special regime, especially regarding their use and registration. It can be seen that the certification mark is a strong instrument for distinguishing products that are certified to possess certain characteristics or qualities from those that are not so certified. Its exploitation model (collectively used), as well as its quality guarantee function, is of special interest for the protection of GIs. However, French and European law precludes the use of certification marks to this end. On the other hand, the regime of certification marks is one of the main instruments used to protect GIs in China. A sub-divisional special regime is used for GI certification marks.

[2] Defence of Certification Marks

Certification marks are protected not only against misleading use but also against any use for products that fail to meet the conditions laid down in the regulations governing the use of the mark. It is thus worthwhile to define the boundary of the protection through the dispositions dedicated to them.

[a] Defence of Collective Certification Marks (Guarantee Marks) in French Law

According to Article L. 715-1 of the IP Code, the provisions for protecting ordinary trademarks apply to collective certification marks (French guarantee marks). Thus acts

356. The procedural rules governing use of the mark are prescribed in the regulations governing use. The permission shall be reported to the Trademark Office for record, and the Office shall publish it. *See* Measures for Collective and Certification Marks, Article 15.
357. Again, the question has been raised of the coherence between the requirements for using the certification mark containing a GI and the conditions for using the GI. Conflicts may arise as a result of their inconsistency.
358. *See* Implementing Regulations of the Trademark Law, Article 4; Measures for Collective and Certification Marks, Article 18(2); *Hangzhou Xihu District Longjing Tea Industry Association v. Beijing Yonghui Supermarket Co. Ltd.*, Beijing Dongcheng District People's Court (14 October 2014).

that constitute an infringement of a certification mark are subject to prosecution on the basis of Article L. 713-1-L. 713-6 of the same code.

French guarantee marks are also protected under Article L. 716-11.[359] Since a certification mark can be used only by persons who supply goods satisfying the conditions set out in the regulations governing the use of that mark (Article L. 715-5, 2°), it is prohibited to (knowingly) use the mark 'under conditions other than that laid down in the regulations accompanying the registration'. It is also prohibited to 'sell or offer for sale a product bearing a collective mark or a guarantee mark employed in an irregular manner'.[360] Such acts shall be liable to imprisonment for a term of three years, together with a fine of EUR 300,000.[361] Just as the '*cahier des charges*' is important for the protection of GIs, the regulations governing usage are critical for the protection of collective certification marks.[362]

[b] Defence of EU Certification Marks

Article 83 of Regulation 2017/1001 provides that 'Chapters I to VII and IX to XIV shall apply to EU certification marks to the extent that this Section does not provide otherwise.' The 'EU certification marks' section does not make any special provision on the scope of the protection for certification marks. Those marks are thus protected in the same way as are individual marks and EU collective marks, under Articles 9-14 of the same Regulation.

[c] Defence of Certification Marks in Chinese Law

Likewise, in China, the provisions regarding what types of acts constitute an infringement of trademark rights that apply to certification marks are no different from those that apply to individual and collective marks.[363] They are contained in Articles 30 and 57 of the Trademark Law,[364] supplemented by Article 76 of its implementation

359. This article applies equally to French collective marks.
360. Article L. 716-11 CPI: '*Sera puni des mêmes peines quiconque: a) Aura sciemment fait un usage quelconque d'une marque collective ou d'une marque de garantie enregistrée dans des conditions autres que celles prescrites au règlement accompagnant le dépôt; b) Aura sciemment vendu ou mis en vente un produit revêtu d'une marque collective ou d'une marque de garantie irrégulièrement employée ....*'
361. Article L. 716-10 CPI; Article L. 716-11 CPI.
362. C.A. Paris, 22 oct. 2010, n° 09/17232.
363. *See* Xie Dongwei, Woguo Dili Biaozhi Zhidu de Lishi yu Fazhan [The History and Development of China's GI Protection System], GONGSHANG XINGZHENG GUANLI [INDUSTRIAL & COMMERCIAL ADMINISTRATION], June 2003, 29.
364. Trademark Law, Article 30: 'Where a trademark application does not comply with the relevant provisions in this Law or is identical with or similar to a registered trademark used in connection with the same or similar goods, its registration shall be refused by the Trademark Office after examination, and the mark shall not be published'; Trademark Law, Article 57: 'Any of the following constitutes an infringement of the exclusive right to use a registered trademark: (1) Using a trademark that is identical with a registered trademark in connection with the same goods without the authorization of the owner of the registered trademark; (2) Using a trademark that is similar to a registered trademark in connection with the same goods,

regulations,[365] and Article 9 of the Judicial Interpretation in the Event of Disputes Relating to the Application of the Trademark Law. One can conclude that the infringement of a certification mark includes the use of a sign identical to the registered mark in relation to goods for which it is registered and the use of a similar sign in relation to identical goods or a similar or identical sign on similar goods to cause a likelihood of confusion.

However, the assessment of the 'likelihood of confusion' concerning GI certification marks is different from traditional approach. The traditional approach is based on Article 9 of the Judicial Interpretation, which prevents consumers from becoming confused as to the commercial source of the goods; in other words, the risk that the public might believe that 'the goods come from the same source of origin' or 'their source has a certain connection to products using the registered mark' is what constitutes a likelihood of confusion.[366] The approach applied to the GI certification mark is based on the view that the GI certification mark does not indicate the specific trade source of the goods but certifies some aspect of the third parties' goods (particularly with regard to the place of origin and the product quality attached to that place). As interpreted by Chinese courts, the likelihood of confusion is 'the risk, not that the public might believe that the goods come from the same undertaking, but that

or that is identical with or similar to a registered trademark in connection with the same or similar goods, without the authorization of the owner of the registered trademark, which may cause public confusion; (3) Selling goods that violate the exclusive right to use a registered trademark; (4) Counterfeiting, or making, without authorization, representations of another party's registered trademark, or selling such representations; (5) Altering another party's registered trademark without authorization and selling goods bearing such an altered trademark; (6) Helping any others to infringe the exclusive right to use its registered trademark with intention to provide convenience for infringing the exclusive right to use its registered trademark; (7) Otherwise causing prejudice to another party's exclusive right to use its registered trademark.'

365. Implementing Regulations of the Trademark Law, Article 76: 'The use of a sign identical with or similar to a registered trademark of any other person on identical or similar goods as the name or decoration of the goods, which misleads the public, shall be within the meaning of infringing upon the right to exclusively use a registered trademark as mentioned in Article 57 (2) of the Trademark Law.'

366. Zuigao Renmin Fayuan Guanyu Shenli Shangbiao Minshi Jiufen Anjian Shiyong Falu Ruogan Wenti de Jieshi [Supreme People's Court's Judicial Interpretation in the Event of Disputes Relating to the Application of the Trademark Law], 12 October 2002 (amended on 29 December 2020), Article 9: 'The phrase "trademark that is identical" in Item (1)(2) of Article 57 of the Trademark Law means that where the suspected infringing trademark is compared with the plaintiff's registered trademark, the two trademarks are essentially without difference visually. The phrase "trademark that is similar" under Item (2) of Article 57 of the Trademark Law means that where the suspected infringing trademark is compared with the plaintiff's registered trademark, the font, pronunciation or meaning of the words or the composition or colouring of the device are similar, or the overall structure of its main combined elements is similar, or where its three-dimensional shape and combination of colours are similar thereby easily leading the relevant public to mistake the source of the products or to believe that their source has a certain connection to products using the plaintiff's registered trademark.' *See also Guzhang Tea Industry Development Research Centre v. Hunan Huaming Tea Industry Co. Ltd.*, *supra* n. 309; *Guannan County Tanggou Town Liangxiangyuan Wines Co. Ltd. v. Jiangsu Tanggou Liangxianghe Wines Co. Ltd.*, Jiangsu High People's Court (13 February 2015); *Guizhou Moutai Liquor Company v. Guizhou Haihang Company and Xiamen Wanshixin Company*, Fujian High People's Court (26 September 2019).

the public might believe that the goods may have the same geographical origin and quality'.[367]

In the '*Zhoushan*' case, the court noted the special function of certification marks and affirmed, 'The fact that the public might be misled as to the geographical origin of the goods may constitute the criterion to establish the likelihood of confusion.'[368] Here, the focus shifted towards determining whether the suspected counterfeit goods came from the area indicated by the GI. If the goods are proved to originate from a place other than the area at issue, the likelihood of confusion is established; however, if they are proved to originate from the given area, the registrant is not entitled to prohibit the defendant from 'fairly' using the geographical name.[369]

Following the same logic, in the application of Article 30 of the Trademark Law, which prevents the registration of an identical or similar mark in relation to identical or similar products, it has been held that 'there is no need to assess the similarity between a GI certification mark and an individual mark'.[370] The court reasoned, 'There would not be any possibility of confusion between these two types of marks because their distinguishing functions are different':[371] one is to distinguish the source of origin; the other is to indicate some aspects of the goods (geographical origin, quality, or other characteristics).[372] The result is that, in cases like '*Enshi Yulu*' and '*Lanshan* Green Tea', GI certification marks were successfully registered, although similar or identical signs had already been registered as individual marks for identical goods.[373]

---

367. *See Zhoushan Fishery Circuits and Processing Industry Association v. Beijing Shenmaren Food Sales Co. Ltd. and Beijing Huaguan Trading Co. Ltd., supra* n. 311; *Hangzhou Xihu District Longjing Tea Industry Association v. Beijing Yonghui Supermarket Co. Ltd., supra* n. 358; *Hangzhou Xihu District Longjing Tea Industry Association v. Beijing Qiruiyuan Tea House*, Beijing Dongcheng District People's Court (9 October 2015).
368. *Zhoushan Fishery Circuits and Processing Industry Association v. Beijing Shenmaren Food Sales Co. Ltd. and Beijing Huaguan Trading Co. Ltd., supra* n. 311. This approach is widely adopted in subsequent cases. *See*, for instance, *Huai'an City Qinghe District Dianmiaofeng Tea Business Department v. Xinyang City Tea Association*, Jiangsu High People's Court (26 April 2021); *Xiaodi Industry Association of Yuping Dong Autonomous County v. Qiannan Xiaodi Musical Instrument Co. Ltd*, Guizhou High People's Court (19 June 2020); *Luanan County Baige Village Heshun Food Processing Plant v. Panjin City Rice Association*, Tianjin High People's Court (13 April 2020); *Zhejiang Province Agricultural Technology Promotion Centre v. Hangzhou Riverside Tesco Life Shopping Co. Ltd*, Zhejiang High People's Court (10 October 2016).
369. The defendant bears the burden of proof. *See also Heilongjiang Yongchao Rice Industry Co., Ltd v. Wuchang Rice Association*, Shandong High People's Court (31 May 2016); *Kaiyuan Jufu Trading Co. Ltd v. Wuchang Rice Association*, Heilongjiang High People's Court (26 February 2018); *Jinan Tea Wholesale Market Lugu Songyang Tea Sales Department v. Hangzhou West Lake District Longjing Tea Industry Association*, Shandong High People's Court (5 March 2018).
370. *See Changsha Yulu Enterprise Marketing Planning Co. Ltd. v. the Trademark Review and Adjudication Board of the State Administration for Industry and Commerce, supra* n. 145.
371. *Ibid.*
372. Zhou Bo, Dili Biaozhi Zhengming Shangbiao Buying yu Shangpin Shangbiao Jinxing Jinsixing Bidui [Geographical Indications Registered as Certification Marks Should Not Be Compared with Trademarks in Similarity], KEJI YU FALU [JOURNAL OF SCIENCE & LAW], April 2014, 340.
373. Xu Bo, Beijing Zhishi Chanquan Fayuan Shouli Lanshan Lucha Zhengming Shangbiao Shenqing Bohui Fushen Xingzheng Jiufen An [Beijing Intellectual Property Court Deals with the Administrative Dispute Concerning 'Lanshan Green Tea' Certification Trademark Application], Zhichanli (15 May 2021), http://www.zhichanli.cn/article/840.html.

Beijing's High People's Court also delivered guidelines in 2014 on dealing with the application of Article 30, which provides that the rights holder of a previously registered individual mark cannot object on the grounds of infringement of Article 30 to a subsequent certification mark containing a GI and vice versa.[374] It actually allows unconnected parties to register the same or similar signs within the trademark regime as long as the signs are registered under different categories of marks. Thus, a subsequent GI may be registered as a certification mark even though the same subject matter, the geographical term, has been already registered as an individual mark for identical or similar goods.

While this may help resolve the classic 'prior trademark, subsequent GI' conflict by opening the door to coexistence, it also appears to weaken the ability of the owner of a registered GI to exercise exclusive rights because it permits cohabitation between a later trademark and a prior GI (already registered as a certification mark).

As observed by Liu Guodong, a Trademark Office official, this solution seems to overlook the functional similarity between GI certification marks and individual trademarks: both indicate the origin of goods (either geographical or commercial), and both differentiate between similar goods on the marketplace.[375] Even where there is a clear division between the two categories, the former could be mistaken by the consumers as the latter (and vice versa), and the two similar signs could both appear to indicate the same origin. This may lead to consumer confusion and ensuing unfair competition. We therefore cannot share the court's optimism that 'there would be no likelihood of confusion' simply because the same sign is registered under different categories of marks.

It should be noted that the approach of denying all likelihood of confusion is not followed by the decision of the Beijing High People's Court of 30 August 2018. In this case, concerning the registration of an individual mark that was similar to the GI 'Napa Valley', the Court concluded that the similarity between the common individual trademark and the 'GI certification mark' may easily lead to consumer confusion and thus disallowed the registration of the later individual trademark.[376] In the guidelines

374. The Supreme People's Court has considered whether to adopt the same provision in its judicial interpretation of the Trademark Law. *See* Zuigao Renmin Fayuan Guanyu Shenli Shangbiao Shouquan Quequan Xingzheng Anjian Ruogan Wenti de Guiding Zhengqiu Yijiangao [Draft Provisions of the Supreme People's Court on Several Issues Concerning the Administrative Cases of Trademark], 14 October 2014, Article 13; *See* Beijing Gaoji Renmin Fayuan Guanyu Shangbiao Shouquan Quequan Xingzheng Anjian de Shenli Zhinan [Beijing High People's Court's Guide to the Trial of Administrative Cases Concerning Trademarks], 22 January 2014, Article 5.

375. Liu Guodong, Dili Biaozhi yu Putong Shangbiao Chongtu de Jiejue Shiyong Jinzhi Hunxiao Yuanze [The Principle of Prohibition of Confusion Applies to the Settlement of the Conflict Between GIs and Trademarks], ZHONGHUA SHANGBIAO [CHINA TRADEMARK], September 2014, 18.

376. *Napa Valley Brewers Association v. State Administration for Industry and Commerce Trademark Review and Adjudication Board and Zhejiang Zhongshang Investment Co. Ltd*, Beijing High People's Court (30 August 2018).

issued in 2019, the Beijing High People's Court has also acknowledged the possibility of consumer confusion.[377]

In summary, although GIs in China may be protected as certification marks, this does not mean that the two instruments have no differences.[378] When attempts are made to reconcile the objectives of GI protection and those of the protection of certification marks containing them, difficulties arise in delimiting the boundaries of the exclusive rights granted to the owners of the marks to prevent confusing uses of identical or similar signs by third parties. While the registration of GIs under the trademark marks regime is endorsed, it poses a range of problems for traditional trademark doctrine.

To conclude this chapter, we have seen two opposing positions: on one side, the European approach, which claims that its sui generis GI regime could be an effective tool and limits the role of the trademark regime so as to avoid interference with the former regime. This approach is reflected in Regulation 2017/1001 (the complete prohibition of the use of EU certification marks to certify geographical origin), the CJEU case law (the rejection of any change in the 'confusion likelihood' assessment for EU collective marks containing geographically descriptive signs), and national laws (the prohibition of registration of purely geographically descriptive signs or indications as trademarks, as in French law).

On the other side, China has demonstrated its ambition to absorb GIs within the trademark regime, via collective or certification marks. This position is reflected in the absence of the 'distinctiveness' requirement for registering GIs as collective or certification marks (GIs alone can be registered as the marks), the addition of the 'product--place link' requirement for the registration of GIs as the marks (product quality, reputation, or other characteristics must be essentially attributed to the place of origin the mark indicates), the understanding of the unique function of the marks, the methodology adopted to assess the 'likelihood of confusion' in cases involving the infringement of the marks, and the permission for the coexistence of earlier ordinary trademarks and later GI collective or certification marks. For these reasons, the regime of collective and certification marks has become a primary instrument for the recognition and protection of GIs, which is in competition with Chinese sui generis GI systems.

Both in Europe and in China, the trademark regime is not the only available tool for protecting GIs. We now move on in Chapter 4 to the study of the other, more important tool (at least for Europe): the sui generis GI regime.

377. Beijing Gaoji Renmin Fayuan Guanyu Shangbiao Shouquan Quequan Xingzheng Anjian de Shenli Zhinan [Beijing High People's Court's Guide to the Trial of Administrative Cases Concerning Trademarks], 24 April 2019, Article 13.

378. *See* Jokuti, *supra* n. 331.

CHAPTER 4

GI Protection under Sui Generis Regime: A Comparison Between the EU and Chinese Approaches

This chapter analyses the sui generis GI regimes in France, the EU, and China, in order to understand Europe's and China's approach to the protection of GIs. It assesses whether China has adopted the European approach to GI (i.e., the basic elements of the EU sui generis regime). It demonstrates the differences in design between the sui generis systems. European sui generis systems are built on a strict and rigorous registration process; a multilayered system with strong state involvement that monitors compliance with established product specifications; and a high level of protection to prevent the misuse, imitation, and evocation of registered GIs. Although China's sui generis systems have similar registration requirements, their monitoring systems are designed differently and, most importantly, their level of protection is much lower. This explains why the EU requires China to provide a higher level of protection for GIs protected under the EU–China GI Agreement, which came into force on 1 March 2021. This chapter concludes that caution should be exercised before discussing the role of sui generis GI systems in achieving private and public interests because the design of the systems can vary greatly from one State to another, which impacts their role.

When talking about the sui generis protection of GIs, one should consider the influential French AOC system.[1] It is one of the earliest special systems for GIs and is

1. In addition to the AOC system, the Law of 1966 has created an administrative procedure to protect ordinary appellations of origin (*non contrôlée*). The relevant provisions can be found in former Article L. 115-2-L. 115-4 of the Consumer Code (since 1 July 2016, Article L. 431-4). However, the practical importance of this regime is limited for two reasons. Firstly, all agricultural, forestry, and alimentary products are exclusively subject to the AOC system. Secondly, industry products can hardly obtain protection under this regime because of the strict definition of AO.

widely regarded as the strictest and most thorough one: 'It is, in this sense, a model of reference for origin labelled products.'[2] Born in the wine sector in 1935, this system involves a rigorous set of controls over the variety of grapes, growing and fermentation methods, and size of the crop and therefore 'straddles both an agricultural regulation role and a certification mark function'.[3]

Today, sui generis GI regimes are no longer solely about French winemakers and farmers. Since the law of 17 March 2014, an analogue of the AOC system has been established in France to protect regional industry and artisanal products (the IGPIA).

Moreover, contrary to what has sometimes been argued, the sui generis regime does not seem to be a 'hard sell'[4] but extends geographically to the entire territory of the EU as well as countries in the Far East, like Japan[5] and China. Derived from French law, sui generis GI protection at the EU level has been established for wines, spirits, aromatized wines, and other agricultural products and foodstuffs. Also influenced by the AOC system, several sui generis frameworks have been or are being developed in China. Among them, the regimes established by the former AQSIQ (since 2018, managed by the CNIPA) and managed by the MOA are the two main instruments in use for the protection of GIs.[6]

The common feature of the French and French-inspired regimes is that they are all based on prior recognition (registration), setting out not only areas of production but also detailed production methods. They are aimed at guaranteeing the link between product and *terroir* (§4.01). However, protection against quality compromise and infringement are not the same or equally powerful in France, the EU, and China (§4.02).

§4.01 RECOGNITION OF GIs

GIs perform a function similar to that of trademarks, by indicating the origin of goods in the marketplace and by protecting the product's reputation against unlawful usurpation. Nevertheless, they differ from trademarks, which safeguard the private

2. Elizabeth Barham, *Translating Terroir: The Global Challenge of French AOC labeling*, 19 J. Rural Stud. 127 (2003).
3. Andrew T. Kenyon, Ng-Loy Wee Loon & Megan Richardson, *The Law of Reputation and Brands in the Asia Pacific* 239 (Cambridge University Press 2012).
4. James Ming Chen, *A Sober Second Look at Appellations of Origin: How the United States Will Crash France's Wine and Cheese Party*, 5 Minn. J. Global Trade 29 (1996).
5. In June 2015, the Act on Protection of the Names of Specific Agricultural, Forestry and Fishery Products and Foodstuffs (Geographical Indication Act, GI Act) entered into force. A new (sui generis) GI protection system is introduced in Japan. Before that, Japan relied on the regional collective trademark system for the protection of GIs. *See Geographical Indication (GI) Protection System*, Ministry of Agriculture, Forestry and Fisheries (15 May 2021), http://www.maff.go.jp/e/policies/intel/gi_act/index.html.
6. In addition, in 2012, the former AQSIQ founded the regime of Protected Eco-Origin Products (PEOP). Furthermore, the former State Forestry Administration (SFA) considered establishing a special system to facilitate the GIs protection of forest products. *See* Chapter 2 *supra*.

interest of its holder, in that they protect the interests of the general public[7] and the interests of all producers working with the product.[8] Thus, their recognition (and registration) requires a dual intervention, by public establishments and collective organizations.

Certain conditions must be met to register a GI. One essential requirement is that the GI needs to have a tie with the *terroir*. First, the GI must have a geographical significance and be capable of evoking a type of product from a specific place. While it is true that some geographical names already evoke the product concerned (like *Champagne* or *Roquefort*), there are many cases where the product name needs to be added to the name of a region (like in *Parma* ham). Second, the product identified by the GI needs to have a specific quality or reputation because of the named origin. The link between the *terroir* and the characteristics of the product is the key element that makes GIs different from simple indications of provenance.

[A] Management Bodies

In France, the EU, and China, the sui generis protection for a GI is granted by a competent authority upon request from a group of producers or an entity.

[1] Public Establishments

The recognition of GIs was founded on a simple, 'peasant' idea:[9] allowing everyone to make products known among consumers according to their place of production. This is 'a good idea but not enough'.[10] The intensity of competition, combined with wine crises in the nineteenth century, led to a traditional response in France: a commitment to provide the public with a guarantee of quality 'through state intervention'.[11] Thus, since the very beginning, the sui generis regime of GIs has been characterized by a greater degree of state involvement in their recognition.[12]

7. *See* Jérôme Passa, *Droit de la propriété industrielle: Tome 1, Marques et autres signes distinctifs, dessins et modèles*, 2e éd., Paris, LGDJ, 2009, p. 763; Dominique Denis, *Appellation d'origine et indication de provenance*, Paris, Dalloz, 1995, p. 78.
8. Case C-478/07 *Budějovický Budvar* [2009] ECR I-07721, para. 82 (AG Opinion).
9. Robert Plaisant, *Le droit français des appellations d'origine, in Les indications de provenance et les appellations d'origine en droit comparé, Actes du colloque de Lausanne*, Genève, Librairie Droz, 1983, p. 72.
10. As demonstrated in Chapter 1, the origin alone does not guarantee the quality.
11. *See* Plaisant, *supra* n. 9, at 76.
12. However, the French/European substantive reform of 2006 provided a step backwards in state involvement and a transfer of activities from the state to the producer organizations. It provided for the disengagement of the INAO in the inspection and control activities. *See* Organization for Economic Co-operation and Development (OECD), *Appellations of Origin and Geographical Indications in OECD Member Countries: Economic and Legal Implications*, COM/AGR/APM/TD/WP(2000)15/FINAL (21 December 2000); Delphine Marie-Vivien, *The Role of the State in the Protection of Geographical Indications: From Disengagement in France/Europe to Significant Involvement in India*, 13 J. World Intell. Prop. 121 (2010); Caroline Le Goffic & Andrea Zappalaglio, *The Role Played by the US Government in Protecting Geographical Indications*, 98 World Dev. 35 (2017).

Today, given the 'public policy nature' of GIs,[13] they are recognized through the adoption of a decree of the *Conseil d'Etat*,[14] an order of the ministers concerned,[15] or a decision of the INPI since France's Law of 2014;[16] an implementing act (commission implementing regulation) at the European level;[17] a notice of approval by the former AQSIQ (the CNIPA since 2018);[18] or a decision of the MOA in China.[19] In each jurisdiction, administrative bodies play an important role in ensuring the full effectiveness of the public intervention.[20]

[a] Public Establishments in French Law

In France, GIs have traditionally been considered a tool of public policy.[21] The recognition of AOC, as well as the control over them, is managed by the INAO. The Law of 2014 created a new category of GIs, IGPIA, which is approved by the INPI.

The INAO is a public administrative body under the Ministry of Agriculture and Food (Ministère de l'Agriculture et de l'Alimentation).[22] It was created by a Decree-Law

---

13. The focus of the policies is on the competition regulation, the regulation of the agricultural market, the rural development, and the protection of traditional *savoir-faire*. *See* Gilles Allaire et al., *Les dispositifs français et européens de protection de la qualité et de l'origine dans le contexte de l'OMC: justifications générales et contextes nationaux*, Symposium international territoires et enjeux du développement régional, 2005.
14. Article L. 641-7(2) C. rur.: '*Cette reconnaissance (d'une appellation d'origine contrôlée) est prononcée par décret en Conseil d'Etat lorsque les propositions de l'Institut national de l'origine et de la qualité comportent l'extension d'une aire de production faisant l'objet d'une délimitation par une loi spéciale ou une révision des conditions de production déterminées par une loi spéciale.*'
15. The former Article L. 641-7 of the Rural Code provides that the recognition of an AOC is declared by the decree. Article 3 of the Order of 2015 replaces the term 'decree' with 'order of the ministers concerned'. *See* Ordonnance n° 2015-1246 du 7 octobre 2015 relative aux signes d'identification de l'origine et de la qualité, J.O. du 8 oct. 2015, p. 18290.
16. Article L. 411-4(1) CPI: '*Le directeur de l'Institut national de la propriété industrielle prend les décisions prévues par le présent code à l'occasion de la délivrance, du rejet ou du maintien des titres de propriété industrielle, ainsi qu'à l'occasion de l'homologation, du rejet ou de la modification du cahier des charges des indications géographiques définies à l'article L. 721-2 ou du retrait de cette homologation.*'
17. Article 52(2) of Regulation 1151/2012; Article 99(1) of Regulation 1308/2013; Article 30(2) of Regulation 2019/787; Article 16 of Regulation 251/2014.
18. Provisions on the Protection of Geographical Indication Products, Article 16 (2005).
19. Measures for the Administration of Geographical Indications for Agricultural Products, Article 12 (2007, amended in 2019).
20. Norbert Olszak notes that the recognition is a kind of official stamp that gives a status of public good to the *terroir*. *See* Norbert Olszak, *Le vin de terroir et la naissance des appellations d'origine*, *in Le droit du vin à l'épreuve des enjeux environnementaux*, Bordeaux, Féret, 2015, p. 56.
21. The French case law has consistently affirmed the public policy nature of geographical indications: '*Une marque ou dénomination commerciale incorporant un nom de lieu ne peut être utilisée pour désigner ou pour commercialiser un produit dont l'origine ne lui donne pas le droit au nom indiqué (AOC), lequel bénéfice d'une protection d'ordre public*'; '*Le statut des appellations d'origine contrôlée est d'ordre public et en interdit toute appropriation privative.*' *See* Cass. com., 9 nov. 1981, n° 80-12.943; Cass. com., 1er déc. 1987, n° 86-11.328; Cass. com., 18 févr. 2004, n° 02-10.576.
22. Article L. 642-5 C. rur.; Article R. 642-1 C. rur.

of 1935[23] to deal with AOC for wines and spirits. Its competence was extended to all agricultural and food products in 1990 and to all SIQOs in 2006.[24]

The composition of the INAO responded to this evolution through the establishment of different national committees. The INAO incorporated three national committees for wines and spirits, dairy products, and other products following the evolution of 1990,[25] which turned the AOC into a framework – 'a kind of box into which one puts what he likes'.[26] This separation is necessary because the 1990 reform brought together AOC of all sorts of agricultural products under the direction of only one body. The INAO staff were at that time mostly experts in wine or dairy product fields, but not in other product fields.[27]

Since the reform of 2006, the composition has undergone extensive changes. There are now five national committees allocated according to different categories of products (the traditional separation) and different SIQOs.[28] Each committee is made up of representatives appointed by a joint order of the ministers responsible for consumer affairs and agriculture[29] to represent professionals, administration, and consumers respectively.[30] In the fields of PDO (AOC)/PGI products, the committees propose the recognition of products eligible for protection and provide advice on the measures necessary for improving their quality or other characteristics.[31] To fulfil this role, the committee appoints a commission of inquiry to examine all aspects of the application, a commission of advisors to perform (where required) a technical analysis on matters relating to the link between the product and the geographical area, and a commission of experts to delimit the place of production.[32] Based on the work of these commissions, the national committee gives its opinion on the draft product specifications.

The INAO also includes an approvals and inspections board, which gives its opinion on the accreditation of control bodies and the control or inspection plans[33] (the accreditation and the plans are required for the recognition of PDO/PGI),[34] and, finally,

23. Décret-loi du 30 juillet 1935 relatif à la défense du marché des vins et au régime économique de l'alcool, J.O. du 31 juill. 1935, p. 8314.
24. L'ordonnance n° 2006-1547 du 7 décembre 2006, Article 2,
25. Décret n° 91-368 du 15 avril 1991 portant organisation et fonctionnement de l'Institut national des appellations d'origine, J.O. du 17 avr. 1991, p. 5051.
26. Denis, *supra* n. 7, at 81.
27. *Ibid.*, 82.
28. The five national committees are: the National Committee for designations of origin for wine, other alcoholic beverages and spirits; the National Committee for designations of dairy, agro-food and forestry product; the National Committee for Protected Geographical Indications PGI, Labels Rouges and Traditional Specialities Guaranteed (TSG); the National Committee for Protected Geographical Indications for Wines and Ciders; the National Committee of Organic Agriculture. *See* Article R. 642-6 C. rur.
29. Article R. 642-12 C. rur.
30. Article L. 642-9 C. rur.; Article R. 642-10 C. rur.
31. Article L. 642-5 C. rur.; Article R. 642-7 C. rur.
32. INAO, *Guide du demandeur d'une appellation d'origine protégée (AOP) ou d'une indication géographique protégée (IGP)*, avr. 2015, p. 36.
33. Article L. 642-7 C. rur.; Article L. 642-10 C. rur.
34. Article L. 642-2 C. rur.: '*Au cahier des charges d'une appellation d'origine ou d'une indication géographique concernant un produit vitivinicole, un produit vinicole aromatisé ou une boisson spiritueuse est associé soit un plan de contrôle, soit un plan d'inspection. Au cahier des charges d'un autre signe d'identification de la qualité et de l'origine est associé un plan de contrôle.*'

a permanent council, which sets and deals with the general policy of the INAO and its budget.[35]

The main difference with the recognition procedure of the IGPIA is the fact that the INPI, not the INAO, is in charge of reviewing application files and supervising the management.[36] Traditionally, the role of the INPI, as a public establishment under the authority of the Minister responsible for industrial property, is to grant (pursuant to an examination of applications) industrial property rights (titles), such as patents, marks, designs, and models. Article 73 of the Law of 2014 makes it the responsibility of the INPI to decide on applications for the approval of the specifications for IGPIA.[37] Article 2 of the Decree of 2015 further specifies that one of the duties of the INPI is to 'review requests or amendment requests related to the specifications for IGPIA, approve and withdraw these specifications'.[38]

While it is clear that the recognition of IGPIA is subject to the jurisdiction of the INPI, the law is silent on the role of the INPI in defending IGPIA. We are familiar with the role of the INAO in defending SIQOs, including AOC/PDO and PGI: it may take legal action, both civil and criminal, against third parties infringing SIQOs, even in a foreign country.[39] However, the role of the INPI in cases of infringement depends on the interpretation of the texts by the Court of Justice.

[b] Public Establishments in EU Law

An application for registration of PDO/PGI involves two phases: the phase at the national level and the phase at the EU level: 'A division of powers between the member states and the European Commission is established.'[40]

Regarding the national phase, the application is addressed to the authorities of the Member State within the territory in which the geographical area in question is situated. Among the four EU GI systems, only the former Regulation 110/2008 for the protection of GIs for spirit drinks has not expressly provided for a preliminary national procedure. In order to register a GI for spirit drinks, both EU countries and non-EU countries must submit an application to the European Commission.[41] However, Article 24 of Regulation 2019/787, which repealed Regulation 110/2008, has eliminated this

35. Article R. 642-3 C. rur.
36. Carole Delga, *Lancement des indications géographiques pour les produits manufacturés et les ressources naturelles*, Ministère de l'économie des finances et de la relance (11 June 2021), https://www.economie.gouv.fr/indications-geographiques-produits-manufactures.
37. Article L. 411-1 CPI; Article L. 721-2 CPI.
38. Article R. 411-1(14) CPI.
39. Article L. 642-5(8) C. rur.: '*… contribue à la défense et à la promotion des signes d'identification de la qualité et de l'origine tant en France qu'à l'étranger*'.
40. Case C-343/07 *Bavaria NV and Bavaria Italia Srl v. Bayerischer Brauerbund eV* [2009] ECR I-05491, para. 64; Case C-269/99 *Carl Kühne GmbH & Co KG and Others v. Jütro Konservenfabrik GmbH & Co KG* [2001] ECR I-09517, para. 51.
41. *See* Article 17(1) of Regulation 110/2008; *Commission Implementing Regulation (EU) No 716/2013 of 25 July 2013 laying down rules for the application of Regulation (EC) No 110/2008 of the European Parliament and of the Council on the definition, description, presentation, labelling and the protection of geographical indications of spirit drinks*, OJ L 201, 26.7.2013, pp. 21-30, Article 6.

exception and requires that the application for spirit drinks also be submitted to the authorities of the Member State.[42]

It is for the Member States to scrutinize the application in order to check whether it is justified with regard to the conditions of the PDO/PGI scheme.[43] In France, the INAO and its line ministries have competence, at the national stage, in relation to the application for registration of PDO/PGI. This procedure partially overlaps that of the AOC. The latter is considered a step prior to PDO/PGI registration.[44]

Where a favourable decision is given, the Member State lodges the application dossier with the Commission. The application then enters the EU-level phase. At this stage, it is the European Commission that plays a central role: it scrutinizes the application;[45] launches the opposition procedure;[46] and finally adopts implementing acts registering the name or rejecting the application.[47] Furthermore, the Commission continues to control the compliance of the registered PDO/PGI with the product specification. If compliance is no longer ensured, the Commission may, on its own initiative or upon request, cancel the registration.[48]

[c] Public Establishments in Chinese Law

The French/European model has become the standard sui generis approach.[49] China, with its traditional product industries, adopted its own version of GI protection in light of the French/European experience. Therefore, one of the central components of Europe's approach – public intervention – is adopted in China, which allows for the registration of a GI as a 'GI product' or 'GI of agricultural product' under the authority of the former AQSIQ (the CNIPA since 2018) and the MOA respectively.

Before the institutional reform in 2018, the former AQSIQ and its local bureaus were in charge of the protection of GI products.[50] The former AQSIQ possessed a

42. *Regulation (EU) 2019/787 of the European Parliament and of the Council of 17 April 2019 on the definition, description, presentation and labelling of spirit drinks, the use of the names of spirit drinks in the presentation and labelling of other foodstuffs, the protection of geographical indications for spirit drinks, the use of ethyl alcohol and distillates of agricultural origin in alcoholic beverages, and repealing Regulation (EC) No 110/2008*, OJ L 130, 17.5.2019, pp. 1-54.
43. Article 49(2) of Regulation 1151/2012; Article 96(3) of Regulation 1308/2013; Article 13(3) of Regulation 251/2014; Article 24(5) of Regulation 2019/787.
44. INAO, *Guide du demandeur d'une appellation d'origine protégée (AOP) ou d'une indication géographique protégée (IGP)*, *supra* n. 32, p. 6.
45. Article 50(1) of Regulation 1151/2012; Article 97(2) of Regulation 1308/2013; Article 26(1) of Regulation 2019/787; Article 14(2) of Regulation 251/2014.
46. Article 51 of Regulation 1151/2012; Article 98 of Regulation 1308/2013; Article 27 of Regulation 2019/787; Article 15 of Regulation 251/2014.
47. Article 52 of Regulation 1151/2012; Article 99 of Regulation 1308/2013; Article 30 of Regulation 2019/787; Article 16 of Regulation 251/2014.
48. Article 54 of Regulation 1151/2012; Article 106 of Regulation 1308/2013; Article 32 of Regulation 2019/787; Article 25 of Regulation 251/2014.
49. Watson K. William, *Reign of Terroir: How to Resist Europe's Efforts to Control Common Food Names as Geographical Indications* (11 June 2021), https://www.cato.org/policy-analysis/reign-terroir-how-resist-europes-efforts-control-common-food-names-geographical.
50. The former General Administration of Quality Supervision, Inspection and Quarantine (AQSIQ) was responsible for exercising the nationwide, uniform administration of the work relating to

competence as broad as, or even broader than, that of the INAO: it could formulate rules and regulations concerning the protection of GI products; it was responsible for the registration procedure;[51] it helped increase awareness of the protection of GI products through promotional and training activities; and it could participate in international cooperation, exchange activities, and WTO negotiations on GIs.[52]

The 2018 Reform transferred the administrative authority from the former AQSIQ to the SAMR – more precisely, to the CNIPA – which is a national office under the supervision of the SAMR.[53] Since the Provisions on the Protection of GI Products issued by the former AQSIQ remain in force, the Provisions constitute the legal basis on which the CNIPA manages the GI product regime[54] and confers a broad competence to the CNIPA.

In September 2020, the CNIPA released the Draft Provisions on the Protection of GIs, which is intended to replace the AQSIQ provisions for GI products. Article 4 of the Draft Provisions is designed to redistribute the managing tasks and responsibilities:

(1) The CNIPA is responsible for the administration and protection of national GIs and the official logo; for the acceptance and examination of the applications for GIs in a unified procedure, and recognize GIs in accordance with the law.
(2) Local administrative departments for IP protection shall be responsible for the administration and protection of GIs and the official logo within their respective administrative areas.
(3) The market regulation departments at or above the county level shall be responsible for the administrative protection of GIs and the official logo within their respective administrative areas.

Regarding the registration of GIs for agricultural products, the competent authorities are the MOA and its agricultural administrative departments at the provincial

the protection of the products of geographical indication. The entry and exit inspection and quarantine bureaus and the quality and technical supervision bureaus of the various localities shall engage ex officio in the protection of the products of geographical indication. *See* Provisions on the Protection of GI Products, Article 4.

51. The former AQSIQ was responsible for proceeding with a formal examination of applications for recognition of GI products, publishing the notice of acceptance, organizing the opposition procedure, appointing the expert panel to carry out the technical review, publishing the notice of approval, coordinating and guiding the administrative law enforcement activities.
52. Dili Biaozhi Chanpin Baohu Gongzuo Xize [Detailed Implementation Rules for the Provisions on the Protection of Geographical Indication Products], 21 May 2009, Article 3.
53. Di Shisanjie Quanguo Renmin Daibiao Dahui Diyici Huiyi Guanyu Guowuyuan Jigou Gaige Fangan de Jueding [Decision of the First Session of the Thirteenth National People's Congress on the Plan for Institutional Reform of the State Council], 17 March 2018.
54. For example, in 2021, the CNIPA registered three names according to the Provisions on the Protection of Geographical Indications. *See* CNIPA, Guojia Zhishi Chanquanju Guanyu Pizhun Guantoushan Jiu deng Liangge Chanpin Shishi Dili Biaozhi Chanpin Baohu de Gonggao [Announcement of Providing the Protection of Geographical Indication Products to Guantoushan Wine and other Two Products], 12 April 2021.

level.[55] Under the MOA, there is an Agricultural Quality Safety Centre (AQSC), whose role is similar to that of the INAO, as several authors have observed.[56]

The main functions of the AQSC include reviewing applications and organizing expert evaluations.[57] To that end, under the AQSC, an expert committee has been established to conduct the review work.[58] The committee consists of experts from various fields[59] and is divided into several working groups according to product category.[60]

[2] Collective Organizations

Both GIs and trademarks are communication and marketing tools and can certainly be considered business assets. However, 'GIs are more than business assets.'[61] The sui generis approach as used in EU countries and China regards GIs as a public asset that cannot be owned by an individual or corporation. Thus, unlike a trademark, which is often more closely associated with individual protection,[62] not everyone can be the owner or 'manager' of a GI.[63] As the protection of the collective interest is conferred on the manager, its qualifications are regulated without exception.

[a] Collective Organizations in French Law

To be eligible in France, applicants must be collective organizations. Prior to the French Ordinance of 2006, producer unions and groups played an important role in the

55. The agricultural administrative department at the provincial level is responsible for accepting and preliminarily examining the applications filed within the administrative region where the GI is located. *See* Measures for the Administration of GIs for Agricultural Products, Article 4.
56. *See* Tian Furong, DILI BIAOZHI FALU BAOHU ZHIDU YANJIU [LEGAL PROTECTION OF GEOGRAPHICAL INDICATIONS], at 270 (Intellectual Property Publishing House, 2009).
57. Measures for the Administration of GIs for Agricultural Products, Article 4.
58. *Ibid.*, Article 11; Nongchanpin Dili Biaozhi Dengji Chengxu [Registration Procedure Concerning Geographical Indications for Agricultural Products], 8 August 2008, Article 9.
59. Experts come from fields such as crop and plant production, animal husbandry, fishery and agricultural quality and safety, etc. *See* Registration Procedure Concerning Geographical Indications for Agricultural Products, Article 9.
60. There are working groups respectively on vegetables, fruits, and grains. *See* Quanguo Nongchanpin Dili Biaozhi Dengji Zhuanjia Pinshen Weiyuanhui Zhangcheng [Statute of the Expert Review Committee for the Registration of Geographical Indications of Agricultural Products], 10 September 2013, Article 6.
61. Daniele Giovannucci et al., *Guide to Geographical Indications: Linking Products and Their Origins* (Organization for an International Geographical Indications Network 11 June 2021), https://www.origin-gi.com/images/stories/PDFs/English/E-Library/geographical_indications.pdf.
62. The trademark can be used by a person other than the proprietor of the mark. If the proprietor itself does not have the right to use the mark, this does not prevent him from registering or owning a trademark. He can grant a person qualified to use the mark. Therefore, a mark can be owned by anyone, even though the latter is not qualified to use it. *See* Cass. com., 16 juin 1964, Bull. civ. III, n° 309.
63. The 'manager' of a GI is also described as the 'guardian of the temple'. *See* Jean-Louis Multon et al., *Traité de droit alimentaire français, européen et international*, Paris, Lavoisier, 2013, p. 581.

recognition and image enhancement of GIs.[64] However, the coexistence of several producers' unions managing the same GI[65] raised doubts as to the representativeness of these groups.[66]

The 2006 reform prioritized the 'Organization for Defence and Management' (ODG) concept. The ODG is a body with a legal personality formed on the initiative of operators (producers, processors, and craftsmen of industrial products) collaborating in a particular production activity, aimed at protecting and adding value to a GI.[67] An AOC or IGPIA can be managed and defended only by one ODG.[68] In cases where several applicants compete for recognition as an ODG regarding the same GI, only one is awarded recognition.[69] It is because of this privilege that both the INAO and INPI require that any request for the recognition of an AOC or IGPIA be filed exclusively by an ODG.[70]

Furthermore, the ODG is assigned the mission of protecting 'general interests', namely the preservation and enhancement of *terroir*, local traditions, *savoir-faire*, and the products obtained therefrom.[71] It thus has the task of preparing the draft product specification; ensuring the application of the product specification by the operators; participating in the implementation of control and inspection plans (i.e., carrying out

---

64. The competent administrative authority may recognize producer unions or groups as the organization responsible for the defence and management of an AOC product. *See* former Article L. 641-25 of the Rural Code (abolished since 1 January 2007): '*Les syndicats ou associations de producteurs d'un produit d'appellation d'origine contrôlée au sens de l'article L. 641-2, ainsi que leurs groupements, peuvent faire l'objet d'une reconnaissance en qualité d'organismes de défense et de gestion par l'autorité administrative compétente, sur une zone de production, pour un produit ou groupe de produits déterminés. A la demande de ces syndicats, associations ou groupements, la reconnaissance peut également viser une association régie par la loi du 1er juillet 1901 et constituée à cet effet pour la réalisation des missions visées au II du présent article. Dans le secteur viticole à appellation d'origine contrôlée, les syndicats ou associations de producteurs ainsi que leurs groupements mènent, conformément à l'intérêt général, leurs actions dans les domaines suivants: connaissance et suivi du potentiel global de production et de ses mécanismes d'évolution; maîtrise de l'évolution de ce potentiel, sous le contrôle de l'Etat; propositions de définition des règles de production, conformément aux dispositions de l'article L. 641-15; protection du nom, de l'image, de la qualité, des conditions de production et de l'aire de l'appellation d'origine conformément aux dispositions des articles L. 115-8 du code de la consommation et L. 641-11 du présent code; participation à la reconnaissance et à la valorisation des appellations.*'
65. An example of several producers' unions managing the same AOC in the pre-2006 period is the AOC '*Lentille verte du Puy*'. *See* Delphine Marie-Vivien, *Le droit des indications géographiques en Inde, un pays de l'ancien monde face aux droits français, communautaire et international*, thèse, Ecole des Hautes Etudes en Sciences Sociales, 2010, p. 395.
66. Norbert Olszak, *Appellations d'origine et indications de provenance*, Répertoire Dalloz de droit pénal et de procédure pénale, 2008 (actualité 2015), para. 192.
67. *See Les organismes de défense et de gestion ODG*, INAO (15 June 2021), http://www.inao.gouv.fr/fre/Espace-professionnel-et-outils/Les-organismes-de-defense-et-de-gestion-ODG; *Qui peut déposer une indication géographique?*, INPI (15 June 2021), https://www.inpi.fr/fr/comprendre-la-propriete-intellectuelle/les-indications-geographiques.
68. However, an ODG can defend and manage different GIs. *See* Article L. 642-17 C. rur.; Article L. 721-4 CPI.
69. INAO, *Guide du demandeur pour la reconnaissance en qualité d'organisme de défense et de gestion*, January 2016, p. 3.
70. The application can also be filed by the representative authorized by the ODG. *See* Article R. 721-1 CPI.
71. Article L. 642-22 C. rur.; Article L. 721-6 CPI.

internal controls); keeping an up-to-date list of operators; and taking part in the defence, protection, and enhancement of the GI, the product, and the *terroir* (or the *savoir-faire* for manufactured products).[72]

Since the ODG is involved in all stages of the life of a GI for the collective benefit of all operators, its representativeness (i.e., relationship with operators) lies at the heart of the system. The ODG is recognized according to its representativeness.[73] Although the French legislation does not require that the ODG have a specific legal form (e.g., a union structure),[74] it must ensure the representativeness of the operators and a balanced representation of different categories of operators under the rules of its composition and functioning.[75] The 'operator' in relation to which the representativeness assessment is performed[76] is defined as 'any person who truly participates in the production, processing, preparation or packaging activities set out in the product specification'.[77] To prove its representativeness, the candidate body must provide information on the number or percentage of operators who are already members of the body and the volumes produced by them.[78] To ensure democratic functioning, it is suggested that the body may function in the form of a general meeting made up of all its members.[79] The body must also represent, in a balanced manner, all categories of operators, including producers, processors, and packagers.

It should be noted that uncertainties remain on the criteria for assessing the representativeness of operators. In the judgment of 25 September 2018, to conclude on the representativeness of the operators within the ODG of the IG '*Porcelaines de Limoges*', the Paris Court of Appeal put forward the number of members of the organization (75 per cent of operators) and its importance in the sector considered (90 per cent of turnover).[80] The question arises as to whether the judges' analysis would

72. Interestingly, Article L. 642-22 of the Rural Code provides that the ODG for AOC products takes part in the common defence and protection actions of the name, the product, and the '*terroir*'. Article L. 721-6 of the Intellectual Property Code uses the same wording in defining the role of the ODG for industrial products, except the term '*terroir*' has been replaced by '*savoir-faire*'.
73. Article L. 642-18 C. rur.; Article L. 721-4 CPI.
74. It only requires that the ODG should be endowed with a legal/civil personality. Article L. 642-17 C. rur.: '*La défense et la gestion d'un produit bénéficiant d'un label rouge, d'une appellation d'origine, d'une indication géographique ou d'une spécialité traditionnelle garantie est assurée par un organisme doté de la personnalité civile.*' *See also* Article L. 721-4 CPI: '*La défense et la gestion d'un produit bénéficiant d'une indication géographique sont assurées par un organisme privé doté de la personnalité morale.*'
75. The representativeness of operators and a balanced representation of different categories of operators are fundamental criteria for the ODG recognition. Other criteria include a balanced representation of professional groups, if it concerns the inter-branch organizations. *See* Article L. 642-18 du C. rur.; Article L. 721-4(3) CPI; Article L. 721-6(4) CPI. *See also* Delphine Marie-Vivien, *Controversies Around Geographical Indications: Are Democracy and Representativeness the Solution?*, 121 Brit. Food J. 2995 (2019).
76. For the wine sector, the representativeness is assessed only on the basis of producers making a harvest declaration. *See* Article L. 644-5 C. rur.
77. Article L. 642-3 C. rur.; Article L. 721-5 CPI.
78. INAO, *Guide du demandeur pour la reconnaissance en qualité d'organisme de défense et de gestion*, 2016, p. 9.
79. *Ibid.*
80. *See* C.A. Paris, 25 sept. 2018, n° 18/00624; *See also* Cass. com., 14 avr. 2021, n° 19-10.327.

have been the same if the minority of operators held the majority of turnover in the sector.[81]

Under the representativeness principle, the ODG has 'compulsory' close ties with operators. First, the operators of a GI must all be members of the ODG.[82] It should consequently not be possible for an ODG to refuse any operator membership.[83] Second, it has been confirmed by the Council of State[84] and subsequently by the Law of 2009[85] that the use of a GI is conditional on membership in the ODG.[86] Thus, the legislation makes it compulsory for all operators to join an ODG.

This compulsory membership enables the ODG to strengthen internal controls and ensure that all actors involved can support the ODG's tasks, such as the drafting of product specifications. However, this obligation has been frequently criticized for 'impairing the freedom of association' and for being 'contrary to the principle of the availability of the PDO/PGI' laid down in EU law.[87]

[b] Collective Organizations in EU Law

The EU law also highlights the role of groups. First, groups 'play an essential role' in the procedure involved in the application for PDO/PGI registration.[88] EU Regulation 1151/2012, Regulation 1308/2013, Regulation 2019/787, and Regulation 251/2014 provide that the application must only be filed by a 'group',[89] namely an association of producers or processors. The legal form of the group is not specified. Regarding its

81. *See* Sylvestre Yamthieu, *Indications géographiques: Représentativité des opérateurs et lieu de production des IGPIA*, Propriété industrielle, n° 5, 2019, étude 12.
82. *See* Article L. 642-21 C. rur.: '*Les opérateurs, au sens de l'article L. 642-3, sont tous adhérents de l'organisme de défense et de gestion, sauf si celui-ci est une organisation interprofessionnelle mentionnée à l'article L. 642-19*'; *See also* Article L. 721-5 CPI: '*Tout opérateur qui en fait la demande est membre de droit de l'organisme de défense et de gestion dès lors qu'il respecte le cahier des charges homologué.*'
83. The fact that the operator is not authorized or has lost his authorization for the concerned production, because of the non-compliance with the product specification, is the only ground for refusal. INAO, *Guide du demandeur pour la reconnaissance en qualité d'organisme de défense et de gestion*, *supra* n. 78, at 7.
84. C.E., 12 févr. 2007, n° 301131.
85. Loi n° 2009-526 du 12 mai 2009 de simplification et de clarification du droit et d'allègement des procédures, J.O. du 13 mai 2009, p. 7920, Article 63.
86. Article L. 642-3(3) C. rur.: '*L'utilisation d'un signe d'identification de la qualité et de l'origine est subordonnée à l'identification des opérateurs auprès de l'organisme de défense et de gestion en vue de leur habilitation, au respect du plan de contrôle ou du plan d'inspection approuvé par l'Institut national de l'origine et de la qualité, et aux résultats des contrôles effectués. Ces contrôles peuvent être réalisés hors de l'aire géographique de production*'; Article L. 721-5(2) CPI: '*Un opérateur ne peut se prévaloir d'une indication géographique que s'il est membre de l'organisme de défense et de gestion de cette indication géographique et est inscrit sur la liste des opérateurs figurant dans le cahier des charges ou sur la liste des opérateurs actualisée et publiée au Bulletin officiel de la propriété industrielle conformément au 5° de l'article L. 721-6.*'
87. GIs should be available to 'any operator marketing a product conforming to the corresponding specification'. *See* Article 12(1) of Regulation 1151/2012; Article 103(1) of Regulation 1308/2013; Article 20(1) of Regulation 251/2014; C.E., 12 févr. 2007, n° 301131.
88. Recital 57 of Regulation 1151/2012.
89. Article 49(1) of Regulation 1151/2012; Article 95 of Regulation 1308/2013; Article 24 of Regulation 2019/787; Article 12 of Regulation 251/2014.

composition, however, the 'group' definition given by the former Regulation 510/2006 is described as 'irrespective of its composition'.[90] This is different from the French law, which expressly requires that the group's composition must ensure the representativeness of all the operators. Regulation 1151/2012 has filled the gap to some extent, by removing the expression 'irrespective of its composition' and by providing that the group shall be 'mainly composed of producers or processors working with the same product'.[91]

In exceptional cases, a single producer may apply for PDO/PGI protection.[92] Regulation 1898/2006 (repealed by Regulation 664/2014), in laying down detailed rules for Regulation 510/2006, first specified the cases in which a single person may be 'treated' as a group: when the person is the only producer willing to be the applicant; when the relevant area possesses features that differ 'appreciably' from those of neighbouring areas; or when the characteristics of the product differ from those of neighbouring areas.[93] The exceptional nature of an application submitted by an individual was then accentuated by the former Regulation 607/2009 (repealed by Regulation 2019/33),[94] which further limited the criteria for legitimate individual applicants, who now had to be 'the only producer in the demarcated geographical area', which had to possess features 'substantially' different from those of the surrounding demarcated areas.[95] Regulation 2019/33 adopted a solution similar to that found in Regulation 1898/2006.[96]

Apart from the function of groups in the application process, Article 45 of Regulation 1151/2012 made a detailed list of their activities under the heading 'Role of Groups'. The group can monitor the enforcement of the protection of registered GIs;[97] develop activities to ensure the compliance of a product with its specification;[98] carry

---

90. Article 5(1) of the former Regulation 510/2006: '"group" means any association, irrespective of its legal form or composition, of producers or processors working with the same agricultural product or foodstuff'.
91. Article 3 of Regulation 1151/2012.
92. Article 49(1)(2) of Regulation 1151/2012; Article 95 of Regulation 1308/2013; Article 12 of Regulation 251/2014.
93. The specific rules for an individual applicant, as set out in Regulation 1898/2006, have been adopted in Regulation 1151/2012 with slight modifications. *See Commission Regulation (EC) No 1898/2006 of 14 December 2006 laying down detailed rules of implementation of Council Regulation (EC) No 510/2006 on the protection of geographical indications and designations of origin for agricultural products and foodstuffs*, OJ L 369, 23.12.2006, pp. 1-19, Article 2.
94. *Commission Delegated Regulation (EU) 2019/33 of 17 October 2018 supplementing Regulation (EU) No 1308/2013 of the European Parliament and of the Council as regards applications for protection of designations of origin, geographical indications and traditional terms in the wine sector, the objection procedure, restrictions of use, amendments to product specifications, cancellation of protection, and labelling and presentation*, OJ L 9, 11.1.2019, pp. 2-45.
95. Article 2 of Regulation 607/2009.
96. Article 3 of Regulation 2019/33.
97. The group contributes to ensuring that the quality, reputation and authenticity of their products are guaranteed on the market, monitors the use of the name in trade, and, if necessary, informs competent authorities. It may take action to ensure adequate legal protection of registered PDO/PGI. It may also take steps to prevent or counter any measures, which are, or risk being, detrimental to the image of those products. *See* Article 45(1)(a), (b), (f) of Regulation 1151/2012.
98. A group is entitled to develop activities related to ensuring compliance of a product with its specification. *See* Article 45(1)(d) of Regulation 1151/2012.

out information and promotion activities;[99] and enhance the value of GIs and improve the effectiveness of the quality scheme.[100]

In the absence of any requirements for legal form or representativeness, the EU law offers a flexibility that can respond to the diversity of the group structures existing in each Member State (e.g., the ODG in France).

[c] *Collective Organizations in Chinese Law*

While it is generally accepted that producers' groups or associations can apply for GI registration under the regimes governed by the former AQSIQ (CNIPA) and MOA, China's regulation focuses on the actions of the governmental administration, ignoring the role of producers' groups, whose activities could support the management and protection of GIs.[101]

Under the 'GI product' regime governed by the CNIPA, the right to apply for the registration of GI products is not exclusive to producers' groups. There are three categories of applicants: the applicant institution (which is usually a local government unit) designated by the government at or above the county level;[102] a professional association appointed by the government; and an enterprise (working with the product) appointed by the government.[103] Thus, a public authority or single producer can act as an applicant only if it is designated/appointed by the government. The most basic applicant requirement as set out in French and EU law – a group structure – is absent, perhaps because groups under the 'GI product' regime play a role much less important than that played by groups in France/the EU.

While it is true that the applicant institution (public authority) can become a management body after registration,[104] it seems that the only function of the producers' group as an applicant is to prepare documentation for its application. It does not turn into a body that manages and protects registered GIs at a later stage.[105]

First, the use of the registered name is conditional neither on prior permission from the group nor on membership in the group. The name is available to any

99. A group develops information and promotion activities aiming at communicating the value-adding attributes of the product to consumers. *See* Article 45(1)(c) of Regulation 1151/2012.
100. Actions may include developing economic expertise, economic analyses, disseminating economic information on the scheme, and providing advice to producers. *See* Article 45(1)(e) of Regulation 1151/2012.
101. Li Xiuli, Liu Shiyi & Xu Weiyuan, Dili Biaozhi Guanli Quewei de Xianshi Kaobian ji Jiejue Fanglue [Realistic Textual Research on and Resolution to Geographical Indication Management Absence], QINGDAO NONGYE DAXUE XUEBAO [JOURNAL OF QINGDAO AGRICULTURAL UNIVERSITY], February 2014, 45.
102. Dong Jingshan, NONGCHANPIN DILI BIAOZHI BAOHU ZHIDU YANJIU [RESEARCH ON THE PROTECTION SYSTEM OF GEOGRAPHICAL INDICATIONS FOR AGRICULTURAL PRODUCTS], at 142 (Intellectual Property Press, 2013); Wang Li, Oumeng Dili Biaozhi Chanpin Guanli Yanjiu [Research on EU Geographical Indications Product Management], Doctoral Thesis, Jilin University, 2015, 32.
103. Provisions on the Protection of GI Products, Article 8.
104. Detailed Implementation Rules for the Provisions on the Protection of GI Products, Article 10(3).
105. Xiuli et al., *supra* n. 101, at 45.

producers whose products are obtained in the production area and conform to the 'GI product standards' and the 'norms regulating GI products'.[106] The delimitation of the production area is proposed 'independently' by the government.[107] Similarly, the product standards and norms are drafted and published by the authorities in charge of standardization.[108] The determination of these two essential issues (the geographical area and production conditions) is not in the hands of the applicant group.[109]

Second, the use of the official logo does not require permission from the group but must be approved by the public authority. The official logo was designed by the former AQSIQ to publicize registered GI products. To use the official logo, producers have to submit another application to a local agency of the former AQSIQ (usually at the municipal or county level),[110] as designated in the AQSIQ announcement about the protection of the GI in question.[111] The application must be examined by provincial agencies and is then forwarded to the former AQSIQ for approval.[112] In other words, applicant groups are involved in the application process as producers who wish to benefit from the official logo.

In April 2020, the CNIPA issued the Administrative Measures for the Use of the Official Logo for GIs, which introduced a new official logo to replace both the logo created by the former AQSIQ (used to publicize GI products) and the logo created by the former SAIC (used to publicize products with GI collective and certification marks). While these new measures have unified the two former official logos, the role of the applicant is not acknowledged.

106. According to Article 21 of the Provisions on the Protection of GI Products, it is prohibited to use the name of the GI product in violation of the GI products standards and norms regulating GI products. The quality and technical supervision department and entry and exit inspection and quarantine department shall investigate and punish those responsible as appropriate.
107. The local government proposes the delimitation of the production area, with no legal obligation to obtain the opinion of the applicant group.
108. In the submission, the applicant shall provide information on the existing standards or norms regulating the GI product, which serves as a basis for the product specification subsequently published by the authorities. However, nothing prevents the authorities from modifying the content of existing standards or norms prepared by the applicant. On the contrary, in French law, the government cannot change the content of a draft decree proposed by the INAO about the delimitation of the production area and the production conditions of an AOC product. It only has the power to veto. *See* Provisions on the Protection of GI Products, Article 18; Detailed Implementation Rules for the Provisions on the Protection of GI Products, Article 18; C.E., 30 juill. 1997, n° 147826.
109. The French Rural Code requires these two elements (the delimitation of the production area and its production condition) to be included in the product specification. *See* Article L. 641-7(1) C. rur.: '*La reconnaissance d'une appellation d'origine contrôlée est prononcée par un arrêté du ou des ministres intéressés qui homologue un cahier des charges où figurent notamment la délimitation de l'aire géographique de production de cette appellation ainsi que ses conditions de production.*'
110. For example, '*Gannan* Tea Oil' has been registered as a GI product in 2016. For producers in the given area who wish to use the official logo, their applications must be submitted to the Ganzhou Entry-Exit and Quarantine Bureau or the Ganzhou Quality and Technical Supervision Bureau. Guojia Zhiliang Jiandu Jianyan Jianyi Zongju Gonggao 2016 Nian di 9 Hao [State General Administration of Quality Supervision, Inspection and Quarantine Announcement No. 9, 2016], 1 February 2016.
111. Detailed Implementation Rules for the Provisions on the Protection of GI Products, Article 23.
112. Provisions on the Protection of GI Products, Article 20.

In short, groups play an essential role in all stages of the life of a GI in France/the EU, but the provisions governing the 'GI product' regime fail to take that role into account, which leads to improper internal management. To remedy this deficiency, several organizations for the defence and management of GI products have recently been created in China. Regrettably, they are not composed of operators but of regional government leaders.[113]

Issued by the CNIPA in September 2020, the Draft Provisions on the Protection of GIs aims to remedy this deficiency by reinforcing the role of the applicant group. Paragraph 32 of the Draft Provisions provides that the applicant shall take measures to control the use of the name of the product's GI and its official logo after the GI is protected.

By contrast, the regime governed by the MOA highlights the role of groups. Under this regime, an application for registration can be filed only by the professional cooperative economic organizations of farmers and industrial associations,[114] selected by the local people's government at or above the county level. However, unlike in French law, where the applicant needs to represent producers working with the same agricultural product, the MOA requires that the applicant be capable of supervising and managing the GI and of providing guidance concerning the production, processing, and marketing of the product.[115]

This difference can be explained by considering the relationship between the producers and the applicant organization after the registration. In China, this relationship is contractual rather than one based on membership in an organization. One of the conditions for using the GI in combination with the official logo is that producers must conclude an agreement with the organization that includes provisions on the use of the GI as well as the obligations and responsibilities.[116] Within the framework of this contract, the organization operates a management system to guarantee long-term regulatory compliance after registration and provide services and consulting.[117] The producers are obliged to accept supervision by the organization.[118]

113. For example, the management committee of the GI wine product in Hexi Corridor comprises governors, municipal mayors, and local authorities. *See* Gansusheng Renmin Zhengfu Bangongting Guanyu Chengli Hexi Zoulang Putaojiu Guojia Dili Biaozhi Chanpin Baohu yu Guanli Weriyuanhui de Tongzhi [General Office of the People's Government of Gansu Province' Notice on the Establishment of the Committee of the Defence and the Management of Hexi Corridor Wine Products], 12 June 2013.

114. The applicant must be a public service organization. Government institutions, individuals and enterprises are not allowed to file an application. *See* Nongchanpin Dili Biaozhi Dengji Shenqingren Zige Queren Pingding Guifan [Guidelines for Examination on the Qualification of the Applicant], 23 October 2015, Article 3.

115. Measures for the Administration of GIs for Agricultural Products, Article 8; Registration Procedure Concerning GIs for Agricultural Products, Article 2.

116. Measures for the Administration of GIs for Agricultural Products, Article 15; Nongchanpin Dili Biaozhi Shiyong Guifan [Regulations on the Use of Geographical Indications for Agricultural Products], 8 August 2008, Article 4.

117. Regulations on the Use of GIs for Agricultural Products, Article 7.

118. Measures for the Administration of GIs for Agricultural Products, Article 17; Regulations on the Use of GIs for Agricultural Products, Article 8.

Moreover, the group is given the task of drafting the technical norms for quality control, which include the geographical area, a description of the production method, and a description of the natural eco-environment.[119] Once the GI is registered, the draft technical norms become mandatory technical specifications, which constitute the basis for product management and quality control.[120] The function of technical norms for quality control is very similar to that of the French *cahier des charges*.

[B] Conditions for Recognition of GIs

In both Europe and China, the sui generis protection of GIs is intended to benefit geographical denominations that meet certain substantive conditions and are recognized in accordance with a special procedure.

[1] Substantive Conditions for Recognition of GIs

Regardless of the subcategories concerned,[121] GIs under both Europe's and China's sui generis regimes serve primarily as an indication of the geographical origin of the product in the form of a place name. In these systems, a place name deserves protection as a specific IP title when a link, close or loose, is established between the product and the place. The link can be constructed in several ways, focusing on either the natural or cultural dimension of the *terroir*. The issue of linkage has been analysed in Chapters 1 and 2 regarding the evolution of the GI notion. In this chapter, we focus on the name and its capacity to constitute a GI.

[a] Substantive Conditions in French Law

The AOC and IGPIA must be formed with verbal indicators (names). Figurative signs, such as symbols or shapes, may also serve to indicate a product's place of origin, and an exclusive right to use a certain figurative sign (e.g., a special type of bottle) may therefore be granted in order to prevent consumers from confusing products of different quality and origin.[122] However, they cannot qualify for AOC or IGPIA status.

---

119. Measures for the Administration of GIs for Agricultural Products, Article 9; Registration Procedure Concerning GIs for Agricultural Products, Article 6.
120. Nongchanpin Dili Biaozhi Zhiliang Kongzhi Jishu Guifan Bianxie Zhinan [Guidelines for Drafting the Technical Norms for Production of GIs for Agricultural Products], 25 May 2010.
121. The subcategories include the AOC and IGPIA in France, the PDO and PGI in the EU, and the GI products and GIs for agricultural products in China.
122. For example, the use of the bottle known as the '*flûte d'Alsace*' was restricted to certain quality wines from specific regions: '*Alsace*', '*Crépy*', '*Château-Grillet*', '*Côtes de Provence*', '*Cassis*', '*Jurançon*', and '*Béarn*'. *See Commission Regulation (EEC) No 997/81 of 26 March 1981 laying down detailed rules for the description and presentation of wines and grape musts*, OJ L 106, 16.4.1981, p. 1, Article 18; Case 16/83 *Criminal proceedings against Karl Prantl* [1984] ECR 01299, para. 26; Cass. com., 11 oct. 1988, n° 87-11.804.

Another substantive condition for constituting an AOC/IGPIA is that the name must carry a geographical (not a generic) connotation.[123] It follows from Article L. 431-1 of the French Consumer Code and Article L. 721-2 of the IP Code that a place name could, on principle, satisfy this condition.[124] An AOC may consist of the name of a tiny parcel of land ('*Romanée*', '*Condrieu*'), of a city ('*Bordeaux*'), of a department ('*Cantal*'), or of a larger region like '*Bretagne*'. Article L. 431-1 expressly provides that an AOC may even consist of the name of a country ('*Cuba*').[125] By contrast, Article L. 721-2 provides, in more general terms, that the name of 'a geographical area' or of 'a particular place' may constitute an IGPIA. The use of the name of a country as an IGPIA is not specifically prescribed by law.

Moreover, it is accepted in practice that a name that is not, strictly speaking, a geographical reference could be recognized as an AOC when that name has been used to describe a product from a specific geographical area.[126] We may mention the AOC '*Muscadet*', which was not a place name but a designation of a variety of grape in the middle of the seventeenth century. Today, the term has lost its original meaning and has acquired a geographical signification designating dry white wines produced in the south of *Nantes*.[127] Its admission as an AOC is justified because it fulfils the same function as that of the 'classic' AOC.[128]

Conversely, a name that has a geographical connotation may lose its original meaning and be no longer viewed as an indication of the origin of a product but rather as an indication of a broad category of a product 'regardless of the geographical origin'.[129] An example of a name that is considered to have become generic is the appellation '*Camembert*':[130] originating as the place name for a community in Normandy where a particular cheese was exclusively manufactured, the term '*Camembert*' now refers to a type of cheese produced throughout the world.[131]

---

123. Joined Cases C-465/02 & C-466/02 *Kingdom of Denmark v. European Commission* [2005] ECR I-09115, para. 86.
124. Article L. 431-1 C. consom.: '*Constitue une appellation d'origine la dénomination d'un pays, d'une région ou d'une localité ...*'; Article L. 721-2 CPI: '*Constitue une indication géographique la dénomination d'une zone géographique ou d'un lieu déterminé ....*'
125. The appellation of origin '*Cuba*' is protected in France for covering tobacco products. Therefore, the public identifies the origin of the products through the term '*Cuba*'. *See* C.A. Paris, 4 juill. 1985, PIBD 1986, n° 383, III, p. 50; Cass. com., 29 mars 1994, n° 92-11.959.
126. The registration of a traditional non-geographical name as the AOC is not expressly provided in French law.
127. Also worth mentioning is the appellation '*gruyère*'. The term '*gruyère*' comes from the Gruyere officer who collected the taxes in the form of cheese during the time of Charlemagne. *See* Cahier des charges de l'appellation d'origine contrôlée Muscadet Coteaux de la Loire homologué par le décret n° 2011-1533 du 14 novembre 2011, J.O. du 16 nov. 2011; Christine Lebel, *Sauvons le Gruyère! À propos de la résolution de l'Assemblée nationale relative à la demande d'enregistrement de la dénomination Gruyère en appellation d'origine protégée*, Droit rural, n° 383, 2010, alerte 73; Norbert Olszak, *Sauvons le gruyère ... générique!*, Droit rural, n° 385, 2010, comm. 105.
128. Denis Rochard, *La protection internationale des indications géographiques*, Paris, Presses Universitaires de France, 2002, p. 73.
129. Caroline Le Goffic, *Dégénérescence des indications géographiques: où situer le point de non-retour?*, Droit rural, n° 424, 2014, étude 11.
130. It has been held otherwise that the term '*Morbier*' did not become a common name for a type of cheese because it traditionally refers to the cheese originating from Jura or Doubs, and it is

The generic status 'breaks the link between the designation and the territory',[132] so that generic terms can no longer perform their function of indicating a product's specific geographical origin. They also 'form part of the general cultural and gastronomic stock and may, in principle, be used by any producer'.[133] The rationale behind the exclusion of generic terms from the scope of the GI is thus clear.[134]

Although French law contains no provision expressly ruling out generic terms, the applicant faces the risk that its name will not be registered because it is generic. French judges have excluded names 'already fallen into the public domain' from the scope of the AO, just as in the case of '*Moutarde de Dijon*'[135] or '*Nougat de Montélimar*'.[136] The Council of State has stated that the generic nature of a name would 'challenge its classification among appellations of origin'.[137]

Nevertheless, this does not exclude the possibility of registering a 'compound designation', associating the generic name of the product with a name that has a geographical signification (e.g., '*Camembert de Normandie*' or '*Époisses de Bourgogne*').[138] However, this type of indicator also raises the question of how to define the protection scope: does the protection cover only the two parts as a whole, or does it also cover each part on its own?[139] In light of the case law, the AO enjoys protection not only in the exact form in which it is registered but also with regard to the elements of the compound structure.[140] Thus, using a part of the registered appellation may constitute

not commonly used in other regions of France as well as other Member States of the EU. The reputation of the name '*Morbier*' remains attached to the traditional cheese manufactured in a *terroir*. *See* C.E., 5 nov. 2003, n° 230438; Denis Rochard, *Retour vers les origines … géographiques*, Droit rural, n° 5, 2005, étude 6.

131. C.A. Orléans, 20 janv. 1926, Ann. propr. ind. 1927, p. 331; Denis Rochard, *De la difficulté de qualifier un terme de générique!*, Droit rural, n° 328, 2004, étude 5.
132. Case C-446/07 *Alberto Severi v. Regione Emilia Romagna* [2009] ECR I-08041, para. 5.
133. Case C-317/95 *Canadane Cheese Trading and Afoi G. Kouri v. Ypourgou Emporiou and Others* [1997] ECR I-04681, para. 28 (AG Opinion)
134. Article 24.6 of the TRIPS Agreement provides that there is no obligation to protect a term, which is 'customary in common language as the common name for such goods or services'.
135. C.A. Paris, 19 mars 1929, Ann. propr. ind. 1930, p. 257.
136. Cass. req., 24 oct. 1928, Ann. propr. ind. 1929, p. 113.
137. C.E., 5 nov. 2003, n° 230438: '*Considérant, en premier lieu, que la circonstance que le morbier figure dans l'annexe du décret du 30 décembre 1988 pris pour l'application de la loi du 1er août 1905 sur les fraudes et falsifications des produits ou services et de la loi du 2 juillet 1935 tendant à l'organisation et à l'assainissement du marché du lait en ce qui concerne les fromages ne saurait faire obstacle à ce qu'à l'occasion de la définition d'une appellation d'origine contrôlée soit désormais réservée aux fromages répondant à cette définition la dénomination de Morbier à condition toutefois que cette dénomination ne revête pas un caractère générique s'opposant à son classement parmi les appellations d'origine.*'
138. Other examples concerning compound designations include: '*dentelles de Calais*', '*tapisserie d'Aubusson*', '*faïence de Moustiers*', '*faïence de Quimper*', '*porcelaine du Berry*', '*granit de Bretagne*', '*porcelaine de Limoges*', '*linge du Pays basque*'. *See* Nicolas Bouche, Professeur de l'université Jean Moulin Lyon 3, *IGPIA Conditions substantielles de la protection*, Présentation au Colloque Les indications géographiques protégeant les produits industriels et artisanaux (IGPIA), 3 févr. 2016, Lyon.
139. Séverine Visse-Causse, *La guerre des camemberts est déclarée … Des conséquences du mauvais usage de l'appellation d'origine*, Droit rural, n° 406, 2012, étude 11; Joanna Schmidt-Szalewski, *Site du feuilleton des Époisses*, Propriété industrielle, n° 3, 2002, comm. 37.
140. C-132/05 *Commission v. Germany* [2008] ECR I-00957.

infringement.[141] Nevertheless, one part alone may not be protected depending on the circumstances (e.g., if that part is a generic term).[142] Regarding this subject, Article L. 721-8 of the IP Code clearly indicates that the use of a generic name does not constitute infringement.[143]

Finally, it has to be noted that a name with only a geographical connotation is just an indication of origin. What makes the AOC and IGPIA different from a simple indication of origin is the internal link that unites the product to the *terroir*.[144]

The link to *terroir* is a fundamental condition for the recognition of an AO.[145] A causal link between the specific nature of the geographical area and the characteristics of the product must be demonstrated in the recognition procedure.

As we have seen in Chapter 1, the concept of *terroir* is traditionally based on the idea that 'the appellation is attributed to the land that has certain characteristics, which gives the product its distinctive features'.[146] Thus, the criteria applied in granting AOC status and, more specifically, in delimiting the authorized production area are based primarily on natural factors, such as the 'geological composition of the soil, gradient of slope, aspect and sunlight'.[147] These factors may influence production methods and can give raw materials their specific characteristics. It is thus believed that products benefiting from the same appellation are always produced in places that share 'geological, pedological and climatic' characteristics.[148] A place that is initially not included in the authorized production zone can be added in the AOC area if it presents the same natural (physical) characteristics[149] and vice versa.[150] It logically follows that

141. Cass. crim., 18 juin 1997, n° 96-83.018.
142. Cass. com., 6 févr. 2001, n° 99-85.218; Joined Cases C-129/97 & C-130/97 *Criminal proceedings against Yvon Chiciak and Fromagerie Chiciak and Jean-Pierre Fol* [1998] ECR I-03315; Caroline Le Goffic, *Le parmesan, c'est râpé!*, Propriété industrielle, n° 7-8, 2008, étude 16; C.E., 21 mars 2001, n° 219809; C.E., 27 juill. 2001, n° 216433; E. Saulnier, *Appellations d'origine et indications géographiques protégées*, Europe, n° 1, 2002, comm. 13.
143. Article L. 721-8(4) CPI: '*Lorsqu'une indication géographique contient en elle-même le nom d'un produit considéré comme générique, l'utilisation de ce nom générique n'est pas considérée comme contraire aux 1° ou 2° du présent I.*'
144. Jacques Azema & Jean-christophe Galloux, *Droit de la propriété industrielle*, 7e éd., Paris, Dalloz, 2012, p. 978.
145. INAO, *Guide du demandeur d'une appellation d'origine protégée (AOP) ou d'une indication géographique protégée (IGP)*, *supra* n. 32, at 23.
146. Anne F. Debrez, *Les tendances jurisprudentielles 'des délimitations' des appellations d'origine contrôlées viti-vinicoles*, Recueil Dalloz, 2005, p. 282.
147. C.E., 20 sept. 1993, n° 112635: '*… en ce qui concerne la composition géologique du sol et du sous-sol, les pentes, l'exposition, l'ensoleillement, différentes parcelles du domaine du Château d'Arsac présentent des caractéristiques de terroir semblables à celles d'unités disséminées au sein de l'appellation d'origine contrôlée Margaux*'.
148. C.E., 30 déc. 2009, n° 311113.
149. *See* C.E., 20 sept. 1993, n° 112635; concerning the PDO, *see Publication of an amendment application pursuant to Article 6(2) of Council Regulation (EC) No 510/2006 on the protection of geographical indications and designations of origin for agricultural products and foodstuffs*, OJ C 198, 22.8.2009, p. 23: 'The municipality of *Militello in Val di Catania* has been added, which borders on the production area and shares the same soil and climate characteristics as well as the same traditions.'
150. A place is likely to be excluded from the authorized AOC area if it presents different natural characteristics. *See* C.E., 29 juin 1998, n° 161674.

the evaluation of potential similarity between areas can be purely scientific and depend largely on judicial expertise.[151]

However, the *terroir* concept has evolved from a model that was targeted only at scientific parameters into a model that also concerns human elements.[152] The constant interactions between soil-climate factors and human contributions 'form the identity of the wine region',[153] which deserves the protection of GIs. The practices and *savoir-faire* shared in the geographical area underpin the link to the *terroir*. The case of the *Champagne* AOC is significant: several elements of the elaboration of *Champagne*, from the harvesting to the bottling process, have been transformed into statutory requirements that must be fulfilled for local producers to become legitimate users of the AOC.[154] Thus, local practices (production and processing practices) and the history of the manufacturing of the product should be codified in the *cahier des charge* (product specification).[155] However, these human factors alone cannot justify AOC recognition or the right to protected designation. The '*Margaux*' judgment of 30 December 2009 posited that the fact that the 'water and soil characteristics (of the land) were at a far distance from requirements' could not be offset by the long-standing and constant use of the lands as a vineyard.[156] Thus, the disputed parcel of land was to be excluded from the defined geographical area.

Regarding IGPIA recognition, the physical environment requirements are further relaxed. In its guild for applicants, the INPI requires that the *cahier des charge* describe the manufacturing process (preparation, production, and processing), which must all take place in the geographical zone and which must guarantee the product's characteristics (quality, reputation, or other characteristics).[157] This could lead one to think that the features of the manufactured product are due simply to its production method and that natural factors are no longer dominant. However, the *terroir* concept is not abandoned. In the IGPIA application process, the INPI ensures not only that the product has certain characteristics but also that these characteristics are 'essentially attributable' to its geographical origin.[158] Here, we can draw a useful parallel with

151. C.E., 2 mars 1979, Rec. CE, 1979, p. 90; C.E., 28 juill. 1995, n° 158609; C.E., 2 oct. 1996, n° 164289.
152. *See* Chapter 1 *supra*.
153. Théodore Georgopoulos, *Le contentieux de la délimitation géographique des AOC*, Droit Administratif, n° 4, 2010, comm. 48.
154. Sylvie Diart-Boucher, *La Réglementation vitivinicole champenoise*, thèse, Université de Reims, 2006.
155. INAO, *Guide du demandeur d'une appellation d'origine protégée (AOP) ou d'une indication géographique protégée (IGP)*, *supra* n. 32, at 25.
156. *See* C.E., 30 déc. 2009, n° 311113; Sylvie Diart-Boucher, *La réglementation vitivinicole champenoise: Une superposition de règles communautaire, nationales et locales*, Paris, Editions L'Harmattan, 2007, p. 142.
157. *See Que doit comporter le cahier des charges?*, INPI (15 June 2021), https://www.inpi.fr/fr/comprendre-la-propriete-intellectuelle/les-indications-geographiques/que-doit-comporter-le.
158. Article L. 721-3 CPI: '*Lorsqu'il instruit la demande d'homologation ou de modification du cahier des charges, l'Institut national de la propriété industrielle s'assure que les opérations de production ou de transformation décrites dans le cahier des charges, ainsi que le périmètre de la zone ou du lieu, permettent de garantir que le produit concerné présente effectivement une qualité, une réputation ou d'autres caractéristiques qui peuvent être essentiellement attribuées à la zone géographique ou au lieu déterminé associés à l'indication géographique.*'

registration for PGI, whose definition is very close to that of IGPIA. Lithuania applied to register the name '*Germantas*' as a PGI for a type of cheese. Having examined the application, the Commission noted that 'specific characteristics of the cheese are due to its production method and they are not attributable to the geographical origin'.[159] As it failed to show 'a link between these factors (production method) and the geographical origin', the application did not meet the basic criteria for registration as a PGI.[160]

Thus, for IGPIA recognition, it is not sufficient to ensure a link between the product's features and human factors; it is also important to show a link between human factors and the place of origin. The latter link could be established by indicating a high concentration in a given area of workshops that possess the same traditional *savoir-faire*.[161] Such a concentration does not happen just by chance but through choices made by several generations of fabricants based, in part, on natural factors in a geographical area. For example, the geographical area of the IGPIA '*Siège de Liffol* (Chair)' is in the centre of a forest of beech trees (*hêtre*). The beech has been the wood most commonly used in the manufacture of stylish chairs for the French nobility since the seventeenth century owning to its physical features, the fineness of its grain, and its ease of workmanship. It is also because of the physical characteristics of the beech that local producers developed their particular methods of production. (For instance, owing to its high density and thus exceptional resistance, the tack has been used in upholstery since the seventeenth century).[162]

[b] Substantive Conditions in EU Law

It is clearly specified in the European regulations on GIs that the PDO/PGI is by its nature 'a name which identifies a product originating in a specific place, region or country'.[163] The use of the term 'name' suggests a willingness to restrict eligible designations to direct GIs. Indirect GIs (figurative signs) are precluded, regardless of their ability to inform consumers of the place of origin of the product.

159. *Commission decision of 19 December 2008 rejecting an application for entry in the register of protected designations of origin and protected geographical indications provided for in Council Regulation No 510/2006 (Germantas) (PGI)*, OJ L 8, 13.1.2009, p. 25.
160. *Ibid.*
161. *Avis relatif à l'ouverture d'une procédure d'enquête publique sur la demande d'homologation d'un cahier des charges pour l'indication géographique 'ESPADRILLE DE MAULÉON – MAULEKO ESPARTINA'*, J.O. du 6 juill. 2016, texte n° 148.
162. Décision n° 2016-221 relative à l'homologation du cahier des charges de l'indication géographique 'Siège de Liffol', Bulletin Officiel de la Propriété Industrielle du 2 décembre 2016; Avis relatif à l'ouverture d'une procédure d'enquête publique sur la demande d'homologation d'un cahier des charges pour l'indication géographique 'Siège de Liffol', J. O. du 2 juin 2016, texte n° 102.
163. Regulation 1151/2012 for agricultural products (Article 5) defines both the PDO and PGI as a name identifying the place of origin. However, it should be noted that Regulation 1308/2013 (Article 93) defines the PDO as the name of a place but describes the PGI as 'an indication referring to a region, a specific place or a country'. Similarly, in both Regulation 2019/787 for spirit drinks (Article 3) and Regulation 251/2014 for aromatized wine products (Article 2), the GIs definitions are formulated as an indication which identifies a product as originating in a specific locality.

The name of which the PDO/PGI is composed does not have to be a 'geographical name' or 'the name of a region, a specific place or a country'.[164] This means that non-geographical names can be registered as a PDO/PGI if they are traditionally used to describe the geographical origin of the product.[165] A 'name' can also legitimately incorporate both geographical and non-geographical references (e.g., the generic name of a product) and form a 'compound designation'.

European law provides clearer rules for the use of generic terms than French law does. First, generic terms are expressly excluded from GI protection. A name that has become generic cannot be registered as a PDO or PGI.[166] Second, although a generic term may form part of a compound designation, it should retain its generic status.[167] The use of a generic name contained within a registered designation is not considered to be contrary to the rules on the protection of PDO/PGI in European law.[168] In the judgment of 4 December 2019, the CJEU considered that the protection of the PGI 'Aceto Balsamico di Modena' does not extend to the use of individual non-geographic components ('Aceto', 'Balsamico', and 'Aceto Balsamico').[169] The court explained:

> First, it is established that the term 'aceto' is a common term, as previously held by the Court. Second, the term 'balsamico' is the Italian translation of the adjective 'balsamic' which has no geographical connotation and which, in the case of vinegar, is commonly used to refer to a vinegar with a bitter-sweet flavour. It is therefore also a common term within the meaning of the case-law referred to in paragraph 26 of this judgment.[170]

Furthermore, after stating that names that have become generic cannot be registered, the EU legislation expressly defines the criteria that apply in the assessment of generic status, 'to shield terms from an easy slide into genericide'.[171] According to Article 41 of Regulation 1151/2012, in establishing whether a name has become generic, account is to be taken of 'all relevant factors', particularly 'the existing situation in areas of consumption' (including the Member State from which the product

164. Article 2 of Regulation 510/2006 defines both PDO and PGI as 'the name of a region, a specific place, or a country'. However, Article 5 of Regulation 1151/2012 only requires the designation to be composed of a name.
165. For example, the word '*feta*' is of Italian origin and was brought into Greece through the influence of Venice. It is derived from '*fetta*', which means 'slice'. The use of the word gained acceptance in Greece in the nineteenth century to designate the traditional white cheese in brine, which has been made in almost the whole area of Greece. *See* Case C-317/95 *Canadane Cheese Trading and Afoi G. Kouri v. Ypourgou Emporiou and Others*, *supra* n. 133, para. 14 (AG Opinion).
166. Article 6(1) of Regulation 1151/2012; Article 101(1) of Regulation 1308/2013; Article 35(1) of Regulation 2019/787; Article 18(1) of Regulation 251/2014.
167. Recital 52 of Regulation 1151/2012.
168. Article 13(1) of Regulation 1151/2012: 'Where a protected designation of origin or a protected geographical indication contains within it the name of a product which is considered to be generic, the use of that generic name shall not be considered to be contrary to points (a) or (b) of the first subparagraph.' *See also* Case C-519/14 P *Schutzgemeinschaft Milch und Milcherzeugnisse eV v. European Commission* (ECJ 6 October 2015) para. 21.
169. Anne Rigaux, *Indications géographiques protégées*, Europe, n° 2, 2020, comm. 52.
170. Case C-432/18 *Consorzio Tutela Aceto Balsamico di Modena* (ECJ 4 December 2019) para. 34.
171. Dev Gangjee, *Say Cheese! A Sharper Image of Generic Use Through the Lens of Feta*, 29 Eur. Intell. Prop. Rev. 172 (2007).

originates and other Member States)[172] and the relevant national or Union legal acts. The EU case law has identified diverse factors that might influence the outcome of the generic status assessment, such as the consumer perception of the alleged generic name, the use of the name by commercial operators in certain Member States, the place of production of the product under the name in question, and the protection of the name in national and European legislation or under other international agreements.[173]

These criteria could be considered a 'high threshold',[174] which makes it difficult to establish the generic status of a name. To begin with, the fact that all relevant factors (which might be 'legal, economic, technical, historical, cultural and social')[175] must be taken into account implies a high burden of proof. Since a generic designation cannot be presumed,[176] the expense of gathering sufficient evidence to establish generic status is high.[177] Even if the party claiming that the name has become generic has submitted evidence suggesting its generic character, the claim would still be dismissed if the proved fact is deemed to be 'only one factor of several which must be taken into account'.[178] For example, a number of attempts to establish the generic status of '*Feta*' have been unsuccessful even though it has been proved that it has been produced in places other than the Hellenic Republic;[179] quotations from dictionaries and specialist literature have been provided to support the generic status of '*Parmesan*';[180] the evidence shows that trademarks and the labels of commercial companies use the term '*Bayerisches*' as a synonym for the old Bavarian bottom-fermentation brewing method;[181] and Internet research has shown the high frequency with which the term '*Grana*' appears online.[182]

As noted by the CJEU, generic status can be established only if 'the direct link between the geographical origin of the product and a specific quality of that product, its reputation or another characteristic of the product, attributable to that origin, has

172. Article 3 of Regulation 2081/92 provides that account shall be taken of the existing situation in the Member State in which the name originates and in areas of consumption and the existing situation in the other Member States. These two factors have been synthesized as the situation in the area of consumption in Regulation 1151/2012.
173. Case T-291/03 *Consorzio per la tutela del formaggio Grana Padano v. OHMI* [2007] II-03081, paras 65-67; Case C-343/07 *Bavaria NV and Bavaria Italia Srl v. Bayerischer Brauerbund eV*, *supra* n. 40, paras 101, 106-107; C-132/05 *Commission v. Germany*, *supra* n. 140, para. 53.
174. Gangjee, *supra* n. 171.
175. Case T-291/03 *Consorzio per la tutela del formaggio Grana Padano v. OHMI*, *supra* n. 173, para. 65.
176. Case C-446/07 *Alberto Severi v. Regione Emilia Romagna*, *supra* n. 132, para. 69.
177. In the absence of sufficient evidence, it has been held that 'it is far from clear that the designation "parmesan" has become generic'. Case C-66/00 *Criminal proceedings against Dante Bigi, third party: Consorzio del Formaggio Parmigiano Reggiano* [2002] ECR I-05917, para. 20.
178. Joined Cases C-465/02 & C-466/02 *Kingdom of Denmark v. European Commission*, *supra* n. 123, para. 87.
179. *Ibid.*, para. 80.
180. Case C-132/05 *Commission of the European Communities v. Federal Republic of Germany* [2008] ECR I-00957, para. 54.
181. Case C-343/07 *Bavaria NV and Bavaria Italia Srl v. Bayerischer Brauerbund eV*, *supra* n. 40, para. 108.
182. Case T-291/03 *Consorzio per la tutela del formaggio Grana Padano v. OHMI*, *supra* n. 173, para. 71.

disappeared'.[183] Again, however, how do we determine if this 'direct link' has disappeared? The case law suggests that the link disappears only when 'no significant part of the public concerned that still considers the indication as a geographical indication'.[184] A judicial conclusion that consumers perceive the name to be associated with the place of origin can even be deduced from the product labels, which refer to the image, culture, and tradition of a place.[185] Thus, the European sui generis GI regimes set a high threshold for generic status, aiming to 'prevent an easy slide into genericide'.[186]

Finally, as in French law, the link to *terroir* is a fundamental condition for the registration of a PDO/PGI. The product specification must include details regarding the link between the characteristics of the product and the geographical environment, with its natural and human factors (PDO); or the links between a given quality, the reputation or other characteristic of the product, and the geographical origin (PGI).[187] Where the link has not been demonstrated, the application to register a name as PDO/PGI will be rejected.[188]

[c] *Substantive Conditions in Chinese Law*

In the same way, the sui generis systems for GI protection in China serve primarily as a scheme to protect 'vocabularies'.[189] Products must be 'named after geographical names' for both the definitions of GI products and the GIs for agricultural products.[190]

---

183. Case C-343/07 *Bavaria NV and Bavaria Italia Srl v. Bayerischer Brauerbund eV, supra* n. 40, para. 107.
184. *Commission Regulation 1829/2002 amending the Annex to Regulation (EC) No 1107/96 with regard to the name 'Feta'*, OJ L 277, 15.10.2002, p. 10, Recital 23.
185. Recital 20 of Regulation 1829/2002: '... those cheeses actually bearing the name "*Feta*" on Community territory generally make explicit or implicit reference to Greek territory, culture or tradition ...'; Joined Cases C-465/02 & C-466/02 *Kingdom of Denmark v. European Commission, supra* n. 123, para. 87: '... *feta* is commonly marketed with labels referring to Greek cultural traditions and civilization. It is legitimate to infer therefrom that consumers in those Member States perceive *feta* as a cheese associated with the Hellenic Republic, even if in reality it has been produced in another Member State'; Case C-132/05 *Commission of the European Communities v. Federal Republic of Germany, supra* n. 180, para. 55: '... in Germany, certain producers of cheese called "*Parmesan*" market that product with labels referring to Italian cultural traditions and landscapes. It is legitimate to infer from this that consumers in that Member State perceive '*Parmesan*' cheese as a cheese associated with Italy, even if in reality it was produced in another Member State'.
186. Gangjee, *supra* n. 171.
187. Article 7(1)(f) of Regulation 1151/2012; Article 5(2) of Regulation 2019/34; Article 22(1)(f) of Regulation 2019/787; Article 10(2)(e) of Regulation 251/2014.
188. *Commission decision of 19 December 2008 rejecting an application for entry in the register of protected designations of origin and protected geographical indications provided for in Council Regulation No 510/2006 (Germantas) (PGI)*, OJ L 8, 13.1.2009, p. 25.
189. Denis Rochard, *L'adoption d'un cadre juridique communautaire de protection de la qualité des produits agro-alimentaires: un système de protection du vocabulaire*, Revue de droit rural, 1996, p. 362.
190. Article 2 of the Provisions on the Protection of GI Products: 'GI products are those products that are named after a geographical name ...'; Article 2(2) of the Measures for the Administration of GIs for Agricultural Products: 'GIs for agricultural products are special agricultural product indications, which are named after geographical names ....'

Article 6 of the Detailed Rules for the Implementation of Provisions on GI Products further specifies that a registered name is to be composed of the geographical name and the common name of the product. The GIs for agricultural products must also be made up of the name of a geographical area and the generic name of an agricultural product.[191] Thus, nearly all of the names registered under the two regimes are compound designations.[192] The generic term alone is excluded from protection[193] since it is not associated with a geographical name capable of indicating the place of origin of the product.

However, China's sui generis legislation on GIs includes neither a definition of a generic term nor a description of the criteria used to determine generic status. This determination is hence left to the judges, who, in practice, have used the criteria laid down by the Supreme People's Court for assessing the generic nature of a trademark. Trademarks are determined as generic where they do not indicate the commercial source or origin of the product, but 'indicate a type of product'.[194] Their generic status can be easily established because there are two different routes by which to reach it: legislation, national standards, and industrial norms may directly stipulate that certain terms are generic; or the relevant public (of the whole nation or in certain markets) may view the term as referring to a certain category of products. The fact that a name is listed as the common name of a product in specialized reference books or dictionaries could also constitute a basis for assessment.[195]

As GIs do not function as a source identifier associating the product with a particular enterprise, they are likely to be considered as 'generic' when the criteria designed to assess the generic status of a mark are applied in the assessment of a GI.[196] The Supreme People's Court has held that the term '*Qinzhouhuang*', already registered as a GI product under the former AQSIQ, 'is the common name of a grain product cultivated in a specific region'.[197] In another case concerning the term '*Jinjunmei*', the Beijing People's Court determined its generic status on the grounds that it refers to a kind of black tea from the Mountain *Wuyi*, rather than a particular commercial origin.[198] While genericide practically means the death of GIs in Europe,[199] GIs are consistently regarded in China as generic terms describing a certain category of product

191. Measures for the Administration of GIs for Agricultural Products, Article 7(1).
192. However, foreign geographical names, such as Bordeaux, Cognac, Scotch whisky, and Tequila, have been registered as GI products without being associated with the product's generic name.
193. Detailed Implementation Rules for the Provisions on the Protection of GI Products, Article 8(2).
194. Zhang Yumin, Kaisa de Gui Kaisa Shangdi de Gui Shangdi [Give back to Caesar what is Caesar's and to God what is God's], RENMIN SIFA [PEOPLE'S JUDICATURE], May 2014, 34.
195. Zuigao Renmin Fayuan Guanyu Shenli Shangbiao Shouquan Quenquan Xingzheng Anjian Ruogan Wenti de Yijian [Opinions of the Supreme People's Court on Several Issues Concerning the Trial of Administrative Cases Involving the Authorization and Determination of Trademark Rights], 20 April 2010, Article 7(1).
196. *See Fuzhou Rice Factory v. Wuchang Jinfutai Agriculture Co. Ltd*, Supreme People's Court (22 December 2017); *Sichuan Bainian Dengying Beef Food Co. Ltd v. Dazhou Honglong Meat Products Co. Ltd*, Supreme People's Court (29 December 2018).
197. *Shanxi Qinzhou Huang Mi (Group) Co. Ltd. v. Shanxi Qinzhou Danshan Huang Mi Development Co. Ltd.*, Supreme People's Court (30 December 2013).
198. *Wuyishan Tongmu Tea Co. Ltd. v. State Administration for Industry and Commerce Trademark Review and Adjudication Board*, Beijing High People's Court (12 December 2013).

from a specific origin. As a result of these findings, registering generic terms as individual marks has been disallowed,[200] and trademark owners have not been entitled to prevent the fair use even of terms that have been registered in connection with other distinctive elements.[201]

This solution is questionable since terms that are generic in a trademark sense may not be able to distinguish certain goods or services from those of other undertakings, but they can indicate the geographical origin of goods and distinguish them in the market. As Professor Zhang Yumin remarks, if such distinctive terms are regarded as generic, they already have one foot in the grave.[202]

Finally, but perhaps most importantly, the product must be linked to the features of the demarcated geographical area: the quality or characteristics of the product must be essentially due to its geographical origin (agricultural GIs registered under the MOA);[203] or a given quality, reputation, or other characteristic of the product must be due to its place of origin (GI products registered under the CNIPA). Thus, application documents must include details on the geographical area (both natural and human factors); details on the quality or characteristics of the product;[204] and a description of the causal interaction between the details on the geographical area and those on the product.[205]

[2] Procedural Conditions for Recognition of GIs

As the French AOC system has been followed as a model in both Europe[206] and in China, the procedural conditions for GI registration have many similarities. From the initial application to final registration, the protection schemes generally encompass similar steps, most commonly a preparatory phase (development of detailed product specifications by applicants), a scrutiny procedure (formality and substantive examination), and an opposition procedure. Nevertheless, the relationship between one scheme and another often varies between the three jurisdictions, creating a lack of comparability across the procedures.

199. Dev Gangjee, *Genericide: The Death of a Geographical Indication?, in Research Handbook on Intellectual Property and Geographical Indications* 508 (Dev Gangjee ed., Edward Elgar Publishing 2016).
200. *Wuyishan Tongmu Tea Co. Ltd. v. State Administration for Industry and Commerce Trademark Review and Adjudication Board, supra* n. 198.
201. *Shanxi Qinzhou Huang Mi (Group) Co. Ltd. v. Shanxi Qinzhou Danshan Huang Mi Development Co. Ltd., supra* n. 197.
202. *See* Yumin, *supra* n. 194, at 37.
203. Measures for the Administration of GIs for Agricultural Products, Article 7(3).
204. *Ibid.*, Article 9.
205. Provisions on the Protection of GI Products, Article 10(3).
206. Bernard Dutoit et al., *La protection des indications de provenance et des appellations d'origine en France, en Italie, en République fédérale d'Allemagne et en Suisse, in Les indications de provenance et les appellations d'origine en droit comparé, Actes du colloque de Lausanne*, Genève, Librairie Droz, 1983, p. 127.

[a] Procedural Conditions in French/EU Law

Concerning the relationship between the European system and national systems, the CJEU has reiterated on several occasions that the aim of the regulations on PDO and PGI was not to establish, alongside national systems, an additional system of protection for qualified GIs[207] but to ensure 'uniform protection' within the EU.[208] The idea is that, because of the exclusive nature of the European regulations,[209] no national protection should operate in the same sphere.[210] Thus, Article L. 641-10 of the Rural Code requires that AOC products, which are covered by the scope of the EU regulations on GIs,[211] apply for PDO/PGI recognition. If the application for European title is refused, the products will lose the national title and no longer be protected as AOC.[212]

However, the exclusivity of the EU system does not preclude the important role of the competent authorities in the Member States.[213] The latter must examine applications to ensure that registered names meet the substantive conditions[214] and monitor official controls to ensure the verification of compliance with the

207. Case C-478/07 *Budějovický Budvar, supra* n. 8, para. 114.
208. Joined Cases C-129/97 & C-130/97 *Criminal proceedings against Yvon Chiciak and Fromagerie Chiciak and Jean-Pierre Fol, supra* n. 142, para. 25.
209. Case C-478/07 *Budějovický Budvar, supra* n. 8, para. 129.
210. In other words, the Member States cannot retain their own systems in the sphere of application of the EU regulation. *See* Case C-478/07 *Budějovický Budvar, supra* n. 8, paras 102-105 (AG Opinion).
211. Article L. 641-10(1) C. rur.: '*Doivent solliciter le bénéfice d'une appellation d'origine protégée les produits agricoles ou alimentaires entrant dans le champ d'application du règlement (UE) n° 1151/2012 du Parlement européen et du Conseil du 21 novembre 2012 relatif aux systèmes de qualité applicables aux produits agricoles et aux denrées alimentaires ainsi que les produits vitivinicoles entrant dans le champ d'application du règlement (UE) n° 1308/2013 du Parlement européen et du Conseil du 17 décembre 2013 portant organisation commune des marchés des produits agricoles et abrogeant les règlements (CEE) n° 922/72, (CEE) n° 234/79, (CE) n° 1037/2001 et (CE) n° 1234/2007 du Conseil auxquels une appellation d'origine contrôlée a été reconnue.*'
212. Article L. 641-10(2) C. rur.: '*Si le produit ne satisfait pas aux conditions posées par les règlements mentionnés à l'alinéa précédent et se voit refuser ou annuler le bénéfice de l'appellation d'origine protégée, il perd celui de l'appellation d'origine contrôlée qui lui a été reconnue.*'
213. Recital 29 of Regulation 1151/2012: 'the means of ensuring that geographical indications and designations of origin are protected should be clarified, particularly as regards the role of producer groups and competent authorities of Member States'.
214. Recital 58 of Regulation 1151/2012: 'applications should be examined by the national authorities of the Member State concerned, in compliance with minimum common provisions, including a national opposition procedure'. The CJEU reasoned that: 'the decision to register a designation as a PDO or as a PGI may only be taken by the Commission if the Member State concerned has submitted to it an application for that purpose and that such an application may only be made if the Member State has checked that it is justified. That system of division of powers is attributable particularly to the fact that registration assumes that it has been verified that a certain number of conditions have been met, which requires, to a great extent, detailed knowledge of matters particular to the Member State concerned, matters which the competent authorities of that State are best placed to check'. *See* Case C-269/99 *Carl Kühne GmbH & Co KG and Others* [2001] ECR I-09517, para. 53.

specifications.[215] They may provide temporary protection to names at the national level until a final decision on registration at the EU level is made,[216] which explains the subsistence of the national title AOC. Member States may also grant protection to products not covered by the scope of the PDO/PGI system, which opens the possibility for creating the IGPIA system.

Thus, while the IGPIA system coexists with the EU system, the AOC system has largely lost its independence, given the increased coverage of the EU regulations on agricultural GIs.[217] The AOC recognition procedure now corresponds only to the national phase of the PDO/PGI application process.[218]

In this national phase, the initial request from the producers is submitted to the INAO and is subject to a formal examination. If the file is complete and admissible, an investigation commission composed of or assisted by experts is then appointed by the national committee to scrutinize the features of the link with the geographical area and prepare a product specification draft. The INAO organizes a national objection procedure that lasts two months[219] before sending the specification draft to the MOA for approval and enactment.[220] The approved specification includes a definition of the geographical area of production and the production conditions.[221] Finally, transitional national protection is granted beginning from the date on which the application was sent to the commission.[222]

The registration procedure at the EU level can be divided into two parts: the scrutiny period (six months) and the opposition period (three months).[223] During the former period, the Commission scrutinizes the applications, with a focus on obvious

215. Recital 46 of Regulation 1151/2012: '... help Member States to better apply provisions of Regulation (EC) No 882/2004 for the controls of geographical indications and traditional specialities guaranteed ...'.
216. Article 9(1) of Regulation 1151/2012: 'A Member State may, on a transitional basis only, grant protection to a name under this Regulation at national level, with effect from the date on which an application is lodged with the Commission.'
217. The sphere of application of the EU regulations expanded. First introduced in agricultural products and foodstuffs, the EU uniform regime is extended to wine, spirit, and aromatized wine products.
218. INAO, *Guide du demandeur d'une appellation d'origine protégée (AOP) ou d'une indication géographique protégée (IGP)*, *supra* n. 32, at 6: '*Dans le cas d'une demande d'enregistrement en AOP, la protection nationale transitoire est automatique: il s'agit de l'AOC ou appellation d'origine contrôlée. Cette dernière est donc une étape préalable à l'enregistrement au niveau européen en tant qu'AOP.*'
219. Article R. 641-13 C. rur.
220. INAO, *Guide du demandeur d'une appellation d'origine protégée (AOP) ou d'une indication géographique protégée (IGP)*, *supra* n. 32, at 36.
221. Article L. 641-7 C. rur.
222. Therefore, the starting date of the national protection can be different from that of the promulgation of the decree that approves the product specification. The starting date will be made available to the public by another notice published in the Official Journal of the Ministry of Agriculture. As an illustration, *See* Arrêté du 16 décembre 2015 relatif à l'appellation d'origine contrôlée Porc noir de Bigorre, J.O. du 26 déc. 2015, p. 24052.
223. These two periods have been shortened in Regulation 1151/2012. In the former Regulation 510/2006, they are twelve months and six months, respectively. *See* Articles 50-51 of Regulation 1151/2012; Articles 6-7 of Regulation 510/2006.

errors.[224] If the commission deems the protection conditions fulfilled, it publishes a document that sets out the main points of the product specification and provides a description of the product-place linkage.[225] Within three months from the date of publication, any natural or legal person (including authorities) may lodge a notice of opposition.[226] On the basis of the above, the commission adopts an implementing act either rejecting the application or registering the name.[227] While in both cases the transitional national protection ceases to exist,[228] the latter confers a uniform protection throughout the EU.

[b] Procedural Conditions in Chinese Law

The sui generis systems for the protection of GI products and of GIs for agricultural products coexist in parallel. Two different procedures, one for each of the two categories, are laid down.

The application for the registration of GI products is submitted to the local bureau of the former AQSIQ (the CNIPA since 2018) for preliminary exanimation,[229] in which the completeness of the dossier[230] and the fulfilment of the protection conditions are scrutinized.[231] Since the preliminary examination focuses on formal requirements, no expert examination board is established, which differentiates the preliminary review from the examination carried out by the CNIPA in the later stage.[232] If the decision is

224. The Commission should subsequently scrutinize applications to ensure that there are no manifest errors. The Commission should verify that the specification contains the required information and that that information does not appear to contain obvious mistakes, and that the designation satisfies the substantial requirements. *See* Recital 58 of Regulation 1151/2012; Case C-269/99 *Carl Kühne GmbH & Co KG and Others, supra* n. 214, para. 54.
225. A single document shall set out the following: the main points of the product specification: the name, a description of the product, including, where appropriate, specific rules concerning packaging and labelling, and a concise definition of the geographical area; a description of the link between the product and the geographical environment or geographical origin, as the case may be, including, where appropriate, the specific elements of the product description or production method justifying the link. *See* Article 8 of Regulation 1151/2012.
226. *Ibid.*, Article 51.
227. *Ibid.*, Article 52.
228. *Ibid.*, Article 9.
229. An application for the protection of a GI product shall be submitted to the competent local authorities. *See* Provisions on the Protection of GI Products, Article 11.
230. The application dossier shall comprise: the proposal of the local government about the boundary of production area for the GI product; the document designating an institution, an association or an enterprise as the applicant; a description of the name, type, boundary of production area, and geographical features; a description of the physical, chemical, sensory and other quality features of the product, as well as the relationship between them and the natural and human factors of the production place; technical norms for the production of the product (including the product processing techniques, safety/sanitation requirements and technical requirements for the processing equipment); a description of the popularity, production, sales and history of the product. *See* Provisions on the Protection of GI Products, Article 10.
231. Shanxisheng Dili Biaozhi Chanpin Baohu Banfa [Provisions on the Protection of GI Products in Shanxi Province], 2 November 2006, Article 15.
232. Detailed Implementation Rules for the Provisions on the Protection of GI Products, Article 12.

favourable, the application dossier is lodged with the CNIPA.[233] The latter shall, after a formal examination, make a public announcement concerning the reception of the application.[234] Within two months from the date of publication, any relevant person or entity may lodge a notice of opposition. If the CNIPA receives no opposition or the opposition has been dismissed,[235] it organizes an expert panel to carry out a technical review.[236] If the conditions are considered fulfilled, the CNIPA issues a public notice informing the public that the product is now protected under its regime.[237]

An application for protecting foreign products as 'GI products' in China shall also be filed with the CNIPA. In this case, the application must be accompanied by the recommendation of the competent department responsible for GI protection in the country or region of origin where the product is located.[238]

A similar procedure is followed to register the GIs for agricultural products. The application is addressed to the administrative departments of agriculture at the provincial level and is subject to a preliminary examination.[239] The dossier is subsequently filed with the AQSC under the MOA for expert review. If the expert committee is in favour of the application, the Centre initiates an opposition procedure that lasts twenty days.[240] If no opposition has been filed, the MOA adopts a decision registering the name, issues a certificate of registration to the applicant, and makes public the technical norms and standards for the product concerned.[241]

Because of the parallel nature of these two sui generis systems, applications from producers who wish to register the name as both a GI product and a GI for agricultural products are subject to two different procedures, which can be bureaucratically and financially burdensome. This explains why the State Intellectual Property Office planned in 2012 to create a more harmonized mechanism, which would allow GIs to be jointly registered by the former AQSIQ, the MOA, and the Trade Office via a single procedure.[242]

233. The local bureau shall forward preliminary examination opinions, the relevant documents and materials to the former AQSIQ (the CNIPA since 2018). *See Ibid.*
234. *Ibid.*, Article 13.
235. *Ibid.*, Article 15.
236. Provisions on the Protection of GI Products, Article 15.
237. *Ibid.*, Article 16.
238. Measures for the Protection of Foreign Geographical Indication Products, Article 7 (2019).
239. Contrary to the preliminary examination conducted by the local bureau of the former AQSIQ (the CNIPA), an expert panel may be brought together to conduct a technical analysis at this stage. *See* Nongchanpin Dili Biaozhi Dengji Shencha Zhunze [Guidelines for the Review of GIs for Agricultural Products], 23 October 2015, Article 4.
240. Measures for the Administration of GIs for Agricultural Products, Article 11.
241. *Ibid.*, Article 12.
242. 2012 Nian Guojia Zhishi Chanquan Zhanlue Shishi Tuijin Jihua [Plan for Promoting the Implementation of the National Intellectual Property Strategy of China in 2012], 10 April 2012, Article 47.

§4.02 CONTROL AND DEFENCE OF GIS

The GI product is not only a quality product but is also a product that is characteristic of the area. It is an expression of *terroir*.[243] Its reputation essentially depends on the specific characteristics and, more generally, the quality[244] acquired through the experience of time and collective production based on the traditional conditions of the region.

If GIs exhibit features of club goods, a producer working with a *terroir* product may face unfair competition from other members who are motivated by the desire to increase productivity at the cost of a reduction in quality and from external producers, who may use the geographical name on products coming from outside to divert potential customers from the GI club members.[245] Thus, there is a need to control common standards of production so that members can collaborate in maintaining quality and prevent the illegal use of a GI.

The French/European sui generis systems for protecting GIs are characterized by high levels of control[246] and protection.[247] However, these features are not found in China's sui generis systems. This explains why the EU requires China to provide a higher level of protection for GIs protected under the EU-China GI Agreement, which came into force on 1 March 2021.

[A] Control of GIs

The control of quality achieved through sui generis systems usually involves different levels and bodies, each with a defined scope and method.

[1] Different Levels of Control

Several solutions for verifying the compliance of a GI product with the common standards of production are possible: the check can be performed by producers on their own initiative (self-control), by producer organizations (internal control), by independent third parties, or by competent authorities (external control). In Europe, the

243. Séverine Visse-Causse, *Pour une défense cohérente de l'appellation d'origine: De la nécessité d'une qualification juridique respectant une institution des terroirs*, Droit rural, n° 380, 2010, étude 2.

244. Joined Cases T-53/04 to T-56/04, T-58/04 & T-59/04 *Budějovický Budvar v. OHMI* [2007] ECR II-00057, para. 189.

245. James Buchanan, *An Economic Theory of Clubs*, 32 Economica 1 (1965); Cerkia Bramley & Kirsten Johann, *Exploring the Economic Rationale for Protecting Geographical Indicators in Agriculture*, 46 Agrekon 47 (2007).

246. Recital 46 of Regulation 1151/2012: 'The added value of the geographical indications and traditional specialities guaranteed is based on consumer trust. It is only credible if accompanied by effective verification and controls.'

247. Recital 32 of Regulation 1151/2012: 'Protection of designations of origin and geographical indications should be extended to the misuse, imitation and evocation of the registered names on goods as well as on services in order to ensure a high level of protection and to align that protection with that which applies to the wine sector.'

preference is external control, particularly control carried out by third parties, intended to provide 'guarantees of competence, impartiality and independence',[248] while control carried out by producer organizations and competent authorities is preferred in China.

[a] Control Bodies in French Law

Prior to the reform of 2006, AOC products were subject to approval procedures, including control over production conditions and control over products.[249] These approval procedures were the INAO's responsibility,[250] but they could be delegated in whole or in part to an authorized body, such as a public administration, a producers' union, or an inter-branch organization.[251] The methods of control were determined by an agreement between the producers' union and the INAO.[252] Therefore, the exercise of control functions was usually provided by the producers' union, which was also responsible for managing and defending the AOC.[253] This approach has a self-management dimension since 'producers establish rules of production and they make sure their production respects every requirement'.[254] It is thus perceived as providing an insufficient guarantee.

In order to strengthen the quality guarantee, the Ordinance of 2006 provided for the establishment of a new monitoring system.[255] While the self-control and the internal control remain,[256] the verification of compliance with common production standards is mainly carried out externally, by an independent third party, not the ODG.[257] The management and defence functions are hence 'strictly separated from the inspection functions'.[258]

248. Article L. 642-27 C. rur.
249. The control over products was usually performed by means of the analytical and organoleptic test. *See* Ancien Article L. 641-2(2) C. rur.; Ancien Article R. 641-8 et Article R. 641-9 C. rur.; Norbert Olszak, *Aspects juridiques de la dégustation d'agrément des vins à appellation d'origine ou indication géographique, in Histoire et actualités du droit viticole La robe et le vin*, Bordeaux, Féret, 2010, pp. 57-72; Norbert Olszak, *Le goût des vins AOP et IGP: description et contrôle des caractéristiques organoleptiques*, Droit rural, n° 371, 2009, étude 5.
250. Ancien Article L. 641-6 C. rur.; Denis Rochard, *AOC, IGP: précisions sur le rôle de l'INAO en matière d'agrément et de contrôle*, Droit rural, n° 4, 2005, comm. 70.
251. Marie-Vivien, *supra* n. 65, at 416.
252. Ancien Article R. 641-8, C. rur.
253. Marie-Vivien, *supra* n. 65, at 416.
254. Laure Bonnaud & Nathalie Joly, *L'alimentation sous contrôle: Tracer, auditer, conseiller*, Versailles, Éditions Quae, 2012, pp. 155-168.
255. One of the goals of the 2006 Law on agriculture is to meet customers' expectations in terms of guarantee for the quality of their products. *See* Loi n° 2006-11 du 5 janvier 2006 d'orientation agricole, J.O. du 6 janvier 2006, texte n° 2.
256. Article R. 642-39 C. rur.
257. Article L. 642-27 C. rur.; Norbert Olszak, *Actualité du droit des signes d'origine et de qualité (indications géographiques, labels)*, Propriété industrielle, n° 9, 2007, étude 18.
258. Norbert Olszak, *Appellations d'origine et indications de provenance (Indications géographiques)*, Répertoire Dalloz de droit pénal et de procédure pénale, 2008 (actualité 2015), para. 225.

In order for the implementation of product specifications to be regularly monitored, all operators must be known in advance of control operations.[259] The operators involved in the production, processing, or packaging of GI products must present the ODG with a statement providing identification and affirming their commitment to respect the production conditions, carry out self-monitoring, and be subject to external controls.[260] The ODG draws up a list of operators, which is periodically sent out to the control body[261] chosen by itself at the GI registration stage.[262]

The control body can be a certification body that ensures the certification of all the SIQOs[263] or an inspection body that monitors the AO and GI concerning wine products, aromatized wine products, or spirits to which the producers have opted to associate the product specification with an inspection plan.[264] Whether a certification or inspection body is involved, it must obtain authorization from the INAO[265] and must be accredited by an accreditation body.[266] The certification body is granted more operational freedom, since it may decide whether to grant, maintain, extend, or even suspend certification in cases of a breach of the specifications.[267] The inspection body does not enjoy this autonomy.[268] It establishes an evaluation report and keeps it at the disposal of the INAO, which then decides on the appropriate measures for sanctioning the breach.[269] In any case, an activity report is submitted to the INAO each year,[270] and all documents relevant to the assessment of the control operation are always at the disposal of the INAO.[271]

The INAO still plays an important role in the control operation. It not only approves control bodies and control plans[272] but also takes steps to ensure a periodic evaluation of the control bodies.[273] To this end, the INAO can perform any verification

259. François Robbe, *Les cahiers des charges des signes de qualité: élaboration et contrôle*, Droit rural, n° 436, 2015, dossier 15.
260. Article D. 644-1 et D. 642-39-1 C. rur.; C.A. Bordeaux, 25 mars 2014, n° 13BX00259.
261. Article L. 642-22 C. rur.
262. Article R. 642-37 C. rur.
263. Article L. 642-28 C. rur.
264. Article L. 642-31 C. rur.: '*Les organismes d'inspection ont pour mission d'effectuer les opérations de contrôle des produits pour lesquels l'article L. 642-2 prévoit que sont associés à leur cahier des charges un plan d'inspection*'; Article L. 642-2 C. rur.: '*Au cahier des charges d'une appellation d'origine ou d'une indication géographique concernant un produit vitivinicole, un produit vinicole aromatisé ou une boisson spiritueuse est associé soit un plan de contrôle, soit un plan d'inspection.*'
265. Article R. 642-41 C. rur.
266. Article R. 642-53 et R. 642-58 C. rur.
267. Article L. 642-30 C. rur.
268. Robbe, *supra* n. 259.
269. Regarding the checks of the IGPIA, the inspection body does not enjoy autonomy, either. While performing the monitoring function, the inspection body shall transmit its report to the ODG, which then adopts adequate measures sanctioning irregularities. *See* Article L. 721-9 CPI; Article L. 642-33 C. rur.
270. Article R. 642-46 C. rur.
271. Article R. 642-48 C. rur.
272. Article L. 642-5(4) C. rur.: '*(INAO) prononce l'agrément des organismes de contrôle et assure leur évaluation*'; Article L. 642-3 C. rur.: '*L'utilisation d'un signe d'identification de la qualité et de l'origine est subordonnée … au respect du plan de contrôle ou du plan d'inspection approuvé par l'Institut national de l'origine et de la qualité ….*'
273. Article L. 642-34 C. rur.

directly with the operators and is allowed access to all premises, lands, and means of transport for professional use.[274] It can also withdraw approval from a control body that no longer satisfies the conditions in accordance with which the approval was granted.[275]

The monitoring function for GIs for industrial products is performed in a similar manner, by a conformity assessment body under the responsibility of the INPI. The latter reserves the right to disqualify the product as an IGPIA in cases where controls have not been carried out.[276]

[b] Control Bodies in EU Law

The obligation to conduct official control over the EU quality scheme devolves onto national authorities, designated by the Member States to 'offer adequate guarantees of objectivity and impartiality'.[277] Regulation 1151/2012 distinguishes between two types of control:[278] control over verification that a product complies with the product specifications before placing it on the market[279] and control over the use of the name in the marketplace.[280] While the former can be carried out by either competent authorities or control bodies, the latter can be carried out only by designated authorities.[281] In France, the competent authorities for marketplace controls are the INAO and the DGCCRF.[282]

Compliance with product specifications is verified by inspection authorities and private bodies operating in the Member States from which the product comes,[283] not by other Member States. This system may be justified given that the control structures of the GI's origin country are best able to monitor compliance.[284] However, since the EU regulations on GIs do not provide for minimum requirements concerning the coverage, frequency, or methodology of these checks, there are discrepancies among the control

274. *Ibid.*
275. The application addressed to the INAO for approval of a control body must specify the activity, sign, and product category, which may serve as a basis for the approval. *See* Article R. 642-42 C. rur.; Article R. 642-49 C. rur.
276. Article L. 721-9 CPI.
277. Article 36 of Regulation 1151/2012; Article 94(2) of Regulation 1308/2013; Article 39 of Regulation 2019/787; Article 23(4) of Regulation 251/2014.
278. Delphine Marie-Vivien, *The Protection of Geographical Indications in India: A New Perspective on the French and European Experience* Part II (SAGE Publishing 2015).
279. Article 37 of Regulation 1151/2012.
280. Article 38 of Regulation 1151/2012.
281. *Ibid.*
282. The DGCCRF *(Direction générale de la concurrence, de la consommation et de la répression des fraudes)* is competent for these checks to prevent and control unfair trading practices between businesses. *See Authorities and/or Bodies Enforcing Compliance with PDO-PGI-TSG Obligations in Respect of Product Placed on the Market (P 2017/0625 Art. 4)*, European Commission (15 June 2021), https://ec.europa.eu/info/sites/default/files/food-farming-fisheries/food_safety_and_quality/documents/national-competent-authorities-food-sector_en.pdf.
283. Case C-132/05 *Commission of the European Communities v. Federal Republic of Germany*, *supra* n. 180, para. 78.
284. Caroline Le Goffic, *Indications géographiques en droit européen*, J.-Cl. Europe Traité, fasc. 1810, 2011, p. 43.

systems set up by the Member States,[285] which may undermine the credibility of the GI quality scheme in consumers' eyes.[286]

[c] Control Bodies in Chinese Law

In China, GIs are subject to monitoring systems. For GI products registered under the former AQSIQ (the CNIPA since 2018), public authorities conduct the verification of compliance with production standards. Local market regulation departments are entitled to: (1) monitor the use of the name to prevent infringement; (2) ensure that production and processing activities take place in the area delimited by the public notice announcing the protection of the product in question; (3) conduct spot checks on the production environment and equipment, and supervise the techniques used to process the product in order to prevent unauthorized modifications of production conditions; (4) organize controls on the quality of the product; and (5) oversee the printing, circulation, and use of the official logo.[287] The CNIPA also conducts random checks annually to verify the compliance of GI products with production standards.[288] However, this regime does not recognize the role of producers, which may impede the potential of groups to develop activities related to surveillance over the use of registered names and product compliance.

By contrast, controls over the GIs for agricultural products rely heavily on internal checks carried out by the specialized farming cooperatives and industry associations that hold the registration certificate. The holder, along with the GI users, 'shall be responsible for the quality of the agricultural product concerned'.[289] To this end, the users must set up a quality control system and accept the supervision carried out by the holder of the registration certificate.[290] Periodically, local agencies of the MOA intervene to provide controls not only on the use of the GI and its production conditions[291] but also on the internal checks and self-controls.[292]

285. European Court of Auditors, *Do the Design and Management of the Geographical Indications Scheme Allow It to Be Effective?* 16 (Publications Office of the European Union 2011).
286. The consumer who buys a PDO or PGI product expects that it complies with the product specification. A robust and uniform system for the checks related to the GI scheme is therefore expected.
287. Provisions on the Protection of GI Products, Article 22; Detailed Implementation Rules for the Provisions on the Protection of GI Products, Article 27.
288. Detailed Implementation Rules for the Provisions on the Protection of GI Products, Article 28.
289. Measures for the Administration of GIs for Agricultural Products, Article 19.
290. *Ibid.*, Articles 17(1), 19.
291. *Ibid.*, Article 18.
292. Henansheng Nongyeting Guanyu Kaizhan 2011 Nian Wugonghai Nongchanpin he Nongchanpin Dili Biaozhi Zonghe Jiancha de Tongzhi [Agriculture Department of Henan Province's Notice on the Comprehensive Inspection over GIs for Agricultural Products], 2 September 2011.

[2] Scope of Control

The use of the GI is reserved for producers who comply with the common production standards. Thus, the scope of control activities should be aimed at ensuring this compliance.

[a] Scope of Control in French Law

The geographical production area of the GI product and its production conditions are defined in the *cahier des charges*, which is drafted by the ODG[293] and subsequently approved by the minister concerned,[294] on the basis of a proposal from the INAO.[295] The production conditions can be very strict. For instance, those for producing *Champagne* include aspects such as variety; vineyard management; the harvest, transport, and ripeness of grapes; and yield, processing, preparation, maturing, packaging, and storage.[296] They may also include measures for preserving the *terroir*.[297]

The *cahier des charges* is associated with a control or inspection plan, on the basis of which control over the compliance of production conditions is carried out.[298] This control/inspection plan, developed by the control body in consultation with the ODG[299] and submitted to the INAO for approval and publication,[300] indicates the self-control performed by producers and the internal control performed under the responsibility of the ODG. It specifies the external control performed, particularly that over the self-control and internal control. It also provides procedures for granting authorization to producers who have the capacity to meet all the requirements of the *cahier des charges*.[301]

The use of GIs is not only subject to the identification of operators by the ODG but is also conditional on the result of the controls carried out.[302] Where the result indicates non-compliance with the *cahier des charges*, administrative measures and penalties may be imposed. These may include a suspension or withdrawal of the right to use the GI on a particular batch or all of the production of the operator in question.[303] In cases of minor breaches, proposals on correction or a formal letter of warning may be sent to the operator.[304]

293. Article L. 642-22(2) C. rur.
294. Article L. 641-7 C. rur.
295. Article L. 641-6(1) C. rur.
296. Décret n° 2010-1441 du 22 novembre 2010 relatif à l'appellation d'origine contrôlée 'Champagne', J.O. du 25 nov. 2010, p. 21013.
297. Article L. 641-6(3) C. rur.
298. Article L. 642-27 C. rur.
299. Article L. 642-32 and L. 642-29 C. rur.
300. Article R. 642-39, R. 642-40, R. 642-54 et R. 642-59 C. rur.
301. Article R. 642-39 C. rur.
302. Article L. 642-3 C. rur.
303. Article L. 642-30 et L. 642-32 C. rur.
304. Article L. 642-33 C. rur.

Rules concerning controls applicable to GIs for industrial products are laid down in Article L. 721-7, L. 721-9, R. 721-9, and R. 721-10 of the IP Code. It is provided that the *cahier des charges* must include information on the attributes of the product and on the control activities. The former defines the geographical area, the characteristic of the product, and its production or processing steps, whereas the latter is used to verify compliance. To this end, the *cahier des charges* sets out the modalities and periodicity of the controls, the type of control body, the methods of funding, and the sanction measures. It can impose declaration and record-keeping obligations on any person engaged in production, processing, or packaging. In cases of non-compliance with the *cahier des charges*, the operator in question is subject to a warning or exclusion procedure.[305] If the controls are not carried out or corrective measures are not implemented, the IP Code explicitly allows for the cancellation of the registration of the GI concerned through a decision issued by the INPI.[306]

[b] Scope of Control in EU Law

As in French legislation concerning the IGPIA, the Commission is entitled to cancel the protection of a PDO/PGI,[307] where compliance with product specifications is not ensured[308] or if no product has been placed on the market for at least seven years.[309] However, the EU GI regulations have not yet provided details on the scope of the control carried out by competent authorities,[310] except for checks related to wine PDO/PGI.[311]

Article 15(5) of Regulation 2019/34 requires each operator to be declared to the control authority, and Article 19 lays down a number of rules concerning the verification of compliance with product specifications. The control conducted in the Member States consists of an organoleptic and/or analytical testing of products and a

305. Article L. 721-7 CPI.
306. Article L. 721-9 et R. 721-7 CPI.
307. *See* Case T-49/14 *Zentralverband des Deutschen Bäckerhandwerks eV v. European Commission* (CFI 7 October 2015).
308. Article 54 of Regulation 1151/2012; Article 106 of Regulation 1308/2013; Article 32 of Regulation 2019/787; Article 25 of Regulation 251/2014.
309. Article 54 of Regulation 1151/2012; Article 32 of Regulation 2019/787.
310. However, Commission Implementing Regulation 809/2014 has provided details on the control system under the common agricultural policy. *See Commission Implementing Regulation (EU) No 809/2014 of 17 July 2014 laying down rules for the application of Regulation (EU) No 1306/2013 of the European Parliament and of the Council with regard to the integrated administration and control system, rural development measures and cross compliance*, OJ L 227, 31.7.2014, pp. 69-124.
311. *Commission Implementing Regulation (EU) 2019/34 of 17 October 2018 laying down rules for the application of Regulation (EU) No 1308/2013 of the European Parliament and of the Council as regards applications for protection of designations of origin, geographical indications and traditional terms in the wine sector, the objection procedure, amendments to product specifications, the register of protected names, cancellation of protection and use of symbols, and of Regulation (EU) No 1306/2013 of the European Parliament and of the Council as regards an appropriate system of checks*, OJ L 9, 11.1.2019, pp. 46-76.

check on the conditions laid down in the product specification.[312] The testing is performed on anonymous samples and carried out at any stage in the production process,[313] whereas control over the production conditions consists in checking both the operator's premises and the products.[314] A tested product can use the GI only if it possesses all the required characteristics and if the production conditions have been met.[315] Any product that fails to meet these conditions may be placed on the market but cannot bear the GI.[316]

[c] Scope of Control in Chinese Law

The production conditions of a GI product registered under the former AQSIQ (the CNIPA since 2018) are prescribed in the relevant national standards, provincial standards, and management norms rather than in a product specification, as required by European law. Such standards and norms are drafted on the basis of the quality and technical requirements of the products,[317] which are contained in the announcement of approval for GI protection. The standards are issued by the State standardization administration[318] and the regional standardization administration, respectively.[319] Where there are difficulties in developing a standard, management norms can be adopted by the local governments above the county level.[320]

Producers who wish to use the official logo of GI products must ensure that their production process conforms to the relevant standards and management norms[321] and must apply for a licence from the CNPIA. The application must be accompanied by a certificate issued by the competent authority of a locality (certifying that the product concerned originates from the area) and an inspection report produced by a quality inspection institution (proving that the product possesses the specific qualities described in the standards or norms).[322] It will then be evaluated by the CNIPA and its local agencies before licensing approval is granted and published. Where compliance with the standards or norms is not ensured or where the licensee has not put the logo

312. The verification shall consist of organoleptic and analytical testing for PDO products, either analytical testing only or both organoleptic and analytical testing for PGI products. *See* Article 19(1) of Regulation 2019/34.
313. *Ibid.*, Article 19(2).
314. *Ibid.*, Article 19(3).
315. *Ibid.*, Article 19(4).
316. *Ibid.*, Article 19(6).
317. Detailed Implementation Rules for the Provisions on the Protection of GI Products, Article 18.
318. Provisions on the Protection of GI Products, Article 18.
319. In practice, regional standardization administrations are often provincial quality inspection departments under the former AQSIQ. *See* Detailed Implementation Rules for the Provisions on the Protection of GI Products, Article 18.
320. Guojia Zhijian Zongju Guanyu Jiaqiang dui Guojia Dili Biaozhi Chanpin Zhuanyong Biaozhi Shiyong Guanli de Zhidao Yijian [Guiding Opinions of the General Administration of Quality Supervision, Inspection and Quarantine on Strengthening the Administration of the Use of the Official Logo for National Geographical Indication Products], 29 December 2015, Article 2.
321. *Zhang Bo v. Jinjiang Metro Co. Ltd. and Guangzhou Tianhe Shopping Mall*, Guangzhou Tianhe District People's Court (21 July 2015).
322. Provisions on the Protection of GI Products, Article 20.

to use within a period of two years or is engaged in the illegal production of counterfeit goods, the licence to use the logo will be revoked.[323]

The scope of control for the GIs for agricultural products is defined in a manner similar to that of the European systems. The producers' group drafts the technical norms for quality control, which include an identification of the geographical area and a description of the natural eco-environment and the production method.[324] Once the GI is registered, the technical norms become mandatory technical specifications, which constitute the basis for product management and quality control.[325] The function of technical norms in quality control closely resembles that of the French *cahier des charges*.

Producers whose production activities are in accordance with the prescribed technical norms can apply to the holder of a GI registration certificate for the right to use the GI.[326] The documents accompanying the application must contain detailed information on the plans for production, marketing, and their own quality control systems.[327] If the application is approved, producers and the registration holder conclude an agreement under which the latter carries out regular inspections to check for conformity in GI use and production methods.[328]

However, neither the GI products regime nor the GIs for agricultural products regime includes a requirement that the plan for the external control of GIs be submitted and approved. The GI regulations also have not addressed detailed questions such as the frequency and method of checks, key control points, and sanction measures. As a result, the extent to which these external controls are realized depends on the ability and willingness of those responsible to monitor the GIs. Where the checks exercised by the local authorities or managers are less strict or less frequent, ideal conditions could be created for compromised quality, as in the case of '*Wuchang* Rice'.[329]

It is worth remembering that the first appellations of origin system, instituted in France in 1905 in response to the wine crisis, proved to be insufficient for ensuring product quality and safeguarding the traditional elements and *terroir* of local products. Later legislation enhanced control over and respect for traditional production methods and led to the AOC system in 1935.[330] The new system turned out to be a huge success

323. Provisions on the Protection of GI Products, Article 23; Guojia Zhijian Zongju Guanyu Jiaqiang dui Guojia Dili Biaozhi Chanpin Zhuanyong Biaozhi Shiyong Guanli de Zhidao Yijian [Guiding Opinions of the General Administration of Quality Supervision, Inspection and Quarantine on Strengthening the Administration of the Use of the Official Logo for National Geographical Indication Products], *supra* n. 320, Article 3(3).
324. Measures for the Administration of GIs for Agricultural Products, Article 9; Registration Procedure Concerning GIs for Agricultural Products, Article 6.
325. Nongchanpin Dili Biaozhi Zhiliang Kongzhi Jishu Guifan Bianxie Zhinan [Guidelines for Drafting the Technical Norms for Production of GIs for Agricultural Products], 25 May 2010.
326. Measures for the Administration of GIs for Agricultural Products, Article 15.
327. Regulations on the Use of GIs for Agricultural Products, Article 3.
328. Guanyu Yinfa Nongchanpin Dili Biaozhi Shiyong Shenqingshu deng Sige Jishu Guifan de Tongzhi [Notice on Publishing Four Technical Specifications such as the Application Form for the Use of GIs for Agricultural Products], 4 July 2008.
329. Yuan Quan & Fang Yuan, Wuchang Zafang Dao Mixiang [How to Prevent the Stealing of Flavour of Wuchang Rice], RENMIN RIBAO [PEOPLE'S DAILY], 11 January 2016.
330. Olszak, *supra* n. 20, at 51-57.

and was expanded to other product sectors and jurisdictions. These developments make clear that effective monitoring measures can play an important role in shaping a more credible GI system. The necessity of these measures can also be demonstrated by considering the negative example of China's GI '*Wuchang*' rice (cited above), whose reputation for quality linked to its place of origin and traditional *savoir-faire* is at risk.

[B] Defence of GIs

It is argued that GIs are conferred with 'near absolute' protection under both French and European sui generis systems.[331] This argument can be supported not only by the fact that the GI cannot be used for any similar product even if this use does not necessarily entail a risk of either confusion or parasitism but also by the fact that its protection is extended to any dissimilar product once the necessary conditions have been met. It can also be supported by the fact that several sanctions can be imposed specifically for the usurpation of a GI.

While the protection afforded under French and European legislation goes beyond conventional 'anti-confusion' and 'anti-parasitism' doctrines, GI regulations in China's sui generis system are in the very early stage of development and provide a clear prohibition only against the 'fraudulent' or 'unauthorized' use of a GI.[332]

We will review the protection of GIs against improper use for, first, identical or similar goods and then for dissimilar products.

[1] Protection of GIs Within the Principle of Speciality

GIs are protected with respect to the particular (or similar) products for which they are used or registered. It must be reiterated that the same rule (i.e., the principle of speciality) applies in the trademark law.[333] However, Article L. 643-1 of the Rural Code related to the protection of AOs makes reference only to 'similar' products, without mentioning 'identical' products as is stated in Article L. 713-2 of the IP Code in delimitating the scope of trademark protection. EU regulations on GIs use the term 'comparable products' to describe the unavailability of the name to third parties. Although it probably would have been preferable to use the same terminology, these

331. For example, in a case concerning the GI *Budějovický Budvar*, one party claims that appellations of origin have a public policy status and absolute protection. In another case, the appellant (*Comité interprofessionnel du gruyère de comté*) considers that the appellations of origin have the right to absolute protection. *See* Joined Cases T-53/04-T-56/04, T-58/04 & T-59/04 *Budějovický Budvar v. OHMI*, *supra* n. 244, para. 29; C.A. Colmar, 8 déc. 2005, n° 1B04/00473.
332. One author observes that GI regulations in China focus on the registration procedure and they do not contain any express provisions defining the scope of the exclusive right of the GI. *See* Zhu Lanye, *An Analysis of China's System of Protecting Geographical Indications*, 1 Asian J. Comp. L. 1, 6 (2006).
333. Like trademarks, geographical indications are subject to the principle of speciality, i.e., they are only protected for the kind of products on which they are actually used. *See* WIPO, *Possible Solutions for Conflict Between Trademarks and Geographical Indications and for Conflicts Between Homonymous Geographical Indications* SCT/5/3 (8 June 2000), para. 20.

descriptions may cover the same ground.[334] Protection for GIs in China's sui generis system is limited to cases where they are used for identical or similar products, although there is no clear mention of this (via terms such as 'identical', 'similar', or 'comparable' products) in the text of the GI regulations.

[a] Protection Within the Principle of Speciality in French Law

The protection of recognized names (including both AO and AOC) is ensured by Article L. 643-1 and L. 643-2 of the Rural Code.[335] The broad wording employed by Article L. 643-1 makes it applicable to any illegal use of appellations of origin for identical or similar products.[336] Article L. 643-2 adds little to this because it addresses only the relationship with the use of indications of origin.[337] We therefore find it appropriate to start with Article L. 643-1 in analysing the content of the protection offered to appellations of origin.[338]

Under Article L. 643-1, 'the name which constitutes an appellation of origin, or any other reference suggesting it, may not be used for any similar product'.[339] At first glance, it seems that this rule falls within the doctrine of trademark protection according to which a sign that is identical to a mark for similar goods or a similar sign for identical or similar goods may not be used if there is a likelihood of confusion. French case law sometimes even borrows the terms 'reproduction' and 'imitation', terms used in the trademark context,[340] when making reference to the misuse of an original appellation[341] and other words suggesting it.[342] The only real difference appears to be linked to the fact that the rule concerning AO protection does not require

334. Alex Tallon, *Les appellations d'origine*, Bruxelles, Larcier, 2016, p. 208.
335. Article L. 431-5 C. consom.: '*Les dispositions applicables aux appellations d'origine contrôlée sont prévues à la sous-section 2 de la section 1 du chapitre Ier du titre IV du livre VI du code rural et de la pêche maritime*'; Ancien Article L. 115-6 C. consom. (ancien, abrogé au 1 juillet 2016): '*La protection des dénominations reconnues est notamment assurée par les articles L. 643-1 et L. 643-2 du code rural et de la pêche maritime.*'
336. Passa, *supra* n. 7, at 775.
337. Article L. 643-2(1) C. rur.: '*L'utilisation d'indication d'origine ou de provenance ne doit pas être susceptible d'induire le consommateur en erreur sur les caractéristiques du produit, de détourner ou d'affaiblir la notoriété d'une dénomination reconnue comme appellation d'origine ou enregistrée comme indication géographique ou comme spécialité traditionnelle garantie, ou, de façon plus générale, de porter atteinte, notamment par l'utilisation abusive d'une mention géographique dans une dénomination de vente, au caractère spécifique de la protection réservée aux appellations d'origine, aux indications géographiques et aux spécialités traditionnelles garanties.*'
338. Article L. 643-1 applies to both ordinary appellations of origin and controlled appellations of origin.
339. Article L. 643-1(2) C. rur.: '*Le nom qui constitue l'appellation d'origine ou toute autre mention l'évoquant ne peuvent être employés pour aucun produit similaire, sans préjudice des dispositions législatives et réglementaires en vigueur le 6 juillet 1990.*'
340. Two modes of infringement of trademark rights are infringement by reproduction and that by imitation. *See* Sylviane Durrande, *Atteintes à la marque: Reproduction et imitation de marque*, J.-Cl. Marques – Dessins et modèles, fasc. 7511, paras 5-15.
341. In a judgment delivered in 2005, the Court of Cassation used the expression 'the reproduction of an AO' to describe 'the use of the name which constitutes the AO'. *See* Cass. crim., 5 avr. 2005, n° 04-85.861, PIBD 2005, n° 814, III, p. 522.

the demonstration of a risk of confusion, as would be the case for trademark infringement.[343]

However, the absence of a 'risk of confusion' in the legislative text does not mean that Article L. 643-1 does not prevent consumer deception or confusion as to origin. On the contrary, there is clear evidence that the misleading use of AOs is covered by the prohibition in this article: French judges have traditionally attempted to establish a risk of confusion before imposing sanctions in cases involving an alleged 'usurpation or evocation' of AOs.[344]

The existence of such a risk is assessed with reference to average consumers of the category of goods in question.[345] The Court of Cassation notes concerning wine with an AO that the benchmark consumers are 'those accustomed to differentiate the goods'.[346] Similarly, it is noted that consideration must be given to 'more or less experienced consumers in this matter'.[347]

The degree of similarity between the products in the minds of the relevant public is the first element of the confusion risk.[348] A lack of similarity would preclude all risk of confusion so that an action brought for an alleged attempt to pass off a different product is likely to be rejected. The Court of Appeal of Pau did not regard the use of the words '*Fleur des Vosges*' as creating a risk of ambiguity with the appellation '*Miel de Sapin des Vosges*' on the grounds that blossom honey was not similar to honeydew honey, for which the AO had been registered.[349] The Court of Cassation nevertheless annulled this ruling, since it was in breach of Article L. 643-1. It confirmed, in a more recent case, that blossom honey and honeydew honey are similar products.[350] Although opinions on the honey diverged, there is a consensus that alcoholic beverages (excluding beer), wines, spirits, liqueurs, and after-dinner liqueurs are similar to the products covered by the appellations *Champagne* and *Bordeaux*.[351]

342. In a judgment of 12 June 1978, the Court of Cassation used the terms 'the illegal imitation of appellations of origin' to describe 'the use of other reference suggesting (evoking) appellations of origin'. Cass. com., 12 juin 1978, n° 76-13.980, Bull. civ. 1978, IV, n° 161.
343. Under Article L. 713-2 of the Intellectual Property Code, certain acts are forbidden even if they do not lead to a risk of confusion. These acts concern the use of an identical mark for goods or services that are identical to those designated in the registration.
344. Caroline Le Goffic, *La protection des indications géographiques*, Paris, LexisNexis, 2011, p. 111.
345. C.A. Bordeaux, 15 sept. 2014, n° 13/04101: '*Le signe évoque le Bordelais de façon claire dans l'esprit du consommateur moyen.*'
346. Cass. com., 6 mars 2007, n° 04-16.815: '*Il n'existe aucun risque de confusion dans l'esprit du consommateur habitué à distinguer, s'agissant de vins d'appellation d'origine contrôlée.*'
347. Cass. crim., 5 avr. 2005, n° 04-85.861: '*Celui d'évoquer de manière subtile, voire subliminale, l'appellation prestigieuse dans les esprits de consommateurs plus ou moins aguerris en la matière.*'
348. In a case concerning the registration of an appellation of origin as a trademark by a third party, the court held that the mark designated the products 'identical' to those covered by the appellation. *See* Cass. com., 31 janv. 2006, n° 04-13.676: '*La marque désignait des produits identiques à ceux couverts par les appellations d'origine protégées.*'
349. Cass. crim., 21 janv. 2003, n° 02-81.660.
350. Cass. crim., 10 janv. 2006, n° 04-87.603.
351. C.A. Paris, 25 avr. 2007, n° 06/03001; C.A. Bordeaux, 15 sept. 2014, n° 13/04101.

It is also a condition for the establishment of a confusion risk that the indicators present a similarity aurally,[352] visually,[353] or conceptually.[354] The use of an isolated element of an AO[355] or its inclusion in a complex combination[356] may be considered as 'imitating'[357] the registered name.

The recognition of the AO in the market is also a factor in the assessment of the likelihood of confusion. The more familiar the public is with the appellation (i.e., the more well-known and thus prestigious it is), the easier it will be to establish this likelihood because the notoriety could strengthen its distinctive function. For example, the use of the term '*Pape*' has not been considered permissible since, given the very high recognition of the AOC '*Châteauneuf du pape*' both in France and abroad, the word '*Pape*' is naturally and immediately associated with the AOC, and a trademark containing '*Pape*' would thus confuse the consumer.[358]

It is worth noting that the likelihood of confusion with the AO is understood as the risk that the public will believe that the goods covered by the indicators used by the alleged infringer have the *same geographical origin*,[359] composition, or method of production[360] as the AO in question or the right to use it.[361] This is different from an assessment between trademarks, in which the risk is that the public will believe that the goods or services come from the same undertaking.

A clear analogy could be made between the norm prohibiting the misleading use of trademarks and that prohibiting the usurpation or evocation of AOs. Both serve to prevent consumer deception or confusion and are assessed based on the consumer reaction to the alleged infringer's use of an identical or similar sign. Nevertheless, AO

352. Cass. crim., 5 avr. 2005, n° 04-85.861: '*Les mots Héritage et Hermitage présentent une ressemblance phonétique.*'
353. The term '*Porthos*' was found to be an evocation or imitation of the term '*Porto*' because of their visual resemblance. *See* Cass. crim., 5 avr. 1954, JCP 1954, II, 8162.
354. The French translation of the Cuban word '*Habana*' is '*Havana*'. The Russian translation of the French word '*Champagne*' is '*Shapanskoe*'. There is some conceptual similarity, which depends on translation. *See* C.A. Paris, 4 juill. 1985, PIBD 1986, n° 383, III, p. 50; C.A. Paris, 25 avr. 2007, n° 06/03001.
355. Cass. com., 26 oct. 1993, n° 91-20.472: '*Il n'est pas nécessaire que la marque reproduise exactement l'AOC.*'
356. Cass. com., 31 janv. 2006, n° 04-13.676 ('*Aoste Excellence*'); Cass. crim., 22 févr. 2011, n° 10-80.723 ('*Enclave des Papes*'); Cass. crim., 5 avr. 2005, n° 04-85.861 ('*Héritage des Caves des Papes*').
357. The word 'imitating' is used by Professor Azéma to indicate the 'evocation' of the AO. *See* Jacques Azéma, *Droit de la propriété industrielle,* 7e éd., Paris, Dalloz, p. 978.
358. Cass. crim., 22 févr. 2011, n° 10-80.723; Cass. crim., 5 avr. 2005, n° 04-85.861.
359. Indicating the word '*Savoie*', a component of an AOC, on the packaging of a table wine may lead consumers to believe that the table wine has been produced in the geographical area where the AOC is produced. Similarly, the trademark '*Enclave des Papes*' would lead one to believe that there was a wine-growing sub-region. The use of the term '*Fourme*' was likely to create confusion in the minds of consumers as to the geographical origin of the product. The use of the company's name '*Cuban Cigar Brands*' on cigars, independent of their place of origin, is likely to cause confusion as to the geographical origin. *See* Cass. crim., 18 juin 1997, n° 96-83.018; Cass. crim., 22 févr. 2011, n° 10-80.723; Cass. com., 26 oct. 1993, n° 91-20.472; Cass. com., 29 mars 1994, n° 92-11.959.
360. C.A. Paris, 4 juill. 1985, PIBD 1986, n° 383, III, p. 50.
361. C.A. Agen, 15 janv. 1998, n° 97/00150: '*L'utilisation de l'expression du Cahors est bien de nature à faire croire à une exclusivité du vin portant l'appellation d'origine.*'

protection moves beyond this conventional anti-confusion doctrine and provides for an 'absolute prohibition' against the use of AOs for identical or similar products.[362]

The French courts point out that Article L. 643-1 prohibits the use of a name that constitutes an AO or its evocation for similar products 'without it being necessary to establish the risk of confusion'.[363] Where the AO or its evocation is used as a mark by the defendant, no demonstration of the misleading nature (as to the geographical origin or essential qualities of the product)[364] of the contested mark is required to trigger AO protection.[365] The company Aoste applied to register the word mark '*Aoste excellence*' to designate various food products. The INPI partially rejected this request for cured meat products, salted meats, and hams, which are products covered by the AOs '*Valle d'Aosta jambon de Bosses*' and '*Valle d'Aosta lard d'Arnad*'. The Court of Appeal of Lyon annulled the INPI's decision, claiming that the contested mark contained a term simply evocative of the AO and that its misleading character was not demonstrated.[366] The Court of Cassation then ruled that the appellate court had violated Article L. 643-1. According to its reasoning, evocation is prohibited for similar products without the need to demonstrate that the public would be likely to be misled.[367]

Since no likelihood of confusion is required, the use of the word '*Shapanskoe*' (the Russian translation of the appellation '*Champagne*') has been held to contravene Article L. 643-1, 'no matter whether the consumer immediately perceives the literal meaning of *Shapanskoe*'.[368] For trademarks, however, consideration must be given to the 'point of view of consumers for whom the two words (original and translated) have a meaning'.[369] The use of the registered sign in the form of a translation is prohibited provided that the targeted public will understand that the two words both refer to the same speciality product from a particular place.[370]

Nevertheless, this does not suggest that what the sign means to a particular audience is no longer the basis for protection. Preventing infringement by evocation is a standard intended to check if consumers make a mental association with the

362. C.A. Paris, 17 mai 2000, Ann. propr. ind. 2000, p. 260: '*L'interdiction absolue de l'appellation d'origine pour produits identiques ou similaires.*'
363. C.A. Paris, 25 avr. 2007, n° 06/03001; Caroline Le Goffic, *Retour sur le cas du Champagne soviétique*, Propriété industrielle, n° 4, 2008, étude 7.
364. Cass. com., 12 juin 1978, n° 76-13.980.
365. C.A. Bordeaux, 15 sept. 2014, n° 13/04101.
366. C.A. Lyon, 26 févr. 2004, Juris-Data n° 2004-287902.
367. Cass. com., 31 Janv. 2006, n° 04-13.676.
368. C.A. Paris, 25 avr. 2007, n° 06/03001: '*Il importe peu que le consommateur n'en perçoit pas spontanément le sens littéral dès lors que l'existence d'un risque de confusion n'est pas requis.*'
369. Case T-534/10 *Organismos Kypriakis Galaktokomikis Viomichanias v. OHMI* (CFI 13 June 2012) para. 39: 'With regard to conceptual similarity, what must be taken into consideration is the point of view of consumers within EU territory for whom the two words have a meaning.'
370. In ruling that the degree of similarity between the trademarks on the conceptual level is sufficiently great for there to be a likelihood of confusion between them, the CJEU notes that consumers who do not immediately recognize the translated word must understand its meaning when they *see* other supplemented images or graphics. *See* Case T-33/03 *Osotspa Co. Ltd v. European Union Intellectual Property Office* [2005] ECR II-00763, para. 51; Case T-138/09 *Muñoz Arraiza v. OHMI* [2010] ECR II-02317, para. 41.

registered name upon seeing the defendant's sign.[371] As interpreted by the CJEU, the concept of evocation covers situations where the term used to designate a product incorporates part of a protected designation,[372] 'so that when the consumer is confronted with the name of the product the image triggered in his mind is that of the product whose designation is protected'.[373] It is essential that 'consumers establish a link between the term and the protected name'.[374]

Moreover, the CJEU has expressly indicated that 'evocation' can occur in the absence of any likelihood of confusion.[375] The name '*Verlados*' may constitute an evocation of the French GI '*Calvados*' because of their phonetic or visual resemblance,[376] even though the beginning of the contested name, '*Verla*', refers directly to the place of manufacture of the drink named '*Verlados*', a village whose name may be recognized by Finnish consumers (the use of the name 'Verlados' is not likely to deceive Finnish consumers), or even if the true origin of the product is indicated or emphasized (it is not likely to deceive consumers in other EU Member States). Even without a phonetic or visual resemblance, the use of an element such as a dissimilar name, figurative image, or product characteristic may constitute evocation.[377] It is clear

371. The court must rely on the presumed reaction of consumers in the light of the term used to designate the product at issue. This is contrary to what has been argued, in a recent case, by the European Commission that 'the finding of an evocation is objective in nature, based solely on an examination of the names at issue' and that it is thus 'not necessary to refer to the concept of consumer'. *See* Case C-75/15 *Viiniverla Oy v. Sosiaali- ja terveysalan lupa- ja valvontavirasto* (ECJ 21 January 2016) para. 18.
372. *See* Case T-828/16 *Consejo Regulador Torta del Casar v. EUIPO* (CFI 14 December 2017) para. 61.
373. *Ibid.*, para. 21; *See also* Joined Cases C-4/10 & C-27/10 *Bureau national interprofessionnel du Cognac v. Gust. Ranin Oy* [2011] ECR I-06131, para. 48; Case C-87/97 *Consorzio per la tutela del formaggio Gorgonzola v. Käserei Champignon Hofmeister GmbH & Co. KG and Eduard Bracharz GmbH* [1999] ECR I-01301, para. 25; Case C-132/05 *Commission of the European Communities v. Federal Republic of Germany, supra* n. 180, para. 44. In the assessment of evocation, the court takes into consideration 'the phonetic and visual relationship between those names and any evidence indicating that such a relationship is not fortuitous'. *See* Case C-75/15 *Viiniverla Oy v. Sosiaali- ja terveysalan lupa- ja valvontavirasto, supra* n. 371, para. 48.
374. Case C-75/15 *Viiniverla Oy v. Sosiaali- ja terveysalan lupa- ja valvontavirasto, supra* n. 371, para. 22.
375. *See* Case C-75/15 *Viiniverla Oy v. Sosiaali- ja terveysalan lupa- ja valvontavirasto, supra* n. 371, para. 45; Case C-87/97 *Consorzio per la tutela del formaggio Gorgonzola v. Käserei Champignon Hofmeister GmbH & Co. KG and Eduard Bracharz GmbH, supra* n. 373, para. 26; Case C-132/05 *Commission of the European Communities v. Federal Republic of Germany, supra* n. 180, para. 45.
376. According to the established case law, it is legitimate to consider that there is an evocation of a protected name where the sales names are phonetically and visually identical. The names '*Verlados*' and '*Calvados*' both contain eight letters, the last four of which are identical, and the same number of syllables, and that they share the suffix '*dos*', which confers on them a certain visual and phonetic similarity. *See* Case C-75/15 *Viiniverla Oy v. Sosiaali- ja terveysalan lupa- ja valvontavirasto, supra* n. 371, para. 38; C-87/97 *Consorzio per la tutela del formaggio Gorgonzola v. Käserei Champignon Hofmeister GmbH & Co. KG and Eduard Bracharz GmbH, supra* n. 373, para. 27; Case C-132/05 *Commission of the European Communities v. Federal Republic of Germany, supra* n. 180, para. 46; Joined Cases C-4/10 & C-27/10 *Bureau national interprofessionnel du Cognac v. Gust. Ranin Oy, supra* n. 373, para. 57; Case T-510/15 *Roberto Mengozzi v. EUIPO* (CFI 2 February 2017) para. 41.
377. *See* Case C-44/17 *Scotch Whisky Association v. Michael Klotz* (ECJ 7 June 2018) para. 41; Case C-614/17 *Fundación Consejo Regulador de la Denominación de Origen Protegida Queso*

that the protection against evocation marks a departure from conventional 'anti-confusion' rules, which seek to safeguard the identification function of distinctive signs.

Having established that the prevention of evocation goes beyond ensuring the classical trademark function of identifying the source of goods, one final question remains: what is the inspiration for such extensive protection? The CJEU has held that what matters is 'that there is not an association of ideas regarding the origin of the products' and 'that a trader does not take undue advantage of the reputation of the protected geographical indication'.[378] This suggests that the wider form of protection is intended to allow producers to reap the fruits of their investment in the image and reputation associated with the GI. However, can it be deduced from the CJEU's opinion that the use of a name evoking the AO must be prohibited because such use, even when not jeopardising the identification function of the AO (i.e., not giving rise to a likelihood of confusion), is liable to affect other functions of the AO, such as that of investment?

We do not consider that the mere misappropriation or freeriding argument could justify the extensive protection of the AO. First, it has to be borne in mind that the protection against the misappropriation of reputation and freeriding on the investment of others is designed to defend AOs with a reputation from being used or imitated for 'any other product or service'[379] (i.e., dissimilar goods), whereas the evocation of the AO that we are discussing here takes place in respect of identical or similar goods. Second, even assuming that this special regime of protection could also apply in relation to identical or similar goods – as has happened in two judgments of the French Council of State[380] – protection against evocation still goes beyond ensuring other functions of AOs (e.g., investment, advertising) because the assessment has no further obligation to determine how those functions may be affected.

Manchego (ECJ 2 May 2019) para. 43; Case C-490/19 *Syndicat interprofessionnel de défense du fromage Morbier* (ECJ 17 December 2020) para. 28 (AG Opinion); Cass. com., 19 juin 2019, n° 17-25822; Jérôme Passa, *Indications géographiques: évocation d'une AOP par l'emploi d'un signe figuratif, Revue trimestrielle de droit commercial et de droit économique*, n° 4, 2020, 897.

378. *See* Case C-75/15 *Viiniverla Oy v. Sosiaali- ja terveysalan lupa- ja valvontavirasto*, *supra* n. 371, para. 45; Joined Cases C-4/10 & C-27/10 *Bureau national interprofessionnel du Cognac v. Gust. Ranin Oy*, *supra* n. 373, para. 46.

379. The second sentence of Article L. 643-1 prohibits the use of the AO and its evocation for different products if that use is likely to misappropriate or weaken the reputation of the appellation of origin.

380. The French Council of State rescinded two decrees creating the AOC '*Chaume-Premier cru des Coteaux du Layon*' and '*Chaume*' for wine products, on the basis that they are likely to '*misappropriate or weaken the reputation*' acquired by the prior AOC in the wine sector, '*Quarts de Chaume*'. In line with this, Article L. 431-2 of the Consumer Code forbids anyone from mentioning the presence of a GI product in the composition of another product (including similar product), where 'that reference misappropriates or weakens the reputation of the GI'. *See* C.E., 27 juill. 2005, n° 261989; C.E., 30 mars 2009, n° 304990; Cass. crim., 30 juin 2009, n° 08-86.919, Bull. civ. 2009, IV, n° 138; Article L. 431-2(7) C. consom.: '*De mentionner sur un produit la présence dans sa composition d'un autre produit bénéficiant d'une appellation d'origine ou d'une indication géographique lorsque cette mention détourne ou affaiblit la réputation de l'appellation ou de l'indication concernée*'; Théodore Georgopoulos, *Les AOC entre notoriété et confusion – Le contentieux autour des vins '(Quarts de) Chaume'*, Droit rural, n° 381, 2010, étude 5.

Here, we can draw useful parallels with trademark law, which establishes a stronger protection against any impairment of the reputation for reputed trademarks.[381] This protection may also apply where the contested marks designate goods or services identical or similar to those for which the trademark with a reputation was registered.[382] As noted by the CJEU, implementation does not require the existence of a likelihood of confusion; it is enough that the public 'makes a connection' or 'establishes a link' between the marks in question, as a consequence of 'a certain degree of similarity' between them.[383] This analysis reminds us of the assessment of the 'evocation' of the AO, in which 'it is essential that consumers establish a link between that term and the protected name'[384] due to 'a certain visual and phonetic similarity' between those names.[385] Furthermore, the contents of the 'link' discussed in the context of trademark infringement and that discussed in the context of AO litigation are very similar: while the link in the former case refers to 'any kind of mental association between those two marks',[386] that in the latter case refers to 'an association of ideas in the mind of the public'.[387] The former covers situations where 'the later mark will bring the earlier mark with a reputation to the mind of the relevant public';[388] the latter covers situations in which the disputed name evokes in the mind of the public the product whose designation is protected. In the French translation of the judgment of 27 November 2008, the word '*évoquer*', the term used in AO protection, is even used to describe the link between two marks.[389]

However, in the trademark infringement context, as the CJEU expressly indicated, 'the existence of such a link constitutes a condition, which is necessary but not,

381. The stronger protection is given when the use of a sign identical or similar to a registered mark would take unfair advantage of or would be detrimental to the distinctive character or the repute of the earlier mark. This is thus specific protection against impairment of the distinctive character or repute of the marks in question. *See* Case C-425/98 *Marca Mode CV v. Adidas AG and Adidas Benelux BV* [2000] ECR I-04861, para. 34; Case C-408/01 *Adidas-Salomon AG and Adidas Benelux BV v. Fitnessworld Trading Ltd* [2003] ECR I-12537, para. 27; Case C-102/07 *adidas AG andt adidas Benelux BV v. Marca Mode CV and Others* [2008] ECR I-02439, para. 40; Case C-252/07 *Intel Corporation Inc v. CPM United Kingdom Ltd* [2008] ECR I-08823, para. 26.
382. *See* Case C-487/07 *L'Oréal and Others* [2009] ECR I-05185, para. 35; Case C-292/00 *Davidoff & Cie SA and Zino Davidoff SA v. Gofkid Ltd* [2003] ECR I-00389, para. 30; Case C-408/01 *Adidas-Salomon AG and Adidas Benelux BV v. Fitnessworld Trading Ltd, supra* n. 381, paras 18-22; Case C-102/07 *adidas AG andt adidas Benelux BV v. Marca Mode CV and Others, supra* n. 381, para. 37.
383. *See* Case C-487/07 *L'Oréal and Others, supra* n. 382, para. 36; Case C-408/01 *Adidas-Salomon AG and Adidas Benelux BV v. Fitnessworld Trading Ltd, supra* n. 381, paras 29-31; Case C-102/07 *adidas AG andt adidas Benelux BV v. Marca Mode CV and Others, supra* n. 381, para. 41.
384. *See* Case C-75/15 *Viiniverla Oy v. Sosiaali- ja terveysalan lupa- ja valvontavirasto, supra* n. 371, para. 22.
385. *See* Case C-75/15 *Viiniverla Oy v. Sosiaali- ja terveysalan lupa- ja valvontavirasto, supra* n. 371, para. 35; Case C-132/05 *Commission of the European Communities v. Federal Republic of Germany, supra* n. 180, paras 47-48.
386. Case C-252/07 *Intel Corporation Inc v. CPM United Kingdom Ltd, supra* n. 381, para. 17.
387. Case C-75/15 *Viiniverla Oy v. Sosiaali- ja terveysalan lupa- ja valvontavirasto, supra* n. 371, para. 45.
388. Case C-252/07 *Intel Corporation Inc v. CPM United Kingdom Ltd, supra* n. 381, paras 44-49.
389. *Ibid.*, para. 80: '*La marque postérieure évoque la marque antérieure renommée dans l'esprit du consommateur moyen, normalement informé et raisonnablement attentif et avisé.*'

of itself, sufficient to establish the existence of one of the types of injury'.[390] In other words, trademark protection cannot be based on a mere association of ideas.[391] The court must also determine whether the use of the sign would impair the distinctive character of the mark (dilution) or the repute of that mark (degradation), or take unfair advantage of the repute of the mark (freeriding).[392] However, this analysis is not required in assessments concerning infringements of the law on the protection of appellations of origin: infringement is constituted once a link is established, 'without it being necessary to demonstrate that those appellations possess a reputation in France, nor that that reputation is liable to be misappropriated or weakened'.[393] In other words, a name can be held to evoke an AO without giving rise to a risk of taking unfair advantage or impairing its reputation.

Therefore, it must be concluded that, while injuries such as dilution, degradation, and freeriding might be covered by the prohibition against evocation in Article L. 643-1,[394] the prohibition also goes beyond the prevention of those injuries and thus represents a *departure* from the conventional 'anti-parasitism' rules.[395] The 'mental link' between the disputed name and the AO does not automatically impair the AO's reputation. It has to be borne in mind that Article L. 643-1 is applicable not only to the French AO but also to the AO registered under the Lisbon Agreement.[396] At the time of writing, there are around 1,000 registered names on the Lisbon register, and half of them are registered by countries other than France.[397] Even if it is true that every AOC

390. *See* Case C-487/07 *L'Oréal and Others*, *supra* n. 382, para. 37; Case C-252/07 *Intel Corporation Inc v. CPM United Kingdom Ltd*, *supra* n. 381, paras 31-32.
391. *See* Case C-425/98 *Marca Mode CV v. Adidas AG and Adidas Benelux BV*, *supra* n. 381, para. 36.
392. *See* Case C-487/07 *L'Oréal and Others*, *supra* n. 382, paras 38-41.
393. Joined Cases T-53/04-T-56/04, T-58/04 & T-59/04 *Budějovický Budvar v. OHMI*, *supra* n. 244, para. 181.
394. The CJEU notes that: 'In the absence of such a link in the mind of the public, the use of the later mark is not likely to take unfair advantage of, or be detrimental to, the distinctive character or the repute of the earlier mark.' Therefore, the link must be found in a situation where there is a likelihood of dilution, tarnishment or freeriding. The prohibition on the link must have the effect of prohibiting any one of those injuries. Given the commonalities between the link in trademark law and that in AO legislation, we assume that this principle would also apply to AOs. Then it follows that in the case of an AO, the prohibition on the link (evocation) would cover the situation where the use is liable to take unfair advantage of or be detrimental to the reputation of the AO. *See* Case C-252/07 *Intel Corporation Inc v. CPM United Kingdom Ltd*, *supra* n. 381, para. 31; Dev Gangjee, *Relocating the Law of Geographical Indications* 163 (Cambridge University Press 2012).
395. As noted above, the existence of the link is not sufficient to establish the existence of one of the types of injury. Thus, the link can also be found in a situation where the likelihood of dilution, tarnishment or freeriding does not exist. Following the same logic, the prohibition on the link (evocation) would encompass a situation in which the use is not liable to take unfair advantage of or be detrimental to the reputation of the AO.
396. C.A. Paris, 4 juill. 1985, PIBD 1986, n° 383, III, p. 50; Cass. com., 29 mars 1994, PIBD 1994, n° 570, III, p. 381; T.G.I. Paris, 7 avr. 2006, PIBD 2006, n° 837, III, p. 633.
397. Registrations can be searched through the Lisbon Express database. Available at (accessed 15 May 2021), https://www.wipo.int/ipdl/en/lisbon/search-struct.jsp.

has a duly established reputation in France,[398] it is highly unlikely that all foreign appellations have such a reputation, convey a positive image, or are able to arouse an immediate association with the product among French consumers. Then, how can external traders take undue advantage of the reputation of the AO if the name is unknown to the relevant public?

In France, the AO is protected to an extent that cannot be justified as a legitimate desire to protect reputations. To take up just one illustration, Article L. 122-3 (the former Article L. 121-10) of the Consumer Code provides that a comparison between AO products is authorized only between products that have the same appellation.[399] The text thus has the effect of prohibiting comparisons between products with AO and those without in order to protect an AO's reputation or image.[400] However, comparative advertising, which aims solely at objectively highlighting the differences between the products of the advertiser and those with AO, would not necessarily be detrimental to the image of the AO or take unfair advantage of it.[401]

The protection given to IGPIAs is also pitched as a high level, which is fixed in Article L. 721-8 of the IP Code.[402] These provisions are very similar to those in the European regulations on PDO and PGI, which will be analysed later in this chapter.

This extensive protection is reinforced further through criminal liabilities for the misuse of GIs (including AO and IGPIA), as enumerated in Article L. 431-2 of the

398. In the recognition procedure applicable to controlled appellations of origin registered in France, the appellation must have a duly established reputation in order to be registered as AOC. *See* Article L. 641-5 C. rur.

399. Article L. 122-3 C. consom.: '*Pour les produits bénéficiant d'une appellation d'origine ou d'une indication géographique protégée, la comparaison n'est autorisée qu'entre des produits bénéficiant chacun de la même appellation ou de la même indication.*'

400. Jean Calais-Auloy & Frank Steinmetz, *Droit de la consommation*, 7e éd., Paris, Dalloz, 2006.

401. According to Article 4 of Directive 2006/114/EC, comparative advertising is to be permitted provided that it does not take unfair advantage of the reputation of a competitor or the AO of competing products. *See Directive 2006/114/EC of the European Parliament and of the Council of 12 December 2006 concerning misleading and comparative advertising*, OJ L376, 27.12.2006, p. 21; Case C-381/05 *De Landtsheer Emmanuel SA v. Comité Interprofessionnel du Vin de Champagne and Veuve Clicquot Ponsardin SA* [2007] ECR I-03115, para. 70.

402. Article L. 721-8 CPI: '*I. Sans préjudice des articles L. 115-16 du code de la consommation et L. 722-1 du présent code, les dénominations enregistrées sont protégées contre: 1° Toute utilisation commerciale directe ou indirecte d'une dénomination enregistrée à l'égard des produits non couverts par l'enregistrement, lorsque ces produits sont comparables à ceux enregistrés sous cette dénomination ou lorsque cette utilisation permet de profiter de la réputation de la dénomination protégée; 2° Toute usurpation, imitation ou évocation, même si l'origine véritable des produits ou des services est indiquée ou si la dénomination protégée est traduite ou accompagnée d'une expression telle que "genre", "type", "méthode", "façon", "imitation" ou d'une expression similaire; 3° Toute autre indication fausse ou fallacieuse quant à la provenance, l'origine, la nature ou les qualités essentielles du produit qui figure sur le conditionnement ou l'emballage, sur la publicité ou sur des documents afférents au produit concerné, ainsi que contre l'utilisation pour le conditionnement d'un récipient de nature à créer une impression erronée sur l'origine du produit; 4° Toute autre pratique susceptible d'induire le consommateur en erreur quant à la véritable origine du produit. Lorsqu'une indication géographique contient en elle-même le nom d'un produit considéré comme générique, l'utilisation de ce nom générique n'est pas considérée comme contraire aux 1° ou 2° du présent I. II. L'indication géographique, dont le cahier des charges a été homologué dans les conditions prévues par la présente section, ne peut jamais être considérée comme présentant un caractère générique et tomber dans le domaine public.*'

Consumer Code:[403] It prohibits 'fraudulently using or attempting to use a GI',[404] 'affixing, through addition, suppression or any other alteration, on natural or manufactured products, offered for sale or intended for sale, a GI, or having it affixed, whilst knowing that this is inaccurate',[405] and 'leading, or attempting to lead the public to believe that the product has a GI'.[406] The list is complemented by Article L. 453-3, which criminalizes the use of any reference prohibited by L. 643-1 of the Rural Code, even in the absence of bad faith.[407]

[b] Protection Within the Principle of Speciality in EU Law

The ability of the PDO/PGI to prevent illegal use is governed by Article 13 of Regulation 1151/2012, Article 103 of Regulation 1308/2013, Article 21 of Regulation 2019/787, and Article 20 of Regulation 251/2014. Despite the differences in wording, these provisions provide protection for registered names against direct or indirect commercial use by comparable products that do not comply with the product specifications. However, none of them defines the concept of 'comparable products'. According to the established case law, the relevant factors in determining the comparability between products include the common objective characteristics, the occasions of consumption, the distribution channels, and the marketing methods.[408] Thus, whiskies could be viewed as comparable to wine spirits, as they have common objective characteristics, are consumed on identical occasions, are distributed through the same channels, and are subject to similar marketing rules.[409] These criteria are different from those applied in interpreting the concept of the 'similarity' between goods or services covered by trademarks.[410] As confirmed by the CJEU, the relevant factors in the assessment of

403. Article L. 431-2 of the Consumer Code applies both to the AO and the IGPIA defined in Article L. 721-2 of the Intellectual Property Code.
404. Article L. 431-2(3) C. consom.: '*D'utiliser ou de tenter d'utiliser frauduleusement une appellation d'origine ou une indication géographique définie à l'article L. 721-2 du code de la propriété intellectuelle.*'
405. Article L. 431-2(4) C. consom.: '*D'apposer ou de faire apparaître, par addition, retranchement ou par une altération quelconque, sur des produits, naturels ou fabriqués, mis en vente ou destinés à être mis en vente, une appellation d'origine ou une indication géographique définie à l'article L. 721-2 du code de la propriété intellectuelle, en la sachant inexacte.*'
406. Article L. 431-2(5) C. consom.: '*De faire croire ou tenter de faire croire qu'un produit bénéficie d'une appellation d'origine ou d'une indication géographique définie au même article L. 721-2.*'
407. Article L. 453-3 C. consom.: '*La violation des interdictions prévues au deuxième alinéa de l'article L. 643-1 du code rural et de la pêche maritime est puni d'une peine d'emprisonnement de deux ans et d'une amende de 300 000 euros.*'
408. These criteria are summarized by the Boards of Appeal of the OHIM (EUIPO) in its decision of 17 May 2013. *See* Case R 757/2012-5 *Decision of the Fifth Board of Appeal of 17 May 2013* (EUIPO) para. 25.
409. Another example refers to cheese and butter. They can be considered comparable since they have a similar appearance, are often consumed together, are both dairy products, have been elaborated in a comparable manner and have the channel of trade. *See* Joined Cases C-4/10 & C-27/10 *Bureau national interprofessionnel du Cognac v. Gust. Ranin Oy*, *supra* n. 373, para. 54; Case R 757/2012-5 *Decision of the Fifth Board of Appeal of 17 May 2013* (EUIPO) para. 25; Case T-387/13 *Federación Nacional de Cafeteros de Colombia v. OHMI* (CFI 18 September 2015) para. 36.
410. Case R 757/2012-5 *Decision of the Fifth Board of Appeal of 17 May 2013* (EUIPO) para. 30.

similarity may include the product's or service's nature, end-users and method of use, and status as competitors or complements.[411] It has been held that tyres and tyre-remoulding services are similar because 'they are both complementary to each other'.[412] Similarly, in the judgment of 21 April 2021, the CJEU held that restaurant services are similar to cheeses because of their complementarity.[413] However, coffee and services that provide coffee have been found to be not comparable due to their inherent difference in nature.[414] Thus, comparability seems to be established in a more restrictive manner.

The direct and indirect use of registered names covers a broad range of situations: the whole GI may be reproduced without modification or addition;[415] some parts of the GI, even parts without geographical significance (e.g., a characteristic root or ending),[416] may be reproduced;[417] the GI may be partially modified by adding words, figurative elements, or qualifying terms;[418] or a translation of the whole or a part of the GI may be used or incorporated in a new combination in any EU language.[419] One author affirms that indirect use can be extended to any mention that refers to a protected name indirectly, even if the name is not used explicitly.[420]

In discussing the scope of PDO/PGI protection, we may also recall the second subparagraph of the aforementioned regulations, which specifies protection against any misuse, imitation, or evocation, even if the true origin is indicated or if the protected name is translated or accompanied by an expression such as 'style', 'type', 'method', 'as produced in', 'imitation', 'flavour', 'like', or any other similar term. These provisions are similar to those in Article 3 of the Lisbon Agreement, which covers cases

411. Case C-39/97 *Canon Kabushiki Kaisha v. Metro-Goldwyn-Mayer* [1998] ECR I-05507, para. 23.
412. C.A. Paris, 7 févr. 2003, PIBD 2003, III, p. 392.
413. *See* Case T-555/19 *Foundation for the Protection of the Traditional Cheese of Cyprus named Halloumi v. EUIPO* (CFI 21 April 2021); Arnaud Folliard-Monguiral, *Arrêt Grilloumi: restauration entre la poire et le fromage*, Propriété industrielle, n° 6, 2021, comm. 38.
414. Case T-387/13 *Federación Nacional de Cafeteros de Colombia v. OHMI*, *supra* n. 409, para. 19.
415. Concerning the scope of the protection conferred on PGIs, the 2014 OHIM Guidelines state that: 'A PGI can prevail if the conditions set out in the provisions preventing use are met, (which) are: the contested (trademark) exclusively consists of the whole PGI or adds other words or figurative elements (direct or indirect use) for comparable products ....' *See* OHIM (EUIPO), *Guidelines for Examination in the Office for Harmonization in the Internal Market (Trade Marks and Designs) on Community Trade Marks and on Registered Community Designs*, 13 June 2014.
416. The term used to designate that product ends in the same two syllables and contains the same number of syllables, with that the phonetic and the result visual similarity between the two names is obvious. For example, '*Cambozola*' and '*Gorgonzola*': the final two syllables are identical. *See* Case C-87/97 *Consorzio per la tutela del formaggio Gorgonzola v. Käserei Champignon Hofmeister GmbH & Co. KG and Eduard Bracharz GmbH*, *supra* n. 373, para. 27.
417. For example, the term '*Chianti*' evokes the PDO '*Chianti Classico*'. *See* Case R 1474/2011-2 *Decision of the Second Board of Appeal of 16 January 2012* (EUIPO) paras 14-15.
418. Qualifying terms include 'type', 'purpose', 'taste' or similar expression. *See* Case C-66/00 *Criminal proceedings Against Dante Bigi*, *supra* n. 177, para. 12.
419. A trademark that contains the term '*Konjakki*' will be considered to evoke '*Cognac*' in Finnish. OHIM (EUIPO), *Guidelines for Examination in the Office for Harmonization in the Internal Market (Trade Marks and Designs) on Community Trade Mark*, Part B, section 4 (1 August 2015) p. 50.
420. *See* Alex Tallon, *Les appellations d'origine*, *supra* n. 334, at 208.

where an AO is usurped or imitated for identical or similar products.[421] Similarly, although EU regulations do not require that the products designated by a protected name be comparable (or similar), Article 13(1)(b) of the former Regulation 2081/92 has been interpreted by the CJEU as being unable to offer protection where the products in question are different.[422] Thus, the principle of speciality still applies.

As described in the review of Article L. 643-1 of the French Rural Code, the concept of 'evocation' refers to a simple connection of images or perceptions in the minds of the consumer, irrespective of whether there is a likelihood of confusion.[423] It follows logically that the indication of the true origin of the products[424] or the modification of the name by adding 'delocalizing' expressions[425] would have no impact on the outcome of the assessment, even if they may be sufficient to avoid misleading consumers.[426]

Moreover, the case law of the CJEU has widened the scope of the protection provided by the evocation law. In the case concerning the designation 'Glen', the CJEU was requested to rule on whether the disputed element must be phonetically and/or visually similar to a protected GI to establish that there is an 'evocation' of the registered GI.[427] In its judgment of 7 June 2018, the CJEU admitted the possibility that an 'evocation' may be found to exist even in the absence of such similarity.[428] In the 'Queso Manchego' case, the CJEU held in its judgment of 2 May 2019, that the use of figurative signs evoking the geographical area with which a designation of origin is

421. Joined Cases T-53/04-T-56/04, T-58/04 & T-59/04 *Budějovický Budvar v. OHMI*, *supra* n. 244, para. 174.
422. The CJEU notes that: 'It does not follow from the case law that Article 13(1)(b) of Regulation No 2081/92 has been interpreted as meaning that the protection conferred under that article applies when the products in question are different, as that situation is governed by Article 13(1)(a) of the same regulation.' *See* Joined Cases T-53/04-T-56/04, T-58/04 & T-59/04 *Budějovický Budvar v. OHMI*, *supra* n. 244, para. 176.
423. Case C-87/97 *Consorzio per la tutela del formaggio Gorgonzola v. Käserei Champignon Hofmeister GmbH & Co. KG and Eduard Bracharz GmbH*, *supra* n. 373, paras 37-38 (AG Opinion).
424. *Ibid.*, para. 29 (AG Opinion).
425. The defendant is likely to be accused of contravening the prohibition on using recognized designations of origin or typical designations, altering or partially modifying them by adding expressions, such as 'type', 'purpose', 'taste' or similar expression. *See* Case C-66/00 *Criminal proceedings Against Dante Bigi*, *supra* n. 177, para. 12. A wine producer cannot be authorized to use, in descriptions relating to the production method of his products (e.g., '*méthode champenoise*'), geographical indications that do not correspond to the actual provenance of the wine. *See* Case C-306/93 *SMW Winzersekt GmbH v. Land Rheinland-Pfalz* [1994] ECR I-05555, para. 25.
426. On the contrary, the Swiss Federal Institute of Intellectual Property considers that delocalizing expressions such as 'style', 'type' or 'method' with an indication of source are not sufficient to avoid misleading consumers about the geographical origin of the products. *See* Alexandra Grazioli, *GIs, Trademarks & Indications of Source: The Swiss Legal Framework and Institutions, in Geographical Indications a Way Forward for Local Development* 29 (AGRIDEA 2008), Available at (accessed 15 June 2021), http://www.fao.org/fileadmin/templates/olq/documents/documents/formationIG%20agrideacirad2007.pdf.
427. Case C-44/17 *Scotch Whisky Association v. Michael Klotz*, *supra* n. 377, para. 41.
428. *Ibid.*, para. 49.

associated may constitute an evocation of that designation.[429] In the 'Morbier' case, the Advocate General noted that the reproduction of the distinctive characteristic of a product covered by a protected name may constitute an evocation of that name.[430] The scope of protection afforded by the evocation law extends from the prohibition on similar names to the prohibition on dissimilar names, figurative elements, and even product characteristics.

The third and fourth subparagraphs cover misleading practices 'liable to covey a false impression as to its origin'. They prohibit any false or misleading indication as to the provenance, origin, nature, or essential qualities of a product on its packaging, advertising material, or other related documents. However, nothing prevents the name of a product from containing geographical references that are not registered as PDO or PGI on the condition that the labelling of the product so named does not mislead the consumer.[431]

In summary, like French law, the EU regulations confer a high level of protection for protected names against direct or indirect use, imitation or evocation, and other false or misleading indications.

[c] Protection Within the Principle of Speciality in Chinese Law

Under the regime governed by the former AQSIQ (the CNIPA since 2018), prohibited acts are prescribed in Article 21 of the Provisions on the Protection of GI Products. They include:

> (1) unauthorized use or reproduction (or falsification) of the name of a GI product and official logo; (2) use of the name of a GI product in respect of products that do not meet the relevant standards and management norms; (3) use of a name or figurative sign that is similar to the official logo, resulting in a likelihood of confusion; (4) and use of any verbal or figurative sign that might mislead consumers and lead them to believe that the product in question is a GI product.[432]

---

429. Case C-614/17 *Fundación Consejo Regulador de la Denominación de Origen Protegida Queso Manchego*, *supra* n. 377, para. 43. *See also* Annalisa Volpato, *On Consumer, Evocation and Cider Spirit*, 11 Eur. Food & Feed L. Rev. 140 (2016); Nicola Coppola, *Viiniverla: Too Much 'Ado' about Nothing*, 11 J. Intell. Prop. L. & Prac. 406 (2016); Johanna Gibson, *Tilting at Windmills: The Law of Evocation in Geographical Indications and Designations of Origin*, 9 Queen Mary J. Intell. Prop. 239 (2019); Vadim Mantrov, *Do You Prefer Scotch or German Whisky? CJEU Judgment in the Scotch Whisky and Glen Buchenbach Dispute*, 9 Eur. J. Risk Reg. 1 (2019).

430. Case C-490/19 *Syndicat interprofessionnel de défense du fromage Morbier*, *supra* n. 377, para. 28 (AG Opinion).

431. Articles 3(1) and 13(3) of Regulation 2081/92, as amended, read with Article 2 of Directive 2000/13, must be interpreted as meaning that the designation of a foodstuff containing geographical references, which is not registered as a PDO or PGI, may legitimately be used, on condition that the labelling of the product so named does not mislead the average reasonably well informed, observant and circumspect consumer. Case C-446/07 *Alberto Severi v. Regione Emilia Romagna*, *supra* n. 132, para. 63.

432. The 'name of a GI product' is necessarily a compound structure, composed of the geographical reference and the generic name of a product of the same type.

These prohibitions deserve several comments. First, the use of the name of a GI is regulated under the same provision that governs the use of the official logo.[433] However, while it is true that the name of the GI product in question is a dominant component of the official logo,[434] the logo itself is not a GI. The counterfeiting of an official logo does not necessarily result in the usurpation of the name of a GI product (e.g., using the logo without displaying the protected name or displaying a place name that does not exist).

Second, in contrast with French and European regulations, which expressly adopt the principle of speciality, Article 21 is silent on whether products must be identical or similar (comparable) to trigger the application of this rule. However, current practice suggests that the name of a GI product will be protected when the products relate to the same product class. In some local rules on the protection of GI products,[435] the act prohibited by Article 21(1) – the unauthorized use of a protected name – is treated as equivalent to the act of 'passing a product (of the same type) from outside off as an authentic product'.[436] The Draft Provisions of the CNIPA issued in 2020 proposed to remedy the lack of clarity by acknowledging that the use of protected names on comparable (or similar) products should be prohibited.[437]

Third, as with the official logo, the law prohibits unauthorized use of the protected name. However, Article 20 imposes only an obligation to obtain approval to

433. Provisions on the Protection of GI Products, Article 1: 'With a view to ... regulating the use of the name of GI products and the official logo ..., these Provisions are hereby formulated pursuant to the relevant provisions of the Law of the People's Republic of China.'

434. Besides the dominant figurative component, the words, which the former AQSIQ's official logo is composed of, include 'GI products of the People's Republic of China' in Chinese at the top, 'The People's Republic of China' in English at the bottom, and the name of the GI product in question in the centre. For example, where the GI product in question is the mature vinegar from *Gaoqiao*, the words '*Gaoqiao* Mature Vinegar' will be displayed in the middle of the logo. However, in 2020, the AQSIQ's official logo has been replaced by the logo designed by the CNIPA. *See* Guojia Zhiliang Jiandu Jianyan Jianyi Zongju Gonggao 2006 Nian di 109 Hao [State General Administration of Quality Supervision, Inspection and Quarantine Announcement No. 109, 2006], 1 August 2006; Gaoqiao Chencu Dili Biaozhi Chanpin Zhuanyong Biaozhi Shiyong Guanli Banfa [Administrative Measures for the Use of the Official Logo of the GI Product Gaoqiao Mature Vinegar], 2 May 2012, Article 9. Administrative Measures for the Use of the Official Logo for Geographical Indications, Article 12 (2020).

435. Within the scope of its jurisdiction, local rules can be enacted by the People's Government of a province, autonomous region, municipality directly under the central government and a major city to implement national law, administrative regulation or local decree. Hundreds of local rules have been enacted to implement the Provisions on the Protection of GI Products (administrative regulation) at the provincial and municipal level. Legislation Law of the People's Republic of China, Article 82 (2000, amended in 2015).

436. For example, local rules for protecting the 'Zhangjiajie Giant Salamander' prohibit 'passing nonlocal giant salamanders off as those from Zhangjiajie'. Another example concerns the administrative measures for 'Gaoqiao Mature Vinegar', which prohibits 'passing nonlocal mature vinegar as vinegar from Gaoqiao'. *See* Zhangjiajie Dani Dili Biaozhi Chanpin Baohu Guanli Banfa [Administrative Measures for the Protection of the GI Product Zhangjiajie Giant Salamander], 1 August 2012, Article 21; Gaoqiao Chencu Dili Biaozhi Chanpin Zhuanyong Biaozhi Shiyong Guanli Banfa [Administrative Measures for the Use of the Official Logo of the GI Product Gaoqiao Mature Vinegar], Article 16.

437. Dili Biaozhi Baohu Guiding Zhengqiu Yijiangao [Draft Provisions on the Protection of Geographical Indications], 24 September 2020, Article 26.

use the official logo.[438] No article in the Provisions sets out an approval procedure for the use of the protected name. However, the question may arise as to what actions amount to an 'unauthorized use' of a protected name if no application obligation is prescribed. Several local rules governing GI products specify that producers who have not been authorized to use an official logo are also forbidden from using the name of the GI product in question.[439] It follows from these rules that the absence of 'the right to the official logo' must result in the loss of 'the right to the protected name',[440] irrespective of whether the product concerned comes from the demarcated place or satisfies the relevant quality standards.

Finally, while Article 21(3) prohibits the use of any sign that is similar to an official logo if it is likely to cause confusion, there is no provision expressly prohibiting the use of signs that are similar to a protected name. In the latter case, sanctions may be imposed, on several grounds. On one hand, some local authorities consider that the use of a term that incorporates part or all of a protected name falls within the ambit of Article 21(4), which prohibits the use of 'any words or signs' likely to mislead the consumer into believing that the product is a GI product.[441] On the other hand, in setting local rules for the implementation of Article 21(3), several local governments modified the original text of Article 21(3) by adding the words 'the protected name' after 'the official logo' in order to make it applicable to the imitation of both official logos and names.[442] These two different approaches adopted by law enforcement authorities illustrate the potential ambiguity in the text.

However, one thing is clear: both approaches set a high threshold for what qualifies as an infringement. Articles 21(3) and 21(4) provide that the use of a word or sign that misleads the public is actionable. As noted by the Supreme People's Court, the risk of confusion here is the risk that the public might believe that the product is a GI

---

438. Provisions on the Protection of GI Products, Article 20: 'A manufacturer using the official logo of the GI product within the limits of its place of origin shall file an application with the local quality and technical supervision bureau or entry and exit inspection and quarantine bureau.'
439. *See* Xinhuang Huangniurou Dili Biaozhi Chanpin Baohu Guanli Guiding [Administrative Regulations on the Protection of the GI Product Xinhuang Yellow Beef], 31 August 2010, Article 20; Fuzhou Moli Huacha Dili Biaozhi Chanpin Baohu Guanli Xize [Detailed Rules for Administering the GI Product Fuzhou Jasmine Tea], 7 April 2011, Article 16.
440. Hexi Zoulang Putaojiu Dili Biaozhi Chanpin Baohu Guanli Banfa [Administrative Measures for the Protection of the GI Product Hexi Corridor Wine], 7 August 2013, Article 15.
441. Market Supervision Administration of Shenzhen Municipality, *Decision of the Administrative Penalty*, Shen Shi Jian Fu Fa Zi 2014 Di 10143 Hao (31 March 2014).
442. Suzhoushi Yangchenghu Dazhaxie Dili Biaozhi Chanpin Baohu Banfa [Measures for the Protection of the GI Product Yangcheng Lake Hairy Crabs], 8 January 2010, Article 21. In an exclusive interview in 2015, the Director of Heilongjiang Bureau of Quality and Technical Supervision said that unauthorized rice production and processing enterprises are not allowed to use names, signs, words or emblems similar to the name of the GI product or the official logo. *See* Zhang Sheng, Baohu Wuchang Dami Yifa Jiejue Dili Biaozhi Chanpin Luanxiang [Protecting Wuchang Rice: Legal Redress for the Chaos of GI Products], HEILONGJIANG RIBAO [HEILONGJIANG DAILY], 10 October 2015. The Heilongjiang Bureau of Quality and Technical Supervision has investigated and punished the use of the words '*Wuchang Daohuaxiang*', which is similar to the protected name '*Wuchang* Rice'. *See* Heilongjiang Sheng Zhiliang Jishu Jianduju Guanyu Wuchang Dami Dili Biaozhi Baohu Chanpin Zhuanxiang Zhifa Jiancha Qingkuang de Tongbao [Heilongjiang Bureau of Quality and Technical Supervision's Inspection Report on the GI Product Wuchang Rice], 14 December 2015.

product (registered under the former AQSIQ).[443] However, it remains an open question as to whether and to what extent the consumer is likely to be misled regarding 'GI product' status in a situation where the protected name is displayed on the product but the official logo is not. In a recent case concerning the use of words containing the protected name '*Ningxia* Wolfberry', Shenzhen Intermediate Court held that the use was not sufficient to create a likelihood of confusion and that 'the consumer would know whether or not the product belongs to a GI product' because 'the wolfberry in question was indeed produced in *Ningxia*' and 'the defendant did not display the official logo on the outer packaging'.[444] By comparison, such conduct can very probably be characterized as a breach of the right to a GI in European law, where a simple association of ideas provides sufficient grounds, independent of any risk of confusion. It appears that the higher the threshold is, the more unlikely it is that the imitation will be sanctioned, and thus the smaller is the scope of GI protection, as is the case in the GI products regime.

Use of agricultural GIs registered under the MOA is reserved for agricultural products that 'meet the requirements on the prescribed place of origin and production specifications'[445] and is also subject to an approval process.[446] It follows that the 'fraudulent use' of agricultural GIs is prohibited by Article 22 of the Measures for the Administration of GIs for Agricultural Products.[447] Nevertheless, aside from this basic prohibition, the Measures have not set out any detailed rules for preventing other forms of misuse (e.g., by addition, suppression, or alteration). Nor does Article 22 specify what would constitute 'fraudulent use'. In an inspection mission carried out in Hefei in 2015 to monitor the use of agricultural GIs, the municipal agriculture commission noted that the focus should be on both the 'fraudulent use' of GIs and 'the use of verbal

443. In a judgment of the Supreme People's Court, The Court then notes that the protection of GI products entitles legitimate operators to prohibit the unauthorized use of any sign that is similar to the official logo if the use is likely to mislead the consumer into believing that is a GI product. *Shanxi Qinzhou Huang Mi (Group) Co. Ltd. v. Shanxi Qinzhou Danshan Huang Mi Development Co. Ltd., supra* n. 197.

444. *Huarun Wanjia Co. Ltd. v. Mai Shuming*, Shenzhen Intermediate People's Court (11 December 2014).

445. Agriculture Law of the People's Republic of China, Article 23 (2012 Amendment): 'For agricultural products that meet the requirements of the prescribed places of origin or production specifications, an application may, in accordance with the provisions of relevant laws or administrative regulations, be made for the use of geographic marks for agricultural products'; Agricultural Product Quality Safety Law of the People's Republic of China, Article 32 (2006): 'The on-sale agricultural products must meet the agricultural product quality safety standards, and the producer may apply for using nuisance-free marks of agricultural products. If the quality of the agricultural products meets the standards prescribed by the state for relevant high-quality agricultural products, the producer may apply for using commensurate quality marks of agricultural products. It is prohibited to imitate the quality marks of agricultural products as prescribed in the preceding paragraph.'

446. An entity or individual may apply to the registration certificate holder for using the registered geographical indication. *See* Measures for the Administration of GIs for Agricultural Products, Article 15; Regulations on the Use of GIs for Agricultural Products, Article 3.

447. *See also* Agricultural Product Quality Safety Law of the People's Republic of China, Article 51 (2018 Amendment): 'Whoever violates Article 32 of the present Law by imitating the quality marks of an agricultural product shall be ordered to make a correction, its/his illegal proceeds shall be confiscated, and it/he shall be fined 2,000 Yuan up to 20,000 Yuan.'

or figurative signs similar to GIs, which are likely to mislead the consumer'.[448] Given the terms employed, the concept of 'fraudulent use' does not necessarily cover a situation where the GI is imitated. It also shows that Article 22 does not provide a clear legal basis on which to combat the imitation of GIs, while local law enforcement authorities are already aware of the danger for GIs such practices pose.

By studying the historical record concerning early French legislation on GIs, we can see that it started to emerge as a reaction to fraudulent wine labelling.[449] The laws of 1905 and 1919 were designed to prohibit 'false designation of origin' or 'indication of a place of origin contrary to its actual origin'.[450] French law gradually moved beyond pure fraud-related provisions and conferred onto GIs a broader scope of protection. Today, any misrepresentation, misappropriation, or dilution is covered by the prohibition in French law (the latter two categories of use will be studied below). By comparison, China's sui generis systems are in the very early stage of development, providing a clear prohibition only for the 'fraudulent' or 'unauthorized' use of GIs.

Given the limited scope of the protection provided by China's sui generis GI systems, widening the protection scope has become one of the objectives of the EU-China GI Agreement, which comes into force on 1 March 2021. Article 4 requires each party to the Agreement to protect GIs against:

(a) the use of any means in the designation or presentation of a good that indicates or suggests that the good in question originates in a geographical area other than the true place of origin in a manner that misleads the public as to the geographical origin of the good;
(b) any use of a GI identifying an identical or similar product not originating in the place indicated by the GI in question, even where the true origin of the goods is indicated or the GI is used in translation, transcription or transliteration, or is accompanied by an expression such as 'kind', 'type', 'style', 'imitation', or the like;
(c) any use of a GI identifying an identical or similar product not compliant with the product specification of the protected name.

The EU and China agree that 'use of any means' or 'any use' used in Article 4 may encompass any 'direct or indirect commercial use' of a protected name, including imitation, or any use that would 'suggest or indicate a connection or an association between the product in question and a protected name. The terms 'suggest or indicate

448. Hefeishi Nongye Weiyuanhui Guanyu Kaizhan Sanpin Yibiao Huozheng Nongchanpin Biaozhi Shiyong Zhuanxiang Jiancha de Tongzhi [Heifei Municipal Agriculture Commission's Notice on Implementation of Concentrated Inspection for the Use of the Logo of Agricultural Products], 20 March 2015.
449. *See* Chapter 1 *supra*.
450. The *loi du 1er août 1905* made it possible to suppress the fraud or deceptive practices as to the origin of goods. Article 1 concerned the punishment for anyone who has 'deceived or attempted to mislead a contracting party as to the origin'. Similarly, Article 1 of the *loi du 6 mai 1919* punishes the use of an appellation of origin, which is 'contrary to the origin of this product (*contrairement à l'origine de ce produit*)'.

a connection or an association' may be considered analogous to the European concept of 'evocation', whose scope of protection is wide.

However, it should be noted that the higher protection level is provided only for GIs listed in Annex III or IV of the Agreement, or for GIs added in the Annex pursuant to Article 3 of the Agreement. It remains to be seen whether China will provide the higher protection level for all GIs or only for GIs listed in the Agreement. It also remains unclear under which of the three GI systems the higher protection level will be legislated.

[2] Protection of GIs Beyond the Principle of Speciality

Although like other distinctive signs, GIs are subject to the principle of speciality, an exception is provided under both French and European law for GIs that have a reputation. However, China's sui generis rules have not yet provided for this extended scope of protection.

[a] Protection Beyond the Principle of Speciality in French Law

While appellations of origin are protected under the principle of speciality, the law of 1990 has extended this scope of protection by providing for an exception to the basic principle,[451] which is now contained in the second sentence of the second paragraph of Article L. 643-1 of the French Rural Code:[452] '(The name which constitutes an appellation of origin or any other reference suggesting it) may not be used for any institution or any other product or service if that use is likely to misappropriate or weaken the reputation of the appellation of origin'.[453] This provision thus allows the AO to be protected against use for goods or services that are not similar to those that the AO covers. 'It is not contrary to the coherence of intellectual property rights of other

451. *See* Loi n° 90-558 du 2 juillet 1990 relative aux appellations d'origine contrôlées des produits agricoles ou alimentaires, bruts ou transformés, J.O. du 6 juill. 1990, p. 7912; Caroline Lampre, *Le champagne ou le parfum de la renommée,* Recueil Dalloz, 1994, p. 213.

452. The Law of 1990 provided that: 'The name which constitutes an appellation of origin, or any other reference suggesting it, may not be used for any similar product, without prejudice to the legislative provisions or regulations in force on 6 July 1990, or for any other product or service if that use is likely to misappropriate or weaken the reputation of the appellation of origin (*Le nom qui constitue l'appellation d'origine ou toute autre mention l'évoquant ne peuvent être employés pour aucun produit similaire, ni pour aucun produit ou service lorsque cette utilisation est susceptible de détourner ou d'affaiblir la notoriété de l'appellation d'origine*).' Subsequently, Article 76 of the Law of 23 February 2005 *(Loi n° 2005-157 du 23 février 2005 relative au développement des territoires ruraux)* has added the expression 'or for any establishment (*ni pour aucun établissement*)'. Therefore, the use of the appellation for an establishment (as a company's name or a business name) is forbidden if the use is likely to misappropriate or weaken the reputation of the AO.

453. Article L. 643-1 C. rur.: '*Ils ne peuvent être employés pour aucun établissement et aucun autre produit ou service, lorsque cette utilisation est susceptible de détourner ou d'affaiblir la notoriété de l'appellation.*'

distinctive signs',[454] since a similar protection is also given to trademarks that enjoy repute.[455]

Like the special regime for trademarks with repute, the enlarged scope of protection for appellations of origin is subject to certain conditions.[456] The similarity between the contested name and the AO is the first condition that needs to be met. The expression 'any other reference suggesting it' indicates that the name the use of which is liable to fall within Article L. 643-1 does not have to be an exact reproduction of the original AO but should at least evoke in the minds of consumers the AO in question. The evocation may occur as a consequence of a certain degree of visual and phonetic similarity between the name and the AO. The Court of Appeal of Pau has held that the use of the mark '*Champomy*' constitutes an act of evocation, ruling that '*the sign is close to that of Champagne*'.[457] Similarly, the beginning of the compound name '*Cham'alal*' has been deemed to 'evoke, visually and phonetically, the appellation *Champagne*'.[458]

The second condition is the existence of a reputation for the AO at issue. Such a reputation cannot be presumed to exist but must be proved[459] since a reputation cannot be misappropriated or weakened if it does not exist. The party claiming AO protection against use on dissimilar products must therefore furnish proof that the AO in question possesses a reputation in France; otherwise, the party's action must be rejected.[460] However, all AOCs could be considered as having 'a duly established reputation'[461] because the latter is one of the main preconditions for obtaining an AOC. However, this does not mean that any assessment regarding the reputation of the AOC is unimportant. The strength of the reputation may vary greatly from one AOC to another. The stronger the AO's reputation is, the easier it will be to accept that it might be misappropriated or weakened.[462] For example, owing to the prestigious image of the goods in the minds of consumers, the AOC '*Champagne*' has obtained protection in several cases wherein the name or other reference evoking it had been used for a

454. C.A. Paris, 15 déc. 1993, JCP 1994. II. 22229, note F. Pollaud-Dulian.

455. Article L. 713-5 also provides penalties for use likely to cause prejudice to the trademark owner and unjustified exploitation of the reputation of the well-known trademark. Article L. 713-5 CPI: '*Ne constitue pas une contrefaçon mais engage la responsabilité civile de son auteur l'usage dans la vie des affaires, pour des produits ou des services, non autorisé par le titulaire d'une marque notoirement connue au sens de l'article 6 bis de la convention de Paris pour la protection de la propriété industrielle: 3° D'un signe identique ou similaire à la marque et utilisé pour des produits ou des services identiques, similaires ou non similaires à ceux pour lesquels la marque est notoirement connue, si cet usage du signe, sans juste motif, tire indûment profit du caractère distinctif ou de la notoriété de la marque, ou leur porte préjudice.*'

456. Joined Cases T-53/04-T-56/04, T-58/04 & T-59/04 *Budějovický Budvar v. OHMI*, *supra* n. 244, para. 182.

457. Cass. com., 7 juill. 2009, n° 08-10.817, PIBD 2009, n° 905, III, p. 1430; Jacques Azéma, *Les dangers de la marque géographique*, RTD Com., 2008, p. 540.

458. C.A. Paris, 3 nov. 2010, n° 09/07276.

459. Joined Cases T-53/04-T-56/04, T-58/04 & T-59/04 *Budějovický Budvar v. OHMI*, *supra* n. 244, para. 194; Joined Cases T-60/04-T-64/04 *Budějovický Budvar v. OHMI – Anheuser-Busch (BUD)* [2007] ECR II-00058, para. 188.

460. *Ibid.*, para. 190.

461. Article L. 641-5 C. rur.: '*Peuvent bénéficier d'une appellation d'origine contrôlée les produits agricoles … (qui) possèdent une notoriété dûment établie.*'

462. Georges Bonet, *Des cigarettes aux parfums, l'irrésistible ascension de l'appellation d'origine Champagne vers la protection absolue*, Propriétés intellectuelles, n° 13, 2004, p. 856.

variety of dissimilar products or services, such as cigarettes,[463] perfumes,[464] pastry products,[465] biscuits,[466] home furnishings,[467] fruit drinks and fruit juices,[468] fatty duck livers,[469] and a website selling spring water for pets.[470]

The third condition concerns the existence of a risk of misappropriation or of a weakening of the reputation of the AO. This condition should not be considered as being automatically met, however, even if the reputation of the AO in question is outstanding. In this regard, we need only mention the '*Champomy*' case, where the judge, after acknowledging the outstanding reputation enjoyed by '*Champagne*', held that there could not be a risk of misappropriation or even of weakening.[471] Again, the party claiming an infringement is bound to demonstrate 'how' the reputation would likely be misappropriated or weakened.[472]

The concept of 'misappropriating the reputation of the AO', corresponding to the notion of 'parasitism' or 'freeriding' in trademark law,[473] relates to the advantage taken by a third party. It covers cases where a third party, through the use of a name evoking an AO, benefits from its power of attraction, its reputation, and its positive image without making any effort of its own. It may even arise if the use is not liable to cause any harm to the reputation of the AO.[474] Thus, in a judgment of 15 December 1993, the Court of Appeal of Paris said, 'in using the name *Champagne* to launch a new luxury perfume ... the appellants wished to create an attractive effect borrowed from the prestige of the appellation'.

When evaluating the likelihood of misappropriation, the French judge will take into account not only the product in question[475] but also the circumstances under which that product is being marketed:[476] these include the shape of the bottle suggesting a cigar,[477] the characteristic *Champagne* cork,[478] the *Champagne* bottle,[479]

463. T.G.I. Paris, 5 mars 1984, PIBD 1984, III, p. 200.
464. C.A. Paris, 15 déc. 1993, D. 1994, jur., p. 145; Cass. com., 18 févr. 2004, n° 02-10.576.
465. T.G.I. Grasse, 18 sept. 1998, PIBD 1998, n° 665, III, p. 570.
466. T.G.I. Paris, 13 oct. 2000, PIBD 2001, n° 715, III, p. 122.
467. T.G.I. Paris, 12 oct. 2001, PIBD 2002, n° 739, III, p. 170.
468. C.A. Paris, 3 nov. 2010, n° 09/07276.
469. Cass. com., 25 nov. 2014, n° 13-19.870.
470. T.G.I. Paris, 7 sept. 2001, PIBD 2002, n° 739, III, p. 169.
471. Cass. com., 7 juill. 2009, n° 08-10.817.
472. C.A. Paris, 26 oct. 2012, n° 12/00612.
473. Article L. 713-5 of the Intellectual Property Code prevents the reproduction or imitation of the reputed trademark, which constitutes an 'unjustified exploitation' of the mark.
474. French legal theorists consider that misappropriation will necessarily result in harm to the AO. However, in a controversial ruling, the court has found that the reputation of the appellation was misappropriated, but not diluted or weakened because of the high quality of goods (luxury perfume) covered by the disputed mark and the prestige of the undertaking marketing them. *See* C.A. Paris, 15 déc. 1993, D. 1994, jurispr., p. 145; Visse-Causse, *supra* n. 243; Marie Malaurie-Vignal, *Parasitisme et notoriété d'autrui*, JCP 1997, I, 3888.
475. Joined Cases T-53/04-T-56/04, T-58/04 & T-59/04 *Budějovický Budvar v. OHMI*, *supra* n. 244, para. 199.
476. Bonet, *supra* n. 462, at 857.
477. C.A. Paris, 17 mai 2000, PIBD 2000, III, p. 518.
478. C.A. Paris, 15 déc. 1993, D. 1994, jurispr., p. 145.
479. C.A. Paris, 3 nov. 2010, n° 09/07276.

the adverting campaign emphasizing the atmosphere of *Cuba*,[480] and the slogan mentioning holidays or birthdays.[481] As noted by the court in the *Cham'alal* case, these 'symbolic accessories', though not exclusively reserved for the AO, invoke in the consumer's imagination the positive image inextricably linked to it.[482]

As regards the 'weakening of the reputation', given the varying degrees of 'weakening', this concept could be considered to encompass at least two forms of harm caused to the AO. The first type, corresponding to the notion of 'degradation' in the parallel context of trademark law,[483] implies a risk that the positive image attached to an AO might be harmed or degraded, which necessarily entails a reduction of its power of attraction. If an AO with a reputation conveys an image of prestige or special quality attributable to its place of origin,[484] a reproduction or evocation of such a well-known AO for dissimilar products might be detrimental to this image if those products are of poor quality.[485] Even if the contested products are of superior quality, a detriment might still arise from the fact that the nature of those products may have a negative impact on the image of the AO. One can easily imagine the impact that using '*Champagne*' on laundry detergent may have in the consumers' minds: they might think of detergent when drinking *Champagne*.[486] Thus, the characteristic or nature of the products offered by the third party necessarily forms part of the assessment of the likelihood of the AO's degradation.[487]

However, the connotation of an AO can be eroded without being tarnished. For this type of harm, it is irrelevant whether the quality of the product in question is poor or whether its nature is incompatible with the product covered by the AO. This is a clear departure from the notion of 'degradation'. It is described as weakening the automatic association in the minds of consumers between the geographical name and the AO product.[488] This corresponds closely to the notion of 'dilution' or 'blurring' in trademark law,[489] which involves a detriment to the distinctiveness of the trademark.[490]

480. C.A. Paris, 17 mai 2000, PIBD 2000, III, p. 518.
481. T.G.I. Paris, 7 sept. 2001, PIBD 2002, n° 739, III, p. 169.
482. C.A. Paris, 3 nov. 2010, n° 09/07276.
483. Article L. 713-5 of the Intellectual Property Code also prevents the reproduction or imitation of the reputed trademark, which is likely to 'cause prejudice' to the trademark owner.
484. As noted by Philippe Le Tourneau, the appellation *Champagne* connects, physically and psychologically, a wine to something rare, precious and happy. *See* C.A. Paris, 15 déc. 1993, D. 1994. 145, note Tourneau.
485. T.G.I. Paris, 25 nov. 1993, PIBD 1994, n° 563, III, p. 185.
486. Case C-252/07 *Intel Corporation Inc v. CPM United Kingdom Ltd*, *supra* n. 381, para. 33 (AG Opinion).
487. Joined Cases T-53/04-T-56/04, T-58/04 & T-59/04 *Budějovický Budvar v. OHMI*, *supra* n. 244, para. 199.
488. Frédéric Pollaud-Dulian, *Droit de la propriété industrielle*, Paris, Montchrestien, 1999, para. 1559.
489. In section 43 of the Lanham Act, detriment to the distinctiveness of the famous mark is referred to as 'dilution by blurring'. *See* 15 U.S.C. § 1125 (c)(2)(B).
490. *See* Xinzhe Song, *A Closer Look at the Elephant in the Room: The Distinctiveness of Geographical Indications*, 11 Queen Mary J. Intell. Prop. 25 (2021).

The classic dilution doctrine prevents the lessening of a famous mark's capacity to 'identify and distinguish goods'[491] or to arouse an 'immediate association with the goods for which it is registered and used'.[492] As argued by Frank Schechter in the 1930s, 'if you allow Rolls Royce restaurants and Rolls Royce cafeterias, and Rolls Royce pants, and Rolls Royce candy, in ten years you will not have the Rolls Royce mark any more'.[493] The distinctive quality of famous marks is therefore the object of protection.

Analogously to trademarks, one of the functions of the AO is to identify and distinguish goods (according to their geographical origin instead of their commercial origin). A well-known AO can also attract the attention of consumers and arouse among them an immediate association with the product covered by it. This ability also needs to be protected. Thus, the rationales behind the trademark law may still be valid in the AO context. In a 2006 judgment, the Court of Appeal of Paris, after noting that the word '*Darjeeling*' identifies the tea originating from the region of the same name, held that 'its use for products other than tea harms this prestigious GI by making it become commonplace and weakening its distinctive nature'.[494] Similarly, in the '*Havana*' case, the court reasoned that 'it is used by a company owning establishments all over the world and having significant advertising means, the spread (of the use of the AO) necessarily destroys the uniqueness and the distinctiveness (of the AO)'.[495] In a more recent case concerning Champagne, the Court of Cassation followed a similar line of reasoning, arguing that 'the spread of the appellation of origin, which could be achieved by a company promoting the goods into a scale, necessarily entails a risk of making the appellation become commonplace'.[496]

It appears, therefore, that preventing the distinctive nature from being reduced is the core focus of anti-dilution rules, both in the trademark and AO context.[497] However, while trademark law expressly mentions 'distinctive character' as the object of protection,[498] AO legislation is silent on the protection of the distinctive nature of the

491. Strasser Mathias, *Rational Basis of Trademark Protection Revisited: Putting the Dilution Doctrine into Context*, 10 Fordham Intell. Prop. Media & Ent. L.J. 375 (1999).
492. Case T-67/04 *Spa Monopole v. OHIM* [2005] ECR II-01825, para. 43; Case T-47/06 *Antartica Srl v. OHMI* [2007] ECR II-00042, para. 55.
493. *Frank Schechter's Testimony: Hearings Before the House Committee on Patents*, 72d Cong., 1st Sess. 15 (1932).
494. C.A. Paris, 22 nov. 2006, PIBD, 2007, n° 845, III, p. 90.
495. C.A. Paris, 17 mai 2000, PIBD 2000, III, p. 518.
496. Cass. com., 25 nov. 2014, n° 13-19.870.
497. There is no definition of dilution in the French legislation, nor does it expressly mention the word 'dilution'. However, the French courts take into account the decisions of the CJEU and generally apply the rules that it lays down. Thus, in compliance with such rules, the risk of dilution is now defined as a violation of distinctiveness, which is considered as having taken place when the trademark's attractive power is diminished, and the trademark becomes commonplace. *See* Christina Berggren, *Protection Against the Dilution of a Trademark*, AIPPI (16 June 2021), https://static1.squarespace.com/static/5bd185694d546e247ed8971c/t/5bdb50db352f53426244acf6/1541099739603/Q214_SE.pdf.
498. Article 10 of Directive 2015/2436: '... where the latter has a reputation in the Member State and where use of that sign without due cause takes unfair advantage of, or is detrimental to, the distinctive character or the repute of the trade mark'.

AO.[499] This silence may be explained by the fact that AO is both descriptive and distinctive: it is descriptive because it indicates the place of production; it is distinctive because it indicates certain products known under this denomination and 'not others'.[500] It is capable of distinguishing between goods in the market when used for a particular kind of product, but, if used for other products or services, AOs may have only a descriptive character. As the Court of Appeal of Paris (rightly) noted, the reference to a region or an ancient province is common in the hotel industry (such as the hotels of *Bourgogne*, of *Bretagne*, or of *Alsace*). The name 'Hotel of *Champagne*' refers only to an old French province, not to the wine that is cultivated in that area. It follows that a clear mention of 'distinctiveness' in the text of Article L. 643-1 may sit awkwardly with the fact that the AO is, in certain cases, only descriptive.[501]

In summary, Article L. 643-1 allows the protection of appellations of origin that possess a reputation against any reproduction or evocation for dissimilar goods or services that is likely to misappropriate or weaken their reputation. One of the three types of injury – 'freeriding', 'degradation,' or 'dilution' – suffices for Article L. 643-1 to apply. This protection is at least somewhat similar to that conferred onto well-known trademarks in that, under bother regimes, the prohibition of uses likely to cause prejudice or unjustified exploitation is not unconditional: it obliges pleaders to prove the existence of a link between the term and the protected sign (evocation), its reputation, and one of the types of injury. Thus, the argument that the AO enjoys absolute protection in France simply on the grounds that the AO is protected beyond the principle of speciality does not hold water.[502]

However, it should be recalled that a misappropriation or weakening of the reputation of a source identifier, whether a trademark or an AO, is also likely to occur when the sign is used for identical or similar products. In the case of a trademark, however, the CJEU confirms that, where a sign is used for identical or similar goods or services, a mark with a reputation must enjoy a protection at least as extensive as that provided in cases where a sign is used for dissimilar goods or services.[503] In other words, the protection against 'freeriding', 'degradation' and 'dilution' may also apply where the contested marks designate identical or similar goods or services. However, this is subject to the same conditions as those that apply beyond the principle of speciality: the existence of a reputation and the likelihood of one of the three types of injury must be assessed. Nevertheless, in the case of an AO, such an assessment would be deemed *unnecessary*. As we have seen in the above section, the use of a term for

499. Article L. 643-1 does not expressly refer to the term dilution, detriment to the distinctive nature, as one of the forms of damage suffered by the AO.
500. On 19 July 1887, the Appeal Court of Angers affirmed that the word *Champagne* is indicative of the place of production of certain wines known under this name. *See* Fabien Barthe, *Le Champagne produit de luxe? Entre AOC et marque notoire*, Revue lamy droit des affaires, n° 66, 2011.
501. Passa, *supra* n. 7, at 782.
502. Certain authors claim that the AO is afforded absolute protection on the ground that it is protected regardless of the principle of speciality. *See* Georges Bonet, *La marque constituée par un nom géographique en droit français*, La semaine juridique entreprise et affaires, n° 50, 1990, 15931; Barthe, *supra* n. 500.
503. Case C-292/00 *Davidoff & Cie SA and Zino Davidoff SA v. Gofkid Ltd*, *supra* n. 382, para. 26.

identical or similar products will constitute an infringement of the rights pertaining to the AO as long as the term evokes the AO in the minds of the relevant public, without the need to assess either a risk of confusion or a risk of a misappropriation or weakening of reputation. In some cases, the reputation itself does not even exist. This shows that absolute and unconditional AO protection is afforded within the principle of speciality. One author observes that by imposing a general prohibition against 'any usurpation or evocation', we seem to be protecting AOs as 'things'[504] rather than as distinctive signs whose protected status depends upon their source-identifying and communicative abilities.[505] The French sui generis system has developed special treatments for these 'things', which incorporate *terroir*, but can the concept of *terroir* provide a rational basis for these special treatments? We explore this further in Chapters 7 and 8.

Article L. 721-8 of the IP Code grants protection for the IGPIA beyond the principle of speciality.[506] Given the similarity between the wording of this article and that of EU regulations on the protection of GIs, the prohibitions on the use of the IGPIA, PDO, and PGI for dissimilar goods will be examined together.

[b] Protection Beyond the Principle of Speciality in EU Law

European GI regulations for agricultural products and foodstuffs, wines, spirit drinks, and aromatized wine products all include a provision prohibiting 'any direct or indirect commercial use of a registered name, where using the name exploits the reputation of the protected name'.[507] This prohibition can be applied to products or services that are not comparable to products registered under that name, thus extending the scope of protection beyond the principle of speciality. It can also be applied in a situation where a PDO or PGI is used as part of the name under which a foodstuff is sold and where that foodstuff does not correspond to the product specifications for that PDO or PGI but contains an ingredient which does correspond to those specifications.[508]

However, the application of the European GI regulations is subject to conditions more severe than those that apply to the extended protection set out in Article L. 643-1 of the French Rural Code. First, the use of the words 'likely to' in Article L. 643-1 suggests that no actual or present injury to the AO needs to be proved. It is only necessary for the pleader to demonstrate that there is a serious risk that such an injury may occur. By contrast, none of the EU regulations mentions the words 'likely to',

504. Gangjee, *supra* n. 394, at 174.
505. For example, the protection afforded to a trademark is limited to cases where the use of the sign by a third party affects or is liable to affect the trademark functions, particularly the function of guaranteeing the origin of the goods. *See* Case C-206/01 *Arsenal Football Club plc v. Matthew Reed* [2002] ECR I-10273.
506. Article L. 721-8(1) CPI: '*(les dénominations enregistrées sont protégées contre) toute utilisation commerciale directe ou indirecte d'une dénomination enregistrée ... lorsque cette utilisation permet de profiter de la réputation de la dénomination protégée*'.
507. Article 13 of Regulation 1151/2012; Article 103 of Regulation 1308/2013; Article 21 of Regulation 2019/787; Article 20 of Regulation 251/2014.
508. *See* Case C-393/16 *Comité Interprofessionnel du Vin de Champagne v. Aldi Süd Dienstleistungs-GmbH & Co.OHG* (ECJ 20 December 2017) para. 36.

which may suggest that the pleader has to wait for the injury to occur in order to be able to prohibit that use. Furthermore, while the effect of Article L. 643-1 is that all three types of injury ('freeriding', 'degradation,' and 'dilution') are banned, the EU regulations expressly prohibit only one type of injury: the actual exploitation of the reputation.

[c] *Protection Beyond the Principle of Speciality in Chinese Law*

The protection afforded by the regulations administered by the former AQSIQ (the CNIPA since 2018) and the MOA does not extend to different products. This allows the third party, under the pretext of 'speciality', to use a well-known GI in the exercise of an activity different from the one the GI producers perform. As an illustration, the term '*Longjing*', the first part of the reputed Chinese GI '*Longjing* tea',[509] has been registered by third parties as a trademark in relation to various dissimilar products and services, including watches,[510] glasses,[511] carpets,[512] toothbrushes,[513] alcohol products,[514] vermicelli noodles,[515] snacks,[516] mineral water,[517] tea sets,[518] tea tables[519] and tea houses.[520] It would stretch credulity to suggest that none of these uses is likely to misappropriate or weaken the reputation of the GI, especially where the GI is used for tea-related products or services. However, neither the AQSIQ regulations nor the MOA administrative measures can be relied upon to protect GIs against detriment caused to them or unjustified exploitation of their reputation.

The protection of GIs in China's sui generis systems is limited to cases where GIs are used for identical or similar products. Furthermore, even in these limited cases, the sui generis regulations do not contain sufficient means to deal with infringements. Here, it would be useful to draw comparisons with French law concerning GI protection. In France, legal action against an alleged GI infringement may be initiated before high courts (*tribunaux de grande instance*)[521] by anyone claiming that an AO

509. Guojia Zhiliang Jiandu Jianyan Jianyi Zongju Gonggao 2001 Nian di 28 Hao [State General Administration of Quality Supervision, Inspection and Quarantine Announcement No. 28, 2001], 26 October 2001.
510. Trademark registration number: 4637147, available at, http://sbj.cnipa.gov.cn/sbcx/, accessed 15 May 2021.
511. Registration number: 11313785.
512. Registration number: 6529879.
513. Registration number: 4637215.
514. Registration number: 9295822.
515. Registration number: 5397515.
516. Registration number: 10393961.
517. Registration number: 1486704.
518. Registration number: 4022527.
519. Registration number: 7218952.
520. Registration number: 4290797.
521. Article R. 431-2 C. consom.: '*L'action est portée devant le tribunal de grande instance du lieu d'origine du produit dont l'appellation est contestée*'; Article L. 722-8 CPI: '*Les actions civiles et les demandes relatives aux indications géographiques, y compris lorsqu'elles portent également sur une question connexe de concurrence déloyale, sont exclusivement portées devant des tribunaux de grande instance, déterminés par voie réglementaire.*'

has been used to their direct or indirect prejudice and in contravention of their right,[522] by unions or associations whose purpose is to defend the appellation,[523] by anyone authorized to use the GI concerned (a local producer),[524] or by any organization to which the law entrusts the defence of GIs (such as the ODG and INAO).[525] However, under China's sui generis regimes, one can report violations of the GI regulations only to the relevant authorities.[526] It then falls to these authorities to impose administrative measures and penalties, specifically under Article 53 of the Product Quality Law[527] and Article 51 of the Agricultural Product Quality Safety Law.[528] Enforcement of GI protection seems to be based on administrative actions rather than lawsuits.

The subjection to the principle of speciality, along with the limited means of intervention, makes China's sui generis GI protection narrower, particularly when compared to the protection afforded by China's trademark law on GIs and on trademarks. One illustration of this narrow scope of protection is a case concerning an order sought by the *Comité Interprofessionnel du vin de Champagne* (CIVC) for the cancellation of the trademark '*Champaign*', registered by a third party for shampoos and cosmetics.[529] The French AOC '*Champagne*' is also a GI product registered under

522. Article L. 431-6(1) C. consom.: '*Toute personne qui prétend qu'une appellation d'origine est utilisée à son préjudice direct ou indirect et contre son droit, à un produit naturel ou fabriqué, contrairement à l'origine de ce produit, peut exercer une action en justice pour faire interdire l'usage de cette appellation.*'
523. Article L. 431-6(2) C. consom.: '*La même action peut être introduite par les syndicats et associations régulièrement constitués, depuis six mois au moins, quant aux droits qu'ils ont pour objet de défendre.*'
524. Article L. 722-2 CPI: '*L'action civile pour contrefaçon est exercée par toute personne autorisée à utiliser l'indication géographique concernée ou tout organisme auquel la législation donne pour mission la défense des indications géographiques.*'
525. Article L. 642-22 et Article L. 642-5 C. rur.; Article L. 721-4 CPI.
526. The violations of Provisions on the Protection of GI Products must be reported to the quality and technical supervision departments and the entry and exit inspection quarantine departments (the CNIPA since 2018). The violations of the Measures for the Administration of GIs for Agricultural Products (administered by the Ministry of Agriculture) should be reported to the competent agricultural departments. *See* Provisions on the Protection of GI Products, Article 21; Measures for the Administration of GIs for Agricultural Products, Article 21; *Zhong Hua v. Beijing Haidian District Food and Drug Administration*, Beijing Haidian District People's Court (6 February 2015).
527. Product Quality Law of the People's Republic of China, Article 53 (2018 Amendment): 'If a producer or a seller is found to have fabricated the place of origin, fabricated or used without authorization the names and addresses of other producers, fabricated or used without authorization quality marks such as certification marks, it shall be ordered to make corrections and be fined an amount of not more than the total value of the products illegal produced or sold with the products illegally produced or sold being confiscated; if any illegal proceeds have occurred, such proceeds shall be confiscated; if the circumstances are serious, the business license shall be revoked.'
528. Agricultural Product Quality Safety Law of the People's Republic of China, Article 51 (2018 Amendment): 'Whoever violates Article 32 of the present Law by imitating the quality marks of an agricultural product shall be ordered to make a correction, its/his illegal proceeds shall be confiscated, and it/he shall be fined 2,000 Yuan up to 20,000 Yuan.'
529. *France Champagne Industry Commission v. Trademark Review and Adjudication Board of the State Administration for Industry and Commerce of the People's Republic of China*, Beijing High People's Court (6 July 2010); *France Champagne Industry Commission v. Trademark Review and Adjudication Board of the State Administration for Industry and Commerce of the People's Republic of China*, Beijing High People's Court (2 March 2012).

the former AQSIQ and is thus protected by the Provisions on the Protection of GI Products.[530] However, the CIVC did not refer to the sui generis regulations because their protection does not extend to different products, and it cannot be invoked through a legal action.[531] Instead, the CIVC made a declaration of invalidity under Article 16 of the Trademark Law, which can be applied to any GI regardless of whether it is registered or not.[532] The Beijing Higher People's Court ruled that the contested mark would not have a negative impact on the image of *Champagne*, simply on the grounds that the products designated by the mark are not similar to the wine products covered by the GI.[533] The court concluded in a subsequent case (also concerning *Champagne*) that the protection of Article 16 is also subject to the principle of speciality.[534] Therefore, in order to protect GIs beyond this principle, the only remaining possibility seems to be the registration of GIs as trademarks in China.[535] Once the trademark becomes well-known, any reproduction, imitation, or translation of it for dissimilar goods would be prohibited.

In short, under China's sui generis systems, GIs are not accorded special treatment different from that of other distinctive signs with regard to their scope of protection. The protection accorded to trademarks is even wider than that accorded to GIs. Then, what is the use of creating the sui generis regimes if GIs enjoy the same or stronger protection under the trademark system?

In conclusion, the adoption of the European sui generis approach in China has not been fully achieved. There is a lack of acknowledgement of the roles played by different actors in the control and defence of GIs: the former AQSIQ ignores the role of producers' groups, while the MOA does not provide for sufficient public intervention for quality control. China's two sui generis GI systems have not set the high level of protection for GIs that European GI laws offer.

530. Guojia Zhiliang Jiandu Jianyan Jianyi Zongju Gonggao 2013 Nian di 51 Hao [State General Administration of Quality Supervision, Inspection and Quarantine Announcement No. 51, 2013], 11 April 2013.
531. In case of violation of the Provisions on the Protection of GI Products, the last sentence of Article 21 only provides that any organization, enterprise and individual may report such violations. It does not endow producers or organizations with the rights of bringing civil actions for damages before the court. In fact, Article 21 has never been applied in legal action for the purpose of punishing those who have committed violations of the Provisions.
532. Trademark Law, Article 16(1): 'It shall be prohibited to register or use a trademark that contains a GI with respect to products not originating in the region indicated, if (use of the indication in the trademark) misleads the public.'
533. *France Champagne Industry Commission v. Trademark Review and Adjudication Board of the State Administration for Industry and Commerce of the People's Republic of China*, Beijing High People's Court (6 July 2010).
534. *France Champagne Industry Commission v. Trademark Review and Adjudication Board of the State Administration for Industry and Commerce of the People's Republic of China*, Beijing High People's Court (2 March 2012).
535. Well-known marks are divided into two kinds, namely well-known marks not registered in China and those registered in China. Well-known marks not registered in China only have exclusive rights over goods or services that are identical or similar, while registered well-known marks have exclusive rights not only on identical or similar goods or services, but also on different or dissimilar goods. *See* An Qinghu, *Well-Known Marks & China's System of Well-Known Mark Protection*, 95 Trademark Rep. 705, 714 (2005).

Our analysis in this chapter has followed two lines. The first line compares the key aspects of the sui generis GI systems in Europe and in China. One simple conclusion that can be drawn from this comparison is that the designing of sui generis GI systems can vary greatly from one state to another. The European systems are built on a strict and rigorous (and, for applicant groups, perhaps burdensome) registration process to make sure that the signs and products they designate meet the requirements prescribed in the GI definitions; this is a multilayer system with strong state involvement intended to monitor compliance with established product specifications and a high level of protection designed to prevent the misuse, imitation, or evocation of the registered GIs. Although China's sui generis systems have similar registration requirements, their monitoring systems are designed differently and, more importantly, their level of protection is much lower.

The second line explores the differences between the trademark regime and the sui generis GI regime, especially in terms of their protection levels. It is well-known that a sui generis regime may have registration requirements and monitoring systems that differ from those in a trademark regime. Thus, we have focused on the protection levels involved. Our results show that the scope of GI protection provided by the French and EU sui *generis* laws is wider than that provided for ordinary trademarks and even for reputed trademarks. The situation is the opposite in China: the scope of the sui generis protection of GIs is less extensive than that enjoyed by ordinary trademarks, collective or certification marks (including those containing GIs) or, of course, reputed trademarks.

Overall, sui generis GI systems should not be arbitrarily stereotyped. Not all have the same degree of state involvement, management structure, quality control measures, or protection level. Furthermore, their differences from trademark systems depend on how both systems are designed.

This chapter, along with Chapter 3, provides a much-needed basis for further discussion on the choice of the instrument to which priority or preference should be given (either the trademark or sui generis regime).

Despite the differences in institutional arrangements between France, the EU, and China, the sui generis GI systems concerned have several features in common, which make them distinct from the trademark systems. Public authorities are generally more involved in the sui generis GI systems, which regard GIs as public assets. The verification of the link between the product and its place of origin in the registration procedure, product manufacture, product quality, and the commercial use of the protected name are all subject to public oversight.

Another major feature of the sui generis systems is the level of protection. The scope of protection provided to GIs is more or less extensive than the protection enjoyed by trademarks. This difference is not surprising, as GIs and trademarks have different justifications for protection (*terroir* logic versus distinctiveness logic). We will take a closer look at these justifications in subsequent sections.[536]

536. *See* Chapter 6 and Chapter 7 *infra*.

When choosing an appropriate instrument for the protection of GIs, account must also be taken of how the instrument is or will be designed. The boundary between the sui generis and trademark systems is not always clear. The experience of China shows that rules often embedded in GI regulations could be inserted into trademark laws (e.g., verification of the link with a place, protection against misleading indications as to the geographical origin, and coexistence between an earlier ordinary mark and a later collective or certification mark containing a GI). This raises the question of whether trademark systems can possibly be tailored to match the needs of GI protection. The choice could be complicated even further in light of this possibility.

CHAPTER 5
The EU Approach Versus the US Approach on the Battlefield of China

China has adopted the EU approach in establishing sui generis systems for GIs and has adopted the US approach by employing the trademark system. The cohabitation of the EU-inspired and US-inspired systems allows a competitive game to develop. This chapter explores the tension between the two types of systems. It shows that the EU-inspired sui generis systems fail to deliver the expected outcomes owing to the competition with the US-inspired trademark system. The two types of systems serve the same purpose, of setting out conditions for the use of GIs. However, the systems offer contrasting solutions to the 'prior trademark, later GI' issue. China's sui generis systems follow the EU approach in allowing for the coexistence of later GIs with prior trademarks, whereas China's trademark system follows the US approach and applies the rule of 'first in time, first in right'. Thus, GIs protected under the sui generis systems are granted only a narrow scope of protection. With this limited protection, operators may lose the right to use GIs acquired under the sui generis systems where conflicting signs are protected as individual, collective, or certification marks.

As Chapter 2 has demonstrated, China has adopted the EU approach and established sui generis systems for GIs. China's sui generis GI regimes, like their European counterparts, serve to link the product to the *terroir* by fixing the definitive boundaries of the production area, determining common standards, providing quality control schemes, and taking legal action against infringement.[1]

China has also adopted the US approach in employing the trademark system to protect GIs. China's trademark system has been adapted to meet GIs' protection needs.[2]

1. *See* Chapter 3 *supra*.
2. *See* Chapter 4 *supra*.

When the two types of systems are employed in the same territory, a cumulative protection of GIs is possible in which a GI can be registered and therefore protected by the two types of systems. The most common way to obtain such a cumulative protection is to register a GI under both the trademark system and one of the sui generis systems. According to a survey report released in September 2020, 1,398 GIs have been registered under at least two systems.[3]

While the use of cumulative protection opens new possibilities for protecting GIs, it also allows a competitive game to develop. China's sui generis systems are often in direct competition with the trademark system since they both serve to identify legitimate GI users and set out the conditions for GI use. For one GI registered under the two types of systems, the authorized users and conditions of use may differ from one system to the other.

There is also competition in terms of the attractiveness of a protection system to its target audiences (producers and consumers). The number of registered GIs is a simple indicator of the interest shown in a system as a tool for protecting and adding value to GIs. The trademark system is the preferred choice for registering GIs. By the end of 2020, the number of GIs registered as collective or certification marks had reached 6,085.[4] By contrast, the number of GIs registered under the GI product regime was 2,391, and the number registered under the MOA was 3,088.[5]

Moreover, the two types of systems have contrasting approaches to the 'prior trademark, later GI' issue. The EU-inspired sui generis GI systems allow for the coexistence of later GIs with trademarks registered before the application date for the GI, while the US-inspired trademark system generally applies the rule of 'first in time, first in right' (FITFIR).

China's law recognizes the validity of individual trademarks composed of geographical names. The same subject matter (geographical names) can therefore be registered under both the trademark and GI regimes. The two regimes operate in parallel with each other, and each regime gives successful applicants the right to exclude certain competitors. A battle occurs when the two regimes permit different parties to claim exclusive rights to the same name. The question then is whether the right conferred by one regime can prevent the name from being registered under the other regime and being used by a third party (§5.01).

China's law also allows GIs to be protected as collective marks and certification marks. Again, the same geographical name can be registered as both a collective or certification mark under the trademark regime and as a GI under the sui generis regime. A battle occurs when persons authorized to use the mark do not include all legitimate producers recognized under the sui generis regime. The right conferred by the latter

3. Beijing Zhongjun Shiji GI Research Group, Di Sici Quanguo Dili Biaozhi Diaoyan Baogao [Report on the Fourth Survey of China's Geographical Indications], 9 September 2020.
4. Shen Changyu zai 2021 Nian Quanguo Zhishi Chanquanju Juzhang Huiyi Shangde Gongzuo Baogao [Shen Changyu's Report at the 2021 National Conference of Directors of Intellectual Property Offices], 25 January 2021.
5. *Ibid. See also* Beijing Zhongjun Shiji GI Research Group, *supra* n. 3.

might be affected to the extent that the recognized legitimate producers could use the geographical name only in a 'descriptive sense' (§5.02).

§5.01 PROTECTING GIs UNDER CHINA'S SUI GENERIS SYSTEMS: A LOSING BATTLE AGAINST INDIVIDUAL MARKS

In theory, the trademark regime regulates the use of signs that identify the commercial origin of products. The sui generis GI regime governs the use of signs that describe the geographical origin of products and a set of characteristics attached to the origin. Geographically descriptive signs cannot perform the function of associating the products with a particular enterprise. Applications for registration of such signs under the trademark regime should normally be rejected since they might be either descriptive or deceptive. Instead, these signs can be registered under the sui generis GI regime once other conditions have been met. There seems to be a clear boundary between the trademark regime and the sui generis GI regime.[6]

However, China's trademark law has not provided a total prohibition of the registration of geographical names as individual trademarks. Since the same subject matter, geographical signs can be protected under both the trademark and GI systems, conflicts between GI registration under the sui generis systems and trademark registration are inevitable. However, China's domestic legislation does not expressly address this issue. Consequently, on the one hand, the existence of a GI previously registered by a sui generis regime does not constitute an 'automatic' obstacle to registering an individual trademark. On the other hand, the existence of a prior individual trademark can limit the use of a GI to a 'descriptive use'. Protecting GIs under China's current sui generis systems puts GI collectives in danger of losing the battle against trademark proprietors.

[A] Unresolved Conflict Between GIs and Subsequent Individual Marks

Although the trademark law imposes several limitations on the registering of geographical names as trademarks, there is still room for individual marks consisting of them. The rights conferred by a GI registration under China's sui generis regime are insufficient to avoid potential interference from subsequent geographical marks.

[1] Validity of an Individual Mark Consisting of a Geographical Name

French and EU law preclude the registration of signs that are descriptive of the geographical origin of the goods[7] or deceive the public as to their geographical origin

6. Bernard O'Connor, *The EC Need Not Be Isolated on GIs*, 29 Eur. Intell. Prop. Rev. 303 (2007).
7. Article L. 711-2(3) CPI: '*Ne peuvent être valablement enregistrés et, s'ils sont enregistrés, sont susceptibles d'être déclaré nuls: 3° Une marque composée exclusivement d'éléments ou d'indications pouvant servir à désigner, dans le commerce, une caractéristique du produit ou du service, et notamment l'espèce, la qualité, la quantité, la destination, la valeur, la provenance*

(in the event that the goods do not come from the place indicated).[8] However, this prohibition is not an insurmountable obstacle to registering geographical names as individual trademarks. The fact that we can find a term on a map does not mean that the term necessarily conveys to the consumer a geographical connotation. Where the term is unknown as a designation of a location, the consumer is unlikely to believe that the goods originate there.[9] Even if the place name is well-known to the consumer, it can be used arbitrarily (e.g., 'Atlantic' in the name of a magazine or Mont-Blanc for pens),[10] as there would be no association in the minds of the consumer between the geographical name and the products concerned.[11] The third possibility is that a geographical term may, through use, acquire a distinctive character it initially lacked and thus identify products from a particular manufacturer.[12] Each of these routes allows a geographical name to satisfy the 'non-descriptiveness' and 'non-deceptiveness' requirements of a

---

géographique, l'époque de la production du bien ou de la prestation du service'; Article 4(1)(c) of Directive 2015/2436: 'The following shall not be registered or, if registered, shall be liable to be declared invalid: trade marks which consist exclusively of signs or indications which may serve, in trade, to designate ... geographical origin ...'; Article 7(1)(c) of Regulation 2017/1001: 'The following shall not be registered: trade marks which consist exclusively of signs or indications which may serve, in trade, to designate ... geographical origin ....' *See also* Chapter 3 *supra*.

8. According to the French case law, a trademark could be invalidated where the trademark registration is fraudulent. The goal is to prevent others from using the geographical name in bad faith (e.g., for the purpose of reserving privileged and monopolistic access to a sign identifying a place, to the detriment of other operators). *See* Article L. 711-2(8) CPI: '*Ne peuvent être valablement enregistrés et, s'ils sont enregistrés, sont susceptibles d'être déclaré nuls: 8° Une marque de nature à tromper le public, notamment sur la nature, la qualité ou la provenance géographique du produit ou du service*'; Article (4)(1)(g) of Directive 2015/2436 and Article 7(1)(g) of Regulation 2017/1001: 'The following shall not be registered: trade marks which are of such a nature as to deceive the public, for instance as to the ... geographical origin of the goods or service'; Cass. com., 23 juin 2009, n° 07-19542; Cass. com., 4 oct. 2016, n° 14-22245; Jacques Larrieu, *Concurrence déloyale laguiole: le match retour*, Propriété Industrielle, n° 12, 2016, p. 37.
9. For example, the word 'Mirabelle' is a place name of a castle in Austria. However, it would not be perceived as such for French consumers but rather seen as a name of a fruit. *See* Georges Bonet, *La marque constituée par un nom géographique en droit français*, La semaine juridique entreprise et affaires, n° 50, 1990, 15931; *See also* Case T-197/13 *Marques de l'État de Monaco (MEM) v. Office for Harmonisation in the Internal Market* (CFI 15 January 2015) para. 51; Case T-379/03 *Peek & Cloppenburg KG v. European Union Intellectual Property Office* [2005] ECR II-04633, para. 38.
10. The CJEU notes that a sign's descriptiveness cannot be assessed other than by reference to the goods or services concerned, on the one hand, and by reference to the understanding which the relevant persons have of it, on the other. Even if it describes precisely the geographical origin of the products, the name can be considered distinctive provided that it is perceived as 'arbitrary' when used in relation to specific goods. For example, the trademark 'Aoste' has been accepted as valid for foodstuffs that come from this area. *See* Case T-295/01 *Nordmilch v. OHIM* [2003] ECR II-4378, para. 34; C.A. Paris, 22 oct. 1979, PIBD 1980, 249, III, p. 287.
11. *See* Joined Case C-108/97 & C-109/97 *Windsurfing Chiemsee* [1999] ECR I-2779, para. 31.
12. Article L. 711-2 CPI: '*Dans les cas prévus aux 2°, 3° et 4°, le caractère distinctif d'une marque peut être acquis à la suite de l'usage qui en a été fait*'; Article 4(4) of Directive 2015/2436: 'A trade mark shall not be refused registration in accordance with paragraph 1(b), (c) or (d) if, before the date of application for registration, following the use which has been made of it, it has acquired a distinctive character'; Article 7(3) of Regulation 2017/1001: 'Paragraph 1(b), (c) and (d) shall not apply if the trade mark has become distinctive in relation to the goods or services for which registration is requested in consequence of the use which has been made of it.'

trademark.[13] It can therefore be concluded that an individual trademark may consist of a geographical name, despite the limitations European legislation imposes on its validity.[14]

Likewise, China's trademark law places two restrictions on geographical marks. First, Article 10 provides that 'the name of any administrative division at or above the county level or the name of any foreign place known by the public may not be used as a trademark, except that the place name has other meanings'. Without mentioning the 'non-descriptiveness' requirement, this article prohibits the registration of the name of an administrative division 'at or above the county level'. That leaves the door wide open for the names of administrative divisions 'below the county level' to constitute a valid individual trademark.[15] It is also possible to register place names that are not names of administrative divisions (e.g., '*Tianya Haijiao*', the name of a scenic area in the southern part of Hainan province).[16]

Even the prohibition on registering the names of administrative divisions at or above the county level is not absolute. It does not apply if the name has 'other meanings'. This 'other meanings' condition does not equate with the 'secondary meaning' in European law.[17] It refers to a situation wherein a word, despite being a division name, does not communicate a geographical meaning to the relevant public but conveys other meanings. '*Hong He*', the name of a county in Yunnan Province, can constitute a valid individual trademark because the literal meaning of the words is 'red river'. Since this place name is not known to the public, it would normally not be understood as such.[18] In China, geographical names are made up of Chinese characters or their combinations. Each character or combination may have a meaning other than

13. Dev Gangjee, *Quibbling Siblings: Conflicts Between Trademarks and Geographical Indications*, 82 Chi.-Kent L. Rev. 1253, 1260 (2007).
14. Ancien Article L. 711-1 CPI: '*Noms géographiques peuvent notamment constituer un tel signe (La marque de fabrique, de commerce ou de service).*'
15. Deng Hongguang, Lun Woguo Diming Shangbiao Falu Zhidu de Wanshan [The Improvement of the Legal System of China's Geographical Trademark], NEIMENGGU SHEHUI KEXUE [INNER MONGOLIA SOCIAL SCIENCES], July 2008, 31.
16. *See Hainan Tianya Haijiao Co. Ltd. v. the Trademark Review and Adjudication Board of the State Administration for Industry and Commerce*, Beijing High People's Court (29 April 2008). However, this type of registration is limited by China's 2019 Trademark Law Amendment that targets bad faith trademark applications.
17. Liu Xiaojun, Shangbiaofa Di Shier Tiao Di Er Kuan Youguan Diming Shangbiao de Wenti Yanjiu [A Study on Trademarks of Geographical Names under Article10(2) of the Trademark Law], ZHONGGUO ZHUANLI YU SHANGBIAO [CHINA PATENTS AND TRADEMARKS], January 2012, 53.
18. For example, the words 'Rui Li', literally meaning 'lucky' and 'beautiful', would not be understood as a place name unless the place bearing the same name becomes well-known to the public. 'Rui Li' has been registered as individual marks for various products by third parties, and some marks have been registered for more than a decade. It is only recently that the phenomenon has attracted attention because of a growing recognition among consumers of the place. *See* Ruan Kaixin, Cong Ruili An Kan Shangbiaofa Zhong de Diming he Dili Biaozhi Wenti [Geographical Names and Geographical Indications in Trademark Law: The Case of Ruili], ZHONGHUA SHANGBIAO [CHINA TRADEMARK], September 2015, 72; *Qin Zhanguo v. Trademark Review and Adjudication Board of State Administration for Industry and Commerce*, Beijing High People's Court (20 July 2010).

a geographical connotation. Thus, in order to serve as a valid trademark, a term's other meanings must be 'stronger' than its geographical connotation.[19]

The prohibition also does not apply to division names that are associated with other words if the combination, taken as a whole, has a distinctive character.[20] Trademarks composed of the abbreviated names of two (or more) administrative divisions are still acceptable.[21]

The second restriction is that the geographical mark must not be 'deceptive'. The 2013 amendment of paragraph 1 of Article 10 of the Trademark Law adds the following clarification: signs that may easily mislead the public regarding the 'geographical origin' of goods shall not be used as trademarks.[22] Trademarks consisting of geographical names may lead to an expectation as to the geographical origin of the goods that is contradictory to the reality (i.e., the goods do not come from the place indicated). Such a circumstance is sufficient to render those marks 'deceptive' and thus not registrable. However, place names unknown to the relevant public can hardly evoke such an expectation. Even if the place name is famous, it would not give rise to such an expectation given the characteristics of the goods (e.g., 'North Pole' for bananas).[23] In addition, by adding other words or figurative elements, the false expectation caused by the famous place name can be corrected and the mark made merely evocative (not misleading).[24] Finally, considering the composition of Chinese place names (wherein their characters have original meanings other than the geographical connotation), place names with strong 'other meanings' are not likely to be understood as such by the relevant public and would thus not mislead the public into believing that the goods come from the particular place.[25]

It must be concluded that the two restrictions imposed by Article 10 of the Trademark Law are not an absolute barrier preventing geographical names from being used as individual marks. However, there is reason to believe that the geographical mark in China could be more widespread than is in Europe. Chinese geographical names always have 'other meanings', and those in less-developed regions are hardly known to the relevant public. China's law does not expressly establish the 'non-descriptiveness' requirement. Only recently has the 'non-deceptiveness' requirement been specified. While the names of administrative divisions at or above the county level are in principle not registrable (except for those with 'other meanings'), names

19. Trademark Office & Trademark Review and Adjudication Board, Shangbiao Shencha ji Shenli Biaozhun [Trademark Review Standard], December 2016, p. 45.
20. *Ibid.*
21. *Ibid.*, p. 47.
22. Before the trademark law amendment in 2013, Article 8(8) only provides that trademarks 'having the nature of exaggeration and fraud in advertising goods' shall not be used.
23. One example of a Chinese trademark is the 'Great Wall' for wines.
24. For example, 'Warsaw', the capital and largest city of Poland, is a foreign place known by Chinese consumers. Therefore, registering 'Warsaw' for shoes may mislead consumers as to the geographical origin of the goods. However, the trademark 'Warsaw Burgrave' is evocative of the Polish city but is not likely to mislead the consumer.
25. An earlier cited example: the trademark '*Ruili*' (meaning 'lucky' and 'beautiful' and also a place name in China) used on magazines would not mislead the consumer into believing that the magazine comes from the place bearing the same name.

below the county level are less protected. Among the latter, many may be qualified as GIs.[26] The threat from subsequent geographical marks to GIs is real, and it is thus important to be more vigilant.

[2] Unavailability of a GI as an Individual Mark

While individual geographical marks are acceptable in Europe, legislators are vigilant in ensuring that they do not infringe a prior GI.[27] First, a GI registered under the European sui generis regime enables its proprietor to prohibit the use and registration of a subsequent trademark.[28] The protection conferred on the GI stems from Article 13(1) of Regulation 1151/2012, Article 103(2) of Regulation 1308/2013, Article 21 of Regulation 2019/787, and Article 20(2) of Regulation 251/2014. Its scope covers any direct or indirect commercial use of a protected name (including use as a trademark) and any misuse, imitation, or evocation. Second, the above mentioned regulations all contain specific provisions governing the conflict between prior GIs and subsequent trademarks. Overall, these provisions specify that the registration of a trademark the use of which falls under the aforementioned articles shall be refused or invalidated.[29] Lastly, the trademark regime offers (or should offer) the same degree of protection to

26. 'Bai Pu' is a name of an administrative division below the county level (a town in Jiangsu Province). It is also a geographical indication for rice wines produced in this area. Therefore, the registration of the words 'Bai Pu' is not objectionable under Article 10, para. 2. *See* Wang Lianfeng, Dili Biaozhi yu Diming Shangbiao de Chongtu ji Falu Shiyong [The Conflict of Geographical Indication with Topographic Trademarks and Its Application of Law], HENAN-SHENG ZHENGFA GUANLI GANBU XUEYUAN XUEBAO [JOURNAL OF HENAN INSTITUTE OF POLITICAL SCIENCE AND LAW], February 2004, 104.
27. *See* Benjamin Fontaine, *L'indisponibilité résultant d'un conflit avec une indication geographique*, Europe, n° 11, 2016, 2.
28. *See* Case T-387/13 *Federación Nacional de Cafeteros de Colombia v. OHMI* (CFI 18 September 2015); Case C-120/08 *Bavaria NV v. Bayerischer Brauerbund eV* [2010] ECR I-13393, para. 36.
29. According to Article 14(1) of Regulation 1151/2012 for agricultural products and foodstuffs, 'where a designation of origin or a geographical indication is registered under this Regulation, the registration of a trade mark the use of which would contravene Article 13(1) and which relates to a product of the same type shall be refused if the application for registration of the trade mark is submitted after the date of submission of the registration application in respect of the designation of origin or the geographical indication to the Commission'. As regards wines, according to Article 102(1) of Regulation 1308/2013, 'the registration of a trade mark that contains or consists of a protected designation of origin or a geographical indication which does not comply with the product specification concerned or the use of which falls under Article 103(2), and that relates to a product falling under one of the categories listed in Part II of Annex VII shall be refused if the application for registration of the trade mark is submitted after the date of submission of the application for protection of the designation of origin or geographical indication to the Commission and the designation of origin or geographical indication is subsequently protected; or invalidated'. As regards spirit drinks, according to Article 36(1) of Regulation 2019/787, 'the registration of a trade mark the use of which corresponds or would correspond to one or more of the situations referred to in Article 21(2) shall be refused or invalidated'. Finally, As regards aromatized wines, according to Article 19(1) of Regulation 251/2014, 'the registration of a trade mark, the use of which falls under Article 20(2) and relates to an aromatized wine product must be refused if the application for registration of the trademark is submitted after the date of submission of the application for protection of the geographical indication to the Commission and the geographical indication is subsequently protected'.

GIs as is provided in the sui generis regime,[30] as is evidenced by the recent EU trademark reform in 2015, especially the amendments to Article 7(1)(j) and (k) of Regulation 207/2009 (replaced and codified by Regulation 2007/1001) and the introduction of Article 4(1)(i) of Directive 2015/2436.[31] At the national level, Article L. 711-2 and Article L. 711-3 of the French IP Code provide that signs may not be registered as trademarks where they infringe earlier rights, particularly 'a protected AO or a GI'.[32] All these efforts are geared toward ensuring that EU sui generis laws protecting GIs are given full effect and that any application to register an individual trademark that contains or consists of a GI (protected under the sui generis regime) will face insurmountable obstacles.[33]

However, in China, neither the Provisions on the Protection of GI Products nor the Measures for the Administration of GIs for Agricultural Products contain a specific provision applicable to trademark applications that may infringe a prior GI. The sui generis law does not address the relationship between GIs previously registered and subsequent trademarks.

Article 16(1) of the Trademark Law provides that 'It shall be prohibited to register or use a trademark that contains a GI with respect to products not originating in the region indicated, if (use of the indication in the trademark) misleads the public.' The application of this article, however, does not require that the GI be registered. The only requirement is that the geographical name or sign in question must meet the definition of GIs as set forth in Article 16(2). It follows that a trademark containing a GI can be objected to under Article 16(1), not because the GI is previously registered under the sui generis regime but because the GI meets the definition established by the trademark

30. European Commission, *Proposal for a Regulation of the European Parliament and the Council Amending Council Regulation 207/2009 on the Community Trade Mark*, 2013/0088 (COD) (27 March 2013) p. 7.
31. Since the reform in 2015, Article 7(1)(j) of EU Trademark Regulation and Article 4(1)(i) of EU Trademark Directive provides that 'trade marks which are excluded from registration pursuant to Union legislation, or the national law of the Member State concerned (applied only in the national trademark system), or to international agreements to which the Union or the Member State concerned is party, providing for protection of designations of origin and geographical indications' shall not be registered.
32. Article L. 711-2(9) CPI: '*Une marque exclue de l'enregistrement en vertu de la législation nationale, du droit de l'Union européenne ou d'accords internationaux auxquels la France ou l'Union sont parties, qui prévoient la protection des appellations d'origine et des indications géographiques, des mentions traditionnelles pour les vins et des spécialités traditionnelles garanties*'; Article L. 711-3(5) CPI: '*Ne peut être valablement enregistrée et, si elle est enregistrée, est susceptible d'être déclarée nulle une marque portant atteinte à des droits antérieurs ayant effet en France, notamment : Une indication géographique enregistrée mentionnée à l'article L. 722-1 ou à une demande d'indication géographique sous réserve de l'homologation de son cahier des charges et de son enregistrement ultérieur.*'
33. A trademark containing a GI could satisfy the 'non-descriptiveness' requirement set out in Article 7(1)(c) of Regulation 2017/1001 by adding other word or figurative elements, which may give the trademark a distinctive character. However, the sign can be acceptable as a whole under Article 7(1)(c) and can still be objectionable according to Article 7(1)(j). Under the latter, it is irrelevant whether or not the other word or figurative elements may give the trademark a distinctive character. What matters is whether the protected name appears in the complex trademark.

regime. Consequently, the Trademark Office is under no obligation to examine whether there is a prior registration of the sign by the sui generis regime.

In a judgment released on 28 July 2015, Beijing Higher People's Court noted that the grounds for refusal provided for in Article 16(1) is not taken into account ex officio by the examiner. The Trademark Office will carry out an examination only at the request of a party. Furthermore, the party opposing the registration of the trademark must demonstrate that the sign contained in the mark constitutes a GI defined in Article 16(2) regardless of whether the sign has already been registered under the sui generis regime.[34] In other words, even if the prior GI registration exists, it will not constitute an 'automatic' obstacle to the registration: the satisfaction of the GI definition must be proved in the opposition proceedings. On the other hand, in the absence of any opposition or solid evidence, the registration of a trademark containing a GI may be approved.

While a GI registration under the sui generis regime theoretically enables its proprietor to exclude the use of that sign by others, China's trademark regime does not offer the same degree of protection to GIs, nor is it willing to do so. Shortly before the promulgation of the Provisions on the Protection of GI Products, the former SAIC wrote a letter to the former AQSIQ expressing its opposition to them.[35] The result is that the trademark regime administered by the former SAIC (specifically, the Trademark Office) refuses to acknowledge the rights conferred by sui generis provisions protecting GIs. Therefore, China's sui generis regime is unable to resolve the conflict between GIs and subsequent individual marks.

The EU-China GI Agreement, which entered into force in March 2021, addresses this conflict. The first two paragraphs of Article 6 of the Agreement govern the relationship between prior GIs and subsequent trademarks. They stipulate as follows:

> (1) The Parties shall, ex officio or at the request of an interested party, refuse or invalidate the registration of a trademark which consists of a GI or its translation or transcription, with respect to identical or similar products not having the origin indicated by that GI, in accordance with their respective rules, provided that the application for registration of the trademark has been submitted after the date of protection for the GIs listed in Annex III or IV, or after the date of application for protection for the GIs referred to in Article 3 of this Agreement, in the territory concerned.
>
> (2) The Parties shall also, at the request of an interested party, refuse or invalidate the registration of a trademark which indicates that the good in question originates in a geographical area other than the true place of origin with respect to identical or similar products, provided that the application for

34. *Chen Jianhua v. Trademark Review and Adjudication Board of the State Administration for Industry and Commerce*, Beijing High People's Court (28 July 2015).

35. Zhang Chuanfeng, Qianxi Dili Biaozhi Baohu Guoji Biaozhun ji Woguo de Kexingxing Xuanze [Discussions on the International Standards of Protection for Geographical Indications and China's Choice], ZHISHI CHANQUAN FA YANJIU [INTELLECTUAL PROPERTY LAW RESEARCH], January 2008, 118.

registration of the trademark has been submitted after the date of protection for the GIs listed in Annex III or IV, or after the date of application for protection for the GIs referred to in Article 3 of this Agreement, in the territory concerned.

The EU and China agree that GI protection may be provided under legislation other than trademark laws and regulations, such as in legislation providing for sui generis GI protection.[36] Therefore, it is foreseeable that GIs registered under China's sui generis systems will constitute prior rights that can be used to challenge a subsequent trademark registration or application for registration. However, since the contractual obligation applies only to the GIs listed or added in the Annexes of the Agreement, it remains to be seen whether all names registered in China's sui generis GI systems will have the same status.

[B] Unresolved Conflict Between GIs and Earlier Individual Marks

Conflicts may also arise between a prior trademark registration and a subsequent GI application under a sui generis regime. There are three possible solutions to this kind of conflict. While the coexistence can be accepted on the basis of the descriptive fair use defence in trademark law, in China, the use of a later GI is not allowed where the GI is used not merely in a 'descriptive sense' but in a 'trademark sense'.[37]

[1] Resolution to the Conflict Between a Later GI and an Earlier Individual Mark

As mentioned,[38] Article 10 of the Trademark Law is not an insurmountable obstacle to the misappropriation of GIs through their registration as individual marks.[39] What is worse, the law provided no restriction of such conduct when it was first adopted in 1982. It was only later that the restriction on the use of geographical names in trademarks was introduced in the Trademark Law (1993) and its implementing regulations (1988).[40] Therefore, numerous individual trademarks that contain or consist of GIs were registered before the date of the application of the amended

36. *Agreement Between the European Union and the Government of the People's Republic of China on Cooperation on, and Protection of, Geographical Indications*, OJ L 408I, 4.12.2020, p. 3, Article 4.
37. The expression 'use in a trademark sense' or 'use as a trademark' means that the use of a GI is not only intended to describe the characteristics of the product but also is intended to differentiate the product from those of other undertakings, and is thus used as a trademark.
38. *See* Chapter 4 *supra*.
39. *Lin Lizhen v. Trademark Review and Adjudication Board of the State Administration for Industry and Commerce of the People's Republic of China*, Beijing First Intermediate People's Court (16 March 2004).
40. China has become a member of the Paris Convention for the Protection of Industrial Property in 1985. The accession has brought China obligations to protect indications of source and appellations of origin. *See* Chapter 2 *supra*.

Trademark Law or before the GI was recognized.[41] This lack of restriction has fuelled tensions and sown the seeds of conflict. Producers working with a GI product may subsequently claim the right to use the same geographical name in order to distinguish between identical or similar products.[42]

Three approaches have been suggested to resolve such conflicts. The first approach, which is advocated by the US,[43] is well-established in trademark law[44] and consists of giving priority to trademarks previously registered over competing GI applications. This is known as the rule of FITFIR. This rule can be demonstrated in two ways. First, an earlier trademark would not be subject to being cancelled or expropriated by virtue of a later protected GI.[45] Instead, it would take precedence over the later GI ('principle of priority'). Second, the sign that is protected first as a trademark would prevent the use of any conflicting subsequent signs ('principle of exclusivity').[46]

The 'principle of priority' has been given a warm reception in China's trademark regime. Legislators clearly applied this principle in amending Article 10 of the Trademark Law in 1993. The second paragraph was added in order to prohibit the use of the name of an administrative region at or above the county level as an individual trademark. One of the exceptions to this rule is any geographical mark registered before the date of the trademark law amendment,[47] which continues to be valid. Therefore, the second paragraph of Article 10 cannot be relied on by GI producers to invalidate a geographical mark that is identical or similar to a GI where that trademark was registered before the amendment came into force.

41. GIs can be recognized under the trademark regime by registering them as collective marks or certification marks. However, while GIs can also be registered under the sui generis regime, the Trademark Office refuses to accept the validity of such a registration.
42. The problem may also occur where the same sign is used by different parties as a trademark and a geographical indication for 'dissimilar goods', since either the trademark or the geographical indication may be well-known. The protection of well-known trademarks can extend beyond the 'principle of speciality'. *See* Chapter 3 *supra*.
43. *See* WTO Panel Report on *European Communities: Protection of Trademarks and Geographical Indications for Agricultural Products and Foodstuffs*, WT/DS174/R, adopted 15 April 2005.
44. The Advocate General Tizzano pointed out, in a case concerning the right to use the words 'Bud', 'Budweiser', that 'the principle of the primacy of the prior exclusive right ... is one of the basic principles of trademark law and, more generally, of all industrial-property law'. *See* Case C-245/02 *Anheuser-Busch Inc v. Budějovický Budvar, národní podnik* [2004] ECR I-10989, para. 98.
45. Frank Z. Hellwig, *A Way Forward for Geographical Indications* (WIPO/GEO/SFO/03/22 9 July 2003) p. 4.
46. The WIPO has suggested that the party, which has first acquired rights in the sign in a given territory, should be entitled to prevent other parties from using that sign. *See* WIPO, *Possible Solution for Conflicts Between Trademarks and Geographical Indications and for Conflicts Between Homonymous Geographical Indications*, SCT/5/3 (8 June 2000) p. 20. *See also* Frank Z. Hellwig, *Why the Principles of Priority and Exclusivity Cannot Be Compromised: The Trademark Owner's Perspective on Geographical Indications and First in Time First in Right* (International Trademark Association, Working Paper 2004).
47. The second paragraph allows three exceptions to the prohibition on the use of the name of administrative divisions at or above the county level: (1) geographical names with other connotations; (2) geographical names contained in collective or certification marks; and (3) trademarks incorporating geographical names registered before the prohibition came into effect.

Article 24.5 of the TRIPS Agreement also establishes a similar grandfather clause in favour of earlier trademarks that are identical or similar to GIs.[48] However, the application of the grandfather clause, which embodies the principle of priority, requires the *good faith* of the trademark owner. The validity of the trademark is not affected if it was acquired 'in good faith' either before the application date of the national provisions as defined in Part VI of the Agreement or before the GI was protected in its country of origin.[49]

The 'good faith' requirement has been included in Article 14(2) of EU Regulation 1151/2012, Article 102(2) of Regulation 1308/2013, and Article 36(2) of Regulation 2019/787.[50] The objective is to prevent the application of the principle of priority to cases where earlier geographical marks were applied for or registered in bad faith.

By contrast, Article 10 of China's Trademark Law does not distinguish between geographical marks registered in good faith and those registered in bad faith. A mark that incorporates the name of administrative divisions, and potentially GIs, can continue to serve as a valid trademark in spite of the willingness of the trademark owner to associate the goods with a place name or a GI that may give rise to a favourable but unjustified consumer response.

Article 6(4) of the EU-China GI Agreement of 2019 explicitly mentions the 'good faith' requirement for the continued use of a prior trademark:

> The protection provided to the geographical indications listed in Annexes III and IV, under this Agreement, is without prejudice to the continued use and renewal of a trademark which, in good faith, has been applied for, registered, or established through use if such possibility is provided for in the legislation of the Party concerned, prior to the date of protection for the geographical indications listed in Annex III or IV, or prior to the date of application for protection for the geographical indications referred to in Article 3 of this Agreement.

Article 16 of China's Trademark Law is more directly relevant to GI protection, as it prohibits the registration and use of trademarks that contain or consist of a false GI. As discussed earlier, this disposition was adopted in 2001 in the context of the major reform of China's Trademark Law intended to meet the requirements of the TRIPS Agreement.[51] Like the latter, there is a grandfather clause in Article 16, which provides that 'where the registration has been obtained in good faith, such registration shall

48. Article 24(5) of the TRIPS Agreement: 'Where a trademark has been applied for or registered in good faith, or where rights to a trademark have been acquired through use in good faith either: (a) before the date of application of these provisions in that Member as defined in Part VI; or (b) before the geographical indication is protected in its country of origin; measures adopted to implement this Section shall not prejudice eligibility for or the validity of the registration of a trademark, or the right to use a trademark, on the basis that such a trademark is identical with, or similar to, a geographical indication.'
49. However, the 'good faith' is not required in Article 24.4 of the TRIPS Agreement concerning GIs for wines and spirits, which have been used 'in a continuous manner with regard to the same or related goods or services in the territory of that Member for at least 10 years preceding 15 April 1994'.
50. The 'good faith' is not required in Regulation 251/2014 concerning aromatized wine products.
51. *See* Chapter 2 *supra*.

continue to be valid'. Thus, Article 16 acknowledges the validity of trademarks containing a false GI if they are registered in good faith before 2001.

Furthermore, Article 16 must be read in conjunction with Article 45 of the Trademark Law. The latter provides for the possibility of seeking the cancellation of trademarks registered in violation of Article 16. It stipulates that 'where a trademark registration violates the provision of Article 16 Paragraph 1, the prior right owner or interested party may, within *five years* from the date registration, request the Trademark Review and Adjudication Board to invalidate the registration'. According to the case law, in the absence of any protection afforded to GIs prior to the contested trademark, GI producers can still come forward as an 'interested party' and submit the application for invalidation.[52] This allows for the cancellation of an earlier trademark (registered after 2001 or in bad faith before 2001) that is in conflict with a GI that was protected (as a collective or certification mark) subsequently. However, there is a five-year time limit for seeking the cancellation of a trademark, even if it is registered or used in bad faith.[53] Therefore, in the event that a trademark containing a false GI has been registered for more than five years (e.g., seven years), the validity of the trademark can no longer be contested on the basis of Article 16.

Regarding the 'principle of exclusivity', the question in the context of the battle between the trademark regime and sui generis regime is whether a sign that is registered first as an individual trademark can prevent a subsequent application for recognition of the sign under the sui generis GI regime and consequently prevent it from being used as a GI by parties other than the trademark owner. Here, it is worth mentioning that, even European counties, which assume 'a certain element of superiority of GIs over trademarks',[54] may grant exclusivity to the prior trademark under certain conditions. EU Regulation 1151/2012 clearly provides that a PDO or PGI shall not be registered 'where, in the light of a trademark's reputation and renown and the length of time it has been used, registration of the name proposed as the PDO or PGI would be liable to mislead the consumer as to the true identity of the product'.[55] Article L. 713-6 of the French IP Code also contains a similar provision, acknowledging that a

52. *Chen Jianhua v. Trademark Review and Adjudication Board of the State Administration for Industry and Commerce*, Beijing High People's Court (28 July 2015).
53. Only the owner of a well-known trademark is not bound by the five-year limitation, where the registration has been obtained in bad faith. *See* Trademark Law, Article 45: 'Where a trademark registration violates the provisions of Articles 10 Paragraph 2 and Paragraph 3, Article 15, Article 16 Paragraph 1, Article 30, Article 31 or Article 32 of this Law, any holder of prior rights or any interested party may, within five years from the date of registration, request that the Trademark Review and Adjudication Board make a ruling to invalidate the trademark's registration. Where the registration was obtained with ill will, the owner of a famous trademark shall not be bound by the five-year limitation.'
54. Burkhart Goebel, *Geographical Indications and Trademarks: The Road from Doha* (WIPO/GEO/SFO/03/11 4 July 2003) p. 8.
55. *See* Article 6(4) of Regulation 1151/2012; Article 35(2) of Regulation 2019/787; Article 101(2) of Regulation 1308/2013; Article 18(2) of Regulation 251/2014; Case C-343/07 *Bavaria NV and Bavaria Italia Srl v. Bayerischer Brauerbund eV* [2009] ECR I-05491.

prior trademark registration can prevent the sign from being used as an IGPIA in some circumstances.[56]

However, China's law does not specifically address this question. Although Article 57 of the Trademark Law gives the trademark owner the right to prevent in the course of trade any use of identical or similar signs,[57] it seems that the interpretation of this article as providing exclusivity to a prior trademark is not uniformly held among China's competent authorities. The Trademark Office claims that Article 57 gives trademark owners the right to enforce their prior trademark against a later GI.[58] Thus, a prior trademark entitles its owner to prevent a GI from being granted protection under the sui generis regime and used in the course of trade. Nevertheless, practice shows that the former AQSIQ may approve the registration of a GI even if competing parties have already acquired trademark rights in the same sign.[59]

The practice of the former AQSIQ relates to the second approach to the 'prior trademark, subsequent GI' conflict. This approach does not seek to cancel the prior trademark but aims at compromising its exclusivity by allowing the 'coexistence' of a later GI with the earlier registered trademark. This solution is promoted by European countries as the next-best alternative. EU Regulations 1151/2012, 1308/2013, 2019/787, and 251/2014 all contain a similar provision indicating that the earlier trademark may continue to be 'used and renewed notwithstanding the (subsequent) protection of a designation of origin or geographical indication'.[60] These four provisions effectively form the legislative basis for coexistence in situations of conflict.

However, such provisions have not been adopted by China's legislators. Only in practice did the former AQSIQ approve the registration of a GI regardless of whether the same name had been registered as a trademark. A famous example is that of '*Jinhua* Ham', which was approved as a GI product under the sui generis regime administered by the former AQSIQ in 2002, although the name had been registered as an individual

56. Ancien Article L. 713-6(c) CPI: '*L'enregistrement d'une marque ne fait pas obstacle à l'utilisation du même signe ou d'un signe similaire comme Indication géographique définie à l'article L. 721-2, sauf lorsque la marque, compte tenu de sa renommée, de sa notoriété et de la durée de son usage, est à l'origine exclusive de la réputation ou de la connaissance par le consommateur du produit pour lequel une indication géographique est demandée.*'
57. Trademark Law, Article 57: 'Any of the following constitutes an infringement of the exclusive right to use a registered trademark: (1) Using a trademark that is identical with a registered trademark in connection with the same goods without the authorization of the owner of the registered trademark; (2) Using a trademark that is similar to a registered trademark in connection with the same goods, or that is identical with or similar to a registered trademark in connection with the same or similar goods, without the authorization of the owner of the registered trademark, which may cause public confusion.'
58. Yao Peng, Dili Biaozhi Chanpin Gai Dedao Zenyang de Baohu [How to Protect Geographical Indication Products], FAZHI RIBAO [LEGAL DAILY], 5 August 2005.
59. However, the Ministry of Agriculture has started in recent years to examine whether the name, which is the subject of the GI registration, has been registered as an individual trademark, collective mark or certification mark. If there are prior identical or similar marks, the GI registration applicant must obtain consent from the proprietor of the mark, which ensures that no conflict will arise. *See* Nongchanpin Dili Biaozhi Dengji Shencha Zhunze [Guidelines for the Review of GIs for Agricultural Products], 23 October 2015, Article 15(1).
60. *See* Article 14(2) of Regulation 1151/2012; Article 102(2) of Regulation 1308/2013; Article 36(2) of Regulation 2019/787; Article 19(2) of Regulation 251/2014.

trademark in 1979 by an enterprise whose products have no connection with the indicated area.[61] Lacking any legislative basis, the former AQSIQ's practice of allowing the coexistence between a prior registered trademark and a subsequent GI registration was contested by the owners of prior trademarks and eventually by the Trademark Office.

Under the EU-China GI Agreement of 2019, China's law should probably insert a clause that allows the coexistence of prior trademarks and GIs. Paragraph 2 of Article 6(4) stipulates that the trademarks registered in good faith before the date of protection for GIs may continue to be used and renewed provided that no grounds for the trademark's invalidity or revocation exist under the legislation.

However, while the EU legislation explicitly mentions that, 'in such cases, the use of the protected designation of origin or protected geographical indication shall be permitted as well as use of the relevant trademarks', the EU-China GI Agreement contains no clause that clarifies whether a coexistence must be permitted 'in such cases'. It remains to be seen whether such a coexistence will be incorporated into China's national legislation.

The third approach concerns the primacy of GIs or, in other words, the cancellation of prior trademarks. The only text that provides for this approach at the international level is the 'old' Lisbon Agreement,[62] Article 5(6)[63] of which allows the removal, within a period of two years, of prior trademarks that conflict with registered AOs.[64] At the national level, EU Member States may afford protection to appellations of

61. *Zhejiang Food Co. Ltd. v. Zhejiang Yongkang Ham Factory*, Shanghai Second Intermediate People's Court (25 August 2005).
62. Daniel J. Gervais, *Irreconcilable Differences? The Geneva Act of the Lisbon Agreement and the Common Law*, 53 Hous. L. Rev. 358 (2015).
63. Article 5(6) of the Lisbon Agreement (amended in 1979): 'If an appellation which has been granted protection in a given country pursuant to notification of its international registration has already been used by third parties in that country from a date prior to such notification, the competent Authority of the said country shall have the right to grant to such third parties a period not exceeding two years to terminate such use, on condition that it advise the International Bureau accordingly during the three months following the expiration of the period of one year provided for in paragraph (3), above.'
64. The 'new' Lisbon Agreement (Article 13.1 of the 2015 Geneva Act) provides more specific conflict rules, allowing for prior trademarks registered in good faith to be protected. According to Article 17, although a Member State still has the option to grant a transitional period for terminating prior use of GIs, it should not prejudice Article 13(1), which safeguards prior trademark rights. *See* Article 13(1) of the Lisbon Agreement (Geneva Act): 'The provisions of this Act shall not prejudice a prior trademark applied for or registered in good faith, or acquired through use in good faith, in a Contracting Party. Where the law of a Contracting Party provides a limited exception to the rights conferred by a trademark to the effect that such a prior trademark in certain circumstances may not entitle its owner to prevent a registered appellation of origin or geographical indication from being granted protection or used in that Contracting Party, protection of the registered appellation of origin or geographical indication shall not limit the rights conferred by that trademark in any other way'; Article 17 of the Lisbon Agreement (Geneva Act): 'Without prejudice to Article 13, where a Contracting Party has not refused the effects of an international registration on the ground of prior use by a third party or has withdrawn such refusal or has notified a grant of protection, it may, if its legislation so permits, grant a defined period as specified in the Regulations, for terminating such use'; *See also* WIPO, *Notes on the Draft Revised Lisbon Agreement on Appellations of Origin and Geographical Indications*, LI/WG/DEV/8/4 (8 November 2013).

origin against conflicting prior trademarks. French courts cancelled the trademarks '*Domaine de la Romanée-Conti*' and '*Romanée-Conti appellation Romanée-Conti contrôlée*' applied for in 1928 on the grounds that they were in conflict with the AOC '*Romanée-Conti*', recognized in 1936.[65]

However, both under the law and in practice, GIs registered under China's sui generis regime are not given the 'superiority' they enjoy in Europe. A prior trademark, even if applied for or registered in bad faith, would not be subject to cancellation simply because a conflicting sign was subsequently protected under China's sui generis regime. Nor is the primacy of GIs required by the EU-China GI Agreement. Article 6(3) of the Agreement stipulates as follows:

> Nothing in this Agreement shall oblige a Party to protect a geographical indication of the other Party under this Agreement where, in the light of a reputed or well-known trademark, the protection would be liable to mislead the consumers as to the true identity of the product.

To conclude, while the 'first in time, first in right' approach advocated by the United States is well-established in trademark law, China's domestic legislation has not yet provided for the 'coexistence' approach or the 'GI superiority' approach advocated by the EU. For this reason, producers working with GI products cannot rely on GI registration under the sui generis regime as a way to contest the validity of a prior trademark. The former AQSIQ allowed, in practice, the coexistence of a later GI with a prior trademark; however, lacking a legislative basis, this coexistence has been the subject of opposition among trademark owners and the trademark regime authority, the former SAIC. Thus, the battle over the exclusive power of the rights conferred has been fought between not only trademark owners and GI producers but also the sui generis GI regime administered by the former AQSIQ and the trademark regime administered by the former SAIC.

In 2018, the former AQSIQ and SAIC merged to become the SAMR. Under the supervision of the SAMR, the CNIPA has become the sole authority responsible for the trademark system and the GI products system established by the former AQSIQ.

However, the merger did not end the battle between the European 'coexistence' approach adopted by the former AQSIQ and the US approach adopted by the former SAIC. The focus of this battle has become the legitimacy of the coexistence: the debate now concerns whether it is lawful to register a GI regardless of prior trademark rights and whether the registered GI can be used without infringing those rights. We will discuss this issue in the subdivision below.

65. *See* Cass. com., 1er déc. 1987, n° 86-11.328. Another case in Europe is the Torres case. The 'Torre' trademark had been registered for wine for many years (first registered in 1911). However, the Portuguese government registered 'Torre' and 'Torre Vedra' as GIs in 1989, under the EU regulation on wine, which would have resulted in prohibiting the use of the prior trademark since it conflicted with a geographical indication. *See* A.G. Skol, *Geographical Indications and International Trade* (WIPO/GEO/SFO/03/15 20 June 2003) p. 2.

[2] Legitimacy of Coexistence

The notion that the 'coexistence' approach adopted by France,[66] the EU, and the former AQSIQ is a solution for conflicts between a later GI and an earlier individual trademark has been met with scepticism by supporters of the US approach. At the international level, the United States and Australia initiated a WTO dispute over the former EU regulations on GIs, Regulation 2081/92,[67] claiming that it could diminish legal protection for trademarks by allowing the coexistence of a later GI and an earlier registered trademark.[68] They contended that Article 14(2), which provides for that coexistence, was in breach of Article 16(1) of the TRIPS Agreement, which requires Members to give trademark owners the exclusive rights to prevent unauthorized uses of identical or similar signs by third parties.[69] The WTO dispute settlement panel explained, however, that the coexistence could be considered as a permitted exception to trademark rights justifiable under Article 17 of the TRIPS Agreement:[70] 'Members may provide limited exceptions to the rights conferred by a trademark, such as fair use of descriptive terms.' Therefore, coexistence was deemed permissible since the use of a GI may fall within the fair use of a term that is descriptive of the geographical origin of the goods.

Regarding China, it should be recalled that the former AQSIQ registered geographical names as GIs regardless of prior trademark rights. In order to use the GI and official logo, producers must be granted approval as GI users by the former AQSIQ. However, the approved GI users often face legal action initiated by the owner of the prior trademark alleging infringement of trademark rights.[71] The '*Jinhua* Ham' case mentioned earlier may serve as a good example. The defendant was one of the enterprises approved in 2003 by the former AQSIQ to use the GI '*Jinhua* Ham' and the official logo. Immediately following the use of the GI in the marketplace, the defendant was charged by the '*Jinhua* Ham' trademark owner with unlawful use of the earlier trademark. The grounds of the trademark owner's claim were contained in the former Article 52 of the Trademark Law,[72] which conferred onto the owner of a registered trademark the exclusive right to prevent all third parties from using identical or similar signs.[73]

66. France has recently partially permitted the coexistence. *See* Ancien Article L. 713-6 CPI; Jacques Larrieu, *Indications géographiques et marques en droit français, in Indications géographiques: perspectives globales et locales* 81, 94 (Jacques de Werra ed., Schulthess Éditions Romandes 2016).
67. *See* Michael Handler, *The WTO Geographical Indications Dispute*, 69 Mod. L. Rev. 70 (2006).
68. *See* WTO Panel Report, *supra* n. 43, at A-14.
69. Article 16(1) of the TRIPS Agreement: 'The owner of a registered trademark shall have the exclusive right to prevent all third parties not having the owner's consent from using in the course of trade identical or similar signs for goods or services which are identical or similar to those in respect of which the trademark is registered where such use would result in a likelihood of confusion.'
70. WTO Panel Report, *supra* n. 43, at 143.
71. *Zhejiang Food Co. Ltd. v. Zhejiang Yongkang Ham Factory, supra* n. 61.
72. This Article became Article 57 of the Trademark Law amended in 2013.
73. Former Article 52 of the Trademark Law (2001 Amendment): 'Any of the following acts shall constitute an infringement on the exclusive rights to the use of a registered trademark: (1) using a trademark that is identical with or similar to the registered trademark on the same or similar

The Shanghai Intermediate People's Court dismissed the action on two grounds. First, the Court noted that 'Both the exclusive rights of the trademark owner and the rights to use the GI granted to GI producers should be protected.'[74] It thus effectively acknowledged the validity of both the prior trademark and the later GI. In justifying this ruling, the court reasoned that:

> From a historical perspective, *Jinhua* Ham (the GI product) has a long history and embodies the hard work and wisdom of several generations of producers in the *Jinhua* area; from another perspective, since becoming the owner of the *Jinhua* Ham trademark, the plaintiff invested in enhancing its reputation.[75]

Second, while acknowledging the exclusive power of the prior trademark registration, the court held that it could not prevent the 'fair use' of the geographical name '*Jinhua*' and the product name 'Ham'. The former Article 49 of the Regulations for the Implementation of the Trademark Law provided that:

> where a registered trademark consists of the generic name, design or model of the goods in question, or directly indicates the quality, raw materials, functions, intended purposes, weight, quantity or other characteristics of the goods in question, or consists of geographical names, the proprietor of the exclusive right to use the registered trademark shall have no right to prohibit the fair use thereof by another person.[76]

Thus, the defendant's use of the name '*Jinhua* Ham' and therefore the coexistence of the GI with the prior trademark could be considered lawful since they fell within the legitimate use of a place name or descriptive term.

Having established that coexistence is possible in both Europe and China under the 'descriptive' fair use defence in trademark law, one question that remains to be answered is whether a defendant's use of a GI could still be permitted where the GI is used not merely in a 'descriptive sense' but also in a 'trademark sense'.[77]

Again, in the '*Jinhua* Ham' case, the court did not presume that every use of a GI was a fair use of a descriptive term. Instead, the court analysed the precise *way* in which the GI was used by the defendant. The court noted that the defendant had displayed its own trademark, '*Zhenfangzong*', prominently on the outer packing and had clearly indicated its own business name, address, and contact information; the term '*Jinhua* Ham' was accompanied by the phrase 'approved by the Appellation of origin Administration Committee'. For these reasons, the court concluded that the

---

goods without permission of the owner of the registered trademark; (2) selling goods that infringe on the exclusive right to the use of a registered trademark; (3) counterfeiting, or making without authorization, representations of another person's registered trademark, or selling such representations; (4) altering a registered trademark without permission of its owner and selling goods bearing such an altered trademark on the market; (5) impairing in other manners another person's exclusive right to the use of its registered trademark.'

74. *Zhejiang Food Co. Ltd. v. Zhejiang Yongkang Ham Factory*, *supra* n. 61.
75. *Ibid.*
76. This Article became Article 59 of the Trademark Law amended in 2013.
77. In addition to describing the product's characteristics, the use of the GI is intended to differentiate the product from those of other undertakings and is thus used in a trademark sense.

defendant's purpose in using the term '*Jinhua* Ham' was to describe the characteristics of the product and that this use constituted fair use.[78]

In another case concerning '*Jinhua* Ham', the Beijing High People's Court confirmed the Trademark Office's position on the boundary between trademark infringement and fair use. After noting that descriptive use of the terms '*Jinhua*' and 'Ham' must be permitted, the court held that these terms should not be 'used prominently'; instead, the product had to be labelled with a phrase like 'Special ham product from *Jinhua*'. The layout, character style, size, and colour of the term '*Jinhua* Ham' had to be no different from those of the other descriptive words.[79] Thus, limitations have been placed on the way in which GIs can be used 'in order to make the GI distinct from the prior trademark'.[80]

China's courts reinforced that position in several subsequent cases. The fact that a defendant has not displayed the GI *prominently* on the packing of the product is always taken into account as an important factor in establishing the fair use defence. In almost all cases that found fair use,[81] the GI in question was held as not being used prominently.[82]

In a case that did not find fair use, the product was marked with the defendant's own trademark in small print and the later protected GI '*Tanggou* Spirit' was marked in larger print.[83] The court found that the GI was used prominently and could serve to differentiate the product from those of other undertakings. The use was thus deemed 'as a trademark' and one that could lead to consumer confusion. Based on this analysis, the court upheld the trademark infringement claim. Remarkably, the court also expressed a view on the rights conferred by a later GI registration under China's *sui generis* regime, noting that:

> Although the sign '*Tanggou* Spirit' is a geographical indication recognized by the former AQSIQ, liquor enterprises in the town of *Tanggou* can only use the sign in

78. *Zhejiang Food Co. Ltd. v. Zhejiang Yongkang Ham Factory, supra* n. 61.
79. *Zhejiang Food Co. Ltd. v. Trademark Office of the State Administration for Industry and Commerce,* Beijing High People's Court (18 May 2005).
80. *Ibid.*
81. However, in a decision of 26 June 2005, the Court considers that the use of the name '*Kuerle*' by the defendant is fair use, without analysing whether it is used prominently or not. *See Korla Pear Association of Bayingolin Mongolian Autonomous Prefecture of Xinjiang Uygur Autonomous Region v. Korla Hebrew Paper Industry Co. Ltd.*, Xinjiang High People's Court (26 June 2005).
82. *Zhou Zhijian v. Xiamen Shanguo Yinyi Tea Industry Co. Ltd.*, Fujian High People's Court (19 July 2012); *Shanxi Qinzhou Huang Mi (Group) Co. Ltd. v. Shanxi Qinzhou Danshan Huang Mi Development Co. Ltd.*, Supreme People's Court (30 December 2013); *Zhejiang Tea Group Co. Ltd. v. Hangzhou Shifeng Tea Co. Ltd.*, Hangzhou Intermediate People's Court (18 December 2014); *Liu Qicai v. Guangdong Shenzhen Simeida Industrial Co. Ltd.*, Guangdong Province Shenzhen Intermediate People's Court (2006).
83. On 30 January 1987, the place name '*Tanggou*' has been registered by one distillery in the town of 'Tanggou' (the town has more than one distillery). Subsequently, in 2010, 'Tanggou Spirit' has been registered as a GI product by the former AQISQ. *See* Guojia Zhiliang Jiandu Jianyan Jianyi Zongju Gonggao 2010 Nian di 104 Hao [State General Administration of Quality Supervision, Inspection and Quarantine Announcement No. 104, 2010], 9 September 2010.

> a descriptive sense to tell that their spirits come from *Tanggou*, and not in a trademark sense to use the place name '*Tanggou*' prominently.[84]

A review of the case law thus suggests that Chinese courts have made a clear division between use that is purely descriptive and use that is 'as a trademark'. The former is permitted since local producers should be legitimately entitled to describe necessary product information. The latter is generally prohibited on the grounds of possible consumer confusion caused by two similar or identical brand-like signs.[85] The fair use defence may be precluded by the possibility of confusion and, more specifically, by the prominence of the sign's display. Several defendants were even held liable for trademark infringement because of the prominence they gave to a descriptive phrase on the package.[86]

We may thus conclude that the scope of the right to use a later GI is not unlimited in China. The coexistence between a prior trademark and a later GI is confined to circumstances where the GI is not used prominently and there is no risk of confusion with the trademark. As noted by one court, 'the fair use of the geographical name should be limited to what is necessary to describe, in good faith, the place of origin of the product'.[87] However, all that is needed to describe the place of origin is a discreet label with, for example, 'Ham produced in *Jinhua*', appearing in small print somewhere on the product packaging.

China adopts the approach advocated by the United States, which confines the legitimate use of a later GI to a *discreet* label.[88] However, GIs are valuable because consumers search for a quality product by reference to its place of origin. Most products are marketed with a bundle of cues that signify quality,[89] such as colour, freshness, aroma, price, store, trademark, popularity, and geographical origin. As consumers may place significant value on geographical origin, why should we hide the name of the origin behind an array of other information cues? A rethink of this approach is needed.

It is worth mentioning the EU's approach to this issue, which is outlined in the CJEU's judgment in the 'Kerry Spring' case.[90] Article 6(1)(b) of Directive 89/104 (which became Article 14(1)(b) of Directive 2015/2436) permits descriptive use by providing that 'the proprietor of the trademark may not prohibit a third party from using, in the course of trade, indications concerning the geographical origin of goods provided the third party uses them in accordance with honest practices in industrial or

84. *Guannan County Tanggou Town Liangxiangyuan Wines Co. Ltd. v. Jiangsu Tanggou Liangxianghe Wines Co. Ltd.*, Jiangsu High People's Court (13 February 2015).
85. *Longquan Longyun Crafts Co. Ltd. and Zhejiang Longquan Baojian Factory Co. Ltd.*, Zhejiang High People's Court (19 May 2010).
86. *See Shangdang Bacon Products Factory v. Changzhi Industry and Commerce Bureau*, Shanxi High People's Court (30 December 2002).
87. *See Longquan Longyun Crafts Co. Ltd. and Zhejiang Longquan Baojian Factory Co. Ltd.*, *supra* n. 85.
88. Gangjee, *supra* n. 13, at 1288.
89. William A. Kerr, *Enjoying a Good Port with a Clear Conscience: Geographic Indicators, Rent Seeking and Development*, 7 Estey Ctr. J. Int'l L. & Trade Pol'y 1, 8 (2006).
90. It should be noted that the terms 'Kerry Spring' are not a GI protected under the European sui generis regime. They constitute, however, an indication of geographical origin. The purpose of citing this case is to show how 'fair use of a geographical indication' is interpreted in Europe.

commercial matters'. According to the judgment, the application of this provision should not be rejected simply because the indication of geographical origin is used by the defendant 'as a trademark'.[91] Nor could a likelihood of confusion prevent a third party from using the indication of geographical origin.[92] Instead, the test is whether it is used in accordance with honest practices.[93] As the Advocate General pointed out, 'the economic value of mineral water primarily consists of this special association between the reference to a particular origin and the consumer's expectation of a particular quality'.[94] The fact that the name of the origin is used prominently may be justified by the need to achieve that value. Thus, a coexisting indication of origin could be used as a trademark provided the use were an honest practice.[95]

The Draft Criteria for Judging Trademark Infringement issued by the CNIPA in 2019 seemed to suggest that the authority responsible for the administrative protection (as compared to the courts that are responsible for the judicial protection) considered the European approach of 'coexistence'. According to Article 44 of the Draft Criteria, in cases where the fair use of a GI is used as a defence against trademark rights, the use should be treated as trademark infringement if the user has not obtained the qualifications for the use of the GI or cannot provide evidence of historical fair use. In other words, if the user has obtained the qualifications or has provided evidence of historical fair use, the use of the GI will not be punished by the administrative authorities.[96] However, Article 44, which implicitly allows for coexistence, has been deleted from the final version of the Criteria for Judging Trademark Infringement issued in July 2020.[97]

The Draft Provisions on the Protection of GIs issued in September 2020 again raise the expectation that the European 'coexistence' approach may be incorporated into China's law. As outlined in Chapter 4, the Draft Provisions were designed by the CNIPA in 2020 to replace the Provisions for GI Products issued by the former AQSIQ. Article 7(3) of the Draft Provisions denies GI protection to names that have been registered as a trademark by third parties or other unregistered well-known trademarks that may mislead the public. In other words, where the name would not be liable to mislead the consumers, it may be protected as a GI despite the registration of a prior mark. The question remains how the misleading character would be assessed. Would it be assessed according to the principles established in the trademark law or in light of 'a trademark's reputation and renown and the length of time it has been used', as set out in the EU GI regulations? If the general principles of the trademark law are applied, the possibility of existence will be limited since a risk of confusion can readily be found

91. Case C-100/02 *Gerolsteiner Brunnen GmbH & Co v. Putsch GmbH* [2004] I-00691, para. 11 (AG Opinion).
92. *Ibid.*, para. 25.
93. *Ibid.*, para. 24.
94. *Ibid.*, para. 71 (AG Opinion).
95. To assess whether the use of an indication in the course of trade is in accordance with honest practices, the CJEU clarified that the circumstances to be taken into account would include in particular the shape and labelling of the bottle. *See Ibid.*, para. 26.
96. Shangbiao Qinquan Panduan Biaozhun Zhengqiu Yijiangao [Draft Criteria for Judging Trademark Infringement], 27 September 2019, Article 44.
97. Shangbiao Qinquan Panduan Biaozhun [Criteria for Judging Trademark Infringement], 17 July 2020.

in situations that involve identical signs for identical goods or identical signs for similar goods.

§5.02 PROTECTING GIS UNDER CHINA'S SUI GENERIS SYSTEMS: A LOSING BATTLE AGAINST COLLECTIVE AND CERTIFICATION MARKS

While it is not uncommon to find different mechanisms of GI protection in a given territory,[98] China is unique in that it employs both the trademark regime and the sui generis regime as the primary means of GI protection.[99] As a result, a GI could be protected jointly by a collective or certification mark, a registered GI product under the former AQISQ (the CNIPA since 2018), and a protected agricultural GI under the MOA,[100] which some scholars describe as 'double protection'.[101]

In China, however, there is a lack of coordination between the trademark regime and sui generis GI systems. While a GI protected under the sui generis regimes *is supposed to* confer on legitimate users the right to use a distinctive sign, GI users do not necessarily have access to a collective or certification mark containing or consisting of the same sign, either because they are not members of the association that is the proprietor of the mark or because their products do not meet the additional requirements imposed by the trademark proprietor. In this case, the rights to use the GI (granted by the sui generis regimes) may be confined to 'descriptive use'. Those GI users would thus have no marketing advantage relative to users of the collective mark or certification mark.

[A] Unclear Relationship Between GIs and Collective Marks

Being different protection mechanisms, collective marks and GIs (protected under sui generis systems) do not necessarily apply on an exclusive basis. In fact, products can be double-branded, by both GIs and collective marks. However, the role of collective marks in protecting GIs varies considerably from one country to another.

In France, the role of collective marks can be described as 'complementary'.[102] Although the joint use of collective marks and GIs in the marketing of the goods is

98. WIPO, *Geographical Indications*, SCT/8/4 (2 April 2002) p. 5.
99. Bradley M. Bashawt, *Geographical Indications in China: Why Protect GIs with Both Trademark Law and AOC-Type Legislation?* 17 Pac. Rim L. & Pol'y J. 73 (2008).
100. In 2011, there were 333 GIs protected under both the trademark regime and the regime established by the former AQSIQ, eighty-nine GIs protected under the trademark regime and the regime established by the Ministry of Agriculture, and nineteen GIs protected under all three regimes. *See* Zhao Xiaoping, ZHONGGUO NONGCHANPIN DILI BIAOZHI FALU BAOHU YANJIU [GEOGRAPHICAL INDICATION PROTECTION OF AGRICULTURAL PRODUCTS IN CHINA], at 113 (Shanxi People's Publishing House, 2012).
101. Shujie Feng, *Geographical Indications: Can China Reconcile the Irreconcilable Intellectual Property Issue Between EU and US?*, 19 World Trade Rev. 424 (2020).
102. Norbert Olszak, *Appellations d'origine et indications de provenance*, Répertoire Dalloz de droit pénal et de procédure pénale, 2008 (actualité 2015), para. 113.

possible,[103] limits have been placed on collective marks containing GIs.[104] First, the collective mark cannot be identical to the corresponding GI;[105] it must consist solely of the GI and therefore be descriptive. Even if the goods for which the mark is used are limited to goods covered by the GI, the mark is still descriptive and can be objected to under Article L. 711-2 of the IP Code unless it is applied for as a 'complex' mark, which associates the GI with other words or figurative elements that give the mark a distinctive character. Second, the complex mark must be registered and used exclusively for products protected by the GI. If all or some of the products covered by the mark do not have the right to the GI, the mark will be considered deceptive or contrary to public order.[106] These limits ensure that the use of collective marks does not interfere with the functions of the GI. While the GI serves to indicate a product's geographical origin and related qualities, a collective mark that incorporates the GI can be used to communicate additional information relating to other aspects of the quality attributes of the goods.

However, in China, one of the primary means of protecting GIs is through collective marks. As discussed in Chapter 3, the GI is considered in China to be fully assimilated into the collective mark containing it, and therefore their functions are regarded as equivalent. The two limits set out in French law do not exist in China. A GI, whether protected under the sui generis regime or not, can be registered as a collective mark without the need to add fanciful or arbitrary works or pictures. In other words, the same sign can be registered both as a GI under the sui generis regime and as a collective mark regardless of priority dates.

Prior rights granted under the sui generis regime would not preclude the registration of the same name as a collective mark or vice versa. The fact that a name has already been registered under one regime is not a barrier to registering the same name under the other regime. A research project conducted in 2020 has shown that a significant number of GIs have been registered under two protection schemes.[107]

---

103. Article L. 643-3 C. rur.: '*Les conditions d'utilisation simultanée d'une marque commerciale et d'un signe d'identification de la qualité ou de l'origine pour l'étiquetage d'une denrée alimentaire ou d'un produit agricole non alimentaire et non transformé, à l'exception des vins, des boissons spiritueuses et des produits intermédiaires, sont, ainsi qu'il est dit à l'article L. 112-4 du code de la consommation, précisées par décret en Conseil d'Etat*'; Article L. 432-7 C. consom. (Ancien Article L.112-4 C. consom.): '*Les conditions d'utilisation simultanée, pour l'étiquetage d'une denrée alimentaire ou d'un produit agricole non alimentaire et non transformé, à l'exception des vins, des boissons spiritueuses et des produits intermédiaires, d'une marque commerciale et d'une référence à l'un des modes de valorisation mentionnés à l'article L. 640-2 du code rural et de la pêche maritime, sont précisées par décret en Conseil d'Etat.*'
104. Producers can use their own distinct trademark along with the GI. The trademark may consist of fancy terms and therefore has nothing to do with the GI. However, once the trademark contains or consists of the GI, some limitation may apply to it.
105. Cass. com., 1er déc. 1987, n° 86-11328; C.A. Paris, 22 avr. 1986, PIBD 1986, n° 397, III, p. 314.
106. Cass. com., 26 oct. 1993, RIPIA 1993, p. 289; C.A. Angers, 17 févr. 1992, PIBD 1992, n° 531, III, p. 554.
107. This study shows that, by September 2020, 16 per cent of GIs have been registered under two different systems, whereas only 3 per cent of GIs have been registered under all three systems. *See* Beijing Zhongjun Shiji GI Research Group, *supra* n. 3; *See also* Zeng Deguo & Ye Peiyin, Woguo Dili Biaozhi Baohu he Fazhan de Nandian ji Duice [Difficulties and Solutions of GI

Under the regimes, the registration is reviewed and approved by different agencies and following different rules.[108] There is no rule requiring the applicants to be one and the same. Nor are there provisions requiring that the regulations governing the use of a collective mark be consistent with the norms regulating GI products or GIs for agricultural products. No coordinated relationship among the different protection systems seems to exist.

However, the use of the collective mark is subject to membership in the group that owns the mark and the satisfaction of certain conditions set out in the regulations governing the use of the mark. Nevertheless, the use of a GI registered by one of the sui generis regimes is subject to approval from the public authority or the holder of the registration certificate of the agricultural GI. Approved users must ensure that their products meet the conditions set out in the product norms established by the former AQSIQ (the CNIPA since 2018) or the MOA.

As the use of the GI and collective mark may be subject to different procedural and substantial conditions, it is not only possible but also inevitable that certain GI users who obtained approval from sui generis regimes might be excluded from the use of the collective trademark, either due to a lack of group membership or because their products are inconsistent with the regulations governing the use of that mark.[109]

The paradox is this: if the sign of which the collective mark is composed is identical with or similar to the GI, how could one producer use the GI without using the mark? Where the GI user does not have the right to use the mark (e.g., where there is no group membership), how could the GI be used without infringing trademark rights?

National law and regulations offer little guidance on this matter. Local governments have made attempts to differentiate use as a GI from use as a trademark. This can be illustrated through the example of '*Zhenjiang* Rice Vinegar', a name recognized as a GI by the former AQSIQ in 2001 and registered as a collective mark in 2007.[110] On 29 July 2016, the administrative head of Jiangsu Province passed local regulations concerning the protection of local vinegar products.[111] Its Article 15 provides that 'Producers who have only obtained the approval of the AQSIQ for the use of the GI official logo (and thus the GI) shall not display prominently the terms "*Zhenjiang* Rice Vinegar" in order to avoid confusion with the "*Zhenjiang* Rice Vinegar" collective mark.' Since the terms in question are protected under both the sui generis regime and

---

Protection and Development in China], ANHUI NONGYE DAXUE XUEBAO [JOURNAL OF ANHUI AGRICULTURAL UNIVERSITY], March 2015, p. 43.

108. Zhang Chi, Bumen Boyi Dili Biaozhi Chanpin Baohu Yu Ganga [A Boxing Match Among Government Bodies: The Riddle of Geographical Indication Protection], FAREN ZAZHI [LEGAL JOURNAL], February 2006, 100.

109. Since no provisions require that regulations governing use of a collective mark must be consistent with norms regulating GI products set out by the former AQSIQ or the Ministry of Agriculture, a product that satisfies the norms of the former AQISQ or Ministry of Agriculture does not necessarily meet the conditions set out in the regulations governing use of the mark.

110. *See* Guojia Zhiliang Jiandu Jianyan Jianyi Zongju Gonggao 2001 Nian di 2 Hao [State General Administration of Quality Supervision, Inspection and Quarantine Announcement No. 2, 2001], 27 April 2001.

111. Zhenjiang Xiangcu Baohu Tiaoli [Ordinance on the Protection of Zhenjiang Vinegar], 29 July 2016.

the trademark regime, it is recommended that producers apply for both approval to use the GI and a trademark licence to use the mark.[112] Where the producer only obtained the approval of the former AQSIQ for the use of the GI, the terms in question can still appear on the package but in small characters and only to convey information about the origin of the product as part of the producer's address. The position and size of the terms must be *limited* to ensure that the terms are not prominently displayed.

This approach has traditionally been applied to address the 'prior trademark, subsequent GI' conflict. It is open to criticism, however, because it fails to recognize the legitimate interest of GI users in highlighting a place name to promote the product. For the same reason, it is also questionable whether this approach can be adopted to make a distinction between the GI and the collective mark. To avoid any confusion, it could be suggested that the owner of the collective mark register a complex mark containing the GI and other distinctive words or pictures. This appears to be a more equitable solution, especially in the example mentioned above, since the mark was registered after the date of GI registration under the sui generis GI system.

Users of a GI who are not members of the group holding the mark could confine their use of it to a discreet label. However, one of the functions of GIs is to add value. For example, a cheese might be desirable because it is *Feta*. Romeo may have believed that a rose by any other name would smell as sweet. Tim Josling asked whether a feta cheese by any other name would sell as well in the supermarket.[113] Likewise, we have to ask if a GI product with a discreet label referring to the geographical origin would sell as well. The inability of a GI user to display the place name prominently would most likely affect the *marketability* of the product.

To conclude, China allows GIs to be protected under both the sui generis regime and the trademark regime (as collective marks). The lack of coordination between the two protection schemes may jeopardize the marketability of some GI products that are not covered by the collective mark. The users of GIs who are recognized only by the sui generis regime (i.e., not authorized by the trademark owner) may be prevented from displaying the place name prominently and would thus lose their competitive advantage over collective mark users.

[B] Unclear Relationship Between GIs and Certification Marks

Like GIs, certification marks can perform a quality assurance function.[114] However, whether GIs can be protected through the concept of certification marks is determined by each country; thus, the role of certification marks in protecting GIs can vary considerably from one state to another.

112. *See Ibid.*, Article 14: 'Producers whose products comply with the national standard of *Zhenjiang* vinegar may apply to use the official logo of the GI (protected as sui generis intellectual property rights) and, at the same time, apply to use the collective mark incorporating the terms "Zhenjiang Vinegar".'
113. Tim Josling, *The War on Terroir: Geographical Indications as a Transatlantic Trade Conflict*, 57 J. Agric. Econ. 337, 339 (2006).
114. Alberto Francisco Ribeiro de Almeida, *Key Differences Between Trademarks and Geographical Indications*, 30 Eur. Intell. Prop. Rev. 406 (2008).

As discussed in Chapter 3, France and the EU are in favour of a sui generis regime, and this limits the use of certification marks for GI protection. Trademark law prevents the registration of certification marks consisting exclusively of a geographical reference because they might be either descriptive or deceptive. The 'non-descriptiveness' and 'non-deceptiveness' requirements that apply to ordinary individual trademarks are equally applicable to certification marks. The latter do not enjoy an exemption from the normal rules of the trademark regime. EU trademark Regulation 2007/1001 even explicitly precludes EU certification marks from certifying the geographical origin of the product. Those measures help keep the sphere of certification marks 'clean' from GIs.

Contrariwise, China's trademark law provides protection for GIs through the notion of 'GI certification marks'.[115] In China, GIs can be registered as certification marks even if they do not meet the 'non-descriptiveness' requirement imposed on individual marks.[116] Prior rights acquired under the sui generis regime would not preclude the registration of the same name as a certification mark or vice versa. Thus, under the sui generis regime, a name registered as a GI can also be registered as a certification mark.

Although the GI and certification mark may serve the same purpose – to guarantee the place of origin and thus the expected quality of the product – there are conflicts as to which group has the right to use the registered name and what constitutes an authentic product. The following two examples will help to illustrate the tensions.

The '*Shaoxing* Rice Wine' GI was first registered by the *Shaoxing* Rice Wine Industry Association as a certification mark in 1999 and subsequently registered by the former AQSIQ as a GI product in 2000.[117] As the proprietor of the mark, the association set out the regulations governing the use of the mark, according to which fifteen enterprises established in Shaoxing were authorized to use it. By a notice of 2 December 2005, the former AQSIQ allowed three enterprises, aside from the fifteen authorized enterprises, to use the GI, which was identical to the mark.[118] The association and the fifteen enterprises responded quickly to the permission of the former AQSIQ by submitting a joint letter to the Legislative Affairs Office of China's State Council claiming that the use of the terms '*Shaoxing* Rice Wine' by the three

115. *See* Chapter 3 *supra*.
116. In a case concerning the registration of the certification mark '*Fiji* Pure Mahogany' in China, the application had been refused by the Trademark Office due to lack of the distinctive character. The Beijing High People's Court annulled this decision. In the judgment, the court noted, in particular, 'the distinctiveness requirement, which serves to ensure the function of ordinary trademarks, does not apply to certification marks'. *See* Yang Xiaoli et al., FIJI Zhengming Shangbiao San'an Pingshu [A Review of Three Cases Concerning FIJI Certification Mark], China Law Insight (18 May 2021), https://www.chinalawinsight.com/2016/10/articles/intellectual-property/.
117. *See* Guojia Zhiliang Jiandu Jianyan Jianyi Zongju Gonggao 2000 Nian di 21 Hao [State General Administration of Quality Supervision, Inspection and Quarantine Announcement No. 21, 2000], 31 January 2000.
118. Guojia Zhiliang Jiandu Jianyan Jianyi Zongju Gonggao 2005 Nian di 158 Hao [State General Administration of Quality Supervision, Inspection and Quarantine Announcement No. 158, 2005], 2 November 2005.

enterprises constituted trademark infringement and thus should be prohibited.[119] They relied primarily on two grounds in support of their plea. First, the three enterprises were established in *Xiaoshan* (a district of the city of *Hangzhou* close to the border with *Shaoxing*), which was not included in the production area defined in the regulations governing the use of the mark.[120] Second, the three enterprises did not have the authorization of the association to use the names.[121] The Trademark Office intervened in support of the trademark owner and users. Due to this pressure, the three enterprises have not marketed their products using the contested GI labelling.

The second case concerns '*Liuyang* Fireworks'. In 2003, the *Liuyang* Municipal Government applied for registration of the '*Liuyang* Fireworks' GI. In the same year, *Liuyang* Fireworks Association applied for registration of a certification mark consisting solely of the GI. The GI was granted protection by the former AQSIQ in July 2003, and the mark was registered in 2004.[122] The association set out conditions for use of the mark, which are less strict than those for use of the GI set out by the former AQSIQ. Consequently, while only about 100 enterprises are authorized by the former AQSIQ to use the GI, more than 300 enterprises are authorized by the association to use the mark.[123] The latter group of enterprises could use the mark consisting solely of the GI (in effect, the GI) without the authorization of the former AQSIQ; this is contrary to the intention of the former AQSIQ, which wanted to establish an instrument to regulate the use of the 'name' of GI products.

These two cases show that the relationship between GIs (protected as sui generis IP rights) and certification marks has not been harmonized in China. There are substantial differences between the two instruments in terms of the conditions and procedures for the use of the sign. Operators cannot rely exclusively on the sui generis GI regime to ensure their rights to use the sign. Where the same sign is protected under both the sui generis regime and the trademark regime (as a certification mark), its use is also subject to the conditions imposed by the trademark owner. Likewise, operators cannot rely solely on the sui generis regime to ensure that third parties are excluded from commercially using the sign since unauthorized third parties can bypass their requirements by using a certification mark containing the GI.

The Draft Provisions on the Protection of GIs issued by the CNIPA in 2020 avoid the difficulty of clarifying the relationship between GIs and collective/certification

119. Shaoxing Intermediate People's Court, Guanyu Shaoxing Huangjiu Chanye Zhishi Chanquan Baohu de Diaoyan Baogao [Investigation Report on the Protection of Intellectual Property Regarding Shaoxing Rice Wine Industry], 23 November 2011.
120. However, the area where the three enterprises' production occurs is included in the geographical area of production defined by the former AQSIQ.
121. Zhou Nengbing, Shaoxing Huangjiu Xiehui Kangyi Xiaoshan Jiuchang Maoda Shangxing Pai [Shaoxing Rice Wine Association Protested Against the Use of 'Shaoxing' by Xiaoshan Wine Enterprises], SHAOXING WANBAO [SHAOXING EVENING NEWS], 26 November 2007.
122. *See* Guojia Zhiliang Jiandu Jianyan Jianyi Zongju Gonggao 2003 Nian di 26 Hao [State General Administration of Quality Supervision, Inspection and Quarantine Announcement No. 26, 2003], 6 March 2003.
123. *See* He Lianhong, Liuyang Huapao Shuangchong Baohu zhi Tong [The Nightmare of Double Protection: Liuyang Fireworks], ZHONGHUA SHANGBIAO [CHINA TRADEMARK], November 2006, 12.

marks. Article 40 of the Draft Provisions provides that the application for the registration of a GI as a collective trademark or certification trademark shall be governed by the relevant provisions of China's Trademark Law. In other words, the Draft Provisions continue to allow for 'double registration', under the sui generis GI system and the trademark system, without harmonizing the roles of the two systems.

As this chapter comes to an end, we must conclude that the introduction of the EU approach in China is not yet a success. We have examined the effect of GI registration under the EU-inspired sui generis regime. The effect is meant to grant an exclusive right for operators to use a denomination identifying the place of origin of a product. However, this right cannot effectively prevent others from registering the same name as an individual, collective, or certification mark. Moreover, where the same or similar name has been registered as a trademark, the 'right to use' granted by the sui generis regime is likely to be confined to use in a 'descriptive sense', instead of in a 'trademark sense'. The effect is also supposed to set out the conditions and minimum requirements for production that must be met in order to be authorized to use the registered name. However, the regime of collective and certification marks has largely undermined this effect, since it allows trademark owners to set out production conditions that might differ from the conditions imposed by the sui generis regime.

Although the sui generis regime provides for the possibility of coexistence between a prior trademark and a later GI, the right to use the later GI (even after the registration of the GI by the sui generis regime) can be subject to opposition based on the earlier trademark and be limited to a purely descriptive use (e.g., a discreet label).

Overall, because of the competition from the US approach applied in China's trademark system, the EU-inspired sui generis GI system cannot achieve the desired effects of granting exclusive rights and laying down rules for the production process. Thus, the question to be asked is this: what is the justification for allowing the trademark regime to serve as a competitor? (Chapter 6)

CHAPTER 6
Criticisms Against Adopting the European Sui Generis Approach in China

China has adopted the European approach in establishing sui generis systems for GIs. However, the rights conferred by China's sui generis GI regulations may be confined to use in a 'descriptive sense' when a conflicting sign is registered in the US-inspired trademark system. This chapter analyses why the European sui generis approach has been accorded low priority in China relative to the US approach. It critically examines the justification for the low priority given to the European approach (i.e., the criticisms of sui generis protection for GIs). It assesses whether the criticisms can be substantiated and justified. The analysis focuses on the following issues, which are those most frequently raised by critics: necessity, cost, the nature of GIs, common practice, and effectiveness. We analyse each of the issues and find the criticisms to be unfounded.

As outlined in Chapter 5, the adoption of European sui generis protection for GIs is subject to challenges from the US approach favouring trademark protection. China's sui generis GI regulations afford only limited protection and may not adequately protect GIs to the extent necessary to avoid interference from ordinary, collective, or certification marks. The rights conferred by China's sui generis GI regulations may be confined to use in a 'descriptive sense' when a conflicting sign is registered in the US-inspired trademark system.

The low priority given to the European sui generis approach is reflected in the fact that China's sui generis systems are governed by administrative rules promulgated by agencies under the State Council, while the trademark system is governed under national laws adopted by a legislative body, the Standing Committee of the National People's Congress. According to the Legislation Law, the sui generis GI rules are 'lower level law',[1] which shall not contravene a 'higher level law', the Trademark Law.[2] In other words, the latter has higher legal authority.[3] This implies that the protection provided by the sui generis rules on GIs should not compromise trademark protection.[4] This partially explains why GIs lose the battle against marks when they are in conflict.

Proponents of sui generis GI protection repeatedly call upon the legislative bodies to enact a national law, a 'higher level law', specifically for the protection of GIs.[5] The State Council has repeatedly expressed its willingness to step up the legislative work necessary to adopt such a law at the right time.[6] Unsurprisingly, opponents criticize sui generis protection and claim that the trademark regime is the best approach for protecting GIs. As a direct consequence of this national debate, no real progress has been made toward the enactment of a GI 'law' since China's accession to the WTO in 2001.

In November 2020, Xi Jinping, General Secretary of the CPC, stressed the need to improve legislation in the field of GIs. However, it remains to be seen whether the trademark law will offer improved GI protection or whether a sui generis law will be enacted.[7]

In September 2021, the CPC and State Council issued the Guidelines for Building a Powerful Country with Intellectual Property Rights (2021-2035), which maps out a number of key tasks, including '*exploring* the formulation of sui generis laws and regulations for GI protection'. However, the term 'exploring' used in the guideline suggests that difficulties and challenges lie ahead and that China may after all choose not to legislate specifically in the field of GIs.

In this chapter, we will critically examine the most common criticisms of the sui generis approach to GIs, which concern the establishment of *the* sui generis systems (§6.01) and their effectiveness (§6.02).

1. Both the Provisions on the Protection of GI Products and the Measures for the Administration of GIs for Agricultural Products are administrative rules promulgated respectively by the former AQSIQ and the Ministry of Agriculture, which are agencies of the State Council.
2. Legislation Law, Article 96 (2000, amended in 2015): 'If a national law, administrative regulation, local decree, autonomous decree and special decree, or administrative or local rule falls into any of the following categories, the relevant body shall amend or cancel it pursuant to the authority granted in Article 97 hereof: ... (ii) A lower level law contravenes a higher level law ....'
3. Legislation Law, Article 88: 'National law has higher legal authority than administrative regulations, local decrees, and administrative or local rules.'
4. Guo Xiushen, Yifa Guifan Dili Biaozhi Baohu Xingzheng Guanli Tizhi [Regulating the Administrative System of Geographical Indication Protection], ZHONGHUA SHANGBIAO [CHINA TRADEMARK], October 2004, 10.
5. Li Hua, Zhiding Dili Biaozhi Baohufa Baohu Ming You Te Chanpin [Adopting GI Law to Protect Famous, Excellent and Special Products], State Council (18 June 2021), http://www.gov.cn/2007lh/content_550110.htm.
6. Guowuyuan Guanyu Yinfa Guojia Zhishi Chanquan Zhanlue Gangyao de Tongzhi [Notice of the State Council on Issuing the Outline of the National Intellectual Property Strategy], 5 June 2008; Guowuyuan Guanyu Xinxingshi xia Jiakuai Zhishi Chanquan Qiangguo Jianshe de Ruogan Yijian [Opinions of the State Council on Accelerating the Development of Intellectual Property Rights under the New Situation], 18 December, 2015.
7. *Xi Focus: Xi Stresses Strengthening Intellectual Property Rights Protection*, Xinhua Net (18 June 2021), http://www.xinhuanet.com/english/2020-12/02/c_139556530.htm.

§6.01 A CRITICAL ANALYSIS OF CRITICISMS OF THE ESTABLISHMENT OF CHINA'S SUI GENERIS SYSTEMS

Regarding the establishment of China's sui generis systems, opponents consistently call into question the necessity of creating a special mechanism for GI protection and its compatibility with IP law as well as international practice. Their concerns appear to be unfounded, however, given the particularity of GIs.

[A] About the Creation of China's Sui Generis Regime

The creation of China's sui generis GI systems has been subject to criticisms based on the unjustified assumption that GIs are 'essentially' no different from trademarks and therefore that modern trademark law can adequately protect them. China's sui generis systems are wrongly deemed unnecessary and not worth the cost.

[1] Is the Sui Generis Regime Unnecessary?

Several Chinese commentators consider the sui generis systems unnecessary, arguing that the trademark regime is a suitable vehicle for protecting GIs. These commentators have offered two theoretical foundations for their argument. First, they argue that GIs and trademarks serve the same functions, as they are both source-identifiers, guarantees of quality, and business interests. Second, they claim that certification marks can be used to certify the origin and quality of the goods, thereby serving the same function as GIs.[8] Thus, they view GIs as a subset of trademarks that can be adequately protected under the trademark regime.[9]

It is true that both GIs and trademarks are indications of origin, telling the consumer where the labelled product comes from. While trademarks enable consumers to distinguish Nike sportswear from sportswear with other commercial origins, GIs allow them to make a choice between *Darjeeling* tea and tea originating from another place. This function of guaranteeing the origin of the product constitutes the essential function of the trademark[10] and the basic function of the GI. Thus, GI protection and trademark protection are rooted in similar concerns about the prevention of consumer

8. *See* Wang Lianfeng, Woguo Dili Biaozhi Lifa Moshi de Xuanze [The Choice of the Legislative Mode of Geographical Indication in China], FALU SHIYONG [LAW APPLICATION], July 2003, 70; *See also* Li Xiaomin, Dili Biaozhi Falu Baohu Jizhi Yanjiu yi Jingdezhen Weili [Protection Mechanism of Geographical Indications: Example of Jingdezhen Geographical Indication], Doctoral Thesis, China University of Political Science and Law, 2005.
9. The treatment of GIs as a subset of trademarks is the cornerstone for the trademark approach for GIs protection, Championed primarily by the US. *See Geographical Indication Protection in the United States*, United States Patent and Trademark Office (USPTO) (10 June 2021), https://www.uspto.gov/sites/default/files/web/offices/dcom/olia/globalip/pdf/gi_system.pdf.
10. *See* Case C-10/89 *SA CNL-SUCAL NV v. HAG GF AG* [1990] ECR I-03711, para. 14: '... essential function of the trade mark ... is to guarantee the identity of the origin of the marked product to the consumer or ultimate user by enabling him without any possibility of confusion to distinguish that product from products which have another origin'; *See also* Case C-39/97 *Canon Kabushiki Kaisha v. Metro-Goldwyn-Mayer Inc* [1998] ECR I-05507, para. 28; Case C-299/99

deception as to the origin of products as well as shielding legitimate producers from unfair competition.[11] Therefore, under both the sui generis GI regime and trademark regime, unauthorized use of a sign that is likely to cause confusion as to the origin of the product and thus create an unfair advantage is prohibited.

Nevertheless, treating GIs as a subset of trademarks overlooks the special element of GIs: the link between the labelled product and the *terroir*. A GI guarantees not only that the products bearing the indication come from a particular place but also that they possess certain qualities or specific characteristics derived from a combination of unique natural and human influences in the place from which they originate.[12] The term 'geographical indications' is the legal expression of the concept of *terroir*,[13] which assumes that a particular place produces particular product characteristics that cannot be imitated by other regions. If this assumption is true or is believed to be true, the purpose of a GI protection scheme should be to define, reinforce, and maintain the qualitative link between the product and the place, to communicate the link to the consumer, and thus to allow the link to generate economic value.[14]

The European (and French) sui generis GI scheme is founded on the concept of *terroir*.[15] The scheme allows for the protection of names on the condition that the applicant has proven a link between the product and its geographical origin.[16] When granting the protection, an act of public authority prescribes the geographical area delimited, quality requirements, and manufacturing standards.[17] This registration aims to define the link between the product and its *terroir*.

Koninklijke Philips Electronics NV v. Remington Consumer Products Ltd [2002] ECR I-05475, para. 30; Case C-273/00 *Ralf Sieckmann v. Deutsches Patent- und Markenamt* [2002] ECR I-11737, para. 35.

11. Ruth L. Okedui, *International Intellectual Property Roots of Geographical Indications*, 82 Chi.-Kent L. Rev. 1329, 1341 (2007).
12. *See* Case C-47/90 *Établissements Delhaize frères and Compagnie Le Lion SA v. Promalvin SA and AGE Bodegas Unidas SA* [1992] ECR I-03669, para. 17: 'The specific function of a registered designation of origin is to guarantee that the product bearing it comes from a specified geographical area and displays certain particular characteristics'; C-3/91 *Exportur SA v. LOR SA and Confiserie du Tech SA* [1992] I-05529, para. 11: 'A designation of origin (appellation d' origine; denominación de origen), for its part, guarantees, not only the geographical provenance of the product, but also that the goods have been manufactured according to quality requirements or manufacturing standards prescribed by an act of public authority and thus that they have certain specific characteristics'; Case C-388/95 *Belgium v. Spain* [2000] ECR I-03123, para. 23: 'The specific function of a registered designation of origin was to guarantee that the product bearing it came from a specified geographical area and displayed certain particular characteristics.'
13. *See* Tim Josling, *The War on Terroir: Geographical Indications as a Transatlantic Trade Conflict*, 57 J. Agric. Econ. 337 (2006).
14. *See* Laurence Bérard & Marchenay Philippe, *From Localized Products to Geographical Indications*, CNRS (18 June 2021), https://www.ethno-terroirs.cnrs.fr/IMG/pdf/Localized_Products_to_GI.pdf.
15. Elizabeth Barham, *Translating Terroir: The Global Challenge of French AOC Labeling*, 19 J. Rural Stud. 127 (2003).
16. *See* Chapter 4 *supra*.
17. *See*, for example, Article L. 641-6 C. rur.: '*La proposition de l'institut porte sur la délimitation de l'aire géographique de production, définie comme la surface comprenant les communes ou parties de communes propres à produire l'appellation d'origine, ainsi que sur la détermination des*

Europe also seeks to reinforce the link even at the risk of imposing restrictions on the free movement of goods. For example, Spanish legislation made it compulsory to bottle wine in the region of production in order to be able to use the GI '*Rioja*'. Belgium brought an action against Spain, declaring that it had failed to fulfil its obligations under Article 34 of the EC treaty (now Article 34 TFEU).[18] The CJEU acknowledged that Spanish rules making use of the GI conditional on bottling in that region had an effect equivalent to quantitative restrictions.[19] It also accepted the argument that a wine's characteristics may be maintained when it has been bottled outside the place of production;[20] in other words, the characteristics of the wine are not due to the place where it is bottled. However, the court noted:

> In the case of bottling, the best conditions are more certain to be assured if bottling is done by undertakings established in the region of those entitled to use the designation and operating under their direct control, since they have specialized experience and, what is more, thorough knowledge of the specific characteristics of the wine in question which must not be impaired or lost at the time of bottling.[21]

The court concluded that the requirement for bottling in the region constituted a necessary and proportionate means of attaining the objective of guaranteeing the wine's quality and preserving its reputation.[22] It can thus be seen that strengthening control over non-essential production steps helps to ensure and reinforce the qualitative link between the product and the place.[23] The strengthening of this link is also one of the purposes of Europe's GI protection scheme.

Regarding the maintenance of the qualitative link, the European GI regime requires any amendment to the product specification – minor or major, temporary or permanent – to be approved by the public authorities.[24] Self-control, internal control, and external control must all be performed to ensure the verification of compliance with the product specification.[25] EU symbols (the official logo) are used in order to communicate the qualitative link to the consumer. Their presence on GI products is obligatory.[26]

---

conditions de production qui figurent dans un cahier des charges. Ces conditions de production peuvent comporter des mesures destinées à favoriser la préservation des terroirs.'

18. Article 34 of the Treaty on the Functioning of the European Union: 'Quantitative restrictions on imports and all measures having equivalent effect shall be prohibited between Member States.'
19. Case C-388/95 *Belgium v. Spain*, *supra* n. 12, para. 42.
20. *Ibid.*, para. 64.
21. *Ibid.*, para. 65.
22. *Ibid.*, paras 75-76.
23. The CJEU confirmed the strengthening of the link to *terroir* in later cases. *See* Case C-108/01 *Consorzio del Prosciutto di Parma and Salumificio S. Rita SpA v. Asda Stores Ltd and Hygrade Foods Ltd* [2003] ECR I-05121, paras 63-64; Case C-469/00 *Ravil SARL v. Bellon import SARL and Biraghi SpA* [2003] ECR I-05053, paras 48-49; Case C-569/18 *Caseificio Cirigliana Srl and Others v. Ministero delle Politiche agricole, alimentari e forestali and Others* (ECJ 17 October 2019) paras 35-36.
24. Article 53 of Regulation 1151/2012; Article 31 of Regulation 2019/787; Article 105 of Regulation 1308/2013; Article 24 of Regulation 251/2014.
25. *See* Chapter 4 *supra*.
26. Nevertheless, the Union symbol is an optional particular for GIs for wines. *See* Article 12 of Regulation 1151/2012; Article 120 of Regulation 1308/2013; Article 16 of Regulation 2019/787.

Finally, to allow the qualitative link to generate value for legitimate operators, the EU sui generis regime excludes the use of terms such as 'kind', 'type', or 'imitation', even if the consumer would likely not be misled as to the origin of the good. The underlying justification is the idea of *terroir*: the combination of natural and human factors in the region of production is so unique that the product's characteristics derived from that place cannot be successfully reproduced or imitated beyond that place.[27] The use of such terms would undermine the distinctiveness of the product by suggesting to consumers that a good produced elsewhere has the same or similar geographically determined attributes.[28]

A brief overview of the European GI system shows that the idea of *terroir* undergirds the special features of the system. Some Western scholars argue that the idea of *terroir* is a myth,[29] that the link between the product's characteristics and the place is not scientifically proven,[30] or that the rapid development of technology has made the natural and human factors transferable so that a product can be perfectly reproduced elsewhere.[31] We will not attempt to demonstrate the scientific basis of the idea of *terroir*. In fact, even China's strongest opponents of the sui generis regime do not question this idea. On the contrary, there is widespread agreement that China has abundant products whose characteristics are due to their place of origin, thanks to its 5,000-year-old civilization, its vast territory with various climatic and geographic conditions, and its long history of farming practices.[32] Even China's trademark regime

---

27. *See* Bérard & Philippe, *supra* n. 14.
28. Kal Raustiala & Stephen R. Munzer, *The Global Struggle over Geographic Indications*, 18 Eur. J. Int'l L. 337 (2007).
29. Justin Hughes, *Champagne, Feta, and Bourbon: The Spirited Debate about Geographical Indications*, 58 Hastings L.J. 299 (2006).
30. James Ming Chen, *A Sober Second Look at Appellations of Origin: How the United States Will Crash France's Wine and Cheese Party*, 5 Minn. J. Global Trade 29 (1996); Michael Blakeney, *Geographical Indications: What Do They Indicate?*, 6 WIPO J. 50 (2014).
31. Hughes, *supra* n. 29; Kees de Roest, *The Production of Parmigiano-Reggiano Cheese: The Force of an Artisanal System in an Industrialized World* 155 (Van Gorcum 2000).
32. *See* Wang Xiaoyan, Lun Woguo Dili Biaozhi de Baohu Moshi [Protection Model of Geographical Indications], ZHISHI CHANQUAN [INTELLECTUAL PROPERTY], November 2019, 66; Xiaomin, *supra* n. 8; Ma Xiaoli, Dili Biaozhi Lifa Moshi Bijiao Fenxi Jianlun Woguo Dili Biaozhi de Lifa Moshi [Comparative Analysis of Legislative Mode of Geographical Indications and China's Legislative Choice], DIANZI ZHISHI CHANQUAN [ELECTRONICS INTELLECTUAL PROPERTY], January 2003, 52; Wang Sumin, Lun Woguo Dili Biaozhi de Baohu Moshi [Protection Mode of Geographical Indications in China], HUABEI SHUILI SHUIDIAN XUEYUAN XUEBAO [JOURNAL OF HUABEI INSTITUTE OF WATER CONSERVANCY AND HYDROELECTRIC POWER], February 2005, 95; Liu Yajun, Wanshan Woguo Dili Biaozhi Falu Baohu Shizheng Fenxi [Positive Analysis on Our Amelioration of Geographical Indication], DANGDAI FAXUE [CONTEMPORARY LAW REVIEW], March 2004, 46; Wang Chunmei, Woguo Dili Biaozhi Siquan Baohu yu Moshi Xuanze [Protection of Private Rights to the Geographical Indications and Choice of Protection Modes in China], BEIFANG FAXUE [NORTHERN LEGAL SCIENCE], September 2009, 95; Wu Bin, Woguo Nongchanpin Dili Biaozhi Falu Baohu de Yiyi ji Wanshan Cuoshi [Legal Protection on Geographical Indications of China's Agricultural Products: Significance and Countermeasures], HUAZHONG NONGYE DAXUE XUEBAO [JOURNAL OF HUAZHONG AGRICULTURAL UNIVERSITY], April 2008, 47; Liu Guoqi, Yuanchan Diyu Baohu he Yuanchandi Zhengming Shangbiao Baohu [Protection of Geographical Origin and Protection of Certification Marks Certifying Geographical Origin], ZHONGHUA SHANGBIAO [CHINA TRADEMARK], April 2002, 42; Gu Xiaodong & Liu Weiming, WTO-TRIPS Xieyi Zhong Dili Biaozhi zai

does not deny the existence of the link between a product and its *terroir*. In China, applicants for the registration of a GI as a collective or certification mark must submit documents proving the correlation.[33]

However, the critics fail to fully appreciate the importance of the idea of *terroir* as a basis for establishing a special protection system for GIs.[34] They argue that GIs can be adequately protected under the trademark regime.

It is undeniable that trademarks can have a *terroir* dimension.[35] An individual mark can be used to designate only local products whose quality is linked to the place of origin. Legitimate operators of products under GIs sometimes choose to use their own individual marks instead of GIs to commercialize their products. An example of such a strategy is a Chinese wine marked with the trademark '*Zhang Yu*' even though the wine is produced in '*Yan Tai*' and benefits from GI protection. The fact that the trademark owner does not sell the wine under the name of the GI does not change the qualitative link between the wine and its place of origin. Moreover, in order to meet the expectations of consumers who want consistency in terms of quality, the owner of the trademark must ensure that the qualitative link is maintained through control of the wine's characteristics and quality.[36] The mark can thus also be an indication of a quality linked to the geographical origin. However, nothing in the trademark law prevents a trademark owner from changing the quality of the trademarked wine. In this case, the qualitative link might disappear, but the trademark would remain valid.[37] The trademark does not 'guarantee' the quality of a product. Defining, strengthening, or maintaining the link is never the responsibility of the trademark protection.[38] Trademarks may have this effect but only because the market drives them.

If there is a market for products linked to *terroir*, the *terroir* argument can be used by any type of trademark owner, ranging from local SMEs to multinational firms. For example, the trademark '*Reflets de France*' from the Carrefour group obviously exploits *terroir* as a marketing strategy, although not all trademarked products have a quality, reputation, or other characteristics attributable to their place of origin.[39] Even in the

Woguo de Falu Baohu Yanjiu [China's Legal Protection of Geographical Indications of the TRIPS Agreement], QIYE JINGJI [ENTERPRISE ECONOMY], July 2006, 172.

33. *See* Chapter 3 *supra*.
34. Wang Xiaobing, Guanlianxing Yaosu yu Dili Biaozhi Fa de Gouzao [The Linkage and the Construction of Geographical Indication Law], FAXUE YANJIU [LEGAL RESEARCH], May 2015, 82.
35. Wang Xiaobing, Woguo Canjia WTO Dili Biaozhi Tanpan de Lichang he Duice [China's Position in WTO Negotiation Protecting GIs], ZHISHI CHANQUAN [INTELLECTUAL PROPERTY], January 2010, 47.
36. Sun Weidong, Yantai Zhongguo Shouge Hongjiu Yuanchandi [Yantai: China's First Wine Appellation of Origin], ZHONGGUO JIANYAN JIANYI [CHINA INSPECTION & QUARANTINE], April 2014.
37. However, the mark might be declared invalid if the mark becomes deceptive after the quality change.
38. By contrast, under the sui generis GI regime, once the qualitative link disappears (e.g., compliance with the conditions of the product specification is not ensured), the GI will be subject to cancellation.
39. *See Des produits régionaux français*, Reflets de France (19 June 2021), https://www.refletsdefrance.fr.

fast-food industry, 'Duck Me' uses the slogan 'Made in *terroir*' to sell their hamburgers.[40] All trademarks can claim to be closely related to *terroir* or be of a high-quality thanks to *terroir*,[41] which means that there might be a divergence between the actual link to *terroir* and consumers' reasonable expectations. However, it is not the responsibility of the trademark law to define what the *terroir* link truly is, or how closely a product should be bonded to *terroir* in order to be labelled as a *terroir* product. The trademark system does not verify the link to *terroir*, nor does it set out legal consequences for a trademark owner who does not maintain the *terroir*-based quality (which may thus diminish without any legal consequences for the owner). Here, we have no intention of recommending that the use of the term '*terroir*' should be subject to certain conditions. The point is that, while sui generis GI regimes regulate at least one kind of *terroir* link (the causal link between quality, reputation, or other characteristics of a product and its place of origin), the trademark system does not.

The same reasoning also applies to certification marks. These can also have a *terroir* dimension if the owners of the marks require, in the regulations governing their use, that the trademarked products possess certain qualities attributable to the place of origin. They provide a legal guarantee of the link between the product and the place, in that only operators who meet this requirement are allowed (and must be allowed) to use the marks. Again, it is up to the mark owners to decide whether to keep the link requirement in the regulations governing use. The *terroir* dimension might disappear, but certification marks will still enjoy the same protection provided by the trademark law.[42] The trademark law does not seem to care about the link between the product and its *terroir*.

To conclude, the *terroir* dimension may be embedded in trademarks depending on the willingness of the trademark proprietors.[43] The trademark regime is not designed to define, reinforce, or maintain the link between the product and the place. In Chapter 7, we will continue to demonstrate that this regime may not be a good tool for enabling the link to generate market value. As GIs differ from trademarks,[44] their particularity (their qualitative link) needs a special treatment that the trademark regime has no intention to offer.

40. *See Made in terroir*, Duck Me (19 June 2021), http://www.duckme.fr.
41. However, the trademark or the practice should not be deceptive.
42. The certification mark will remain valid as long as it still certifies something.
43. Li Hua & Wang Zhaoke, Dili Biaozhi yu Shangbiao de Benzhi Qubie [The Essential Difference Between Geographical Indications and Trademarks], SHIJIE NONGYE [WORLD AGRICULTURE], January 2006, 48.
44. Nancy Kremers, *Speaking with a Forked Tongue in the Global Debate on Traditional Knowledge and Genetic Resources: Is US Intellectual Property Law and Policy Really Aimed at Meaningful Protection for Native American Cultures*, 15 Fordham Intell. Prop. Media & Ent. L.J. 1 (2004); Leigh Ann Lindquist, *Champagne or Champagne-An Examination of US Failure to Comply with the Geographical Provisions of the TRIPS Agreement*, 27 Ga. J. Int'l & Comp. L. 309 (1998); Molly Torsen, *Apples and Oranges (and Wine): Why the International Conversation Regarding Geographic Indications Is at a Standstill*, 87 J. Pat. & Trademark Off. Soc'y 31 (2005).

[2] *Is the Sui Generis Regime Not Worth the Cost?*

Chinese academics and legal practitioners who oppose protecting GIs as sui generis IP argue that doing so requires additional resources in order to modify the existing trademark system and develop a new GI system.[45] It is argued that, since there is already a trademark law that addresses GI protection, creating a special regime involves additional legislation and operating costs (e.g., for staff and a database for GI registration to avoid infringing prior third party rights, especially trademark rights).[46]

However, protecting GIs as trademarks cannot be justified simply on the basis of cost savings. While it is true that the Trademark Law (amended in 1993) is the first law in China to provide protection for GIs, neither 'geographical indications' nor 'appellations of origin' has been mentioned in any of the provisions associated with the 1993 amendment. It was not until the 2001 amendment that the Trademark Law provided a definition of 'geographical indications', though this definition is actually a faithful copy of the TRIPS definition. Research shows that, even in 2001, the concept of GIs was still vague and sometimes confusing to many Chinese legal practitioners.[47] Given the low awareness of the GI concept, one must wonder if protecting GIs as trademarks at this early stage was a *conscious* choice made by China's government.

There is evidence to suggest that China's government had a rather ambiguous attitude regarding how GIs should be protected. On the question of whether the 'additional protection' for wines and spirits provided by Article 23.1 of the TRIPS Agreement should be extended to other products, a number of European countries and developing countries with a strong interest in GIs advocated for the extension of the protection in two papers submitted in 2000 and 2001 to the TRIPS Council.[48] New

45. The Trademark Law amended in 1993, its implementing regulations (1993) and the Measures for the Registration and Administration of Collective Marks and Certification Marks (1994) are believed to be China's first laws protecting GIs. *See* An Qinghu, Former director, Trademark Office of the People's Republic of China, *Legal System on Geographical Indication Protection in China and Related Issues*, Speech at the International Symposium on Geographical Indications (25 June 2007).
46. *See* Xiaomin, *supra* n. 8, at 59; Sumin, *supra* n. 32, at 97; Yu Jinkui, Dili Biaozhi Falu Baohu Moshi de Tantao [Discussion of the Protection Mode of Geographical Indications], ZHONGGUO HAIYANG DAXUE XUEBAO [JOURNAL OF OCEAN UNIVERSITY OF CHINA], January 2006, 91; Peter K. Yu, *From Pirates to Partners (Episode II): Protecting Intellectual Property in Post-WTO China*, 55 Am. UL Rev. 901 (2005).
47. Wu Chunqi, Dili Biaozhi ji Yuanchandi Mingcheng deng Xiangguan Gainian de Tanjiu [The Relationship among Geographical Indications, Indications of Source, and Appellations of Origin], SHANDONG DAXUE XUEBAO [JOURNAL OF SHANDONG UNIVERSITY], August 2003, 94.
48. Countries advocating or supporting the extension include Bulgaria, the Czech Republic, Iceland, India, Liechtenstein, Slovenia, Sri Lanka, Switzerland, Turkey, Cuba, Egypt, Georgia, Hungary, Kenya, the Kyrgyz Republic, Moldova, Mauritius, Nigeria, Pakistan, and Venezuela. *See* WTO, *Communication from Bulgaria et al.*, IP/C/W/204/Rev.1 (2 October 2000); WTO, *Proposal from Bulgaria et al.*, IP/C/W/247/Rev.1 (17 May 2001); WTO, *Communication from Bulgaria et al.*, IP/C/W/353 (24 June 2002).

World countries later argued the opposite position.[49] China seemed to be a silent and disinterested onlooker in this debate; it did not provide a clear position until later.[50]

China's silence during the international debate at the early stage was not due to a lack of interest in GIs. Quite the opposite: Chinese scholars believe that the GI constitutes an asset for China and that GI protection can be of great benefit.[51] The silence could be attributed to the fact that there was no consensus or clear understanding as to what legal protection should be granted to GIs.[52]

Thus, it must be concluded that protecting GIs through trademarks was not China's conscious choice:[53] How could China choose the trademark regime as a primary tool when it was still hesitant about the level of protection GIs should have? What is more, as China has recently acquired a better understanding of the protection GIs require, it is actively working with the EU and other 'Old World' countries to extend the additional protection provided by the TRIPS Agreement to GIs for all products. This higher level of protection, which is characterized as a 'dilution plus' standard of protection,[54] does not fit with existing trademark doctrines. It seems more appropriate to grant GIs additional protection under a special regime, built on a different rational basis.

It then follows that simply maintaining the status quo (prioritizing trademark law) would be inadequate in the face of China's growing consciousness of the need for a higher level of protection for national GIs.

It might be true that introducing a sui generis system of GIs could be costly. The system, by definition, involves allowing special treatment to accommodate the special characteristics of GIs, which requires more financial and human resources than are needed to simply employ the existing trademark regime. Nevertheless, the cost savings argument is not persuasive because GIs protected as collective or certification marks have also been given special treatment by the trademark law since 2001, and this also has incurred costs.

We recall that according to Article 7 of the Collective and Certification Marks Measures, an application for the registration of a GI as a collective or certification mark should be accompanied by documentation demonstrating how the given quality,

49. Those opposing the extension include, in particular, Argentina, Australia, Canada, Chile, Guatemala, New Zealand, Paraguay, and the United States. *See* WTO, *Communication from Argentina et al.*, IP/C/W/289 (29 June 2001).
50. It is only at a later stage that China's position becomes clear. In 2011, along with the EU and other Old World countries, China submitted a draft amendment to the TRIPS Agreement to realize the extension of the protection of Article 23 of the TRIPS Agreement to GIs for all products. *See* WTO, *Draft Decision to Amend Section 3 of Part II of the TRIPS Agreement (Communication from Albania et al.)*, TN/C/W/60 (19 April 2011).
51. Zheng Chengsi, Cong Rushi ji Faxue Yanjiu Jiaodu Kan Zhongguo Liangbu Fa de Xiugai [Two Laws Modified: Insights from Acceding WTO and Legal Research], ZHONGHUA SHANGBIAO [CHINA TRADEMARK], December 2001, 13.
52. Xiaobing, *supra* n. 35, at 51.
53. China's conscious choice needs to be discussed in the light of Chinese culture, political system, or features of Chinese society. *See* Chapter 7 *infra*.
54. Hughes, *supra* n. 29.

reputation, or other characteristics of the goods are linked to the place of origin.[55] The Trademark Office verifies the existence of the link and will reject the application if the applicant fails to prove it.[56] Verifying the link is not merely a question of examining the distinctiveness or availability of the signs: the product–place nexus is studied. However, under the systems administered by the former AQSIQ (the CNIPA) and the MOA, an expert committee is responsible for verifying this nexus, based on a scientific and objective approach. Under the trademark regime, it appears necessary that a team of experts be available to assist the Trademark Office with all technical matters relating to the registration of marks that incorporate GIs, including the assessment of the place–quality nexus.[57] Such an expert team does not come free and may even cost more than the search database for GI registrations that is required for a sui generis GI regime.

Moreover, the former SAIC established the official logo for GIs registered as collective or certification marks in 2007. The use of the logo was subject to the Measures for the Administration of the Special Logo for Geographical Indications.[58] Unauthorized use of a sign that is identical or similar to the official logo will be prosecuted by offices of the former SAIC at the regional and municipal levels.[59] Again, the enactment and enforcement of the administrative measures incur expenses. Although a new official logo replaced the 2007 logo in 2020, the enforcement of the administrative measures for the use of the new official logo also requires supervision and expenses.[60]

This is not to deny that there are many features of the trademark regime that can be used to protect GIs (e.g., application, registration, opposition, cancellation, modification, and enforcement) and that employing those features could be cost-effective. The main point is that GIs are given special treatment in China by both their sui generis systems and trademark regime. The only difference is that, under the latter, special treatment is not granted in a systematic or structured manner: while the place–quality nexus is required at the time of registration, there are no mandatory requirements for trademark owners to maintain that nexus;[61] further, while additional conditions are

55. Measures for the Registration and Administration of Collective Marks and Certification Marks, Article 7; *See also* Chapter 3 *supra*.
56. *See Shandong Tourism Industry Association v. Trademark Review and Adjudication Board of State Administration for Industry and Commerce*, Beijing High People's Court (19 August 2015); Zhou Bo, Ruhe Shencha Butong Leixing de Jiti Shangbiao [How to Examine Different Types of Collective Trademarks], ZHONGGUO ZHISHI CHANQUAN BAO [CHINA INTELLECTUAL PROPERTY NEWS], 11 September 2015.
57. Contrary to our expectations, there is no expert review process to which the registration of GIs as collective or certification marks should be subject. The verification of the place/quality nexus is only carried out by trademark examiners, who might be incompetent in view of a lack of technical, topical, and geographical expertise.
58. Dili Biaozhi Chanpin Zhuanyong Biaozhi Guanli Banfa [Measures for the Administration of the Official Logo for Geographical Indication Products], 30 January 2007.
59. *Ibid.*, Article 9.
60. Administrative Measures for the Use of the Official Logo for Geographical Indications, Article 11 (2020).
61. Certification marks and collective marks do not necessarily have to certify the product's unbreakable link with the geographical area from which it comes.

added to the registration of GIs as collective or certification marks,[62] there are no additional rights above and beyond those enjoyed by other ordinary marks.[63]

This unstructured approach entails a risk that the applicant might choose to directly register a 'simple' collective or certification mark without declaring the sign at issue to be a GI, thus bypassing the additional conditions relating to 'GI marks' while enjoying the same level of protection.[64] An example of this is the registration of the collective mark '*Jingpohu* (a place name) Soybean'. The Trademark Office rejected the application on the grounds that the goods in respect of which that mark has been applied for did not have a firm, proven link with the natural and human factors in the region of origin. The trademark applicant appealed the decision denying its registration of the mark as a 'GI mark'.[65] The former Trademark Review and Adjudication Board (TRAB) rejected the appeal, finding that, although the applicant intended to register a 'simple' collective mark, the consumer may have perceived it as being a 'GI mark' and thus have been misled into believing that a given quality, reputation, or other characteristics of the goods were due to the place of origin.[66] Here, the Board revealed the real danger of protecting GIs as a subset of trademarks: ordinary marks composed of geographical names could be mistaken for GIs. However, the Board's decision was later annulled by the Beijing IP Court, which noted that, even if the contested sign contained a GI, it could constitute a valid collective mark as long as it did not mislead the consumer as to the geographical origin of the goods.[67] It actually allowed GIs to be registered as a 'simple' collective mark. Then, what is the point of these special rules and obligations imposed on 'GI marks' when trademark applicants can evade them?

In conclusion, the cost savings argument is just a pretext for maintaining the status quo (prioritizing trademark law), which is neither a conscious choice nor an adequate one. This argument is also unfounded: the trademark regime contains special rules for GIs registered as collective marks and certification marks; the enforcement of these rules is not free of charge.

62. *See* Measures for the Registration and Administration of Collective Marks and Certification Marks, Article 4 (additional conditions regarding the applicant for a collective mark with GI status), Article 5 (additional conditions regarding the applicant for a certification mark with GI status), Article 6 (prior approval by the people's government), and Article 7 (information regarding the link between the product and the place of origin).
63. However, the legitimate users of the registered marks with GI status can use the official logo on their goods to publicize the GI status.
64. All geographical indications recognized under the trademark regime are trademarks, but not all registered trademarks have GI status. GIs protected as collective or certification marks are referred to as 'GI marks', whereas trademarks without GI status are ordinary or simple trademarks. Nevertheless, this distinction may become blurred when the trademarks deny the GI status at the time of registration, although they could be classified as GIs in reality.
65. The applicant argued that the registration was not based on a GI but based on a simple geographical name. In other words, while a GI can be registered as a collective or certification mark, this does not prevent other ordinary place names from being registered as valid marks.
66. *State Administration for Industry v. Commerce Trademark Review and Adjudication Board and Ning'an Jingpo Lake Soybean Association*, Beijing High People's Court (12 June 2016).
67. *Ibid.*

[B] About the Inconsistency of China's Sui Generis Regime

Critics also argue that the sui generis approach is inconsistent with the nature of GIs and that it does not conform to commonly accepted practices. These criticisms are unjustified.

[1] Is the Sui Generis Regime Inconsistent with the Nature of GIs?

Questions about the nature of GIs (whether they are private rights or public goods) lies at the heart of the debate about China's choice of GI protection model.[68] Many critics of the sui generis approach argue that GIs are private IP rights, as outlined in the TRIPS Agreement.[69] They argue that GI protection should therefore be dealt with through the trademark system, which is designed to safeguard private business interests,[70] whereas the sui generis regime, characterized by a high degree of state or public involvement, is incompatible with the private nature of GIs.[71]

Indeed, a GI can be described as a business asset. Distinguishing origin-based goods from those that are not can be beneficial to local players as long as the origin is a clear quality signal in the minds of consumers. As it is a distinctive sign like a trademark, a GI certainly has a brand dimension[72] and forms the basis of such a product-differentiation strategy.[73] Put simply, GIs can act as commercial brands, just as trademarks do. Given their functional similarity to trademarks, GIs are often (but wrongly) thought of as a subset of trademarks and therefore part of private rights.[74]

However, this classification obviously overlooks the multifunctional dimension of the GI. To begin, there is the *terroir* dimension, the place–quality nexus, which underpins the concept of GIs. GIs are a guarantee of both geographical origin and

68. Zhang Yumin, Dili Biaozhi de Xingzhi he Baohu Moshi Xuanze [Nature and Protection Mode of Geographical Indications], FAXUE ZAZHI [LAW JOURNAL], November 2007, 6. French scholar Jacques Audier also underlines that the protection of GIs depends on their legal nature. *See* Jacques Audier, *De la nature juridique de l'appellation d'origine*, Bulletin de l'OIV, n° 743-744, 1993, p. 21.
69. Preamble of the TRIPS Agreement: 'recognizing that intellectual property rights are private rights'.
70. *See* Xiaoli, *supra* n. 32, at 56; Xie Dongwei, Rushi yu Woguo Yuanchandi Mingcheng Dili Biaozhi de Baohu [WTO and the Protection of China's Geographical Indications], ZHONGGUO GONGSHANG BAO [CHINA BUSINESS NEWSPAPER], 17 May 2001; Chunmei, *supra* n. 32, at 101.
71. *See* Guoqi, *supra* n. 32, at 44; Xiaomin, *supra* n. 8, at 60.
72. Norma Dawson claims that GIs should be regarded as a 'sign' in that the prevention from deception and unfair competition underpins the legal protection of both geographical indications and (geographical) trademarks. *See* Norma Dawson, *Locating Geographical Indications: Perspectives from English Law*, 90 Trademark Rep. 590, 599 (2000).
73. *See* Daniele Giovannucci et al., *Guide to Geographical Indications: Linking Products and Their Origins* (Organization for an International Geographical Indications Network 11 June 2021), https://www.origin-gi.com/images/stories/PDFs/English/E-Library/geographical_indications.pdf; Dev Gangjee, *Protecting Geographical Indications as Collective Trademarks: The Prospects and Pitfalls* (Institute of Intellectual Property 10 June 2021), https://www.iip.or.jp/e/summary/pdf/detail2005/e17_14.pdf
74. *See* Caroline Le Goffic, *La protection des indications géographiques*, Paris, LexisNexis, 2011, p. 236.

quality.[75] In order to ensure this function, the exclusive power conferred by GIs must be justified as being essential for guaranteeing the place–quality nexus (although, on a superficial level, the function of GIs, like that of trademarks, is exclusionary).[76] This requires an equitable access to GIs: everyone whose products meet the nexus requirement must be entitled to use them, even a total stranger from a faraway community who has just moved into the region.[77] The importance of equity considerations provides a clue about their 'public good' nature.[78]

Furthermore, thanks to their intrinsic anchorage to *terroir*, GIs are expected to do other kinds of work that are not trade-related. As explored in Chapter 1, GIs can serve a number of public policy interests, such as benefiting rural economies; fostering sustainable agricultural development; and preserving TK, cultural heritage, biological diversity, and the environment.[79]

These 'public service' considerations challenge the conclusion drawn from the TRIPS Agreement that GIs are concerned only with clean-cut private rights. In fact, an extensive body of literature expresses doubts not only about this conclusion but also about whether GIs can ever be treated as a form of IP.[80] Arguments against the inclusion of GIs under the 'IP' umbrella concept include the fact that the TRIPS Agreement is the product of negotiation and political compromise,[81] the difference between the rationale for IP protection and that for GI protection,[82] the difference

75. *See* Chapter 1 *supra*.
76. If a sign is recognized as a GI or registered as a trademark, certain operators may use it while others may not. Both a GI and a trademark will grant a power of exclusivity.
77. Raustiala and Munzer observe that: 'It is hard … to see why a perfect stranger from a far-away community can move into the region and thus avail him or herself of the GI. Yet this is precisely what current GI law permits'. *See* Raustiala & Stephen, *supra* n. 28, at 359.
78. The 'public good' nature of GIs is reiterated by a survey report of the AIPPI, according to which the majority of countries that participated in this study confirmed that GIs are not generally associated with 'ownership'. *See Summary Report on Question Q191: Relationship Between Trademarks and Geographical Indications*, AIPPI (18 June 2021), https://www.aippi.fr/upload/Gothenburg%202006%20Q189%20190%20191%20192/sr191english.pdf.
79. *See also* Junko Kimura & Cyrille Rigolot, *The Potential of Geographical Indications (GI) to Enhance Sustainable Development Goals (SDGs) in Japan: Overview and Insights from Japan GI Mishima Potato*, 13 Sustainability 961 (2021); Wang Xiaobing, JINGJI FAZHAN FANGSHI ZHUANBIAN SHIJIAO XIA DE DILI BIAOZHI BAOHU [GEOGRAPHICAL INDICATION PROTECTION FROM THE PERSPECTIVE OF ECONOMIC DEVELOPMENT MODE CHANGE] (China Social Sciences Publishing, 2019).
80. *See* Marie-Christine Piatti, *L'appellation d'origine: essai de qualification*, RTD Com., 1999, p. 557; Marie-Christine Piatti, *Nature juridique de l'AOC: une propriété démembrée*, Revue lamy droit des affaires, n° 68, 2004, p. 5; Dorothée Franjus-Guigues, *Nature et protection juridiques des indications géographiques: l'avènement d'un droit à l'épreuve de sa mise en œuvre*, thèse, Université d'Aix-Marseille, 2012.
81. The negotiation and compromise may sometimes result in incorrect legal classification of certain facts. This is especially true for GIs, to which the TRIPS Agreement provides two levels of protection (Article 22 base level and Article 23 high level) without further justification. *See* Daniel Gervais, *Geographical indications under TRIPS, in Research Handbook on Intellectual Property and Geographical Indications* 130 (Dev Gangjee ed., Edward Elgar Publishing 2016).
82. Erik W. Ibele argues that IP protection aims to award the invention of new products and processes and create new artistic works. However, GIs involve much less human inventiveness that IP law seeks to reward. What GIs encourage is the maintenance and preservation of the relationship between the place of origin and the products. Likewise, Caroline Le Goffic contends that, while trademarks involve intellectual effort (either creating a new sign or creatively

between rights *to* something (public policy) and rights *on* something (rights similar to ownership),[83] the non-transferability of GIs,[84] the infinite lifespan of GIs,[85] and the collective interest in the use of the sign.[86]

This chapter does not focus on the justification for removing GIs from the IP field,[87] nor does it intend to deny all the private interests that GIs may represent. It would be naïve to believe that anyone would be motivated to register a GI if they were likely to be excluded from legitimate use after registration.[88] It is also hard to imagine that anyone would participate in the GI scheme if the costs arising from inspections (or the need to adapt production methods to respect the product specification) exceeded the premium price derived from joining the scheme.[89] Simply put, producers, attempting to make optimal choices, are unlikely to register or use a GI at the cost of their own

---

associating an existing sign to a certain type of goods), GIs are not the fruit of intellectual work. The choice of the geographical term, region of production, and production methods is not a creative work of current producers but simply follows a historical evolution. *See* Erik W. Ibele, *The Nature and Function of Geographical Indications in Law*, 10 Estey Ctr. J. Int'l L. & Trade Pol'y 36 (2009); Le Goffic, *supra* n. 74, at 238.

83. Jacques Audier advocated separating 'the right on the appellation of origin' from 'the right to the appellation of origin'. The latter corresponds to the use of the name by all legitimate producers, whereas the first relates to the ownership of the name. However, who owns the appellation of origin? State? Producers' group? Individual producers? It seems that none of them could qualify as an 'owner' since they do not have all the prerogatives that can be derived from the 'ownership'. Teshager W. Dagne notes that rights holders do not own GIs in the same context as trademarks. The term 'property' in the context of GIs is construed in a strict sense of 'rights to something rather than to the thing that is owned'. From another perspective, it is hard to imagine how the 'property' or 'the right on property' exists without any owner. If the law regulates only 'the right to the appellation of origin' to maintain the link between place and product, it is essentially a public policy. *See* Audier, *supra*. 68, at 27; Teshager W. Dagne, *The Identity of Geographical Indications and Their Relation to Traditional Knowledge in Intellectual Property Law*, 5 WIPO J. 137 (2014).
84. GIs cannot be sold, licensed, or transferred through a mortgage as opposed to most IP rights. *See* Stephen Stern, *Are GIs IP?*, 29 Eur. Intell. Prop. Rev. 39 (2007).
85. While most IP rights have a limited period, the rights to GIs are not bound to a fixed term. Trademark rights are valid for ten years, and the renewal is necessary to extend the duration. The rights can be revoked or invalidated where needed. In contrast, registered GIs can never become generic (at least in the EU). *See* Andras Jokuti, *Where Is the What If the What Is in Why? A Rough Guide to the Maze of Geographical Indications*, 31 Eur. Intell. Prop. Rev. 118 (2009).
86. It is commonly accepted that rights stemming from GI protection are collective rights that cannot be a subject of private ownership.
87. Séverine Visse-Causse identified three characteristics common to all intellectual property types: the intangible nature of the subject matter of the IP rights, the creation or innovation required for protection, and the limited duration of the rights. She argued that, while the AO has intangible nature and is protected by infringement action, it can hardly be classified as IP because of the lack of creation or innovation and the unlimited duration of rights. *See* Séverine Visse-Causse, *L'appellation d'origine*, thèse, Université de Reims, 2004, pp. 303-313.
88. From the delimitation of the geographical area to the drafting of the specifications, the registration efforts are by nature exclusive. Individual actors may disagree on these constructions, leading to conflicts since they may promote different constructions to pursue specific goals. It is doubtful that one actor would propose a construction that would potentially result in his exclusion (e.g., setting a working practice that he cannot respect). *See* Angela Tregear et al., *The Impact of Territorial Product Qualification Processes on the Rural Development Potential of Small-Scale Food Productions* (XI World Congress of Rural Sociology 2004).
89. G. Belletti shows that direct certification costs emerge as an important but not as the main element in the firms' decision whether to use or not a PDO or PGI. *See* Giovanni Belletti et al.,

private interests. It is not a surprise that many winemakers in Tuscany abandoned the prestigious appellation '*Chianti Classico*' because of the estimated financial loss that the GI strategy could have caused.[90]

Based on the above considerations, we opt for a middle-of-the-road approach in identifying the true nature of GIs. Their nature would be more appropriately considered as a blend of private and public interests. The GI protection regime can be either designed to maximize private interests or be oriented towards public interests. The 'privately oriented' GI scheme, such as a trademark regime, focuses on traditional producer- and consumer-protection concerns. The 'publicly oriented' GI scheme, such as the EU PDO/PGI scheme, pays more attention to rural development and *terroir* preservation. If maximizing individual liberty were to automatically bring all the potential public benefits that are expected from GIs, there would be no legal basis for public intervention, not to mention the sui generis GI regime. However, empirical evidence suggests that GIs do not produce miracles. Some producers' incomes have benefited (at least for short periods) from a self-determined marketing strategy that, however, resulted in the loosening of the *terroir* linkage. One illustration of this is the case of *Darjeeling* tea, which was initially protected as a certification mark. The Tea Board, the trademark owner, had set out the regulations governing the use of that mark, providing that blends containing at least sixty per cent of tea from the Darjeeling region could be certified as Darjeeling tea.[91] While tea growers' and merchants' incomes might be safeguarded with the help of the increased yield resulting from the outsourced tea, the term 'Darjeeling' lost its capacity to guarantee the origin and typicality linked to it. Only when the Indian GI Act[92] later established a sui generis regime was this capacity restored through public intervention.[93]

In conclusion, since GIs are expected to benefit both private and public interests, systems governing GIs can be either privately oriented or publicly oriented. The advantages of these two types of protection will be considered in Chapter 7. This chapter does not try to convince anyone of the need to support one model over the other. In the light of the topics discussed above, however, it is probably not too audacious to reject the argument that China must adopt a privately oriented approach simply because the TRIPS Agreement said that IP rights are private rights.

The Effects of Certification Costs on the Success of a PDO/PGI, in Quality Management in Food Chains 107-121 (Wageningen Academic Publishers 2007).

90. *See* Tomer Broude, *Taking Trade and Culture Seriously: Geographical Indications and Cultural Protection in WTO Law*, 26 U. Pa. J. Int'l Econ. L. 623 (2005).
91. *See* Cerkia Bramley, Marie-Vivien Delphine & Biénabe Estelle, *Considerations in Designing an Appropriate Legal Framework for GIs in Southern Countries, in Developing Geographical Indications in the South* 15 (Cerkia Bramley ed., Springer 2013).
92. Geographical Indications of Goods (Registration and Protection) Act (1999).
93. The regulations governing use of the mark were amended in 2002 to provide that only 100 per cent of Darjeeling tea may be certified as Darjeeling and that blends may only claim to contain Darjeeling if the teas included in the blends are certified as Darjeeling. *See Ibid.*, at 45.

[2] *Is the Sui Generis Regime Inconsistent with the Commonly Accepted Practice?*

The sui generis regime is often viewed with suspicion because it is not as widespread as the trademark regime. Xie Dongwei, an in-house lawyer for the Trademark Office, noted when China joined the WTO (2001) that:

> Most countries, such as the UK, the US, Canada, Australia, Germany, Italy, protect AOs and GIs in the form of collective or certification marks, whereas only a handful of countries like France has specialized agencies working on GIs' registration and protection ... Hence, the trademark approach fits in with the current practice of most countries.[94]

Although this argument has been used by opponents of the sui generis regime for many years,[95] it has never been substantiated. In fact, this argument cannot be substantiated. It is based on a false perception that the use of the sui generis regime is a very rare exception. The opposite is true. A 2003 WTO paper on the types of national protection provided for GIs suggests that a significant number of countries have put special regimes in place.[96] A more recent study concludes that, among 167 countries that protect GIs as a form of IP, 111 have specific or sui generis GI systems and 56 rely on their trademark systems.[97] Thus, neither of the two approaches is overwhelmingly predominant.

Furthermore, even if the trademark approach were more widely accepted, as is argued by some sceptics, we see no rationale as to why China has to follow that practice. One of the very few justifications is that 'China's main trading partners, such as the US, the UK, Germany, Australia, Canada, and Italy, protect GIs by the trademark law. The same approach taken by China is important to foster international trade.'[98] This justification ignores the international conflict of interests between the 'Old' and 'New' worlds.[99] It is no coincidence that New World countries that are in favour of weaker protection for GIs (and oppose the 'GI extension')[100] in debates at the

94. Dongwei, *supra* n. 70.
95. *See* Yajun, *supra* n. 32, at 131; Sumin, *supra* n. 32, at 97; Chen Jintao, Xi TRIPS Xieyi yu Woguo Dili Biaozhi de Falu Baohu [TRIPS Agreement and Legal Protection of Geographical Indications in China], DANGDAI FAXUE [CONTEMPORARY LAW REVIEW], April 2003, 131.
96. WTO, *Review under Article 24.2 of the Application of the Provisions of the Section of the TRIPS Agreement on Geographical Indications*, IP/C/W/253/Rev.1 (24 November 2003).
97. Daniele Giovannucci et al., *Guide to Geographical Indications: Linking Products and Their Origins*, Organization for an International Geographical Indications Network (11 June 2021), https://www.origin-gi.com/images/stories/PDFs/English/E-Library/geographical_indications.pdf.
98. Jinkui, *supra* n. 46, at 91.
99. Felix Addor & Alexandra Grazioli, *Geographical Indications Beyond Wines and Spirits: A Roadmap for a Better Protection for Geographical Indications in the WTO TRIPS Agreement*, 5 J. World Intell. Prop. 865, 883 (2002); Jose Manuel Cortes Martin, *The WTO TRIPS Agreement: The Battle Between the Old and the New World over the Protection of Geographical Indications*, 7 J. World Intell. Prop. 287 (2004).
100. The term 'GI extension' refers to the attempt to extend to other products the higher level of protection for geographical indications beyond wines and spirits.

international level advocate the trademark regime as an appropriate means of protecting GIs at the national level. The underlying reason is that the endowment of traditional GIs is limited in New World nations and their companies would be threatened by a policy that gives GIs special status.[101] Why should China, with a rich variety of traditional localized products, follow the approach championed by New World countries such as the US, Australia, and Canada? Is such an approach really the best suited to China's national interests?[102]

In fact, due to the long-standing economic and cultural exchange between China and neighbouring countries or regions, the latter have imitated certain processing techniques used to produce China's local products. The imitation of techniques is accompanied by an imitation of original names for those products. In other words, traditional products originating in China are now imitated in neighbouring countries or regions, with the imitations called by the same names.[103] '*Shaoxing* Wine' provides a good illustration of this situation. In the 1950s, the migration of people from Mainland China to Taiwan due to the civil war between the Kuomintang and Communists brought demand for the drink and the technology used to make it. Emigrant populations quickly learned how to make a similar wine in Taiwan with familiar manufacturing techniques. The substitute drink was called by the familiar terminology '*Shaoxing*'.[104] It was reported in 2000 that two-thirds of the '*Shaoxing* Wine' sold in the world market was produced in Japan and Taiwan.[105] Therefore, China is experiencing 'another round of "Old World–New World" conflicts'.[106]

The battle between the Old and New worlds reminds us of the need to be cautious about the possible outcomes of GI protection approaches. The EU claimed that the problem of protecting their GIs at the international level was due to 'the lack of an appropriate level of protection' and 'the "sins" of the past'.[107] Presumably, the same is true for China, part of the 'Old World'. China's negotiating efforts at the WTO intended to improve the level of protection for GIs could benefit from national protection measures that provide a sufficient level of protection and allows earlier trademarks to be challenged by, or coexist with, subsequent GIs. However, we do not find it appropriate to craft such special measures under the trademark regime, which is bound by established doctrines such as 'the consumer confusion-based protection' and 'first in time, first in right'. This again touches upon the need to provide an enhanced

---

101. Lina Montén, *Geographical Indications of Origin: Should They Be Protected and Why: An Analysis of the Issue from the US and EU Perspectives*, 22 Santa Clara Computer & High Tech. L.J. 315 (2005).
102. Regarding the discussion on China's interests, *see* Chapter 7 *infra*.
103. Min-Chiuan Wang, *Asian Consciousness and Interests in Geographical Indications*, 96 Trademark Rep. 906, 932 (2006).
104. Li Houdun, TANFANG ZHONGGUO PUTAO JIUZHUANG [VISITING THE WINE VILLAGE OF CHINA], at 150 (Shanghai Scientific and Technical Press, 2012).
105. Mark J. Calaguas, *Rosé by Any Other Name: Protecting Geographical Indications for Wines and Spirits in China*, 3 Loy. U. Chi. Int'l L. Rev. 257, 278 (2006).
106. Wang, *supra* n. 103, at 932.
107. European Commission, *Why Do Geographical Indications Matter to Us?*, MEMO/03/160 (30 July 2003).

protection through sui generis GI protection, as will be unpacked further in the next chapter.[108]

In conclusion, the trademark approach is in the interests of New World countries.[109] It is highly questionable whether that approach would bring China more benefits. This offers more proof of the need to revise our understanding of the different approaches and their roles in China's GI industry.

§6.02 A CRITICAL ANALYSIS OF CRITICISMS OF THE EFFECTIVENESS OF CHINA'S SUI GENERIS SYSTEMS

It is worthwhile for China to use the experience of French sui generis GI regulations as a reference, not simply because France was the first country to implement such regulations but also because they are believed to have significantly contributed to the success of the French wine industry. However, what if the French wine industry were to encounter a major crisis? Critics might say, 'The French may not necessarily know which measures are the most suitable for protecting their GIs, and it is therefore premature to learn from the French experience and adopt AOC-type legislation.'[110] This criticism requires a response.

Like their French counterparts, Chinese *sui generis* systems – particularly the GI product system and the system for GIs for agricultural products – have always been suspected of being ineffective. Some accuse them of having caused 'institutional chaos'.[111] Nevertheless, this suspicion is not enough to justify the abandonment of the sui generis regime.

[A] About the Effectiveness of the French AOC Regime

The French wine industry was said to have again been in a state of crisis as this century began, just about one hundred years after the phylloxera crisis.[112] Faced with the rapid development of new vineyards (New World producers and new players like China and Brazil), the French industry has struggled to maintain its position as the top provider of wine.[113] Since 1999, French wine exports have been following a steep downward trend,

108. *See* Chapter 7 *infra*.
109. Dong Binghe, DILI BIAOZHI ZHISHI CHANQUAN ZHIDU YANJIU GOUJIAN YI LIYI FENXIANG WEI JICHU DE QUANLI TIXI [INTELLECTUAL PROPERTY SYSTEM OF GEOGRAPHICAL INDICATIONS CONSTRUCTING THE RIGHTS OF BENEFIT SHARING BASED SYSTEM] (China University of Political Science and Law Press, 2005).
110. Xiaomin, *supra* n. 8, 59.
111. Yao Fan, Yiyou Shangbiaofa You Lingjian Xin Guizhang Liangzhong Zhuce Qudao Weinan Quanliren [Existing Trademark Law and Other New Rules: Two Kinds of Registration Channels for Right Holders], FAZHI RIBAO [LEGAL DAILY], 5 August 2005.
112. *See* Chapter 1 *supra*.
113. Bernard Pomel, *Réussir l'avenir de la viticulture de France*, Vie publique (15 June 2021), https://www.vie-publique.fr/sites/default/files/rapport/pdf/064000298.pdf.

and national wine consumption has also dropped.[114] Though production also decreased, sales were still a problem due to the overproduction of wine.[115] Small vineyards have been hit particularly hard. Some of them are confronting bankruptcy.[116]

While the phylloxera crisis gave rise to the AOC system,[117] the latest crisis might put an end to it; the system is, in fact, believed to have helped provoke the crisis. The pre-2006 AOC system has been criticized for being too 'lenient' or 'permissive'.[118] First, the number of protected AOCs has been growing quickly over the last few decades.[119] The fact that so many products (not only wines) could claim to have AOC status meant that AOC lost its superiority for some,[120] who contend that the benefits of AOC protection were diminished through the increased number of AOCs protected.[121] Second, quality, which is meant to be a reflection of *terroir*, was not always guaranteed[122] for various reasons, including excessive laxity in monitoring, insufficient control of yields, and undue extensions of production areas.[123] Finally, many other

114. Paul Amadieu, Jean-Pierre Couderc & Jean-Laurent Viviani, *Financial Reaction to the Business Cycle in Periods of Difficulties: The Case of French Wine Companies, in Wine Economics: Quantitative Studies and Empirical Applications* 200 (Marie-Claude Pichery ed., Palgrave Macmillan 2013).
115. Tyler Colman, *Wine Politics: How Governments, Environmentalists, Mobsters, and Critics Influence the Wines We Drink* 64 (University of California Press 2008).
116. Frank J. Prial, *Much of Bordeaux Goes Begging* (N.Y. Times, 11 August 2004).
117. Alberto Alemanno & Enrico Bonadio, *The New Intellectual Property of Health: Beyond Plain Packaging* 286 (Edward Elgar Publishing 2016).
118. Andy Smith, Jacques de Maillard & Olivier Costa, *Vin et politique: Bordeaux, la France, la mondialisation*, Paris, Presses de Sciences Po, 2007, pp. 321-364; Mélanie Gros, *Les signes d'origine et de qualité des vins*, thèse, Université de Toulouse, 2009, pp. 115-125.
119. In 2004, Philippe Roudié noted that a substantial part (60 per cent) of French wines had AOC status, while only 8 per cent of Italian wines were sold under appellation. He commented: 'When all will belong to AOC, it (AOC) does not mean anything *(à partir du moment où tout sera en appellation, ça ne veut plus rien dire)* ... when the elite becomes the rule, what is elite? *(à partir du moment où l'élite devient la règle, qu'est-ce que c'est qu'une élite).' See* Chantal Crenn & Isabelle Techoueyres, *Vin et mondialisation, le point de vue d'un géographe: conversation avec Philippe Roudié, in Wine and Globalization*, para. 66 (Chantal Crenn ed., 2004).
120. Geneviève Teil, *The French Wine 'Appellations d'Origine Contrôlée' and the Virtues of Suspicion*, 13 J. World Intell. Prop. 253 (2010).
121. Ben Shepherd, *Costs and Benefits of Protecting Geographical Indications: Some Lessons from the French Wine Sector* 6 (European Centre for International Political Economy 2006).
122. In a survey published in 2007 by the consumer organization 'UFC-Que Choisir', seventy-five professionals from the field of AOC wine claimed that a third of French wines with AOC did not deserve this appellation because of the low-quality level and the lack of connection with the terroir. Likewise, a 2001 governmental report highlighted that 'under the big umbrella AOC, particularly under those that are most widely recognized, some (AOC) wines are average or even unfit for the appellation (*sous les grandes ombrelles que sont nos appellations d'origine contrôlée, surtout sous celles qui jouissent de la plus grande notoriété, s'abritent des vins moyens voire indignes de l'appellation*)'. *See Réforme des AOC viticoles: le tiers de la production doit sortir de l'appellation!*, Que Choisir (18 June 2021), https://www.quechoisir.org/action-ufc-que-choisir-reforme-des-aoc-viticoles-le-tiers-de-la-production-doit-sortir-de-l-appellation-n11953/; Jacques Berthomeau, *Comment mieux positionner les vins français sur les marchés d'exportation?*, Rapport remis à J. Glavany, ministre de l'agriculture et de la pêche, 2001.
123. *See Le salon des refusés*, L'Expressmag, 2839, 1er déc. 2005, p. 71: '*pour mentionner une appellation sur ses étiquettes, les vignerons doivent soumettre leur vin en cours d'élaboration à une dégustation collective, sous l'égide de l'Institut national des appellations contrôlées (INAO), qui en délègue l'organisation à un comité agréé, souvent un syndicat d'appellation, dont le jury*

indicators aside from AOC can be used to inform the consumer about the link with *terroir*, such as VDP and AOVDQS, not to mention the European titles QWpsr and WT. It is argued that consumers can be confused by them.[124]

The pre-2006 AOC system has also been criticized for being too 'strict' or 'constraining'.[125] The process of AOC recognition was accompanied by the establishment of a set of production methods in the *cahier des charges*, which cannot be changed without approval from the authorities. Critics have argued that this rigidity had prevented producers from adapting to changing technologies and consumer tastes.[126]

A number of AOC reform proposals for solving the crisis have been put on the table. These take two different positions, demanding either tighter rules or looser rules. The first option would be to 'tighten' the AOC system. Its advocates argue that the wine crisis occurred because the rules governing AOC were not strenuous enough. According to René Renou, former president of the committee of wines of the INAO, product differentiation based on the *terroir* was the right positioning for French wines to adopt to tackle the challenges arising from globalization.[127] Therefore, he claimed that compliance with stricter production conditions was at the root of the quality and competitive force of the *vigneron*. With this aim in mind, the INAO promoted reforms relating to the approval procedure (to assure batch traceability),[128] the monitoring of

est majoritairement composé des viticulteurs de l'appellation, à la fois juges et parties. Cette procédure très lourde aboutit à des aberrations: 98% des vins, y compris de bien mauvais, sont agréés'; *AOC: appellation d'origine contestée*, Le Guide du Nouvel observateur, 2000, p. 12: '*(les rendements) ... ne cessent d'augmenter depuis trente ans, au point d'être presque multipliés par deux*'.

124. Shepherd, *supra* n. 121, at 5.
125. Smith et al., *supra* n. 118, at 337; Gros, *supra* n. 118, at 125.
126. Shepherd, *supra* n. 121, at 14.
127. René Renou, *cité dans* L'avenir du Libournais, 23 mars 2001: '*Les vignerons français n'ont qu'une chance d'être compétitifs par rapport à ceux du Nouveau Monde, c'est de ne pas se situer sur les mêmes marchés qu'eux. Si je vends du vin de cépage chardonnay ou merlot, je dois lutter avec tous les chardonnay et merlot du monde, presque tous moins chers et dont certains sont aussi bons que les vins français. En revanche, si je vends du Chablis ou du Bordeaux, le client étranger ne les retrouvera que chez moi, et pratiquement à mes conditions.*'
128. Arrêté du 7 décembre 2001 relatif aux examens analytique et organoleptique pour les vins à appellation d'origine contrôlée à l'exception des vins mousseux et pétillants, J.O. du 9 déc. 2001, p. 19619, Article 2: '*Pour l'obtention du certificat d'agrément prévu par le décret du 7 décembre 2001 susvisé, chaque producteur de vins effectue auprès des services de l'Institut national des appellations d'origine, dans un délai fixé par le règlement intérieur, une demande de certificat d'agrément. La demande de certificat d'agrément indique notamment: l'appellation revendiquée; le volume de vin pour lequel est demandé le certificat d'agrément ainsi que la surface correspondante si cette dernière n'est pas exigée dans la déclaration de récolte; le numéro EVV (entreprise vitivinicole); le nom et l'adresse du demandeur; le lieu d'entrepôt du vin et le lieu de vinification si celui-ci est différent. Pour être recevable, cette demande est accompagnée notamment de: une copie de la déclaration de récolte et, selon le cas, une copie de la déclaration de fabrication ou d'un extrait de la comptabilité matières pour les acheteurs de raisins et de moûts; une déclaration d'encépagement ou de modification d'encépagement validée par la direction générale des douanes et des droits indirects (DGDDI) dans le cas où l'encépagement de l'exploitation tel qu'enregistré dans le casier viticole informatisé (CVI) n'est pas à jour; un titre de paiement représentant le montant de la cotisation dû au titre de l'article L. 641-10 du code rural et du droit dû au titre de l'article L. 641-8 du code rural. La demande de certificat d'agrément est non recevable en cas de non-respect de la réglementation vitivinicole, et notamment d'une condition de production de l'appellation d'origine revendiquée.*'

compliance with the production conditions laid down in the *cahier des charges* (to ensure a more precise follow-up of production),[129] and the creation of a new category of AOC, the AOCE (*Appellation d'Origine Contrôlée d'Excellence*) with the maximum level of constraint (to establish stricter production criteria for the link to *terroir*).[130]

The second option constitutes a departure from the *terroir* logic. As the relation to history and *terroir* was considered to have hindered the necessary adaptation to new global competition, the alternative strategy proposed a relaxation of the *terroir*-based AOC rules that were, according to its advocates, no longer necessary or even harmful.[131] For instance, it was proposed to allow the use of wood chips (*copeaux de bois*) in winemaking in order to add oak flavour (*boiser*) to the wine and thus satisfy consumer tastes without incurring high investment costs.[132] However, some believe that this practice is 'a trick which masks the taste of *terroir*'.[133]

Although the solution will involve difficult choices, it is very unlikely that France would abandon its most potent weapon: the *terroir* (provenance, traditional *savoir-faire*, and distinctive quality). The reforms undertaken since 2006 show that policy-makers have chosen to redesign, rather than discard, the *terroir*-based schemes by improving efficiency through consolidation as well as reducing complexity.

The 2006 AOC reform aimed at helping AOC to restore its credibility as an indicator of both origin and quality. It introduced an additional layer of control: external control by the independent *organisme de contrôle* (OC). Some argue that only when monitoring practices are carried out by an independent body can the monitoring system be fully credible.[134] However, quality requires guarantees 'whose credibility required guarantees that again required new guarantees'.[135] Thus, the proper functioning of the OC should also be guaranteed. For this reason, the OC must not only be accredited by the COFRAC on the basis of its competence, impartiality, and independence but must also be approved by the INAO. The monitoring plan according to which the external control is performed must be approved by the INAO. The INAO should be able to assess the functioning conditions of the OC, the regularity of its activities, and

129. Décret n° 2002-1325 du 5 novembre 2002 relatif aux conditions de production et au rendement des vignobles produisant des vins à appellation d'origine contrôlée, J.O. du 6 nov. 2002, p. 18337, Article 11: '*Les services de l'Institut national des appellations d'origine, ladite commission technique, de façon concomitante ou séparément, peuvent examiner par parcelle les conditions de production définies pour l'appellation d'origine contrôlée concernée et l'état cultural global de la vigne, notamment son état sanitaire et l'entretien de son sol, et apprécier sa production potentielle de raisins au regard du rendement agronomique maximum à la parcelle prévu à l'article 10 du présent décret.*'
130. This proposal was rejected. *See* Marie-France Garcia-Parpet, *Le marché de l'excellence: le classement des grands crus à l'épreuve de la mondialisation*, Genèses, n° 56, 2004, p. 72.
131. Yves Bénard, *cité dans* L'avenir du Libournais, 23 mars 2001: '*Notre système est sclérosé là où le Nouveau Monde est en train de faire preuve de sa réussite pour n'avoir pas de contraintes historiques dans lesquelles nous sommes enfermés.*'
132. Smith et al., *supra* n. 118, at 340.
133. *Copeaux de chêne dans le vin*, La Revue du vin de France (18 May 2021), https://www.larvf.com/,video-vin-copeaux-de-chene-arome-boise,10366,4022974.asp.
134. Nuria Ackermann & Fabio Russo, *Adding Value to Traditional Products of Regional Origin: A Guide to Creating a Quality Consortium* 38 (United Nations Industrial Development Organization 2010).
135. Teil, *supra* n. 120.

the effectiveness of its controls.[136] Based on the assessment, approval to carry out monitoring practices could be withdrawn.[137] The introduction of an independent control body and a 'control of control' process would contribute to the overall credibility of the AOC system.

Other reforms have reduced the complexity of the various GI schemes and labelling terms. At the EU-wide level, the distinction between QWpsr and TW has disappeared. A new scheme has been established around 'wines with GIs', which in turn can be further divided into PDO and PGI. Nationally, diverse wine categories have been simplified by removing AOVDQS[138] and VDP[139] in 2007 and 2009, respectively.

Although the long-term effects of those reforms on the French wine industry require further study, at least two conclusions can now be drawn from them. First, like any other system, the AOC system is effective only if properly designed. Its effectiveness does not simply depend on its sui generis status. A sui generis system will be a good tool for GIs not simply because it is sui generis; its design must allow it to be effective. Second, building and maintaining an effective system demand constant change. The system must be constantly adapted to changing circumstances. This need was at the origin of the successive reforms that have tried to solve the French wine crisis. Despite those changes, the sui generis approach has not been abandoned, as the concept of *terroir* is still viewed as a powerful weapon.

It is useful to look at the lessons that China and other countries can learn from the AOC reforms. In order to design an appropriate legal framework for GIs, careful consideration must be given to key issues, such as the importance of *terroir* to China's agricultural products and the characteristics of the sui generis framework and trademark law. Those questions will be explored in the following chapters.[140]

[B] About the Effectiveness of China's GI Regime

The sui generis regime is a relative latecomer to China. The GI product system was not introduced until 1999, while the trademark system provided protection (collective and certification marks) for GIs starting in 1995. Since the introduction of the sui generis system, its effectiveness has been the subject of considerable criticism. It is criticized for being either a root cause of conflicts (i.e., between the former AQSIQ and the Trademark Office, particularly regarding rights owners and permitted users) or a duplication of effort (i.e., rendering decisions that are largely identical or only slightly different).[141]

---

136. Article R. 642-48 C. rur.
137. Article R. 642-49 C. rur.
138. Loi n° 2007-1821 du 24 décembre 2007 ratifiant l'ordonnance n° 2006-1547 du 7 décembre 2006 relative à la valorisation des produits agricoles, forestiers ou alimentaires et des produits de la mer, J.O. du 27 déc. 2007, p. 21210.
139. Loi n° 2009-526 du 12 mai 2009 de simplification et de clarification du droit et d'allègement des procédures, J.O. du 13 mai 2009, p. 7920.
140. *See* Chapter 7 *infra*.
141. Xiaodong & Weiming, *supra* n. 32, p. 172; Fan, *supra* n. 111; Zhang Jin & Dong Fang, Dili Biaozhi de Guoji Baohu ji Woguo Baohu zhong Cunzai de Wenti [The International Protection

As the conflict regarding rights was considered in the previous chapter,[142] only the inconvenience that the duplicated protection has caused will be addressed here. With the intervention of the MOA, there are three main parallel systems for the protection of GIs. This situation creates confusion among producers regarding which system should be chosen to register GIs. Finding a more suitable choice requires extensive market research and legal analysis of all the complex GI schemes. Producers may lose market opportunities while seeking the best choice for their products.[143] The most common alternative is to register a single GI under two or three systems, which results in duplicated administrative tasks and increased operating costs for enterprises.[144]

The duplicated protection also creates confusion among consumers. Three GI systems all have their own GI definitions and official logos for publicizing GI status. Certain professionals working in the GI field cannot even tell the difference, let alone average consumers.[145] In some cases, producers register the GI under one regime but use an official logo from another.[146]

It appears that none of these protection mechanisms can provide an efficient way of guaranteeing a product's authenticity. This can be illustrated by the different and even contradictory understandings in the media about what an authentic product should correspond to. For instance, both '*Zhenjiang* Vinegar' and '*Wuchang* Rice' are GIs protected under more than two systems. About '*Zhenjiang* Vinegar', a journalist pointed out that only products with the collective mark were authentic, while another reporter commented on the authenticity of '*Wuchang* Rice' and recommended the former AQSIQ's logo as a reliable quality identifier.[147]

Although the inefficiency is undeniable, it should be emphasized that the sui generis regime, the latecomer, should not be made a scapegoat. As the inefficiency is caused by the duplicated effort, the solution lies in structuring those efforts better. In

---

of Geographical Indications and the Problems in the Protection of China], ZHONGGUO ZHISHI CHANQUAN BAO [CHINA INTELLECTUAL PROPERTY NEWS], 22 May 2001.

142. *See* Chapter 5 *supra*.
143. Wang Miao, Dili Biaozhi yu Shangbiaoquan de Chongtu Jiqi Falu Xietiao [The Conflict Between Geographical Indication and Trademark Right and Its Legal Coordination], CHANGCHUN SHIFAN DAXUE XUEBAO [JOURNAL OF CHANGCHUN NORMAL UNIVERSITY], July 2005, 112-115.
144. Zeng Deguo & Ye Peiyin, Woguo Dili Biaozhi Baohu he Fazhan de Nandian ji Duice [Difficulties and Countermeasures of the Protection and Development of Geographical Indications in China], ANHUI NONGYE DAXUE XUEBAO [JOURNAL OF ANHUI AGRICULTURAL UNIVERSITY], March 2015, 43.
145. *Ibid.*
146. Li Cheng, Zuohao Dili Biaozhi Gongzuo Tuidong Zhuanyong Biaozhi Shiyong Zhongguo Dili Biaozhi Chanpin Zhuanyong Biaozhi Shiyong Jingyan Jiaoliu Zuotanhui Zongshu [A Summary of the Exchange of Experience in the Use of Official Logos for Geographical Indications in China], GONGSHANG XINGHENG GUANLI [INDUSTRIAL AND COMMERCIAL ADMINISTRATION], July 2012, 17.
147. *See* Han Fei, Zhenjiang Xiangcu Jiangyou Shenfenzheng Sun Tian Xiang Gongyi Xieru Fagui [Zhenjiang Vinegar Will Have the 'Identity Card' and Sour Sweet and Fragrance Process Will be Written in the Legislation], YANGZI WANBAO [YANGTZE EVENING], 26 July 2016; Qiang Yong, Harbin Yanda Jia Wuchang Dami Zhengfu Guanwang Jiang Jizhong Zhanshi [Harbin Combats Counterfeiting of Wuchang Rice], XINHUA WANG [XINHUA NEWS], 24 October 2015.

other words, if the sui generis regime proves to be a more useful tool and a necessity for China's GIs, the role of the trademark regime must be adjusted accordingly and be made to be complementary. Contrariwise, if the trademark regime proves to be more useful, then there is no reason to give the latecomer a warm welcome. It is thus necessary to determine which regime better suits China's needs.

To conclude this chapter, we have undertaken an analysis of whether the criticisms of China's sui generis regime are justified. The analysis has focused on the issues most frequently raised by critics: necessity, cost, the nature of GIs, common practice, and effectiveness.

Our goal is not to provide definitive answers to all these issues, which may go beyond the scope of this chapter. Moreover, there may be no simple, non-controversial answers. What we find is that the critics' responses to the issues do not demonstrate that the trademark regime is sufficient for the protection of GIs; thus, China should abandon the European approach to establishing a *sui generis* regime.

However, our findings in this chapter do not lead to the conclusion that there is a need to establish or give preference to a sui generis regime. This need depends on other considerations (e.g., the consumption habits of Chinese consumers). At the very least, however, we can conclude that the criticisms of China's sui generis regime are unjustified and that further discussion on which approach should be taken (trademark or sui generis) is required.

The adoption of the EU approach to sui generis GI protection is currently mired in problems caused by competition from the trademark approach and mired in arguments as to why the EU approach should be adopted in China and why sui generis systems should function as the main instrument of GI protection in China. The sui generis regime is losing the battle against the trademark regime, in terms of both decisions concerning rightful users and conditions for use as well as external attractiveness to target audiences (as the number of GI registrations under the trademark regime is growing more rapidly). It is also suspected of wasting administrative resources, creating conflicts, and causing the whole GI scheme to be ineffective.

These two factors are tightly linked. Suspicions of the sui generis approach are impeding legislative progress concerning it, which has led to a significant competitive disadvantage against the trademark regime. Since, as we have seen, these suspicions are unfounded, the status quo of China's GI protection should not be the preferred option (Chapter 7).

CHAPTER 7

Benefits of Adopting the European Sui Generis Approach in China

China's sui generis and trademark systems are used as the main instruments for the protection of GIs. To achieve a coherent framework that delivers effective support to GIs, China is faced with the choice of either following the European approach and strengthening the role of China's sui generis GI systems or following the US approach and strengthening the role of trademark system and eliminating the sui generis systems. This chapter shows the need to reform China's legal framework for GIs by strengthening the sui generis systems. A practical and economic analysis is carried out comparing the sui generis and trademark systems in terms of their estimated benefits to producers, consumers, rural development, and traditional knowledge. We conclude that choosing the sui generis regime as the main mechanism for the protection of GIs would be the best option for China.

Chapters 5 and 6 have illustrated the irreconcilability between China's sui generis GI systems and trademark system, both of which are used as the main instruments of GI protection. This practice shows that 'one plus one does not always equal two'. Adopting the EU and US approaches to regulate the same field impairs the effectiveness of both. What is needed is a coherent framework that delivers effective support to GIs.

If it were true that the trademark system is sufficient for effectively protecting GIs, there would be no need for sui generis systems. To achieve a coherent approach to GI protection, China is faced with the choice of either eliminating the sui generis systems or strengthening them by preventing the trademark system from running a similar, competing regime and making them more harmonized, effective, and operational.

Thus, Chinese legislators must choose one, and only one. This choice involves the question of whether there should be a special mechanism tailored to the unique attributes of GIs (§7.02). This in turn raises another fundamental question: do China's products possess attributes that are so unique that the trademark regime cannot cater to them? (§7.01)

§7.01 A DIMINUTION OF THE ROLE OF THE TRADEMARK REGIME

It should be recalled that the difference between the sui generis approach propounded by the EU and the trademark approach championed by the United States lies in whether the concept of *terroir* is taken as the foundation of GI regulation measures.[1]

Therefore, we must not lose sight of the fact that China has an abundance of products whose characteristics are closely linked to the *terroir* in a specific area. However, the trademark regime is inadequate for adding value to *terroir* products or providing suitable responses to several issues related to their protection. The regime should thus not remain the primary instrument for protecting GIs.

[A] China's Interest in Protecting GIs

Chinese commentators generally recognize the importance of taking into account national conditions while designing rules and policies around GIs.[2] A critical aspect of China's conditions is that many Chinese products have a *terroir* dimension, which affects Chinese consumers' purchase decisions and has a positive impact on their willingness to pay for those products.

[1] Abundance of Terroir Products in China

As Elizabeth Barham observes, '*Terroir* is a French word without a suitable English translation.'[3] It cannot be easily translated into Chinese either. However, this does not mean that Chinese products do not reflect *terroir* attributes.

The EU-China GI Agreement concluded in 2019 might serve as an illustration of an element of *terroir* in Chinese agricultural products and foodstuff.[4] Briefly stated, this

---

1. *See* Chapter 6 *supra*.
2. Zhao Xiaoping, ZHONGGUO NONGCHANPIN DILI BIAOZHI FALU BAOHU YANJIU [GEOGRAPHICAL INDICATION PROTECTION OF AGRICULTURAL PRODUCTS IN CHINA], at 131 (Shanxi People's Publishing House, 2012); Tian Furong, DILI BIAOZHI FALU BAOHU ZHIDU YANJIU [LEGAL PROTECTION OF GEOGRAPHICAL INDICATIONS], at 280 (Intellectual Property Publishing House, 2009).
3. Elizabeth Barham, *Translating Terroir: The Global Challenge of French AOC Labeling*, 19 J. Rural Stud. 127 (2003).
4. The cooperation between the EU and China on the mutual recognition of GIs started from the '10 plus 10 project', followed in 2017 by a '100 plus 100 project'. The '10 plus 10 project' allows ten European product names to be registered under China's 'GI product' regime established by the former AQSIQ. The ten European names are *Comté, Grana Padano, Priego de Córdoba, Prosciutto di Parma, Pruneaux d'Agen/Pruneaux d'Agen mi-cuits, Roquefort, Scottish Farmed Salmon, Sierra Mágina, West Country Farmhouse Cheddar* and *White Stilton Cheese/Blue Stilton Cheese*. The ten Chinese names that have been added to the EU GI register are *Pinggu Da Tao* (peach), *Yancheng Long Xia* (crayfish), *Zhenjiang Xiang Cu* (rice vinegar), *Dongshan Bai Lu Sun* (asparagus), *Jinxiang Da Suan* (garlic), *Longjing cha* (tea), *Guanxi Mi You* (honey pomelo), *Shaanxi ping guo* (apple), *Lixian Ma Shan Yao* (yam) and *Longkou Fen Si* (vermicelli/noodles). *See* European Commission, *EU-China Geographical Indications: '10 Plus 10' Project Is Now Complete*, Press Release (30 November 2012); European Commission, *100 European Geographical Indications Set to Be Protected in China*, Press Release (2 June 2017).

agreement ensured protection for several EU GIs in China, while the same number of Chinese food names receive protected status in the EU as PDO or PGI.[5]

The PDO concept is closely related to that of AOC, and the philosophy behind PDO regulation is *terroir*, aimed at protecting a unique product that is demonstrably connected with and influenced by a specific geographical area.[6] If Chinese products can be protected as a PDO, their *terroir* attributes will be proven.

Longjing tea, which obtained PDO registration, can be taken as a case study to analyse the importance of *terroir* in this product.[7] The tea's distinctive characteristics are its green colour, rich aroma, sweet aftertaste, and attractive appearance.[8] Those features depend on, first, the biophysical elements of the locality (e.g., microclimate, soil, geology).[9] Although the farming and roasting skills needed to produce the tea can be replicated in many places other than the original locality, the difference in taste and quality is significant. Tea experts believe that the physical elements in the West Lake region make it the most suitable area for growing *Longjing* and that they have a significant impact on quality.[10] For this reason, regardless of the fact that a substantial number of tea makers in *Yunnan* and *Guizhou* are using similar skills and producing similar tea, the Chinese government defines authentic *Longjing* by reference to a demarcated area: only those teas produced in three areas (*Xihu*, *Qiantang*, and *Yuezhou*) are eligible to be labelled as *Longjing* tea.[11] Any tea sharing the same seedling and roasting techniques but produced outside the three areas will be considered counterfeit if it is labelled as *Longjing*. It can be seen that the physical aspect of *terroir* is the backbone of this tea.

As stated in Chapter 1, *terroir* encompasses not only physical aspects but also human contributions (production, manufacture techniques, *savoir-faire* arising out of

5. *Agreement Between the European Union and the Government of the People's Republic of China on Cooperation on, and Protection of, Geographical Indications*, OJ L 408I, 4.12.2020, p. 3, Article 1.
6. *See* Laurence Bérard & Marchenay Philippe, *From Localized Products to Geographical Indications*, CNRS (18 June 2021), https://www.ethno-terroirs.cnrs.fr/IMC/pdf/Localized_Products_to_GI.pdf.
7. Selina Ching Chan, *Terroir and Green Tea in China: The Case of Meijiawu Dragon Well (Longjing) Tea, in Geographical Indications and International Agricultural Trade: The Challenge for Asia* 226 (Louis Augustin-Jean ed., Palgrave Macmillan 2012).
8. *Publication of an application pursuant to Article 6(2) of Council Regulation (EC) No 510/2006 on the protection of geographical indications and designations of origin for agricultural products and foodstuffs*, OJ C 254, 22.9.2010, p. 6.
9. The growing regions of Longjing are mainly in the basins of the *Qiantang* River and *Cao'e* River, with many mountains, hills, rivers and lakes. *Xihu* and *Qiandao* lakes are in this area, as are *Tianmu* and *Kuaiji* Mountains. It has a typical mild subtropical monsoon climate, with four distinct seasons. It has warm and humid air and plentiful rainfall. All of this makes for good natural conditions with an optimized combination of climate, soil, water and vegetation, beneficial to the growth of tea trees. They provide a good and stable ecological environment for the physiological process and the substance metabolism of bud-leaves, which is conducive to the formation and accumulation of nitrogen compounds including amino acids and aromatic substances. *See Ibid.*
10. *See* Chan, *supra* n. 7, at 230.
11. Guojia Zhiliang Jiandu Jianyan Jianyi Zongju Gonggao 2001 Nian di 28 Hao [State General Administration of Quality Supervision, Inspection and Quarantine Announcement No. 28, 2001], 26 October 2001.

the interaction between inhabitants and their environment).[12] *Savoir-faire* (e.g., picking, slight withering, cooling, moisturizing) is essential in the processing of *Longjing* tea.[13] There is also a cultural aspect, as the roasting production technique was listed in 2008 as a Chinese national-level ICH.[14] Zhou Enlai, the first Premier of China, explained the importance of production techniques to a foreign visitor: 'the tea processing of Longjing is an *artwork* that guarantees the colour, taste and appearance'.[15] It follows that the combination of the natural, human, and even cultural elements in the locality makes up the unique characteristics of *Longjing* tea. The *terroir* dimension is thus evident.

Several Chinese products have been registered as PGI. The PGI definition treats 'reputation' as being equally significant for protection as product 'quality' and 'other characteristics'. However, this does not imply that those PGI products are only reputation-based, without any *terroir* dimension. They do reflect the concept of *terroir* but a 'loosening' interpretation of it.[16] Taking *Zhenjiang* vinegar (a registered PGI) as an example, the fact that *Zhenjiang* City is renowned as the 'Home of Vinegar' is not a coincidence. The humid monsoon climate in Zhenjiang helps the yield and reproduction of acetic acid bacteria. Water from hills and springs produces a rich content of mineral materials, which leads to a strong and slightly sweet flavour.[17] While the soil and climate factors make the place suitable for brewing vinegar, the use of traditional methods in the fermentation of brewing mass, the extraction of the vinegar, and the steaming and storage/maturing of the raw vinegar[18] creates the conditions that permit the geographical resources to express themselves. Those traditional methods form an integral part of *terroir* and have helped to build the reputation of the products for which the term is registered.

The Chinese products protected as European PDO or PGI serve as a showcase to the outside world proving that products from China can be *terroir*-based. However, they are not the only Chinese goods that can benefit from GI protection. The EU-China GI Agreement of 2019 opens a path for other Chinese products to be added to the

12. *See also* Bronwyn Parry, *Geographical Indications: Not All 'Champagne and Roses', in Trade Marks and Brands: An Interdisciplinary Critique* 361 (Lionel AF Bently et al. eds, Cambridge University Press 2008).
13. *See Publication of an application pursuant to Article 6(2) of Council Regulation (EC) No 510/2006, supra* n. 8.
14. Guowuyuan Guanyu Gongbu Dierpi Guojiaji Feiwuzhi Wenhua Yichan Minglu he Diyipi Guojiaji Feiwuzhi Wenhua Yichan Kuozhan Xiangmu Minglu de Tongzhi [Notice of the State Council on Announcing the List of the Second Batch of National Intangible Cultural Heritage and the Extension of the First Batch of National Intangible Cultural Heritage], 7 June 2008.
15. Chen Lisha, Hangzhou Jiushisi Sui Dangyuan Yi Zhou Enlai Heying Cunmin Zhan Zhongjian Zongli Zhan Pangbian [Hangzhou 94-Year-Old Party Member Recalled Zhou Enlai], Zhongxin Net (19 May 2021), https://www.chinanews.com/gn/2016/07-23/7949483.shtml.
16. *See also* Irene Calboli, *Geographical Indications in the Global Arena: Observations and Recent Developments, in Geographical Indications: Global and Local Perspectives* 176 (Jacques de Werra ed., Schulthess Éditions Romandes 2016).
17. *See Publication of an application pursuant to Article 6(2) of Council Regulation (EC) No 510/2006, supra* n. 8, para. 5.3.
18. Zhenjiang Xiangcu Baohu Tiaoli [Ordinance on the Protection of Zhenjiang Vinegar], 29 July 2016.

Annexes of the Agreement and thus obtain GI status in the EU.[19] Furthermore, according to the Beijing *Zhongjun Shiji* GI Research Team, 8,421 GIs had been registered in China by the end of 2020,[20] which is more than twice the number of GIs registered in the EU.[21] Thus, it is reasonable to conclude that China has an abundant wealth of GI resources that have been, or have the potential to be, protected under a classification/certification system inextricably linked with the French concept of *terroir*.

[2] A Deeply Rooted Terroir Philosophy in the Minds of Chinese Consumers

Most Chinese consumers probably do not know the word '*terroir*', but they would not consider the idea alien. This idea, though conveyed by a French expression, is embedded in Chinese culture and customs. Since as early as 2000 B.C., the Chinese have relied upon the place of origin as a means of judging the quality of agri-food products. They believe that agri-food products planted in certain locales possess unique natural qualities, which contribute to medicinal properties, personal health, and disease prevention.[22] Many localized foods thus form a basis of Chinese 'food therapy'.[23]

Not surprisingly, the idea has long been appreciated in the field of traditional Chinese medicine (TCM).[24] It is captured by the Chinese expression '*Daodi Yaocai*' ('Geo-authentic Crude Drugs'). China's Food and Drug Administration defined this in 2002 as 'traditional Chinese crude drugs with specific germ plasma, production sites, or with specific production techniques and processing methods'.[25] Recent publications tend to elaborate on a definition that more closely resembles that of GIs.[26] For instance,

19. EU-China GI Agreement, Article 3.
20. *See* Beijing Zhongjun Shiji GI Research Group, Di Sici Quanguo Dili Biaozhi Diaoyan Baogao [Report on the Fourth Survey of China's Geographical Indications], 9 September 2020.
21. Over 3300 geographical indications have been registered in the European Union. *See* European Commission, *EU-China Agreement Protecting Geographical Indications Enters into Force,* Press Release (1 March 2021).
22. Ping Zou, *Traditional Chinese Medicine, Food Therapy, and Hypertension Control: A Narrative Review of Chinese Literature,* 44 Am. J. Chinese Med. 1579 (2016).
23. Xing Zhao, Donald Finlay & Moya Kneafsey, *The Effectiveness of Contemporary Geographical Indications (GIs) Schemes in Enhancing the Quality of Chinese Agrifoods: Experiences from the Field,* 36 J. Rural Stud. 77 (2014).
24. Sun Zhiguo et al., Sichuansheng Daodi Yaocai Lei Guojia Dili Biaozhi Chanpin de Baohu Fenxi [Protection Situation of National Products of Geographical Indication of Geo-authentic Crude Drugs in Sichuan Province], XINAN NONGYE XUEBAO [SOUTHWEST CHINA JOURNAL OF AGRICULTURE], April 2010, 532.
25. Good Agricultural Practice for Chinese Crude Drugs (interim), Article 55 (2002).
26. *See* Sun Zhiguo et al., Anhuisheng Daodi Yaocai Lei Guojia Dili Biaozhi Chanpin de Baohu Xianzhuang ji Duice [Protection Situation and Countermeasures of National Geographical Indication Products of Genuine Medicinal Materials in Anhui Province], ANHUI NONGYE KEXUE [JOURNAL OF ANHUI AGRICULTURAL SCIENCES], May 2010, 7353-7355; Liu Lihe, Daodi Yaocai de Dili Biaozhi Baohu [The Geographical Mark Protection of Genuine Medical Materials], NANHUA DAXUE XUEBAO [JOURNAL OF UNIVERSITY OF SOUTH CHINA], April 2009, 64.

Zhao Zhongzhen described '*Daodi* medicinal material' as 'medicinal material that is produced and assembled in specific geographic regions with designated natural conditions and ecological environment, with particular attention to cultivation technique, harvesting and processing'.[27]

The TCM theory considers geo-authentic crude drugs superior in terms of quality and clinical effect to the same species produced in other regions. Qian Xinzhong, a former Minister of Health, stressed that 'we would rather respect *Daodi* crude drugs in a specific region than induce the herd to other regions blindly'.[28] The underlying aim is the preservation of medicine quality that is regarded as being linked to a given place. Thus, it is no wonder that Western scholars put the *Daodi* concept on an equal footing with the French *terroir* concept.[29]

'*Daodi*' as a term was officially recorded in the *Collected Essentials of Species of Materia Medica* during the Ming Dynasty (1505). This concept soon took root in the minds of the Chinese and began appearing in their literary works.[30] The number of species of *Daodi* crude drugs is estimated to be between 300 and 400.[31] Many names are well-known to Chinese consumers, such as '*Huai* (located in Henan province) *Dihuang* (Rehmannia glutinosa)', '*Chuan* (Sichuan province) *Lian* (Rhizoma coptidis)' and '*Ningxia* (an autonomous region of China) *Gouqi* (Lycium barbarum)'.[32]

Having established that a concept similar to *terroir* has existed throughout China's history, it is necessary to take a closer look into the contemporary consumer's perception of the concept. The extent to which producers can obtain a price premium depends on the consumer's behaviour in response to *terroir*-based labels and marketing strategies.[33] Simply put, at issue is whether the concept affects Chinese consumers' purchase decisions.

As Wang Xiaobing points out in his article comparing GI protection in the EU and China, general consumer awareness of GI labels is low in China: 'Most Chinese consumers are accustomed to being guided and give preference to famous brands and trademarks.'[34] Empirical research conducted in recent years has confirmed this low

27. Zhao Zhongzhen et al., *The Formation of Daodi Medicinal Materials*, 48 J. Ethnopharmacology 476 (2012).
28. Hu Shilin, ZHONGGUO DAODI YAOCAI [CHINESE GENUINE MEDICAL MATERIALS], at Foreword Page (Heilongjiang Science and Technology Press, 1989).
29. *See* Josef A. Brinckmann, *Geographical Indications for Medicinal Plants: Globalization, Climate Change, Quality and Market Implications for Geo-authentic Botanicals*, 1 World J. Traditional Chinese Med. 16 (2015).
30. *See* Shilin, *supra* n. 28, at 3.
31. *See* Wang Qiang & Xu Guojun, DAODI YAOCAI TUDIAN [THE DICTIONARY OF GEO-AUTHENTIC CRUDE DRUGS] (Fujian science and Technology Press, 2003).
32. Song Xiaoting, ZHONGGUO DAODI YAOCAI DE ZHISHI CHANQUAN BAOHU [INTELLECTUAL PROPERTY PROTECTION OF CHINA'S GEO-AUTHENTIC CRUDE DRUGS], at 5 (Intellectual Property Press, 2014).
33. *See* Marianna Bicskei et al., *Reform Proposals on the Geographical Indications of the European Union for the Protection of Traditional Knowledge*, 3 WIPO J. 222 (2012).
34. Wang Xiaobing & Irina Kireeva, *The Protection of Geographical Indication in the EU and China: Tracing Causes of Delays in the Ongoing Negotiation on the Co-operative Agreement on Geographical Indications*, 2 Intell. Prop. Q. 125 (2014).

level of general awareness.[35] However, a wide range of individual GI-denominated products are renowned among and consumed by Chinese consumers. One can purchase a GI product without knowing either the legally binding definition of GIs or the product's GI status.[36] In this case, it is the reputation of individual GI products (rather than the reputation of GIs in general) that generates a favourable attitude among consumers. This reputation, in turn, depends essentially on the quality and, more importantly, the particular characteristics of the product. As the latter is due essentially to the place of origin (*terroir*), it is ultimately on *terroir* that the product's reputation is based. Briefly stated, in the absence of adequate general awareness of GIs, *terroir* can still have an impact on consumers' willingness to pay for GI products.

If it is true that 'commercial imitation is a particularly costly form of flattery',[37] the reputation that individual GI products enjoy can be partially measured by the number of infringement cases involving those seeking to profit from that reputation. From 2010 to 2015, more than 1,000 such cases were investigated and dealt with by the local authorities of the former SAIC.[38] These data do not represent the whole GI infringement market, since the former SAIC is not the only authority responsible for investigations, and some infringements could have gone unnoticed.[39] Nevertheless, they support the argument that *terroir* plays a role in generating added value for products. No one is willing to imitate the name of a little-known rock in the centre of the *Gobi* desert, especially considering the legal sanctions of such behaviour. A GI product's name will be imitated only if the name (often a place name) can serve as an indication of the quality and/or other characteristics and may influence consumer choices.

35. *See* Shang Xudong et al., Xiaofeizhe Dui Dili Biaozhi Nongchanpin Zhifu Yiyuan de Shizheng Fenxi [An Analysis of Payment Intention of Consumers to Geographical Indication Agricultural Products], JISHU JINGJI YU GUANLI YANJIU [JOURNAL OF TECHNICAL ECONOMICS & MANAGEMENT], January 2014, 123-128; Yang Jianhui & Ren Jianlan, Xiaofeizhe dui Nongchanpin Dili Biaozhi Renzhi de Pingjia ji Yingxiang Yinsu Fenxi [Analysis of Consumers' Recognition of Geographical Indications of Agricultural Products and Influence Factors], DIAOYAN SHIJIE [THE WORLD OF SURVEY & RESEARCH], January 2015, 19-23; Hao Jianqiang et al., Xiaofeizhe Dui Nongchanpin Dili Biaozhi Renzhidu he Goumai Xingwei de Fenxi [Analysis of Consumers' Recognition and Purchase Behavior of Geographical Indications of Agricultural Products], NONGCHANPIN ZHILIANG YU ANQUAN [QUALITY AND SAFETY OF AGRO-PRODUCTS], August 2012, 18-21.
36. A case study on the consumers' purchase intention to the GI product 'Anxi Tieguanyin Tea' indicates that, among a sample of 447 consumers, 80 per cent have consumed the tea, and 78 per cent have purchased it, whereas only 53 per cent have heard of the GI concept. This means that a large number of consumers bought the GI product without knowing its legal status. *See* Wang Qiangcai, Xiaofeizhe dui Dili Biaozhi Chanpin de Goumai Yiyuan ji Yingxiang Yinsu Yanjiu Yi Anxi Tieguanyin Weili [An Analysis of Consumers' Purchase Intention to Geographical Indication Products and Influencing Factors: Taking Anxi Tieguanyin Tea as an Example], Dissertation, Fuzhou University, 2014, p. 32.
37. James Ming Chen, *A Sober Second Look at Appellations of Origin: How the United States Will Crash France's Wine and Cheese Party*, 5 Minn. J. Global Trade 29, 63 (1996).
38. *See* China National Intellectual Property Administration, Zhongguo Zhishi Chanquan Baohu Zhuangkuang [Intellectual Property Protection in China], 2010-2015.
39. The former AQSIQ, the Ministry of Agriculture, and holders of GI labels can also take action for infringement. The cases brought by them are not included in the data mentioned above.

Perhaps the best evidence of how the *terroir* concept functions among Chinese consumers can be found in the marketing of Bordeaux wine in China. When the wine was introduced in China, the *Union des Grands Crus de Bordeaux* organized advertising and promotion activities aiming at selling both the *terroir* product (the wine) and the *terroir* concept. It educated Chinese consumers about the linkage between the wine's quality and place of origin and, in doing so, tried to convince them that '*Bordeaux* wine' meant 'good wine'.[40] Are Chinese consumers insensitive to or ignorant of the way in which the AOC *Bordeaux* expresses that linkage? The answer must be 'no'. Chinese consumers have become the top foreign buyers of *Bordeaux* wine in terms of both volume and value.[41] Thus, marketing strategies building upon *terroir* can be effective in the Chinese market, and, more importantly, the *terroir* concept does indeed produce a favourable response.

[B] Difficulties in Protecting GIs Through the Trademark Regime

Reflecting upon Japan's experience reveals that the problems arising from the use of the trademark regime to protect GIs may constitute a major constraint on the valorization of the products. Similar problems also exist in China.

Under the framework of China's trademark law, considerable efforts have been made to remedy the weaknesses in the product control system, increase the level of protection, and permit the coexistence of later GIs with prior trademarks. Nevertheless, the results so far cannot be considered satisfactory.

[1] Difficulties in Adding Value to Terroir Products: Experience from Japan

In the previous subdivision, we looked at the abundance of Chinese products that reflect *terroir* attributes and discussed the emergence of a Chinese concept similar to *terroir*. We concluded that *terroir* (climate, soil, and human contribution) form unique products and that value can be added to them by highlighting *terroir* and its linkage with their quality.

Before turning to the role of the trademark regime in this value-adding process, it is worth noting that no form of legal protection (trademark, consumer protection, unfair competition, sui generis GI protection, or other laws) is a 'magic potion'[42] that

40. *See* Xiaobing & Kireeva, *supra* n. 34, at 134.
41. *See* Zhongguo Jixu Chengwei Faguo Boerduo Putaojiu Zuida Haiwai Shichang [China Remains as Top Export Market of French Bordeaux Wines in 2015], Xinhua Net (19 June 2021), http://www.xinhuanet.com/2018-03/14/c_1122537653.htm.
42. Daniele Giovannucci et al., *Guide to Geographical Indications: Linking Products and Their Origins* 20 (International Trade Centre 2009).

can create market demand for the product or overturn disappointing results out of nothing,[43] but a suitable instrument can make it easier to reach those goals.[44]

The question of whether the trademark regime is such a suitable instrument has barely been discussed by Chinese policymakers and academics. Since the protection of GIs in China is fairly 'young',[45] GI issues are mainly discussed from a legal perspective, rather than an economic perspective.[46] Given the paucity of studies, we find it useful to take a look at Japan's experience with this issue during its GI system reform.

Before the reform, Japan relied on its 'regional collective trademark' system to protect its *terroir* products. This system allows groups to register a regional collective mark, which consists of the name of the region and the common name of the product.[47] The requirements for registration include a close relationship between the place name and the product, a certain degree of fame among consumers, and the applicant's intention to allow its members to use the mark.[48] When the registration is approved, the owner of the mark has an exclusive right to use the mark for the designated goods.[49] Furthermore, the owner is allowed to prevent the use of the mark by another person (within the scope of similarity).[50] Initiated in 2006, this system has had much success; the number of registration had reached 592 by the end of February 2016.[51]

Nevertheless, some problems have been identified concerning the effectiveness of the system. The first is the quality control issue. The trademark law accords a great deal of freedom to the trademark owners in the managing of their own business. Efforts to ensure product quality are merely voluntary. The weakness of this approach is that not every mark owner takes effective measures in setting up and implementing unified quality standards. The quality of products designated by the same mark can vary vastly among producers. Low-quality products cannot possibly meet the expectations of demanding consumers willing to pay for high quality and *terroir* attributes. Disappointed consumers will lose their willingness to pay for products designated by the same mark or simply switch to alternatives. As a result, no value is added due to varying product standards and insufficient quality control.[52]

43. Nuria Ackermann & Fabio Russo, *Adding Value to Traditional Products of Regional Origin: A Guide to Creating a Quality Consortium* 2 (United Nations Industrial Development Organization 2010).
44. *See* Bicskei et al., *supra* n. 33, at 223.
45. *See* Xiaobing & Kireeva, *supra* n. 34, at 133.
46. *See* Wang Yafeng & Jiang Hezhong, Dili Biaozhi Nongchanpin Xiaofeizhe Goumai Yiyuan he Goumai Xingwei Yanjiu Zongshu [Synthesis of Researches on Consumers' Purchase Intention and Behavior of Geographical Indications of Agricultural Products], ZHONGXIAO QIYE GUANLI YU KEJI [MANAGEMENT & TECHNOLOGY OF SME], September 2016, 114.
47. Trademark Act (Act No. 127 of 13 April 1959), Article 7(2).
48. Other registration requirements are the same as those for regular trademarks. *See Ibid.*
49. *Ibid.*, Article 25.
50. *Ibid.*, Article 51.
51. *The System of Regional Collective Trademarks*, Japan Patent Office (18 June 2021), https://www.jpo.go.jp/e/system/trademark/gaiyo/chidan/document/index/pamphlet_e.pdf.
52. *See Establishment of Japan's Geographical Indication (GI) Protection System*, Ministry of Agriculture, Forestry and Fisheries (MAFF) (18 June 2021), https://www.eu-japan.eu/sites/eu-japan.eu/files/SAKA_EN_0.pdf.

Second, as trademark rights are private rights, infringements are dealt with independently by each mark owner. Mark owners with a limited ability to take anti-infringement action face the problem wherein third-party products are bought as if they were theirs (or, more precisely, the members of the mark owner), and their poorer quality has adverse effects on the reputation of their products. This may impair the favourable attitude of consumers, which constitutes an essential condition for better product valorization.[53]

This problem could be overcome by either amending the regional collective mark system or establishing a new system. The first option was considered difficult because the trademark system regulates signs, rather than product quality. It deals with registering the name of the product but is not responsible for filing a lawsuit against alleged unlawful users on behalf of trademark owners.[54] Japan therefore opted to establish a new sui generis GI system.

In 2014, the Japanese parliament adopted the Act on the Protection of the Names of Specific Agricultural, Forestry and Fishery Products and Foodstuffs,[55] also known as the 'GI Act'.[56] One of the main features of the GI Act is that both the 'name' and the 'product' are the objects of regulation. According to the Act, the registration application must include a product specification that specifies the name of the GI product,[57] the place of production, the characteristics of the product, and the method of protection.[58] Both the availability of the name as well as the link between the product and the place of production are then examined. The registration will be refused where the name is a generic term;[59] where it is identical with or similar to a prior trademark for identical or similar products;[60] where the product is not produced in the specific region; or where the product's quality, reputation, or other characteristics are not essentially attributable to the place of production.[61] The goal is to ensure that only products with specified *terroir*-linked quality standards can receive GI status, which guarantees the quality of the GI-denominated product.[62]

53. *See Ibid.*
54. *Ibid.*
55. The Act entered into force in June 2015.
56. *See* Steven van Uytsel, *Geographical Indications in Japan: A New Start*, 2015, SSRN (18 June 2021), https://papers.ssrn.com/sol3/papers.cfm?abstract_id=2692450; Steven van Uytsel, *The New Japanese Act on Geographical Indications: An Intangible Cultural Heritage Perspective*, SSRN (18 June 2021), https://papers.ssrn.com/sol3/papers.cfm?abstract_id=2692449.
57. It should be mentioned that the GI Act uses the term 'Specific Agricultural, Forestry and Fishery Products and Foodstuffs', instead of the term 'GI Products'. The Act defines those products as any agricultural, forestry and fishery products and foodstuffs 'produced in a specific place, region or country; products whose quality, reputation or other established characteristic is essentially attributable to the place of production'. *See* Act on Protection of the Names of Specific Agricultural, Forestry and Fishery Products and Foodstuffs (GI Act), Act No. 84 of 25 June 2014, Article 2(2).
58. *Ibid.*, Article 7(1).
59. *Ibid.*, Article 13(1)(iv)(a).
60. *Ibid.*, Article 13(1)(iv)(b).
61. *Ibid.*, Article 13(1)(iii)(a).
62. *Geographical Indication (GI) Protection System in Japan*, Ministry of Agriculture, Forestry and Fisheries (MAFF) (18 June 2021), https://www.maff.go.jp/e/policies/intel/gi_act/attach/pdf/index-2.pdf.

Another feature is the mechanism for quality control. The GI Act allows public authorities to intervene in the management of the compliance of the registrant's[63] members with the product specification. While 'production process management'[64] is conducted by the registrant, the rules governing that management are to be attached to the registration application.[65] The legibility and practicability of the proposed rules are evaluated by the Ministry of Agriculture, Forestry and Fisheries (MAFF), the body in charge of the GI Act. An unfavourable evaluation may lead to an application refusal.[66] For registered products, the MAFF must be notified of any change to the production process management rules.[67] The MAFF may also order the mark owner to change the rules under certain circumstances.[68] It may also revoke all or part of the registration if the registrant fails to manage the product's quality.[69]

Not only does the MAFF monitor if the production process management is conducted effectively, but it may also carry out, *directly*, onsite inspections. The Act gives the MAFF the authority to send officials to the offices, warehouses, farms, factories, or any other place operated by the registrant, manufacturer, or related persons and have them inspect the business situation, products, documents, and other articles.[70]

The last significant feature is the enforcement action against the illegal use of a registered name. Any person who considers that there has been an unlawful use of a name may report it to the MAFF and request it to take appropriate measures.[71] The MAFF must conduct the necessary investigation after receiving the report and must take appropriate measures when the allegation is found to be true.[72] As the injunction against illegal use is made by the MAFF, producers can protect their GIs without incurring legal expenses.[73]

This brief description of the features of Japan's new GI system shows that it is designed to overcome the problems that have arisen in trademark protection. In doing

63. The term 'registrant' refers to the applicant group who has received a registration.
64. The term 'production process management' as used in the GI Act means '... guidance, examination and other operations that are necessary to accord the production of the producer as member of said group of producers with the (product) specification'. *See* GI Act, Article 2(6).
65. *Ibid.*, Article 7(2).
66. *Ibid.*, Article 13(1)(ii): '(The Minister of Agriculture, Forestry and Fisheries must refuse registration), when the production process management falls under any of the following: ... (b) when the method of production process management provided for by the production process management rules does not accord with the standards provided by Ordinance of the Ministry of Agriculture, Forestry and Fisheries as a way necessary to ensure that the production conducted by a producer as a member of said group of producers accords with the specification; (c) when the group of producers do not have sufficient financial basis to conduct accurate and smooth production process management; (d) when a system necessary to ensure fair conduct of production process management is found not to be established.'
67. *Ibid.*, Article 18.
68. *Ibid.*, Article 21.
69. *Ibid.*, Article 22(1)(ii); *See also* Uytsel, *supra* n. 56.
70. *Ibid.*, Article 24(1).
71. *Ibid.*, Article 25(1).
72. *Ibid.*, Article 25(2).
73. MAFF, *Geographical Indication (GI) Protection System in Japan*, *supra* n. 62.

so, Japan expects to retain and increase the value inherent in its high value-added *terroir* products and protect their authenticity.[74]

While Japan has distanced itself from the trademark system, China still uses it as one of the main mechanisms for protecting GI-denominated products. Does this mean that the problems identified by Japan occur exclusively in Japan? No, it does not. China's trademark mark regime is experiencing the same (or even worse) problems. One could argue that China's certification mark system serves as a remedy since it requires unified quality standards to be established by the mark applicant. Nevertheless, again, the implementation of these standards (including ensuring the compliance of the product covered by the mark with the prescribed standards and taking measures to prevent infringement) depends on the mark holder's will and capacity. As not all mark holders are equally competent, product standards cannot be implemented equally effectively. Not surprisingly, while the holder of the certification mark '*Xihu Longjin*' took a number of infringement actions against illegal users,[75] the holder of another certification mark, '*Zhangqiu* Scallion', tolerated widespread unauthorized use of the mark by local farmers.[76] Such a *laissez-faire* policy does not help maintain the reputation of the products.

China's trademark system has its own specific problems. It is worth recalling that both 'simple indications of origin' and 'geographical indications' can be registered as collective or certification marks.[77] They are composed in the same way[78] and governed by essentially the same regime. Thus, the consumer might misidentify an indication of origin (without a quality–place nexus) as a GI. This risk has actually been identified by the TRAB in the case of '*Jingpohu* Bean'.[79] In such a case, no true quality–place nexus exists; it is mixed with illusions of strong *terroir* roots created through other geographical marks. Based on the above considerations, we conclude that the trademark regime may not be an effective tool for maintaining and highlighting the *terroir* link based on which added value is generated.

74. Article 1 of the GI Act provides that its purpose is to 'secure the profits of producers of specific agricultural, forestry and fishery products and foodstuffs by establishing a system concerning the protection of the names ..., and thereby to contribute to the development of agricultural, forestry and fishery industries and relevant industries as well as to protect the interests of customers'. *See also* MAFF, *Establishment of Japan's Geographical Indication (GI) Protection System*, *supra* n. 52.
75. *See* Liu Xue & Wang Ziwen, Mingcha Xihu Longjin Weiquan 150 Jia Chashang Zao Diaoyushi Suopei [The Famous Tea 'Xihu Longjing' Claims Its Rights], NANFANG DUSHI BAO [SOUTHERN METROPOLITAN DAILY], 2 June 2015.
76. *See* Wang Xiaobing, Woguo Canjia WTO Dili Biaozhi Tanpan de Lichang he Duice [China's Position in WTO Negotiation Protecting GIs], ZHISHI CHANQUAN [INTELLECTUAL PROPERTY], January 2010, 48.
77. *See* Chapter 3 & Chapter 7 *supra*.
78. Both indications of origin and geographical indications are composed of the name of the place and the product's common name.
79. *State Administration for Industry v. Commerce Trademark Review and Adjudication Board and Ning'an Jingpo Lake Soybean Association*, Beijing High People's Court (12 June 2016).

[2] Difficulties in Crafting Specific Responses to Several Issues

Chinese authorities have made efforts, under the framework of the trademark law, to accommodate the needs of GIs. However, they have not been successful due to the tensions between liberalism and public intervention, between trademark protection and a higher level of protection, and between later GIs and prior trademarks.

[a] Tension Between Liberalism and Public Intervention

The trademark regime gives great freedom to the trademark owner in the management of the quality of the marked product. The law does not assure consumers of a constant *terroir*-based quality for the products sold under the same brand identity, except in the case of certification marks. Whether the later marks constitute a guarantee of *terroir*-based quality depends on the judgement of the mark owner. To ensure this quality, the owner must integrate the quality-place nexus requirement into the regulations governing the use of that mark, prevent it from being removed or inappropriately modified even in the face of market pressure, place effective controls over mark users' compliance with the regulations, and take the necessary measures against infringements. As those efforts are independent and voluntary[80] and are limited by the resources available to each trademark owner, the *terroir*-based quality may be missing or substantially compromised.

One solution to this problem is public intervention. In revising the Measures for Collective Marks and Certification Marks in 2003,[81] the former SAIC imposed the obligation on applicants seeking to register a GI as a collective or certification mark to submit a document specifying the quality-place nexus.[82] It is assumed that the applicant is then obliged to include the nexus requirement as one condition of the use of the mark. The reality is, however, that the applicant could evade compliance with the obligation by simply not declaring the GI status, as there is nothing preventing them from registering a simple indication of origin as a collective or certification mark.[83] Even if everyone duly respects the obligation, how will the nexus be scientifically verified? It is highly doubtful that the trademark examiners, usually in charge only of 'signs', are competent for the task.

The former SAIC's intervention regarding quality control is even more problematic. This is based on Article 21 of the Measures, which stipulates as follows:

80. Although the owner of the certification mark should take reasonable steps to prevent the mark from being used in a manner that is incompatible with the conditions of use laid down in the regulations, each trademark owner enjoys great freedom in determining the methods and frequency of the supervision of the use.
81. The Measures for Collective Marks and Certification Marks issued in 1994 is repealed and replaced by the new Measures issued in 2003. *See* Chapter 2 *supra*.
82. Measures for Collective Marks and Certification Marks, Article 7; *See also* Chapter 4 *supra*.
83. *See State Administration for Industry v. Commerce Trademark Review and Adjudication Board and Ning'an Jingpo Lake Soybean Association*, *supra* n. 79.

> Where the registrant of a collective mark or a certification mark fails to exercise effective governing of, or control on, the use of the mark and, as a result, the goods to which the said mark applies fail to meet the requirements of the regulation governing the use of the mark, causing damages to consumers, the administrative authority for industry and commerce shall order him or it to rectify the situation within a time limit.

Thus, by the time the authority decides to intervene, it might be too late, and consumers may already have suffered damage. In order to avoid this situation, the authority should conduct regular onsite product inspections, monitor the implementation of regulations governing use, and modify the regulations where required. However, on what basis can such actions be justified? Is it appropriate to stipulate such actions, characterized by a high level of public intervention, for a law governing private rights?

Furthermore, the trademark regime gives great freedom to operators in the choice of the sign to be registered.[84] Even if the proprietor of the trademark does not have the right to engage in the production and marketing of the designated products,[85] nothing prevents them from applying for, owning, or defending the trademark that they license to another person qualified to work with the products.[86] This registrability allows trademarks containing GIs to be owned by entities with no connection with the region. In theory, even a foreign entity could register a certification mark for a Chinese GI product. This raises a serious concern regarding whether the proprietor of the mark, who might theoretically be an 'outsider', could represent or serve the interests of the 'insiders' (the GI producers).

The trademark system addresses the 'insider–outsider' concern by providing that only organizations composed of operators from within the indicated area may apply to register a GI as a collective mark.[87] However, this limitation does not address the concern over trademark owners' representativeness. One example will suffice here. *Qixia* is an area within *Yantai*, and apples from *Yantai* (including the former subarea) are GI products. It seems that the trademark law does not prevent *Qixia* Apple Industry Association from owning the collective mark '*Yantai* Apple', since its initial members reside within the larger area of '*Yantai*' (though they are only a subset of the group of operators). With a membership composed primarily of people from the subarea, the Association does not truly represent the whole industry, and they may find it difficult to manage/inspect the production of apples from the area of *Yantai*.

One may argue that the trademark law could impose the representativeness requirement on the applicant group. It should be mentioned that the assessment of representativeness involves identifying the number of operators (both of all operators

84. *See* Jacques Larrieu, *Indications géographiques et marques en droit français, in Indications géographiques: perspectives globales et locales* 80 (Jacques de Werra ed., Schulthess Éditions Romandes 2016).
85. For example, an entity, which does not have the necessary qualifications to follow the profession of hospital pharmacist, owns a trademark for drugs.
86. *See* Frédéric Pollaud-Dulian, *Droit de la propriété industrielle*, Paris, Economica, 2010, p. 717.
87. This limitation does not apply to certification marks. Any party, regardless of where it is situated, can become a mark holder as long as it has the capacity of supervising the particular quality of the goods.

in the field and of those who are already members of the applicant group), the volumes produced by the members relative to the overall volume, and the functioning of the structure of the applicant group (i.e., whether the functioning is democratic enough to allow operators to express their views).[88] Those tasks go beyond the evaluation of distinctive 'signs' in the context of trademark registration. It is doubtful if the Trademark Office's scope of activities should be widened by the inclusion of these tasks and if it is justifiable to place the burden (of lumping all the operators into one group) on the applicant seeking simply to register a distinctive sign.

[b] Tension Between Trademark Protection and a Higher Level of Protection for GIs

Article 23 of the TRIPS Agreement provides for a higher level of protection for GIs identifying wines and spirits. This protection is not dependant on meeting the 'misleading test' and applies even if the true place of origin is indicated, the use is accompanied by qualifying terms such as 'type' or 'kind', or the use is in translation. In the international debate over whether to expand this protection to other products, China is among the proponents of extension.[89] This implies that a higher level of protection for GIs is needed in China's legislation to support its efforts to enhance the protection at a multilateral level in the WTO.

However, this additional protection can hardly find a rightful place in the trademark law, which is bound by established doctrines. Admittedly, the prohibitions provided for in Article 23 may partially be justified by the need to protect the reputation of GIs. The representative of Switzerland illustrated in a submission to the TRIPS Council that:

> Rice that was sold under the Indian geographical indication '*Basmati*', but which was clearly marked as originating from another region or country, would not mislead the public as to the place of origin of that product; nevertheless, such use would free-ride on the worldwide famous and therefore commercially valuable GI '*Basmati*'.[90]

The same applies to the well-known Chinese '*Longjing*' tea, for instance. This rationale is similar to that of the dilution protection for famous marks, which also precludes non-confusing commercial uses of signs.

However, not all uses would tarnish or unduly exploit the reputation of the GI. First, not all GIs have significant reputations outside their regional borders. Justin Hughes observes that 'Most of the world's consumers do not know most of the world's

88. *See* INAO, *Guide du demandeur pour la reconnaissance en qualité d'organisme de défense et de gestion*, 2016, p. 9; *See also* Chapter 4 *supra*.
89. *See* Chapter 6 *supra*.
90. *See* Michael Blakeney, *Geographical Indications and TRIPS, in Extending the Protection of Geographical Indications: Case Studies of Agricultural Products in Africa* 17 (Michael Blakeney et al. eds, Routledge 2012).

GIs.'[91] If it is true that most Chinese consumers do not know most of the Chinese GIs, then a higher level of protection, which would be granted to all relevant GIs, cannot be justified on the basis of reputation protection, since no reputation may have been built, at least for some GIs. Second, labelling such as '*Longjing*-imitation' or '*Longjing*-style' may truthfully inform consumers as to some similar product features. This benefits consumers who are searching for substitute products originating from other places. Such labelling is not very different from comparative advertising or the nominative fair use of trademarks, which are permitted under certain conditions in the trademark regime. It would be contradictory for the same law (i.e., the trademark law) to prohibit all 'comparative phrases' (e.g., 'X-like', 'X-style') in labelling while permitting them in advertising.

[c] Tension Between Earlier Trademarks and Subsequent GIs

As stated earlier,[92] the FITFIR rule has been adopted in China's trademark regime as the solution for conflicts arising because two parties are making competing claims to the same sign. As no exceptions are made for GIs, the rule applies to conflicts between earlier trademarks and subsequent GIs. This means that trademarks that are protected first can prevent the registration and use of conflicting subsequent GIs.

The application of the FITFIR rule to such categorical conflicts may lead to inequity.[93] In a dispute concerning attempts to register '*Enshi Yulu*' (a GI for tea) as a certification mark, Chinese courts provided a new solution to the difficult task of resolving the tension between earlier trademarks and later GIs. The application for registration was objected to by the holder of an earlier trademark, '*Yulu*', for tea. The Beijing High People's Court ruled that 'The function of "GI certification marks" is clearly distinct from that of ordinary trademarks and service marks ... any assessment of similarity between those certification marks and ordinary marks should not be conducted. The contested mark could not give rise to consumer confusion.'[94]

This solution is questionable, however. For instance, the function of corporate names is also different from that of trademarks. They are not used to distinguish the products or services of a business but to identify legal entities. The use of a sign that is similar or identical to a prior trademark as a corporate name could mislead consumers as to the source of the products or into the belief that there was some connection between the legal entity and the mark holder.[95] In fact, once the corporate name is used

---

91. Justin Hughes, *Champagne, Feta, and Bourbon: The Spirited Debate about Geographical Indications*, 58 Hastings L.J. 299, 382 (2006).
92. *See* Chapter 5 *supra*.
93. *See* Xinzhe Song, *The Role Played by the Regime of Collective and Certification Marks in the Protection of Geographical Indications: Comparative Study of Law and Practice in France, the EU and China*, 21 J. World Intell. Prop. 437 (2017).
94. *Changsha Yulu Enterprise Marketing Planning Co. Ltd. v. the Trademark Review and Adjudication Board of the State Administration for Industry and Commerce*, Beijing High People's Court (5 July 2013).
95. Zuigao Renmin Fayuan Guanyu Shenli Shangbiao Minshi Jiufen Anjian Shiyong Falu Ruogan Wenti de Jieshi [Supreme People's Court's Judicial Interpretation in the Event of Disputes

in trade, it could be perceived by the consumer as a source identifier.[96] The same applies to certification marks.

Perhaps the most desirable solution is to provide for an exception to the FITFIR rule allowing later GIs to coexist with earlier trademarks under certain conditions. However, it would be paradoxical if the trademark law provided for such an exception. On the one hand, China's trademark law is relied on as a primary means of protecting GIs; the argument is that trademarks and GIs are functionally equivalent. On the other hand, if the trademark law provided for such an exception, would the argument be, conversely, that the function of GIs is distinct from that of trademarks? There is a gap between the trademark law and the protection needs of Chinese GIs, and the efforts to close it are neither sufficient nor appropriate. If a satisfactory solution cannot be found in the trademark system, the potential use of sui generis GI systems must be considered. We will discuss this in the following section.

§7.02 A STRENGTHENED ROLE FOR THE SUI GENERIS REGIME

GIs are expected to benefit both private and public interests. An acknowledgement of their potential benefits can be found not only in the context of the sui generis regime (for instance, Recitals 1-5 of Regulation 1151/2012) but also in the context of the trademark regime.[97] However, by virtue of their inherent characteristics,[98] GIs alone (without state involvement establishing a legal regime) cannot meet these expectations.[99]

A well-designed, well-implemented sui generis GI regime may offer many advantages that the trademark regime cannot provide. Those advantages could help unleash the benefits, both private and public, associated with GIs.[100] We thus consider that the sui generis regime should become the primary instrument used for GIs

Relating to the Application of the Trademark Law], 12 October 2002 (amended on 29 December 2020), Article 1: 'The following acts shall be the acts of causing other damages to the registered trademark ... Using the words that are identical or similar to the registered trademark of any other person as the name of one's enterprise on identical or similar commodities so that the relevant public is liable to be misled.'

96. *See* Jérôme Passa, *Droit de la propriété industrielle: Tome 1, Marques et autres signes distinctifs, dessins et modèles*, 2e éd., Paris, LGDJ, 2009, p. 332.

97. Lu Zhihua (Deputy Director General of China Trademark Office), Zhongguo Shangbiao Tixi Xia de Dili Biaozhi Baohu [Protection for Geographical Indications under the Trademark System in China], IPKEY (13 February 2017), http://www.ipkey.org/en/ip-law-document/download/3253/3760/23: 'Geographical indications promote the development of farmers, rural areas and agriculture; increase the added value of agriculture products and the income of farmers; optimize the industrial structure of agriculture and facilitate the formation and development of featured agriculture industry (local specialities); improve the agriculture technology level and industrialization level; further the socialized service system of agriculture and drive the simultaneous development of other industries; expand the market share of agriculture products and accelerate the process of selling them to the international market.'

98. For example, they can be characterized as club goods and experience goods.

99. *See* Xing Zhao, *Food Safety and Chinese Geographical Indications*, 118 Brit. Food J. 217 (2016).

100. However, it should be noted that GI protection, no matter what methods we choose, is not a sufficient condition for the success of GIs. Other factors such as marketing strategies also matter.

[A] Benefits of the Sui Generis Regime for Private Interests

A well-designed sui generis GI regime can better safeguard the interests of producers and protect the interests of consumers.

[1] Benefits of the Sui Generis Regime for Producers

Faced with growing competition for commodities, producers are finding ways to escape commodity markets and enter more lucrative niche markets.[101] For those working with GI products, their entry ticket is *terroir*-based quality, which allows their products to achieve differentiation.[102] *Terroir*-based quality is a potent weapon[103] because consumers with growing disposable income are demanding[104] and are willing to pay a premium price for quality, tradition, typicality, and authenticity in their products.[105] The producers, in turn, benefit from the premium paid by consumers.

However, the price–quality correlation is not always as high as expected.[106] Quality does not always give rise to a price premium.[107] Most GI products are not search goods, whose quality attributes are readily observable prior to purchase. For example, when purchasing a bottle of wine, consumers observe quality cues (rather

101. Dermot J. Hayes et al., *Geographic Indications and Farmer-Owned Brands: Why Do the US and EU Disagree?*, 4 EuroChoices 28, 30 (2005).
102. Louis Augustin-Jean, *The Globalization of Geographical Indications: The Challenge for Asia, in Geographical Indications and International Agricultural Trade: The Challenge for Asia* 1, 4 (Louis Augustin-Jean ed., Palgrave Macmillan 2012).
103. European Commission, *Green Paper on Agricultural Product Quality: Product Standards, Farming Requirements and Quality Schemes*, COM(2008)641 final (15 October 2008) p. 4.
104. *Ibid.*
105. There is extensive empirical literature indicating that consumers are willing to pay the premium for typical products closely linked to a specific place of origin, although the willingness varies and is influenced by many factors (e.g., education level, age, income). *See*, for instance, Pascale Bazoche et al., *Willingness to Pay for Appellation of Origin: Results of an Experiment with Pinot Noir Wines in France and Germany, in Wine Economics: Quantitative Studies and Empirical Applications* 129 (Eric Giraud-Héraud et al. eds, Palgrave Macmillan 2013); Pierre Combris et al., *Does Taste Beat Food Safety? Evidence from the 'Pêra Rocha' Case in Portugal*, 16 J. Food Prod. Marketing 60 (2009); Dimitris Skuras & Aleka Vakrou, *Consumers' Willingness to Pay for Origin Labelled Wine: A Greek Case Study*, 104 Bri. Food J. 898 (2002); Luisa Menapace et al., *Consumers' Preferences for Geographical Origin Labels: Evidence from the Canadian Olive Oil Market*, 38 Eur. Rev. Agric. Econ. 193 (2011); Leonardo Cei et al., *From Geographical Indications to Rural Development: A Review of the Economic Effects of European Union Policy*, 10 Sustainability 3754 (2018); Christian Garavaglia, *How Much Do Consumers Value Protected Designation of Origin Certifications? Estimates of Willingness to Pay for PDO Dry-Cured Ham in Italy*, 33 Agribusiness 403 (2017); Xudong et al., *supra* n. 35; Zhou Anning & Ying Ruiyao, Xiaofeizhe Dui Dili Biaozhi Nongchanpin Zhifu Yiyuan Jiqi Yingxiang Yinsu Yanjiu [Consumer's Willingness to Pay Considering Geographical Indication Product and the Influential Factors: From the Perspective of Consumer's Behavioral and Psychological Factors and Positive Examination], XUESHU TANSUO [ACADEMIC EXPLORATION], May 2012, 110-113.
106. Stuart Landon & Smith E. Constance, *The Use of Quality and Reputation Indicators by Consumers: The Case of Bordeaux Wine*, 20 J. Consumer Pol'y 289 (1997).
107. A case study on the relationship between the price and quality of Bordeaux wine shows that price differences are primarily explained by the information appearing on the bottle's label rather than the characteristics of the wine (taste, texture, or odour). It concludes that quality

than quality attributes) such as vintage year, château name, ranking, store, and the popularity of the wine. It is only after consumption that they are able to decide whether the taste of the wine is really special. Even if they have tried wines with the same quality cues, the purchase decision still does not depend on current quality attributes but on expectations arising from past consumption. The traditional *savoir-faire* used in the winemaking process may not be verified even after consumption.[108]

As they formalize the nexus between a product's quality attributes and its place of origin, GIs can act as a signalling device to reduce the asymmetric information problem. If it is true that 'an effective label may transform a product from being an experience good to a search good',[109] a GI label may make quality attributes more observable by transmitting information on quality and reducing consumers' search costs.[110]

The ability of a GI to signal quality depends on the credibility associated with the sign: 'Credibility is a key variable to the extent that it gives the signalling its power.'[111] If a GI is not deemed credible by consumers, they will pay more attention to other cues, such as vintage ratings by independent critics (for wine) or trademarks.[112] Thus, consumers' trust in the GI as a cue signalling quality is of paramount importance.[113] Empirical studies have found that consumers are generally willing to pay a higher price in order to have greater guarantees,[114] which can be achieved through the strengthening of quality control via state intervention.

As indicated previously, such state intervention is in tension with the freedom the trademark law accords to proprietors of marks.[115] The alternative is to rely on the sui generis regime to institutionalize state intervention so as to increase the credibility of the GI and consequently help the producers to obtain the price premium.

Once the price premium is created, it will not go unnoticed by potential competitors. Quality attributes valued by consumers may be imitated; they will only

---

does not play a role in the determination of the market price. *See* Pierre Combris et al., *Estimation of a Hedonic Price Equation for Bordeaux Wine: Does Quality Matter?*, 107 Econ. J. 390 (1997).

108. Maria L. Loureiro & Jill Mccluskey, *Assessing Consumer Response to Protected Geographical Identification Labelling*, 16 Agribusiness 309 (2000).
109. Julie A. Caswell & Daniel I. Padberg, *Toward a More Comprehensive Theory of Food Labels*, 74 Am. J. Agric. Econ. 460 (1992).
110. Cerkia Bramley, *A Review of the Socio-Economic Impact of Geographical Indications: Considerations for the Developing World* (WIPO Worldwide Symposium on Geographical Indications, Lima, Peru 22-24 June 2011).
111. Marie Carpenter & Fabrice Larceneux, *Label Equity and the Effectiveness of Values-Based Labels: An Experiment with Two French Protected Geographic Indication Labels*, 32 Int'l J. Consumer Stud. 499, 501 (2008).
112. Geneviève Teil, *The French Wine 'Appellations d'Origine Contrôlée' and the Virtues of Suspicion*, 13 J. World Intell. Prop. 253 (2010).
113. Giovanni Belletti et al., *The Effects of Protecting Geographical Indications: Ways and Means of Their Evaluation* 53 (Swiss Federal Institute of Intellectual Property 2011).
114. Bertil Sylvander, *DOLPHINS Concerted Action: Development of Origin Labelled Products: Humanity, Innovation and Sustainability* 82 (WP7 Final Report, 2004).
115. *See* §7.01 *supra*.

have to be marketed in a different way.[116] That is why Chinese '*Xuan* Paper'[117] is produced in Japan. Japanese firms have made efforts to convince consumers that their new products are close substitutes by advertising them using appeals such as 'For *Xuan* Paper, which can be produced all over the world, (China) *Anhui* (Province) Jing County the first, Japan the second, *Zhengjiang* (Province) the third and *Taiwan* the fourth.'[118] In marketing 'Japanese *Xuan* Paper', the firms have met some success in creating a new association in consumers' minds. Another example is a 'Port-style wine' called 'Pipe', marketed by Canadian vintner Sumac Ridge.[119] Over time, such marketing efforts are likely to change or erode consumers' perceptions of the linkage of a product's attributes with its place of origin,[120] and thus limit or erode any premium that can be gained from the *terroir*-based quality.[121]

If anchorage to *terroir* is a competitive advantage for local producers, other agro-food economies will try to erode or devalue it by making the geographical location irrelevant or at least secondary to objective production standards that can easily be delocalized.[122] Trademark protection against confusion is of little help in combating this challenge since it does not prohibit the labelling of any hard cheese with a gritty texture as 'Parmesan-type'.

It is therefore necessary to provide for a level of protection that prevents consumers from being misled into a belief that quality attributes are not based on *terroir* but can be duplicated somewhere else. This enhanced level of protection will help educate consumers about the existence of the link to *terroir* that makes the difference between authentic products and imitations (e.g., authentic Basmati rice from *Punjab* (India) and 'Uncle Ben's' [trademark] *basmati* rice made in Belgium).[123] In other words, it would decrease the degree of substitutability between GI products and imitated products by helping keep the *terroir* concept in the minds of consumers:[124] 'Better educated consumers would become more aware of, and perhaps more sensitive to, the characteristics and qualities that are embodied in the authentic GI-denominated

116. William A. Kerr, *Enjoying a Good Port with a Clear Conscience: Geographic Indicators, Rent Seeking and Development*, 7 Estey Ctr. J. Int'l L. & Trade Pol'y 1, 10 (2006).
117. Xuan paper is named after its production location Xuancheng City in Anhui Province. Its softness and fine texture make it suitable for conveying the artistic expression of Chinese calligraphy and painting. Xuan Paper has been recognized as a 'GI product' by the former AQSIQ. *See* Guojia Zhiliang Jiandu Jianyan Jianyi Zongju Gonggao 2002 Nian di 75 Hao [State General Administration of Quality Supervision, Inspection and Quarantine Announcement No. 75, 2002], 6 August 2002.
118. Hu Ping, QINGBAO RIBEN [INFORMATION-GATHERING JAPAN], at 355 (Twenty-First Century Publishing, 2011).
119. Kerr, *supra* n. 116, at 10.
120. Consumers may be misled into believing that the quality attributes are 'duplicated' elsewhere.
121. Felix Addor & Alexandra Grazioli, *Geographical Indications Beyond Wines and Spirits: A Roadmap for a Better Protection for Geographical Indications in the WTO TRIPS Agreement*, 5 J. World Intell. Prop. 865 (2002).
122. Gustavo Ghidini, *Innovation, Competition and Consumer Welfare in Intellectual Property Law* 199 (Edward Elgar Publishing 2010).
123. Daniel J. Gervais, *International Intellectual Property: A Handbook of Contemporary Research* 457 (Edward Elgar Publishing 2015).
124. Luisa Menapace & Gian Carlo Moschini, *Strength of Protection for Geographical Indications: Promotion Incentives and Welfare Effects*, 96 Am. J. Agric. Econ. 1030 (2014).

products.'[125] Their demand for those products, if it did not increase, would at least be less likely to decrease due to the marketing efforts made for the imitated products. The corollary is that GI producers would be better off.[126]

That level of protection has, in fact, already been conferred on GIs under European GI regimes. The French Consumer Code (Article L. 122-3) prohibits comparative advertising in so far as products compared do not benefit from the same appellation. The EU Regulation on GIs protects registered names against any misuse, imitation, or evocation, even if the true origin is indicated or if the names are translated or accompanied by qualifying terms. Those provisions correspond to the higher level of protection for GIs set out in Article 23 of the TRIPS Agreement.[127]

Again, as indicated earlier, such a level of protection is not compatible with trademark doctrines.[128] It can be more readily achieved in the sui generis GI regime.

Finally, our discussion must allude to the matter of protection implementation, which also has an impact on the value that *terroir*-based quality adds to a product. There might be a gap between legal protection and the quality of enforcement. Legal protection (under the 1953 Tea Act and 1958 Trademarks Act) seems not to have improved *Darjeeling* tea prices very much between 1972 and 2002[129] due to the inadequacy of the fight against counterfeiting.[130]

Given that GI producers (especially SMEs) may have limited resources available for use in dealing with infringements, the state may share this burden (e.g., INAO in France and MAFF in Japan). The sui generis law could entrust the defence of GIs to public authorities, allowing them to initiate legal actions against infringements.

[2] Benefits of the Sui Generis Regime for Consumers

Terroir-based quality may be an important factor in the purchase decision for consumers choosing between a *Bordeaux* and a *Chianti* based on expectations as to their taste.[131] This type of quality exists not only in wines but in a wide range of products (e.g., agricultural products, foodstuffs, industrial products). On the demand side, there is growing interest among consumers in products closely linked to the place of origin, and this interest is not limited to wines.[132] It is thus not inconceivable that, for example,

125. Gervais, *supra* n. 123, at 458.
126. *Ibid.*
127. The level of protection that the EU and France give to GIs is even higher than the level of protection required by Article 23.
128. *See* §7.01 *supra*.
129. WTO, *Exploring the Linkage Between the Domestic Policy Environment and International Trade* 86 (World Trade Report, 2004).
130. In 2000, it was estimated that 40,000 tons of tea were sold every year as *Darjeeling* tea in the world market, whereas production of Darjeeling tea in the area had not exceeded 10,000 tons in any year since 1976. *See Ibid.*
131. *See* Pawel Bryla, *The Perception of EU Quality Signs for Origin and Organic Food Products among Polish Consumers*, 9 Quality Assurance & Safety Crops & Foods 345 (2017).
132. Dimitris Skuras & Efthalia Dimara, *Regional Image and the Consumption of Regionally Denominated Products*, 41 Urb. Stud. 801 (2004).

some '*terroir* wine consumers' might value that quality and search for other products (e.g., rice, mineral water) with the same type.

A GI can reduce consumers' search costs if the consumers know it and understand its meaning. If they have never heard of it, however, the GI can be of little help. The name '*Chasselas de Moissac*' would convey very little quality-related information to Chinese consumers because they may not even be aware of the existence of *Moissac*. Promotion and advertising are required to make a single GI a well-known, credible sign of origin and quality, but individual GIs are not equally capable of mustering the necessary resources toward that end.[133]

The sui generis regime can be a useful aid to consumers' decision-making. Knowing that '*Chasselas de Moissac*' is subject to the same regime as '*Champagne*' tells you a great deal about the product, and knowing that the regime is specifically tailored to protect *terroir* products can be highly informative about the requisite quality attributes and authenticity.[134] This process is usually achieved through public authorities' efforts to make available an official logo that can be used along with registered names, to raise consumers' awareness of the logo, and to help them understand its meaning. Protection status under the sui generis regime conveys a message to consumers about the *terroir*-based quality of the product.[135]

European research finds that official logos signifying protection status under the PDO/PGI regime are the main purchasing motivation for consumers with excellent knowledge of EU quality classification/certification systems.[136] Chinese studies showed that a large percentage of consumers expressed a willingness to purchase a tea after learning that it was protected under China's sui generis regime, even though many of them had little knowledge of the tea.[137]

However, consumers will suffer a detriment if they pay a price premium in the belief that a product with GI status has qualities or a reputation attributable to the region of origin when it does not. Therefore, to protect the interests of consumers, the sui generis regime should be designed to effectively verify the quality attributes of the protected products. This is why the AOC regime obliges applicants to submit a product specification containing details about the quality–place nexus. The nexus must then be examined by advisors and experts through technical analysis.

133. GianCarlo Moschini et al., *Geographical Indications and the Competitive Provision of Quality in Agricultural Markets*, 90 Am. J. Agric. Econ. 794 (2008).
134. This requires that sufficient information should be available for consumers, enabling them to understand the meaning of the GI regime and the guarantees it offers. *See* Ivo A. van der Lans et al., *The Role of the Region of Origin and EU Certificates of Origin in Consumer Evaluation of Food Products*, 28 Eur. Rev. Agric. Econ. 451 (2001).
135. Dev Gangjee, *Proving Provenance? Geographical Indications Certification and Its Ambiguities*, 98 World Dev. 12 (2017).
136. Riccardo Vecchio & Azzurra Annunziata, *The Role of PDO/PGI Labelling in Italian Consumers' Food Choices*, 12 Agric. Econ. Rev. 80 (2011).
137. Zhan Huibin & Chen Chao, Xiaofeizhe Dui Dili Biaozhi Chanpin de Renzhi Chengdu Yiji Goumai Yiyuan Yanjiu [A Study on Consumers' Cognition and Purchase Intention of Geographical Indication Products], XIAOFEI JINGJI [CONSUMER ECONOMICS], August 2010, 55-57.

Delphine Marie-Vivien argues that the substantive examination in sui generis systems is the foundation of GIs' value proposition to consumers.[138] The lack of substantive examination in trademark regimes can lead to tenuous links between registered names and product quality.[139] Simply stated, the name will hardly be understood as guaranteeing quality elements.

Introducing substantive examination to trademark regimes is not a reasonable option because trademark examiners are not scientific or technical experts, and they usually do not possess the knowledge, experience, or means required for proper substantive examination. This further confirms the need for a sui generis regime.

Another advantage of the sui generis regime is that public authorities conduct quality control to ensure that the use of the GI complies with the product specification. These inspections may increase product safety and help guarantee product authenticity.[140]

[B] Benefits of the Sui Generis Regime for the Public

A well-designed sui generis regime can better support rural development, particularly agricultural SMEs, and preserve traditional *savoir-faire*.[141]

[1] Benefits of the Sui Generis Regime for Rural Development

GIs are often considered to exert positive effects on rural development.[142] The underlying assumption is that GI products are produced in traditional, small-scale farms in marginalized rural areas,[143] and the mass production of agro-industrial products at low cost is difficult in these areas.[144] Thus, GIs provide an alternative way for farmers and SMEs to compete with large companies producing cheap, standardized

138. Cerkia Bramley, Delphine Marie-Vivien & Estelle Biénabe, *Considerations in Designing an Appropriate Legal Framework for GIs in Southern Countries*, *in Developing Geographical Indications in the South* 25 (Cerkia Bramley ed., Springer 2013).
139. Stephan Marette, Roxanne Clemens & Bruce Babcock, *Recent International and Regulatory Decisions about Geographical Indications*, 24 Agribusiness 453 (2008).
140. Burkhard Schaer, Claudia Strauch & Karlheinz Knickel, *Marketing Sustainable Agriculture: An Analysis of the Potential Role of New Food Supply Chains in Sustainable Rural Development* (Tegut Case Study Report, QLK5-CT-2002-01349, 2002).
141. *See also* Filippo Arfini, *Are Geographical Indication Products Fostering Public Goods? Some Evidence from Europe*, 11 Sustainability 272 (2019).
142. Yu Bo, DILI BIAOZHI BAOHU ZHIDU [PROTECTION SYSTEM OF GEOGRAPHICAL INDICATIONS], at 28 (Shanghai People Press, 2018); Giovanni Belletti & Andrea Marescotti, *Strengthening International Research on Geographical Indications: From Research Foundation to Consistent Policy* 34 (D2-WP2 Report, 2006); Fatima Lambarraa-Lehnhardt, *Geographical Indications for Supporting Rural Development in the Context of the Green Morocco Plan: Oasis Dates*, 67 Agric. Econ. 70 (2021); Giang Hoang et al., *The Impact of Geographical Indications on Sustainable Rural Development: A Case Study of the Vietnamese Cao Phong Orange*, 12 Sustainability 4711 (2020).
143. Belletti & Marescotti, *supra* n. 142, at 30.
144. Ackermann & Russo, *supra* n. 43, at 21.

products, as they encourage product differentiation,[145] which gives rise to price premiums.[146] Farmers and SMEs reap the benefits, and rural areas can therefore revitalize.[147] In addition, GI products cannot be delocalized; they therefore help sustain economic activity, and thus jobs and populations, in rural areas.[148] The *theoretical* effects of GIs on rural development have been recognized by the EU, as reflected in its GI regulations:

> The promotion of products having certain characteristics could be of considerable benefit to the rural economy, in particular to less-favoured or remote areas, by improving the incomes of farmers and by retaining the rural population in these areas.[149]

Nevertheless, a growing number of case studies have shown that GIs cannot by themselves guarantee benefits for rural development.[150] In the *Tequila* case, the rules governing the GI are limited to demarcating the boundary of production, without specifying quality requirements for raw materials (agave) and appropriate practices for agave cultivation (traditional cultivation practices are not required). The delimited area is too large and includes areas that have neither a cultivation tradition nor natural conditions for agave cultivation. As a consequence, tequila companies source agave from a large area and base their decisions on purchase prices without worrying if the low-price agave meets any quality requirements (which do not exist). Thus, farmers cultivating high-quality agave in traditional areas struggle to earn extra income. Furthermore, tequila companies value mechanized, chemically intensive production methods over traditional methods. Traditional agave farmers are forced to 'modernize' their practices and in many cases are pushed out of the supply chain.[151] It appears that

145. Studies confirm that GIs generate independent demands and consumers' preferences within the market. *See* Antonio Stasi et al., *Italian Wine Demand and Differentiation Effect of Geographical Indications*, 23 Int'l J. Wine Bus. Res. 49 (2011); Ramona Teuber, *Geographical Indications of Origin as a Tool of Product Differentiation: The Case of Coffee*, 22 J. Int'l Food & Agribus. Mark. 277 (2010).
146. Dominique Barjolle et al., *Organization and Performance of the Origin Labelled Food Alliances, in Focus on Agricultural Economics* 91 (Ami R. Bellows ed., Nova Science Publishers 2005).
147. Bruce A. Babcock & Roxanne Clemens, *Geographical Indications and Property Rights: Protecting Value-Added Agricultural Products* 14 (MATRIC Briefing Paper 04-MBP 7, 2004).
148. Jean-Louis Rastoin, *The Concept of Terroir as the Basis of Corporate Strategy in Agribusiness: The European Social, Economic and Institutional Model, in Geographical Indications and International Agricultural Trade* 128 (Louis Augustin-Jean et al. eds, Palgrave Macmillan 2012).
149. The second recital in the preamble to Regulation 2081/92.
150. *See also* Dominique Barjolle & Erik Thevenod-Mottet, *Ancrage territorial des systèmes de production: le cas des appellations d'origine contrôlée*, Industries alimentaires et agricoles, Vol. 121, 2004, pp. 19-27; Christophe Bontemps et al., *Quality Labels and Firm Survival: Some First Empirical Evidence*, 40 Eur. Rev. Agric. Econ. 413 (2013); Áron Török et al., *Understanding the Real-World Impact of Geographical Indications: A Critical Review of the Empirical Economic Literature*, 12 Sustainability 9434 (2020).
151. Sarah Bowena & Ana Valenzuela Zapata, *Geographical Indications, Terroir, and Socioeconomic and Ecological Sustainability: The Case of Tequila*, 25 J. Rural Stud. 108 (2009).

the *Tequila* GI benefits powerful actors (*Tequila* companies) while excluding farmers and rural areas.[152]

Similarly, in a case concerning the Nicaraguan cheese *Queso Chontaleño*, GIs seem to exclude farmers in marginalized areas from their benefits. The code of practice of the GI requires that the cheese be processed in the Chontales Department, but it places no restrictions on the sourcing of raw materials (milk), which may thus come from anywhere. The requirements for measurable parameters (percentage of humidity, fat, and sodium chloride), rather than traditional production techniques, are specified as conditions for using the GI. Thus, while foreign enterprises and multinationals – with processing plants in the Chontales Department and the necessary technological, production, and trade tools – can easily make a cheese in compliance with the code of practice, farmers and artisan enterprises using authentic production techniques cannot due to their low level of technology and lack of research centres.[153]

A relevant Chinese case concerns *Nanfeng* Mandarins. The characteristics of the product are defined very flexibly in the product specification, in the hope that all local mandarin producers would be able to benefit from the GI. However, the 'flexible' specification has contributed to a rapid expansion of the planting area. This enabled the Fuzhou government to allow all ten counties it governs (*Nanfeng* is one of them) to produce *Nanfeng* mandarins. Not surprisingly, the increase in supply resulting from the expansion of the planting area has reduced prices (from RMB 3.2 per kg in 2006 to RMB 1.8 per kg in 2009).[154]

These cases reveal the danger whereby large agribusinesses and out-of-area actors can capture the rents embedded in GIs without letting any benefits flow to small, rural actors who are the original custodians of the local sources.[155] Surbhi Jain argued that, if the benefits of a GI flow to a few powerful actors in the supply chain and are not shared equitably among the stakeholders, the GI is likely to have a limited impact on rural development.[156] Several authors have highlighted the increasing risk that out-of-area actors will capture GI benefits in an increasingly globalized environment,[157] particularly in developing countries.[158] Policies around GIs should therefore address that concern.

The advantage of the sui generis regime regarding this issue is that the contents of the product specification (code of practice) can be regulated. As many commentators

152. Dominique Barjolle et al., *Impacts of Geographical Indications: Review of Methods and Empirical Evidences*, Presentation at the International Association of Agricultural Economists Conference, Beijing, China (16-22 August 2009), p. 11.
153. Maria Cecilia Mancini, *Geographical Indications in Latin America Value Chains: A 'Branding from Below' Strategy or a Mechanism Excluding the Poorest?* 32 J. Rural Stud. 295 (2013).
154. Zhao et al., *supra* n. 23.
155. Rokiah Alavi et al., *The Economics of Intellectual Property: Suggestions for Further Research in Developing Countries and Countries with Economies in Transition* 119 (WIPO Publication 2009).
156. Surbhi Jain, *Effects of the Extension of Geographical Indications: A South Asian Perspective*, 16 Asia-Pacific Dev. J. 65 (2009).
157. Sarah Bowen, *Development from Within? The Potential for Geographical Indications in the Global South*, 13 J. World Intell. Prop. 231 (2010).
158. Alavi et al., *supra* n. 155.

have noted, the effects of GIs on rural development depend on the contents of the codes of practice.[159] Different types of wording in the codes may have different effects.[160] For example, the code of practice may require that the raw materials be sourced in a given area or that the products be processed in traditional ways,[161] which would create demand for local resources and skilled local labour.[162] The sui generis regime regulates the code of practice by, first, enumerating the elements that must be included in it (e.g., product characteristics, raw materials, geographical area, production methods, authentic and unvarying local methods, a link between the quality of the product and the geographical origin).[163] The link established in the code of practice must, in turn, meet the definition of a GI, which is also usually prescribed by the sui generis regime.[164]

Second, the sui generis regime can regulate the code of practice by determining by whom the code of practice is drawn. The importance of the 'writer' can be seen from the intense conflicts between the artisan producers and more industrial producers in the drawing up of the code of practice for *Culatello di Zibello* (salami).[165] One can easily imagine the disastrous consequences if the code of practice were drawn up only by the industrial producers.[166] Under the sui generis regime, it could be stipulated that the code of practice must be prepared by the GI applicant group, which should represent the interests of different types of operators equitably. The AOC regime, for instance, requires that the draft code of practice be prepared by the ODG. Two criteria must be met in order for a group to be recognized as an ODG: the representativeness and balanced representation of all categories of operators.[167] These provisions may serve to ensure the widest participation of all categories of operators while respecting their different and specific interests.

159. Belletti et al., *supra* n. 113, at 23.
160. Alessandro Pacciani et al., *The Role of Typical Products in Fostering Rural Development and the Effects of Regulation (EEC) 2081/92*, the 73rd Seminar of the European Association of Agricultural Economists ANCONA (2001).
161. However, these requirements must be justified as essential to ensure the specific quality, characteristics and uniqueness of the product.
162. For example, various traditional techniques are required in the code of practice for *Comté* Cheese. As a result, *Comté* generates five times more jobs than that of the generic, completely industrially produced *Emmentaler* cheese in the same area. *See* Petra van de Kop, Denis Sautier & Astrid Gerz, *Origin-Based Products: Lessons for Pro-poor Market Development* 83 (The Royal Tropical Institute-KIT 2006).
163. Article 7 of Regulation 1151/2012.
164. For example, Article 5 of Regulation 1151/2012 lays down two definitions for the PDO and the PGI.
165. Angela Tregear et al., *The Impact of Territorial Product Qualification Processes on the Rural Development Potential of Small-Scale Food Productions* 12 (XI World Congress of Rural Sociology 2004).
166. Decisions on the code of practice can be a source of conflict between different actors. Therefore, it is essential to encourage all qualified producers to engage in collective actions (reach compromise, draft code of practice). *See* Angela Tregear, *Regional Foods and Rural Development: The Role of Product Qualification*, 23 J. Rur. Stud. 12 (2007).
167. Article L. 642-18 C. rur.

Finally, the sui generis regime can regulate the code of practice by enabling public intervention to examine the contents of the draft, propose revisions to the draft, and approve or reject the draft or revisions of the approved code of practice.[168]

By contrast, protecting GIs as private rights under the trademark regime may not provide the advantages the sui generis regime can offer, since trademark protection implies that few requirements are placed on how and by whom the code of practice is defined, and little public control is exercised in the decision process. It is possible for an industry to define a code of practice in a way that runs counter to the quality–place nexus and fails to recognize the contribution of different operators to it.[169]

[2] Benefits of the Sui Generis Regime for the Preservation of Traditional Savoir-Faire

GIs are often considered to support the sustainability of traditional *savoir-faire*.[170] One explanation is that GI-denominated products frequently embody a component of traditional *savoir-faire*, which relates to the traditional methods by which the localized products are made.[171] Those methods, combined with local natural resources, lead to particular product characteristics, which may be valued by the consumer, who then becomes willing to pay a price premium. Thus, GIs help producers using those methods to obtain the price premium by differentiating products according to their place of origin and conveying information about quality.[172] The increased price constitutes the incentive for the producers to engage in the sustainable utilization of traditional *savoir-faire*.[173]

However, the truth is that, once the product's quality has been acknowledged (and the price premium has been obtained), the producers will try to take advantage of it by increasing their production volume. Where there is a strong demand for products, producers are encouraged to do so in order to meet market demand and maximize profits. Once the expected increased production exceeds the production capacity, the producers will search for ways to increase efficiency and productivity. In this process, traditional production methods may be seen as an obstacle, as they are often more time-consuming than modern high-tech methods.

168. For example, Article L. 642-5 of the Rural Code provides that the INAO may propose revisions to the code of practice drafted by the ODG.
169. Daniele Giovannucci et al., *Guide to Geographical Indications: Linking Products and Their Origins* 54 (International Trade Centre 2009); Estelle Biénabe et al., *Private Versus Public Quality Schemes for Origin-Labelled Products: Insights from the Karakul Pelts and Camdeboo Mohair Industries, in Developing geographical indications in the South* 73, 89 (Cerkia Bramley ed., Springer 2013).
170. Irene Calboli, *Of Markets, Culture, and Terroir: The Unique Economic and Culture-Related Benefits of Geographical Indications of Origin, in International Intellectual Property: A Handbook of Contemporary Research* 454 (Daniel J. Gervais ed., Edward Elgar Publishing 2015).
171. Teshager Worku Dagne, *Harnessing the Development Potential of Geographical Indications for Traditional Knowledge-Based Agricultural Products*, 5 J. Intell. Prop. L. & Prac. 441 (2010).
172. Jonathan Curci, *The Protection of Biodiversity and Traditional Knowledge in International Law of Intellectual Property* 317 (Cambridge University Press 2010).
173. *See* Bicskei et al., *supra* n. 33, at 223.

In fact, many reputed Chinese GIs are considering modifying or replacing traditional techniques, some of which are conductive or even essential to the characteristics of the products. For example, traditional methods of fermentation have been used for centuries to process '*Pixian* Chili Bean Paste'[174] and give the paste its brick red colour, smooth texture, and rich, blended flavour (a spiciness with subtle notes of sweetness). However, the drawback is that a long fermentation period is required (of at least one year).[175] This long period makes it difficult to increase production capacity. Producers have therefore financed or co-financed several studies in order to speed up the fermentation process via biological technology (e.g., by co-culturing lactobacillus with yeasts in the fermentation).[176] Similarly, studies have also been carried out on '*Fuling* Hot Pickled Mustard Tuber' with the aim of replacing traditional methods and thus shortening the long fermentation period.[177]

The sui generis GI regime may be useful for countering the trend towards the marginalization and exclusion of traditional *savoir-faire*. Although, like the trademark regime, it does not directly protect the underlying contents of traditional *savoir-faire*,[178] it achieves this by identifying the contents in the code of practice that must be respected by all producers who wish to be authorized GI users.[179] This does not imply the 'freezing' of production methods. The regime may allow for production techniques to evolve by permitting amendments to the code of practice.[180] Furthermore, under the regime, it can be stipulated that any amendment to the code of practice must be approved by the public authorities.[181] State involvement in this decision-making process may help to strike a balance between producers' interests (to take advantage of new technology) and the public interest (to preserve traditional *savoir-faire*, which may constitute China's ICH).

By contrast, protecting GIs as private property under the trademark regime would leave the question as to whether the tradition should be maintained entirely to the discretion of individual producers.

---

174. Yang Xiao, Pixian Douban Naogeming Jiyao Hao Haiyao Kuai [Revolution of Pixian Chili Bean Paste], SICHUAN RIBAO [SICHUAN DAILY], 19 March 2007.
175. Guojia Biaozhun GB/T 20560-2006 Dili Biaozhi Chanpin Pixian Douban [National Standard GB/T 20560-2006 for the Product of Geographical Indication: Pixian Bean Chili Paste], 18 September 2006.
176. Liu Chaolan et al., Rusuanjun he Jiaomu Gong Peiyang Jishu Suoduan Pixian Doubanjiang Chenniang de Yingyong Yanjiu [Reduction of Ripening Period of Pixian Bean Chili Pastes by Conculturing of Salt-Tolerance Lactobacillus and Yeasts], ZHONGGUO NIANGZAO [CHINA BREWING], March 2009, 105-109.
177. Chongqing University, Yizhong Zhacai Zhitoushi Fajiaoji Jiqi Zhibei Fangfa [Fermentation Agents for Hot Pickled Mustard Tuber and Preparation Method], Patent Application n° CN200910103925.8 (25 May 2009).
178. For example, Spanish producers of *Cava* can learn and utilize techniques similar to the *méthode champenoise*.
179. *See*, for example, Article 7 of Regulation 1151/2012.
180. David R. Downes, *How Intellectual Property Could Be a Tool to Protect Traditional Knowledge*, 25 Colum. J. Envtl. L. 253 (2000); Xiomara Fernanda Quinones-Ruiz et al., *How Are Food Geographical Indications Evolving?: An Analysis of EU GI Amendments*, 120 Brit. Food J. 1876, 1884 (2018).
181. For example, Article L. 721-3 of the Intellectual Property Code states that the modification of the cahier des charges must be approved by the INPI.

To conclude, in this chapter, we have looked into the choice of one regime over the other, which can be made only according to practical, technical, and economic considerations. The first step is recognizing the reality that China has a large number of products that are identified by the name of their geographical origin, from which a given quality, reputation, or other characteristics are derived. We have also recognized the importance of geographical origin to Chinese consumers when making purchases, which is both a contemporary reality and rooted in history.

Since the link to *terroir* means a lot to consumers, the second step is the identification of a strong need for specific rules in order to maintain, reinforce, and add value to this link. From a technical viewpoint, it is difficult to craft these rules in trademark law.

The choice is not only a technical matter; it also has important implications for producers, consumers, rural development, and TK. The last step is thus a practical and economic analysis comparing the two regimes in terms of their estimated benefits to the above-mentioned areas.

The above considerations lead to the conclusion that choosing the sui generis regime as the main mechanism for the protection of GIs would be the best option for China. A reform of China's GI scheme thus needs to be considered (Chapter 8).

CHAPTER 8

Improvement of China's GI Legislation at the Crossroads of the EU and US Approaches

Having established that Chinese legislators should make a choice in favour of the European sui generis approach, one closing question remains: how to reform the existing systems in order to strengthen the role of China's sui generis systems and reduce the role of the trademark regime in the protection of GIs. This chapter provides recommendations for the reconstruction of China's GI framework and the design of a sui generis system. The parallel GI systems should be unified through a merger of the former authorities responsible for GI protection. Collective organizations should replace trademark owners as those responsible for the management and defence of GIs. The unified sui generis system should enhance quality control measures and defence mechanisms. This improvement requires, in particular, a higher level of protection for all GIs.

In November 2020, General Secretary of the CPC Xi Jinping stressed that China should improve legislation in the field of GIs.[1] Several indications enable us to predict that the European sui generis approach will be promoted in China. The 2019 EU-China GI Agreement requires China to establish the essential elements for the procedure for the registration and protection of GIs,[2] which are also the essential elements of the European sui generis GI systems. In other words, the EU-China GI Agreement will bring China's GI protection approach closer to the European approach. Moreover, China's

1. Xi Focus: Xi Stresses Strengthening Intellectual Property Rights Protection, Xinhua Net (19 June 2021), http://www.xinhuanet.com/english/2020-12/02/c_139556530.htm.
2. *Agreement Between the European Union and the Government of the People's Republic of China on Cooperation on, and Protection of, Geographical Indications*, OJ L 408I, 4.12.2020, p. 3, Article 2.

Civil Code adopted in 2020 lists GIs as separate IP rights, independent from trademarks.[3] It follows the European approach of giving GIs an independent legal status, rather than the US approach of considering GIs as a subset of trademarks.

However, the US-China Economic and Trade Agreement, concluded in January 2020, contains several provisions designed to undermine the EU's GI (i.e., *terroir*) philosophy and efforts in China. As a countermeasure against the EU's efforts, Article 1.16(1)(b) of the US-China Trade Agreement stipulates that any GI may become generic over time and be subject to cancellation on that basis. Article 1.16(1)(b) can be relied on to cancel GIs that have been 'recognized pursuant to an international agreement or otherwise'. Article 1.16(1)(a) identified consumer perception as the determining factor in testing whether a term is generic, unlike the EU's approach, which also takes *terroir* into account.[4] The Agreement sets out a list of factors that may indicate how consumers understand a term: dictionaries, newspapers, websites, trade usage, standard rules (such as the Codex Alimentarius), use of the term on imported goods from a place other than the indicated origin, and consumer confusion resulting from such use. Factors such as consumer confusion resulting from the use of imported goods were 'invented' to confront the EU's trade agenda against the US food industry.

At the crossroads of the EU and US approaches, China's legislators have not yet decided which system should be employed as the primary means of improving GI legislation. The choice consists of determining whether the existing sui generis GI systems should be abolished (if the trademark protection is deemed sufficient) or whether the GI systems should be maintained and function as the main instrument for GI protection (if the European sui generis approach is proven necessary). Although the former authorities responsible for GI protection (the former SAIC and former AQSIQ) were merged in 2018, the Draft Provisions on the Protection of GIs issued in 2020 by the new authority (the CNIPA) contain no indication of how the three parallel GI systems will be unified or harmonized.

Chapter 7 has explored the question of which approach (trademark or sui generis protection) better serves the needs of China. It considered the possibility of absorbing certain sui generis rules within the trademark system, which turns out to be unfeasible. After having compared the benefits that could be obtained from the two approaches, we concluded that the sui generis regime should play the primary role in the protection of GIs, and the trademark regime should play a complementary role. Chinese legislators should make a choice in favour of the European sui generis approach.

In this chapter, we outline our recommendations on how to reform the existing framework in order to harmonize China's parallel GI systems (§8.01) and improve national legislation in the field of GIs (§8.02).

3. China's Civil Code, Article 123 (2020).
4. *See* Chapter 4 *supra*.

§8.01 REFORM TOWARDS A UNIFIED GI REGIME

China's current systems responsible for protecting GIs are composed of the trademark system and two separate sui generis systems. The reform should aim first at unifying these systems. Along with that unification, the roles of the existing management bodies should be adjusted.

[A] Restructuring of China's GI Scheme

The trademark system should be reformed so that it would no longer remain a primary mechanism to protect GIs and become a complementary tool. The two special systems should be unified so as to simplify GI legislation.

[1] Revision of the Trademark System

As illustrated in the previous chapter, the trademark system's role in GI protection should be reduced to eliminate duplication with the sui generis regime, which is more suitable for unleashing the benefits, both private and public, associated with GIs. However, this does not mean that trademarks (including collective and certification marks)[5] could no longer be used as a marketing tool for promoting GI products.

In fact, as GIs, trademarks also encourage product differentiation and help producers obtain price premiums.[6] Their marketing power has long been recognized by market players, as is reflected in the constantly growing number of new applications for trademark registration.[7] Unlike GIs, however, trademarks more often take the form of images, pictures, and combinations of images or pictures and words, or even sound, colours, and three-dimensional shapes.[8] In certain situations, these forms would be easier for consumers to memorize and more evocative than mere geographical names. Moreover, trademarks are not linked to a particular kind of product but can be used to designate a wide variety of products. The 'umbrella marks' can cover different GIs and make a 'basket of products' easily recognizable,[9] which is particularly important for

5. In this chapter, except where otherwise specified, the term 'trademarks' encompasses collective marks and certification marks.
6. David Higgins, *The Making of Modern Trade Mark Law: The UK, 1860–1914, A Business History Perspective, in Trademarks and Brands: An Interdisciplinary Critique* 42 (Lionel AF Bently et al. eds, Cambridge University Press 2008); William M. Landes & Richard A. Posner, *Trademark Law: An Economic Perspective,* 30 J.L. & Econ. 265 (1987).
7. Some commentators compare trademarks and official logos for GIs and infer that trademarks appear to be more relevant information in the consumer's valuation of the available products. *See* Céline Bonnet & Michel Simioni, *Assessing Consumer Response to Protected Designation of Origin Labelling: A Mixed Multinomial Logit Approach,* 28 Eur. Rev. Agric. Econ. 433 (2001).
8. GIs may also include images, expressions or three-dimensional shapes, which refer to a specific geographical area, such as a bulbous shape *Bocksbeutel* bottle. However, in most cases, GIs are denominations or names referring to a specific area. *See* Case 16/83 *Criminal proceedings against Karl Prantl* [1984] ECR 01299.
9. For example, the umbrella mark '*Sud de France*' designates a wide range of products and covers various GIs. *See* Chapter 3 *supra*.

GIs that are not yet widely known and have a low production volume.[10] Furthermore, from a legal perspective, the Madrid System allows applicants to obtain trademark protection in multiple territories (up to 114 territories across its 98 members) by filing one application, instead of filing separately in the trademark offices of the various contracting parties. The convenience the system offers cannot be overlooked by GI operators, as no system is in place for expanding the geographical coverage of GI protection in an equally efficient way.[11]

It is thus important to achieve a balance between the need to avoid duplication and the need to avoid depriving GI operators of a powerful marketing tool. This is feasible since GIs and trademarks are not in competition but are complementary as long as they fulfil different functions.[12]

The separation of their functions can be realized by the 'non-descriptiveness' requirement that must be met in order for a GI to constitute a valid trademark. A sign composed exclusively of a GI is normally descriptive,[13] and thus an application for registration of the sign as a trademark should be rejected. However, nothing prevents a sign containing the GI from being registered by operators who have rights to use the GI if the sign is associated with other elements (pictures, images, or words) that give the whole structure a distinctive character. As the complex mark can serve to distinguish products according to a particular commercial source or provide additional information to consumers, it would not be in competition with the GI but be complementary to it.

It is also worth recalling that China's trademark law does not explicitly prohibit the registration of a trademark that is geographically descriptive. Instead, it explicitly allows a GI to be registered as a collective or certification mark without the need to add any distinctive elements or acquire distinctiveness through use.[14]

Based on the above considerations, we propose amending Article 11, paragraph 1 of the Trademark Law by replacing the sentence '(the following shall not be registered as trademarks): (2) those having direct reference to the quality, main raw materials, function, use, weight, quantity or other features of the goods in respect of which the trademarks are used' with the following: 'trademarks that consist exclusively of signs or indications that may serve, in trade, to designate the quality, main raw materials, function, use, weight, quantity, geographical origin, or other characteristics of the goods or services'. The amended article shall apply equally to collective marks and certification marks. Accordingly, the current exemptions for collective marks and certification marks should be removed,[15] and the special rules for 'GI

10. Thomas Debril, *Interactions des marchands et qualifications des marchandises: le cas du marché des vins de Bourgogne, in Sociologie de l'action organisée, Nouvelles études de cas*, Bruxelles, De Boeck, 2011, pp. 215-233.
11. The ability of the Lisbon System (for the international registration of AOs and GIs) is conditioned by the limited number of contracting parties.
12. Bertil Sylvander, *DOLPHINS Concerted Action: Development of Origin Labelled Products: Humanity, Innovation and Sustainability* 43 (WP7 Final Report, 2004).
13. However, if it has acquired a secondary meaning through consistent use, it is not descriptive.
14. *See* Chapter 3 *supra*.
15. Collective marks and certification marks will not be subject to a statutory derogation from the prohibition on registering signs that serve to designate geographical origin.

collective marks' and 'GI certification marks' (provided in the Measures for Collective Marks and Certification Marks)[16] should be abolished.

Finally, this proposed amendment does not prevent the trademark system from protecting sole GIs. The system can still play a defensive role, ensuring that the level of protection afforded to GIs by the sui generis regime is applied in the examination of absolute and relative grounds for refusal.

[2] Unification of Sui Generis Systems

The former AQSIQ and the MOA have both engaged in the protection of GIs, and each has established its own sui generis system. The two systems overlap[17] but also have considerable differences in terms of quality control measures and protection mechanisms.[18] This makes it difficult for producers to activate the GI application process (they must choose one or both of the systems) and for consumers to understand the distinction between products that are protected by one system and those that are not.[19]

Many commentators have pointed out the negative effect that the complex sui generis GI rules produce,[20] including wasting administrative resources,[21] creating conflicts of interest,[22] adding costs for producers,[23] confusing consumers,[24] and constraining the development of China's GI industry. They have therefore advocated a merger of the systems.[25]

One may argue that GIs are not governed by a unified system even in France and the EU, where sui generis regulations are highly developed. The French systems consist mainly of the AOC regime for agricultural products and the IGPIA regime for industrial products. The EU-level systems include four regulations – for agricultural products and foodstuffs, wine, spirits, and aromatized wine. However, those regimes do not overlap

16. *See* Chapter 3 *supra*.
17. It is possible to register a GI under both systems.
18. *See* Chapter 4 *supra*.
19. Products 'that are not so protected' include products protected by the other GI system and products that do not belong to neither of the two systems.
20. Wang Lianfeng, Dili Biaozhi de Falu Baohu [Legal Protection of Geographical Indications], ZHENGZHOU DAXUE XUEBAO [JOURNAL OF ZHENGZHOU UNIVERSITY], October 2003, 66; Lu Guoqiang & Wu Denglou, Woguo Dili Biaozhi Falu Zhidu de Wanshan [Improvement of the Legal System of Geographical Indications in China], FAXUE [LAW SCIENCE], 20 January 2006, 154; Xiong Ying, Lun Woguo Dili Biaozhi Baohu Moshi de Danyizhi [The Unitary System of Geographical Indication Protection in China], ZHONGHUA SHANGBIAO [CHINA TRADEMARK], January 2017, 59-62; Fu Zimei, Chandi Baohu Ting Shui de? [Protection of Place of Origin: To Whom Should We Listen?], PEOPLE'S DAILY, 23 July 2007.
21. The overlap of the two systems is considered a waste of administrative resources.
22. The conflicts arise where a GI has been registered under both systems, but the applicants are not the same party or the authorized users are not the same.
23. Where producers have obtained the rights to use the sign under both systems, they must comply with the rules of both systems.
24. Chinese consumers have a tough time distinguishing between brands, GI products protected by the former AQSIQ and agricultural GIs by the Ministry of Agriculture.
25. Wang Xiaobing, Guanlianxing Yaosu yu Dili Biaozhi Fa de Gouzao [The Linkage and the Construction of Geographical Indication Law], FAXUE YANJIU [LEGAL RESEARCH], May 2015, 100.

at the national and EU levels.[26] They are divided according to product category. Their relationship is different from that between the GI products system established by the former AQSIQ and the system established by the MOA. Furthermore, the EU has also considered the possibility of merging the four systems of GI protection and creating a single GI legislation aiming at improving its GI scheme through simplification.[27] China does not have to tread the same old path that the EU is now trying to evade.

The simplification of the sui generis GI systems appears to be more important to China, since a simplified structure would help Chinese consumers, most of whom have little knowledge of GI protection, to recognize the GI regime and understand its core pillars, which would in turn have a positive impact on consumers' preference for GI-denominated products.[28]

On the basis of the above considerations, we propose simplifying China's GI framework by merging the sui generis GI systems and creating a single 'GI law'. The unified GI system should cover not only agricultural, forestry, fishery, and food products but also industrial and artisanal products. The idea of establishing a separate system for forest products, as proposed by the former SFA of China, should be discarded, as those products fall within the protection scope of the unified system.

One remaining concern is how to define GIs in the unified system. We will recall that the trademark system and the two sui generis GI systems each have a specific definition of GIs. The definition given in the trademark system resembles the TRIPS definition of GIs, while the definitions elaborated in the sui generis GI systems are similar to the French definition of AOs.[29] Does the merger necessarily entail a merger of the GI definitions? Although a single GI definition would be more understandable, there would be a risk of de-emphasizing the closer link between the products and the *terroir* from which the products originate and derive their characteristics if a broader definition of GIs (such as the TRIPS definition) were adopted. Conversely, if a narrow definition (such as the AO definition) were adopted, there would be a risk of excluding products that have a looser link to their region of origin from protection. This risk is particularly high for industrial products and crafts. Thus, as a compromise, the unified system may retain two categories of geographical indicators – AOs and GIs. The AO could be defined as any denomination consisting of or containing the name of a geographical area, or another denomination known as referring to such area, any name that serves to designate a good as originating in that geographical area, where the quality or characteristics of the good are due exclusively or essentially to the geographical environment, including natural and human factors. The GI could be defined as any indication consisting of or containing the name of a geographical area, or another indication known as referring to such area that identifies a good as originating in that

26. The EU-level systems also do not overlap with national systems because of the exclusive nature of the European regulations. *See* Chapter 4 *supra*.
27. European Commission, *Proposal for a Regulation of the European Parliament and of Council on Agricultural Product Quality Schemes*, COM(2010)733 final (10 December 2010) p. 5.
28. Li Yuping et al., Zhongguo Dili Biaozhi Baohu Fazhan Yanjiu [Research on the Protection and Development of Geographical Indications in China], GUANGDONG NONGYE KEXUE [GUANGDONG AGRICULTURAL SCIENCES], October 2012, 213-232.
29. *See* Chapter 2 *supra*.

geographical area, where a given quality, reputation or other characteristic of the good is essentially attributable to its geographical origin.[30] The former category could be used to highlight a tight product-place nexus, which may give rise to higher added value, while the latter would be more suitable for industrial products.

[B] Reallocation of the Roles of Management Bodies

The restructuring of the GI systems implies the need to harmonize the competing, duplicated efforts of the public authorities and to recognize and clarify the roles of collective organizations.

[1] Harmonization of the Roles of Public Establishments

The existing systems for GI protection (the trademark system, GI product system, agricultural GI system) are managed in parallel by the former SAIC (the CNIPA since 2018), the former AQSIQ (the CNIPA since 2018), and the MOA. With the revision of the trademark system and the unification of the sui generis systems, a unified regime would replace the existing systems, giving rise to the need to adjust the roles of the public establishments.

The first question to be discussed is which body should be the competent authority in charge of the operating of the unified regime. The CNIPA and MOA have each gained management experience in running their respective systems. Nevertheless, the MOA appears to be the most suitable for achieving the objectives of the sui generis GI regime and should therefore be charged with the supervision and operation of the regime. The regime should not be limited to the protection of products closely linked to *terroir* but should also deal with the protection of *terroir* itself. For example, Article L. 643-4 of the French Rural Code enables organizations responsible for the defence and management of AOCs to refer the matter to the competent administrative authority where 'the content of a planning or an urban planning document in the process of being drawn up, a project for equipment, construction, use of land or subsoil and establishing commercial activities is likely to prejudice the area or conditions of production, the quality or the image of the AOC product'.[31] This administrative authority is obliged to obtain, prior to any decision, the opinion of the minister responsible for agriculture.[32] Similarly, China's MOA, one of whose functions is to

30. The proposed definitions have borrowed the TRIPS language common to all WTO members and the Lisbon Agreement language common to countries with a tradition of protecting AOs.
31. Article L. 643-4(1) C. rur.: '*Tout organisme de défense et de gestion d'une appellation d'origine peut saisir l'autorité administrative compétente s'il estime que le contenu d'un document d'aménagement ou d'urbanisme en cours d'élaboration, un projet d'équipement, de construction, d'exploitation du sol ou du sous-sol, d'implantation d'activités économiques est de nature à porter atteinte à l'aire ou aux conditions de production, à la qualité ou à l'image du produit d'appellation.*'
32. Article L. 643-4(2) C. rur.: '*Préalablement à toute décision, cette autorité administrative doit recueillir l'avis du ministre chargé de l'agriculture, pris après consultation de l'Institut national de l'origine et de la qualité.*'

guide the exploitation of agricultural land and other land suitable for agricultural purposes, would be the most appropriate body to charge with protecting *terroir*.[33]

Furthermore, the purposes of establishing a special regime for GIs include facilitating the valorization of products and supporting rural development.[34] These objectives fall within the mandate of the MOA.[35] Regarding the valorization of products, many authors have pointed out that the legal protection of product names alone is insufficient to achieve this goal.[36] Other factors are important in product success. For instance, the construction of a highway passing through the production area of an AOC may help promote it.[37] Conversely, the production and marketing of products may be constrained by underdeveloped water, energy, and transport infrastructure in rural areas.[38] Improvements in infrastructure and other basic services in those areas need the support of the MOA.[39] Regarding rural development, the MOA can help farmers update production activities so as to adapt to hygienic and quality requirements set by the code of practice through educational, scientific, and technical assistance.[40] Finally, 95 per cent of registered GIs are related to agricultural, forestry, and fishery products.[41] It also falls within the responsibility of the MOA to provide quality and certification schemes for those products.[42]

We thus consider it appropriate to entrust the MOA with the mission of managing the system. An administrative public body could be established under the supervision and direction of the MOA to implement the mission, receive and review GI applications, initiate opposition procedures, organize expert panels for further assessment, and propose the registration of the GIs to the MOA for approval. The mission of the body would be similar to that of the INAO.

---

33. One of the Ministry's primary functions is to take the lead in preparing and implementing strategies, mid-term and long-term plans and major policies related to agriculture, rural areas and farmers. *See Institutional Functions*, MARA (19 May 2021), http://english.moa.gov.cn/Institutional/.
34. *See* Chapter 7 *supra*.
35. The MOA is responsible for drawing up rural development plans and organizing their implementation. It should direct the rational structural adjustment of agricultural industries, rational allocation of agricultural resources, and product quality improvement.
36. Cerkia Bramley, *A Review of the Socio-Economic Impact of Geographical Indications: Considerations for the Developing World* (WIPO Worldwide Symposium on Geographical Indications, Lima, Peru 22-24 June 2011).
37. Chantal Pégaz, *La défense de l'AOC*, Revue lamy droit des affaires, n° 68, 2004.
38. WTO, *Exploring the Linkage Between the Domestic Policy Environment and International Trade* 86 (World Trade Report, 2004).
39. Office of the Science Committee of the Ministry of Agriculture, XIANDAI NONGYE YU XINNONGCUN JIANSHE [MODERN AGRICULTURE AND NEW RURAL CONSTRUCTION], (China Financial & Economic Publishing House, 2010).
40. The MOA is responsible for guiding agricultural education and the development of agricultural vocational skills.
41. Wang Yafeng & Jiang Hezhong, Dili Biaozhi Nongchanpin Xiaofeizhe Goumai Yiyuan he Goumai Xingwei Yanjiu Zongshu [Synthesis of Researches on Consumers' Purchase Intention and Behavior of Geographical Indications of Agricultural Products], ZHONGXIAO QIYE GUANLI YU KEJI [MANAGEMENT & TECHNOLOGY OF SME], September 2016, 114.
42. The MOA is entrusted with the task of organizing the implementation of quality supervision and certification of various agricultural products and green food products.

The second issue is the need for harmonized efforts from other public establishments that would play important roles in the unified system. The CNIPA, which merged with the former AQSIQ, has strong expertise in quality inspection. Its quality and technical supervision function is performed through provincial-level bureaus and various lower-level bureaus. Therefore, the CNIPA can play the same role played by the certification and inspection bodies in the French AOC regime, carrying out the monitoring of compliance with the code of practice.

Moreover, the CNIPA, which is also responsible for registering trademarks, can protect the names of GI products in a defensive way. It would ensure that the protection afforded to GIs by the sui generis regime is applied via the examination of absolute and relative grounds for the refusal of trademark applications.

[2] Strengthening of the Roles of Collective Organizations

While tasks could be reallocated among public authorities in light of the multiple benefits GIs can bring, we must not lose sight of the fact that state involvement in the form of a protection system can enhance the socioeconomic impacts of GIs but cannot create them.[43]

European experience has shown that GI protection does not necessarily secure a price premium for producers. '*Ternasco de Aragon*' faces stiff competition from typical substitutes; the offer of hand-made cheddar is insufficient to convince UK consumers to buy farm products; apricot '*Luizet du Valais*' is not sufficiently favourably perceived by distributors or consumers; and the list goes on.[44] One study commissioned by the European Commission suggests that GI protection alone cannot overcome the disappointing results that usually flow from inadequate production and marketing methods.[45]

Thus, additional gross margins are directly linked to the collective actions of producers.[46] Since GIs exhibit the characteristics of public goods that in many cases cannot be provided by single producers, their success depends on the ability of several producers to collectively 'codify' product quality and production practices on the basis of individual competencies (e.g., technology, know-how, financial resources, flexibility in production), ensure compliance with the codified rules, and seize market

43. Cerkia Bramley & Kirsten Johann, *Exploring the Economic Rationale for Protecting Geographical Indicators in Agriculture*, 46 Agrekon 47 (2007); Astrid Gerz et al., *Geographical Indications: A Way Forward for Local Development*, Summary of the International Training Module, Prangins, Switzerland (14-25 May 2007), p. 38.
44. Dominique Barjolle & Bertil Sylvander, *Some Factors of Success for Origin Labelled Products in Agri-food Supply Chains in Europe: Market, Internal Resources and Institutions, in Agri-food Supply Chains in Europe: Market, Internal Resources, and Institutions* 1441 (Economies et Sociétés 2002).
45. Areté & Directorate-General for Agriculture and Rural Development, *Study on Assessing the Added Value of PDO/PGI Products* 11 (Final Report, KF-02-14-448-EN-N, 2014).
46. *See* Susana López-Bayón et al., *In Search of Agri-food Quality for Wine: Is It Enough to Join a Geographical Indication?*, 36 Agribusiness 568 (2020); Thanasis Kizos et al., *The Governance of Geographical Indications: Experiences of Practical Implementation of Selected Case Studies in Austria, Italy, Greece and Japan*, 119 Brit. Food J. 2863, 2874 (2017).

opportunities (e.g., to collectively negotiate a premium price with large distribution channels).[47]

In Europe, collective actions are usually undertaken by producers' groups. Most GI projects are initiated collectively by professionals who are personally involved in production and commercial transactions.[48] The sui generis GI recognition scheme may foster and reinforce collective action by, for example, requiring a democratic decision-making process or imposing discipline on the code of practice.[49] The AOC registration process requires that applications be presented by groups representing operators.[50] The procedural conditions could help operators by making it compulsory for them to meet together, come to know each other and set up collective strategies.[51]

In China, by contrast, GI projects are usually initiated by public authorities and Non-governmental Organizations. A local government unit, a professional association, or even an individual enterprise can apply for the recognition of GI products. Although the MOA requires that the application be filed by a collective organization of farmers or an industrial association, there is no requirement as to the applicant's representativeness.[52] Such a top-down approach is seldom successful since it may not sufficiently consider operators' concerns and commercial risks.[53] Hence, it is not surprising when only a few operators actively participate in a GI scheme after registration.[54] A study conducted by the *Shaoxing* Intermediate People's Court shows that big leading firms seldom use the registered GI '*Shaoxing* Rice Wine' because they fear that the image and reputation that they build around the GI through their individual efforts would only benefit others and open opportunities for free-riders. SMEs are interested in using the GI but find themselves unable to join the party because of their incapacity to fully meet the quality and large-scale requirements.[55] The operators simply have no desire to work together based on shared goals and objectives.

---

47. Francesco Vanni, *Agriculture and Public Goods: The Role of Collective Action* 24 (Springer 2014); Guido Van Huylenbroeck, *Market and Rural Policy Institutions to Stimulate Multifunctional Food and Fibre Production, in The Multifunctional Role of Forests: Policies, Methods and Case Studies* 57 (European Forest Institute 2008); Barjolle & Sylvander, *supra* n. 44.
48. Sophie Reviron, Erik Thevenod-Mottet & Nadja El Benni, *Geographical Indications: Creation and Distribution of Economic Value in Developing Countries* 19 (Swiss National Centre of Competence in Research (NCCR), Working Paper 14, 2009).
49. Sophie Réviron & Jean-Marc Chappuis, *Geographical Indications: Collective Organization and Management, in Labels of Origin for Food: Local Development, Global Recognition* 45 (Elizabeth Barham et al. eds, CABI Publishing 2011).
50. *See* Chapter 4 *supra*.
51. Giovanni Belletti & Andrea Marescotti, *Strengthening International Research on Geographical Indications: From Research Foundation to Consistent Policy* 36 (D2-WP2 Report, 2006).
52. *See* Chapter 4 *supra*.
53. *See* Reviron et al., *supra* n. 48.
54. Shang Xudong & Li Binlong, Woguo Dili Biaozhi Nongchanpin Baohu he Fazhan Wenti yu Duice [Protection and Development of Agricultural Products of Geographical Indications in China: Problems and Countermeasures], JIAGE LILUN YU SHIJIAN [PRICE THEORY & PRACTICE], November 2011, 73; Zhao Wenming, Dili Biaozhi Zhong Zhuce Qing Shiyong Difang Tute Nongchanpin Nan Tuiguang [Emphasizing Registration but De-emphasizing Usage: Geographical Indications Are Difficult to Promote Local Special Agricultural Products], FAZHI RIBAO [LEGAL DAILY], 25 December 2009; Yuping et al., *supra* n. 28, at 217.
55. Shaoxing Intermediate People's Court, Guanyu Shaoxing Huangjiu Chanye Zhishi Chanquan Baohu de Diaoyan Baogao [Investigation Report on the Protection of Intellectual Property

One commentator employed the metaphor of 'building a house from the roof down' to describe the situation in which a GI project is started when the necessary organizational infrastructure is not yet in place.[56] In this scenario, collective organizations can be regarded as the foundation. China's GI regime should thus be designed to promote collective actions by the operators and foster collective organizations.[57]

Based on the above considerations, we propose that China's GI regime should require that a GI be applied for, defended, and managed by a *single* collective organization that represents all operators concerned. The use of the registered GI should be conditional on membership in the organization. In order to consolidate the network, all operators should have an equal chance to express their objectives and express opinions on the future of the products. It is therefore necessary for the organization to represent, in a balanced manner, all types of operators.

Furthermore, the role of collective organizations can be stipulated in the 'GI law'. A collective organization for the defence and management of a GI should be entitled to help ensure that the quality, reputation, and authenticity of their products are guaranteed in the market by monitoring the use of the name in trade; take action to ensure adequate legal protection of the GI; develop information and promotion activities aimed at communicating the value-adding attributes (*terroir*) of the product to consumers; develop activities to ensure product compliance with the specification; take action to improve the performance of the scheme; take measures to enhance the value of products; and, where necessary, take steps to prevent or counter any measures that are detrimental to the image of those products.[58]

§8.02 REFORM TOWARDS AN EFFECTIVE SUI GENERIS REGIME

As demonstrated in Chapter 7, like any other system, the sui generis GI system is not effective per se but only when properly designed. It is not a good tool for GIs simply because it is 'sui generis'. The design of the system must allow it to be effective.[59]

It is beyond the scope of this chapter to discuss all the elements that an effective GI system needs. These proposals are based on the comparative study of the sui generis systems in France, the EU, and China carried out in Chapters 3 and 4.

Regarding Shaoxing Rice Wine Industry], 23 November 2011; Zhan Ailan & Mao Shanshan, Shaoxing Huangjiu Dili Biaozhi Guanli Shijian ji Qishi [Practice and Enlightenment of the Geographical Indication Management of Shaoxing Yellow Rice Wine], ZHEJIANG NONGYE KEXUE [JOURNAL OF ZHEJIANG AGRICULTURAL SCIENCES], May 2012, 770-774.

56. Nuria Ackermann & Fabio Russo, *Adding Value to Traditional Products of Regional Origin: A Guide to Creating a Quality Consortium* 2 (United Nations Industrial Development Organization 2010).
57. Yi Jiming, Dili Biaozhi Baohu Renzhong Daoyuan [The Protection of Geographical Indications Has a Long Way to Go], ZHONGGUO ZHISHI CHANQUAN BAO [CHINA INTELLECTUAL PROPERTY NEWS], 15 July 2020.
58. This proposal transposes Article 45 of Regulation 1151/2012, which recognizes and clarifies the role of groups.
59. *See* Dev Gangjee, *Sui Generis or Independent Geographical Indications Protection, in The Cambridge Handbook of International and Comparative Trademark Law* 256 (Irene Calboli & Jane Ginsburg ed., Cambridge University Press 2020).

A high level of control and protection characterize the French/EU sui generis systems. The lack of these two features in China's sui generis systems has had a negative impact on their effectiveness. In order for the future unified GI regime to be effective, reforms should be undertaken to enhance quality control measures and protection levels.

[A] Enhancement of Control Measures

Quality control could be strengthened by multiplying the control levels and organizing the control activities according to an approved control plan.

[1] Multiplication of Control Levels

Unlike French GI systems, which provide multiple control levels to verify the compliance of products with their specifications, China's sui generis GI systems each rely extensively on one control level. Under the system managed by the former AQISQ (the CNIPA since 2018), quality control for GI products is undertaken by public authorities (the CNIPA and its local bureaus). Under the MOA, however, monitoring is mainly carried out by farmers' groups or industry associations that are GI holders.[60]

Each approach has disadvantages. While the public authorities may offer guarantees of independence, impartiality, and competence, they have difficulty implementing the checks due to financial and human constraints, especially when it comes to supervising numerous small production units, which prefer to produce and sell their products individually.[61] Nor is it easy for farmers' groups and industry associations to carry out effective checks. Those groups are often established with the support of the local government for the purpose of registering a GI and are therefore not likely to have adequate training or experience. In addition, they are not entitled to charge fees to GI users.[62] Their activities are financed by the local government, but the funds are usually very limited.[63]

---

60. *See* Chapter 4 *supra*.
61. Xing Zhao, Donald Finlay & Moya Kneafsey, *The Effectiveness of Contemporary Geographical Indications (GIs) Schemes in Enhancing the Quality of Chinese Agrifoods: Experiences from the Field*, 36 J. Rural Stud. 77, 84 (2014).
62. Article 15 of the Measures for the Administration of Geographical Indications for Agricultural Products: 'To use a geographical indication, an entity or individual shall conclude an agreement on the use of geographical indication with the registration certificate holder of the indication on the basis of production and operation year, and the agreement shall bear the quantity and scope of use as well as the relevant responsibilities and obligations. The registration certificate holder of a geographical indication of agricultural products may not charge fees for use against users of the indication.'
63. Li Xiuli, Liu Shiyi & Xu Weiyuan, Dili Biaozhi Guanli Quewei de Xianshi Kaobian ji Jiejue Fanglue [Realistic Textual Research on and Resolution to Geographical Indication Management Absence], QINGDAO NONGYE DAXUE XUEBAO [JOURNAL OF QINGDAO AGRICULTURAL UNIVERSITY], February 2014, 49; Wang Xiaobing, Woguo Canjia WTO Dili Biaozhi Tanpan de Lichang he Duice [China's Position in WTO Negotiation Protecting GIs], ZHISHI CHANQUAN [INTELLECTUAL PROPERTY], January 2010, 49.

Thus, neither approach, alone, can function efficiently. Over the last decade, many GI-labelled products have been reported by the media as having serious quality problems: pesticide-poisoned *Jinhua* ham,[64] adulterated *Pingyao* beef,[65] *Baiyangdian* duck eggs containing Sudan red,[66] and the list continues to grow.[67] Media coverage of such sub-standard products is likely to give the consumer the impression that the products' quality cannot be guaranteed by the GI systems.[68]

We thus propose that China's future unified GI regime should adopt a mixed approach, using the efforts of both public and collective organizations. Quality control could take place at three levels. The first level can be referred to as 'internal control': individual operators should perform checks on their own products and create documents allowing the traceability of the products; producers' groups should verify the traceability of the products, compile the documents prepared by operators for further checks by external bodies, and monitor if critical production phases meet the requirements set forth in the specifications. The second level can be referred to as 'external control': the CNIPA and its local bureaus should carry out control over the production conditions and be responsible for verifying if the products conform to the parameters set forth in the specifications. The third level is the control carried out by the MOA, which should periodically evaluate the effectiveness of the internal and external controls.

[2] Submission of Control Plan

Having considered the bodies that should be responsible for undertaking controls, it is also useful to consider how the controls should be carried out. In France, this question is addressed by Article L. 642-2 of the Rural Code, which requires that the code of practice be associated with a control or inspection plan.[69] It is the control or inspection plan that specifies detailed rules for the implementation of quality controls, including monitoring plans, monitoring frequency, monitoring points, target values, control methodologies, and sanction measures.[70]

China's sui generis GI systems require GI applicants to submit documents containing the name to be protected, the geographical area delimited, a description of the method of obtaining the product, and proof of the link between the quality or

64. Huotui Zao Wuran Baoguo Li You Nongyao [Ham Contaminated by Pesticides], CCTV MEIZHOU ZHILIANG BAOGAO [CCTV WEEKLY QUALITY REPORT], 6 December 2003.
65. Luomarou Maochong Pingyao Niurou [Passing Horsemeat off as Pingyao Beef], CCTV MEIZHOU ZHILIANG BAOGAO [CCTV WEEKLY QUALITY REPORT], 15 February 2004.
66. Sudanhong Zaochu Hongxin Yadan [Sudan Red Makes Red Egg Yolk], CCTV MEIZHOU ZHILIANG BAOGAO [CCTV WEEKLY QUALITY REPORT], 13 December 2006.
67. Zhao Xiaoping, DILI BIAOZHI DE FALU BAOHU YAOJIU [RESEARCH ON LEGAL PROTECTION OF GEOGRAPHICAL INDICATIONS], at 286 (Law Press China, 2007).
68. Wang Lei, Jiedu Meizhou Zhiliang Baogao de Pingheng Baodao [Interpretation of the Weekly Quality Report: Balanced Media Coverage], DANGDAI CHUANBO [CONTEMPORARY COMMUNICATIONS], May 2005, 90; Xiuli et al., *supra* n. 63, at 47.
69. *See* Chapter 4 *supra*.
70. Adrien Trucas, *Le rôle des organismes de contrôle*, Intervention au colloque 'Les indications géographiques protégeant les produits industriels et artisanaux (IGPIA)', Lyon, 3 févr. 2016.

characteristics of the product and the geographical environment.[71] These documents are similar to the code of practice. However, there is no requirement that a plan for external control of the GI be submitted and approved.[72]

We consider the submission of the control plan an essential step towards effective verification and controls. The submitted and approved control plan helps clarify the roles, rights, and responsibilities of all parties - individual producers, groups, and public bodies. It allows the public body in charge of the GI regime to evaluate the results of the quality scheme. Once published, the control plan can increase the transparency of the system and demonstrate to consumers how the quality controls are carried out and thus why product quality is guaranteed.

Therefore, we propose that China's future GI regime should require the submission of a control plan during the registration process. The control plan shall be drafted by the applicant group concerned. It shall specify the control performed by individual producers, the internal control, and the external controls. Subsequently, it should be submitted to the MOA for approval and publication.

[B] Enhancement of Protection Level

The protection of GIs could be enhanced if protection levels were raised as set out in Article 23 of the TRIPS Agreement, for both all products and particularly for reputed GIs. The coexistence of subsequent GIs with prior trademarks under certain conditions should be formalized and embodied in GI law.

[1] Introduction of 'Absolute' Protection Standard for All GI Products

To fulfil the obligations of Article 23 of the TRIPS Agreement, China uses the trademark regime to provide a higher level of protection but only for GIs designating wines and spirits.[73] The EU-China GI Agreement requires China to provide a similar high level of GI protection, but only for names added to the Annexes of the Agreement. The existing sui generis GI systems contain no provision concerning this additional protection.[74]

Chapter 4 has discussed why GIs (not only those for wines and spirits protected under the trademark regime) are worth the additional protection, often referred to as an 'absolute' form of protection.[75] This additional protection could be partially explained on the basis that the use of a GI, though accompanied by the true origin of the products and/or certain qualifying terms such as 'type' or 'kind' to avoid the risk of confusion, is likely to misappropriate or weaken the reputation of the GI. However, this explana tion

71. Provisions on the Protection of GI Products, Article 10; Detailed Implementation Rules for the Provisions on the Protection of GI products, Article 11; Measures for the Administration of GIs for Agricultural Products, Article 9; Registration Procedure Concerning GIs for Agricultural Products, Article 6.
72. *See* Chapter 4 *supra*.
73. *See* Chapter 2 *supra*.
74. *See* Chapter 4 *supra*.
75. Dwijen Rangnekar, *Geographical Indications: A Review of Proposals at the TRIPS Council* 33 (UNCTAD-ICTSD Project on IPRs and Sustainable Development, Issue Paper No. 4, 2002).

does not hold true for the many GIs that possess only a regional reputation but whose geographical coverage of protection is much wider. If the GI is unknown outside its regional border, there can be no dilution or freeriding. Moreover, no assessment of the risk of dilution or freeriding is required in the application of the rule, but not all uses of the GI are harmful (e.g., the use of the trademark 'Champomy' on non-alcoholic sparkling beverages for children).[76] We have explored an alternative justification: absolute protection is needed because, otherwise, GIs risk losing consumers who are misled into believing that the product's characteristics are not based on the *terroir* in a particular area but can be duplicated elsewhere. Nevertheless, this justification does not apply in respect of GIs whose reputation is attributable to the region of origin rather than to specific characteristics.[77]

It is beyond the scope of this chapter to work through all other supporting rationales for absolute protection. However, one rationale deserves our attention: the rationale of traditional *savoir-faire*.[78] We have retraced the history of how the AOC notion made its appearance and found that the importance of collectively generated and intergenerational *savoir-faire* through which the products are produced has been gradually acknowledged. The concept of *terroir* has been reinterpreted by putting more emphasis on human contributions, TK, local *savoir-faire*, and other practices of producers. It is the traditional *savoir-faire* component in *terroir* that paved the way for the creation of other GI concepts (e.g., IGPIA) and regimes (e.g., the potential EU GI regulation for industrial products), which are designed to designate or protect products that have a looser link with the climate and soil of a given place.[79]

The traditional *savoir-faire* component in *terroir* may also serve as an explanation for absolute GI protection. The rules and principles of the current IP system have largely been developed in response to inventions and original works.[80] The need to

76. The French Supreme Court admitted that the term evoked 'Champagne' but held that the evocation was harmless or even beneficial in this case. According to the reasoning, when consumers of 'Champomy' leave the world of childhood, they will naturally be inclined to celebrate the happy circumstances with exceptional wine products from the Champagne region, under the influence of childhood memories. *See* Cass. com., 7 Juill. 2009, n° 08-10.817.
77. *See* Chapter 1 *supra*.
78. Daniel Gervais, *Traditional Knowledge & Intellectual Property: A TRIPS-Compatible Approach*, Mich. St. L. Rev. 137 (2005); Daniel Gervais, *Traditional Innovation and the Ongoing Debate on the Protection of Geographical Indications, in Indigenous Peoples' Innovation: Intellectual Property Pathways to Development* 121 (Peter Drahos ed., ANU Press 2012); Dev Gangjee, *Relocating the Law of Geographical Indications* 275-295 (Cambridge University Press 2012); Teshager W. Dagne, *The Identity of Geographical Indications and Their Relation to Traditional Knowledge in Intellectual Property Law*, 5 WIPO J. 137 (2014); Michael Blakeney, *Protection of Traditional Knowledge by Geographical Indications*, 3 Int'l J. Intell. Prop. Mgmt. 357 (2009); Teshager W. Dagne, *Law and Policy on Intellectual Property, Traditional Knowledge and Development: Legally Protecting Creativity and Collective Rights in Traditional Knowledge-Based Agricultural Products Through Geographical Indications*, 11 Estey Ctr. J. Int'l L. & Trade Pol'y 68 (2010).
79. *See* Chapter 1 *supra*.
80. *Intellectual Property Needs and Expectations of Traditional Knowledge Holders* 32 (WIPO Report on Fact-Finding Missions, 2001), https://www.wipo.int/edocs/pubdocs/en/tk/768/wipo_pub_768.pdf; Gerard Bodeker, *Traditional Medical Knowledge, Intellectual Property Rights & Benefit Sharing*, 11 Cardozo J. Int'l & Comp. L. 785 (2003); Gregory Younging, *Traditional Knowledge Exists; Intellectual Property Is Invented or Created*, 36 U. Pa. J. Int'l L. 1077 (2014); Brad

protect traditional forms of creativity and innovation is largely ignored. Thus, this system can hardly be expected to satisfy the objective of local producers to obtain a monopoly right (e.g., a patent, copyright, or design right) over their traditional production methods. Nor does the GI system enable them to exercise control over use and benefits derived from commercial exploitation by other parties. That is why *Guizhou* producers can learn and exploit *Longjing* tea seedling and roasting techniques without obtaining permission from those making 'real' *Longjing* tea or paying any fees to them. *Guizhou* producers sold their tea under the name 'Imitated *Longjing*' until 1958, but they have continued to compare their tea with authentic *Longjing* in advertising and to tell consumers that the quality of their tea is very close to (or even better than) that of *Longjing* because the same techniques are used.[81] The transmission of traditional techniques brings no direct benefits (licensing fees) to *Hangzhou* farmers producing true *Longjing*. Instead, it may bring them new competitors.[82]

Therefore, providing GIs with a high level of protection could be seen as a compensation for the lack of protection offered to the traditional *savoir-faire* embedded in GIs.[83] This does not mean that the GI system with an enhanced scope of protection would be a desirable tool for protecting traditional *savoir-faire*. It may never be. Nor does this mean that traditional *savoir-faire* should be left unprotected. What we would like to propose is that, although a higher level of protection for GIs might contribute *only marginally* to the protection of traditional *savoir-faire*, rewarding traditional forms of creativity and innovation may justify a higher level of protection for GIs.

The rationale of traditional *savoir-faire* can be applied in the context of China. As mentioned, China has an abundance of *terroir* products.[84] While particular soil and climate conditions in the region of origin do matter, the role of traditional *savoir-faire* in shaping those products cannot be overlooked. In fact, those human contributions are increasingly being given due recognition. One need only look at the long list of national ICH elements recognized by China (in the traditional *savoir-faire* category) to see that a considerable number of them are anchored in a specific place and are used to produce GI products (e.g., *Yixing zisha* ceramic making skills, *Sichuan* brocade weaving skills, *Moutai* spirit brewing techniques). Under the current IP system, those regional techniques can be learnt, borrowed, and used by out-of-area actors *free of charge*. The IP system does not grant monopoly rights such as patents or copyright to reward efforts associated with traditional *savoir-faire*. The alternative may be to reserve the use of the sign to the area, instead of reserving the *savoir-faire* itself, in order to strike a balance.

Sherman, *Regulating Access and Use of Genetic Resources: Intellectual Property Law and Biodiscovery*, 25 Eur. Intell. Prop. Rev. 301 (2003); *Traditional Knowledge and Intellectual Property: Background Brief*, WIPO (28 June 2021), https://www.wipo.int/pressroom/en/briefs/tk_ip.html.

81. Zhou Zhijiang, Lonjingcha Weihe Chanzai Guizhou [Why Longjing Tea Is Produced in Guizhou?], XINHUA WANG [XINHUA NET], 2005.
82. On the free movement of traditional *savoir-faire*, *see* Alexandra Mendoza-Caminade, *Ethique et voyage: la circulation des savoir-faire traditionnels*, *in Variations juridiques sur le thème du voyage*, Toulouse, Presses de l'Université Toulouse 1 Capitole-LGDJ, 2015, p. 251.
83. *See* Gangjee, *supra* n. 78, at 287.
84. *See* Chapter 7 *supra*.

Furthermore, from a global perspective, Chinese producers, like their French counterparts, already have a significant export market and are seeking new opportunities. This explains why the Chinese government has resolved to support the EU's agenda in the 'GI extension debate' at the WTO.[85] The Chinese government is aware of the effects the amendment of Article 23 will have on WTO members: they will be obliged to afford a higher level of protection to all GIs (not just wines and spirits) under their domestic laws, and Chinese GIs will thus enjoy protection in those countries. Thus, demanding the amendment of Article 23 is equivalent to demanding that other countries afford additional protection. However, how can China expect others to grant Chinese GIs the additional protection that China does not grant to them in its domestic law?

Likewise, the Chinese government is not unaware of the potential value of the WIPO Lisbon Agreement to Chinese GIs. The system offers a means of obtaining protection for AOs from the contracting parties through a single registration. The Geneva Act could be deemed even more beneficial, as the Act expands the scope of the treaty beyond AOs to all GIs. This means that more Chinese GIs could be covered by the system. However, one major obstacle to the accession of China to the Agreement, as pointed out by China's representative at the Geneva diplomatic conference,[86] is that China's law is incompatible with the Agreement, which provides absolute protection for GIs. Thus, China's efforts to enhance the protection of its GIs in the global market are constrained by a lack of domestic laws offering the same level of protection.

Finally, our discussion must allude to another important matter: protection beyond the principle of speciality. We recall that the protection of GIs in China's sui generis systems is limited to cases where the disputed signs are used for identical or similar products.[87] Furthermore, Article 16 of the Trademark Law, transposing Article 22(2)(a) of the TRIPS Agreement, is also subject to the principle of speciality.[88] This allows unauthorized third parties to use a GI in relation to dissimilar products or services even if such use is likely to misappropriate or weaken its reputation. While reputed trademarks enjoy wider protection, surpassing the principle of trademark speciality, reputed GIs do not. This disparity should not be permitted to continue.

Based on the above considerations, we suggest that China's future unified GI system should transpose Article 13 of EU Regulation 1151/2012, which both provides a higher level of protection (as set out in Article 23 of the TRIPS Agreement) and protects reputed GIs beyond the principle of speciality. Therefore, names registered in the system shall be protected against any direct or indirect commercial use in respect

85. Michael Handler, *Rethinking GI Extension, in Research Handbook on Intellectual Property and Geographical Indications* 150 (Dev Gangjee ed., Edward Elgar Publishing 2016).

86. China participated in the diplomatic conference as observers without voting rights. *See Revised WIPO Lisbon Agreement to Cover Geographical Indications*, International Centre for Trade and Sustainable Development (29 June 2021), https://ictsd.iisd.org/bridges-news/bridges/news/revised-wipo-lisbon-agreement-to-cover-geographical-indications.

87. *See* Chapter 4 *supra*.

88. Article 12 of the Measures for Collective and Certification Marks, transposing Article 23(1) of the TRIPS Agreement, also only applies to GIs used for wines and spirits, not including dissimilar goods.

of products not covered by the registration where those products are similar (or comparable) to the products registered under that name or where using the name exploits the reputation of the protected name; and any misuse, imitation or evocation, even if the true origin of the products or services is indicated or if the protected name is translated or accompanied by expressions such as 'style', 'type', 'method', 'as produced in', or 'imitation'.

[2] Coexistence of Earlier Trademarks and Subsequent GIs

Unlike in the EU, China's sui generis GI systems provide no specific provisions allowing for the coexistence of prior trademarks and subsequent GIs.[89] In practice, however, this coexistence can be achieved through three routes.

The first path is to apply for GI protection under the former AQSIQ. The latter approved the recognition of the GI despite the fact that competing parties had already acquired trademark rights in the same sign. This practice is strongly opposed by large numbers of trademark owners, as it may compromise the rights (to use the trademarks) that the owners are supposed to have.[90]

The second path can be found in earlier court decisions.[91] Coexistence is permitted if the GI is used in a descriptive sense, not in a trademark sense (e.g., to label a product with the descriptive expression 'produced in a place' instead of using the GI directly; the size of the characters on the labels must be very small and the position must not be prominent). This limitation will severely restrict the GI's function. Suppose the later GI '*Bayerisches* Bier' is allowed to be used only in a strictly descriptive sense (e.g., a discreet label with 'produced in Bavaria' in small print). To order it, the consumer would have to ask for 'beer produced in the German Land of Bavaria, in accordance with a particular method of production that originated during the nineteenth century in Bavaria; and there is a direct link between the quality of the beer and the place Bavaria' in order to avoid buying a beer produced elsewhere via the 'Bavarian method', a beer that is produced in Bavaria but not in accordance with the 'Bavarian method', or a beer whose characteristics are not attributable to Bavaria because the later beers can also be labelled 'produced in Bavaria' or 'beer by the Bavarian method'. He may also need to add 'not the one that bears the trademark "Bavaria"'. It can be observed that the 'use in descriptive sense' limitation works against the interests of GI producers (to distinguish their products from those of the competitors by simply mentioning a name) and does not reduce consumer search costs.

89. The French legislators have only recently planned the coexistence. *See* Ancien Article L. 713-6 CPI: '*L'enregistrement d'une marque ne fait pas obstacle à l'utilisation du même signe ou d'un signe similaire comme ... c) Indication géographique définie à l'article L. 721-2, sauf lorsque la marque, compte tenu de sa renommée, de sa notoriété et de la durée de son usage, est à l'origine exclusive de la réputation ou de la connaissance par le consommateur du produit pour lequel une indication géographique est demandée.*'
90. *See* Chapter 5 *supra*.
91. *Ibid.*

The judges of the Beijing High People's Court have opened up a third path.[92] They consider that the registration of a later GI as a collective or certification mark will not lead to consumer confusion since the function of GI certification marks and GI collective marks is clearly distinct from that of ordinary trademarks. Thus, they have generally allowed a coexistence of early trademarks with subsequent GIs if the latter are registered as collective or certification marks. This insight overlooks the fact that the use of an earlier trademark as a corporate name, a trade name, or a website name could still cause confusion in the minds of consumers, although these signs obviously function in a different way (they are not even meant to identify products). Similarly, individual trademarks may be perceived by consumers as a 'label of quality' (i.e., certification marks), and vice versa.[93] The frontiers between individual marks, collective marks, and certification marks (including those containing GIs) are not easy to draw.[94] They depend on the perceptions of consumers. We cannot artificially simplify the task by categorizing the marks according to the choices trademark applicants make about which box to tick during the registration process.

Thus, the coexistence should not be allowed in all cases, especially where the later GI is likely to cause confusion and render the consumer unable to discern the true identity of the product, as can happen when the prior trademark has been used in the market for a long period and has a considerable reputation. Otherwise, both signs would be unable to perform their distinguishing function.

Nevertheless, this does not mean that any degree of confusion should be tolerated. Practical efforts can be made to reduce the risk, for instance by using an official logo identifying all CIs in general along with the specific GI.

Based on the above, we consider that primary consideration should be given to consumers in the decision on whether to permit coexistence. In light of a trademark's reputation and renown and the length of time it has been used, the GI should not be registered where registration of a (subsequent) GI would be liable to mislead the consumer as to the true identity of the product.[95] Otherwise, GI producers should be allowed to use the GI not only in a 'descriptive sense' but also in a manner that would enable the GI to perform its essential function.

Paragraph 6(4) of the EU-China GI Agreement deals with the relationship between prior trademarks and GIs. This paragraph borrows words from the EU GI Regulation 1151/2012. However, unlike the EU GI Regulation, it does not explicitly clarify whether 'the use of the protected designation of origin or protected geographical indication shall be permitted as well as use of the relevant trademarks'.[96] We propose that, where the registration of a subsequent GI would not be misleading, coexistence with prior trademarks should be expressly allowed to avoid legal uncertainty.

92. *Ibid.*
93. Case C-689/15 *W. F. Gözze Frottierweberei GmbH and Wolfgang Gözze v. Verein Bremer Baumwollbörse* (ECJ 8 June 2017) para. 51.
94. *See* Chapter 3 *supra.*
95. This proposed provision draws inspiration from Article 6(4) of Regulation 1151/2012. It complies with Article 6 of the EU-China GI Agreement.
96. Article 14(2) of Regulation 1151/2012.

The recommendations presented in this chapter are based on the recognition of the need to adopt the sui generis approach in order to highlight the link to *terroir* and thus unleash the associated benefits.

Along with the partial disengagement of the trademark regime from GI protection and the unification of the current sui generis systems, the CNIPA should transfer its role as a governing body to the MOA, as the latter is the most appropriate body to charge with verifying the link to *terroir*, protecting it, and supporting its valorization. Responsibility for the management and defence of GIs should be given to collective organizations rather than trademark owners.

To ensure *terroir* protection (i.e., to allow *terroir* to be a quality parameter and reward its traditional *savoir-faire* component), the unified sui generis regime should be improved through an enhancement of control measures and defence mechanisms. This improvement requires a higher level of protection for all GIs.

The scope of these recommendations is defined by the research presented earlier in this book. They cannot possibly cover every aspect and detail of a good GI scheme. Additional research on topics such as how to increase public awareness of the scheme would be necessary if the proposed reform were to be implemented.

Conclusion

At the national level, GIs are protected by a diversity of approaches adopted by different countries. There is a divide between countries that regard GIs as a subset of trademarks and thus protect them as collective and certification marks (e.g., the US) and those that view GIs as independent IP rights and prefer a separate, sui generis regime (e.g., the EU). This divide has attracted much attention from both academics and political decision-makers because it is believed to be the reason behind the limited number of signatories to the former Lisbon Agreement for the Protection of Appellations of Origin, continued disagreements over the proposed revision of the TRIPS Agreement, and the difficulty many countries face in choosing an appropriate legal framework (sui generis or trademark system) for GIs under their domestic laws.

The evidence presented in the first four chapters of this book shows that China's sui generis systems for GI protection have been established under the influence of the European approach. The former AQSIQ and the MOA established their own separate sui generis system for protecting GIs, whose definitions closely resemble the definition of 'appellations of origin', a subcategory of GIs to which France and other pioneer countries traditionally paid more attention. Each system builds upon some elements of Europe's sui generis regime, including a register specifically for GIs, a process verifying if denominations to be registered meet the GI definition, a requirement that a registered name may be used only by operators who conform to the corresponding standard, and the enforcement of GI protection via administrative action by public authorities.

However, other evidence indicates that the adoption of the European approach in China has not been fully achieved. The former AQSIQ used the terminology 'appellations of origin' borrowed from French legislation, but that terminology was soon abandoned and replaced by a more widely accepted term, 'geographical indications'. The role of different actors in the control and defence of GIs has not been sufficiently acknowledged. China's two sui generis GI systems have not set a level of protection for GIs as high as what European GI laws offer.

Chapters 5 and 6 discuss the challenges of adopting the European sui generis approach in China, primarily the competition provided by trademark protection (the approach advocated by the United States). China does not give preference to the sui generis GI systems. Instead, the trademark system is designed to compete with them:

it allows GIs to be registered as collective or certification marks without imposing a 'distinctiveness' requirement (in other words, GIs per se can be registered as those marks); it defines GIs and verifies if the mark for which registration is sought meets the GI definition; and the function of the marks consisting of or containing a GI is regarded as equivalent to that of the GI. Moreover, the rights conferred by China's sui generis GI regulations may be confined to use in a 'descriptive sense' where a conflicting sign is registered in the US-inspired trademark system. We have thus concluded that the introduction of the EU approach in China has not been a success.

If it is true that the *terroir* concept underpins the sui generis system of GIs, countries with an interest in valorizing the link to *terroir* should have a similar attitude towards the sui generis system. Strangely enough, although China and Europe both have a large number of products with a strong tradition and they are anchored in the *terroir* of their place of origin, the sui generis GI regime has received considerably less priority in China.

Our findings indicate that this discrepancy stems from differences in the way GI laws have been made and evolved. The European approach is more bottom-up. France's modern GI regime was initiated in 1905 at the request of producers to suppress fraudulent practices that distorted competition. It became more sophisticated with the creation of the AOC in 1935, aimed at guaranteeing the quality of products (a protection for consumers), and then became more comprehensive with the recent establishment of the IGPIA in order to accommodate the needs of handcrafters who keep traditional *savoir-faire* alive. The development of the EU-wide GI scheme was driven by the Member States, which represent the interests of their national stakeholders. Europe has come a long way in building its sui generis GI regime, from a few clauses in the French Law of 1905 to today's significant body of laws and regulations. Its choice in favour of a sui generis regime was not made based on a single law, decree, or decision from a policy designer. Instead, producers' participation, consumers' trust, and past experiences of using sui generis GI laws to fight against challenges facing agriculture (e.g., the phylloxera crisis) all helped to lead to this choice.

By contrast, the Chinese approach has been almost purely top-down. Although the *produits de terroir* have a counterpart in China, called 'local special products', there was no counterpart in Chinese culture to the legal concept of 'geographical indications', let alone a special set of rules drawn up to protect them. After China's reform and opening-up policy began, foreign bodies made several early attempts to prevent third parties from using some GIs. It is hard to imagine that any Chinese local producers would have claimed 'property rights' on place names, especially considering that the planned distribution system (i.e., planned economy) was not replaced by the market system until 1992. Thus, when accession to international treaties forced China to implement a GI scheme conforming to the requirements laid down in those treaties that would enable Chinese producers to benefit, there was no past local experience on which to base decisions. The lack of input from local actors further complicated the task of looking for a suitable approach (sui generis or trademark). Furthermore, this task not only concerned the need to enact a few articles, as the 1905 Law did, but required a complete and fully operational system that incorporated all the elements necessary for GI registration and protection. It was thus much harder for China to choose which regime to build than it was for France and the EU.

Faced with these challenges, China's highest decision-making body made a choice by making no choice. It allowed the Trademark Office to register and manage GIs through the regime of collective and certification marks while also allowing the former AQSIQ and the MOA to import European GI laws and establish sui generis systems. While the trademark regime and sui generis regime have both been used to protect GIs in a given jurisdiction (e.g., the EU), the particularity of China's scheme is that no clear preference is given to either regime. Chinese laws regarding GIs could therefore be said to be inspired by foreign policies and experiences without much deliberation going into the decision.

This means that 'choosing not to choose' may probably not be the choice most suited to China's interests. Three decades after the introduction of the GI laws, there is growing evidence to support this assumption. The ongoing battle between China's sui generis systems and trademark system is a manifestation of the unsustainability of the status quo.

It is never too early to jump off a sinking ship, and it is never too late to entirely rethink a legislative approach. The objective of our research is to reflect on the type of GI protection instrument that could best respond to China's demands. The key insights we have gained from our research are as follows.

Giving preference to the sui generis GI regime would be the best approach for China. Endowed with abundant products that are closely linked to their place of origin, China needs a comprehensive body of rules that require, or provide support for, the upholding of the link to *terroir* (product-place nexus) and the communication of information about the link, and that allow the link to generate value for producers, consumers, rural development, and traditional *savoir-faire*. It is inappropriate and technically impossible for the regime of trademarks to include such rules. The best alternative is to develop them under a sui generis regime. Giving preference to the sui generis GI regime also means giving the regime sufficient authority and resources to register and manage GIs, while reducing the involvement of the trademark regime in these activities.

The conceptual framework could be based on the link to *terroir*. There are two kinds of links: first, a combination of material and immaterial *terroir* components (natural and human factors) results in particular characteristics or desirable qualities in a product; second, immaterial components (traditional *savoir-faire*, cultural values, traditions) help to build the reputation of a product from a given area. Thus, China's sui generis regime could provide for two categories of indicators: appellations of origin and GIs. The former category can be used to highlight a product's inimitable quality due to a product-place nexus, while the latter better meets the needs of producers, particularly craftworkers, who keep the traditional *savoir-faire* alive and make the localized product famous.

A high level of GI protection could also be justified on the basis of this link. Where a product possesses a quality or specific characteristic resulting from the *terroir* of its geographical origin, a prohibition on qualifying terms such as 'type' or 'kind' may prevent consumers from being misled into believing that the specific quality is not due to *terroir* but can be duplicated elsewhere. According to the traditional *terroir* logic, the natural and human conditions of a place are inimitable, so that no out-of-area operators can truly imitate the product with equivalent specifications. Where the immaterial component of *terroir* is the main reason behind the creation of a GI, a high level of protection can be viewed as a reward for the traditional forms of creativity used in its production and compensation for the IP system's failure to provide protection to the traditional *savoir-faire* embedded in the GI. Thus, China should adopt the absolute protection standard set out in Article 23 of the TRIPS Agreement and as implemented in the EU for all protected names.

The recommendations presented above deal with GI protection in China, but questions regarding GI protection are being asked in other 'Old World' countries such as the EU Member States, 'New World' countries such as New Zealand, and countries without a tradition of protecting GIs (e.g., India, Japan, the Philippines). These discussions usually lead to shifts in GI policy and sometimes result in the development or improvement of a sui generis regime. The *terroir* in the Champagne region cannot be reproduced anywhere else, but every place can have its own unique *terroir*. This means that products from other places in the world can also join 'France's wine and cheese party'. As long as the link to *terroir* exists and consumers place a value on it, there is good reason to ask if special rules are needed for its verification (a special registration system?), its maintenance (a special control system?), and its valorization (a special defence system?). If the 'likelihood of confusion' test is the standard that protects a distinctive sign as an information-transmission device, what should be the protection standard to safeguard the link's capacities? By stepping into local *terroir*, are we getting close to a global consensus?

Bibliography

Books

Adrien Bouvel, *Principe de spécialité et signes distinctifs*, Paris, Litec, 2004.
Alberto Alemanno & Enrico Bonadio, *The New Intellectual Property of Health: Beyond Plain Packaging* (Edward Elgar Publishing 2016).
Alex Tallon, *Les appellations d'origine*, Bruxelles, Larcier, 2016.
Alfred Bedel, *Traité complet de manipulation des vins*, Paris, Garniers frères, 1887.
Amy B. Trubek, *The Taste of Place: A Cultural Journey into Terroir* (University of California Press 2008).
André-R Bertrand, *Droit des marques: Signes distinctifs, Noms de domaine*, Paris, Dalloz, 2005.
Andrew T. Kenyon, Ng-Loy Wee Loon & Megan Richardson, *The Law of Reputation and Brands in the Asia Pacific* (Cambridge University Press 2012).
Andy Smith, Jacques de Maillard & Olivier Costa, *Vin et politique: Bordeaux, la France, la mondialisation*, Paris, Presses de Sciences Po, 2007.
Annie J. De Roo & Robert W. Jagtenberg, *Yearbook Law and Legal Practice in East Asia (1997-1998)* (Kluwer Law International 1998).
Auguste Brachet, *Dictionnaire étymologique de la langue française*, 3e édition, Paris, J. Hetzel, 1870.
Bernard O'Connor, *The Law of Geographical Indications* (Cameron 2004).
Carlos M. Correa, *Intellectual Property Rights, the WTO and Developing Countries: The TRIPS Agreement and Policy Options* (Zed Books 2000).
Carlos M. Correa, *Intellectual Property Rights, the WTO and Developing Countries: The TRIPS Agreement and Policy Options* (Zed Books 2000).
Carlos M. Correa, *Trade-Related Aspects of Intellectual Property Rights: A Commentary on the TRIPS Agreement* (Oxford University Press 2007).
Catherine Aubertin, Florence Pinton & Valérie Boisvert, *Les marchés de la biodiversité*, Paris, IRD éditions, 2007.
Catherine Seville, *EU Intellectual Property Law and Policy* (Edward Elgar Publishing 2009).

Charles Gielen & Verena Von Bomhard, *Concise European Trademark and Design Law* (Kluwer Law International 2011).

Christophe Geiger, *Constructing European Intellectual Property: Achievements and New Perspective* (Edward Elgar Publishing 2013).

Christopher Heath & Anselm Kamperman Sanders, *New Frontiers of Intellectual Property Law: IP, Cultural Heritage, Geographical Indications, Enforcement and Overprotection* (Hart Publishing 2005).

Claude Blumann, *Politique agricole commune: Droit communautaire agricole et agro-alimentaire*, Paris, Litec, 1996.

Daniel Gervais, *The TRIPS Agreement: Drafting History and Analysis* (Sweet & Maxwell 3rd ed. 2008).

Daniel J. Gervais, *International Intellectual Property: A Handbook of Contemporary Research* (Edward Elgar Publishing 2015).

Davide Gaeta & Corsinovi Paola, *Economics, Governance, and Politics in the Wine Market: European Union Developments* (Palgrave Macmillan 2014).

Delphine Marie-Vivien, *La protection des indications géographiques: France, Europe, Inde*, Paris, Quae, 2012.

Delphine Marie-Vivien, *The Protection of Geographical Indications in India: A New Perspective on the French and European Experience* (SAGE Publishing 2015).

Dev Gangjee, *Relocating the Law of Geographical Indications* (Cambridge University Press 2012).

Dominique Denis, *Appellation d'origine et indication de provenance*, Paris, Dalloz, 1995.

Dong Binghe, DILI BIAOZHI ZHISHI CHANQUAN ZHIDU YANJIU GOUJIAN YI LIYI FENXIANG WEI JICHU DE QUANLI TIXI [INTELLECTUAL PROPERTY SYSTEM OF GEOGRAPHICAL INDICATIONS CONSTRUCTING THE RIGHTS OF BENEFIT SHARING BASED SYSTEM] (China University of Political Science and Law Press, 2005).

Dong Jingshan, NONGCHANPIN DILI BIAOZHI BAOHU ZHIDU YANJIU [RESEARCH ON THE PROTECTION SYSTEM OF GEOGRAPHICAL INDICATIONS FOR AGRICULTURAL PRODUCTS] (Intellectual Property Press, 2013).

Du Ying, SHEHUI JINBU YU SHANGBIAO GUANNIAN SHANGBIAO FALU ZHIDU DE GUOQU XIANZAI HE WEILAI [SOCIAL DEVELOPMENT AND TRADEMARK CONCEPT: THE PAST, PRESENT AND FUTURE OF TRADEMARK SYSTEM] (Peking University Press, 2012).

Étienne Clémentel, *Un drame économique, les délimitations, le passé, l'avenir*, Paris, Pierre Lafitte & Cie, 1914.

Eugène Pouillet, *Traité des marques de fabrique de la concurrence déloyale en tous genres*, 2e éd., Paris, Marchal et Billard, 1883.

Fan Baomin, ZHONGGUO LINYE SIXIANG YU ZHENGCE SHI [CHINESE FORESTRY IDEOLOGY AND POLICY HISTORY (1644-2008)] (Science Press, 2009).

Feng Shoubo, LUN DILI BIAOZHI DE GUOJI FALU BAOHU [INTERNATIONAL LEGAL PROTECTION OF GEOGRAPHICAL INDICATIONS] (Peking University Press, 2008).

Feng Xiaoqing & Yang Lihua, ZHONGGUO SHANGBIAOFA YANJIU YU LIFA SHIJIAN [RESEARCH AND LEGISLATIVE PRACTICE ON TRADE MARKS IN CHINA] (China University of Political Science and Law Press, 2013).

Feng Xiaoqing, ZHISHI CHANQUAN LIYI PINGHENG LILUN [THEORY OF BALANCE OF INTERESTS OF INTELLECTUAL PROPERTY] (China University of Political Science & Law Press, 2006).

Francesco Vanni, *Agriculture and Public Goods: The Role of Collective Action* (Springer 2014).

Frédéric Pollaud-Dulian, *Droit de la propriété industrielle*, Paris, Economica, 2011.

Gary Myers, *Principles of Intellectual Property Law* (Concise Hornbook Series 2nd ed. 2012).

Giovanni Belletti et al., *The Effects of Protecting Geographical Indicators: Ways and Means of Their Evaluation* (Swiss Federal Institute of Intellectual Property 2011).

Gustavo Ghidini, *Innovation, Competition and Consumer Welfare in Intellectual Property Law* (Edward Elgar Publishing 2010).

Hector Mac Queen & Charlotte Waelde, *Contemporary Intellectual Property: Law and Policy* (Oxford University Press 2nd ed. 2011).

Hélène Gaumont-Prat, *Droit de la propriété industrielle*, 4e éd., Paris, LexisNexis, 2017.

Henry G. Schermers & Niels M. Blokke, *International Institutional Law: Unity Within Diversity* (Martinus Nijhoff Publishers 5th ed. 2011).

Hu Ping, QINGBAO RIBEN [INFORMATION-GATHERING JAPAN] (Twenty-First Century Publishing, 2011).

Hu Shilin, ZHONGGUO DAODI YAOCAI [CHINESE GENUINE MEDICAL MATERIALS] (Heilongjiang Science and Technology Press, 1989).

Huang Guilin, DILI BIAOZHI DE GUOJI BAOHU JI ZHONGGUO XIANZHUANG [INTERNATIONAL PROTECTION OF GEOGRAPHICAL INDICATIONS AND ITS SITUATION IN CHINA] (People's Court Press, 2005).

Hugh Johnson & Claude Dovaz, *Une histoire mondiale du vin: de l'Antiquité à nos jours*, Paris, Hachette literatures, 2009.

Hugh Johnson & Jancis Robinson, *The World Atlas of Wine* (Mitchell Beazley 7th ed. 2013).

Irene Calboli & Jane C. Ginsburg, *The Cambridge Handbook of International and Comparative Trademark Law* (Cambridge University Press 2020).

J. Thomas McCarthy, *McCarthy on Trademarks and Unfair Competition* (Thomson West 5th ed. 2021).

Jacques Azema & Jean-christophe Galloux, *Droit de la propriété industrielle*, 7e éd., Paris, Dalloz, 2012.

Jacques de Werra, *Indications géographiques: perspectives globales et locales*, Zürich, Schulthess Verlag, 2016.

Jacques Larrieu, *Les métamorphoses de la marque*, Paris, LGDJ, 2011.

Jacques Raynard et al., *Droit de la propriété industrielle*, Paris, LexisNexis, 2016.

Jan Rosén, *Individualism and Collectiveness in Intellectual Property Law* (Edward Elgar 2012).

Jean-Louis Multon et al., *Traité de droit alimentaire français, européen et international*, Paris, Lavoisier, 2013.

Jeffrey Belson, *Certification and Collecitve Marks* (Edward Elgar Publishing 2017).

Jérôme Passa, *Droit de la propriété industrielle: Tome 1, Marques et autres signes distinctifs, dessins et modèles*, 2e éd., Paris, LGDJ, 2009.

Jiang Lin, DILI BIAOZHI GUOJI BAOHU WENTI YANJIU LIYI FENZHENG JI ZHONGGUO ZHIDU XUANZE [INTERNATIONAL PROTECTION OF GEOGRAPHICAL INDICATIONS: CONFLICTS AND CHINA'S CHOICE] (Harbin Institute of Technology Press, 2013).

Joanna Schmidt-Szalewski, *Droit de la propriété industrielle*, 7e éd., Paris, Dalloz, 2009.

Joanna Schmidt-Szalewski, *Le droit des marques*, Paris, Dalloz, 1997.

Jonathan Curci, *The Protection of Biodiversity and Traditional Knowledge in International Law of Intellectual Property* (Cambridge University Press 2010).

Josef Drexl et al., *EU Bilateral Trade Agreements and Intellectual Property: For Better or Worse?* (Springer 2013).

Joseph Capus, *L'évolution de la législation sur les appellations d'origine : Genèse des appellations contrôlées*, Paris, Louis larmat, 1947.

Kong Xiangjun, SHANGBIAOFA SHIYONG DE JIBEN WENTI [FUNDAMENTAL ISSUES ON APPLICATION OF THE TRADEMARK LAW] (2nd ed., China Legal Publishing House, 2015).

Konrad E. Zweigert et al., *Droit de la propriété intellectuelle et de la concurrence*, Alphen aan den Rijn, Sijthoff & Noordhoff, 1979.

Kym Anderson & Vicente Pinilla, *Wine Globalization: A New Comparative History* (Cambridge University Press 2018).

Laure Bonnaud & Nathalie Joly, *L'alimentation sous contrôle: Tracer, auditer, conseiller*, Versailles, Éditions Quae, 2012.

Laure Marino, *Droit de la propriété industrielle*, 8e éd., Paris, Mémentos, 2013.

Li Houdun, TANFANG ZHONGGUO PUTAO JIUZHUANG [VISITING THE WINE VILLAGE OF CHINA] (Shanghai Scientific and Technical Press, 2012).

Li Mingde, OUMENG ZHISHI CHANQUAN FA [INTELLECTUAL PROPERTY LAW IN THE EUROPEAN UNION] (Law Press, 2010).

Li Yi, NONGCHANPIN DILI BIAOZHI GUANLI SHIWU [MANAGEMENT PRACTICE OF AGRICULTURAL GEOGRAPHICAL INDICATIONS] (Hunan Science and Technology Press, 2011).

Li Zuming, DILI BIAOZHI DE BAOHU YU GUANLI [PROTECTION AND MANAGEMENT OF GEOGRAPHICAL INDICATIONS] (Intellectual Property Publishing House, 2009).

Lin Xiuqin, YIDAI YILU SHANGBIAO FALU ZHIDU YANJIU [TRADEMARK LEGAL SYSTEM UNDER ONE BELT AND ONE ROAD], (Intellectual Property Press, 2018).

Liu Chuntian, ZHISHI CHANQUAN FAXUE [INTELLECTUAL PROPERTY LAW] (Higher Education Press, 2019).

Liu Wentai, BENCAO PINHUI JINGYAO [COLLECTED ESSENTIALS OF SPECIES OF MEDICAL MATERIALS] (Beijing Science and Technology Press, 2019).

Liu Yinliang, GUOJI ZHISHI CHANQUAN ZHENGZHI WENTI YANJIU [POLITICAL ISSUES OF INTERNATIONAL INTELLECTUAL PROPERTY RIGHTS] (Intellectual Property Press, 2014).

Ludwig Krämer, *La CEE et la protection au consommateur*, Bruxelles, Story Scientia, 1988.

Martine Tabeaud, *Le changement en environnement: Les faits, les représentations, les enjeux*, Paris, Publications de la Sorbonne, 1995.

Michael Blakeney, *Extending the Protection of Geographical Indications: Case Studies of Agricultural Products in Africa* (Routledge 2012).

Michael Blakeney, *The Protection of Geographical Indications: Law and Practice* (Edward Elgar 2014).

Michael G. Mullins et al., *Biology of the Grapevine* (Cambridge University Press 1992).

Michel Menjucq & Jean-Marc Bahans, *Droit de la vigne et du vin*, 2e éd., Paris, Litec, 2010.

Nicolas Bouche, *Intellectual Property Law in France* (Kluwer Law International 2nd ed. 2014).

Norbert Olszak, *Droit des appellations d'origine et indications de provenance*, Paris, Tec & Doc, 2001.

Nuria Ackermann & Fabio Russo, *Adding Value to Traditional Products of Regional Origin: A Guide to Creating a Quality Consortium* 1 (United Nations Industrial Development Organization 2010).

Paul Mathé, *Marques collectives et de certification, Mélanges offerts à Albert Chavanne*, Paris, Litec, 1990.

Paul Roubier, *Le droit de la propriété industrielle*, Tome 2, Paris, Sirey, 1954.

Paul Torremans et al., *Intellectual Property and TRIPs Compliance in China: Chinese and European Perspectives* (Edward Elgar Publishing 2007).

Peter-Tobias Stoll, Jan Busche & Katrin Arend, *WTO: Trade-Related Aspects of Intellectual Property Rights* (Martinus Nijhoff Publishers 2009).

Raymond Dusolier, *Les Marques collectives et les marques de qualité dans l'ancien droit et dans le droit moderne*, Paris, Librairies techniques, 1974.

Roger Dion, *Histoire de la vigne et du vin en France: des origines au 19e siècle*, Paris, CNRS, 2010.

Séverine Visse-Causse, *Droit de la propriété intellectuelle*, Paris, Lextenso, 2015.

Sheldon W. Halpern, Craig Allen Nard & Kenneth L. Port, *Fundamentals of United States Intellectual Property Law: Copyright, Patent, and Trademark* (Kluwer Law International 2nd ed. 2006).

Song Xiaoting, ZHONGGUO DAODI YAOCAI DE ZHISHI CHANQUAN BAOHU [INTELLECTUAL PROPERTY PROTECTION OF CHINA'S GEO-AUTHENTIC CRUDE DRUGS] (Intellectual Property Press 2014).

Stephen P. Ladas, *Patents, Trademarks, and Related Rights: National and International Protection* (Harvard University Press 1975).

Stewart Lockie & David Carpenter, *Agriculture, Biodiversity and Markets: Livelihoods and Agroecology in Comparative Perspective* (Earthscan 2009).

Tian Furong, DILI BIAOZHI FALU BAOHU ZHIDU YANJIU [LEGAL PROTECTION OF GEOGRAPHICAL INDICATIONS] (Intellectual Property Publishing House, 2009).

Toshiyuki Kono, *Intellectual Property and Private International Law: Comparative Perspectives* (Hart Publishing 2012).

Tyler Colman, *Wine Politics: How Governments, Environmentalists, Mobsters, and Critics Influence the Wines We Drink* (University of California Press 2008).

Vadim Mantrov, *EU Law on Indications of Geographical Origin: Theory and Practice* (Springer 2014).

Wang Dong, *China's Unequal Treaties: Narrating National History* (Lexington Books 2005).

Wang Qian, ZHISHI CHANQUAN FA JIAOCHENG [TEXTBOOK ON INTELLECTUAL PROPERTY LAW] (6th ed., Renmin University Press, 2019).

Wang Qiang & Xu Guojun, DAODI YAOCAI TUDIAN [THE DICTIONARY OF GEO-AUTHENTIC CRUDE DRUGS] (Fujian science and Technology Press, 2003).

Wang Xiaobing, DILI BIAOZHI FALU BAOHU XINLUN YI ZHONG'OU BIJIAO WEI SHIJIAO [NEW DISCUSSION ON LEGAL PROTECTION OF GEOGRAPHICAL INDICATIONS: CHINESE AND EUROPEAN PERSPECTIVES] (China University of Political Science and Law Press, 2013).

Wang Xiaobing, JINGJI FAZHAN FANGSHI ZHUANBIAN SHIJIAO XIA DE DILI BIAOZHI BAOHU [GEOGRAPHICAL INDICATION PROTECTION FROM THE PERSPECTIVE OF ECONOMIC DEVELOPMENT MODE CHANGE] (China Social Sciences Publishing, 2019).

Wang Xiaobing, LUN DILI BIAOZHI DE FALU BAOHU [LEGAL PROTECTION OF GEOGRAPHICAL INDICATIONS] (China Renmin University Press, 2006).

Wang Yingchao & Zhang Hui, ZHONGHUA RENMIN GONGHEGUO SHANGBIAOFA SHIYI [INTERPRETATION OF THE TRADEMARK LAW OF THE PEOPLE'S REPUBLIC OF CHINA] (China Industry and Commerce Press, 2013).

Weinian Hu, *Dinner for Three: EU, China and the US Around the Geographical Indications Table* (Centre for European Policy Studies 2021).

William R. Cornish, *Intellectual Property: Patents, Copyright, Trade Marks and Allied Rights* (Sweet & Maxwell 8th ed. 2013).

Wu Handong, ZHISHI CHANQUAN JIBEN WENTI YANJIU [BASIC ISSUES OF INTELLECTUAL PROPERTY RIGHTS] (2nd ed., Renmin University Press, 2009).

Yu Bo, DILI BIAOZHI BAOHU ZHIDU [PROTECTION SYSTEM OF GEOGRAPHICAL INDICATIONS] (Shanghai Renmin Press, 2018).

Zeng Deguo, DILI BIAOZHI LILUN YU SHIWU [THEORY AND PRACTICE OF GEOGRAPHICAL INDICATIONS] (Intellectual Property Press, 2014).

Zhao Xiaoping, DILI BIAOZHI DE FALU BAOHU YAOJIU [RESEARCH ON LEGAL PROTECTION OF GEOGRAPHICAL INDICATIONS] (Law Press China, 2007).

Zhao Xiaoping, ZHONGGUO NONGCHANPIN DILI BIAOZHI FALU BAOHU YANJIU [GEOGRAPHICAL INDICATION PROTECTION OF AGRICULTURAL PRODUCTS IN CHINA] (Shanxi People's Publishing House, 2012).

Zhou Bo & Liu Yong, DILI BIAOZHI SHANGBIAO DIANXING ANLI PINGSHU [A REVIEW OF TYPICAL CASES OF GEOGRAPHICAL INDICATIONS TRADEMARKS] (China Industry and Commerce Press, 2018).

Theses and Dissertations

Caroline Le Goffic, *La protection des indications géographiques*, Paris, LexisNexis, 2011.

Delphine Marie-Vivien, *Le droit des indications géographiques en Inde, un pays de l'ancien monde face aux droits français, communautaire et international*, thèse, Ecole des Hautes Etudes en Sciences Sociales, 2010.

Denis Rochard, *La protection internationale des indications géographiques*, Paris, Presses Universitaires de France, 2002.

Dorothée Franjus-Guigues, *Nature et protection juridiques des indications géographiques: l'avènement d'un droit à l'épreuve de sa mise en œuvre*, thèse, Université d'Aix-Marseille, 2012.

Gabrielle Rochdi Talbot, *L'harmonisation européenne des législations nationales relatives aux produits agro-alimentaires*, thèse, Université de Poitiers, 1994.

Henry Sempé, *Régime économique du vin*, thèse, Université de Bordeaux, 1898.

Li Xiaomin, Dili Biaozhi Falu Baohu Jizhi Yanjiu yi Jingdezhen Weili [Protection Mechanism of Geographical Indications: Example of Jingdezhen Geographical Indication], Doctoral Thesis, China University of Political Science and Law, 2005.

Liang Fei, Daodi Yaocai Kao [Daodi Chinese Medicinal Materials], Doctoral Thesis, Beijing University of Chinese Medicine, 2013.

Mélanie Gros, *Les signes d'origine et de qualité des vins*, thèse, Université de Toulouse, 2009.

P. Max Bernard, *Le régime des vins à appellation d'origine*, thèse, Université de Montpellier, 1932.

Rokiah Alavi et al., *The Economics of Intellectual Property: Suggestions for Further Research in Developing Countries and Countries with Economies in Transition* (WIPO Publication 2009).

Séverine Visse-Causse, *L'appellation d'origine*, thèse, Université de Reims, 2004.

Sylvestre Yamthieu, *Indications géographiques: Représentativité des opérateurs et lieu de production des IGPIA*, Propriété industrielle, n° 5, 2019, étude 12.

Sylvie Diart-Boucher, *La réglementation vitivinicole champenoise: Une superposition de règles communautaire, nationales et locales*, Paris, Editions L'Harmattan, 2007.

Sylvie Diart-Boucher, *La Réglementation vitivinicole champenoise*, thèse, Université de Reims, 2006.

Teiji Takahashi, *La sécurité et la qualité des denrées alimentaires: étude comparée, Japon: UE – Etats-Unis: de la science à la confiance*, thèse, Université de Toulouse, 2011.

Wang Han, Woguo Dili Biaozhi Chuji Nongchanpin Fazhan Moshi Yanjiu [Study on Development Mode of our Country's Elementarily Agricultural Products Concerning Geographical Indications], Doctoral Thesis, University of Tianjin, 2008.

Wang Li, Oumeng Dili Biaozhi Chanpin Guanli Yanjiu [Research on EU Geographical Indications Product Management], Doctoral Thesis, Jilin University, 2015.

Wang Qiangcai, Xiaofeizhe dui Dili Biaozhi Chanpin de Goumai Yiyuan ji Yingxiang Yinsu Yanjiu Yi Anxi Tieguanyin Weili [An Analysis of Consumers' Purchase Intention to Geographical Indication Products and Influencing Factors: Taking Anxi Tieguanyin Tea as an Example], Dissertation, Fuzhou University, 2014.

Xavier Kalinda, *La protection des indications géographiques et son intérêt pour les pays en développement*, thèse, Université de Strasbourg, 2010.

Yanhai Zhao, *L'insertion de la Chine dans la mondialisation, les flux d'investissements directs étrangers et la disparité économique régionale en Chine*, thèse, Université Sorbonne Nouvelle-Paris 3, 2009.

Yann Basire, *Les fonctions de la marque: essai sur la cohérence du régime juridique d'un signe distinctif*, Paris, LexisNexis, 2015.

Articles

Adriano Profeta et al., *The Protection of Origins for Agricultural Products and Foods in Europe: Status Quo, Problems and Policy Recommendations for the Green Book*, 12 J. World Intell. Prop. 622 (2009).

Albert Chavanne, *La loi du 4 janvier 1991 sur les marques de fabrique*, La semaine juridique entreprise et affaires, n° 16, 1991, p. 45.

Alberto Francisco Ribeiro de Almeida, *Key Differences Between Trademarks and Geographical Indications*, 30 Eur. Intell. Prop. Rev. 406 (2008).

Alberto Francisco Ribeiro de Almeida, *The Legal Nature of Geographical Indications and Designations of Origin*, 36 Eur. Intell. Prop. Rev. 640 (2014).

Alberto Francisco Ribeiro de Almeida, *The TRIPs Agreement, the Bilateral Agreement Concerning Geographical Indications and the Philosophy of the WTO*, 4 Eur. Intell. Prop. Rev. 150 (2005).

Alberto Ribeiro de Almeida, *Geographical Indications Versus Trade Marks and Generic Terms: The US-China Agreement*, 51 IIC-Int'l Rev. Intell. Prop. & Competition L. 277 (2020).

Alessandro Pacciani et al., *The Role of Typical Products in Fostering Rural Development and the Effects of Regulation (EEC) 2081/92*, the 73rd Seminar of the European Association of Agricultural Economists ANCONA (2001).

Alessandro Stanziani, *La falsification du vin en France, 1880-1905: un cas de fraude agro-alimentaire*, Revue d'histoire moderne et contemporaine, 2003, p. 172.

Alessandro Stanziani, *Wine Reputation and Quality Controls: The Origin of the AOCs in 19th Century France*, 18 Eur. J.L. & Econ. 149 (2004).

Amel Benkahla et al., *Enjeux de la Certification d'Origine et Stratégies d'Acteurs: le Cas de l'AOC Pélardon*, 27 Économies et Sociétés 817 (2005).

Amy P. Cotton, *123 Years at the Negotiating Table and Still No Dessert: The Case in Support of TRIPS Geographical Indication Protections*, 82 Chi.-Kent L. Rev. 1295 (2007).

An Qinghu, *Well-Known Marks & China's System of Well-Known Mark Protection*, 95 Trademark Rep. 705 (2005).

Andras Jokuti, *Where Is the What if the What Is in Why? A Rough Guide to the Maze of Geographical Indications*, 31 Eur. Intell. Prop. Rev. 118 (2009).

Angela Tregear et al. *The Impact of Territorial Product Qualification Processes on the Rural Development Potential of Small-Scale Food Productions* (XI World Congress of Rural Sociology 2004).

Angela Tregear, *Regional Foods and Rural Development: The Role of Product Qualification*, 23 J. Rur. Stud. 12 (2007).

Angelo Zago, *La réputation collective sur les marchés agricoles*, Économie rurale. Agricultures, alimentations, territoires, Vol. 345, 2015, p. 29.

Anna G. Micara, *The Geneva Act of the Lisbon Agreement for the Protection of Appellations of Origin and Their International Registration: An Assessment of a Controversial Agreement*, 47 IIC-Int'l Rev. Intell. Prop. & Competition L. 673 (2016).

Annalisa Volpato, *On Consumer, Evocation and Cider Spirit*, 11 Eur. Food & Feed L. Rev. 140 (2016).

Anne F. Debrez, *Les tendances jurisprudentielles 'des délimitations' des appellations d'origine contrôlées viti-vinicoles*, Recueil Dalloz, 2005, p. 282.

Anne Rigaux, *Indications géographiques protégées*, Europe, n° 2, 2020, comm. 52.

Annette Kur & Sam Cocks, *Nothing but a GI Thing: Geographical Indications under EU Law*, 17 Fordham Intell. Prop. Media & Ent. L.J. 999 (2006).

Annette Kur, *Quibbling Siblings: Comments to Dev Gangjee's Presentation*, 82 Chi. -Kent. L. Rev. 1317 (2007).

Antonio Stasi et al., *Italian Wine Demand and Differentiation Effect of Geographical Indications*, 23 Int'l J. Wine Bus. Res. 49 (2011).

Antony Taubman, *Thinking Locally, Acting Globally: How Trade Negotiations over Geographical Indications Improvise 'Fair Trade' Rules*, 3 Intell. Prop. Q. 231 (2008).

Arnaud Folliard-Monguiral, *Arrêt Grilloumi: restauration entre la poire et le fromage*, Propriété industrielle, n° 6, 2021, comm. 38.

Arnaud Folliard-Monguiral, *Arrêt Gözze: marques de certification et fonction essentielle*, Propriété industrielle, n° 9, 2017, alerte 52.

Arnaud Folliard-Monguiral, *Arrêt Teflon: l'usage en tant que composant d'un produit final*, Propriété Industrielle, n° 9, 2015, comm. 6.

Arnaud Folliard-Monguiral, *TPICE, arrêt Port Louis: caractère descriptif et noms géographiques*, Propriété industrielle, n° 12, 2008, comm. 97.

Arnaud Folliard-Monguiral, *Un an de jurisprudence sur les motifs absolus de refus de marques communautaires*, Propriété industrielle, n° 3, 2015, chron. 3.

Áron Török et al., *Understanding the Real-World Impact of Geographical Indications: A Critical Review of the Empirical Economic Literature*, 12 Sustainability 9434 (2020).

B. Brett Heavner & Michael R. Justus, *Worldwide Certification-Mark Registration: A Certifiable Nightmare*, 2 Landslide 21 (2009).

Bai Huiying, Woguo Dili Biaozhi Zhidu Ruogan Wenti Tanxi [Several Issues of the System of Geographical Indications in China], HENANSHENG ZHENGFA

GUANLI GANBU XUEYUAN XUEBAO [JOURNAL OF HENAN ADMINISTRATIVE INSTITUTE OF POLITICS AND LAW], July 2006, 143.

Becki Graham, *Ten Years Later: Compromise or Conflict over Geographical Indications*, 1 Syracuse Sci. & Tech. L. Rep. (2005).

Ben Shepherd, *Costs and Benefits of Protecting Geographical Indications: Some Lessons from the French Wine Sector* (European Centre for International Political Economy 2006).

Ben Shepherd, *Regulating Access and Use of Genetic Resources: Intellectual Property Law and Biodiscovery*, 25 Eur. Intell. Prop. Rev. 301 (2003).

Benedetta Ubertazzi, *EU Geographical Indications and Intangible Cultural Heritage*, 48 IIC-Int'l Rev. Intell. Prop. & Competition L. 562 (2017).

Benjamin Fontaine, *L'EUIPO prépare l'arrivée de la marque de certification de l'Union européenne, le 1er octobre 2017*, Propriété industrielle, n° 7, 2017, alerte 44.

Benjamin Fontaine, *L'indisponibilité résultant d'un conflit avec une indication geographique*, Europe, n° 11, 2016, 2.

Benjamin Fontaine, *L'opposabilité des indications géographiques dans le système de la marque communautaire: une course d'obstacles?*, Propriété industrielle, n° 12, 2014, étude 26.

Benjamin Fontaine, *La défense des indications géographiques protégées à titre de marques communautaires collectives: Quelques réflexions inspirées du jugement du Tribunal de l'Union européenne du 9 juin 2010*, Propriété industrielle, n° 2, 2011, étude 4.

Bernard O'Connor, *Protecting Traditional Knowledge: An Overview of a Developing Area of Intellectual Property Law*, 6 J. World Intell. Prop. 677 (2003).

Bernard O'Connor, *Sui Generis Protection of Geographical Indications*, 9 Drake J. Agric. L. 359 (2004).

Bernard O'Connor, *The EC Need Not Be Isolated on GIs*, 29 Eur. Intell. Prop. Rev. 303 (2007).

Bernard O'Connor, *The European Union and the United States Conflicting Agendas on Geographical Indications: What's Happening in Asia?*, 9 Global Trade & Cust. J. 66 (2014).

Bradley M. Bashawt, *Geographical Indications in China: Why Protect GIs with Both Trademark Law and AOC-Type Legislation?* 17 Pac. Rim L. & Pol'y J. 73 (2008).

Burkhart Goebel & Manuela Groeschl, *The Long Road to Resolving Conflicts Between Trademarks and Geographical Indications*, 104 Trademark Rep. 829 (2014).

Burkhart Goebel, *Geographical Indications and Trademarks: The Road from Doha*, 93 Trademark Rep. 964 (2003).

Camille Guthmann, *Marques. Réglementation. Réforme. Contenu.*, La semaine juridique entreprise et affaires, n° 4, 1991, act. 89.

Cao Jianming, Jiaru WTO dui Zhongguo Sifa Gongzuo de Yingxiang ji Sikao [The Impact of the WTO on China's Judicial Work], FAXUE [SCIENCE OF LAW], June 2001, 59.

Cao Xinming, Woguo Dili Biaozhi Baohu Zhidu zhi Wanshan [On Improving the System of Geographical Indications in China Based on Promoting China's Agricultural Economy Development], ZHISHI CHANQUAN [INTELLECTUAL PROPERTY], January 2007, 26.

Caoimhin MacMaolain, *Eligibility Criteria for Protected Geographical Food Names*, 31 Eur. L. Rev. 579 (2006).

Caoimhin MacMaolain, *Free Movement of Foodstuffs, Quality Requirements and Consumer Protection: Have the Court and the Commission Both Got It Wrong?*, 26 Eur. L. Rev. 413 (2001).

Carlos Correa, *Trade-Related Aspects of Intellectual Property Rights: A Commentary on the TRIPS Agreement* (Oxford University Press 2007).

Carlos M. Correa, *Protection of Geographical Indications in CARICOM Countries* (Caribbean Regional Negotiating Machinery Technical Papers 2002).

Caroline Lampre, *Le champagne ou le parfum de la renommée*, Recueil Dalloz, 1994, p. 213.

Caroline Le Goffic & Andrea Zappalaglio, *The Role Played by the US Government in Protecting Geographical Indications*, 98 World Dev. 35 (2017).

Caroline Le Goffic, *Dégénérescence des indications géographiques: où situer le point de non-retour?*, Droit rural, n° 424, 2014, étude 11.

Caroline Le Goffic, *L'appellation d'origine, reconnaissance juridique du concept géographique de terroir*, Droit rural, n° 358, 2007, étude 37.

Caroline Le Goffic, *Le parmesan, c'est râpé! (Commentaire de l'arrêt de la CJCE du 26 février 2008)*, Propriété industrielle, n° 7-8, 2008, étude 16.

Caroline Le Goffic, *Les apports de la loi du 17 mars 2014 au Code de la propriété intellectuelle*, Propriété intellectuelle, n° 5, 2014, p. 3.

Catherine Verneret, *Évolution jurisprudentielle en matière d'appréciation de la contrefaçon de marque*, La semaine juridique entreprise et affaires, n° 12, 2001.

Céline Bonnet & Michel Simioni, *Assessing Consumer Response to Protected Designation of Origin Labelling: A Mixed Multinomial Logit Approach*, 28 Eur. Rev. Agric. Econ. 433 (2001).

Cerkia Bramley & Estelle Bienabe, *Developments and Considerations Around Geographical Indications in the Developing World*, 2 Queen Mary J. Intell. Prop. 14 (2012).

Cerkia Bramley & Kirsten Johann, *Exploring the Economic Rationale for Protecting Geographical Indicators in Agriculture*, 46 Agrekon 47 (2007).

Cerkia Bramley, *A Review of the Socio-Economic Impact of Geographical Indications: Considerations for the Developing World*, at the WIPO Worldwide Symposium on Geographical Indications, Lima, Peru (22-24 June 2011).

Chantal Pégaz, *La défense de l'AOC*, Revue lamy droit des affaires, n° 68, 2004.

Charles Lister, *Protectionism and Integration: Designations of Origin for Foodstuffs in the European Community*, 47 Food & Drug L.J. 639 (1992).

Chen Jintao, Xi TRIPS Xieyi yu Woguo Dili Biaozhi de Falu Baohu [TRIPS Agreement and Legal Protection of Geographical Indications in China], DANGDAI FAXUE [CONTEMPORARY LAW REVIEW], April 2003, 129.

Christian Garavaglia, *How Much Do Consumers Value Protected Designation of Origin Certifications? Estimates of Willingness to Pay for PDO Dry-Cured Ham in Italy*, 33 Agribusiness 403 (2017).

Christian le Stanc, *Agitation legislative*, Propriété industrielle, n° 5, 2014, repère 5.

Christian le Stanc, *Laguiole Bazar*, Propriété industrielle, 2013, repère 4.

Christine Lebel, *Agriculteur: quelle liberté d'entreprendre demain?*, Droit rural, n° 411, 2013, alerte 37.

Christine Lebel, *Sauvons le Gruyère! À propos de la résolution de l'Assemblée nationale relative à la demande d'enregistrement de la dénomination Gruyère en appellation d'origine protégée*, Droit rural, n° 383, 2010, alerte 73.

Christophe Bontemps et al., *Quality Labels and Firm Survival: Some First Empirical Evidence*, 40 Eur. Rev. Agric. Econ. 413 (2013).

Christophe Charlier & Mai-Anh Ngo, *An Analysis of the European Communities: Protection of Trademarks and Geographical Indications for Agricultural Products and Foodstuffs Dispute*, 10 J. World Intell. Prop. 171 (2007).

Christophe Dernoncourt, *Marques et collectivités territoriales: enregistrement et protection contre les usurpations en droit européen et en droit français*, Propriété industrielle, n° 7-8, 2014, étude 18.

Christophe Geiger et al., *Toward a Flexible International Framework for the Protection of Geographical Indications*, 1 WIPO J. 147 (2010).

Claude Garcia et al., *Geographical Indications and Biodiversity in the Western Ghats, India*, 27 Mountain Res. & Dev. 206 (2007).

Claude Ménard & Egizio Valceschini, *New Institutions for Governing the Agri-food Industry*, 32 Eur. Rev. Agric. Econ. 421 (2005).

Daniel Gadbin, *Le système communautaire des indications géographiques, rattrapé par le droit des marques: la Commission consulte*, Droit rural, n° 367, 2008, repère 9.

Daniel Gervais, *The Lisbon Agreement's Misunderstood Potential*, 1 WIPO J. 87 (2009).

Daniel Gervais, *Traditional Knowledge & Intellectual Property: A TRIPS-Compatible Approach*, Mich. St. L. Rev. 137 (2005).

Daniel Gervais, *Traditional Knowledge: Are We Closer to the Answer(s) – The Potential Role of Geographical Indications*, 15 ILSA J. Int'l & Comp. L. 551 (2008).

Daniel J. Gervais, *Irreconcilable Differences? The Geneva Act of the Lisbon Agreement and the Common Law*, 53 Hous. L. Rev. 358 (2015).

Daniel J. Gervais, *Reinventing Lisbon: The Case for a Protocol to the Lisbon Agreement (Geographical Indications)*, 11 Chi. J. Int'l L. 67 (2010).

Daniel Rogits, *EU Geographical Indications v US Trade Marks: TKO against the International Harmonization of the Protection of Geographical Indications*, 4 Intell. Prop. Q. 403 (2010).

Daniele Giovannucci et al., *Guide to Geographical Indications: Linking Products and Their Origins*, Organization for an International Geographical Indications Network (11 June 2021), https://www.origin-gi.com/images/stories/PDFs/English/E-Library/geographical_indications.pdf.

Danielle Da Palma et al., *La protection des marques et des noms de domaine des collectivités publiques*, La semaine juridique administrations et collectivités territoriales, n° 35, 2015, 2250.

Danielle Dudding, *The Lisbon Agreement: Why the United States Should Stop Fighting the Geneva Act*, 18 Vand. J. Ent. & Tech. L. 167 (2015).

David R. Downes, *How Intellectual Property Could Be a Tool to Protect Traditional Knowledge*, 25 Colum. J. Envtl. L. 253 (2000).

Deborah J. Kemp & Lynn M. Forsythe, *Trademarks and Geographical Indications: A Case of California Champagne*, 10 Chap. L. Rev. 257 (2006).

Delphine Marie-Vivien et al., *Are French Geographical Indications Losing Their Soul? Analyzing Recent Developments in the Governance of the Link to the Origin in France*, 98 World Dev. 25 (2017).

Delphine Marie-Vivien et al., *Marques, indications géographiques et certifications: comment valoriser la biodiversité dans les Ghâts occidentaux (Inde)?*, Autrepart, 2, 2009, p. 93-115.

Delphine Marie-Vivien et al., *Trademarks, Geographical Indications and Environmental Labelling to Promote Biodiversity: The Case of Agroforestry Coffee in India*, 32 Dev. Pol'y Rev. 379 (2014).

Delphine Marie-Vivien, *Controversies Around Geographical Indications: Are Democracy and Representativeness the Solution?*, 121 Brit. Food J. 2995 (2019).

Delphine Marie-Vivien, *Le choix d'un régime juridique spécifique en question, Contrats concurrence consommation*, n° 12, 2013, étude 15.

Delphine Marie-Vivien, *Protection of Geographical Indications in ASEAN Countries: Convergences and Challenges to Awakening Sleeping Geographical Indications*, 23 Journal World Intell. Prop. 328 (2020).

Delphine Marie-Vivien, *The Protection of Geographical Indications for Handicrafts or How to Apply the Concepts of Natural and Human Factors to All Products*, 4 WIPO J. 191 (2013).

Delphine Marie-Vivien, *The Role of the State in the Protection of Geographical Indications: From Disengagement in France/Europe to Significant Involvement in India*, 13 J. World Intell. Prop. 121 (2010).

Delphine Marie-Vivien, *Trademarks, Geographical Indications and Environmental Labelling to Promote Biodiversity: The Case of Agroforestry Coffee in India*, 32 Dev. Pol'y Rev. 382 (2014).

Deng Hongguang, Lun Woguo Diming Shangbiao Falu Zhidu de Wanshan [The Improvement of the Legal System of China's Geographical Trademark], NEIMENGGU SHEHUI KEXUE [INNER MONGOLIA SOCIAL SCIENCES], July 2008, 31.

Denis Rochard, *AOC, IGP: précisions sur le rôle de l'INAO en matière d'agrément et de contrôle*, Droit rural, n° 4, 2005, comm. 70.

Denis Rochard, *AOP-IGP: Protection communautaire – Évolution de la réglementation*, Revue de droit rural, n° 314, 2003, p. 357.

Denis Rochard, *De la difficulté de qualifier un terme de générique!*, Droit rural, n° 328, 2004, étude 5.

Denis Rochard, *L'adoption d'un cadre juridique communautaire de protection de la qualité des produits agro-alimentaires: un système de protection du vocabulaire*, Revue de droit rural, n° 246, 1996, p. 362.

Denis Rochard, *Retour vers les origines ... géographiques*, Droit rural, n° 5, 2005, étude 6.

Dev Gangjee, *Geographical Indications and Cultural Heritage*, 4 WIPO J. 92 (2012).

Dev Gangjee, *Melton Mowbray and the GI Pie in the Sky: Exploring Cartographies of Protection*, 3 Intell. Prop. Q. 291 (2006).

Dev Gangjee, *Protecting Geographical Indications as Collective Trademarks: The Prospects and Pitfalls*, Institute of Intellectual Property (10 May 2021), https://www.iip.or.jp/e/summary/pdf/detail2005/e17_14.pdf.

Dev Gangjee, *Proving Provenance? Geographical Indications Certification and Its Ambiguities*, 98 World Dev. 12 (2017).

Dev Gangjee, *Quibbling Siblings: Conflicts Between Trademarks and Geographical Indications*, 82 Chi.-Kent L. Rev. 1253 (2007).

Dev Gangjee, *Say Cheese! A Sharper Image of Generic Use Through the Lens of Feta*, 29 Eur. Intell. Prop. Rev. 172 (2007).

Dimitris Skuras & Aleka Vakrou, *Consumers' Willingness to Pay for Origin Labelled Wine: A Greek Case Study*, 104 Bri. Food J. 898 (2002).

David Snyder, *Enhanced Protections for Geographical Indications under TRIPs: Potential Conflicts under the US Constitutional and Statutory Regimes*, 18 Fordham Intell. Prop. Media & Ent. L.J. 1297 (2008).

Dimitris Skuras & Efthalia Dimara, *Regional Image and the Consumption of Regionally Denominated Products*, 41 Urb. Stud. 801 (2004).

Dominique Barjolle & Bertil Sylvander, *Some Factors of Success for Origin Labelled Products in Agri-food Supply Chains in Europe: Market, Internal Resources and Institutions*, 25 Economies et Sociétés 1441 (2002).

Dominique Barjolle & Erik Thevenod-Mottet, *Ancrage territorial des systèmes de production: le cas des appellations d'origine contrôlée*, Industries alimentaires et agricoles, Vol. 121, 2004, p. 19.

Dominique Barjolle et al., *Création et Distribution de Valeur Economique dans les Filières de Fromages AOP*, 41 Economies et sociétés 1507 (2007).

Dominique Barjolle et al., *Impacts of Geographical Indications: Review of Methods and Empirical Evidences*, Presentation at the International Association of Agricultural Economists Conference, Beijing, China (16-22 August 2009), p. 11.

Dorothée Boyer-Paillard, *Essai sur les notions d'origine et de provenance en droit du commerce: la reconnaissance juridique des 'territoires des productions typiques'*, Droit rural, n° 435, 2015, étude 16.

Dwijen Rangnekar, *Geographical Indications: A Review of Proposals at the TRIPS Council* 33 (UNCTAD-ICTSD Project on IPRs and Sustainable Development, Issue Paper No. 4, 2002).

E. Saulnier, *Appellations d'origine et indications géographiques protégées*, Europe, n° 1, 2002, comm. 13.

Elizabeth Barham, *Translating Terroir: The Global Challenge of French AOC Labeling*, 19 J. Rural Stud. 127 (2003).

Elizabeth Ferreira da Silva & Patrícia Pereira Peralta, *Collective Marks and Geographical Indications: Competitive Strategy of Differentiation and Appropriation of Intangible Heritage*, 16 J. Intell. Prop. Rts. 246 (2011).

Elmer William Hanak III, *The Quality Assurance Function of Trademarks*, 43 Fordham L. Rev. 363 (1974).

Emily C. Creditt, *Terroir v. Trademarks: The Debate over Geographical Indications and Expansions to the TRIPS Agreement*, 11 Vand. J. Ent. & Tech. L. 425 (2008).

Erik W Ibele, *The Nature and Function of Geographical Indications in Law*, 10 Estey Ctr. J. Int'l L. & Trade Pol'y 36 (2009).

Eva Gutierrez, *Geographical Indicators: A Unique European Perspective on Intellectual Property*, 29 Hastings Int'l & Comp. L. Rev. 29 (2005).

Fabien Barthe, *L'harmonisation des signes de qualité*, Droit rural, n° 396, 2011, dossier 21.

Fabien Barthe, *Le Champagne produit de luxe? Entre AOC et marque notoire*, Revue lamy droit des affaires, n° 66, 2011.

Fan Shengming, Wang Zhongming & Zhou Dawei, Woguo Linchanpin Dili Biaozhi Zhishi Chanquan Baohu Wenti Tantao [Discussions on the Protection of Forestry Products' Intellectual Property of Geographical Indications], GUANGDONG NONGYE KEXUE [GUANGDONG AGRICULTURAL SCIENCES], January 2012, 186.

Fatima Lambarraa-Lehnhardt, *Geographical Indications for Supporting Rural Development in the Context of the Green Morocco Plan: Oasis Dates*, 67 Agric. Econ. 70 (2021).

Felix Addor & Alexandra Grazioli, *Geographical Indications Beyond Wines and Spirits: A Roadmap for a Better Protection for Geographical Indications in the WTO TRIPS Agreement*, 5 J. World Intell. Prop. 865 (2002).

Filippo Arfini, *Are Geographical Indication Products Fostering Public Goods? Some Evidence from Europe*, 11 Sustainability 272 (2019).

Florence Chaltiel, *La protection de l'identité des produits en Europe, À propos des règlements européens de 2006*, Contrats concurrence consommation, n° 7, 2006, étude 16.

François Barque, *Le droit communautaire des appellations d'origine et indications géographiques en matière vinicole*, Revue trimestrielle de droit européen, 2009, p. 743.

François Robbe, *Les cahiers des charges des signes de qualité: élaboration et contrôle*, Droit rural, n° 436, 2015, dossier 15.

Frank I. Schechter, *Rational Basis of Trademark Protection*, 40 Harv. L. Rev. 813 (1926).

Frederic Wallet, *La protection des produits sous indication géographique en Chine: une analyse du processus d'émergence d'une régulation de la qualité agro-alimentaire*, Colloque SFER Toulouse, 2012.

Frederick Breitenfeld, *Collective Marks: Should They Be Abolished?* 47 Trademark Rep. 1 (1957).

Friederike Frantz, *Twenty Years of TRIPS, Twenty Years of Debate: The Extension of High Level Protection of Geographical Indications: Arguments, State of negotiations and Prospects*, 21 Ann. Surv. Int'l & Comp. L. 93 (2016).

Gail E. Evans & Michael Blakeney, *The Protection of Geographical Indications after Doha: Quo Vadis?*, 9 J. Int'l Econ. L. 575 (2006).

Gail E. Evans, *The Comparative Advantage of Geographical Indications and Community Trade Marks for the Marketing of Agricultural Products*, 41 IIC-Int'l Rev. Intell. Prop. & Competition L. 645 (2010).

Gail E. Evans, *The Protection of Geographical Indications in the European Union and the United States under Sui Generis and Trade Mark Systems: Signs of Harmonization?*, 1 Intell. Prop. Q. 18 (2013).

Gail E. Evans, *The Simplification of European Legislation for the Protection of Geographical Indications: The Proposed Regulation on Agricultural Product Quality Schemes*, 34 Eur. Intell. Prop. Rev. 770 (2012).

Gail E. Evans, *The Strategic Exploitation of Geographical Indications and Community Trade Marks for the Marketing of Agricultural Products in the European Union*, 1 WIPO J. 159 (2010).

Gail Evans & Michael Blakeney, *The International Protection of Geographical Indications Yesterday, Today and Tomorrow*, 9 J. Int'l Econ. L. 575 (2006).

Geneviève Teil, *Nature, The Co-author of Its Products? An Analysis of the Recent Controversy over Rejected AOC Wines in France*, 17 J. World Intell. Prop. 96 (2014).

Geneviève Teil, *The French Wine 'Appellations d'Origine Contrôlée' and the Virtues of Suspicion*, 13 J. World Intell. Prop. 253 (2010).

Georges Bonet, *Des cigarettes aux parfums, l'irrésistible ascension de l'appellation d'origine Champagne vers la protection absolue*, Propriétés intellectuelles, n° 13, 2004, p. 856.

Georges Bonet, *La marque constituée par un nom géographique en droit français*, La semaine juridique entreprise et affaires, n° 50, 1990, 15931.

Gerard Bodeker, *Traditional Medical Knowledge, Intellectual Property Rights & Benefit Sharing*, 11 Cardozo J. Int'l & Comp. L. 785 (2003).

GianCarlo Moschini et al., *Geographical Indications and the Competitive Provision of Quality in Agricultural Markets*, 90 Am. J. Agric. Econ. 794 (2008).

Giang Hoang et al., *The Impact of Geographical Indications on Sustainable Rural Development: A Case Study of the Vietnamese Cao Phong Orange*, 12 Sustainability 4711 (2020).

Gilles Allaire et al., *Les dispositifs français et européens de protection de la qualité et de l'origine dans le contexte de l'OMC: justifications générales et contextes nationaux*, Symposium international territoires et enjeux du développement régional, 2005.

Giovanni Belletti et al., *Geographical Indications, Public Goods, and Sustainable Development: The Roles of Actors' Strategies and Public Policies*, 98 World Dev. 45 (2017).

Giulia Meloni & Johan Swinnen, *Trade and Terroir: The Political Economy of the World's First Geographical Indications*, 81 Food Pol'y 1 (2018).

Giulia Melonia & Johan Swinnena, *The Political Economy of European Wine Regulations*, 8 J. Wine Econ. 244 (2013).

Grégoire Salignon, *La jurisprudence et la réglementation communautaire relatives à la protection des appellations d'origine, des dénominations géographiques et des indications de provenance*, Revue du marché unique européen, 1994, p. 108.

Gregory Younging, *Traditional Knowledge Exists; Intellectual Property Is Invented or Created*, 36 U. Pa. J. Int'l L. 1077 (2014).

Guo Xiushen, Yifa Guifan Dili Biaozhi Baohu Xingzheng Guanli Tizhi [Regulating the Administrative System of Geographical Indication Protection], ZHONGHUA SHANGBIAO [CHINA TRADEMARK], October 2004, 10.

Hao Jianqiang et al., Xiaofeizhe Dui Nongchanpin Dili Biaozhi Renzhidu he Goumai Xingwei de Fenxi [Analysis of Consumers' Recognition and Purchase Behavior of Geographical Indications of Agricultural Products], NONGCHANPIN ZHILIANG YU ANQUAN [QUALITY AND SAFETY OF AGRO-PRODUCTS], August 2012, 18-21.

Harvinder Singh & Rashmi Aggarwal, *Marketing of Geographical Indications in India: An Analysis*, 35 Eur. Intell. Prop. Rev. 667 (2013).

He Lianhong, Liuyang Huapao Shuangchong Baohu zhi Tong [The Nightmare of Double Protection: Liuyang Fireworks], ZHONGHUA SHANGBIAO [CHINA TRADEMARK], November 2006, 12.

Hogan Lovells, *Pratique contentieuse. Contentieux de la concurrence déloyale et parasitisme. – L'extension de la protection des indications géographiques aux produits industriels et artisanaux*, Communication commerce électronique, n° 12, 2014, 20.

Hu Shen et al., Shengtai Yuanchandi Renzheng Tanxi [Analysis on Ecology Origin Certification], XIANDAI NONGYE KEJI [MODERN AGRICULTURAL SCIENCE AND TECHNOLOGY], September 2013, 301-302.

Hu Shilin, Daodi Yaocai yu Fangzhi he Gongpin [Geo-herbals with Geographies and Medical Tributes], ZHONGGUO YAOXUE ZAZHI [CHINESE PHARMACEUTICAL JOURNAL], August 1996, 496.

Huang Huajun, Nongye Xiandaihua yu Dili Biaozhi de Zhishi Chanquan Baohu [The Modernization of Agriculture and Geographical Indication Protection], SHEHUI KEXUE ZHANXIAN [SOCIAL SCIENCE FRONT], January 2006, 224-227.

Inessa Shalevich, *Protection of Trademarks and Geographical Indications*, 6 Buff. Intell. Prop. L.J. 67 (2008).

Irene Calboli, *Expanding the Protection of Geographical Indications of Origin under TRIPS: Old Debate or New Opportunity?*, 10 Marq. Intell. Prop. L. Rev. 181 (2006).

Irene Calboli, *In Territorio Veritas: Bringing Geographical Coherence in the Definition of Geographical Indications of Origin under TRIPS*, 6 WIPO J. 57 (2014).

Irina Kireeva, *Overview of the EC Case Law Protecting Geographical Indications: The Slicing of Parma Ham and the Grating of Grana Padano Cheese*, 26 Eur. Intell. Prop. Rev. 313 (2004).

Ivo A. van der Lans et al., *The Role of the Region of Origin and EU Certificates of Origin in Consumer Evaluation of Food Products*, 28 Eur. Rev. Agric. Econ. 451 (2001).

Jacques Audier, *Accord ADPIC: indication géographique*, Office des publications officielles des communautés européennes, 2000, p. 29.

Jacques Audier, *De la nature juridique de l'appellation d'origine*, Bulletin de l'OIV, n° 743-744, 1993, p. 21.

Jacques Audier, *Réflexions juridiques sur la notion de terroir*, Bulletin de l'OIV (747-748), 1993, p. 21.

Jacques Azéma, *Législation: Loi relative à la consommation*, RTD Com., 2014, p. 355.

Jacques Azéma, *Les dangers de la marque géographique*, RTD Com., 2008, p. 540.

Jacques Azéma, *Marque collective de certification*, RTD Com., 2014, p. 358.

Jacques Azéma, *Propriété industrielle, Marques, Marque collective, Nullité*, RTD Com., 1998, p. 142.

Jacques Larrieu, *Laguiole: le match retour*, Propriété industrielle, n° 12, 2016, comm. 89.

Jacques Larrieu, *Guerre des étoiles contre la fraude à Laguiole*, La semaine juridique entreprise et affaires, n° 10, 2018, 1124.

Jacques Larrieu, *À couteaux tirés*, Propriété industrielle, n° 4, 2013, comm. 29.

Jacques Larrieu, *Concurrence déloyale laguiole: le match retour*, Propriété industrielle, n° 12, 2016, p. 37.

Jacques Larrieu, *La concurrence déloyale prête main-forte au label*, Propriété industrielle, n° 10, 2011, comm. 75.

Jacques Larrieu, *Un an de protection des noms des communes*, Propriété industrielle, n° 4, 2008, chron. 3.

James M. Treece, *Trademark Licensing and Vertical Restraints in Franchising Arrangements*, 116 U. Pa. L. Rev. 435 (1967).

Jean Foyer, *Commentaire de la loi du 4 janvier 1991 relative aux marques de fabrique, de commerce et de service*, Actualités législatives Dalloz, 1991, p. 69.

Jean-Christophe Galloux, *Les lois n° 2014-315 du 11 mars 2014 renforçant la lutte contre la contrefaçon et n° 2014-344 du 17 mars 2014, relative à la consommation*, RTD Com., 2014, p. 579.

Jean-François Belhoste, *La maison, la fabrique et la ville. L'industrie du drap fin en France (XVe-XVIIIe siècles)*, Histoire, économie et société, Vol. 13, n° 3, 1994, p. 460.

Jean-François Gautier, *Le droit vitivinicole*, Revue de droit rural, n° 212, 1993, p. 175.

Jean-Jacques Burst & Jean-Marc Mousseron, *Droits et accords industriels (suite)*, La semaine juridique entreprise et affaires, n° 8, 1990, 15706.

Jean-Marc Bahans, *La nouvelle OCM vitivinicole: une réforme communautaire sous l'inspiration de l'OMC.: (commentaire des titres II, III et IV du règlement (CE) n° 479/2008 du Conseil du 29 avril 2008 et du règlement (CE) n° 555/2008 de la Commission du 27 juin 2008)*, Droit rural, n° 366, 2008, dossier 33.

Jean-Marc Bahans, *Un an de jurisprudence en droit de la vigne et du vin (2013 -2014)*, Droit rural, n° 429, 2015, chron. 1.

Jean-Marie Bailly, *Appellation d'origine protégées et indications géographiques protégées*, Revue de droit rural, n° 215, 1993, p. 319.

Jeremy Reed, *ECJ Protects Simple Geographical Indications for Their Bud-dy*, 27 Eur. Intell. Prop. Rev. 25 (2005).

Jeremy Reed, *Water from Kerry Spring and Honest Practices*, 26 Eur. Intell. Prop. Rev. 429 (2004).

Jérôme Ferrando, *La consécration d'un nouveau droit de propriété industrielle – Embouteillages à l'INPI*, Revue Lamy droit de l'immatériel, n° 102, 2014, p. 89.

Jérôme Passa, *Indications géographiques: évocation d'une AOP par l'emploi d'un signe figuratif*, Revue trimestrielle de droit commercial et de droit économique, n° 4, 2020, 897.

Jim Chen, *A Sober Second Look at Appellations of Origin: How the United States Will Crash France's Wine and Cheese Party*, 5 Minn. J. Global Trade 29 (1996).

Joanna Schmidt-Szalewski, *La propriété intellectuelle dans la mondialisation*, Propriété industrielle, n° 6, 2006, étude 20.

Joanna Schmidt-Szalewski, *La protection des noms géographiques en droit communautaire*, La semaine juridique entreprise et affaires, n° 44, 1997, p. 703.

Joanna Schmidt-Szalewski, *Site du feuilleton des époisses*, Propriété industrielle, n° 3, 2002, comm. 37.

Johanna Gibson, *Tilting at Windmills: The Law of Evocation in Geographical Indications and Designations of Origin*, 9 Queen Mary J. Intell. Prop. 239 (2019).

Jose Manuel Cortes Martin, *The WTO TRIPS Agreement: The Battle Between the Old and the New World over the Protection of Geographical Indications*, 7 J. World Intell. Prop. 287 (2004).

Jose Manuel Cortes Martin, *Trips Agreement: Towards a Better Protection for Geographical Indications*, 30 Brook. J. Int'l L. 117 (2004).

Josef A. Brinckmann, *Geographical Indications for Medicinal Plants: Globalization, Climate Change, Quality and Market Implications for Geo-authentic Botanicals*, 1 World J. Traditional Chinese Med. 16 (2015).

Julie A. Caswell & Daniel I. Padberg, *Toward a More Comprehensive Theory of Food Labels*, 74 Am. J. Agric. Econ. 460 (1992).

Junko Kimura & Cyrille Rigolot, *The Potential of Geographical Indications (GI) to Enhance Sustainable Development Goals (SDGs) in Japan: Overview and Insights from Japan GI Mishima Potato*, 13 Sustainability 961 (2021).

Justin Hughes, *Champagne, Feta, and Bourbon: The Spirited Debate about Geographical Indications*, 58 Hastings L.J. 299 (2006).

Justin M. Waggoner, *Acquiring a European Taste for Geographical Indications*, 33 Brook. J. Int'l L. 569 (2007).

Kal Raustiala & Chris Sprigman, *Eat, Drink and Be Wary: Why the U.S. Should Oppose the WTO's Extending Stringent Intellectual Property Protection of Wine and Spirit Names to Other Products*, Findlaw (11 June 2021), https://supreme.findlaw.com/legal-commentary/eat-drink-and-be-wary.html.

Kal Raustiala & Stephen R. Munzer, *The Global Struggle over Geographic Indications*, 18 Eur. J. Int'l L. 337, 340 (2007).

Karl H. Pilny, *Germany: Trade Marks: Appellations of Geographical Origin: Use for Products not Manufactured in Geographical Region*, 24 Eur. Intell. Prop. Rev. 110 (2002).

Kees de Roest, *The Production of Parmigiano-Reggiano Cheese: The Force of an Artisanal System in an Industrialized World* 155 (Van Gorcum 2000).

Kevin M. Murphy, *Conflict, Confusion, and Bias under TRIPs Articles 22-24*, 19 Am. U. Int'l L. Rev. 1181 (2003).

Koert Van Ittersum et al., *Consumers' Appreciation of Regional Certification Labels: A Pan-European Study*, 58 J. Agric. Econ. 1 (2007).

Kong Xiangjun & Su Yuejuan, Dili Biaozhi Baohu yu Shengtai Yuanchandi Baohu Buke Hunxiao [GIs and Protected Eco-Origin Products Are Not to Be Confused], ZHONGGUO JIANYAN JIANYI [CHINA INSPECTION AND QUARANTINE], December 2014, 78-79.

Kong Xiangjun, Xia Junli & Zhou Yunchuan, Guanyu Shenli Shangbiao Shouquan Quequan Xingzheng Anjian Ruogan Wenti de Lijie yu Shiyong [Understanding and Application of the Opinions on Several Issues Concerning the Trial of Administrative Cases Involving the Authorization and Determination of Trademark Rights], RENMIN SIFA [PEOPLE'S JUSTICE], June 2010, 21.

Laurence Bérard & Marchenay Philippe, *From Localized Products to Geographical Indications*, CNRS (June 18, 2021), https://www.ethno-terroirs.cnrs.fr/IMG/pdf/Localized_Products_to_GI.pdf.

Laurence Bérard & Philippe Marchenay, *Les produits de terroir. Entre cultures et règlements*, Paris, CNRS, 2004.

Laurence Bérard & Philippe Marchenay, *Local Products and Geographical Indications: Taking Account of Local Knowledge and Biodiversity*, 58 Int'l Soc. Sci. J. 109 (2006).

Laurence Bérard & Philippe Marchenay, *Produits de terroir: comprendre et agir*, Ressources des terroirs – Cultures, usages, sociétés, 2007.

Laurence Bérard, *Savoirs et savoir-faire naturalistes locaux: l'originalité française*, La revue en sciences de l'environnement, Vol. 6, 2005, p. 8.

Laurence Bineau, *Une extension attendue de l'indication géographique protégée aux produits manufacturés*, Contrats concurrence consommation, n° 2, 2013, étude 3.

Laurence Boy, *Propriété intellectuelle, l'agriculture en première ligne avec l'accord ADPIC*, Déméter, 2002, p. 67.

Lee Bendekgey & Caroline H. Mead, *International Protection of Appellations of Origin and Other Geographical Indications*, 82 Trademark Rep. 765 (1992).

Leigh Ann Lindquist, *Champagne or Champagne-An Examination of US Failure to Comply with the Geographical Provisions of the TRIPS Agreement*, 27 Ga. J. Int'l & Comp. L. 309 (1998).

Léon Vandermeersch, *La Chine et la mondialisation*, Archives de Philosophie du Droit, Vol. 47, 2003, p. 99.

Leonardo Cei et al., *From Geographical Indications to Rural Development: A Review of the Economic Effects of European Union Policy*, 10 Sustainability 3754 (2018).

Li Hua & Wang Zhaoke, Dili Biaozhi yu Shangbiao de Benzhi Qubie [The Essential Difference Between Geographical Indications and Trademarks], SHIJIE NONGYE [WORLD AGRICULTURE], January 2006, 48.

Li Xiuli, Liu Shiyi & Xu Weiyuan, Dili Biaozhi Guanli Quewei de Xianshi Kaobian ji Jiejue Fanglue [Realistic Textual Research on and Resolution to Geographical Indication Management Absence], QINGDAO NONGYE DAXUE XUEBAO [JOURNAL OF QINGDAO AGRICULTURAL UNIVERSITY], February 2014, 49.

Li Yahong, *The Wolf Has Come: Are China's Intellectual Property Industries Prepared for the WTO*, 20 UCLA Pac. Basin L.J. 77 (2002).

Li Yaqin, Lun Dili Biaozhi de Falu Baohu [Legal Protection of Geographical Indications], KEJI YU FALU [SCIENCE & LAW], April 2008, 54.

Li Yuping et al., Zhongguo Dili Biaozhi Baohu Fazhan Yanjiu [Research on the Protection and Development of Geographical Indications in China], GUANGDONG NONGYE KEXUE [GUANGDONG AGRICULTURAL SCIENCES], October 2012, 213-232.

Liang Siya & Liu Guining, Shengtai Yuanchandi Chanpin Baohu Zhidu de Fazhan yu Zhanwang [Development and Prospect of Protection System of PEOP], DI SHIYI JIE ZHONGGUO BIAOZHUNHUA LUNTAN LUNWENJI [THE ELEVENTH CHINA STANDARDIZATION FORUM], September 2014, 739-743.

Lilian V. Faulhaber, *Cured Meat and Idaho Potatoes: A Comparative Analysis of European and American Protection and Enforcement of Geographic Indications of Foodstuffs*, 11 Colum. J. Eur. L. 623 (2004).

Lina Montén, *Geographical Indications of Origin: Should They Be Protected and Why: An Analysis of the Issue from the US and EU Perspectives*, 22 Santa Clara Computer & High Tech. L.J. 315 (2005).

Lionel Bently & Brad Sherman, *The Impact of European Geographical Indications on National Rights in Member States*, 96 Trademark Rep. 850 (2006).

Liu Chaolan et al., Rusuanjun he Jiaomu Gong Peiyang Jishu Suoduan Pixian Doubanjiang Chenniang de Yingyong Yanjiu [Reduction of Ripening Period of Pixian Bean Chili Pastes by Conculturing of Salt-Tolerance Lactobacillus and Yeasts], ZHONGGUO NIANGZAO [CHINA BREWING], March 2009, 105-109.

Liu Guodong, Dili Biaozhi yu Putong Shangbiao Chongtu de Jiejue Shiyong Jinzhi Hunxiao Yuanze [The Principle of Prohibition of Confusion Applies to the Settlement of the Conflict Between GIs and Trademarks], ZHONGHUA SHANGBIAO [CHINA TRADEMARK], September 2014, 18.

Liu Guoqi, Yuanchan Diyu Baohu he Yuanchandi Zhengming Shangbiao Baohu [Protection of Geographical Origin and Protection of Certification Marks Certifying Geographical Origin], ZHONGHUA SHANGBIAO [CHINA TRADEMARK], April 2002, 42.

Liu Lihe, Daodi Yaocai de Dili Biaozhi Baohu [The Geographical Mark Protection of Genuine Medical Materials], NANHUA DAXUE XUEBAO [JOURNAL OF UNIVERSITY OF SOUTH CHINA], April 2009, 64.

Liu Yajun, Wanshan Woguo Dili Biaozhi Falu Baohu Shizheng Fenxi [Positive Analysis on Our Amelioration of Geographical Indication], DANGDAI FAXUE [CONTEMPORARY LAW REVIEW], March 2004, 47.

Liu Zhaobin, Faguo Dili Biaozhi Chanpin Baohu Zhidu de Qishi [Inspirations from the French Instruments for Geographical Indication Protection], GUANGMING RIBAO [GUANGMING DAILY], 25 January 2015, 5.

Liu Zhaobin, Woguo Yuanchan Diyu Chanpin Baohu Zhidu Shishi de Xianzhuang yu Fazhan [The Status Quo and Development of the Protection System of Appellations of Origin Products in China], ZHONGGUO BIAOZHUNHUA [CHINA STANDARDIZATION], December 2001, 7.

Lu Guoqiang & Wu Denglou, Woguo Dili Biaozhi Falu Zhidu de Wanshan [Improvement of the Legal system of Geographical Indications in China], FAXUE [LAW SCIENCE], 20 January 2006, 154.

Lu Qi, Zhongfa Dili Biaozhi Falu Baohu Bijiao Yanjiu [Comparative Study on Geographical Indications Protection: France-China], FAZHI LUNCONG [LAW FORUM], March 2004, 25.

Luisa Menapace & Gian Carlo Moschini, *Quality Certification by Geographical Indications, Trademarks and Firm Reputation*, 39 Eur. Rev. Agric. Econ. 539 (2011).

Luisa Menapace & Gian Carlo Moschini, *Strength of Protection for Geographical Indications: Promotion Incentives and Welfare Effects*, 96 Am. J. Agric. Econ. 1030 (2014).

Luisa Menapace et al., *Consumers' Preferences for Geographical Origin Labels: Evidence from the Canadian Olive Oil Market*, 38 Eur. Rev. Agric. Econ. 193 (2011).

Lynne Beresford, *Geographical Indications: The Current Landscape*, 17 Fordham Intell. Prop. Media & Ent. L.J. 979 (2006).

Ma Xiaoli, Dili Biaozhi Lifa Moshi Bijiao Fenxi Jianlun Woguo Dili Biaozhi de Lifa Moshi [Comparative Analysis of Legislative Mode of Geographical Indications and China's Legislative Choice], DIANZI ZHISHI CHANQUAN [ELECTRONICS INTELLECTUAL PROPERTY], January 2003, 52.

Mai-Anh NGO, *L'apposition obligatoire de l'origine géographique des produits: une harmonisation entraînant le déclin des indications géographiques et le triomphe des marques*, Propriété industrielle, n° 4, 2011, étude 10.

Mai-Anh NGO, *Quel avenir pour les labels au regard de la libre circulation des marchandises?*, Droit rural, n° 356, 2007, étude 34.

Maria Cecilia Mancini, *Geographical Indications in Latin America Value Chains: A 'Branding from Below' Strategy or a Mechanism Excluding the Poorest?*, 32 J. Rural Stud. 295 (2013).

Maria L. Loureiro & Jill Mccluskey, *Assessing Consumer Response to Protected Geographical Identification Labelling*, 16 Agribusiness 309 (2000).

Marianna Bicskei et al., *Reform Proposals on the Geographical Indications of the European Union for the Protection of Traditional Knowledge*, 3 WIPO J. 222 (2012).

Marie Blanchart, *L'optimisation du patrimoine immatériel des collectivités territoriales: la protection offerte par le droit des marques*, Revue Lamy collectivités territoriales, 2014, p. 101.

Marie Carpenter & Fabrice Larceneux, *Label Equity and the Effectiveness of Values-Based Labels: An Experiment with Two French Protected Geographic Indication Labels*, 32 Int'l J. Consumer Stud. 499 (2008).

Marie Malaurie-Vignal, *La protection des savoir-faire et motifs traditionnels: Pour la défense d'une mode éthique*, Propriété industrielle, n° 2, 2019, étude 4.

Marie Malaurie-Vignal, *Parasitisme et notoriété d'autrui*, La semaine juridique édition générale, n° 49, 1995, I. 3888.

Marie-Christine Piatti, *L'appellation d'origine: essai de qualification*, RTD Com., 1999, p. 557.

Marie-Christine Piatti, *Nature juridique de l'AOC: une propriété démembrée*, Revue lamy droit des affaires, n° 68, 2004, p. 5.

Marie-France Garcia-Parpet, *Le marché de l'excellence: le classement des grands crus à l'épreuve de la mondialisation*, Genèses, n° 56, 2004, p. 72.

Marina Kolia, *Monopolising Names: EEC Proposal on the Protection of Trade Descriptions of Foodstuffs*, 14 Eur. Intell. Prop. Rev. 238 (1992).

Marion Desquilbet & Sylvette Monier-Dilhan, *Are Geographical Indications a Worthy Quality Signal? A Framework with Endogenous Quality Choice*, 42 Eur. Rev. of Agric. Econ. 129 (2015).

Mark J. Calaguas, *Rosé by Any Other Name: Protecting Geographical Indications for Wines and Spirits in China*, 3 Loy. U. Chi. Int'l L. Rev. 257 (2006).

Marsha A. Echols, *Food Safety Regulation in the European Union and the United States: Different Cultures, Different Laws*, 4 Colum. J. Eur. L. 525 (1998).

Martijn Huysmans & Julian Swinnen, *No Terroir in the Cold? A Note on the Geography of Geographical Indications*, 70 J. Agric. Econ 550 (2019).

Martin Senftleben, *The Trademark Tower of Babel: Dilution Concepts in International, US and EC Trademark Law*, 40 Int. Rev. Intellect. Prop. Compet. L. 45 (2009).

Martine Dehaut & Natalie Pacaud, *Les marques de certification: apports du décret du 1er mars 2007 modifiant le Code de la propriété intellectuelle*, Propriété industrielle, n° 6, 2007, alerte 79.

Maryline Boizard, *Régime communautaire de protection des indications géographiques et des appellations d'origine protégées et dispositifs nationaux de protection des dénominations géographiques: une application distributive stricte*, Droit rural, n° 429, 2015, comm. 17.

Maryline Filippi & Pierre Triboulet, *Coordination des acteurs et valorisation de produits liés à l'origine, Les signes d'identification comme signes d'exclusion?*, Revue d'économie régionale & urbaine, n° 1, 2006, p. 103.

Matteo Gragnani, *The EU Regulation 1151/2012 on Quality Schemes for Agricultural Products and Foodstuffs*, 8 Eur. Food and Feed L. Rev. 376 (2013).

Matteo Gragnani, *The European Union and the Lisbon Agreement for the Protection of Appellations of Origin and Their International Registration*, Centre d'études juridiques européennes (11 June 2021), https://www.ceje.ch/fr/actualites/

action-exterieure/2010/08/european-union-and-lisbon-agreement-protection-appellations-origin-and-their-international-registration/.

Matthew J. Rippon, *Traditional Foods, Territorial Boundaries and the TRIPS Agreement: The Case of the Melton Mowbray Pork Pie*, 16 J. World Intell. Prop. 262 (2013).

Matthijs Geuze, *The Provisions on Geographical Indications in the TRIPS Agreement*, 10 Estey Ctr. J. Int'l L. & Trade 50 (2009).

May T. Yeung & William A. Kerr, *Are Geographical Indications a Wise Strategy for Developing Country Farmers? Greenfields, Clawbacks and Monopoly Rents*, 14 J. World Intell. Prop. 353 (2011).

Michael Blakeney, *Geographical Indications: What Do They Indicate?*, 6 WIPO J. 50 (2014).

Michael Blakeney, *Geographical Indications and Environmental Protection*, 12 Frontiers L. China 162 (2017).

Michael Blakeney, *Protection of Traditional Knowledge by Geographical Indications*, 3 Int'l J. Intell. Prop. Mgmt. 357 (2009).

Michael Handler, *The WTO Geographical Indications Dispute*, 69 Mod. L. Rev. 70 (2006).

Michel Lecerf, *Les produits agricoles et les denrées alimentaires présentant des caractéristiques particulières quant à leur mode de production ou leur origine.: Articulation des Règlements communautaires avecle nouveau Code de la consommation*, La semaine juridique entreprise et affaires, n° 47, 1994, 402.

Min-Chiuan Wang, *Asian Consciousness and Interests in Geographical Indications*, 96 Trademark Rep. 906 (2006).

Mohammad AI-Shammari & Rasha Hattab, *La Notoriété de l'Appellation d'Origine et du Nom Commercial, Deux Signes Distinctifs. Étude Comparée de Droit Français et Jordanien*, 26 Arab L.Q. 47 (2012).

Molly Torsen, *Apples and Oranges (and Wine): Why the International Conversation Regarding Geographic Indications Is at a Standstill*, 87 J. Pat. & Trademark Off. Soc'y 31 (2005).

Molly Torsen, *Apples and Oranges: French and American Models of Geographic Indications Policies Demonstrate an International Lack of Consensus*, 95 Trademark Rep. 1415 (2005).

Nancy Kremers, *Speaking with a Forked Tongue in the Global Debate on Traditional Knowledge and Genetic Resources: Is US Intellectual Property Law and Policy Really Aimed at Meaningful Protection for Native American Cultures*, 15 Fordham Intell. Prop. Media & Ent. L.J. 1 (2004).

Nicola Coppola, Viiniverla: *Too Much 'Ado' about Nothing*, 11 J. Intell. Prop. L. & Prac. 406 (2016).

Nicolas Binctin, *Marque collective et marque de garantie: Ordonnance et décret d'application issus de la transposition du 'Paquet Marques'*, Communication commerce électronique, n° 5, 2020, étude 10.

Nicolas Bouche, *Les indications géographiques protégeant les produits industriels et artisanaux*, Propriété industrielle, n° 4, 2016, étude 7.

Nina Resinek, *Geographical Indications and Trade Marks: Coexistence or 'First in Time, First in Right' Principle?*, 29 Eur. Intell. Prop. Rev. 446 (2007).

Norbert Olszak, *Acteurs et méthodes de la politique de qualité du produit agricole: Rapport de synthèse*, Droit rural, n° 396, 2011, dossier 24.

Norbert Olszak, *Actualité du droit des signes d'origine et de qualité (appellations d'origine, labels)*, Propriété industrielle, n° 6, 2006, étude 18.

Norbert Olszak, *Actualité du droit des signes d'origine et de qualité (indications géographiques, labels)*, Propriété industrielle, n° 9, 2007, étude 18.

Norbert Olszak, *Appellations d'origine et indications de provenance*, Répertoire Dalloz de droit pénal et de procédure pénale, 2008 (actualité 2015).

Norbert Olszak, *La constitutionnalité de la défense de la notoriété des appellations d'origine*, Droit rural, n° 423, 2014, comm. 102.

Norbert Olszak, *Le goût des vins AOP et IGP: description et contrôle des caractéristiques organoleptiques*, Droit rural, n° 371, 2009, étude 5.

Norbert Olszak, *Les nouveaux règlements européens sur les appellations d'origine et indications géographique protégées et les spécialités traditionnelles garanties*, Revue de droit rural, 2006, p. 9.

Norbert Olszak, *Sauvons le gruyère … générique!*, Droit rural, n° 385, 2010, comm. 105.

Norbert Olszak, *Une demande d'annulation d'une indication géographique protégée de bière*, Propriété industrielle, n° 1, 2013, alerte 1.

Norma Dawson, *Locating Geographical Indications: Perspectives from English Law*, 90 Trademark Rep. 590 (2000).

Olivier Thrierr, *Les conflits entre indications géographiques et marques*, Propriété industrielle, n° 6, 2007, étude 14.

Olivier Thrierr, *Quel(s) nouveau(x) droit(s) des marques dans l'Union européenne?*, Propriété industrielle, n° 7, 2016, étude 14.

Olivier Thrierr, *Quel(s) nouveau(x) droit(s) des marques dans l'Union européenne?*, Propriété industrielle, n° 7, 2016, étude 14.

Olivier Thrierr, *Vers une réforme du droit des marques dans l'Union européenne*, Propriété industrielle, n° 10, 2013, étude 13.

Onno Brouwer, *Community Protection of Geographical Indications and Specific Character as a Means of Enhancing Foodstuff Quality*, 28 Common Mkt. L. Rev. 615 (1991).

Onno Brouwer, *Free Movement of Foodstuffs and Quality Requirements: Has the Commission Got It Wrong?*, 25 Common Mkt. L. Rev. 237 (1998).

Pascale Tréfigny, *Conditions d'obtention du droit de marque*, J.-Cl. Marques Dessins et modèles, fasc. 600.

Pascale Tréfigny, *D'utiles précisions: déchéance et intérêt légitime à l'action …*, Propriété industrielle, n° 7-8, 2006, comm. 55.

Pascale Tréfigny, *L'incidence de la fonction sur la portée de la protection de la marque*, Propriété industrielle, n° 10, 2010, dossier 5.

Pascale Tréfigny, *L'usage de la marque, sa qualification et sa portée …*, Propriété industrielle, n° 11, 2014, comm. 75.

Pascale Tréfigny, *Le régime particulier des marques appliqué au vin*, Propriété industrielle, n° 7-8, 2007, comm. 63.

Pascale Tréfigny, *Les principe du droit, brève histoires juridique*, Lamy droit des affaires, n° 68, 2004, p. 17.

Pascale Tréfigny, *Palace pour tous …*, Propriété industrielle, n° 1, 2014, comm. 3.

Pawel Bryla, *The Perception of EU Quality Signs for Origin and Organic Food Products among Polish Consumers*, 9 Quality Assurance & Safety Crops & Foods 345 (2017).

Pei Xiaoying, Liu Hongchun & Qiao Hong, Dili Biaozhi Diyu Techan de Huwei Shen [Geographical Indications: Guardian of Local Products], ZHONGGUO ZHILIANG JISHU JIANDU [CHINA QUALITY SUPERVISION], March 2006, 48.

Peter K. Yu, *From Pirates to Partners (Episode II): Protecting Intellectual Property in Post-WTO China*, 55 Am. UL Rev. 901 (2005).

Petra van de Kop, Denis Sautier & Astrid Gerz, *Origin-Based Products: Lessons for Pro-poor Market Development* 83 (The Royal Tropical Institute-KIT 2006).

Philip Whalen, *'Insofar as the Ruby Wine Seduces Them': Cultural Strategies for Selling Wine in Inter-war Burgundy*, 18 Contemp. Eur. Hist. 67 (2009).

Philippe Zylberg, *Geographical Indications v. Trademarks: The Lisbon Agreement: A Violation of TRIPS*, 11 U. Balt. Intell. Prop. L.J. 1 (2002).

Pierre Combris et al., *Does Taste Beat Food Safety? Evidence from the 'Pêra Rocha' Case in Portugal*, 16 J. Food Prod. Marketing 60 (2009).

Pierre Combris et al., *Estimation of a Hedonic Price Equation for Bordeaux Wine: Does Quality Matter?*, 107 Econ. J. 390 (1997).

Pierre Mérel & Richard J. Sexton, *Will Geographical Indications Supply Excessive Quality?*, 39 Eur. Rev. Agric. Econ. 567 (2012).

Pilar Fernández-Ferrín et al., *Geographical Indication Food Products and Ethnocentric Tendencies: The Importance of Proximity, Tradition, and Ethnicity*, 241 J. Cleaner Production 118-210 (2019).

R. Van Der Stappen, *L'OCM vitivinicole: genèse, évolution et défis actuels*, Revue du droit rural, n° 335, 2005, p. 22.

Ramona Teuber, *Consumers' and Producers' Expectations Towards Geographical Indications: Empirical Evidence for a German Case Study*, 113 Brit. Food J. 900 (2011).

Ramona Teuber, *Geographical Indications of Origin as a Tool of Product Differentiation: The Case of Coffee*, 22 J. Int'l Food & Agribus. Mark. 277 (2010).

Ramona Teuber, *Protecting Geographical Indications: Lessons Learned from the Economic Literature*, Presentation at the EAAE 2011 Congress (30 August 2011).

Rhonda Chesmond, *Protection or Privatisation of Culture? The Cultural Dimension of the International Intellectual Property Debate on Geographical Indications of Origin*, 29 Eur. Intell. Prop. Rev. 378 (2007).

Riccardo Vecchio & Azzurra Annunziata, *The Role of PDO/PGI Labelling in Italian Consumers' Food Choices*, 12 Agric. Econ. Rev. 80 (2011).

Ritika Banerjee & Mohar Majumdar, *In the Mood to Compromise? Extended Protection of Geographical Indications under TRIPS Article 23*, 6 J. Intell. Prop. L. & Prac. 657 (2011).

Robert Brauneis & Roger E. Schechter, *Geographic Trademarks and the Protection of Competitor Communication*, 96 Trademark Rep. 782 (2006).

Robert Heuser, *The Chinese Trademark Law of 1904: A Preliminary Study in Exterritoriality, Competition, and Late Ch'ing Law Reform*, 22 Oriens Extremus 183 (1975).

Robert Stoll & Wang Ze (trans.), TRIPS Youguan Dili Biaozhi Guiding de Shishi [TRIPS Implementation on Geographical Indications], ZHONGHUA SHANGBIAO [CHINA TRADEMARK], March 2000, 38-41.

Ruan Kaixin, Cong Ruili An Kan Shangbiaofa Zhong de Diming he Dili Biaozhi Wenti [Geographical Names and Geographical Indications in Trademark Law: The Case of Ruili], ZHONGHUA SHANGBIAO [CHINA TRADEMARK], September 2015, 72.

Rudolf Callmann, *Trademark Infringement and Unfair Competition*, 14 L & Contemp. Probs. 185 (1949).

Ruth L. Okedui, *International Intellectual Property Roots of Geographical Indications*, 82 Chi.-Kent L. Rev. 1329 (2007).

Sarah Bowen, *Development from Within? The Potential for Geographical Indications in the Global South*, 13 J. World Intell. Prop. 231 (2010).

Sarah Bowena & Ana Valenzuela Zapata, *Geographical Indications, Terroir, and Socioeconomic and Ecological Sustainability: The Case of Tequila*, 25 J. Rural Stud. 108 (2009).

Séverine Visse-Causse, *L'appellation d'origine arrachée à son terroir*, Recueil Dalloz, 2010, p. 309.

Séverine Visse-Causse, *La guerre des camemberts est déclarée ... Des conséquences du mauvais usage de l'appellation d'origine*, Droit rural, n° 406, 2012, étude 11.

Séverine Visse-Causse, *Pour une défense cohérente de l'appellation d'origine: De la nécessité d'une qualification juridique respectant une institution des terroirs*, Droit rural, n° 380, 2010, étude 2.

Shang Xudong & Li Binlong, Woguo Dili Biaozhi Nongchanpin Baohu he Fazhan Wenti yu Duice [Protection and Development of Agricultural Products of Geographical Indications in China: Problems and Countermeasures], JIAGE LILUN YU SHIJIAN [PRICE THEORY & PRACTICE], November 2011, 73.

Shang Xudong et al., Xiaofeizhe Dui Dili Biaozhi Nongchanpin Zhifu Yiyuan de Shizheng Fenxi [An Analysis of Payment Intention of Consumers to Geographical Indication Agricultural Products], JISHU JINGJI YU GUANLI YANJIU [JOURNAL OF TECHNICAL ECONOMICS & MANAGEMENT], January 2014, 123-128.

Shao Weijie, Nongchanpin Dili Biaozhi Baohu de Yiyi ji Lujin [The Significance of Protecting GIs for Agricultural Products and How to Protect], QILU XUEKAN [QILU JOURNAL], January 2009, 105-110.

Shen Feilong, Tutechan Pinpai de Chengwei Tanxi [Appellation of Local and Special Products], FAZHAN [DEVELOPMENT], November 2007, 111.

Shujie Feng, *Geographical Indications: Can China Reconcile the Irreconcilable Intellectual Property Issue Between EU and US?*, 19 World Trade Rev. 424 (2020).

Stacy D. Goldberg, *Who Will Raise the White Flag: The Battle Between the United States and the European Union over the Protection of Geographical Indications*, 22 U. Pa. J. Int'l Econ. L. 107 (2001).

Stephan Marette, Roxanne Clemens & Bruce Babcock, *Recent International and Regulatory Decisions about Geographical Indications*, 24 Agribusiness 453 (2008).

Stephen Stern, *Are GIs IP?*, 29 Eur. Intell. Prop. Rev. 39 (2007).

Steven A. Bowers, *Location, Location, Location: The Case Against Extending Geographical Indication Protection under the TRIPS Agreement*, 31 AIPLA Q.J. 129 (2003).

Strasser Mathias, *Rational Basis of Trademark Protection Revisited: Putting the Dilution Doctrine into Context*, 10 Fordham Intell. Prop. Media & Ent. L.J. 375 (1999).

Strasser Mathias, *Rational Basis of Trademark Protection Revisited: Putting the Dilution Doctrine into Context*, 10 Fordham Intell. Prop. Media & Ent. L.J. 375 (1999).

Stuart Landon & Smith E. Constance, *The Use of Quality and Reputation Indicators by Consumers: The Case of Bordeaux Wine*, 20 J. Consumer Pol'y 289 (1997).

Su Ping, Yu Dili Biaozhi Xiangguan de Falu Shuyu Yujing Kaobian (Textual Research on the Contexts for Legal Terms Related to Geographical Signs), CHONGQING GONGXUEYUAN XUEBAO [JOURNAL OF CHONGQING INSTITUTE OF TECHNOLOGY], January 2007, 123.

Sumner J. La Croix & Denise Eby Konan, *Intellectual Property Rights in China: The Changing Political Economy of Chinese-American Interests*, 25 World Econ. 759 (2002).

Sun Weidong, Yantai Zhongguo Shouge Hongjiu Yuanchandi [Yantai: China's First Wine Appellation of Origin], ZHONGGUO JIANYAN JIANYI [CHINA INSPECTION & QUARANTINE], April 2014.

Sun Zhiguo et al., Anhuisheng Daodi Yaocai Lei Guojia Dili Biaozhi Chanpin de Baohu Xianzhuang ji Duice [Protection Situation and Countermeasures of National Geographical Indication Products of Genuine Medicinal Materials in Anhui Province], ANHUI NONGYE KEXUE [JOURNAL OF ANHUI AGRICULTURAL SCIENCES], May 2010, 7353-7355.

Sun Zhiguo et al., Sichuansheng Daodi Yaocai Lei Guojia Dili Biaozhi Chanpin de Baohu Fenxi [Protection Situation of National Products of Geographical Indication of Geo-authentic Crude Drugs in Sichuan Province], XINAN NONGYE XUEBAO [SOUTHWEST CHINA JOURNAL OF AGRICULTURE], April 2010, 532.

Surbhi Jain, *Effects of the Extension of Geographical Indications: A South Asian Perspective*, 16 Asia-Pacific Dev. J. 65 (2009).

Susana López-Bayón et al., *In Search of Agri-food Quality for Wine: Is It Enough to Join a Geographical Indication?*, 36 Agribusiness 568 (2020).

Susy Frankel, *The Mismatch of Geographical Indications and Innovative Traditional Knowledge*, 29 Prometheus 253 (2011).

Taj Kunwar Paul, *Geographical Indications Before and Beyond TRIPS: An Asian Perspective*, 30 Int'l Bus. Law. 127 (2002).

Tanguy Chever et al., *Value of Production of Agricultural Products and Foodstuffs, Wines, Aromatised Wines and Spirits Protected by a Geographical Indication (GI)* (AND International 2012).

Tania G. Albuquerque et al., *25 Years of European Union (EU) Quality Schemes for Agricultural Products and Foodstuffs Across EU Member States*, 98 J. Sci. Food & Agric. 2475 (2018).

Teshager W. Dagne, *Harnessing the Development Potential of Geographical Indications for Traditional Knowledge-Based Agricultural Products*, 5 J. Intell. Prop. L. & Prac. 441 (2010).

Teshager W. Dagne, *Law and Policy on Intellectual Property, Traditional Knowledge and Development: Legally Protecting Creativity and Collective Rights in Traditional Knowledge-Based Agricultural Products Through Geographical Indications*, 11 Estey Ctr. J. Int'l L. & Trade Pol'y 68 (2010).

Teshager W. Dagne, *The Identity of Geographical Indications and Their Relation to Traditional Knowledge in Intellectual Property Law*, 5 WIPO J. 137 (2014).

Thanasis Kizos et al., *The Governance of Geographical Indications: Experiences of Practical Implementation of Selected Case Studies in Austria, Italy, Greece and Japan*, 119 Brit. Food J. 2863 (2017).

Théodore Georgopoulos, *La protection renforcée des appellations d'origine à l'égard des marques viticoles.: À propos de l'arrêt 'Abadía Retuerta' du Tribunal de l'Union européenne*, Droit rural, n° 387, 2010, étude 28.

Théodore Georgopoulos, *Le contentieux de la délimitation géographique des AOC*, Droit Administratif, n° 4, 2010, comm. 48.

Théodore Georgopoulos, *Les AOC entre notoriété et confusion: Le contentieux autour des vins '(Quarts de) Chaume'*, Droit rural, n° 381, 2010, étude 5.

Thibault Lancrenon, *Ballade dans la brume des marques collectives*, Propriété intellectuelle, n° 13, 2004, p. 848.

Tilman Becker & Alexander Staus, *European Food Quality Policy: The Importance of Geographical Indications, Organic Certification and Food Quality Assurance Schemes in European Countries*, 10 Estey Ctr. J. Int'l L. & Trade Pol'y 111 (2009).

Tim Josling, *The War on Terroir: Geographical Indications as a Transatlantic Trade Conflict*, 57 J. Agric. Econ. 337 (2006).

Tomer Broude, *Culture, Trade and Additional Protection for Geographical Indications*, 9 Bridges 20 (2005).

Tomer Broude, *Taking Trade and Culture Seriously: Geographical Indications and Cultural Protection in WTO Law*, 26 U. Pa. J. Int'l Econ. L. 623 (2005).

Ulrike Grote, *Environmental Labelling, Protected Geographical Indications and the Interests of Developing Countries*, 10 Estey Ctr. J. Int'l L. & Trade Pol'y 99 (2009).

Vadim Mantrov, *The Cases of Edam Holland and Gouda Holland: Continuing Road Back Home as Protected Indications of Geographical Origin*, 7 Eur. J. Risk Reg. 44 (2016).

Vadim Mantrov, *Do You Prefer Scotch or German Whisky? CJEU Judgment in the Scotch Whisky and Glen Buchenbach Dispute*, 9 Eur. J. Risk Reg. 1 (2019).

Vincent Ruzek, *La stratégie communautaire de protection des indications géographiques en question*, Droit rural, n° 373, 2009, étude 7.

Von Heydebrand, *Free Movement of Foodstuffs, Consumer Protection and Food Standards in the European Community: Has the Court of Justice Got It Wrong?*, 16 Eur. L. Rev. 391 (1991).

Wang Chunmei, Woguo Dili Biaozhi Siquan Baohu yu Moshi Xuanze [Protection of Private Rights to the Geographical Indications and Choice of Protection Modes in China], BEIFANG FAXUE [NORTHERN LEGAL SCIENCE], September 2009, 95.

Wang Han & Chen Tong, Woguo Nongchanpin Dili Biaozhi Fazhan Xianzhuang Fenxi [Development of Geographical Indications of Agricultural Products in China], XIAN DIANZI KEJI DAXUE XUEBAO [JOURNAL OF XIDIAN UNIVERSITY], July 2008, 101-105.

Wang Lianfeng, Dili Biaozhi de Falu Baohu [Legal Protection of Geographical Indications], ZHENGZHOU DAXUE XUEBAO [JOURNAL OF ZHENGZHOU UNIVERSITY], October 2003, 66.

Wang Lianfeng, Dili Biaozhi yu Diming Shangbiao de Chongtu ji Falu Shiyong [The Conflict of Geographical Indication with Topographic Trademarks and Its Application of Law], HENANSHENG ZHENGFA GUANLI GANBU XUEYUAN XUEBAO [JOURNAL OF HENAN INSTITUTE OF POLITICAL SCIENCE AND LAW], February 2004, 104.

Wang Lianfeng, Woguo Dili Biaozhi Lifa Moshi de Xuanze [The Choice of the Legislative Mode of Geographical Indication in China], FALU SHIYONG [LAW APPLICATION], July 2003, 70.

Wang Miao, Dili Biaozhi yu Shangbiaoquan de Chongtu Jiqi Falu Xietiao [The Conflict Between Geographical Indication and Trademark Right and Its Legal Coordination], CHANGCHUN SHIFAN DAXUE XUEBAO [JOURNAL OF CHANGCHUN NORMAL UNIVERSITY], July 2005, 112-115.

Wang Sumin, Lun Woguo Dili Biaozhi de Baohu Moshi [Protection Mode of Geographical Indications in China], HUABEI SHUILI SHUIDIAN XUEYUAN XUEBAO [JOURNAL OF HUABEI INSTITUTE OF WATER CONSERVANCY AND HYDROELECTRIC POWER], February 2005, 95.

Wang Xiaobing & Irina Kireeva, *Protection of Geographical Indications in China: Conflicts, Causes and Solutions*, 10 J. World Intellect. Prop. 79 (2007).

Wang Xiaobing & Irina Kireeva, *The Protection of Geographical Indication in the EU and China: Tracing Causes of Delays in the Ongoing Negotiation on the Co-operative Agreement on Geographical Indications*, 2 Intell. Prop. Q. 125 (2014).

Wang Xiaobing, Guanlianxing Yaosu yu Dili Biaozhi Fa de Gouzao [The Linkage and the Construction of Geographical Indication Law], FAXUE YANJIU [LEGAL RESEARCH], May 2015, 82.

Wang Xiaobing, Woguo Canjia WTO Dili Biaozhi Tanpan de Lichang he Duice [China's Position in WTO Negotiation Protecting GIs], ZHISHI CHANQUAN [INTELLECTUAL PROPERTY], January 2010, 47.

Wang Yafeng & Jiang Hezhong, Dili Biaozhi Nongchanpin Xiaofeizhe Goumai Yiyuan he Goumai Xingwei Yanjiu Zongshu [Synthesis of Researches on Consumers'

Purchase Intention and Behavior of Geographical Indications of Agricultural Products], ZHONGXIAO QIYE GUANLI YU KEJI [MANAGEMENT & TECHNOLOGY OF SME], September 2016, 114.

Wang Zhiben, Yuanchan Diyu Chanpin Baohu yu Tigao Woguo Nongchanpin Guoji Jingzhengli [Protecting Appellations of Origin and Improving the International Competitiveness of Agricultural Products in China], SHIJIE NONGYE [WORLD AGRICULTURE], May 2002, 7.

Warren Moran, *The Wine Appellation as Territory in France and California*, 83 Annals Ass'n Am. Geographers 694 (1993).

Watson K. William, *Reign of Terroir: How to Resist Europe's Efforts to Control Common Food Names as Geographical Indications* (11 June 2021), https://www.cato.org/policy-analysis/reign-terroir-how-resist-europes-efforts-control-common-food-names-geographical.

William A. Kerr, *Enjoying a Good Port with a Clear Conscience: Geographic Indicators, Rent Seeking and Development*, 7 Estey Ctr. J. Int'l L. & Trade Pol'y 1, 10 (2006).

William M. Landes & Richard A. Posner, *Trademark Law: An Economic Perspective*, 30 J.L. & Econ. 265 (1987).

William van Caenegem, *Registered Geographical Indications: Between Intellectual Property and Rural Policy: Part 2*, 6 J. World Intell. Prop. 861 (2003).

Wim Verbeke et al., *Consumers' Awareness and Attitudinal Determinants of European Union Quality Label Use on Traditional Foods*, 1 Bio-based & Applied Econ. 213 (2012).

Wu Bin, Woguo Nongchanpin Dili Biaozhi Falu Baohu de Yiyi ji Wanshan Cuoshi [Legal Protection on Geographical Indications of China's Agricultural Products: Significance and Countermeasures], HUAZHONG NONGYE DAXUE XUEBAO [JOURNAL OF HUAZHONG AGRICULTURAL UNIVERSITY], April 2008, 47.

Wu Chunqi, Dili Biaozhi ji Yuanchandi Mingcheng deng Xiangguan Gainian de Tanjiu [The Relationship among Geographical Indications, Indications of Source, and Appellations of Origin], SHANDONG DAXUE XUEBAO [JOURNAL OF SHANDONG UNIVERSITY], August 2003, 94.

Wu Shan, Dili Biaozhi he Chiming Shangbiao Chongtu de Falu Tiaozheng [The Resolution of the Conflict Between Geographical Indications and Geographical Marks], ZHONGGUO LUSHI [CHINA LAWYER], October 2008, 23.

Xia Liyan, Nongcun Laodongli Liushi dui Nongcun Jingji Fazhan de Yingxiang ji Duice [Negative Effects of Labor Force Drain on Rural Economy], NANJIN NONGYE DAXUE XUEBAO [JOURNAL OF NANJING AGRICULTURAL UNIVERSITY], March 2009, 14-19.

Xiao Xiaohe et al., Zhongguo Daodi Yaocai Yanjiu Ershinian Gailun [Survey of Investigations on Daodi Chinese Medicinal Materials in China Since 1980s], ZHONGGUO ZHONGYAO ZAZHI [CHINA JOURNAL OF CHINESE MATERIA MEDICA], March 2009, 519.

Xie Dongwei, Rushi yu Woguo Yuanchandi Mingcheng Dili Biaozhi de Baohu [WTO and the Protection of China's Geographical Indications], ZHONGHUA SHANGBIAO [CHINA TRADEMARK], May 2001, 14-16.

Xie Dongwei, Woguo Dili Biaozhi Zhidu de Lishi yu Fazhan [The History and Development of China's GI Protection System], GONGSHANG XINGZHENG GUANLI [INDUSTRIAL & COMMERCIAL ADMINISTRATION], June 2003, 29.

Xinzhe Song, *A Closer Look at the Elephant in the Room: the Distinctiveness of Geographical Indications*, 11 Queen Mary J. Intell. Prop. 25 (2021).

Xinzhe Song, *The Role Played by the Regime of Collective and Certification Marks in the Protection of Geographical Indications: Comparative Study of Law and Practice in France, the EU and China*, 21 J. World Intell. Prop. 437 (2017).

Xing Zhao, Donald Finlay & Moya Kneafsey, *The Effectiveness of Contemporary Geographical Indications (GIs) Schemes in Enhancing the Quality of Chinese Agrifoods: Experiences from the Field*, 36 J. Rural Stud. 77 (2014).

Xing Zhao, *Food Safety and Chinese Geographical Indications*, 118 Brit. Food J. 217 (2016).

Xiomara F. Quinones-Ruiz, *Why Early Collective Action Pays Off: Evidence from Setting Protected Geographical Indications*, 32 Renewable Agric. & Food Sys. 179 (2016).

Xiomara Fernanda Quinones-Ruiz et al., *How Are Food Geographical Indications Evolving?: An Analysis of EU GI Amendments*, 120 Brit. Food J. 1876 (2018).

Xiong Ying, Lun Woguo Dili Biaozhi Baohu Moshi de Danyizhi [The Unitary System of Geographical Indication Protection in China], ZHONGHUA SHANGBIAO [CHINA TRADEMARK], January 2017, 59-62.

Xu Fang & Wu Guoying, Mingyoute Chanpin Dili Biaozhi de Baohu Zhanlue Yanjiu [Geographical Indications Protection for Famous, Excellent and Special Products], JIANGSU SHANGLUN [JIANGSU FORUM], February 2005, 15.

Xu Zengwen, Nongcun Laodongli de Liudong yu Nongye Laodongli de Liushi [Rural Labor Movement and Rural Labor Drain], ZHONGGUO NONGCUN JINGJI [CHINESE RURAL ECONOMY], January 1995, 51-53.

Yang Jianhui & Ren Jianlan, Xiaofeizhe dui Nongchanpin Dili Biaozhi Renzhi de Pingjia ji Yingxiang Yinsu Fenxi [Analysis of Consumers' Recognition of Geographical Indications of Agricultural Products and Influence Factors], DIAOYAN SHIJIE [THE WORLD OF SURVEY & RESEARCH], January 2015, 19-23.

Yann Basire, *La réforme du droit des marques en Europe: quid novi?* Europe, n° 5, 2016, étude 4.

Yann Basire, *Quel futur pour le régime des marques nationales?*, Propriété industrielle, n° 7-8, 2013, alerte 51.

Yao Fan, Yiyou Shangbiaofa You Lingjian Xin Guizhang Liangzhong Zhuce Qudao Weinan Quanliren [Existing Trademark Law and Other New Rules: Two Kinds of Registration Channels for Right Holders], FAZHI RIBAO [LEGAL DAILY], 5 August 2005.

Yu Jinkui, Dili Biaozhi Falu Baohu Moshi de Tantao [Discussion of the Protection Mode of Geographical Indications], ZHONGGUO HAIYANG DAXUE XUEBAO [JOURNAL OF OCEAN UNIVERSITY OF CHINA], January 2006, 91.

Zeng Deguo & Ye Peiyin, Woguo Dili Biaozhi Baohu he Fazhan de Nandian ji Duice [Difficulties and Countermeasures of the Protection and Development of Geographical Indications in China], ANHUI NONGYE DAXUE XUEBAO [JOURNAL OF ANHUI AGRICULTURAL UNIVERSITY], March 2015, 43.

Zhan Ailan & Mao Shanshan, Shaoxing Huangjiu Dili Biaozhi Guanli Shijian ji Qishi [Practice and Enlightenment of the Geographical Indication Management of Shaoxing Yellow Rice Wine], ZHEJIANG NONGYE KEXUE [JOURNAL OF ZHEJIANG AGRICULTURAL SCIENCES], May 2012, 770-774.

Zhan Huibin & Chen Chao, Xiaofeizhe Dui Dili Biaozhi Chanpin de Renzhi Chengdu Yiji Goumai Yiyuan Yanjiu [A Study on Consumers' Cognition and Purchase Intention of Geographical Indication Products], XIAOFEI JINGJI [CONSUMER ECONOMICS], August 2010, 55-57.

Zhang Chi, Bumen Boyi Dili Biaozhi Chanpin Baohu Yu Ganga [A Boxing Match Among Government Bodies: The Riddle of Geographical Indication Protection], FAREN ZAZHI [LEGAL JOURNAL], February 2006, 100.

Zhang Chuanfeng, Qianxi Dili Biaozhi Baohu Guoji Biaozhun ji Woguo de Kexingxing Xuanze [Discussions on the International Standards of Protection for Geographical Indications and China's Choice], ZHISHI CHANQUAN FA YANJIU [INTELLECTUAL PROPERTY LAW RESEARCH], January 2008, 118.

Zhang Huiping, Yuanchandi Mingcheng yu Diming de Bianxi Guizhou Maotai yu Maotai Zhen de Falu Dingwei [Analysis of Appellation of Origin and Place Name: Legal Definition of Guizhou Maotai Liquor and Maotao Town], NIANGJIU KEJI [LIQUOR MAKING SCIENCE & TECHNOLOGY], April 2007, 142.

Zhang Jin & Dong Fang, Dili Biaozhi de Guoji Baohu ji Woguo Baohu zhong Cunzai de Wenti [The International Protection of Geographical Indications and the Problems in the Protection of China], ZHONGGUO ZHISHI CHANQUAN BAO [CHINA INTELLECTUAL PROPERTY NEWS], 22 May 2001.

Zhang Weijun, Diming Shangbiao yu Dili Biaozhi Chongtu de Falu Tiaozheng [The Legal Adjustment of the Conflict Between Trademarks Containing Geographical Names and Geographical Indications], ZHONGHUA SHANGBIAO [CHINA TRADEMARK], August 2002, 44.

Zhang Weike, Liu Zhenlei & Gao Dacheng, Dili Biaozhi Baohu yu Mingyoute Nongchanpin de Fazhan [The Geographical Indication Protection and the Development of Famous Agricultural Products], QINGDAO XINGZHENG XUEYUAN XUEBAO [JOURNAL OF QINGDAO ADMINISTRATIVE INSTITUTE], August 2004, 85.

Zhang Yumin, Dili Biaozhi Baohu de Jige Guanxi [Several Relations on Geographical Indications Protection], GONGSHANG XINGZHENG GUANLI [BIWEEKLY OF ADMINISTRATION FOR INDUSTRY AND COMMERCE], March 2012, 12-13.

Zhang Yumin, Dili Biaozhi de Xingzhi he Baohu Moshi Xuanze [Nature and Protection Mode of Geographical Indications], FAXUE ZAZHI [LAW JOURNAL], November 2007, 6.

Zhang Yumin, Kaisa de Gui Kaisa Shangdi de Gui Shangdi [Give back to Caesar what is Caesar's and to God what is God's], RENMIN SIFA [PEOPLE'S JUDICATURE], May 2014, 34.

Zhao Junqi, Jianshe Meili Zhongguo Shengtai Yuanchandi Chanpin Baohu Dayou Kewei [Building a Beautiful Country: The Role of Protected Eco-origin Products], ZHONGGUO JIANYAN JIANYI [CHINA INSPECTION AND QUARANTINE], May 2013, 16.

Zhao Wenming, Dili Biaozhi Zhong Zhuce Qing Shiyong Difang Tute Nongchanpin Nan Tuiguang [Emphasizing Registration but De-emphasizing Usage: Geographical Indications Are Difficult to Promote Local Special Agricultural Products], FAZHI RIBAO [LEGAL DAILY], 25 December 2009.

Zhao Yuanguo, Huigu Zhongguo Zhuanlifa de Yunyu yu Dansheng [The Birth of China's Patent Law], ZHONGGUO FAMING YU ZHUANLI [CHINA INVENTION & PATENT], February 2007, 24.

Zhao Yuanguo, Zhongguo Jiaru Baohu Gongye Chanquan Bali Gongye Huimou [A Retrospective Analysis of China's Accession to the Paris Convention], ZHONGGUO ZHISHI CHANQUAN BAO [CHINA REPORT OF INTELLECTUAL PROPERTY], 19 March 2010, 1-5.

Zhao Zhongzhen et al., *The Formation of Daodi Medicinal Materials*, 48 J. Ethnopharmacology 476 (2012).

Zheng Chengsi, Cong Rushi ji Faxue Yanjiu Jiaodu Kan Zhongguo Liangbu Fa de Xiugai [Two Laws Modified: Insights from Acceding WTO and Legal Research], ZHONGHUA SHANGBIAO [CHINA TRADEMARK], December 2001, 13.

Zheng Chengsi, Manzu Zuidi Yaoqiu Zhongguo Rushi yu Zhishi Chanquan Baohu [Fulfilling Minimum Requirements: WTO and the Protection of Intellectual Property Rights], GUOJI MAOYI [INTERNATIONAL TRADE], January 2001, 38.

Zheng Chengsi, WTO Zhong de Shangbiao yu Dili Biaozhi [Trademarks and Geographical Indications in the WTO], ZHONGHUA SHANGBIAO [CHINA TRADEMARK], April 1997, 10.

Zhong Changyuan, Qianxi Yuanchandi Biaoji he Dili Biaozhi Jiqi Xiangguan Gainian [Analysis on the Marks of Origin and Geographical Indication and Relevant Concepts], KEJI QINGBAO KAIFA YU JINGJI [SCI-TECH INFORMATION DEVELOPMENT & ECONOMY], September 2009, 124.

Zhou Anning & Ying Ruiyao, Xiaofeizhe Dui Dili Biaozhi Nongchanpin Zhifu Yiyuan Jiqi Yingxiang Yinsu Yanjiu [Consumer's Willingness to Pay Considering Geographical Indication Product and the Influential Factors: From the Perspective of Consumer's Behavioral and Psychological Factors and Positive Examination], XUESHU TANSUO [ACADEMIC EXPLORATION], May 2012, 110-113.

Zhou Bo, Dili Biaozhi Zhengming Shangbiao Buying yu Shangpin Shangbiao Jinxing Jinsixing Bidui [Geographical Indications Registered as Certification Marks Should Not Be Compared with Trademarks in Similarity], KEJI YU FALU [JOURNAL OF SCIENCE & LAW], April 2014, 340.

Zhou Bo, Jiaqiang Shenli Zhidao Tongyi Shenpan Chidu Zhiyi [Strengthening the Guide of Trials and Unifying Judgment Standard], ZHONGGUO ZHISHI CHANQUAN BAO [CHINA INTELLECTUAL PROPERTY NEWS], 7 March 2014.

Zhou Bo, Ruhe Shencha Butong Leixing de Jiti Shangbiao [How to Examine Different Types of Collective Trademarks], ZHONGGUO ZHISHI CHANQUAN BAO [CHINA INTELLECTUAL PROPERTY NEWS], 11 September 2015.

Zhu Jinqing & Zhao Yuanguo, Zhongguo Zhuanlifa yu Bali Gongyue [China's Patent Law and Paris Convention], FAXUE YANJIU [CHINESE JOURNAL OF LAW], February 1987, 24.

Zhu Lanye, *An Analysis of China's System of Protecting Geographical Indications*, 1 Asian J. Comp. L. 1, 6 (2006).

Collected Works

Albert Chavanne, *Caractère facultatif ou obligatoire de la marque collective, in Les Marques collectives, Journée d'étude, Faculté de droit, Lyon, 12 janvier 1979*, Paris, Librairies techniques, 1979, p. 59.

Bernard Dutoit et al., *La protection des indications de provenance et des appellations d'origine en France, en Italie, en République fédérale d'Allemagne et en Suisse, in Les indications de provenance et les appellations d'origine en droit comparé, Actes du colloque de Lausanne*, Genève, Librairie Droz, 1983, p. 127.

Bronwyn Parry, *Geographical Indications: Not All 'Champagne and Roses', in Trade Marks and Brands: An Interdisciplinary Critique* 361 (Lionel AF Bently et al. eds, Cambridge University Press 2008).

Cerkia Bramley, Marie-Vivien Delphine & Biénabe Estelle, *Considerations in Designing an Appropriate Legal Framework for GIs in Southern Countries, in Developing Geographical Indications in the South* 15 (Cerkia Bramley ed., Springer 2013).

Daniel Gervais, *Geographical indications under TRIPS, in Research Handbook on Intellectual Property and Geographical Indications* 130 (Dev Gangjee ed., Edward Elgar Publishing 2016).

Daniel Gervais, *Traditional Innovation and the Ongoing Debate on the Protection of Geographical Indications, in Indigenous Peoples' Innovation: Intellectual Property Pathways to Development* 121 (Peter Drahos ed., ANU Press 2012).

Daniel J. Gervais & Matthew Slider, *The Geneva Act of the Lisbon Agreement: Controversial Negotiations and Controversial Results, in The Importance of Place: Geographical Indications as a Tool for Local and Regional Development* 15 (William van Caenegem ed., Springer International Publishing 2017).

Daniel Richard & Laurent Rieutort, *Les processus récents de valorisation de la qualité et de l'origine des produits agroalimentaires: marques territoriales ou labels? in Labellisation et mise en marques des territoires*, Clermont-Ferrand, Presses Universitaires Blaise Pascal, 2014, p. 24.

David Higgins, *The Making of Modern Trade Mark Law: The UK, 1860–1914, A Business History Perspective, in Trademarks and Brands: An Interdisciplinary Critique* 42 (Lionel AF Bently et al. eds, Cambridge University Press 2008).

Dev Gangjee, *Sui Generis or Independent Geographical Indications Protection, in The Cambridge Handbook of International and Comparative Trademark Law* 256 (Irene Calboli & Jane Ginsburg eds, Cambridge University Press 2020).

Dominique Barjolle et al., *Organization and Performance of the Origin Labelled Food Alliances, in Focus on Agricultural Economics* 91 (Ami R. Bellows ed., Nova Science Publishers 2005).

Eduardo Ramos Real & Dolores Garrido Garcia, *Towards a Second Generation of Quality Labels: A Proposal for Evaluation of Territorial Quality Marks, in Labellisation et mise en marques des territoires*, Clermont-Ferrand, Presses Universitaires Blaise Pascal, 2014, p. 71.

Estelle Biénabe et al., *Private Versus Public Quality Schemes for Origin-Labelled Products: Insights from the Karakul Pelts and Camdeboo Mohair Industries, in Developing geographical indications in the South* 73 (Cerkia Bramley ed., Springer 2013).

Giovanni Belletti et al., *The Effects of Certification Costs on the Success of a PDO/PGI, in Quality Management in Food Chains* 107-121 (Wageningen Academic Publishers 2007).

Guido Van Huylenbroeck, *Market and Rural Policy Institutions to Stimulate Multifunctional Food and Fibre Production, in The Multifunctional Role of Forests: Policies, Methods and Case Studies* 57 (European Forest Institute 2008).

Hélène Ilbert, *Products with Denominations of Origin and Intellectual Property Rights: The International Bargaining Process, in Geographical Indications and International Agricultural Trade: The Challenge for Asia* 91, 92 (Louis Augustin-Jean ed., Palgrave Macmillan 2012).

Irene Calboli, *Geographical Indications in the Global Arena: Observations and Recent Developments, in Geographical Indications: Global and Local Perspectives* 176 (Jacques de Werra ed., Schulthess Éditions Romandes 2016).

Jacques Larrieu, *Indications géographiques et marques en droit français, in Indications géographiques: perspectives globales et locales* 81 (Jacques de Werra ed., Schulthess Éditions Romandes 2016).

Jean-Louis Rastoin, *Créer un label méditerranéen Pour les produits agroalimentaires d'origine: quelques justifications théoriques et empiriques, in Les produits de terroir, les indications géographiques et le développement local durable des pays méditerranéens*, Paris, CIHEAM, 2009, p. 19.

Jeanne Boucourechliev, *Presentation de la marque collective, in Les Marques collectives, Journée d'étude, Faculté de droit, Lyon, 12 janvier 1979*, Paris, Librairies techniques, 1979, p. 16.

Julien Frayssignes, *Marques territoriales et développement rural: lecture critique pour la construction d'un programme de recherche, in Labellisation et mise en marques des territoires*, Clermont-Ferrand, Presses Universitaires Blaise Pascal, 2014, p. 56.

Louis Augustin-Jean, *The Globalization of Geographical Indications: The Challenge for Asia, in Geographical Indications and International Agricultural Trade: The Challenge for Asia* 1 (Louis Augustin-Jean ed., Palgrave Macmillan 2012).

Michael Handler, *Rethinking GI Extension, in Research Handbook on Intellectual Property and Geographical Indications* 146 (Dev Gangjee ed., Edward Elgar Publishing 2016).

Norbert Olszak, *Aspects juridiques de la dégustation d'agrément des vins à appellation d'origine ou indication géographique, in Histoire et actualités du droit viticole La robe et le vin*, Bordeaux, Féret, 2010, p. 57.

Norbert Olszak, *Le vin de terroir et la naissance des appellations d'origine, in Le droit du vin à l'épreuve des enjeux environnementaux*, Bordeaux, Féret, 2015, p. 56.

Norbert Olszak, *Marques et indications géographiques, in Les défis du droit des marques au XXIe siècle: Actes du colloque en l'honneur du Professeur Yves Reboul*, Paris, Lexis Nexis, 2011, p. 76.

Pascale Bazoche et al., *Willingness to Pay for Appellation of Origin: Results of an Experiment with Pinot Noir Wines in France and Germany, in Wine Economics: Quantitative Studies and Empirical Applications* 129 (Eric Giraud-Héraud et al. eds, Palgrave Macmillan 2013).

Paul Amadieu, Jean-Pierre Couderc & Jean-Laurent Viviani, *Financial Reaction to the Business Cycle in Periods of Difficulties: The Case of French Wine Companies, in Wine Economics: Quantitative Studies and Empirical Applications* 200 (Marie-Claude Pichery ed., Palgrave Macmillan 2013).

Robert Plaisant, *Le droit français des appellations d'origine, in Les indications de provenance et les appellations d'origine en droit comparé, Actes du colloque de Lausanne*, Genève, Librairie Droz, 1983, p. 72.

Selina Ching Chan, *Terroir and Green Tea in China: The Case of Meijiawu Dragon Well (Longjing) Tea, in Geographical Indications and International Agricultural Trade: The Challenge for Asia* 226 (Louis Augustin-Jean ed., Palgrave Macmillan 2012).

Sophie Réviron & Jean-Marc Chappuis, *Geographical Indications: Collective Organization and Management, in Labels of Origin for Food: Local Development, Global Recognition* 45 (Elizabeth Barham et al. eds, CABI Publishing 2011).

Thomas Debril, *Interactions des marchands et qualifications des marchandises: le cas du marché des vins de Bourgogne, in Sociologie de l'action organisée, Nouvelles études de cas*, Bruxelles, De Boeck, 2011, p. 215.

Zheng Haiyan, *Geographical Indications Protection in China, in Research Handbook on Intellectual Property and Geographical Indications* 327 (Dev Gangjee ed., Edward Elgar Publishing 2016).

Table of Cases

Cases from Chinese Courts

Cases from the Court of Justice of the European Union

Cases from French Courts

Other Cases

Table of Legislation

Treaties and Conventions

Chinese Statutes, Regulations, and Rules

Statutes

Regulations and Rules

Judicial Interpretations

French Codes, Statutes and Decrees

Codes

Statutes

Decrees

Directives

Others

Index

www.ingramcontent.com/pod-product-compliance
Lightning Source LLC
LaVergne TN
LVHW010654300926
849161LV00005B/1118
* 9 7 8 9 4 0 3 5 3 4 0 0 8 *